Shoal of Time

A HISTORY OF THE HAWAIIAN ISLANDS

GAVAN DAWS

Shoal of Time

A HISTORY OF THE HAWAIIAN ISLANDS

University of Hawaii Press
Honolulu

TO MY WIFE

Contents

CHAPTER 4: THE NATION 1839–1854

CHAPTER 5: A NEW SOCIETY, A NEW ECONOMY 1855–1876

CHAPTER 6: OUT IN THE NOONDAY SUN 1876–1887

Prologue

THE EXISTENCE of the Hawaiian Islands became known to Europeans late in the eighteenth century, at the end of the great age of exploration in the Pacific. It had been a lengthy era: merely to locate the major island groups took two and a half centuries. The reason was simple. The ocean was immense—the biggest single feature of the earth's surface—and the islands were tiny. So it was not surprising that the explorers ran into difficulties.

The first Westerner to enter the Pacific, Ferdinand Magellan, set the tone. Early in the sixteenth century he sailed from Cape Horn to the Philippines without encountering a single island on the way. Among the navigators who followed him—Spaniards, Dutchmen, Frenchmen, and Englishmen—were many who made useful discoveries, but more who spent years at a time sailing blindly after nothing.

The Pacific, then, was unreasonably large, an ocean so big that whole groups of islands, once found, might easily be lost again for decades at a time. It was easy to imagine, as well, that in such a place marvelous discoveries remained to be made. Here the closest attention was given to the ocean south of the equator. Theoretical geographers were especially intrigued with the idea of a Great Southern Continent somewhere in the Pacific. As more and more islands were located and mapped, the imagined land mass changed its dimensions and shifted its boundaries, and in the end it disappeared altogether, leaving the enthusiasts with Australia, New Zealand, Antarctica, and a quota of islands for consolation. But the myth was a sturdy one, still flourishing as late as the middle of the eighteenth century, and it took the work of a practical genius to lay it to rest.

Two brilliant voyages to the South Pacific established the Englishman James Cook as the greatest seagoing explorer produced by a nation of explorers. In less than a decade he made systematic traverses of seas covering about a quarter of the earth's surface, and found answers to all sorts of problems that had vexed explorers ever since Magellan's time. If the Great Southern Continent was gone for good, at least the modern map of the South Pacific had taken its place. This was more than a fair exchange, and it made Cook's name.

So much for the ocean south of the equator. To the north, the Spanish controlled the seas around the Philippines, and they were growing familiar with a few of the thousands of small islands in the western Pacific that became known collectively as Micronesia. In the extreme north, an arctic sea was known to exist; and on the eastern side of the ocean, the Spanish and others had explored the coast of the American continent as far north as California. But points of information about the western part of North America were few and far between, and there another great geographic problem awaited a solution. Was there a sea passage joining the Pacific and the Atlantic? Like the Southern Continent, it was a perennial puzzle.

Obviously Cook was the man to discover the passage, if it existed to be discovered. His government commissioned him to take a third expedition to the Pacific for this purpose, and it was during this voyage that he discovered the Hawaiian Islands.

The word "discovery," of course, is a conventional one. Wherever Cook went on his first and second voyages to the South Pacific he found populated islands, clearly settled long ago, and he found the same situation in the Hawaiian archipelago. So he was really a rediscoverer. The Pacific islanders had made his voyages in advance, and they had done so without the benefit of big ships or navigating instruments.

Given the distances involved, this was a formidable accomplishment, and naturally Cook was intrigued. He never settled the question of the islanders' navigating skills to his own satisfaction. Nor, indeed, has anyone else done so since then. The greatest mystery, then and now, lay in the realization that in places as far apart as New Zealand, Easter Island, and Hawaii people of a common physical stock could be found, speaking much the same kind of language, and living much the same kind of life. Obviously they had a common origin. Where was it? How long ago had they dispersed? And by what means?

The islanders, who were given the general name Polynesians, could not answer these questions themselves. By the time Westerners came to the Pacific the natives' long-distance canoe voyages had stopped. Legendary tales of migratory expeditions were still told, and the Polynesians could reel off genealogical chants that went back to the creation of the earth. But it was difficult to get the traditions of one group of islands to agree exactly with the traditions of another, and harder still to get the Polynesian idea of time to fit the Western historical calendar.

As far as the Hawaiian Islands were concerned, archeology (a science only of the mid-twentieth century in the Pacific) was finally able to suggest some tentative answers. Evidently, Hawaii was settled from the

Marquesas and the Society Islands, probably as early as the eighth century A.D., possibly earlier still; and there was another wave of migration in the twelfth and thirteenth centuries, this time from Tahiti. After that, apparently, there were no more voyages back and forth to the South Pacific, and the Hawaiians lived in isolation until the arrival of Cook.

The discovery of new islands was no part of Cook's official task on his third voyage. The sea passage from Pacific to Atlantic was the sole object of search. Cook, with his two ships, HMS *Resolution* and HMS *Discovery,* was to go directly from the South Pacific to the coast of North America. But Cook was a man to whom things happened, and it was his gift to turn the most matter-of-fact instructions to interesting account.

Early in December 1777, his expedition headed north from the Society Islands toward the equatorial Pacific. The two ships crossed the line before the month was over, and in the last week of the year they made their first new landfall, a tiny, uninhabited, crescent-shaped coral atoll. Cook named it Christmas Island.

He set sail for the north again on January 2, 1778, and every day took him farther into unfamiliar waters. He had never before been north of the equator in the Pacific, and neither he nor any other Englishman knew much about the central part of the ocean. For more than two hundred years the Spanish had been sailing between Mexico and the Philippines, but they were notoriously close-lipped about their activities. If they had sighted the Hawaiian Islands they made no use of the discovery, and certainly they told no one else. Any information about the track followed by the Spanish galleons had to be collected at swordpoint, and even so the best charts available to the English were crude. They showed little more than the imperfectly mapped coastlines of Asia and America, separated from each other in the far north by a narrow strait, and then parting, in the lower latitudes, like ragged curtains on vast and empty seas.

A Note on the Use of the Hawaiian Language

THE HAWAIIAN LANGUAGE has always confused Westerners coming upon it for the first time. The Europeans who put native words on paper in the late eighteenth century resorted to a bewildering variety of spellings. In the eighteen twenties the written language was standardized with an alphabet of only twelve letters (a, e, i, o, u, h, k, l, m, n, p, w), and from then on, to the uninstructed eye, most words looked too much alike. Names of people and places, especially, seemed often to begin with a K and then go on indefinitely. So that the general reader will not be subjected to undue strain, all Hawaiian words in the text of this book, including those in quotations, have been given standard spellings. Scholars wishing to find out how early travelers spelled Hawaiian words may trace quotations through the Notes.

CHAPTER ONE

Captain Cook

1778–1779

High Islands at Daybreak

AT DAWN on January 18, 1778, a high island, deep blue in the early light, appeared to the northeast, and shortly afterward another to the north. Occasional calms held the *Resolution* and the *Discovery* offshore all day, and at sunset they were still nine or ten leagues from land. During the night the ships drifted west, leaving the first island quite a distance to windward. Next morning, while Cook was steering for the second island, yet a third came into view on the northwest horizon. So far the watch had seen no sign of life on shore, but as the *Resolution* worked closer to the beach some sturdy brown-skinned men launched canoes and made their way out through the surf. Cook's native friends in the South Pacific had not mentioned islands as far to the north as this, and so he was "agreeably surprised" to hear the paddlers hail his ship in what sounded like a dialect of the familiar language of the Society Islands. Although Cook had no way of knowing it, he was at the apex of the great Polynesian triangle, based on New Zealand in the southwest and Easter Island in the southeast and including within its boundaries most of the islands he himself had discovered and named. He had now come upon Oahu, Kauai, and Niihau, at the western end of the Hawaiian chain.

The natives of Kauai who approached the *Resolution* were friendly, though very timid at first. They had brought no weapons except a few stones, and these they threw away after Cook convinced them he meant no harm. They would not come aboard, but they were willing to trade or at least to exchange gifts. Some brass medals were lowered to them on the end of a rope, then some small pieces of iron, and they sent up fish and sweet potatoes in return.

Cook could not see a likely anchorage close by, so he turned his ships along the southwestern side of Kauai where the land sloped gently down to the sea from the base of high wooded mountains in the interior. On the uplands bananas and sugarcane grew, and dotted about the grassy open plains were villages of steep-sided thatch huts, with large cultivated gardens and plantations, and here and there strange insubstantial white towers, like nothing Cook had ever seen before, standing as high as fifty feet. As the ships passed crowds of natives gathered on the hills and at the water's edge; more canoes came out to trade, and Cook was able to barter iron nails for live pigs and sweet potatoes.

By the end of the day the *Resolution* and the *Discovery* were close to the village of Waimea, a cluster of about sixty huts near the beach and another forty or so farther inland. The ships spent the night standing off the coast, and next morning some natives nerved themselves to come aboard. It was an overwhelming experience for them. "Their eyes," wrote Cook, "were continually flying from object to object, the wildness of their looks and actions fully express'd their surprise and astonishment, at the several new objects before them and evinced that they never had been on board of a ship before." Some prayed as they came on deck; others asked anxiously where they might seat themselves, and if it was proper to spit.

This was only right, Cook thought. It was a sensible primitive who bowed before a superior civilization. Cook had seen more of life in a "state of nature" than all the salon philosophers of Europe together, and experience taught him not to follow the London vogue of overrating Noble Savages at the expense of civilized men. He had spent several years among the savages of the Pacific, "Indians," as he and everyone else called them, and they seemed to him noble and ignoble in about equal parts. Polynesians he knew best of all. They were a handsome race, fortunate enough to live on beautiful islands. Nature had been kind to them and they ought to have responded by developing a perfect humanity, but they had not. Sometimes Cook found them the most attractive of people, impulsively warm, welcoming, open, hospitable, and frank—a philosopher's delight. Just as often they were deceitful, even treacherous, and occasionally one set of attitudes cloaked the other.

A practical explorer could not afford the luxury of regarding atolls and archipelagoes as islands of the mind, and Cook had to cope with savages as they were. Landfalls were interesting to him for geographical reasons and important as places of refreshment for his men; islanders were useful mainly as providers of food. Over the years Cook had worked out fairly reliable methods of getting what he wanted. He would begin, as he did at Kauai, by offering gifts to establish good relations, and usually this was sufficient. Almost always he let the natives set the tone of the dealings. If they were friendly so was he, because things were easier that way. If he could impress them without injuring them he tried to do so. He would perhaps fire a demonstration shot or two, but he was forbearing up to the point where the success of his expedition might be threatened.

Some of his officers disagreed with this lenient policy, arguing that it was best to make an early example and save trouble later on. Cook's view was rather less simple. He too relied in the end on guns and he fired them when he had to, which was quite often, but at the same time he gave Polynesians credit for an intelligence of their own. They might be savages, but they were also men, not mere animals to be terrified by loud noises and the sight of blood. "Three things," he wrote, "made them our fast friends, Their own good Natured and benevolent disposition, gentle treatment on our part, and the dread of our Fire arms; by our ceaseing to observe the Second the first would have wore of[f] of Course, and the too frequent use of the latter would have excited a spirit of revenge and perhaps have taught them that fire Arms were not such terrible things as they had imagined, they are very sencible of the superiority they have over us in numbers and no one knows what an enraged multitude might do."

One thing more than most gave Cook trouble with Polynesians—they were thieves, and in this the Hawaiians of Kauai were like the rest. As soon as they came aboard the *Resolution,* even before the strangeness of the encounter died away, they began to pick things up with the idea of keeping them. At first it was only powerful curiosity, but after Cook's men mounted a close watch it became a matter of cunning and daring. Just as an armed party was setting out in the *Resolution*'s pinnace to look for a landing place at Waimea a native stole a butcher's cleaver, jumped over the side to a waiting canoe, and made for the shore. The pinnace and a boat from the *Discovery* gave chase. The lieutenant in charge, an Irishman named John Williamson, fired a pistol shot, and his excited men, against his instructions, let go a volley. Some of the Hawaiians leaped overboard from the canoe in fright, but when Williamson came up to them the thief had disappeared ashore with the cleaver.

Nothing would be gained at the moment by hunting him down, and the natives were beginning to pelt the pinnace with stones. Williamson withdrew and went back to the business of finding a landing place. The first time he tried to go ashore a great crowd of natives splashed out into the shallows and surrounded his boats, climbing on board and tugging at oars, muskets, and everything else they could lay their hands on. Williamson did not think they meant to kill or even harm his men, and a few of them seemed satisfied with an iron nail or two, but the others were so boisterous that they almost turned the pinnace over. One man in the bow got hold of a boat hook, and he would not let go even for a nail. Williamson believed that the best way of handling situations such as this was not to fire unless it was absolutely necessary, and then to "do execution."

With the "greatest reluctance" he shot the man. Even this did not frighten the natives away entirely. They took the bleeding body back to the beach and stood there signaling for the boats to come in. Williamson understandably thought it safer to look for a landing somewhere else.

Cook, who had not seen the shooting, went ashore some hours later with a guard of armed marines. The Hawaiians had no doubt that they were in the presence of an important man. On the beach in front of the village hundreds of natives waited with gifts, and when Cook stepped from his boat they fell to the ground and lay face down until he encouraged them to get up. He accepted their offerings of pigs, bananas, and kapa or bark cloth, distributed presents of his own, and then went to inspect a fresh-water pool picked out by Lieutenant Williamson to supply the ships. Next morning Cook came in again, and once the watering was under way he left Williamson in charge at the beach and walked inland with his ship's surgeon, William Anderson, and the expedition's artist, John Webber.

About half a mile away stood one of the towers they had seen from the ships. Their guide led them toward it, past irrigated plantations of the edible root kalo or taro, groves of coconut trees and banana plants, and stands of the paper mulberry whose bark was used in making kapa cloth. The tower had a wooden frame, partly covered with the same kind of grayish kapa that the natives had given Cook at the beach. At head-height was a board on which some bananas had been laid as an offering to one of the Hawaiian gods. The whole structure stood on a raised stone platform, a burying place like those Cook had seen at Tahiti and other Polynesian islands in the South Pacific, with sacred stones and carved wooden images. Inside a long thatched hut they saw the graves of several chiefs, marked by more wooden images. Except for the unusual tower, the comparison between this heiau or temple and those of Tahiti was irresistible, and Cook and his companions, who had learned about human sacrifice in the Societies, were not really surprised when their guide showed them where the kanaka kapus, the tabooed men or sacrificial victims, were buried outside the hut. On this spot they counted four kanaka kapu graves, and they had already seen several other towers in the district, some much bigger than the one they were examining. Among the noble savages of Kauai, then, human sacrifice was common.

By sunset the ships' work parties and their native helpers at the beach had rolled a good supply of fresh water in casks down to the boats. The day's trading had gone well too; once the Hawaiians were convinced that they could not get away with stealing, most of them settled down to steady barter. In exchange for nails and pieces of iron Cook's men got sweet potatoes, some of which weighed as much as fourteen pounds, bananas, taro roots, fowls, and between sixty and eighty pigs. The natives also showed the visitors some rich feather cloaks and helmets, red and yellow, beautifully made, as thick and glossy as velvet. These they seemed to value very highly.

From the first the Hawaiians were fascinated by iron, almost to the exclusion of other things from the ships. They did not mine any metals themselves and they had no real name for iron, but they knew what it was. Cook had come across this paradox in the South Pacific. He surmised that early explorers left iron as they went from place to place there, and natives then took it with them on trips between islands, or at least told others about it. Admittedly Kauai was very isolated, and there was no indication that European ships had put in there before the *Resolution* and the *Discovery*. Even so, the Spanish had been sailing the North Pacific for two hundred and fifty years; no doubt pieces of wreckage and discarded ships' stores had drifted ashore. It turned out that the people of Kauai did have some iron of their own—two small pieces—and they said it came from the eastward, or from the sea. They were avid for more. Captain Charles Clerke of the *Discovery* found that a moderate sized nail would supply his ship with pork for a day, and sweet potatoes and taro were even cheaper. The market at Kauai was the best he had ever seen.

As news of Cook's iron-bearing ships spread around the island natives flocked to Waimea to trade. Strong winds were whipping up a heavy surf along the beach, but the canoes continued to bring out hogs and vegetables. After a few days the *Resolution* and the *Discovery* had as much food aboard as they could handle and their barter goods were running low. On the morning of January 23 Cook weighed anchor with the idea of taking the *Resolution* farther out beyond the breaking surf. Once he was out he found he could not get in again, and for the next six days he was reduced to tacking back and forth in the channel between Kauai and Niihau.

Though Cook had been welcomed with honors usually reserved for high-ranking aliis or chiefs, including prostration, no Kauai chief made his appearance at the beach until after the *Resolution* was forced out into the channel. The *Discovery* remained at Waimea a little longer, and while she was still at anchor a young chief and his retinue visited Captain Clerke. Most of the commoners on board jumped over the sides of the ship when they saw the alii coming, and the rest prostrated themselves on the deck. The great man seemed friendly enough, but his attendants were stultifyingly formal. They would not let their master come all the way on deck, much less go below, and they were disturbed when Clerke clapped him on the shoulder in greeting. Clerke offered presents and got in return a large, handsome wooden bowl with carved human figures as supports, for serving the Hawaiians' ceremonial drink, a mild narcotic called awa, made from the root of a kind of pepper plant. Then the chief was ushered down the gang plank by his attendants, with the greatest care, "as tho'," wrote

Clerke, " a drop of Salt Water wou'd have destroyed him." Later, another high chief came out and ordered the commoners away from the *Discovery* once more. Even on the water the natives had to prostrate themselves, and as they lay in their drifting outrigger canoes they ran the risk of being rammed and capsized by the chief's big double-hulled canoe. The chief waved the commoners off the decks and then invited Clerke to land and receive more presents. Clerke was almost ready to leave Waimea; he declined politely, and the disappointed chief went back to shore, scattering canoes on either side.

By January 29 Cook had given up trying to return to Kauai, and he began searching the coast of Niihau for an anchorage with fresh water. The Niihauans were just as impressed by his big ship as the people of Kauai and just as interested in iron, for which they traded enthusiastically, bringing their canoes out to the *Resolution* through surf so heavy that Cook's boats could not handle it. On January 30, yet another rough day, Lieutenant John Gore went with three armed boats to check a landing place. Cook was going to follow but the surf became too high, and Gore and twenty men stayed ashore that night rather than chance the short passage back to the *Resolution*.

This was something Cook had hoped to avoid, because the *Resolution*, like almost all European ships, carried venereal disease, and a shore party would be certain to infect the Hawaiians. At Kauai and Niihau native women, bare-breasted and more than friendly, wanted to come aboard with their menfolk. Cook ordered them kept off. This proved a near impossibility, so Thomas Edgar, master of the *Discovery*, said, because the common sailors perfected "Schemes to deceive the Officers by dressing them up as Men." Cook also set strict limits on the size of landing parties, allowing only men who appeared free of disease to go ashore. Even this was no guarantee, Cook realized; a man might be diseased and not know it, and once the sailors got ashore, as Edgar wrote, the women "used all their arts to entice them into their Houses & even went so far as to endeavour to draw them in by force."

That was how things went with Gore's men at Niihau. They were ashore two days and two nights, and, according to Lieutenant Williamson, "ye extreme reservedness of the party excited so great a curiosity in the women, that they were determined to see wether our people were men or not, & us'd every means in their power to provoke them to do that, which ye dread of punishment would have kept them from."

Cook himself was abstemious. On Saturday nights, at dinner with his officers, he might unbend and drink an extra glass in honor of the distant ladies of England, but he left the ladies of the islands alone, and he wished his men would do the same. His concern in trying to keep native girls and sailors apart was not puritanical—far from it. He was a man of broad sympathies, and he did not want to be responsible for spreading disease. It hurt him to think that he had failed in his hopes so many times in the Pacific. He failed again at Niihau, where the weather set his orders aside.

Cook was finally able to go ashore in his pinnace on February 1. He took with him three goats, a male and two females; a boar and a sow; and melon, pumpkin, and onion seeds, all of which he gave to a Hawaiian who had been helping Gore load water. This native and several others accompanied Cook on a short walk about the island. Carrying the pigs and chanting prayers, they circled around Cook, and wherever they went they ordered commoners to prostrate themselves until the party was out of sight.

Niihau was small, low lying, seemingly poor except for yams and salt, and thinly populated. Gore's men thought only about five hundred people lived there, compared with possibly thirty thousand on Kauai. Cook meant to stay and see some more of the place, but after he went back to the *Resolution* that evening the anchor worked free of the bottom and his ship began to drift. Next morning Niihau was three leagues away. The island really offered very little, and Cook was behind schedule. He signalled to the *Discovery* to join him, and about noon on February 2 the two ships set off to the north once more.

It had been Cook's experience in the Pacific that islands generally came in clusters. So far he had seen five here, all between 21° 30′ and 22° 15′ North, and 199° 20′ and 201° 30′ East: Oahu, the first one sighted; Kauai and Niihau, where he had landed; and two small, rocky, uninhabited islets off Niihau called Lehua and Kaula. The natives told him of others to east and west, inhabited and uninhabited. Cook had to leave these for future investigation; in the meantime he named the whole archipelago the Sandwich Islands, after his patron at the Admiralty.

The Hawaiians impressed Cook and his men quite favorably, apart from their early disposition to steal. Perhaps not the handsomest or most intelligent natives the explorers had encountered, they were still strong and active, especially as swimmers, surfers, and canoe handlers. The climate of the islands was pleasant, with temperatures in the seventies and low eighties, so the Hawaiians did not need much in the way of clothes, and they spent more time in the open air than in their small, closed thatch huts. Kauai seemed less luxuriant than Tahiti in the Societies or Tongatapu in the Friendly Islands, but all the same land and sea yielded plenty of food and the Hawaiians ate copiously, though one of their favorite dishes, poi, a paste-like pudding made from taro, struck at least one of the visitors as "a disagreeable mess from its sourness." Around Waimea life appeared tranquil, but the men were well equipped for fighting with wooden spears and daggers. Cook thought war might account for the fact that the population looked small in relation to the amount of usable land. On matters of religion and government, Cook and his officers did not have time to make sound judgments. Kahunas or priests were numerous and officious, but the extent of their authority was not clear. Apparently the despotism of the aliis, the chiefs, was reinforced by a powerful kapu or taboo that could bring commoners to the ground in their presence, and veneration did not end with death, as the burying places with their offerings and sacrificial graves showed. The outward trappings of religion seemed to be similar to those of Tahiti, but what the gods of the Hawaiians were really like and how worshippers approached them Cook could not tell; and he was experienced enough to realize that such important questions could hardly be understood by a passing visitor.

Kealakekua Bay

Cook spent several difficult and disappointing months in the far north. The spring and summer of 1778 went by and still a sea passage from the Pacific to the Atlantic eluded him. The last stage of his search took him through Bering Strait into the Arctic sea, and there the *Resolution* and the *Discovery* encountered a frozen half-world of fog and snow, of trumpeting walruses and howling wolves. Finally in the latitude of 70° 44′ a dazzling and impenetrable wall of pack ice put an end to further investigation. There was no point in trying to wait out the cold weather on the spot. The *Resolution* was badly in need of overhauling, and food was so short that the men were reduced to hunting sea animals on the ice. Cook decided to winter at the Sandwich Islands and come north again in the summer of 1779.

For a month after the two ships left the northern American coast and headed back into the open Pacific very little was seen: an occasional bird, a single dolphin. At last the variable winds of the middle latitudes gave way to steady northeast trades, and Cook entered the tropics again late in November, a few hundred miles east of the islands he had discovered on his way north in January. On November 25 he turned his ships westward, and at daybreak next morning, in the latitude of 20° 55′, land was sighted. It was an island new to Cook—Maui: large, well-wooded and watered, dominated by a saddle-shaped volcanic mountain ten thousand feet high, whose summit was visible above a layer of cloud.

About noon the first native canoes came out. "As soon as they got a long side," wrote Cook, "many of the people who conducted them came into the Ships without the least hesitation. They were of the same Nation as those of the leeward islands, and if we did not misstake them they knew of our being there. Indeed it appeared rather too evident as these people had got a mongst the veneral distemper, and I as yet knew of no other way they could come by it."

Clerke was visited on the *Discovery* by Kahekili, principal chief of Maui, who brought with him as a gift a fine red feather cloak. One day of trading seemed to exhaust the natives' food. Another island was visible in the west (this was Molokai, and it in turn obscured a small island called Lanai), but Cook decided to make use of a strong current flowing eastward to get round to the leeward side of Maui. By November 30 he was at the northeast end of the island. That afternoon a strange looking chief named Kalaniopuu, elderly, scaly skinned and red-eyed, his body racked by spasms of trembling, came alongside with several canoes and gave Cook a cloak and several small pigs. A party of Kalaniopuu's people stayed overnight on the *Resolution,* their double canoe trailing astern at the end of a rope. Some of them had venereal sores; they were given medicine. The same evening yet another big island appeared in the east. Next morning Cook abandoned his plan to go to the protected side of Maui and made instead for the new island, which his native visitors called Hawaii.

It proved to be the last of the group to windward, and the largest, with two volcanic peaks more than thirteen thousand feet high. Surprisingly, even in this mild tropical "winter" the summits were covered with snow. For a month Cook sailed along offshore looking for a safe anchorage, with the northern and then the eastern shore on his starboard bow, but he was frustrated at every new turn of the land by winds or currents or pounding surf in the shallows.

The people who came out to trade were just as friendly and trusting as those of Kauai had been. The men were quite happy to stay alongside in their outrigger canoes and send their hogs and vegetables up for sale on board. With venereal disease already visible among the natives there was no reason to keep the women away. They came on board and made love spiritedly below decks, even though the rolling of the ships made some of them seasick.

Cook got out of the way of the blustering winds early in January 1779, when he rounded the south point of the island, at about 18° 55′ North latitude. There he came upon a large village near the beach, in the midst of a region devastated by volcanic eruptions. Beyond the village, slag and ash lay everywhere. Just an occasional plant pushed through the black and barren surface, and the only fresh water stood in brackish rain pools on the lava. The inhabitants, wrote Cook, "thronged off to the Ship with hogs and Women. It was not possible to keep the latter out of the Ship and no Women I ever met with were more ready to bestow their favours, indeed it appeared to me that they came with no other view."

The *Discovery* had fallen behind the *Resolution* some days before, and Cook was pleased to see Clerke's ship round the point on January 6. The village offered no anchorage; half a mile from shore a line of a hundred and sixty fathoms did not reach bottom. For several days the ships stood off and on to trade, until at last the canoes were coming out empty of goods, though filled with men and women. Cook and Clerke turned their ships up the western coast. From time to time canoeloads of natives stayed on board all night, and once some obliging girls sang and danced for the sailors.

At daybreak on January 17 a curving bay came into view, and Cook sent his sailing master, William Bligh, to look it over. Steep cliffs came down to the water's edge in some places. The shoreline, of black volcanic rock, looked dangerous except at one spot, where the village of Kekua* stood on a sandy beach. Near the barren north point of the bay, about a mile and a half from Kekua, was a smaller village, Kaawaloa. Inland, on rising ground above Kekua, native huts were scattered among groves of coconut trees, and loose rocks had been cleared and piled into fences so that sweet potatoes and paper mulberries could be cultivated. Still higher up, breadfruit trees flourished.

Bligh needed all day to make his examination. In the meantime a tremendous crowd of natives took to the water. "Canoes now began to come off from all parts," wrote Cook, "so that before 10 oclock there were not less than a thousand about the two Ships, the most of them filled with people, hogs and other productions of the Island. Not a man had with him a Weapon of any sort, Trade and curiosity alone brought them off. Among such numbers as we had at times on board it is no wonder that some betrayed a thievish disposition, one man took out of the Ship a boats Ruther, he was discovered but too late to recover it. I thought this a good oppertunity to shew them the use of fire arms, two or three muskets and as many four pound shot were fired over the Canoe which carried off the Ruther. As it was not intended that any of the Shot should take effect, the Indians seemed rather more surprised than frightened." After dark most of the Hawaiians went ashore again, but some who remained on the *Resolution* stayed to steal. Cook decided "not to entertain so many another night."

Next morning, as the two ships made ready to anchor, the Hawaiians came singing and shouting down to the bay in thousands. Nowhere in all his travels had Cook seen such a crowd. They swam about the ships like shoals of fish, and his men were helpless to keep them off. So many

---

* Its modern name is Napoopoo.

clambered up one side of the *Discovery* that she began to heel over. At eleven in the morning the *Resolution* let out her anchor about a quarter mile from the shore. The sails were unbent, the yards and top masts struck. Captain Cook had come to Kealakekua Bay.

Lono

Amid all the excitement and confusion two chiefs, an exceptionally handsome six-footer named Kanaina and a friendly young man named Palea, made themselves useful by ordering canoes out of the path of the ships and stoning the more importunate commoners from the decks. Once the *Resolution* was at anchor a third dignitary appeared, the priest Koa. "This," wrote Lieutenant James King, "was a little old man, had sore eyes & a Scaly body, the effects of the awa . . ." Koa approached Cook respectfully and threw over his shoulders a piece of red cloth; then, stepping back, he presented a small pig and made a long speech. Koa stayed on board to dine and ate heartily, but addicted to awa as he was he could not be persuaded to do more than take a sip of the captain's wines and spirits.

In the evening Cook, King, and the astronomer William Bayly went ashore with Koa at Kekua. They were met by four men carrying short sticks tipped with dog's hair, who went before them chanting over and over a sentence in which only the word "Orono" or Lono could be made out. The commoners had cleared the beach; only a few remained in sight, lying prostrate near their huts. The escorts led Cook's party along the south side of the beach to a high platform of levelled stones with a wooden scaffolding, like the heiau on Kauai except that here the skulls of sacrificial victims were lined up on a railing.

This was not just a casual sight-seeing tour. Koa and the priests had planned an elaborate ceremony. "We enterd the Area on one side near the houses," wrote King, "& the Captn was made to stop at two rude images of Wood, the faces only were Carved, & made to represent most distort'd mouths; with a long piece of Carved Wood on the head. these Images had pieces of old Cloth wrap'd round them, & at the foot was dry hay & a few old Coco nut husks. After Koa & a tall grave young man with a long beard whose name was Keliikea repeated a few words, we were led to the end of the Area where the Scaffold was; At the foot of this were 12 Images ranged in a semicircular form, & fronting these opposite the Center figure was a corrupt'd hog, placed on a stand, supportd by post 6 feet high, exactly resembling the haka of Tahiti, & at the foot were many pieces of Sugar Cane. Coco nuts. breadfruit &c. Koa led the Captn under this Stand, & after handling the hog & Repeating a prayer, he let it drop, & conducted him, to the Scaffolding which they asscended, not without great risk of tumbling, Koa kept hold of the Captns. hand;

"We now saw coming round the Rail, a procession of 10 men, who brought with them a hog & a large piece of Red Cloth. they approachd to where a piece of a wall, & the Scaffolding of a house which together, seperates this part of the Area from the rest, & there prostrated themselves. Keliikea taking the Red Cloth, & carrying it to Koa, who wrapt it round the Captn: afterwards the hog was handed up to him.

"For some time Keliikea & Koa kept repeating sentences in concert & alternately, & many times appeard to be interrogating; at last Koa let the hog fall, & he & the Captain descended, & Koa led him to different images, said something to each but in a very ludicrous & Slighting tone, except to the Center image; which was the only one coverd with Cloth, & was only three feet high, whilst the rest were Six; to this he prostrated himself, & afterwards kiss'd, & desird the Captn to do the same, who was quite passive, & sufferd Koa to do with him as he chose . . ."

Still more was to come. A procession of natives entered carrying a meal of baked pig, breadfruit, coconut, vegetables, and poi. For fifteen minutes the priests performed chants and responses, ending again with the word "Lono." The awa makers chewed their pepper root and spat it mouthful by mouthful into a drinking bowl. Cook and King tasted it, and then a young priest rubbed the visitors' faces, heads, shoulders, and hands with chewed coconut wrapped in cloth. When it came to the pig the visitors were fed by hand. "I had no objection to have the hog handled by Palea," wrote King, "but the Captn recollecting what offices Koa had officiated when he handled the Putrid hog could not get a morsel down, not even when the old fellow very Politely chew'd it for him." A midshipman once described Cook's taste as "surely, the coarsest that ever mortal was endued with," but even for such an insensitive palate this was too much, and as soon as he could Cook distributed his own gifts and went back to the *Resolution*.

What did it all mean? No one could be sure. The priests were clearly identifying Cook with something or someone called "Orono" or Lono; the commoners, after the tumultuous welcome in the bay, treated him with awe; and, as King observed, the business at the stone platform far exceeded the chants and food offerings that Cook was used to: it seemed almost like religious adoration. At any rate it was an apparent guarantee of good treatment. Cook was invited to a second ceremonial feast, this time at the "house of Lono" in a secluded part of the village where many priests lived. From then on he was accompanied on all his excursions by a priest who announced his presence and ordered the commoners to prostrate themselves, and wherever he went he was plied with gifts.

When Captain Clerke came ashore from the *Discovery* he too was received with extravagant honors, though he found it, as he said, a disagreeable amusement to be worshipped as a being of "Superior nature," and tried to avoid it. All the other members of the expedition shared in the reflected glory. Lieutenant King was allowed to set up the astronomical observatory in a patch of sweet potatoes next to the heiau at Kekua, and the obliging priests of Lono placed a kapu on the site to keep trespassers away. The ban was evidently a powerful one; no canoes were beached there and natives dared not cross the wall without permission. King and his marine guard, in fact, had a little too much privacy to suit them. On board ship at night, wrote Surgeon David Samwell, so many beautiful women gathered "that there is hardly one among us that may not vie with the grand Turk himself." But not at the observatory. "The Gentlemen who sleep on shore are mortified at this as no Women will on any Account come to them." Elsewhere it was a happier story. The villagers competed for the attention of the officers and men. Little children capered about them, householders gave them coconut milk to drink, and young women sang and danced for them.

All this sociability came to an abrupt halt on January 24, when the natives would not venture out of their houses and no canoes were allowed on the bay. Some hours passed before the ships' officers learned that a kapu had been ordered for the arrival of the great alii Kalaniopuu, ruler of the island of Hawaii, the same decrepit chief who had visited Cook off Maui. The suddenness of the imposition left the ships short of vegetables, and the men urged a few natives to break the kapu and bring out food. A chief interfered, but a musket fired over his canoe drove him away and the trade was completed.

Kalaniopuu arrived on January 25 and paid an informal visit to the *Resolution* before going ashore at Kaawaloa. A formal exchange of courtesies took place next day about noon. Lieutenant King watched from the observatory at Kekua as three big canoes set out for the ships. Kalaniopuu was accompanied by one of the principal priests of Lono, named Kaoo. "In the first Canoe," wrote King, "was Kalaniopuu. In the Second Kaoo with 4 Images, the third was fill'd with hogs & Vegetables as they went along those in the Center Canoe kept Singing with much Solemnity; from which we concluded that this procession had some of their religious ceremonys mixt with it. but instead of going on board they came to our side, their appearance was very grand, the Chiefs standing up drest in their Cloaks & Caps, & in the Center Canoe, where the busts of what we supposd their Gods made of basket work, variously coverd with Red, black, white, & Yellow feathers, the Eyes represent'd by a bit of Pearl

Oyster Shell with a black button, & the teeth were those of dogs, the mouths of all were strangely distorted, as well as other features."

King called out his guard to receive Kalaniopuu at the observatory. Cook arrived almost at the same time, and as soon as both parties were inside King's tent Kalaniopuu took off his feather cloak and helmet, robed Cook in them, and pledged his friendship in an exchange of personal names. Cook invited Kalaniopuu on board the *Resolution* to receive gifts in turn.

The ruler of Hawaii was now Cook's fast friend; the priests of the house of Lono had done everything they could to make the expedition welcome (Cook's irreverent men began to call Kaoo "the bishop" and the young priest Keliikea "the rector"); the commoners, and especially the women, seemed delighted with the company of white men. Just one uncomfortable fact kept intruding: the Hawaiians continued to steal. They were determined and ingenious thieves, and an occasional exemplary whipping did nothing to stop them. "These people," wrote David Samwell, "are so eager after our Iron that they pick the Sheathing Nails out of the Ship's bottom." (They were not alone in this, Samwell noted: "our Men pull as many as they can conveniently on the inside to give to the Girls so that between them was there not a strict Eye kept over them we should have the Ships pulled to pieces at this place.") Not just nails but bigger items such as knives disappeared, and when the stolen goods were traced the trail sometimes led to a chief. The alii Kanaina had been helpful from the first; so had young Palea, even after the men of the *Resolution* spoke sharply to him and manhandled him when he encouraged a commoner to ask a high price for a pig. But apparently some of the other chiefs were not so respectful of the dignity and the property of the visitors—one alii was bold enough to appear on board ship sporting a stolen knife tied to his wrist with a string. As for old Koa, the red-eyed awa drinker who had been the first priest to visit the ships, he was detected in something very like a confidence trick, and though he continued to be attentive, going so far as to adopt the name of "Brittanee" in honor of the Englishmen, his credit with the officers was strained.

For the moment, however, such things were only a nuisance, and the good times continued. By invitation the visitors watched a Hawaiian boxing match, which they found amusing. The combatants looked each other over contemptuously, strutted about flexing their muscles for the spectators, then stood and swung roundhouse blows at each other's head without trying to dodge or parry. When one was beaten into ignominy the other would "turn his backside" on him arrogantly and walk away. The Hawaiians good humoredly invited their guests to stand the buffet, but there were no takers. Some of the sailors had tried it at Tonga earlier in the voyage, and they still carried in their heads the memory of ringing punches delivered by husky Friendly Islanders. Instead the Englishmen put on a fireworks display, to the terror and delight of the natives.

On the day of the boxing contest William Watman, an old seaman on the *Resolution*, died of a paralytic stroke. Kalaniopuu wanted him buried on the stone platform or heiau at Kekua, and after the naval service was read and the grave was being filled the priests of Lono threw in sacrificial pigs, coconuts, and bananas. For three nights they continued to chant and pray and sacrifice hogs.

More than two weeks had gone by since the *Resolution* and the *Discovery* dropped anchor at Kealakekua, and their galley fuel was exhausted. Good wood was scarce along the water, so Cook directed King to ask the priests of the house of Lono if he could take the wooden railing from the heiau. They agreed unhesitatingly. A work party of sailors dismantled the railing and then uprooted the wooden images as well. Some natives who were watching helped them carry the carved statues down to the boats, and the priests asked only that the central image be returned. Evidently the trappings of the heiau were not sacred, at least in the European meaning of the word. Or perhaps the priests, who identified Cook with their special deity, saw nothing wrong in giving him images from a heiau dedicated to Lono.

Cook's two ships had about a hundred and eighty men aboard, and they had been eating heartily at Kealakekua Bay for a fortnight. This did not diminish Kalaniopuu's good feeling. He was engaged in collecting tribute from the people of the district—ironware and hatchets bought by commoners from the ships, vegetables, kapa cloth in bundles, a large herd of hogs, and red and yellow feathers of the kind used to make cloaks and helmets. He kept the iron and about a third of the native goods, and gave the rest to Cook and King. It was a gift of astonishing generosity, far more lavish than anything they had been offered at the Friendly Islands or the Societies.

On February 3 the ships began making ready to leave. The Hawaiians wanted to keep King with them. "In all the islands," he wrote, "although they have wishd the Ships away, yet they have been desirous of Retaining Individuals, often from no better motive, than what Actuates Children, to be possess'd of a Curious play thing." If not a ship's officer, then any plaything would do. Once the observatory tent and the astronomical instruments were taken back to the *Resolution* the force of the priests' kapu disappeared from the sweet potato field. All through the day and on into the night the natives scoured the place, looking for things the Englishmen might have overlooked, and in their enthusiasm they accidentally set one or two huts on fire with a torch.

A Broken Mast

A host of canoes followed the ships as they left Kealakekua on the morning of February 4 and set sail along the coast to the north. Cook was hoping to find a more protected anchorage on Hawaii; failing that, he would head for the southeast coast of Maui where, so the natives said, there was a good harbor. All day on February 5 the canoes stayed with the *Resolution,* and Kalaniopuu sent Cook a last handsome gift of food. Rounding the west point of Hawaii on February 6, Cook sighted the shallow bay of Kawaihae. The little priest Koa, who was on board, had described this place as having a good anchorage, and he went in ahead of the ships to act as a guide for William Bligh. Bligh reported that Kawaihae offered nothing. Koa, wrote King, was "afraid of being abus'd for deceiving us, & did not return."

At Kawaihae the weather turned foul, forcing the native canoes to flee before strong offshore winds. A great many women were left aboard the *Resolution,* and they grew more and more disenchanted with life among the white men as the hours went by and the coastline slipped farther and farther away; they were leaving their families behind, they were seasick, and there was nothing they could do about any of it. Twice the *Resolution* came across canoes in difficulties and rescued the occupants, adding to the crowd already on board an old woman, four men, and a small child.

By midnight on February 7 the winds had risen to gale force and the *Resolution* was miles from shore. She was able to ride out the storm under shortened sail, but in the morning it was discovered that she had sprung her foremast. It would have to be unstepped and repaired—but where? Should Cook run before the wind and chance finding a safe harbor at one of the windward islands? Or should he try to beat back to Kealakekua? The bay there was exposed to strong winds and its food supply was probably close to exhaustion, but at least it was a familiar place, and nothing but uncertainty lay to leeward. Cook chose the devil he knew.

After the gale died down he sent the bedraggled native women ashore at Kawaihae in the ship's pinnace, and the *Resolution* turned to make her way down the coast to Kealakekua once more. At the western tip of the island she ran into a strong northward current and changeable winds, and a heavy squall drove her dangerously close to the breakers on the point. By the night of February 10, after another day spent beating to windward, she was around the point and only a mile from Kealakekua, and next morning she came into the bay and dropped anchor again close to Kekua, where she was joined by the *Discovery.*

The natives did not turn out a second time in glad welcome; in fact the bay was deserted. Cook sent off a boat and it returned with the news that Kalaniopuu had gone away, leaving the villages under a kapu. This did not seem a sufficient reason for delaying the work that had to be done on the *Resolution*. The head of the foremast was damaged and the rotted heel had a hole in it the size of four or five coconuts; it looked as if repairs would take several days of work on shore. With time to spare, Lieutenant King set up the observatory on the heiau at Kekua. Nearby the carpenters and the sailmakers went to work on the mast under the double protection of an armed guard from the ship and a kapu imposed by the priests of Lono. When Kalaniopuu returned and lifted the general kapu on the bay natives in canoes began to barter food for iron at the ships, and soon the women "were also trading in their way," as Surgeon's Mate William Ellis put it.

Things seemed normal again, but what was normal—the dignified expansiveness of Kalaniopuu, the constant helpfulness of the priests of Lono and the apparent friendliness of Kanaina and Palea, or the deviousness of old Koa and some of the chiefs? Commoners all bowed down when Cook came ashore, and the women willingly gave their bodies to the sailors, but the men stole iron from the ships and the aliis encouraged them. How could a stranger be certain about the goodwill of a people among whom one kind of behavior flowed without apparent consistency into another, turning curiosity into turbulence and near violence at Kauai, adoration into calculated theft at Kealakekua?

Cook, of course, was well aware that it must have been equally difficult for natives to fathom the intentions of white men. During an earlier voyage in the South Pacific he had reflected on this: "Its impossible for them to know our real design, we enter their Ports without their daring to make opposition, we attempt to land in a peaceable manner, if this succeeds its well, if not we land nevertheless and mentain the footing we thus got by the Superiority of our fire arms, in what other light can they than at first look upon us but as invaders of their Country; time and some acquaintance with us can only convince them of their mistake."

This sequence of events was normal in its own way, and Cook had learned how to manage it. At Kealakekua Bay, for reasons unknown, normality was stood on its head. Cook's expedition had been overwhelmed from the start not by hostility but by friendship, and although "time and some acquaintance" revealed a darker side in the character of some Hawaiians there was hardly any need to use firearms. The year before at Kauai Lieutenant John Williamson had shot a man, but that was long ago and far away. In the eighteen days of the first visit at Kealakekua, pistols, muskets, and four-pounders were fired, but without any intention of drawing blood. Earlier, on the east coast of Hawaii, some natives had seen the sailors hook a shark and finish it off with a gun; they had not reacted strongly one way or another. No one at Kealakekua had seen a man killed or even wounded by gunfire.

On the evening of Saturday, February 13, a party from the *Discovery* was getting water from the well at Kekua with the help of some hired natives, when several chiefs came up and drove the commoners away. Lieutenant King sent a marine from the observatory to the well. The commoners became "insolent" and picked up stones. King himself went to the well, accompanied by a marine armed with a musket. This time, wrote King, the Hawaiians "threw away their Stones, & upon speaking to some of the Chiefs present, the mob were driven away, & those who chose, suffer'd to assist in filling the Casks; I left . . . to meet the Capt . . . coming on shore, to whom I told what had just pass'd, he gave orders to me, that on the first appearance, of throwing stones or behaving insolently, to fire ball at the offenders. This made me give orders to the Corporal, to have the Centries pieces loaded with Ball instead of Shot."

No sooner had Cook and King gone back to the observatory than they heard musket fire from the *Discovery* and saw a canoe heading for shore at high speed, followed by a boatload of sailors pulling hard. Captain Clerke had been entertaining the young chief Palea on board. Earlier in the day a commoner had been caught trying to steal something; now a native had seized a pair of armorer's tongs and a chisel, jumped overboard, and made off with them. Muskets fired from the ship did not stop him, and his pursuer, the *Discovery*'s sailing master Thomas Edgar, was in such a hurry to lower away that he and his men left without guns or swords.

Cook and King saw the fleeing paddlers beach their canoe ahead of Edgar and run inland. They did not know quite what had happened, and they did not see the thief pass the stolen tools to another canoe; and so their hunt was hampered from the start, indeed pointless. This time Cook had no priestly escort, and the commoners, far from prostrating themselves, followed him in a jeering crowd as he and King and their two supporting marines began their futile search. Cook was at the stage of making threats. He told the natives he would fire on them if they did not produce the thief, and the crowd retreated when one of the marines raised his gun, but when Cook did not give the order to shoot they laughed. Darkness fell; Cook gave up and went back to the beach.

More bad news was waiting for him there. Edgar had got the stolen tools back from the second canoe in the shallows. Then, seeing the *Resolution*'s pinnace coming to support him, he decided to seize the thief's canoe, even though neither ship's boat was armed. As it happened the canoe really belonged to the alii Palea, who came ashore from the *Discovery* just then. Palea disclaimed any connection with the theft and tried to get his canoe back. He and Edgar came to grips, a sailor took an oar and hit Palea on the head, and within seconds the natives were hailing stones at the ships' boats and smashing oars and fittings. Most of the sailors managed to scramble safely onto some rocks, but Edgar and Midshipman George Vancouver were caught and beaten badly. Finally Palea called off his people, and as the boats' crews collected themselves Palea asked if he would be allowed to visit the ships again.

Back on the *Resolution* Cook "expressd his sorrow," according to King, "that the behaviour of the Indians would at last oblige him to use force; for that they must not he said imagine they Have gaind an advantage over us." He ordered all natives, men and women, off the ships. That night at the observatory, where a double guard was posted, a sentry heard a prowler and fired over his head to frighten him away.

Early next morning, Sunday, February 14, Captain Clerke learned that his large cutter was missing. It had been moored to a buoy close to the *Discovery* and filled with water up to its gunwales to keep the sun off. During the night natives cut the rope and spirited the boat away. Clerke went to the *Resolution* and told Cook. King, coming on board after a night at the observatory, saw a detachment of marines arming and "the Captⁿ loading his double Barreld piece." Cook was preparing to put into effect a two-edged strategy, both parts of which he had used elsewhere in the Pacific. He sent armed boats to blockade the bay and seize any canoes that tried to escape, with the idea that if the cutter was not returned he would have the canoes destroyed. As the boats moved into position one of the ships fired its four-pounders at two big canoes making for the mouth of the bay. At the same time Cook led an armed party ashore to make a hostage of the great chief Kalaniopuu. This might very well provoke the natives, but Cook was confident that they would not stand up against the fire of "a single Musquet."

King went back to the observatory and ordered his marines to load their muskets with ball and stay inside the tents. The priests of Lono, at their huts nearby, were greatly alarmed. They had seen the armed boats in the bay, and they asked anxiously if Cook meant to harm Kalaniopuu. King explained that Cook wanted nothing but the recovery of the cutter and the punishment of the thieves, and they seemed reassured.

Cook's three boats—a pinnace, a cutter, and a launch under the command of Lieutenant Williamson—made for the village of Kaawaloa at the north point of the bay. Cook went ashore there with Lieutenant Molesworth Phillips and nine armed marines. Two of the boats moved back into the shallows; the third covered the point.

Cook and his ten men made their way to Kalaniopuu's hut through a crowd of natives, who behaved respectfully enough. It was still early in the morning and Kalaniopuu had just been awakened. Cook talked to him about the theft of the cutter, and Kalaniopuu made it clear that he had nothing to do with it. Then Cook invited him to visit the *Resolution*. Kalaniopuu was willing, and they began to walk back to the beach. The chief's two young sons ran on ahead. Cook's strategy seemed to be working well.

Before Kalaniopuu reached the boats, however, Kanekapolei, one of his favorite wives and the mother of his boys, caught up with him and begged him tearfully not to go. Two chiefs took hold of him, and Kalaniopuu, looking dejected and frightened, so Phillips thought, sat down on the ground about thirty yards from the water. A great crowd had gathered—two or three thousand, Phillips estimated—and they pressed so close that the marines had no room to move. With Cook's agreement Phillips ordered his men down to the rocks at the water's edge, and they lined up there facing the crowd.

Cook urged Kalaniopuu to his feet, but the chiefs were just as insistent that the old man should stay where he was. Cook concluded that it would be best to give up his plan to take Kalaniopuu hostage. According to Phillips, he said: "We can never think of compelling him to go on board without killing a number of these People." Cook did not seem to regard his situation as dangerous, but it was certainly time to leave. As he turned to walk the few yards to the boats a native messenger from across the bay came ashore. Some sailors had fired on a big canoe trying to run the blockade at the south point, and they had killed a chief. Two Hawaiians went on board the *Resolution* to complain. Not finding Cook there, they set out to take the bad news to Kaawaloa.

The crowd's mood turned ugly in a flash; the women and children retreated; one man came out ahead of the others and menaced Cook with a stone and a long iron spike. Cook warned him off. The Hawaiian was unafraid. Cook fired the first barrel of his musket, but the charge (either small shot or blank) struck the native's heavy body mat harmlessly. Some of the crowd started to throw stones at the marines lined up at the water's edge. A chief made a pass at Phillips with a dagger, and Phillips hit him with the butt of his musket. Cook fired his second barrel, loaded with ball, and killed a man. The Hawaiians threw more stones. Cook ordered his marines to fire. After one volley they had to reload, and in the pause the Hawaiians pushed forward again. Cook turned toward the boats and was struck from behind. He swung his empty musket once and was stabbed in the back of the neck. He fell face down in the shallows, and there he was overwhelmed, stabbed and clubbed to death.

Phillips had been knocked down and stabbed too, but he managed to shoot his attacker dead and clamber on board the pinnace. Four of his marines were already dead, killed between the rocks and the boats, and the rest were struggling in the water. Phillips jumped in again to save one who was drowning. The pinnace was closest to shore; it took the survivors and pulled away; the men in the cutter kept firing. All this time Lieutenant Williamson in the launch had been out beyond the rocks. If ever there was a time to "do execution" it was now, but Williamson did not bring his boat close enough to be of real help.

The Hawaiian warriors had attacked ferociously, standing their ground under fire even after several of them were killed. It was impossible to try to take Cook's body from the beach. The boats were forced to turn about, leaving the corpse of their commander floating in the shallows.

King, down the coast at the observatory, heard the gunshots and saw the fighting. He and the priests of Lono were in consternation, and King had just repeated his assurances of friendship when Captain Clerke, watching from the *Discovery,* saw a crowd gathering at King's tents and ordered two four-pounders fired in their general direction. Fifteen minutes later King was told to strike camp and send aboard the sails that were being repaired. The *Resolution*'s foremast was still on the ground and King had only six marines to guard it. He left to confer with Clerke, and while he was gone the marines had to fire in self-defense. King hurried back. The natives were arming and several large groups were coming along the high ground from Kaawaloa. Reinforcements from the ships arrived, led by the indestructible Molesworth Phillips, and King was able to arrange a truce. He got the mast, the remaining sails, and the astronomical instruments off safely, and abandoned the heiau to the natives. By noon all the men of the shore parties were back aboard ship.

Clerke could see through his telescope the bodies of the dead being taken inland. The officers discussed their next move. They agreed to try to recover Cook's body and the stolen cutter that was the cause of the morning's carnage. King and some others urged reprisals at first, but Clerke decided on moderation. Cook's death was a disaster, and nothing would be gained by compounding it. At the very best a major battle would delay the repair of the *Resolution* and the departure of the expedition; at the worst the fearless natives might win.

Moderation on the quarterdeck was one thing, but it was hard for officers and men to keep their tempers when canoe loads of natives came out from the crowded shore and paddled up within pistol shot, shouting and making insulting gestures. King was chosen to arrange a parley. He took a small boat in under a white flag, and the priest Koa swam out to meet him. Koa was the last person King wanted to see. His record was one of deceit, and some of the men thought they had caught sight of him in the crowd that attacked Cook. Closer to the shore, a chief told Midshipman George Vancouver that Cook's body had been taken inland, but that Kalaniopuu said it would be returned. On Clerke's orders the natives were warned that if the body was not brought next morning the village would be destroyed. As King was being rowed back to his ship a native standing on a rock "had the Insolence to turn up his backside, & make other signs of Contempt," and King had to be restrained from shooting him.

That night the ships lay under double guard. Fires flared in the darkness of the hills, and unearthly "howlings and lamentations" drifted across the bay. Next morning the blowing of conch-shell horns along the cliffs signalled the arrival of more warriors. Koa came out again, without Cook's body, but with glib assurances that the chiefs were to blame for everything, and that if Clerke and King would only go ashore Kalaniopuu would settle with them. (The officers found out later that after Cook was killed Kalaniopuu had taken refuge in a cave on the cliff and was being kept alive with food let down to him on ropes.)

At night two natives, one of them a priest who had been Cook's escort, approached the ships under cover of darkness. They brought a bundle containing part of Cook's body. "Our horror will be barely conceiv'd, than can possibly be describ'd," wrote King, "when the bundle was open'd to see in it a piece of human flesh from the hind parts, this the man said was all he could get of the body; that the rest was cut to pieces & all burnt, but that the head & bones, excepting what belongd to the trunk of the body; were in the possession of Kalaniopuu, & other Chiefs, that the flesh before had been sent to Kaoo (to perform with it as we suppose some Religious ceremony,) but that he had sent it to us, as we had desir'd so ardently the body." The two men were afraid for their lives if the chiefs found out where they were and what they had done. They went ashore while it was still dark, asking anxiously when Lono would come again and what he would do to them.

A good many of the natives left the bay at sunrise, blowing their conch-shells and gesturing defiantly as their canoes passed close to the ships. One man came almost within musket shot and stood up, slinging stones and twirling Cook's hat. This was too much. Clerke ordered the four-pounders fired at the crowd still on shore. After a half dozen shots Koa came out to ask Clerke to stop. Kalaniopuu's nephew Kamehameha had been injured, others killed, he said; the chiefs were the officers' friends; there would be no more insults.

But when the *Discovery*'s watering party went ashore the natives harassed them, slinging stones from behind the protection of their huts, and darting in and out of the caves that honeycombed the hills to find rocks to roll down on the heads of the sailors. A barrage from the four-pounders did not get rid of them, and the officers decided to burn a few huts in the village where some of the stone throwers were hiding. Once the sailors got torches in their hands they did not want to stop. They set the whole village afire, including several huts belonging to King's friends, the priests of Lono, and as the natives fled they chased them, shooting some and bayoneting others. When it was over they cut off two heads and took them back to the ships as trophies. All this time, in fact ever since Cook's death, there had been native women on the ships. They watched the attack on the village with interest, and they liked the look of the flames, exclaiming that they were maikai, very fine.

Keliikea, the "rector" from the house of Lono, led about twenty natives down to the beach with white flags and peace offerings, but the sailors fired at them from the ships. Eventually the party's good intentions were honored and they made it clear how hurt they were that the priests' huts had been burned along with the others. The insufferable Koa also came out, carrying his standard offering of hogs and bananas. King ordered him to keep away and told him that if he turned up again without Cook's body he would be killed. Koa, wrote King, "minded us so little that he went where, the Waterers were, & joind some Indians, who were pelting stones, unluckily one of the Midshipmens piece mist fire, as he aim'd at him." King would have been delighted to see Koa dead.

At last the stalemate was resolved when Kalaniopuu told the aliis to give back Cook's bones. A procession with drums and white flags came down to the beach to meet Clerke and King. A chief handed over the remains, which were wrapped in kapa cloth and covered with a spotted cloak of black and white feathers. "On opening it," wrote King, "we found the Captns. hands (which were well known, from a remarkable Cut) the Scalp the Skull, wanting the lower jaw, thigh bones & Arm bone; the hands only had flesh on them, & were cut in holes, & salt cramed in; the leg bones, lower jaw, & feet, which were all that remain'd & had escaped the fire, he said were dispers'd among other Chiefs."

A few of Cook's belongings were returned—his gun, with both barrels beaten flat, and other trifles. The *Discovery's* stolen cutter, which started it all, had been taken away and burned for its iron by Palea's men, so the officers were told. Cook's sea chest of effects had already been sold among the men of his ship. (This was the usual practice after a sailor died; it was less usual in the case of a commander, but the expedition had been away from home for a long time and the men must have been running short of clothes.)

The chiefs put a kapu on the bay, the naval burial service was read, the ships' cannon were fired in salute, and Cook's bones were let down into the silent waters. As soon as the kapu was lifted the ships were surrounded by canoes, and a party of aliis came aboard to express their sorrow at what had happened and their happiness at the belated reconciliation.

The *Resolution's* foremast was in place; everything was ready for the sea. At about eight o'clock in the evening of February 22 Clerke gave orders to hoist anchor, and the two ships stood away to the open ocean. "Thus left we Kealakekua bay," wrote King, "a place become too remarkably famous, for the very unfortunate, & Tragical death of one of the greatest Navigators our nation or any nation ever had . . ."

The End of Lono

Along the shore the coconut groves remained. Well into the nineteenth century visitors were able to find trees scarred in 1779 by musket shots and cannon balls. At Kaawaloa energetic sightseers could scramble up a hill to the small heiau where Cook's body had been dismembered and burned, and in 1825 some British naval officers from the warship HMS *Blonde* marked the place with an engraved metal plate nailed to a post. At the beach almost every visitor went down to the water's edge and prospected for a small stone or two or a chip of rock from the "exact spot" where the great navigator fell. A coconut tree there was sawed off short in 1837 by a party from HMS *Imogene,* and on the stump a plate was fixed, the first of several left by British commanders. Not until the eighteen seventies was a somewhat more dignified monument, an inscribed obelisk, erected at Kaawaloa.

These observances, all arranged by Britishers, might seem unduly modest remembrances of the man whose life and death ushered the Hawaiian Islands into the modern world. The fact was that by the middle of the nineteenth century Cook's reputation had sunk very low in the place that was his last great discovery. It was a curious fate for him to have suffered, and one not altogether the fault of the Hawaiians. Natives at Kealakekua Bay and elsewhere looked back on Cook's death with a mixture of genuine sorrow and mournful relish, the kind of feeling shared by people who have survived a great catastrophe and cannot stop talking about it. They loved to point out the warrior who struck the first blow, the one who finished Cook off, and the man who, mistaking Cook's intestines for the entrails of an animal, stole them from the heiau and ate them. As late as mid-century old Hawaiians would claim to have seen Cook killed, and even after that, storytellers could command fascinated audiences for their tales of the return of Lono long ago, with his men who breathed fire and smoke from their mouths and his great masted ships that looked like floating forests. They even took the trouble in their stories to provide Cook with a native princess for a lover.

In the meantime, however, a different spirit had been at work upon the legend of Cook. A few of the more rigorous American Protestant missionaries who came to the islands in the eighteen twenties were upset by Cook's "blasphemy" in allowing himself to be venerated as a god. They found a useful parable in his death: Cook was not a properly devout Christian, but a presumptuous worm who accepted the worship of ignorant savages at the same time as he infected them with venereal disease, and for this the true God struck him down. It was a powerful and dramatic argument, and when the native historian Kamakau, a Christian convert, described the affair later in the century he picked up the refrain, adding some fine Hawaiian flourishes to the missionaries' bleak censure. Cook's entrails, wrote Kamakau, "were used to rope off the arena, and the palms of his hands used for fly swatters at a cock fight. Such is the end of a transgressor."

Traces of arid and fretful bitterness lingered on into the twentieth century, but they had faded away for the most part by 1928, and the sesquicentennial celebration of the discovery of the islands was the most amiable of affairs. Cook's supreme accomplishment as the explorer who added a hemisphere to the civilized world had always been properly valued elsewhere, and dignitaries from Great Britain, the United States, Australia, and New Zealand came by battleship to the islands for the ceremonies. Monuments were unveiled at Waimea and Kealakekua; commemorative coins were struck; pigs were cooked and eaten at elaborate luau feasts; and the first landing in January, 1778, was reenacted in a pageant staged at Waikiki, where Hawaiian beach boys in malos, or loin cloths, played warriors and the part of Cook was taken by an actor fresh from a great local success as Admiral Porter in Gilbert and Sullivan's "HMS *Pinafore.*"

In several of the speeches and papers read during the celebrations the old, sad, unanswerable question was raised again—why did the Hawaiians kill Cook? Cook's companions at Kealakekua in 1779 all had their reasons. Some thought they had seen an obscure but menacing change in the Hawaiians' attitude from the moment the ships appeared in the bay a second time. Others discounted this idea, saying that the disastrous fight at the water's edge was a sudden storm, rising out of nowhere, passing quickly, and leaving white men and natives at a loss to understand what had really happened. It was much easier to find heroes and villains among the officers on February 14 than it was to explain away the larger question of Cook's death. Molesworth Phillips came out of the affray with a fine reputation for bravery in an impossible situation. John Williamson was blamed for everything from indecisiveness and stupidity to craven cowardice, and he never managed to redeem himself: he was disgraced again after the battle of Camperdown in 1797 when a naval court of inquiry found him wanting in courage in action. But though Williamson may have let Cook die he did not kill him; the Hawaiians did, a people from whom Cook had once received adoration. Where were the heroes and villains there? Or were there any?

Without meaning to, Cook had impressed the Hawaiians as the reincarnation of one of their principal gods, Lono. Every new year Lono returned symbolically from his travels to preside over a festival called the makahiki, in which images representing Lono were paraded through each coastal district while the great chiefs collected annual taxes in produce and the commoners celebrated the fruitfulness of the earth with holidays, athletic contests, and feasting. As it happened, Cook's two major landfalls in the Hawaiian Islands came during the makahiki months. His reception at Kauai in January 1778, was reverent without being tumultuous. By the time he appeared again off Maui in November the Hawaiians had had almost a year to consider who he might be, and as the *Resolution* and the *Discovery* coasted the island of Hawaii for six weeks, stopping occasionally to collect native goods in trade, the evidence grew stronger and stronger that this was Lono. Cook came from the sea, as Lono had promised he would, and Cook's ships had tall masts and white sails, shaped very like the upright sticks and swaths of kapa cloth that were carried in the makahiki procession to announce the presence of Lono. Cook's course followed that of the main procession, which always went around the island in a clockwise direction, and he chose to put in for a long stay at Kealakekua, the home of a chief whose exploits had become part of the Lono myth and the site of an important heiau dedicated to Lono. There had never been a makahiki season like this, and the priests of Lono made the most of it.

The chiefs, however, did not have the same powerful incentive for treating Cook with veneration. Several of Cook's men caught glimpses of what Captain Clerke called "party matters" between "clergy" and "laity," and though the Englishmen did not grasp the fact of chronically divided authority between secular and sacred factions in Hawaiian society, it seemed clear to them that the priests were more affable and reliable than the chiefs (with a very few exceptions—on one side the untrustworthy priest Koa, on the other the ruler of Hawaii, Kalaniopuu, and two apparently friendly chiefs, Kanaina and Palea). For warrior chiefs, indeed, the makahiki might be nothing but a breathing space in the year, a pause to gather strength before the serious preoccupations of politics returned to center stage and the luakini heiaus or state temples could be dedicated once again to the war god Ku. The coming of Lono, then, might not impress them greatly, especially as Lono came to Kealakekua in 1779 not once, but twice. The second time was in mid-February, when the makahiki season was all but over. By then chiefs and commoners alike had had time enough to see far more humanity than divinity among Cook's men. The second time, too, Lono was in distress, and he dismantled his tall mast and white sails, just as the sticks and kapa sheets of the makahiki procession were dismantled when Lono's annual reign came to a close.

At this point in the makahiki each year a ceremony was held at the beach in which warriors took a leading part. When Lono's procession returned from its circuit of the coastal districts the ruler of the island was challenged at the water's edge by armed fighting men, and the protectors of the great chief had to ward off this attack on their master. On the day before Cook was killed Kanaina, a chief who had been friendly up to that stage, asked the ships' armorers for a pahoa, an iron dagger, as long as his arm; and another chief wanted to know if any of the officers of the *Resolution* were fighting men. Cook, the only one with a visible wound, held up his badly scarred right hand, and the chief displayed his own marks of battle. Next day Cook and his armed marines landed at Kaawaloa and menaced Kalaniopuu, great chief of the island. Across the bay at the same time a chief was killed by Cook's gunners, and another chief brought the news to Kaawaloa, where Kalaniopuu's warrior chiefs, armed with pahoas, turned a defense of their ruler into an attack on Cook, the insulter of chiefs.

It was not the Hawaiians as a people who deified Cook, but the priests of Lono. It was not the Hawaiians as a people who killed him, but the chiefs and their fighting men, devotees of Ku, the war god, acting as protectors of their ruler, Kalaniopuu, against the incursions of a god who might very well not be a god, and whose period of ascendancy was in any case drawing to an end. Cook died in a distorted realization of the symbolic conflict that marked the close of the makahiki season.

Cook could hardly have known of the delicate seasonal shifts in the balance of power between political and religious factions in Hawaiian society. But why, even so, did he allow himself to be caught on the beach at Kaawaloa without the possibility of an orderly retreat, once he gave up his plan to take Kalaniopuu hostage? He anticipated no difficulty. The day's work was hardly a routine one, but neither was it unique in his experience. He was placing his reliance on tested methods. He had used armed marines before in the Pacific to confiscate property and capture hostages, and he was accustomed to take the responsibility of leading shore parties when there was a possibility of danger.

Of course, Cook was getting older—he was in his fifty-first year, still physically strong but a little shorter of patience than he had once been, and given to more frequent outbursts of the temper for which he had always been famous. On his hurried way to Kaawaloa he should perhaps have noticed something that neither he nor any of his officers seems to have regarded as significant—he was beginning a harsh punitive action on shore, with only ten men to back him up, and without having first shown the Hawaiians of Kealakekua Bay that firearms could kill men. He had had no occasion to do this, because the scale of thefts and annoyances on his first visit there had been relatively small when set beside the overwhelming warmth of the welcome to Lono. But his officers might have been right after all—those of them, at least, who said that native blood ought to be shed early and publicly.

Even this might have been no assurance of safety. There were times in Cook's life when threats backed by the demonstrated power of gunfire produced what he wanted, but there were times when they did not, and yet other times when Cook really did not know how lucky he was. On his most recent visit to the Friendly Islands some chiefs had prepared to ambush and kill him; only a disagreement on tactics delayed them until too late. And in the Societies, just before Cook sailed north to the Hawaiian Islands, three of his men deserted and he seized a chief's family as hostages; the other chiefs planned to ambush Cook and Clerke at their bathing pool on shore, and the Englishmen escaped only because a native girl told them of the plot.

All this, of course, only throws the question of Cook's death into the wider arena of chance, but perhaps that is where it belongs. The probabilities were not altogether favorable that any Englishman of the eighteenth century would live to be fifty years of age, much less a man who between the ages of forty and fifty traveled scores of thousands of miles at sea, traversing the oceans from antarctic to arctic and going ashore in innumerable strange places peopled by savages. In the life of every great man critical junctions leading either to fame or extinction are easily found. To take three celebrated cases from Cook's own half century: Robert Clive, a lowly clerk on his way to India for the first time, was washed overboard by a wave and saved only by a miracle; Midshipman Horatio Nelson was attacked by a polar bear on the ice at Spitzbergen; and the French explorer of the Pacific who followed Cook, Jean François de Galaup, Comte de Lé Pérouse, turned down the application of a young military cadet named Napoleon Bonaparte for a place in an expedition that ended in shipwreck and death for all hands. Cook had such moments in his life. Before he went to the Pacific, before he ever had command of a ship, a gunpowder flask blew up in his hands; a worse explosion and he might have been maimed and retired from service, or even killed. On his second voyage in the Pacific he fell ill and almost died, ignominiously, of a "Billious colick." More than once in face-to-face encounters with armed natives his gun misfired, and a moment either way might have meant his life. Cook's death at Kealakekua Bay was as unlucky as could be imagined; but his life until then was filled with good fortune of all kinds. He once spoke of himself as a man "who had Ambition not only to go farther than any one had done before, but as far as it was possible for man to go." In the service of his country he found a way to do this. He died at the height of his fame, leaving his successors, as Lé Pérouse remarked, little to do but admire him.

CHAPTER TWO

Kamehameha

1779—1819

Enter Kamehameha

COOK'S SHIPS had not been gone much more than a year when the aging alii Kalaniopuu, shrunken with age and palsied by a lifetime of awa drinking, called a halt to his last nostalgic season of hula dancing and brought his retainers together for the disposition of his domains on Hawaii. He named as his political heir his son Kiwalao. To his nephew Kamehameha he entrusted the war god Kukailimoku, a feathered image with a snarling mouth full of sharp teeth. This was a fitting enough bequest. Kamehameha, at about thirty years of age, was far from handsome; James King thought he had "as savage a looking face as I ever saw." He was already an experienced fighter—tall, strong, physically fearless—and he moved in an aura of violence. Aboard ship at Kealakekua he had traded a feather cloak for several iron daggers; some of the British officers thought they saw him in at the death of their commander; they were told he was wounded in the bombardment of the beach; and he was said to have added further to his warrior's mana, his power and prestige, by claiming and keeping the hair of Captain Cook. Already he had a considerable notoriety, and he paraded it with an imperiousness that matched and even exceeded his rank as a high chief.

By descent Kamehameha was junior to Kiwalao, but on the island of Hawaii seniority was not everything. On the smaller islands to leeward, power for generations past had been in the hands of chiefs who were indisputably in the senior line of succession; but on Hawaii half a dozen large districts were controlled by various descendants of the earliest ruler, and quarrels over precedence often turned into war. If a chief's bloodlines were broadly satisfactory, skill and good fortune might raise him to great power. A division such as the one Kalaniopuu had just made was a likely occasion for strife.

Kamehameha soon showed his hand. One of Kalaniopuu's chiefs rebelled and was killed, and his body was prepared for sacrifice. Kiwalao, as the designated heir of Kalaniopuu, had the privilege of performing the ceremony at the heiau, and he laid a hog and some bananas on the altar in good form, but before he could complete the rituals Kamehameha stepped forward boldly, picked up the body of the dead chief, and presented it to the gods. This was a serious breach of decorum, to say the least, and a tremendous insult to Kiwalao. It left not much doubt that after Kalaniopuu died his successors would come to blows over their inheritance.

Kamehameha withdrew to bide his time in his home district of Kohala, and he was there when Kalaniopuu died in 1782. Kiwalao took the stripped bones of his father to be placed with the remains of other aliis in the royal burial house, Hale o Keawe, at Honaunau on the west coast of Hawaii. Kamehameha and several of his fellow chiefs from western Hawaii followed and settled watchfully at Kealakekua close by. The rivals met to drink awa and mourn the death of Kalaniopuu, but this was only ritual politeness. The heart of the matter was in the redistribution of lands which always took place after the death of an important chief, and that was what everyone was waiting for. Kiwalao's uncle Keawemauhili took affairs into his own hands and made a division, enriching himself greatly at the expense of Kamehameha and the western chiefs. Then Keoua, the younger brother of Kiwalao, dressed himself for war and attacked Kamehameha's men. The sovereignty of the island of Hawaii was at stake, and some of Kamehameha's allies deserted him for the more powerful party of Kiwalao, Keoua, and Keawemauhili.

The crisis came after a few days of inconclusive skirmishing. Kamehameha was consulting the auguries when his ally Keeaumoku encountered Kiwalao. At first things went badly for Keeaumoku. He lost several of his men, and then he himself tripped and fell. Two warriors hacked at him, but they could not kill him. Just then Kiwalao was brought down by a sling stone, and the wounded Keeaumoku crawled over and cut his enemy's throat with a shark-tooth dagger. Kiwalao was dead; his younger brother Keoua ran away; his uncle Keawemauhili was captured, but managed to escape.

This battle, fought at Mokuohai in mid-1782, established the usurper Kamehameha as a contestant for power on equal terms with his two surviving opponents, but in the four years of campaigning that followed no one gained a decisive advantage. In fact the most powerful alii in the islands during the early eighties was not on Hawaii at all, but on Maui. He was Kahekili, one of the last of the older generation of chiefs, raised in the tradition of warriors who roasted their enemies and "used the skulls of the dead for filth pots." Kahekili had always been strong enough on Maui to resist invasions from the island of Hawaii, and he added to his strength when he took the island of Oahu from his own foster-son, killed him and sacrificed him to his war god, tortured most of the Oahu chiefs to death, and left their skeletons to be built into the walls and doorways of a gruesome house of bones. By 1786 Kahekili was all powerful on Oahu; he ruled Maui and its subordinate islands of Molokai and Lanai; and he had a working agreement with his half-brother Kaeokulani on Kauai. If the islands were ever to come under one chief, it looked as though Kahekili would be the man.

The Arts of War

Kahekili, Kamehameha, and the other great chiefs fought their battles along traditional lines. The aliis first had to go through the laborious ritual of building and consecrating a luakini heiau or state temple, and when that was done they continued to consult their kahunas or priests to make sure of the best time to launch an attack. Clever and unscrupulous men might strike at night or lie in wait to ambush their opponents, and the ingenious Kahekili once won a battle simply by cutting off his enemies' water supply, but for the most part war was a very formal business. On the field the chief's advisers helped to deploy the trained warriors, usually in a crescent-shaped formation on open ground and in clusters on broken terrain. Often the campaign opened in a leisurely manner, with sacrifices, prayers, exhortations by spear-flourishing orators, and individual combat between champions, before the agreed moment of general attack. In the early stages the chiefs, resplendent in feather cloaks and helmets, directed the battle under the protection of a phalanx of warriors carrying long spears, but once the fight was fairly under way and javelins and sling stones began to break up the stylized formations, the aliis joined their near-naked subjects in sweaty, hard-breathing personal combat. At close quarters it was a war of daggers and clubs and even bare hands, and life or death depended on swiftness of hand and foot, and, in the last moments, spine-breaking brute strength.

All this was well understood. Every chief had his experts in war, seasoned fighting men who taught the young bloods of the district how to sling stones, hurl and dodge spears, and how to trip, paralyze, and strangle; and the most skillful warriors of all were great chiefs like Kahekili and Kamehameha. In peacetime exhibition fights, single combats, and mock battles kept the military skills sharp. Mettlesome men fought enthusiastically before big crowds of spectators, and deaths were not uncommon.

By the middle of the eighteenth century the predatory great chiefs were exploring the farthest reaches of their power. They had outgrown single islands and were engaging in raids between islands, campaigns that cost a great deal in men and materials. The fruits of the rites of husbandry and fertility were devoted increasingly to the service of the gods of war. Gradually but irresistibly the initiative shifted to the chiefs of the biggest islands, Hawaii and Maui. Even so, war had natural limits dictated by primitive weapons and an economy that could not survive prolonged turmoil.

When Cook came he gave the chiefs their first sight of weapons that might transform war and turn an enterprising alii into a king. The iron pahoas or daggers that Cook's armorers hammered out were coveted, even though they were only a new version of an old weapon. Firearms were the great prize, but the only guns the Englishmen left behind were those the natives took from the bodies of Cook and his murdered marines, the only cannon balls those that splintered rocks and smashed tree trunks at Kealakekua Bay. On their way westward along the Hawaiian chain for the last time the *Resolution* and the *Discovery* put in for water at Kauai and found the island in a state of civil war. The natives wanted guns, and more than once the shore parties had to use their muskets in order to keep them. Many of the Hawaiians were marked with venereal sores, and they made it clear that their delight in owning a gun would be doubled if they could get one by killing a white man.

As it happened the islanders did not have to wait long for weapons. Cook's discoveries on the northwest coast of America opened up a new trade in furs, and ships came to rendezvous and refresh at the Sandwich Islands between voyages to the hunting grounds and the market at the Chinese port city of Canton—one in 1785, several in 1786, and more every year after that. The fur traders wanted much the same things as Cook: meat, fruit, vegetables, firewood, salt, and water. The aliis, especially at Kealakekua, greeted the first of them with a strange mixture of respect and suppressed guilt over the murder of Cook, but once this uneasiness was put to rest they went ahead to bargain for guns.

Among the early traders were several who saw nothing wrong in arming one Hawaiian chief against another. They sold guns to as many factions as they could find and then encouraged them to fight. If they could peddle gunpowder adulterated with charcoal they would do it, and when they came upon an unsophisticated alii they might leave him a consignment of defective guns likely to blow up when the trigger was pulled and take off a hand or the side of a face. None of this discouraged the chiefs, who hardly needed to be taught how to settle with white men on equal terms. For several seasons on the west coast of Hawaii hogs were kapu to foreign vessels unless they were paid for in arms, and when this did not bring results quickly enough more direct methods were tried. On every island shore parties from merchantmen and warships were attacked; sailors were killed, and anchors and boats were stolen with the idea that they could be ransomed for guns and ammunition or kept so that their iron could be turned into hand weapons.

Despite these risks the ships continued to come, and more often than not, to be sure, they were able to fill their water casks and salt down their hogs without trouble. The common Hawaiian women were sublimely indifferent to politics and war, and they went out to the ships in droves, which was pleasant enough (though by the turn of the nineteenth century at least one commander was keeping them off, not because his sailors would infect the women, but because the women would infect his sailors). The native men were more devious, and among those amphibians a captain could never be certain whether a frayed hawser was cut by coral and not by a knife, or if copper sheathing which lifted and let water into the hold overnight had really worked loose by itself. When the midnight raiders were faced with their misdeeds they blamed their chiefs, and one alii was always ready to blame another. Kahekili was a master of ambiguity, and on Hawaii Kamehameha and the dashing chief Kaiana raised evasion and contradiction to a high art.

Into these troubled waters sailed the American merchantman *Eleanora,* commanded by Simon Metcalfe. At the end of January 1790, he was at Honuaula, on the island of Maui, bartering for food. One night natives killed a sailor on watch, cut loose a boat tied astern of the ship, took it ashore, and burned it for the iron fittings. Next day, when Metcalfe discovered what had happened, he turned all the native women out of his ship and shot at a trading canoe, killing or wounding a few Hawaiians. Later a man was caught swimming underneath the ship. Metcalfe wanted to hang him, but his officers dissuaded him.

Ashore, the whole district had armed, but Metcalfe saw no reason to withdraw before he was ready. He bombarded the village of Honuaula with grapeshot and then sent his men to set fire to the huts and heiaus. The *Eleanora* moved on to complete her watering farther down the coast at Olowalu, and there a chief offered to bring back the boat and the missing sailor. Metcalfe promised him a musket, eight cartridges, a bar of iron, and a piece of Bengal cloth in return for the boat, and the same for the man, but all he got was a piece of the boat's keel and a pair of stripped thighbones. Now all the officers of the *Eleanora* were in a hanging mood; it would make a good example, they thought, to string a few chiefs to the yardarm in front of their subjects. Metcalfe had a better idea. He encouraged the trading canoes to come out again, and when several score were crowded around the ship he got them all to go to starboard. Then he dropped his gun ports. The *Eleanora* carried swivels and brass guns on deck and seven cannon below, almost at water level. Metcalfe's men fired methodically. Within minutes the sea was red with blood. Honor was satisfied; Metcalfe weighed anchor and sailed for the island of Hawaii, leaving the natives to drag for their dead with fishhooks. More than a hundred natives were killed or wounded, and dozens of bodies were never found.

The *Eleanora* had a companion ship, the tiny schooner *Fair American,* commanded by Metcalfe's son Thomas. The two had lost contact some months before on the northwest coast of America. Now the younger Metcalfe had reached the islands and was looking for the *Eleanora* along the west coast of Hawaii. By chance the *Fair American* sailed into the territory of the chief Kameeiamoku, who had been beaten and insulted not long before by the high-handed Simon Metcalfe of the *Eleanora.* Kameeiamoku had sworn to revenge himself on the next foreign ship that appeared. Without knowing who Thomas Metcalfe was, and without knowing anything of the massacre at Olowalu on Maui, Kameeiamoku and his men went aboard the *Fair American* and heaved her six crewmen over the side. Thomas Metcalfe and four others, floundering in the sea, were beaten to death with canoe paddles. The lone survivor was an Englishman named Isaac Davis, a strong man and a strong swimmer. Kameeiamoku's men pulled him into a canoe, half-naked, half-drowned, half-blinded, and they were choking him to death when a chief less callous than Kameeiamoku intervened and took him ashore.

The natives stripped the *Fair American* of its guns, including a small cannon which they christened Lopaka, a Hawaiian version of the name Robert. Kamehameha, using his rank to advantage, took possession of the arms and the schooner itself. While all this was happening, the elder Metcalfe in the *Eleanora* put in a short way down the coast at Kealakekua. Kamehameha laid a kapu on the bay so that Metcalfe would not find out a foreign ship had been attacked, and when the *Eleanora*'s boatswain, the Englishman John Young, came ashore on an excursion, Kamehameha kept him there. The *Eleanora* waited a few days, firing guns every so often for Young, and finally sailed without him. Old Simon Metcalfe was killed some time later by natives of the Tuamotu archipelago in the South Pacific.

Isaac Davis and John Young attracted the attention and the calculating eye of Kamehameha. Now that he had a foreign ship, the *Fair American,* a pair of skilled seamen would be more than useful, especially since several of the other major chiefs had white men working for them by then. Young and Davis did not want to stay. At the very first opportunity they tried to escape to a visiting merchant ship. Kamehameha had them brought back, and he made sure that they were not allowed to go out on the water together again. Within a few years they were reconciled to their fate, and in time they came to prefer the islands to their home country.

The Lord of Hawaii

Kamehameha had done very well in the first Hawaiian arms race. His enemies were still strong on his home island, but all the same he felt confident enough to launch an attack on Maui. Twice in the last decade the great chief Kahekili had been able to turn back armies from Hawaii, but now he was away on Oahu. Kamehameha's judgment was sound: when his forces landed on Maui in 1790 the feathers of the war god Kukailimoku bristled and stood up straight, a good omen.

Kamehameha defeated the first army sent against him, killing its leader in personal combat. Then he took his war canoes to Kahului, where the son of Kahekili, the alii Kalanikupule, was waiting. The invaders came ashore and marched inland, pushing Kalanikupule's men back into the narrow and steep-sided valley of Iao. While women, children, and old men watched from the hills, Isaac Davis and John Young with their big gun Lopaka cannonaded the Maui army into flight. Kalanikupule escaped over the mountains and took the disastrous news to his father on Oahu.

A messenger from Kamehameha followed, carrying two stones, one black and one white. At Waikiki Kahekili read the symbols of challenge correctly: the white stone stood for peace, the black for war. "Go back," he said, "and tell Kamehameha to return to Hawaii, and when the black kapa covers Kahekili and the black pig rests at his nose, then is the time to cast stones." In fact Kahekili had no intention of letting his own death close the issue. On the contrary—he began at once to consolidate his alliance with his half-brother Kaeokulani of Kauai.

When Kamehameha went home to Hawaii it was not because he had been ordered to, but because war had broken out there. Keawemauhili, the chief who had started the troubles on Hawaii in 1782 with his grasping land division, was dead, killed by his former ally Keoua; and now Keoua was ravaging Kamehameha's lands on the east coast of the island, burning villages and destroying taro patches and fish ponds. After two fierce battles that decided nothing Kamehameha withdrew, and Keoua and his warriors and their families prepared to go home to Kau, at the south end of Hawaii.

Keoua's path took him close to the volcanic crater of Kilauea, and as his three companies entered the domain of the unpredictable goddess Pele the volcano erupted. Before Keoua and his men could make their way out of danger a terrible eruption trapped them, throwing a cloud of scorching, suffocating smoke across the sun and raining hot cinders on the bare backs of the travelers. According to an account taken from some of Keoua's men, "the rear body, which was nearest the volcanoe at the time of the eruption, seemed to suffer the least injury, and after the earthquake and shower of sand had passed over, hastened forward to escape the dangers which threatened them, and rejoicing in mutual congratulations that they had been preserved in the midst of such imminent peril. But what was their surprise and consternation, when on coming up with their comrades of the centre party, they discovered them all to have become corpses. Some were lying down, and others were sitting upright clasping with dying grasp, their wives and children, and joining noses (their form of expressing affection) as in the act of taking a final leave. So much like life they looked, that they at first supposed them merely at rest, and it was not until they had come up to them and handled them, that they could detect their mistake."

Neither the volcano nor the cannon of Kamehameha destroyed Keoua. After nine years in the field he was still far from victory, but so, it seemed, was Kamehameha. War was not their only weapon. Genealogists on both sides were always busy exalting the purity of their champion's bloodlines and deriding the mean ancestry of the enemy. At the same time Kamehameha was following the advice of his kahunas and building a new heiau for his war god at Puukohola. It was a great undertaking. All his retainers, even the senior chiefs, were set to carrying stones. His specialists designed the heiau, fixed its location to best advantage, built its stone walls, carved its images, and erected its tall kapa-covered oracle tower. Every step was accompanied by successful prayers, and when the heiau was complete down to the hole dug for the kanaka kapus, the sacrificial victims, two of Kamehameha's men went to Keoua and invited him to a parley.

Keoua accepted the ominous overture, although it is hard to see why. His preparations showed that he suspected Kamehameha might kill him. He gathered all his feather cloaks and helmets and chose his "companions in death," chiefs of high rank and old friends. Twenty-six men sailed with him on his double canoe to Kawaihae, and others followed. They came around the point into the bay to find the war canoes of Kamehameha riding in a formidable crescent offshore and his fighting men massed on the beach with their cannon and muskets. Keoua could see the storm clouds flying. Kamehameha's lieutenant Keeaumoku, the slayer of Kiwalao, advanced with a party of armed men to surround Keoua's canoe when it beached. Keoua called, "Here I am!" and Kamehameha answered, "Stand up and come forward that we may greet each other." Keoua stepped down, and Keeaumoku sank a spear into him, wounding him fatally. The warriors on shore fired their muskets, and all but two of Keoua's companions joined him in death. Keoua's body was carried to Puukohola and placed in sacrifice on the altar of Kamehameha's heiau there. Keoua's retainers mourned him: "The rain drives down from the cliffs above, the tears for my chief drop down on the heads of the people." Kamehameha had no need to weep: he was lord of the island of Hawaii.

On Oahu, Kahekili, lord of the leeward islands, decided that no better time could be chosen for the harassment of Kamehameha. He and his half-brother Kaeokulani of Kauai sailed for Hawaii, carrying with them on their war canoes a foreign gunner known as Mare Amara (Mare the Armorer), some trained dogs, and a special group of fighting men called the pahupus. Kahekili had taken his own name from a thunder god, and as a reminder of this he had tattooed one side of his body black from head to toe. The pahupus were tattooed in the same way, "with eyelids turned inside out and held up by props and only their eyeballs and teeth left in their natural state," according to a native historian. These outlandish warriors skirmished along Kamehameha's coastal lands, looting villages and defiling the graves of the island's rulers. Finally Kamehameha's canoes and ships caught up with them off Waimanu, not far from the beautiful valley of Waipio. For the first time a Hawaiian sea battle was fought in which both sides had foreign gunners—Mare Amara with Kahekili, and Isaac Davis and John Young with Kamehameha. The engagement was bloody enough to be called Kepuwahaulaula, the battle of the red-mouthed gun, but it was indecisive, and Kahekili was able to break off and withdraw safely to Oahu.

The Way to Nuuanu

During the breathing space that followed, events of the greatest importance took place on Oahu: the harbor of Honolulu was discovered by the English merchant captain William Brown, and he became the first foreigner to involve himself heavily in the affairs of the island. Brown was a fur trader and gun seller, and in one or another of his three ships he made several voyages from the northwest coast of America to the Sandwich Islands in the early seventeen nineties. Possibly in 1792, almost certainly before March 1793 (the exact date is unknown), Brown found what others had missed, and led his ships through a narrow channel on the south coast of Oahu into the safe waters of Honolulu harbor—Fair Haven, as he called it.

Honolulu was not an attractive place. Down by the sea the weather was hot, humid, and unpleasant, and the sparsely covered hinterland of the district stretched back an uncomfortable distance to cooler valleys. The beaches were indifferent, mostly mud flats and raised coral reefs. Not many common natives lived there, and the district had never really interested the great chiefs; they preferred the surfing beaches and coconut groves of Waikiki, or the rich lands of Kailua on windward Oahu. But Brown could see a commercial future for Honolulu harbor. It was the one place in the islands with a navigable channel through the reef, a protected anchorage inside, and deep water close to the shore; more than a hundred ships could ride safely there.

Brown took advantage of his discovery to make an agreement with Kahekili in which the chief "ceded" Oahu (and perhaps Kauai) in return for promises of military assistance. What Kahekili understood by a cession is not at all clear, but very likely he was prepared to give Brown the use of Honolulu harbor if Brown would help him against Kamehameha. The battle of Kepuwahaulaula in 1791 had been inconclusive. More red-mouthed cannon might settle matters, and Brown's thirty-gun frigate *Butterworth* was the biggest ship in Hawaiian waters.

Kamehameha was almost certainly thinking along the same lines when he "ceded" the island of Hawaii to Great Britain in February 1794. Captain George Vancouver, who had been at the Sandwich Islands as a midshipman with Cook, returned in command of HMS *Discovery* in the early nineties, and after prolonged discussions he was able to convince Kamehameha that it would be a good idea to put his domains under the protection of Great Britain. Vancouver took a genuine interest in the well-being of all the natives of the archipelago. He hated seeing villages laid waste by warring chiefs, and he spent some time trying, unsuccessfully, to bring Kahekili and Kamehameha together peacefully. He was also a conscientious man of empire; hence the cession of Hawaii. Kamehameha, who knew less than nothing of international law, was interested only in an alliance against his enemies to leeward. Vancouver left some cattle and sheep to breed on Hawaii, but Kamehameha wanted gifts more useful than these; as the price of the cession he demanded and got enough stores to build a fair-sized ship, and the help of Vancouver's men to do it. Vancouver refused on principle to give weapons to any Hawaiian chief, but Kamehameha insisted then and later that he had been promised an armed vessel loaded with goods as a gift from the king of England. No doubt Kamehameha wished the ship would come soon. There had been peace for three years, and war would not wait forever.

As it happened the two rival chiefs never met again. Kahekili died at Waikiki in mid-1794, leaving his son Kalanikupule on Oahu and his half-brother Kaeokulani in control of Kauai, Maui, Lanai, and Molokai. Almost at once the heirs turned on each other.

The first collision came almost by accident. Kaeokulani had been away from his home island of Kauai for some time, and he decided to pay a visit there. Kalanikupule, unsure of what was happening but suspecting the worst, went to windward Oahu where Kaeokulani's canoes would pass and dug trenches and put up earthworks ready for war. A severe battle was fought on land while Kaeokulani's canoes lay offshore. Once more foreign weapons worked devastation on the old methods of waging war: Kaeokulani's gunner Mare Amara picked off an enemy chief where he stood, feather-cloaked, directing his warriors with sweeping gestures. In the end Kalanikupule halted the fighting and the two chiefs met for a day of "mingled joy and weeping—joy for the ending of the war, weeping for the dead in battle and also for the death of Kahekili."

Kaeokulani never reached Kauai. He discovered a plot among his chiefs to throw him overboard when his canoes left the west coast of Oahu. He resolved not to die like a drowned dog. To turn aside the disaffection he proposed war against Kalanikupule. His chiefs, attracted by the prospect of loot, were ready to follow. Kaeokulani ordered his canoe fleet hauled up on shore, and an overland march on Kalanikupule began.

Kaeokulani may have been hoping for a repetition of the recent battle in which Mare Amara had shot and killed an Oahu war chief. He had only to raise his sights a little to be rid of Kalanikupule, and then he would be master of all the leeward islands. Kaeokulani pushed through the Ewa district as far as Aiea in the early part of December 1794. There he was confronted by Kalanikupule, and by the men and muskets of the Englishman William Brown. Kaeokulani was outnumbered and out-maneuvered. At the end of a day's fighting his forces scattered and fled. He and his party took to the uplands, and he might have escaped there, but his feather cloak stood out brightly, and Brown's boats inside the eastern arm of Puuloa (Pearl Harbor) fired on him, pinpointing him for Kalanikupule's soldiers. They came down on him from high ground, and there he was killed, together with his wives and warrior chiefs.

Back at Honolulu harbor Captain Brown celebrated the victory. Two of his ships, the *Prince Lee Boo* and the *Jackall,* lay at anchor close to a third foreign vessel, the *Lady Washington* of the American John Kendrick, another pioneer trader in the islands. Kendrick was the last casualty of the campaign. He was having dinner on board when the cannon of Brown's ships were fired in salute. One gun proved to be loaded; grape and roundshot smashed into the *Lady Washington,* killing Kendrick and some of his crew. Kendrick was taken ashore and buried, and the same night natives dug open the grave and stole his winding sheet.

Victory on Oahu led Kalanikupule to think of victory to windward, on Hawaii. On January 1, 1795, while his white allies were scattered, some inland and others at the harbor, the natives attacked them, killing

Brown, his second in command, and several sailors. Then Kalanikupule forced the mates of the *Prince Lee Boo* and the *Jackall* to navigate for him. With several of their shipmates dead and Brown's body stripped and slung on a pole ashore, they had not much choice. George Lamport took the *Jackall* out of Honolulu harbor, carrying Kalanikupule and his wife and about forty warriors. The *Prince Lee Boo* and a fleet of canoes followed. But instead of sailing down the coast Lamport steered abruptly out to sea, and in a few minutes crowded with violence, bravery, and luck, he and his skeleton crew seized guns and drove the Hawaiians overboard. The humiliated Kalanikupule was sent ashore ignominiously in a canoe. Lamport and the mate of the *Prince Lee Boo,* William Bonallack, headed for Hawaii, where they wrote a laconic note to John Young and Isaac Davis describing the plot and its outcome, and sailed for Canton.

Kalanikupule's military advantage was gone and Kamehameha knew it. Kamehameha himself was as strong as he would ever be. He was unopposed on Hawaii; he had a tested army and a fleet of canoes and small ships to move his warriors from island to island. In the early months of 1795 he invaded and took Maui and Molokai, and then prepared to cross to Oahu.

At this point his ally Kaiana deserted him. There had been bad blood between them for a long time. Kaiana was handsome and widely traveled, with a following and foreign arms of his own. Kamehameha might well have regarded him as a threat. What was more, Kaiana had committed adultery with Kamehameha's favorite wife, Kaahumanu. On Molokai Kaiana was systematically excluded from the war councils, and he came to think that Kamehameha's chiefs might be plotting his death. As the fleet crossed from Molokai to Oahu, Kaiana and a number of his men chose a separate course, landed on the windward side, and joined Kalanikupule.

Kamehameha took his fleet around to the leeward coast and came in over the reefs between Waialae and Waikiki, where he drew his canoes up on the sand and advanced across the plains. The Oahuans and Kaiana's men made a stand in Nuuanu valley, fighting with their faces to the sea, but even with the advantage of high ground they could not stop Kamehameha. Toward the head of the valley the hills grew steeper on either side, and at the rear the sheer drop of a thousand-foot cliff called the Nuuanu Pali prevented any orderly retreat or regrouping. The Oahuans broke, scattering along the cold and windy mountain tops, some to make their way out of Nuuanu by the highest ridges, some to find a path to safety down the dangerous trail to windward, some to leap to bloody death on the rocks at the foot of the Pali. Kaiana stood fast and was killed. Kalanikupule wandered miserably in the highlands for several months, until eventually he was cornered and put to death.

For years afterward, Hawaiians passing over the battleground of Nuuanu would point out what they called the footprints of Kaiana; they would plant their feet as he had done and stand where he had stood, as he turned to hurl his last spear into the smoke of Kamehameha's guns. From that spot they could see the valley of Nuuanu spread out below them, the harbor of Honolulu in the distance, and all the landmarks of the final victory of Kamehameha.

Reach and Grasp

Oahu after the battle of Nuuanu was a great prize, a flourishing island with well-stocked fish ponds on the lower plains and inside the reefs, and rich valleys planted in taro. For Kamehameha, however, it was little more than a stepping stone to westward, to the last big island of the chain, Kauai, which now seemed almost within reach. He readied his cannon-carrying canoes again and ordered his English carpenters at Honolulu to build him a forty-ton ship. The Britisher William Broughton, who visited Honolulu twice in the first half of 1796, tried to dissuade Kamehameha from attacking Kauai, but the king rejected his advice and asked instead for rigging and equipment to finish his new ship.

In mid-1796 the war fleet was ready. Offerings were made at the heiau of the war god Kukailimoku, whose staring eyes had witnessed all Kamehameha's victories, and in the dark of night the invaders set off for Kauai. Out in the rough channel strong winds and waves began to buffet the canoes and many were swamped and overturned. Kamehameha was forced to turn back.

Before he could mount a second attack news came from Hawaii of a revolt led by Namakeha, brother of Kaiana, the renegade chief killed at Nuuanu. The king's presence was needed at home. He decided to leave Oahu in charge of his own trusted men rather than chiefs of senior rank who might take advantage of his absence to follow the example of the rebellious Namakeha. Kamehameha sailed for Hawaii in September 1796; within a few months the rising there was crushed, its leader defeated and sacrificed.

With no pressing reason of state to take him back to Oahu, Kamehameha remained on Hawaii for six years. Everywhere along the archipelago there was peace, and time for him to perfect a government that would bridge the islands, maintain his security, and promote an orderly flow of wealth in his direction. Kamehameha approached the task in the

manner of the most sensible of conservatives. All his life he was prepared
to make changes so that things might remain the same. He drew on the
best of old and new, incorporating novelty without letting it become
heresy or anarchy. He was a devoted supporter of the old gods, a constant
builder of heiaus. He encouraged the yearly makahiki festivals, built storehouses for the harvest of tax goods, and then used his riches in lucrative
trade with foreigners. The high chiefs, possible competitors for power,
were politely invited to dwell at Kamehameha's court, under his surveillance. He gathered around him, as well, skilled and talented men and
women of every kind, beginning with his trusted advisers, his carefully
chosen wives and a handful of reliable white men, and including warriors,
canoe makers, athletes, surfers, feather workers, wood carvers, healers,
masseurs, chanters, dancers, orators, diviners, and genealogists. Over each
island he set a governor, and between Hawaii and Oahu he dispatched
canoeloads of strong paddlers under master navigators to carry saluta-
tions and commands to his appointees.

It was an impressive feat of government. There was nothing like it
anywhere in the islands of the Pàcific. And yet the independent island of
Kauai blighted the symmetry of the scheme. Upon this reminder of his
one great failure Kamehameha turned his warrior king's rage, summoning
his war gods, his fighting chiefs, and the concentrated energies of all the
subjects of his kingdom to the destruction of Kauai.

Even before his peacetime regime was well established Kamehameha
began preparations for a conclusive strike against Kauai. He came home
to Hawaii in 1796 dissatisfied with the war canoes that had sunk in the
Kauai channel, and he set his chiefs to building peleleu canoes—twin-
hulled, broad and deep, with a covered platform, some of them rigged
with a main sail and a jib. This new fleet, eight hundred vessels strong,
able to carry an army of several thousand, was five years in the making.
All this time Kamehameha's foreign carpenters were at work building him
more schooners, and from his growing trade with merchant ships he put
together a large armory of muskets and cannon. Very little was left to
chance, and if the effort was disproportionate to the possible reward this
did not matter to Kamehameha. His success had been unprecedented, but
not complete. He fiercely wanted total power, and the extension of his
wish, the peleleu fleet, was like nothing ever seen before in Hawaiian
waters.

In 1802 the armada was ready, and it left Hawaii under the com-
mand of Kamehameha, who took with him his son and heir, the small boy
Liholiho. They put ashore at Lahaina on Maui for more than a year, while
Kamehameha sent threatening messages to the ruler of Kauai, Kaumualii.
No answers came back. Kaumualii was preparing to defend his island and
then, if beaten, to take to the western Pacific in a ship being built for him

by his foreign carpenters. About the turn of the year 1804 the peleleu fleet moved on to Oahu.

In the majesty of his departure from Hawaii Kamehameha had paid no heed to the warning of a prophet: "A man-made canoe you have to sail away from Hawaii, but a god-made canoe it will be that brings you back again, and there will be a great pestilence." Then in the spring or summer of 1804 an epidemic struck with dreadful effect on Oahu. Kamehameha survived, but the disease killed many of his war leaders, chiefs, and soldiers. The victims fell quickly—a man out walking might become ill and die before he reached home—and the corpses turned black.

The epidemic was probably cholera or typhoid fever, perhaps brought by an American ship. To Kamehameha's kahunas it was clear only that the gods were angry. Offerings were prepared: hundreds of hogs, coconuts, and bananas. Three men who had broken an eating kapu had their eyes scooped out, their arms and legs broken, and at the appointed time they were killed and laid on the altar of a heiau at Waikiki. Regardless of ritual the epidemic ran its course, leaving Kamehameha's army decimated. The disaster on Oahu saved Kauai from invasion. The peleleu fleet never sailed. The expedition was called off, the dead were buried, and along the shore at Waikiki the war canoes were left to rot in the sun.

Kamehameha stayed at Oahu several years longer. He did not give up altogether his plans for the conquest of Kauai. In 1805 he bought the one hundred and seventy-five ton *Lelia Byrd* as a flag ship, and he kept carpenters, smiths, and ropemakers busy in his thatch-roofed workshops. But at the same time he let it be known that he would be satisfied if Kaumualii merely acknowledged his sovereignty in person and paid him tribute. As a practical matter, both chiefs stood to lose by war and gain by peace. Peace was profitable, war was wasteful. More and more trading ships were coming to the islands every year. Kamehameha, perhaps considering this, perhaps discouraged by his two previous failures, perhaps less obsessed with total power as he grew older, was ready to compromise. Kaumualii on his side was willing to pay tribute and even to bow to superior strength if he had to, but he was reluctant to make his acknowledgments on Kamehameha's soil, and with good reason. The last chief to accept such an invitation had been murdered while Kamehameha looked on. Delicate negotiations were begun, with canoeloads of gifts passing back and forth across the Kauai channel. In the end the aliis were brought together by an American trader, Nathan Winship. Early in 1810 his ship carried Kaumualii and his retinue to Honolulu. Kamehameha met them and escorted them to the royal compound on the beach, and after several days of celebration the diplomatic issue was broached and settled. Kaumualii would continue to govern Kauai as a tributary king under Kamehameha. So the conqueror rounded out his domains and Kaumualii escaped with his domestic rule intact, also with his life, though for a time this was threatened. A group of Kamehameha's chiefs conspired to poison Kaumualii, but Isaac Davis warned him and the thwarted plotters turned on Davis and poisoned him instead.

The Arts of Peace

For Kamehameha the agreement with Kaumualii marked the end of war and thoughts of war. He never fought another campaign, and one of his most famous decrees, Ka Mamalahoe Kanawai, kept his subjects safe from bloody and capricious death—"Let the old men, the old women, and the children sleep in safety by the roadside." Hundreds, even thousands of men had been killed in battle at his orders, but now that he was king he wanted tranquillity. He set his people the good example of hard labor in the taro patches, and his retainers had to work just as hard for him when he wanted to enjoy himself on a fishing expedition.

More than most things he seemed to relish the business of haggling with ships' captains over supplies and cargoes. His presence was not really needed in the details of bargaining with foreigners. Trade was a royal monopoly. The king normally gave permission for incoming ships to visit other islands, and he provided their commanders with "confidential men" to relay orders to his governors. In this way he could arrange simple provisioning, or the more complicated matters of ship buying and salvage, and even the transport of his own tax goods on foreign vessels. Wherever he was, though, Kamehameha immersed himself in trading, and with great gusto. A visiting ship would anchor and wait for clearance from the king's harbor masters. For merchant vessels and naval ships alike the royal guards fired their cannon in salute, and then Kamehameha came out on his platformed canoe, sometimes wearing only a loin cloth and alone except for an interpreter and a few attendants, sometimes dressed in European magnificence, seated on a gun chest with his hand on a silver sword, and surrounded by feather-cloaked chiefs and courtiers, but always with his tooth-edged calabash spittoon beside him. While his buxom queens lolled on deck or threw off their kapa dresses and swam about the ship he would discuss quantities and terms with the merchant captain. Tall, strongly built, stern faced, taciturn, Kamehameha in late middle age was a most impressive figure, a shrewd, hard trader, able to match even the sharpest New Englander; and after a bargain was struck he was not above using his royal prerogative to help himself to small things that caught his eye—mirrors, handkerchiefs, pen knives, small casks of wine, and so on.

Kamehameha was well aware of the worth of the hogs, fruit, vegetables, firewood, salt, and water his people brought to the shore at his orders, and of the miscellany of European goods they got in return. In practice much of his trading was by barter, but whenever he could take his price in Spanish dollars or other coins he did so, and he was unwilling to let this hard cash go. Toward the end of his life his closely guarded storehouses contained thousands of dollars as well as pile upon pile of Western goods. Kamehameha was in fact a persistent, even selfish accumulator, a king whose feeling for royal largesse was stunted, a great consumer only of other people's goods, food, and liquor. His only weakness as a businessman-king was his appetite for ships. His plans for the invasion of Kauai had led him to buy and build foreign vessels far beyond his normal needs, and even after he made his peace with Kaumualii, abandoning dozens of schooners to the worms rather than see them fall into other hands, he continued to be fascinated by the idea of a fleet of Western vessels.

One other trade linked ship and shore. This was the intercourse of sailors and Hawaiian women, which had been going on steadily ever since Cook first touched at Kauai and Niihau in 1778. It was a lively business, restrained only by the periodic kapus that halted all contact with the ships, occasional prohibitions by martinet captains, and a tax payable to Kamehameha, who enriched himself from every form of commerce. Husbands and fathers would bring their flower-bedecked women to the ships in canoes, or the women would swim out by themselves, naked, carefully holding their soluble kapa clothes in the air with one hand. The Hawaiians saw no particular harm in this. "The husbands and parents, not knowing that it would bring trouble," wrote the educated Hawaiian John Ii later in the century, "permitted such association with foreign men because of a desire for clothing, mirrors, scissors, knives, iron hoops from which to fashion fishhooks, and nails."

Some merchant captains deplored the way women clustered in the rigging, on deck, below decks, everywhere, and the custom arose of firing a gun at sunup to clear them from the ship and another at sunset to bring them back once the day's work was done. Philosophizing scientists attached to exploring expeditions were led to wonder whether feminine shame was an inborn human attribute or merely a European trait. Such questions did not concern common sailors greatly. They were happy enough to enjoy a few days at the islands after weeks and months on the womanless waste of the dreary ocean. Pleasant companionship made them forgetful of the time, and evenly marked watches on board were likely to dissolve alcoholically into hazy days on shore. One liberty party that failed to return to Honolulu harbor on schedule was found by officers "descending a hill near the village, each with a lass under his arm, their hats decorated with flowers, ribbons, and handkerchiefs, and a fifer and fiddler at their head, playing away merrily. They were all nearly 'half-seas over,' and were on their way to the ship when they perceived us. They insisted in a humble good-natured manner on our taking the lead; and as we were anxious to get them on board, we accordingly joined them, and marched on at their head. We had not proceeded far when the Iolani [Liholiho, son and heir of Kamehameha] met us, and he appeared so much pleased with the procession, that he fell into the ranks."

Many sailors never came back at all, and no doubt Hawaiian women were among the several powerful persuaders leading them to jump ship. Cook did not lose any of his crew this way, but a good many of the traders who followed him had trouble keeping a full roster of men. By the turn of the nineteenth century almost every district on the larger islands had a white man or two, and by 1810 several dozen foreigners were living on Oahu, especially around the harbor at Honolulu. Most were miserable loafers, human flotsam and jetsam. Some, such as the escapees from the British prison colony at Botany Bay on the east coast of Australia, had no great love for the islands, except that to them any place was better than the one they came from. Alcohol was the beachcombers' social bond. A Botany Bay man set up one of the first stills on Oahu, and, according to the resident Archibald Campbell, "it was no uncommon sight to see a party of them broach a small cask . . . and sit drinking for days" until they emptied it.

Kamehameha was understandably eager to hurry this class of men off the islands, and he encouraged captains to recruit amongst them. But he and other chiefs were always ready to make an offer to a skilled navigator, sailmaker, blacksmith, armorer, or carpenter. A good tradesman could depend on a gift of land and a native wife or two or three if he stayed. Understandably, many men preferred this arrangement to life at sea. The only thing they were giving up was civilization, and for sailors who had shipped out of the waterfront sinkholes of Britain and the United States that was no great pain.

Kamehameha's favor could be worth a great deal. John Young—called by the natives Olohana, their version of "all hands"—lived on Hawaii, near Kawaihae, where he had an estate with several white stone houses. He survived Kamehameha by a generation, and his style of life deteriorated as he got older. In his last years he contented himself with a dirty adobe house filled with rusty muskets, swords, and bayonets, and he fed his visitors goat meat and fried taro on pewter plates in a room decorated by a coffin slung from the ridge pole. But his will listed more than thirty substantial pieces of land on Hawaii and others elsewhere.

Isaac Davis, who had been with Kamehameha since 1790, apparently spent a good deal of time on Oahu after the battle of Nuuanu, and as early as 1798 he was "supreme" at Honolulu, handling all trade with visiting ships. Despite a quarrel of some sort with Kamehameha in 1808 he was allowed to keep his lands and property, and at the time of his death at the hands of the poisoning chiefs in 1810 he was a wealthy man. He lived simply in a native style house spread with mats, but nearby he had a storehouse for his European trade goods and his native cloth, mats, and feathers; and on Oahu alone four or five hundred commoners worked his lands and paid him rent.

After Davis' death Oliver Holmes, an American, impressed visitors as the most important man on Oahu next to the king. Like Davis, Holmes served as governor, and he was addressed by the natives as Alii Homo or Chief Holmes. Ever since his arrival in the islands in 1793 he had been accumulating lands on Oahu and Molokai. At Honolulu he had a hundred and eighty retainers living around him, including some to wait on table, napkin over arm, malo at the loins, as he served roast pig and roast dog to his guests. His part-Hawaiian daughters grew up to be beautiful, intelligent, and spirited, the delight and the despair of Honolulu for a generation.

Another notable foreigner at Honolulu in the early days was Don Francisco de Paula Marin, whose adventures had led him from Spain to Mexico, California, and then the islands. He spoke Spanish, French, and English. To these he quickly added Hawaiian, and for a time he served the king as interpreter and manager of trade. In his stone house near Honolulu harbor he lived with one female chief after another, sired numerous children, entertained visiting ships' captains with wine from his vineyards and highly colored stories of his past, and directed the cultivation of his lands, which included large gardens in the rear of the village and an entire small island at Puuloa (Pearl Harbor).

Davis, Young, Holmes, Marin, and many lesser known men all managed to make their accommodations with native life. All spoke Hawaiian. All had married one or more native women (Kamehameha's Welsh gardener even suffered the indignity of being cuckolded by a native, who took his wife away from him). Those whose wives were of high rank found themselves inside the kapu system with all its intricate prohibitions and permissions. Davis was a convinced thatch house dweller and poi eater, and Marin, a curious Christian who owned religious pictures bought in Canton that slid apart to reveal "subjects of a far different nature," entered at least some way into the native psychic world and began to see Hawaiian apparitions and ghosts.

Without doubt, the best place for an interested Hawaiian to look closely at the haole, the stranger or foreigner, was at Honolulu. By the turn of the nineteenth century the harbor was known all over the Pacific, and scarcely a month passed without a merchant ship beating its way around Leahi (Diamond Head) and coasting past Waikiki to drop anchor inside the reef at Honolulu, where a village of several hundred native thatch huts was springing up on the muddy beach front.

One observer of life at the port in the early days was the small boy John Ii. When he was still young he was frightened by two haoles, who said jokingly that they would take him away from his family because he was crying, but he soon lost his fears, for, as he wrote later, "there were many who constantly passed through the town from visiting ships. As he learned to associate with them, he found them pleasant. . . . Thus the boy began to lose his country ways. . . . It was customary for the children to follow the haole men, who made friends with them and took them by the hand, in the daytime. But they avoided these men at night." Sundown held no terrors for the native women; they waited impatiently for the cannon shot that signaled the start of the evening's pleasures. And as young Ii and his friends played around the harbor, sailing toy boats in the fish ponds and drawing ships in the sand, full grown Hawaiian men were signing on for voyages to Canton and the northwest coast of America.

With all this traffic back and forth Honolulu produced some strange juxtapositions of old and new. Kamehameha lounged all but naked outside a European house being built for him. Native chiefs had Western names tattooed on their arms—a visitor in 1812 saw Billy Pitt (Kamehameha's prime minister Kalanimoku), William Cobbett, Charley Fox, Thomas Jefferson, James Madison, Bonaparte, and Tom Paine at Honolulu. A Lascar tended the king's rope walk, which was laid out over an old maika or native bowling course. The American traders held Fourth of July celebrations with rockets and fireworks in the royal yam patch.

Those who looked a little more closely could see that learning was advancing well beyond the sometimes ludicrous imitations which added cartridge belts to kapa loin cloths and windsor coats to bare legs, and put beaver hats on women's heads. As a sign of the times the Hawaiians, always great gamblers, took up foreign card games and quickly became very skillful; and these same illiterate primitives, who were not generally credited with much in the way of reasoning power, drew on the experience of their traditional checkers game, konane, and could soon beat foreigners at draughts, as the "scientific amateurs" of one ship discovered when they played a tournament against Kamehameha's queens at Honolulu.

Perhaps more important, along the shore from Waikiki to Honolulu Hawaiians were working at foreign trades. While Kamehameha was on Oahu he had a smithy at Waikiki run entirely by natives, and they learned other crafts with ease. This, together with the king's appetite for foreign ships and his subjects' enthusiasm for travel all over the Pacific, moved one or two of the king's privileged haoles to try to slow down the rate of change. When Kamehameha wanted some new sails, his sailmaker Archibald Campbell asked the English carpenter Boyd to build him a loom, and Boyd refused on the ground that if the natives found out how to do everything there would be no place at the islands for foreign traders and artisans. Campbell also discovered that Isaac Davis did not want the natives to learn English, for much the same reason.

There was certainly no lack of industry about the Hawaiians. Cook and Vancouver had been most impressed by the labor that went into the irrigated taro plantations, and Archibald Campbell, who lived on Oahu for a year in 1809-1810, thought Hawaiians worked harder than any people he had ever seen. The Hawaiians themselves thought so too, reasonably enough, since most of the foreigners they encountered were beachcombers and sailors on leave. One indefatigable haole, the king's gardener William Davis, was so different from the others of his race that the natives suspected he was really a Hawaiian whose spirit after death had gone to England and returned in a foreigner's body.

The Hawaiians' capacity for work was tested and given some new outlets by the things they learned from foreigners. But hard productive labor had been the normal lot of the Hawaiian, and the port had not yet turned him into a client of the haole: the good health of agriculture was the good health of the nation. Western visitors might be impressed by Kamehameha's carefully guarded storehouses at Honolulu on Oahu, Lahaina on Maui, and Kailua on Hawaii, but the true source of wealth and strength in the islands was still the earth itself. As long as the passing seasons were observed in the old way and the makahiki festival guaranteed good times to come, any changes brought in at the ports could be seen as superficial, perhaps curious and entertaining, but easily put off like Western clothes, not touching the heart of things, which was as carefully planted in the soil as the buried navel strings and dead bones of centuries of Hawaiians.

Schäffer of Schäfferthal

In the forests of the Hawaiian Islands grew a tree that the natives called iliahi. Under the ax and the adze it yielded a yellowish aromatic timber, laau ala or fragrant wood. The Hawaiians used sticks of it to make bows for their simple stringed musical instrument, the ukeke, and they ground the heart wood into a powder and sprinkled it on kapa clothes as a perfume. Westerners recognized the iliahi as sandalwood. The Pacific traders who opened up a market in furs at Canton in the seventeen eighties found sandalwood in demand there as well, and soon afterward one or two merchant captains dropped men at the Sandwich Islands to prospect for it in the hills.

The experiment turned out badly. The first cargoes sent to Canton were of poor quality and the Chinese would not buy them. After this Hawaiian sandalwood was left alone for twenty years while the forests of several islands in the southwest Pacific were exploited. Then in 1810 three American traders, William Heath Davis and the brothers Jonathan and Nathan Winship, put together an agreement with Kamehameha under which the king granted them a monopoly of the islands' sandalwood in return for a quarter of the proceeds. The haole partners gave up their voyages to the fur grounds of the American northwest in favor of taking a convoy of sandalwood ships to Canton in 1812. There they heard the news that the United States and Great Britain had gone to war. Washington and London were thousands of miles away from the Sandwich Islands, but the War of 1812 reached into the Pacific just the same, and when the Winships came back to the islands in the fall of 1813 they found several American ships taking refuge while British men of war patrolled the open ocean. Kamehameha did not honor his contract (the Winships blamed the British for this, but Kamehameha claimed his partners had bilked him). A new arrangement with Kaumualii, ruler of Kauai, lasted no longer: Englishmen at the islands saw to that. The Winships considered using force to get their rights but in the end they gave up the idea. Their monopoly netted them hardly anything, and after the war several big American mercantile houses came to control the sandalwood trade Davis and the Winships had revived.

Neither the War of 1812 nor the new traffic in sandalwood made much difference to the pattern of ship movements in the Pacific. Traders continued to load furs and other goods on the northwest coast of America or at California; they usually wintered there and made only brief stops at the islands on the way to and from Canton. Along the American coast the old Spanish hegemony had been broken by Great Britain, the United States and Russia, and ships of all those countries were represented in the ports of the islands early in the nineteenth century. Great Britain had begun to drop behind the United States in the Hawaiian trade, but a strong sense of royal fraternity lingered in the mind of Kamehameha, dating from the time of Vancouver's visits in the seventeen nineties. Until the end of his life Kamehameha continued to alternate requests for British ships with protestations of good will for the rulers of Great Britain; and on Kauai the tributary chief Kaumualii referred to himself as King George and gave his family names from the British royal house.

Britain for brotherhood, then, the United States for trade, and Kamehameha over all. A flag of red, white, and blue stripes, with a Union Jack in one corner, was Kamehameha's royal standard. With these relationships well established, it was upsetting to find an adventurer employed by the Russians trying to take over the sandalwood trade and bring about a division of the Hawaiian kingdom. Russian ships had touched at the Sandwich Islands as early as 1804, and from time to time the possibility of a settlement had been discussed. No action was taken, however, and certainly nothing of the kind was planned officially when in 1815 Georg Anton Schäffer, a German-born doctor working for the Russian-American Company, was sent to the islands on a simple salvage mission by Alexander Baranov, chief manager of the company in Alaska. Schäffer's orders were to recover the cargo of a Russian ship wrecked on Kauai or, failing that, to get compensation from the island's ruler, Kaumualii. The instructions were quite clear, and they had quite precise limits, but once Schäffer reached Hawaii he was seized by that peculiar vision of realms and islands which was to seduce a long line of political fantasts in the Pacific during the nineteenth century.

Schäffer arrived at Kamehameha's court on Hawaii in November 1815. The plan was that he should present himself as an enquiring naturalist. Only after gaining the king's confidence was he to raise the question of salvage; then he was to try to secure trading privileges and a sandalwood monopoly for the company. In all this Schäffer succeeded for the moment. Kamehameha waved aside the cautions of John Young and the American traders and arranged for Schäffer to have the use of one of the royal storehouses at Honolulu. Kamehameha's principal wife Kaahumanu and her brother the high chief Kuakini went further, granting the Company large estates on windward and leeward, Oahu. Schäffer, sped on his way by fears that Americans might be getting ready to take his life, made a visit to Honolulu and then sailed for Kauai to transact his salvage business with Kaumualii.

Kaumualii, as it turned out, still nursed a grievance against Kamehameha. He admitted Kamehameha's overlordship, but he was an unwilling subordinate and a quiet irredentist. Schäffer himself affected to consider Kamehameha a dreadful tyrant, and this led the discontented Kaumualii to bring up the subject of a possible alliance with his newfound friend. The two disposed of the salvage case and went on to conclude an agreement promising the Russian-American Company land and a monopoly of sandalwood on Kauai. Kaumualii told Schäffer further that Maui, Oahu, Lanai, and Molokai belonged to him. If Russia would help him get them back, "he would give her half the island of Oahu, and all of the sandalwood forever, and also whatever provinces I might want to select on the other islands." This was heady talk. With the Russian flag already waving on Kauai and great things in prospect on Oahu, Schäffer sailed to Honolulu.

At once he came up sharply against John Young and the entrenched American traders. They insulted him, harassed his men, encouraged the natives to burn his buildings, and then followed him back to Kauai, where they set about to haul down his Russian flag. Kaumualii's guard had to drive them off with fixed bayonets.

Schäffer spent a good part of 1816 surveying his domains on Kauai, giving his lands Russian names (the beautiful valley of Hanalei, however, became Schäfferthal), raising fortifications, and calculating revenues from the cotton, taro, maize, sandalwood, salt, and tobacco he would harvest some day. He looked forward to approval from the Russian-American Company, but it did not come. Baranov disavowed his dealings, and when a Russian naval expedition visited the islands late in 1816 its commander, Lieutenant Otto von Kotzebue, pointedly had nothing to do with Schäffer. Von Kotzebue told Kamehameha that Imperial Russia was not responsible for Schäffer's alliance with Kaumualii, and he confirmed this by leaving the islands without visiting Kauai.

Reality was beginning to close in on Schäffer. Kamehameha knew about his alliance with Kaumualii and knew also that the scheme was not endorsed by the Russian government. Kaumualii must have been dismayed to find that his partner's political credit was not good. To make things even worse the Americans at Honolulu were busy spreading rumors of war between the United States and Russia, and they were threatening, so Schäffer heard, that if Kaumualii "did not chase the Russians from the islands there were now eight ships at Oahu to come to Kauai and kill not only every Russian but all the Indians."

In the circumstances it was surprising that Schäffer managed to hold his precarious position as long as he did. The end, when it came, was acutely embarrassing. In May 1817, before a huge crowd of natives at Waimea, Schäffer was bundled into a boat and told that he must leave Kauai. He tried to make a stand at Fort Alexander at Hanalei, but the determined Hawaiians drove the Russians off into the two company ships. Schäffer sent word to Alaska in the *Il'mena,* the sounder of his two vessels, and sailed for Oahu in the *Kad'iak,* which was leaking like a sieve.

When he reached Honolulu Kamehameha's chiefs would not let him come inside the reef. They offered safe conduct to the Russians and Aleuts aboard the *Kad'iak* if Schäffer would go as a prisoner to Hawaii. "It seemed a little early to me to be a caught fish," wrote Schäffer, "so I refused . . ." The chiefs told the Russians that anyone trying to go ashore would be shot, but finally on July 1 they relented and had the *Kad'iak* towed into the harbor, nearly running her on the reef in the process. Schäffer pro-

ceeded to enrage the Americans by flying his flag upside down on July 4 as
a signal of distress.

His distress was real enough. The *Kad'iak* was useless, and the only
friend Schäffer had at Honolulu was Captain Isaiah Lewis of the ship
Panther. Lewis owed Schäffer a debt of gratitude for medical treatment
the year before, and now he offered him an escape—passage to Canton.
With the agreement of his party Schäffer left the *Kad'iak* in charge of a
lieutenant, and on July 7 the *Panther* carried him down the coast of Oahu,
past the abandoned (indeed never occupied) company land grants. Next
day the *Panther* anchored at Waimea on Kauai and there, within sight of
valleys and rivers he had explored and named for Russia and himself,
Schäffer knew the humiliation of having to hide in his cabin so that
Kaumualii's men would not see him. On the way west to Canton Schäffer
filled his journal with fulminations against the villainy of the American
traders, but this was after the fact. For a few years more the Russians kept
up a desultory correspondence about Schäffer's Hawaiian adventure, but
for practical purposes their interest in the islands soon returned to its
normal low level. Kamehameha ruled still, Kaumualii was confined to
Kauai, and every year on July 4 the Americans at Honolulu flew their
flags and fired their rockets.

The King Is Dead

When Schäffer sailed Kamehameha had less than two years of life
left to him. He was old, and sometimes his reflections on his own rise to
power led him to think that his chiefs might be conspiring against him, but
as far as anyone could see his royal orders continued to be obeyed without
question. At his court on Hawaii he managed to make great chiefs and
high priests serve him and not themselves. And in case a chief living at a
distance should feel tempted to test the king's strength, the royal governors, whose loyalties to Kamehameha were not diminished by ties of
kinship on the islands where they served, were in a position to see that no
ambitious man put together a following of soldiers and an arsenal of
weapons. Kamehameha's son Liholiho had been named heir to the throne
when he was a small child. He had been instructed in his royal duties and
responsibilities, and now that he was a young man Kamehameha turned
over to him a good supply of arms. Kamehameha was king, and his son
was learning to be king.

Kamehameha had begun his pursuit of power as one of many chiefs bound by the sacred rituals of the kapu system; he ended as an absolute king who could make ritual work for him. The kapus served his needs admirably. Hawaiians lived in constant awareness of the presence of the gods, and the gods gave high-ranking chiefs their mana, their power and prestige. Royal incest kept the most valuable bloodlines pure, and the highest chiefs, with the authority of the gods behind them, could demand the kapu moe, prostration, from everyone. Elaborate prohibitions and regulations were enforced to make sure that superior and inferior elements in life were kept at a proper distance from each other, because only defilement and danger could result if they came in contact. So kapu pervaded all of life—politics, religious worship, sex, landholding, the cultivation and eating of food, even play. It was a fixed principle, always there, just as shadow was an inevitable part of a sunlit day. To step into the shadow to violate the kapus, even accidentally, was to forfeit the right to live.

Much as Kamehameha had benefited from his experience with Westerners, he was by no means ready to abandon his own gods. Several of his foreign visitors talked to him about the superior merits of the Christian God, and late in his reign he heard that the chiefs of Tahiti had become Christians, but in this as in most other matters Kamehameha was a practical man. As he said to one haole, he would need good evidence of the power of this god: if the Christian would jump off a cliff Kamehameha would watch to see if his god saved him.

As far as government was concerned kapu was a fine instrument of terror in the hands of an absolutist, and in comparison with its dreadfulness Western penalties, once the use of firearms was understood, must have seemed effete. Kamehameha and his fellow chiefs had seen how foreigners enforced their own laws. Cook led the first punitive expedition in the islands, and several foreigners after him killed natives in defense of property and life. Quarterdeck justice of the most elaborate sort came to Oahu as early as 1793, when the English commander George Vancouver demanded the execution of some Hawaiians who had murdered a party of men from his store ship *Daedalus* the year before. The aliis produced three victims, very likely not the killers at all, and Vancouver, who wanted to make the "ceremony" as "solemn and awful as possible," had them shot to death by a chief armed with a pistol. He then proposed to hang the bodies on a tree by the shore at Waikiki, but was told that this was very improper, and would "greatly offend the whole of the priesthood." Vancouver's spavined sense of ritual drama, apart from its offensiveness, was rudimentary compared with that of the Hawaiian kahunas, whose silent stranglings and bloody clubbings and sacrificial burials in support of the kapus had about them nothing of the merely exemplary. Vancouver was both before and after his time. Cook was long dead, and no other white man shared his aura of divinity; and it would be another two generations before Hawaiians could be brought to appreciate the spare style of a Western public hanging performed to the tune of Protestant hymns. In the meantime the haole's daily round of kickings, cursings, beatings, and whippings aboard merchant ships at the port villages struck the Hawaiians as whimsical.

In the last year of Kamehameha's life, 1819, Hawaiian society still seemed to be soundly based. Only at the ports, and most noticeably at Honolulu, was the social surface much abraded, and even there the laws of the kingdom were enforced. Kamehameha seemed well able to take what he wanted from the haole and leave the rest alone. No one could have suspected that the traditional order was on the brink of collapse; yet six months after Kamehameha died the kapu system was overthrown.

The king was at one of his favorite places, Kailua on Hawaii, when he fell ill for the last time. The great chiefs came from everywhere to attend him, the medical kahunas did their best, and when it was clear that their best was not good enough the Spaniard Don Francisco de Paula Marin was brought from Honolulu to try his skills. Nothing could save Kamehameha; he died on May 8, 1819, at about seventy years of age. His heir, Liholiho, left Kailua to escape the defilement of death, and those who remained began their ritual mourning under a special kapu while the king's body was prepared for burial. When at last the prayers were completed two of Kamehameha's old companions took his bones and buried them secretly. They did their work well; "the morning star alone knows where Kamehameha's bones are guarded."

The twenty-two-year-old Liholiho, son of the greatest Hawaiian of all, now became king with the title of Kamehameha II. He appeared before the chiefs and commoners at Kailua "in great splendor," according to the native historian Kamakau, "wearing a suit presented him from England with a red coat trimmed with gold lace and a gold order on his breast, a feather helmet on his head and a feather cloak worn over his shoulders." The high chiefess Kaahumanu, Kamehameha's favorite among his twenty-one wives, spoke to Liholiho, announcing the will of the dead king: "O heavenly one! . . . Here are the chiefs, here are the people of your ancestors, here are your guns; here are your lands. But we two shall share the rule over the land."

In this quite spectacular way Kaahumanu created for herself the new post of kuhina nui (roughly, executive officer), and placed herself at the center of political affairs. She claimed to be voicing the will of her dead husband, and whether this was strictly true or not no one gainsaid her. Her imposing presence gave her words irresistible force.

Kamehameha had in fact dissipated his absolutism somewhat in death. As well as leaving the way open for Kaahumanu to proclaim herself kuhina nui, he had decreed that his nephew Kekuaokalani should be custodian of the war god Kukailimoku. So once again formal authority was divided: the son of a king was to rule and the nephew of a king was to have charge of the war god. The feathered image of Kukailimoku had not been carried into battle for a generation, but Kekuaokalani could hardly have been unaware of the possibilities of his position; he was strong and ambitious, and he stood where Kamehameha had stood a lifetime before.

He was not the only one who had designs on Liholiho's inheritance. The young king, still unsure of his powers, was unable to resist some of the demands the high chiefs made upon him. He was allowed to keep his father's lands for the time being, but he was persuaded to surrender the royal sandalwood monopoly to the chiefs.

Kaahumanu, the kuhina nui, had even more daring things to suggest. As soon as Kamehameha died she began to urge Liholiho to abandon the kapu system. She had her reasons. Among the strictest kapus were those barring women of whatever rank from the luakini heiaus, where political as well as religious decisions were made. Thus Kaahumanu's high rank as a female chief and her special relationship to the Kamehamehas, father and son, guaranteed her a position of power, but her sex kept her from exercising that power to the utmost.

From the time of her marriage to Kamehameha, Kaahumanu had been almost ungovernable. She ran away from her husband several times, she argued with him constantly and tempestuously, and even after Kamehameha put a kapu on her body she slept with other chiefs, one of whom, a nephew of Kamehameha, paid for this transgression with his life. She was a close observer of the white man's ways and a great drinker of his liquor, and for her as for other Hawaiians liquor was a solvent of guilt. As early as 1810 she was known to be breaking the kapu on the eating of pork and shark's meat by women, even though discovery might put her life in jeopardy. Fairly clearly she had come to the conclusion by then that she need not fear the retribution of the gods, but only the penalties exacted by male chiefs on behalf of the gods, and these at last she was prepared to challenge altogether.

Faced with a tremendous decision, Liholiho hesitated. His cousin Kekuaokalani was against any change in the old ways: if the kapus fell, the war god would lose his potency. Kaahumanu was insistent. She and Liholiho's mother, a chiefess of very high rank named Keopuolani, arranged a feast at Kailua and suggested that Liholiho eat there with the women, thus breaking one of the most obvious and onerous kapus and dramatizing the overthrow of the whole system. Liholiho remained uncertain up to the last moment. While the food was being prepared he went out to sea with a boatload of liquor and drank for two days. Then, when the feast was well under way, he took the irrevocable step and ate with the female chiefs. Ai noa, free eating, was a fact; the kapu system was broken.

Liholiho sent messengers to all districts of Hawaii and to the leeward islands, ordering the heiaus desecrated and the images of the gods overthrown. Kaahumanu and Keopuolani had won; Kamehameha's prime minister Kalanimoku supported them; so, oddly enough, did the high priest Hewahewa; but Kekuaokalani, champion of the war god, resisted. The king's forces had more guns than Kekuaokalani did, and nothing could save the old religion. Kekuaokalani and his wife were killed on the battle field; Liholiho's chiefs went on to put down stirrings of rebellion in other districts, and within a few weeks peace was restored. Liholiho was still king, even though his right to rule was no longer guaranteed by the gods.

Actually, religious doubts had appeared among the Hawaiians long before 1819. Forty years passed between the time of Cook's death and the overthrow of the kapus. Most Hawaiians alive in 1819 would have been born into a world in which the haole was already a familiar figure, and, in point of fact, from the very beginning natives could be found who were willing to break the kapus to please the white man. During Cook's first visit to Kealakekua Bay commoners brought food out to his ships in the face of a kapu, and this sort of infringement continued to occur.

Women in particular became stealthy and successful breakers of the kapus. They could have all sorts of interesting and exciting experiences aboard ship, and that was enough to lead them to take risks. In the early seventeen nineties Vancouver found some of them arguing that there was really no risk: kapus could not possibly apply on ships owned by people who were outside Hawaiian law. Archibald Campbell in 1810 found the risk admitted but dismissed. He noted that although the kapus were "generally observed" at Honolulu, "the women very seldom scruple to break them, when it can be done in secret; they often swim off to ships at night during the taboo; and I have known them eat of the forbidden delicacies of pork and sharks' meat." Within the knowledge of white men, women were put to death for these offences; others were saved by the efforts of haoles; and an unknown number were never discovered in their transgressions. So, with luck, women were able to break the kapus and escape punishment whether by the gods or by the chiefs. At the same time these members of the inferior sex, condemned by kapu to a hopelessly subordinate position in society, were able to command a new source of power and influence—Western goods—more readily than men, because a woman's body was the most saleable of commodities; and this in itself was a quiet but real revolution.

The aliis themselves often had trouble deciding where kapus began and ended in connection with haoles. The picture was confused. Cook was the only early visitor treated consistently like a kapu chief, but Westerners such as Isaac Davis and John Young, who married female aliis, were placed within the kapu system and required to submit to its regulations. In the course of day to day business at the port captains who wanted to clear their ships of natives could declare a kapu, and the chiefs would see to it that the prohibition was enforced. In the same way a general kapu announced by a chief would halt all but illicit contact with the ships. One thing remained constant: the Hawaiians did not kill foreigners even when they infringed the gravest kapu. While the Englishman James Colnett was at Waikiki in 1788 his ship was crowded with natives, including the ruler of Oahu, Kahekili. At one point Colnett "took hold of the man they called their king he push'd me from him, which I laugh'd at, as a jest, the supercargo going on deck after dinner, the King was going to force himself into the Cabin, & on being told he should not, gave the Supercargo a Shove, which he return'd and the King went off much displeas'd." This insulting physical contact would have cost a Hawaiian commoner his life.

By the last years of Kamehameha's reign there was evidence of considerable disarray in the chiefs' observance of the kapus. When the Russian Otto von Kotzebue visited Honolulu in 1816 he found a common woman's body floating in the harbor. She had been killed for breaking the eating kapu; but then male and female chiefs came on board Kotzebue's ship to eat together—a most irregular arrangement, although some other prohibitions still held. The chiefs arrived well dressed and well mannered, but as it turned out they did not eat much. The pig served by the Russians had not been consecrated, and it had contaminated all other food cooked at the same fire. So the Hawaiians watched while the Russians ate, and themselves merely nibbled at biscuits, cheese, and fruit. Toasts were drunk back and forth to the Emperor of Russia and Kamehameha, and all were the best of friends. The female chiefs were at table, where they really should not have been, and they drank heavily enough to become tipsy.

On the same day, Kotzebue's naturalist Adelbert von Chamisso was allowed to enter a heiau with the chiefs and priests, remain there throughout a kapu period, and watch religious ceremonies. The happenings were familiar to Von Chamisso from the accounts of earlier explorers. What surprised him was the atmosphere of gaiety and merry making, which, he said, was so extreme as to make a European masked ball look like a funeral. Entertainments filled up the pauses between rituals; Von Chamisso reclined on a woven mat and was served baked taro and poi. He asked to inspect a feathered basket work image of a god, and when, curious, he ran his fingers over its teeth, the young man carrying it moved it suddenly to make it appear as if it had swallowed Von Chamisso's hand, and exploded in laughter when the naturalist pulled his arm back.

The same lightheartedness about serious religious matters was noticed by the merchant Peter Corney, who was an interested observer of native ways. Some chiefs told him just a few years before the overthrow of the kapus that they went to the heiau "more to feast than to pray, which I believe to be really the case"; and Corney also remarked that the common people appeared to know "nothing more about their religion than a stranger who never saw the islands." Corney thought it was more than just a playful attitude to religion he saw—it was frivolous trifling. One alii he talked to "sets the wooden gods and priests at defiance; he says, that they are all liars, and that the white-men's God is the true and only God."

Before the first Christian missionaries arrived no chief could have had a very clear idea of the white man's god. But anyone could see that the haole was wealthy and powerful and that he did not owe this happy state to his observance of the kapus. Western wealth helped Kamehameha overcome his ritual disabilities and become a king. He virtually turned a tribal society into a state. After he died a good number of the chiefs might have had dreams of taking his place, dreams that they could realize only by breaking the bounds of rank. Kekuaokalani, guardian of the war god and champion of the old ways, knew dimly what he was saying when he advocated killing all the white men in the islands as a way of keeping the old system intact. The other chiefs, perhaps, knew something of what they were doing when they abandoned the kapus. The haole offered the seductive example of the powerful man who did not need the kapu to sustain him; and the chiefs' occasional drunken flirtations with "free eating" on board foreign ships did not seem to bring down the wrath of the gods. Their conclusion might well have been that they could neglect the kapus and concentrate on amassing political power by secular means.

All the important decisions for or against the breaking of the kapus were taken by a handful of chiefs. The commoners, as usual, followed where their aliis led. Certainly the ordinary Hawaiians had good reason to be relieved when the life and death burden of religious observance was lifted, but just as certainly they did not abandon their old faith completely. Many images from the heiaus were hidden and worshipped secretly; the bones of dead chiefs in the mausoleum at Honaunau were venerated as before; the gods of fishing and planting continued to be given first fruits; Pele, the goddess of the volcano, had her devotees for decades after 1819; travelers' shrines were piled with offerings; and the spirit world of the Hawaiians was still filled with powerful supernatural beings.

The fact that the chiefs had tested the patience of the gods did not cost them the support of the commoners; whether or not the gods withdrew their approval from the chiefs ordinary Hawaiians continued long after 1819 to treat the aliis, from kings and queens down to minor chiefs, with unswerving respect. The fall of the kapus, then, was an incomplete revolution. It left relations between chiefs and commoners more or less as they had been, but changed relations between chiefs, freeing each of them to try his skill at amassing and using political power in new ways. This rearrangement suited Kaahumanu and Keopuolani because now they were emancipated women; it suited chiefs of whatever rank because there was no longer an upward limit on their aspirations.

That was how matters stood in 1819. The chiefs, however, could not see very far ahead, any more than men of other societies could, and it was not surprising that once the kapus were overthrown a number of the aliis came to fear the future. The same chief who belittled his religion in conversation with Peter Corney had terrifying dreams later on: he saw all the islands in flames, and was greatly alarmed, but was unable to find a way to escape or a place to hide from the dreadful conflagration.

CHAPTER THREE

Missionaries and Merchants

1820—1839

Go Ye Forth Into all the World

OPUKAHAIA was a Hawaiian boy born before the turn of the nineteenth century, brought up at Kealakekua Bay, and orphaned during the wars of Kamehameha. In 1809 an American sea captain offered him passage to the United States along with another island boy, Hopu. A Yale man on board ship taught Opukahaia some English, just enough to show him his terrible ignorance, and when the young Hawaiian went ashore he looked for more instruction at Yale, a tearful supplicant making a praiseworthy acknowledgment of heathen dependency upon Christian good will.

Samuel J. Mills, one of the leaders in the growing movement to send American Protestant missionaries overseas, heard about Opukahaia and got the idea of having him trained and returned home as a Christian teacher. Opukahaia was willing. He spent several years perfecting his English and then enrolled in the Foreign Mission School at Cornwall, Connecticut, a living testament to the benevolent impulses of New England Calvinists and to the transforming power of their religion. "His form, which at sixteen was awkward . . . had become erect, graceful, and dignified," wrote one of his sponsors approvingly. "His countenance had lost every mark of dullness; and was, in an unusual degree, sprightly and intelligent."

Opukahaia was an exemplary convert. He took delight in praying, publicly and privately, and wherever he went he exhorted people in the name of God. He kept a model Christian journal, translated the Book of Genesis into Hawaiian, and began to work on a Hawaiian grammar, dictionary, and spelling book. His teachers were sure that he was marked out for a useful life among his own people, but before the first Protestant mission to the Sandwich Islands could be organized he fell fatally ill with typhus. On his death bed Opukahaia admonished the students of the Foreign Mission School to love God, and he died secure in Christ, so the anxious watchers noted: "The spirit had departed—but a smile, such as none present had ever beheld—an expression of the final triumph of the soul, remained upon his countenance."

Opukahaia's "interesting death" only made the supporters of the American Board of Commissioners for Foreign Missions more eager than ever to see the Sandwich Islands evangelized as part of a worldwide program to save the heathen from himself. A good many serious-minded Protestants thought they could detect signs in the disturbed and changing world about them that the Second Coming of Christ was near, and if this was true there was no time to waste. Sinners everywhere must be confronted with the choice of accepting Christ or suffering the terrors of God's judgment.

Repent or burn—what could be more simple? The saving of souls was the important thing; complicated questions of doctrine and church organization took second place. The Lord in His divine wisdom had led the American Board to set up its headquarters at Boston, and New Englanders could not refrain from applauding the good sense of a God who saw to it that most of the men chosen for the Sandwich Islands were Yankees by birth and Congregationalists by persuasion. But the Board was generous enough to hear applications from any inspired Calvinist, whatever his formal denomination, and the first ministers ordained and set apart for the islands—Hiram Bingham of Vermont and Asa Thurston of Massachusetts—understood that they were to preach only the truths that "every good Christian" could agree upon.

Hawaiians, of course, were savages as well as sinners; the missionaries would have to civilize and save them all at once. As Hiram Bingham interpreted events, forty years of experience with white men had only confirmed the Hawaiians in vice and deepened their depravity. From now on, however, the Gospel would be the civilizing instrument, and Hawaiian civilization would be Christian civilization.

Bingham and his fellow workers were instructed to take a broad view of their mission, to aim at nothing short of covering the islands with "fruitful fields and pleasant dwellings, and schools and churches." It was assumed that in time they would create a community of saints who would accept the Law of God as the law of the land, and it was understood that this would mean social revolution; just the same the evangelists were warned by their masters at the American Board rooms not to interfere directly in politics. But what should a missionary do if, for example, he found a Hawaiian chief—whether through ignorance, weakness, or viciousness—permitting public outrages against morality that would never have been tolerated in the small towns of New England? Surely it would be difficult for a conscientious Christian to refrain from making helpful suggestions. So where was the line against intervention to be drawn, or could it be drawn at all?

When it came to the test most of the missionaries discovered in themselves a contempt for caution. For all that they liked to describe themselves as humble servants of the Prince of Peace they humbled themselves only before God, and they came to the islands prepared for war—far outnumbered, yet clothed in invulnerable self-righteousness and convinced that against the Truth they preached no enemy, however powerful or high born, could stand. Their victory was to be a bloodless one, but they were armed with the Sword of the Spirit and their minds were teeming with the images of struggle and violence in which their beloved Bible abounded. The heathen must "die to sin" and be reborn in Christ, and God would glory in the spiritual slaughter of the wicked.

The American Board's first mission to the Sandwich Islands was organized in 1819. In place of the dead Opukahaia four other Hawaiians educated at the Foreign Mission School were chosen to be sent home: Opukahaia's old shipboard companion, Hopu (who had been given the baptismal name of Thomas), William Kanui, John Honolii, and George Kaumualii, son of the ruler of Kauai. George had not yet been converted, but at least he would go back to his family with some idea of Christianity. The other three, more pious if less aristocratic, were to work with Bingham and Thurston, the ordained ministers.

The mission family also included several lay specialists. Daniel Chamberlain, the farmer, was in his late thirties, with five children. The rest were younger, some of them barely out of their teens: Elisha Loomis the printer, Samuel Ruggles and Samuel Whitney the teachers, and Thomas Holman the physician. Bingham and Thurston were just entering their thirties. Only Chamberlain was married when the call came. The American Board did not want to send unmarried workers into the field, and so the six bachelors had to make a quick search of New England for maiden ladies of high principle to share their lives on short notice. In the space of two months brides were found, the engagements were announced, the marriages performed. Then the missionaries assembled at Boston to form a church, and on October 23, 1819, they boarded the brig *Thaddeus* for the long trip around Cape Horn and across the Pacific to Hawaii—eighteen thousand miles away.

The missionaries knew the voyage would be slow and miserable. They were sure, too, that five months of seasickness in embarrassingly cramped common quarters would be only the beginning of their trials. The real struggle lay before them in the islands. Hiram Bingham knew very well what kind of place he was going to—not an earthly paradise where noble savages dwelled, but a dark and ruined land whose people were filled with "unrighteousness, fornication, wickedness, murder, debate, deceit, malignity . . . whisperers, backbiters, haters of God, despiteful, proud, boasters, inventors of evil things, disobedient to parents, without natural affection, implacable, unmerciful."

On March 30, 1820, one hundred and fifty-nine days out of Boston, the *Thaddeus* raised the snow-capped mountain peak of Mauna Kea on the island of Hawaii. Bingham and the rest were quite unable to look at Hawaiians with the eyes of Cook; for months they had been preparing themselves to see dreadful sights, and they were not disappointed. "The appearance of destitution, degradation, and barbarism, among the chattering, and almost naked savages, whose heads and feet, and much of their sunburnt swarthy skins, were bare, was appalling," wrote Bingham. "Some of our number, with gushing tears, turned away from the spectacle. Others, with firmer nerve, continued their gaze, but were ready to exclaim, 'Can these be human beings! . . . Can we throw ourselves upon these rude shores, and take up our abode, for life, among such a people, for the purpose of training them for heaven?'"

The answer was yes, though "faith had to struggle for the victory." Even so, a more immediate question was not yet answered—would the missionaries be allowed to stay? When a shore party landed and brought back the astonishing news that Kamehameha was dead and the idols overthrown, the evangelists were quick to praise God for helping to clear their way.

A king who had just disposed of one repressive religion might not, however, see the urgent need for another. Liholiho accepted the missionaries' gifts readily enough, but then he kept the company waiting several days before he made his pleasure known. Perhaps the missionaries, being Americans, would cause trouble with the British government, or they would go into business for themselves, or they would criticize Liholiho's political arrangements and his traditional incestuous and polygamous private life (he had five wives, two of them wives of Kamehameha the Great, another his own half-sister). All these things had to be considered, and then of course the chiefs had other important matters to attend to—a card game, a fishing expedition, a hula dance. In the end the king gave the missionaries permission to stay for a year on probation. It was better than nothing.

Then the question of locations arose. Kailua, where Liholiho was living for the moment, was unattractive to the New Englanders—it was lava country, hot and dry, without good land or pure water. But Liholiho was not sure he could trust the missionaries anywhere out of his sight. Foreigners seemed to like Oahu too much, he said; perhaps the Americans wanted to take the island. Finally he decided to keep some missionaries with him and let the rest go to Honolulu. Then who should go? By the vote of the mission company Asa Thurston was chosen to stay at Kailua, together with Dr. Thomas Holman, William Kanui, and Thomas Hopu. Hiram Bingham was to lead the others in setting up the Honolulu station.

During the outward voyage Bingham, by sheer personal force, had become a kind of unofficial leader among his brothers and sisters in Christ; now he had been called to the most public place in the mission scheme. The *Thaddeus* dropped anchor at Honolulu on April 14, and Bingham and his party went ashore for a day of sight-seeing in the sleepy village, with its taro gardens and fish ponds and clusters of grass huts. Bingham lost no time in taking emotional possession of his field of work, imagining "toil and privation . . . various conflicts, and probably . . . death to us, but . . . triumphs to the gospel . . ." He thought himself more blessed than Moses, who had been allowed to look upon but not enter the promised land.

The Isles Shall Wait for His Law

The first months in the promised land were difficult. Outdoor sermons preached in halting Hawaiian by Bingham and Thurston might draw a few hundred curiosity seekers, but so might the sight of the missionaries' wives doing their cooking or washing. Natives young and old came to the mission schools to see what was to be seen; some stayed, but most found the constraint of clothing and the pain of literacy unbearable, even after the benefits of Christian civilization were patiently explained to them. The example of the mission's native helpers was not altogether happy. Thomas Hopu did well, working against heavy odds, but he was no Opukahaia; neither was John Honolii; and William Kanui turned into a drunkard and had to be excommunicated from the tiny church.

All things considered, the missionaries found it hard at first to understand Hawaiians and harder still to love them. By New England standards the islanders' style of life seemed unhealthy and sluggish, and Hawaiian women in particular thought work "rather a disgrace." Yet when it came to a frivolous diversion such as a hula they would practice energetically in the hot sun for days on end. The court of Laka, goddess of the hula, was set up on the dancing ground; drums pounded, gourds rattled, singers chanted, and hundreds of dancers garlanded with green leaves and flowers and adorned with dog-tooth anklets moved endlessly to and fro in serried ranks, their bare brown flesh glistening with sweat—and there was never a sign of boredom or fatigue.

As if "lewd dancing" and public nakedness were not bad enough there was evidence of polygamy everywhere, not to mention even more upsetting sexual arrangements such as royal incest. Worst of all were the repeated stories of abortion and infanticide, appalling to the determinedly fecund mission ladies, four of whom had conceived and borne babies before the end of 1820. Then too, though the kapus were supposed to have died with Kamehameha, kahunas could still be found practicing their black arts, "praying people to death," and warning villagers that if they ignored the kapus everything would dry up for want of rain. The Christians were pleased every time heavy showers fell, but they needed allies more directly responsive than the weather.

From the beginning they had planned to enlist the aid of the chiefs. The missionaries, as good American republicans, had no interest in propping up a savage despotism based on inherited rank, and as good Christians they certainly did not believe that the soul of a chief was worth more to God than the soul of a commoner. All the same there could be nothing wrong in trying to turn the influence of powerful men and women to good purposes, provided this could be done without undue interference in politics.

The early results were mixed. Kaumualii, ruler of Kauai, was more than pleased when Samuel Whitney and Samuel Ruggles appeared at his court, bringing with them his favorite son, George. Whitney and Ruggles declined Kaumualii's offer of a chieftainship apiece and accepted instead the use of some land and the promise of protection for a mission station at Waimea. This was an excellent start. But at Honolulu, Governor Boki of Oahu went from apathy to empty amiability and back again. He was slow to give the missionaries permission to build houses, and slower still to take up serious study of the Bible. His brother Kalanimoku, prime minister of the kingdom, went to school on Hawaii with his wife and a number of young men from his train. The high chief Kuakini, Governor of Hawaii, was an attentive and intelligent scholar, but it soon became clear that he was only experimenting with Christianity as a possible substitute for the kapus, a new means of dragooning his people into obedience. Kuakini's sister, the powerful and haughty Kaahumanu, was willing to give the missionaries a little finger to touch in greeting and nothing more, so that they could not hope for help from her, at least for the moment.

The king himself, Liholiho, was such an erratic young man that it was hard to tell what he really thought about anything. He allowed the missionaries to stay on indefinitely, but then he went his own strange way. He would announce that he had to be the most accomplished scholar in the kingdom, and then he would assign intelligent young men like John Ii and David Malo to the schoolroom in his palace, telling them to do his learning for him—it would be the same thing, he said. He was unreceptive to new ideas. When the missionaries showed him his name on a piece of paper he said it looked neither like him nor any other man. Most of the chiefs were able to grasp the fact that the world was round, but Liholiho persisted in saying that it was flat, like a plain, and that sailing around the world would be like sailing around an island. He made a joke of the whole thing, warning his people to be careful of their calabashes as the earth turned over.

One of the things that made Liholiho such an unsatisfactory pupil was that he could hardly bear to stay still. When the missionaries arrived he was at Kailua on Hawaii. Six months later he decided to move to Oahu, but no sooner had he landed at Honolulu in a bedlam of barking dogs, shouting commoners, pealing ships' bells, and booming cannon, than he was off again—to the windward islands, back to Honolulu, then to Kauai, all in the course of a few months.

The king's journey to Kauai in July, 1821, was made on impulse, but at least it had a purpose. Kaumualii of Kauai had never really given the Kamehameha dynasty convincing evidence of his loyalty. Liholiho, on the spur of the moment, set out to clear up the problem. His small schooner almost foundered in the dangerous Kauai channel, but after some anxious moments he and his party arrived safely. The trip was worth the trouble. Kaumualii, without hesitating, put his island and his army at the king's disposal.

Liholiho brought Kaumualii back to Oahu with him. It was politely done, but Kaumualii was a virtual prisoner of state from then on, and soon he was put in another kind of captivity when Kaahumanu, husbandless since the death of Kamehameha in 1819, married him. Kaahumanu took Kauai further into her keeping by marrying as well one of Kaumualii's sons, a handsome young chief named Kealiiahonui who stood almost seven feet tall.

Not long after she consummated this triumphant piece of sexual diplomacy Kaahumanu fell seriously ill. Hiram Bingham's wife Sybil nursed her back to health, and she emerged much more receptive to Christian teaching—"the new Kaahumanu," as the missionaries began to call her. She made a tour of the windward islands and burned a good many carved images of the old gods that had come back into the open there. In Honolulu once more she picked up her studies, took part in the mission school examinations (where she wrote that she repented her sins), and came to church each Sunday driving a carriage pulled by a dozen natives, with Kaumualii inside and Kealiiahonui riding postilion.

All this time King Liholiho refused to be pinned down to church attendance. He would visit the missionary houses at Kawaiahao, east of Honolulu proper, utter a few encouraging platitudes, and then be off, drawn by running natives in the borrowed mission handcart, trailing dust and shouts down the road to Waikiki. When he did appear at the thatch church at Kawaiahao it was always in the midst of a cluster of noisy wives and attendants flourishing fans of imported peacock feathers; he might stay until the sermon was over, he might not.

Regrettably but obviously, Liholiho drank too much—so much, in fact, that foreigners who kept diaries at Honolulu found it simplest to note the days when the king was sober. In his cups he might limit himself to ordering some feux de joie from the battery at the fort on the harbor, or he might set off on a long carouse and be unmanageable for weeks on end. One drinking bout almost killed him. Bingham found the king in dreadful condition at his beach house at Waikiki—rigid, shaken by convulsions, bleeding from the mouth. He recovered, but for days afterward he was deranged, and he amused himself by picking up straws and presenting them with a great deal of dignity to people around him.

Sober, and in the right mood, Liholiho was capable of giving a good impression. He and the other chiefs were buying lavishly on credit from the foreign merchants of Honolulu, with the promise of payment in sandalwood, and the king's "grass palace" near the waterfront was filling up with chairs, writing desks, bedsteads, and pier glasses, in imitation of the things Liholiho and his wives found interesting or pleasant about the mission buildings. He could set a table for twenty with blue china, cut glass, and spermaceti candles, for meals of turtle soup, meat, and vegetables, washed down with fine wine. He and his court could turn out dashingly dressed in clothes fitted to them by the Western tailors of Honolulu or cut to their measurements at Canton: suits and waistcoats of satin or good broadcloth, silk stockings and elegant pumps for the men, and for the women long dresses of velvet, satin, damask, and crepe.

For the most part, however, life at the royal court was lived in traditional Hawaiian style, on the floor and without clothes. Visitors brushed aside in the course of Liholiho's drunken dashes to and from Waikiki might come upon him later at home, snoring on a mat with a pet hog stretched out beside him, a naked queen stroking his brow, the inevitable attendants singing monotonously as they fanned away the flies, and on the walls obscene drawings left by feckless white men. The king often seemed not to know what to do with himself, and his flower-bedecked, six-foot queens were even more at loose ends, lounging on luxurious piles of woven mats, diverting themselves with interminable arguments over card games, drinking great quantities of wine and spirits, fondling their pet hogs, and inspecting their lapdogs for lice.

Liholiho lived in two worlds—an old world dying, a new world being born. He did not have to rule by ritual and he did not know how to rule by law, and so he ruled by whim, alternately despotic and delinquent. A young chief was beheaded in his sleep for dallying with one of the queens; for the same offense another chief was merely banished to the island of Molokai; one unlucky commoner caught stealing was flogged through the royal fleet and then drowned in the harbor; another was dismissed with a wave of the hand.

Even a decent respect for his own position seemed to be beyond the king. Though most of the old royal ceremonies binding together the living and the dead of the Hawaiian community had fallen into disuse with the abolition of the kapus, a few days of the year kept a heightened significance. One of these was the anniversary day of the death of Kamehameha the Great, which the Hawaiians celebrated with all the pageantry they could muster. In part, of course, the observance represented a kind of yearning for the lost past, but the Hawaiians did not hesitate to add new and showy foreign elements to the ceremonies whenever such things caught their eye. The mixture of old and new reached bizarre and spectacular heights in the early eighteen twenties, and only Liholiho, son of Kamehameha and heir to his kingdom, seemed unable to find a place in the proceedings.

While preparations were under way for the celebrations of 1823, a second company of American Board missionaries from Boston arrived at Honolulu. One of the evangelists, Charles Stewart, confronted with a new experience of almost overwhelming richness and strangeness, wrote a half-shocked, half-infatuated account of what he saw.

A fortnight of activity at Honolulu began with hulas and a European style feast for several hundred guests. The climax, wrote Stewart, came with the formal processions of the final days. Kamamalu, Liholiho's half-sister and his favorite wife, was "a conspicuous object. The *car of state,* in which she joined the processions passing in different directions, consisted of an elegantly modelled *whale boat,* fastened firmly to a platform or frame of light spars, thirty feet long by twelve wide; and borne on the heads or shoulders of seventy men . . . formed into a solid body, so that the outer rows only, at the sides and ends, were seen; and all forming these, wore the splendid scarlet and yellow feather cloaks and helmets . . . The only dress of the queen was a scarlet silk pau, or native petticoat, and a coronet of feathers. She was seated in the middle of the boat, and screened from the sun by an immense Chinese umbrella of scarlet damask, richly ornamented with gilding, fringe, and tassels, and supported by a chief standing behind her in a scarlet malo or girdle, and feather helmet. On one quarter of the boat stood Kalanimoku, the prime minister; and on the other, Naihe the national orator; both also in malos of scarlet silk and helmets of feathers, and each bearing a kahili or feathered staff of state, near thirty feet in height. The upper parts of these kahilis were of scarlet feathers, so ingeniously and beautifully arranged . . . as to form cylinders fifteen or eighteen inches in diameter, and twelve or fourteen feet long; the lower parts or handles were covered with alternate rings of tortoise shell and ivory, of the neatest workmanship and highest polish. . . . Pauahi, another of the wives of Liholiho, after passing in procession with her retinue, alighted from the couch on which she had been borne, set fire to it and all its expensive trappings, and then threw into the flames the whole of her dress, except a single handkerchief to cast around her. In this she was immediately imitated by all her attendants: and many valuable articles, a large quantity of kapa, and entire pieces of broadcloth, were thus consumed. . . . It was to commemorate a narrow escape from death by fire, while an infant . . . The dresses of some of the queens-dowager were expensive, and immense in quantity. One wore *seventy-two* yards of kerseymere of double fold: one half being scarlet, and the other orange. It was wrapped round her figure, till her arms were supported horizontally by the bulk; and the remainder was formed into a train supported by persons appointed for the purpose.

"The young prince and princess [Kauikeaouli and Nahienaena] wore the native dress, malo and pau, of scarlet silk. Their *vehicle* consisted of *four field-bedsteads* of Chinese wood and workmanship, lashed together side by side, covered with handsome native cloth, and ornamented with canopies and drapery of yellow figured moreen. Two chiefs of rank bore their kahilis: and Hoapili and Kaikioewa, their stepfather and guardian, in scarlet malos, followed them as servants: the one bearing a calabash of *raw fish,* and a calabash of poi, and the other, a *dish of baked dog,* for the refreshment of the young favourites. . . .

"The king and his suite made but a sorry exhibition. They were nearly naked, mounted on horses without saddles, and so much intoxicated as scarce to be able to retain their seats as they scampered from place to place in all the disorder of a troop of bacchanalians. A body-guard of fifty or sixty men, in shabby uniform, attempted by a running march to keep near the person of their sovereign, while hundreds of ragged natives, filling the air with their hootings and shoutings, followed in the royal chase.

"Companies of singing and dancing girls and men, consisting of many hundreds, met the processions in different places, encircling the highest chiefs, and shouting their praise in enthusiastic adulations. The dull and monotonous sounds of the native drum and calabash, the wild notes of their songs in the loud choruses and responses of the various parties, and the pulsations, on the ground, of the tread of thousands in the dance, reached us even at the Missionary enclosure."

Liholiho in London

How to coax the capering king inside the missionary enclosure? The question was never answered. Late in 1823 Liholiho began to talk about a voyage to England, to see his "friend" King George IV, to discuss British-Hawaiian affairs, but mostly just to look at the world.

The missionaries thought a properly conducted tour might be very good for the king, but they wanted him to go to the United States instead. Bingham wrote that he for one would rather see the king exposed to the bracing morality of New England than have him debauched and swindled by the British. Liholiho, a convinced anglophile, was unresponsive; he decided to bypass Boston.

For the Hawaiians, who could produce tears and wails at a parting of just a few days, the king's farewell was a harrowing experience. On November 27 he went aboard his chartered ship, the British whaler *L'Aigle*, with several members of his suite, including Governor Boki and his wife Liliha, and the royal "secretary," a dwarfish Frenchman named Jean Rives who had been a member of Liholiho's train since about 1810. The king's favorite wife, Kamamalu, stayed ashore a little longer, wailing, throwing up her hands, and chanting:

> *O Heaven! O earth!*
> *O mountains and sea!*
> *O commoners and people!*
> *Farewell to you all.*
> *O soil farewell.*
> *O land for which my father suffered,*
> *Farewell,*
> *O burden that my father strived for.*
> *We two are leaving your labors.*
> *I go in obedience to your command,*
> *I will not desert your voice.*
> *I go in accordance with the words you spoke to me.*

Scores of Hawaiian seamen each year made long cruises in the Pacific on merchant ships and whalers, but for a king a voyage half way around the world seemed risky. The commoners of Honolulu, watching the masts of *L'Aigle* sink below the horizon, believed they were seeing their ruler lowered into his grave.

The missionaries could take comfort in the thought that the king's absence might actually strengthen Christianity in the islands. The chiefs who came to Honolulu to say goodby to Liholiho stayed on to discuss political affairs with their accepted leaders, Kaahumanu the kuhina nui and Kalanimoku the prime minister, both of whom were strong friends of the mission by then.

The beginnings of a new moral law soon appeared. In December a crier ordered the people of Honolulu not to work, travel, or even light fires on the Sabbath, and the orders were repeated on the other islands. A few months later Kaahumanu and Kalanimoku told chiefs and head men to see that their people observed the Sabbath, attended school and church, and in general obeyed God's word, especially as it concerned the reckless gambling that was one of the natives' great passions. The announcements were greeted with black looks and evasions in some places, but all the same the missionaries thought they could see improvements during the early part of 1824—more people at church and at school on Oahu, Maui, Kauai, and Hawaii, more requests for books from the mission press.

At least one chief took no part in these activities—George Kaumualii, son of the ruler of Kauai. George had been baptized a Christian not long after he came home from the United States, but this did not keep him from drinking and wasting time with a handful of worthless white men who lolled about his run-down estate. He was a great disappointment to his father, and when the elder Kaumualii died at Honolulu in May, 1824, he left all his lands to King Liholiho and nothing to George. Some of the Kauai chiefs argued belatedly that the old custom of settling the ownership of land in battle ought not to be pushed aside by the will of a single chief. The aggrieved George joined them in an armed attack on the government's fort at Waimea.

The rebels were beaten off, and they withdrew to George's lands at Wahiawa. Two companies of volunteers came up from Honolulu to restore the peace. They assembled at the fort, paused to honor the Sabbath, and then engaged the rebels, killing some and driving the rest into the mountains. George was found and taken prisoner a few weeks later, naked and exhausted, with nothing to sustain him but a bamboo joint full of rum. A new governor was put in charge of Kauai and most of the high-ranking rebels were taken to Honolulu. Less than two years later George fell ill there during an influenza epidemic, and he died in the throes of a dreadful nightmare of swords and devils.

The missionaries were more than pleased with the way things had turned out. The chiefs had asked for reassurance that God would consider their cause a just one, they had prayed before battle, and they had been merciful in victory (except for one lapse at the start of the campaign, when they bound a rebel leader and threw him overboard from a boat in the Kauai channel). The defeat of the rebels showed, too, that the government was strong even when the king was on the other side of the world. Then in March 1825, not long after the capture of the last dissidents on Kauai, the shocking news reached the islands that Liholiho would never come home. He and his wife were dead.

It was a disastrous end to a voyage that began uncertainly. The British government had not been given advance notice of the visit of Their Sandwich Islands Majesties, and when *L'Aigle* appeared at Portsmouth in May 1824, a personage from Foreign Minister Canning's office, the Honorable Frederick Gerald "Poodle" Byng, was hurriedly assigned to the royal party as guardian and adviser.

One look at Queen Kamamalu and Governor Boki's wife Liliha, dressed in loose trousers and velveteen bed gowns and playing whist with a pack of dirty cards, convinced Byng that it would be hard to make the Hawaiians presentable. He began by arranging new wardrobes for everybody, but by 1824 no savage, however noble, could create a furor in London by his presence alone, and not even clothes were certain to make the man. Some of the city's journalists found Liholiho handsome enough —copper colored, no darker than a quadroon or a creole. The fashionables were more cruel, describing the king as a "vulgar-looking man, perfectly black," and his wife as a "tall, fine, masculine figure."

Color, like beauty, was evidently in the eye of the beholder. The Hawaiians soon got over their first awkwardness and learned to handle public occasions without too much embarrassment, and once this happened their skins began to look lighter too. The *Times* relented and allowed them a certain simple dignity, and only a few incorrigibles persisted in making fun of the visitors. "The King's name is Dog of Dogs," wrote the aristocratic diarist Harriet Arbuthnot, "so Mr. Canning has put *Poodle Byng* about them as their chamberlain & placed their money in *Dog* Dent's bank. Very bad jokes and not very dignified in a minister, but he is very much pleased with his own wit."

King George was less than willing to submit to a social meeting with Liholiho and Kamamalu, that "pair of d—d cannibals," as he was heard to call them. A formal audience was arranged for June 21, but Liholiho did not keep the appointment. The royal party had been taken ill with measles, a serious disease for Hawaiians who had never been exposed to it. For the king and queen it was fatal. Kamamalu died on July 8. Liholiho was depressed by his wife's death, and he seemed sure that he too would die. He dictated a will, confirming a decree made before he left the islands. His throne was to go to his younger brother Kauikeaouli, last son of Kamehameha the Great, under the protection of the kuhina nui Kaahumanu and the prime minister Kalanimoku. The end came for Liholiho on July 14.

Boki took charge of the royal party. On September 11 he met King

George at Windsor Castle, and several discussions with Canning followed. Britain had at least the rudiments of a title to the Sandwich Islands, dating from Kamehameha's "cession" of Hawaii to Vancouver in 1794. Byng of the Foreign Office suggested that if Britain sent a representative there he ought not to be called a consul, because this would be an open acknowledgment of the independence of the islands. Britain, however, had never acted to ratify Vancouver's cession, and she did not do so now. A consul was duly commissioned; the independence of the Sandwich Islands was tacitly recognized.

Liholiho had asked to be taken home with his wife for burial. In the meantime their coffins lay under guard at St. Martin's Church. Rumors were heard that body snatchers coveted the royal curiosities (a dwarf's body had recently brought £100 in London, and a price of £500 was quoted for either Hawaiian). Three men skulking about St. Martin's late one night were driven off when a passerby raised the alarm, and nothing more came of the macabre story.

The ship that brought the Hawaiians to London did not carry them back again. Captain Valentine Starbuck of *L'Aigle* was dismissed and then sued by his masters for leaving the rich whaling grounds of the Pacific to carry Liholiho to Britain. Starbuck tried to enlist the sympathy of King George, but he hardly deserved a hearing. He and Liholiho's secretary, the Frenchman Jean Rives, had been dipping into the royal strongboxes. Liholiho left the islands with $25,000 in sealed chests, $3,000 was allegedly spent at Rio de Janeiro on the way up the Atlantic, and when the money was counted at London only $10,000 could be found. Rives, under a cloud for this and other peccadilloes (he was suspected of stealing Liholiho's gold watch), departed for Paris. Late in September the remainder of the royal suite embarked on a ship provided by the British government, the forty-six gun frigate *Blonde,* commanded by Lord George Byron, cousin of the poet.

In mid-April 1825, the newly appointed British consul, a merchant captain named Richard Charlton, arrived at Honolulu with word that the *Blonde* was close at hand. On May 6 she dropped anchor in Honolulu harbor, and the bodies of the king and queen were taken to funeral services at Kawaiahao Church in a procession led by twenty kahili bearers and a marine band from the ship.

The lesson of the king's life and death was not lost on the Hawaiians. Liholiho was buried by the missionaries but he had died outside the church. On the first Sabbath in June 1825, several chiefs, including Kaahumanu and Kalanimoku, requested membership in the church. This moment of humility was something the Congregationalists had waited five years to see, but even though they were eager to sport the most prestigious chiefs in the kingdom as communicants they did not admit the petitioners immediately. Instead the chiefs were placed on probation for six months.

A good many commoners followed the example of their rulers, and soon Kawaiahao Church had a hundred candidates for baptism. Hiram Bingham preached to three thousand natives each Sunday. On all the major islands the schools were crowded, and the mission press at Honolulu was working day and night. For the first time it began to look as if the future might belong to the Protestants.

Foreigners and French Priests

Not long after the visit of the *Blonde* the old white chief Oliver Holmes, a survivor of the great days of Kamehameha, died at Honolulu. All the grog shops of the town lowered their flags in memory of Holmes, who had been a steady customer, and a big crowd turned out for his funeral. Some of the missionaries from Kawaiahao were about to join the procession to the burial ground when they took a closer look at their fellow mourners and drew back: Holmes' pretty part-native daughters were being squired by their white lovers, and several other foreigners were arm in arm with "notorious prostitutes."

This was only the latest in a long series of distressing encounters between missionaries and foreigners. The evangelists had been greeted in a friendly enough way on their arrival in 1820, but they had been quick to observe—and perhaps too quick to point out publicly—that only a handful of white men among the scores at the port could have claimed respectability in New England. At Lahaina on Maui the moral climate was worse if anything, and among foreigners like the bullock hunters who lived with natives for months on end in the mountains of Hawaii the question of propriety simply did not arise.

Strictly speaking, unchurched white men were no concern of the missionaries, whose call was to the Hawaiians, but foreigners could hardly be ignored, especially since they too showed an interest in the natives. As the American merchant captain Dixey Wildes remarked, the white man's day at Honolulu was divided into three parts—drinking, gambling, and sleeping. Without a woman life was empty, and the only white women in view were missionaries' wives, so it was not surprising that many foreigners took Hawaiian mistresses. Some preferred educated half-caste girls from the mission schools, and this was as close as they ever came to acknowledging that Protestantism was a force for improvement. The missionaries hated them for it. White men who chanced to visit Kawaiahao on a Sunday were likely to be met with a blast from the pulpit aimed at drunkards, gamblers, and fornicators.

Hiram Bingham and his fellow workers did their best to save the Hawaiian women of the ports, but it was an impossible task. Not many native girls had made up their minds that they really wanted to be saved, whether from foreigners who lived at the islands or from sailors passing through. The missionaries were especially embarrassed in the spring and the fall when the northern Pacific whaling fleet put in at Honolulu and Lahaina for supplies, crowding the harbors with ships and the streets with boisterous liberty parties.

Until the middle eighteen twenties the chiefs put controls on women only as they did on other trade goods. In the mind of Governor Boki, for example, morality was not an issue: he let women board ships at Honolulu after a dollar a head was paid at the fort. But with foreign residents and sailors pulling one way, the missionaries another, and the Hawaiian chiefs in the middle, serious strife was always a possibility. It was not long in coming.

Kaahumanu and Kalanimoku began their religious probation by ordering the suppression of "vice, such as drunkenness, debauchery, theft and the violation of the Sabbath." Almost immediately the Englishman William Buckle, captain of the whaler *Daniel,* ran up against a Christian "kapu" on women at Lahaina. On an earlier visit to Maui, Buckle had been able to buy a Hawaiian girl outright from a female chief for $160, but now he and his men were denied even the hire of women. They blamed it all on William Richards, the resident missionary at Lahaina. A boatload of sailors came ashore under a black flag, armed with knives and out for Calvinist blood. Richards, barricaded in his house, spent some hours in fear for his life before friendly natives drove the *Daniel's* men back to their ship. Buckle sailed for Honolulu, and there his men marched on the missionaries' houses at Kawaiahao. The Christian chiefs turned the sailors back by threatening to lock them up in the fort, and to keep the peace hundreds of armed natives were put on the streets.

The chiefs had completed their probation with a sturdy defense of morality. On the first Sunday in December, 1825, Kaahumanu, Kalanimoku, and several others received communion at Kawaiahao for the first time. Kalanimoku's next step was to suggest that the Ten Commandments would make a good fundamental law for the kingdom.

The idea was discussed at a noisy public meeting. Kaahumanu and Kalanimoku made it clear that they wanted the law of God to bind everybody who lived in the islands. Hiram Bingham encouraged the Christian chiefs, reminding them that the King of England had told Governor Boki the Word of God was worthy of attention. The foreigners used Boki's voyage to England as a weapon against the Commandments—he had been to London, they said, he knew how things were done there. Boki became agitated, and finally he told the king he would not support him if the laws were enforced. Kauikeaouli, not yet in his teens, obviously did not know what to say or do. At last he said that he was afraid, and that it would be best to defer the laws.

The foreigners had carried their point by sheer vehemence. All the same the missionaries were convinced that it was God's purpose to establish His laws despite the "malice and rage" of the enemy. Next day at the mission printing house Elisha Loomis published the Ten Commandments in Hawaiian together with fourteen rules by which Christians could be identified, and natives crowded around his door to take the sheets wet from the press.

The missionaries found it painful to be opposed in God's work among the heathen by men who came from Christian countries. And it was even more galling to learn that they could not expect moral support from the official representatives of Great Britain and the United States in the islands. British Consul Richard Charlton and United States Commercial Agent John Coffin Jones hated each other cordially, but they hated the mission more.

An appointment to a village in the middle of the Pacific was hardly a plum in the British consular service, and it would have been too much to look for a man of superior talent at Honolulu, but by any standard, and especially from a missionary point of view, Richard Charlton was a miserable choice. He suffered from an ingrained hostility to the United States, and he spun wild fantasies about the alleged secret political purposes of the American Protestant mission. He was rough, obtuse, foul-mouthed, and choleric; he advocated temperance and drank to excess; he was a fornicator; he was chronically litigious; he menaced white men with pistols or had his bully boys beat them; he lassoed a Hawaiian and dragged him along the ground for a mile behind his horse; he threatened other natives with flogging or beheading; he spoke wildly of killing Kaahumanu and tearing down the fort at Honolulu; he gratuitously and publicly accused a British merchant of sodomy, and when he was convicted of slander he broadened the accusation to include the jurymen; he horsewhipped a newspaper editor; he slaughtered trespassing cows and chickens without mercy. For two decades he laid about him savagely and clumsily at Honolulu, and from the wreckage of his personal life he constructed huge and baseless diplomatic causes. The strange thing was that the British Foreign Office allowed him to go on like this for so long. When at last the Hawaiian government succeeded in having him removed he departed leaving his consular archives in shambles, his illegitimate offspring unprovided for, and in the courts of Honolulu a major case of land litigation, one of the most involved and acrimonious in all Hawaiian history.

The New Englander John Coffin Jones, by contrast, impressed the missionaries as a pleasant young man when he arrived at the islands in 1821. But the favorable impression did not last. Jones was an agent of the Boston firm of Marshall & Wildes as well as United States Commercial Agent. Business was bad at Honolulu during the eighteen twenties; the sandalwood trade was coming to an end and whaling had not yet taken up the slack. Jones, who happened to be a Unitarian, concluded that Calvinism was at the bottom of his financial troubles. He began writing home to Marshall & Wildes about "canting, hypocritical missionaries" who stood in the way of good profits. Honolulu was a doomed place, where "nothing but the sound of the church going bell is heard from the rising to the setting Sun and religion is cramed down the throats of these poor simple mortals whilst certain famine and destruction are stareing them in the face." Work and grace were obsessive themes with Jones: many of the chiefs were heavily in debt to Marshall & Wildes and would not pay, and Hannah, the oldest and most attractive of the daughters of Oliver Holmes, alternately shared Jones' bed and deserted him for Christ.

In January 1826, the first American warship to visit the islands arrived at Honolulu: USS *Dolphin,* commanded by Lieutenant John "Mad Jack" Percival, who had orders to investigate the Hawaiian chiefs' indebtedness to American traders. He did nothing to settle that complicated question, but he managed to add to the missionaries' troubles by advocating a free trade in women.

Percival found a Christian "kapu" on women in effect at Honolulu, and no matter how hard he tried he could not convince the chiefs that civilized countries allowed prostitution. The chiefs consulted the missionaries, the missionaries quoted the Bible, the chiefs kept women away from the *Dolphin,* and after two months of deprivation the *Dolphin*'s men became unruly.

On Sunday, February 26, a crowd of sailors surrounded Kalanimoku's stone house, where Hiram Bingham was getting ready to hold divine service. They demanded women, and to lend point to their demand they smashed all the windows in the building. Bingham left hastily for his home at Kawaiahao. Some natives joined him there just as the sailors caught up with him. He lifted his umbrella to ward off a blow from a club, and the female chief Lydia Namahana put out her arm to help him and was hit. At that the Hawaiians threw themselves on the sailors. They knocked several down and seized and bound others. Bingham had to stop one overenthusiastic native from braining a fallen seaman with a rock. Finally Lieutenant Percival and his officers arrived and caned their men into silence.

Percival locked up the ringleaders and made some muted apologies for the riot, but then he asked the chiefs again to lift the kapu on women.

This time Governor Boki yielded and his fort commander, Manuia, supported him. Once again boatloads of women passed back and forth in the harbor, and the downcast Christians set aside a day to fast and pray that Percival would see the light.

The chiefs were not sure how far they could go in resisting evil. They put guards on the streets immediately, and by the beginning of April they felt strong enough to overrule Boki and reimpose the kapu. There was no more rioting, perhaps because the sailors found ways to get around the prohibition. At a dinner for the chiefs Percival read a passage from the Bible about Solomon, who was a wise man with a thousand wives; in private he tried to persuade one of Oliver Holmes' daughters to live with him. Finally, to the unbounded relief of the missionaries and the chiefs, the *Dolphin* sailed on May 11, leaving the Christians of Kawaiahaö to count their losses.

A second American naval commander came to Honolulu later in 1826: Lieutenant Thomas ap Catesby Jones of USS *Peacock*. Jones had orders to clean up the rat's nest of beached sailors at Honolulu. Once he had got this salutary operation under way he looked into the question of the chiefs' long-standing debts to American traders. For years the chiefs had been buying all sorts of luxury goods and contracting to pay in sandalwood. Now the big stands of sandalwood were disappearing, but the debts remained. On December 27 the chiefs acknowledged debts amounting to fifteen thousand piculs of wood, worth between $120,000 and $160,000. The burden of collecting more wood passed as a matter of course to the commoners, under a new tax law.

Jones took advantage of his stay at Honolulu to sign an informal treaty of commerce and friendship with the chiefs. He had no authority to do this, and his home government did not ratify the convention, but the chiefs willingly observed the terms of these "articles of agreement" for a good many years.

Ever since the unfortunate visit of Lieutenant Percival the Christians had been working to recover their influence. Governor Kaikioewa of Kauai, Governor Hoapili of Maui, and Governor Kuakini of Hawaii were building churches or otherwise encouraging their people to attend to the word of God, and in mid-1826 Hiram Bingham and Kaahumanu toured Oahu together with two or three hundred followers, telling natives in the rural districts about the Ten Commandments.

At their general meeting in September the missionaries agreed that although they could not interfere in politics, they could properly give the chiefs advice and information about the laws and political institutions of Christian countries. In October they published a circular discussing the aims and principles of the mission, the rights of chiefs, and the duties of subjects under a government based on Christian morality.

They were inviting a confrontation. At Honolulu the foreigners rose excitedly to the bait. Lieutenant Jones of the *Peacock* was in town; he would make a good independent judge. Jones, at a public meeting on December 8, listened to all sides of every question in dispute, and then announced that he found the mission's circular "full and fair." Both before and after he left the islands Jones repeated his general approval of the missionaries, and the Christians made the most of this, but of course as soon as the *Peacock* sailed things went back to where they had been.

In July 1827, French Catholic missionaries arrived at Honolulu, adding another disturbing element to the volatile situation there. The idea for a Catholic mission dated from the time of Liholiho's voyage to London. When Jean Rives left the royal party in disgrace and went to Paris he began to drum up support for a French settlement in the islands, where, so he claimed, he was a person of great importance. With the help of the Ministry of Foreign Affairs and the Bureau of Commerce and Colonies an expedition was outfitted, consisting of several "agriculturists" and six missionaries from the order of the Sacred Hearts of Jesus and Mary, three of them ordained priests under Father Alexis Bachelot.

Rives was not at Honolulu to smooth their way. He had taken another ship out from Europe. On the California coast he learned that he was no longer welcome in the islands, and he never came back to Honolulu. This put the Catholics in a bad position. They landed without permission from Kaahumanu, who sent for Governor Boki to put them back on board their ship, the *Comète*. But Boki was away in the country, and by the time he reached Honolulu the *Comète* had sailed, leaving the Catholics ashore.

Even one active Catholic in the islands would have been enough to upset the Protestant missionaries. Hiram Bingham wrote at once for advice from his superiors at the American Board rooms in Boston. In the meantime the Congregationalists preached against "idolatry" and began work on a Hawaiian language geography book designed to point out the relative progress of various parts of the world under Protestantism and Catholicism.

The fall whaling season of 1827 followed closely on the arrival of the Catholics. At Honolulu native women went on board ship as usual. On Maui Governor Hoapili, a good Christian, did his best to keep the port of Lahaina clean, but some women flouted his orders and visited the English whaler *John Palmer*. Her captain, an American named Elisha Clarke, was detained ashore by Hoapili, and before he was released his men fired half a dozen cannon at the village. Two shots fell, hardly by accident, close to the house of the missionary William Richards.

The *John Palmer* went on to Honolulu. She was joined there by the *Daniel*, whose captain, the Englishman William Buckle, had crossed swords with Richards two years before over the question of women. Since then Richards had written home to the United States about Buckle and his purchase of a Hawaiian girl, and the letter had found its way into a New York newspaper. Buckle was furious: Richards, he said, was accusing him of slave owning and piracy. Most of the foreigners at Honolulu agreed that the letter should never have been published, and British Consul Charlton fell into one of his ready made rages on behalf of Buckle.

The chiefs asked Richards to come to Honolulu, and the whole business was thrashed out. Charlton wanted to send Richards to England for trial. Money, said the consul, could never salve the wounds of Captain Buckle; libeling missionaries ought to be pilloried or chained to a block for ten years. Buckle wanted Richards to swear an oath to the contents of the published letter; Richards said he had not seen the newspaper and could not guarantee the accuracy of the version that appeared there. He wrote Buckle a conciliatory note and got an angry answer. The chiefs heard everybody out, decided that in fact Buckle had bought the Hawaiian girl for $160 (though she now claimed she went with him willingly), and dismissed the charges against Richards. Levi Chamberlain, the Protestant mission's secular agent at Honolulu, a quiet, sensible man with a genius for understatement, remarked that perhaps the brethren should be more careful before they made public observations about public characters.

The chiefs stayed at Honolulu to take up once again the question of a fundamental moral law for the kingdom. They drafted some regulations and showed them to Bingham to make sure that they conformed with God's will. Six crimes were proscribed: murder, theft, adultery, prostitution, gambling, and the sale of liquor. Governor Boki, who had a vested interest in all but the first two activities, was strongly against the laws. Richard Charlton wanted the text sent to England for approval. Kaahumanu suggested that Governor Kuakini of Hawaii should go to London and talk with King George. Boki said, accurately enough, that King George would not be interested in seeing Kuakini; besides, the British had left law making to the chiefs.

After more discussion the chiefs decided to impose only the laws against murder, theft, and adultery. On December 17 a crowd gathered in a coconut grove by the waterfront at Honolulu to hear the proclamation. Bingham opened the meeting with a prayer but left before the laws were read, so that the missionaries would not be accused of stage managing the occasion. The decrees against selling liquor, gambling, and prostitution (the ones that would involve foreigners most directly) were postponed; they were to be studied by the common natives with the aid of handbills printed at the mission press.

The Troubles of Boki

Among the high chiefs of the eighteen twenties the young alii Boki was something of an odd man out. On the face of things there was no reason for this. He had been chosen as Governor of Oahu by Kamehameha the Great himself. His voyage to England had given him immense prestige; chiefs and commoners listened respectfully to his tales of high life in London. On formal occasions at Honolulu he shone, portly but handsome, in the full dress uniform of a British major general, and he saw to it that his retainers were well supplied with colorful clothes. He was generous with patronage, and with land, to the point of giving away tracts that belonged to other people. Best of all, Boki was close to King Kauikeaouli. The two went everywhere together—to church whenever they felt like it, on sandalwood cutting expeditions, on sailing jaunts between islands, up to the quiet retreat of Manoa valley behind Honolulu for drunken hula parties, down to the billiard saloons and grogshops of the waterfront.

It seemed almost as if Boki could have anything he wanted. But he could never decide just what it was that he wanted. Life had dealt him an unkind blow in making him a chief of a junior line, forced to live in the shadow of his older brother Kalanimoku. After 1819 there was no need for him to brood over this—the kapus no longer operated. Just the same, the memory of the heavy primeval ban weighed on Boki. He was free, and yet he could not feel free. So he became a chronic malcontent for whom the times were perpetually out of joint. At every moment he felt himself pulled in several directions, and he could never settle on a consistent course of action. So he frittered away his life, paying less attention than he should have to the governorship, running himself deeply into debt as a merchant and sugar planter, toying with Protestantism, then giving it up as too much trouble and becoming, mostly out of perversity, the protector of the Catholic priests at Honolulu. As one of the chiefs put it, in the earthy Hawaiian idiom, Boki was a calabash of poi that fermented, turned sour, pushed off the lid, and overflowed.

The danger was that Boki might make political trouble, and the problem seemed more real than ever early in 1827. Kalanimoku was dying, and his death might touch off a crisis. Boki might try to dislodge Kaahumanu from the regency and turn his personal influence over the king into control of the kingdom.

Kalanimoku died in February, and immediately rumors were heard in Honolulu that Boki was massing armed men at the fort. But he could not nerve himself to act. The issue came into the open at a meeting of the chiefs, and Kaahumanu quickly made it clear that it was she who ruled. A question was raised about a state visit to Hawaii. Boki wanted to go, Kaahumanu challenged him, and he knuckled under. "It is with you—if you wish to go—go and take along the king and his sister," he said. "It is with you to exercise authority. Kamehameha at his death committed his son to your charge & the kingdom to your care—and it was the wish of Kalanimoku that you should still have the charge. The mana is yours."

Kaahumanu was determined to exercise her mana on behalf of Protestant morality. A few months later she charged Boki, his wife Liliha, and several members of the king's train with misconduct, intemperance, fornication, and adultery, and had them fined—just a few days after the facile Boki had told Levi Chamberlain that he wanted to turn to the pono (the good) and that the king had acquired a Christian teacher.

What kind of pono Boki had in mind he did not say. For the rest of 1827 and throughout 1828 he attended Mass with the French priests, and in general stood between them and Kaahumanu, who wanted them removed. In fact it was only Boki's quiet support that made it possible for them to stay in the islands. He was moving farther and farther outside the circle of Protestant chiefs and their missionary advisers, and any tactic that might embarrass the government was potentially useful to him.

Kaahumanu continued on her Christian way. Early in 1829 she went to Honaunau on the west coast of Hawaii, to the crowded burial house of Hale o Keawe, where she took the bones of the ancient chiefs from their netted baskets and set fire to the debris, all in the name of her new god, and had the bones re-buried with a Christian service. At the same time the foreigners at Honolulu heard that she was going to poison Boki, unseat the king, and place either the king's half-sister Kinau or Kinau's son on the throne. Boki was busy spreading his own rumors; he went around telling the foreigners that the Christian chiefs were plotting to kill every white man in the islands. In April the foreigners heard that Boki was getting ready to attack Kaahumanu when she came back from the windward islands.

This was one story that was true. Boki was assembling his men at Waikiki. He had the king with him, and he also had in his possession the mana-laden bones of two ancient chiefs, Liloa and Lonoikamakahiki. The high chief Kekuanaoa tried unsuccessfully to get him to give up his plans for war. Then Hiram Bingham, stretching (not for the first time) the American Board's injunction against interference in politics, arranged a meeting with Boki and the king at Boki's Blonde Hotel, a dive like the others in downtown Honolulu where "noisy swine gathered . . . drunken-

ness and licentious indulgence became common, and people gathered . . .
for hulas and filthy dances."

In these uncongenial surroundings Bingham tried to calm Boki down.
It was surprisingly simple. Once more Boki found himself unable to translate his mixed ambitions into action, and Bingham left him willing enough
to put aside the sword he had never really unsheathed. Later, Boki and the
king joined Kaahumanu in a "social cup of tea" at Bingham's house. "The
king being desirous to use his good voice in singing," wrote Bingham, "we
sang together . . . not war songs, but sacred songs of praise to the God of
peace."

All well and good, but within a few months Boki disturbed the peace
again. This time he got noisily drunk and tried to persuade Princess
Nahienaena to marry her brother the king. Levi Chamberlain overheard
Boki's incoherent outburst: "Three native schooners arrived from Lahaina this morning. . . . They were met by Boki who had been drinking;
and he said to the Princess do you kill Kaahumanu & all her family & take
your brother for a husband. . . . If you and your brother marry and have a
child he will be the rightful heir to the kingdom. The princess replied,
What you say is foolish.—Boki took her by the ear to pull her along
saying what did you come down here for; did you come down as a god to
be worshipped?—He endeavoured to separate her from her attendants
in order to retain her into the house alone with the king. . . . She however
got out of the hands of the Governor and went to the house of some of the
other chiefs."

The king and his sister, in fact, had slept with each other as early as
1824, according to reports that reached Elisha Loomis. The foreigners of
Honolulu came to take the incestuous union for granted. Once the question came up at the dinner table of an American merchant who was
entertaining Charles Stewart, a former missionary turned naval chaplain.
Stewart, who had known the princess when she was a little girl, was told
that Kauikeaouli and Nahienaena were "mutually and strongly attached,
and that they themselves and all the chiefs wished a marriage to take place
between them, according to former usages in the royal family, but were
prevented by the missionaries: adding that the ceremony, however might
as well be performed, for, it was well known, that they were already living
in a state of licentiousness and incest!

"As you may readily imagine," wrote Stewart, "the boldness of this
assertion, which I was persuaded was utterly false, caused me to drop my
knife and fork, with a surprise bordering on indignation; and to demand . . .
whether Mr.—— believed the assertion to be true? To which he replied,
'most assuredly nothing is more notorious—everybody knows it!' while
two other Americans at the table, corroborated the charge with the strongest asseverations."

The Christian chiefs denied the scandalous talk, and most of the missionaries were content to think of the king and the princess as they appeared at the dedication of a new church building at Kawaiahao, a huge thatch hut with a floor area of more than twelve thousand square feet. During the inaugural services Kauikeaouli and Nahienaena joined in the singing of the Hundredth Psalm and offered spontaneous prayers, much to the gratification of the Christians.

In September 1829, Kaahumanu ordered all couples in the islands who had not been married in a Christian ceremony to dissolve their alliances, whether native and native or native and foreigner. This would have been a blow to many important people—Kauikeaouli, Nahienaena, Boki, and Liliha included, not to mention United States Commercial Agent Jones, who was involved just then in a three-cornered menage with Hannah Holmes and Lahilahi, one of the daughters of Don Francisco de Paula Marin. But before any action was taken the attention of the town was diverted by an explosion from British Consul Charlton.

Charlton was a great legalist on matters of his own property rights, if not those of others. Any straying cow that wandered onto Charlton's land risked death, but his own cattle grazed everywhere. At last, in October 1829, a native annoyed by a trespassing cow of Charlton's took a gun, chased the animal, caught up with it on a common, and shot it dead. The chiefs offered to assess damages if the native proved to be in the wrong, but Charlton wanted vengeance. He and John Coffin Jones hunted down the cow killer, put a noose around his neck, and dragged him behind a horse to the village.

Charlton puffed up the case into a general windy complaint that foreigners' lives and property were always in danger at Honolulu, and he threatened to take the matter to the British government unless the chiefs put things right. He got forty-five of his fellow Britishers to sign a paper supporting him, and sixteen illiterates added their marks. The chiefs' answer came quite soon, in the form of an edict printed for them at the mission press. Charlton was offered no sympathy at all. His cow, the chiefs pointed out, had trespassed on clearly marked property; his angry handling of the Hawaiian had been rash and criminal; the laws of the islands, previously published, held for foreigners as well as natives.

While the "cow case" was still being discussed an American war ship, USS *Vincennes,* arrived. Its commander, Captain W. C. B. Finch, carried a letter addressed to the chiefs from the Secretary of the Navy, praising the Hawaiians for their progress toward civilization through Christianity. Finch could not have come at a better time, and the missionaries and the Christian chiefs glowed at the happy accident that brought him to Honolulu just when they needed him.

Some of the glow faded when Finch re-opened the question of the sandalwood debts. According to the American merchants a great deal of wood had been harvested in the hills since the visit of the *Peacock* in 1826—about twenty-five thousand piculs altogether. But the chiefs disregarded their debts and squandered their new wealth on new purchases. At Finch's insistence the king, Boki, and four other chiefs signed two fresh notes, one for 4,700 piculs, representing the balance of the debt owed since 1826, and the other for 2,165 piculs, an amount they owed for a ship bought in 1828.

The *Vincennes* agreements bound Boki very tightly, and sandalwood was not his only problem. He lived high, he gambled heavily, and his various business enterprises—a sugar plantation in Manoa valley, trading voyages to ports around the Pacific, dry goods stores and taverns in Honolulu—were doing poorly.

Life, in fact, was on the verge of becoming unbearable for Boki. He was over his head in debt; the Christian chiefs, coached by Bingham, were openly contemptuous of him; Kaahumanu stood in the way of his political ambitions; his plans for the marriage of Kauikeaouli and Nahienaena would probably be thwarted. He was beaten at every turn.

Boki signed the *Vincennes* notes in November 1829. In the same month a ship arrived at Honolulu with news of an island rich in sandalwood in the south west Pacific—Erromanga in the New Hebrides. Here was a way out. Boki hired two foreign seamen to direct an expedition for him, and as soon as the contracts were signed he set about recruiting men. About two hundred and fifty, most of them armed with muskets, went aboard his ship, the *Kamehameha;* the *Becket,* under Manuia, Boki's fort commander at Honolulu, carried one hundred and eighty, among them a hundred soldiers from Boki's following at Honolulu and his home district of Waianae, in leeward Oahu. Not stopping even for the Sabbath, Boki's men loaded all kinds of supplies, including gunpowder for the armed force. By December 3 everything was ready; the two ships fired their cannon in salute and stood away to the south.

Clearly Boki had more on his mind than sandalwood alone. The contracts he signed with his foreign navigators mentioned taking islands under protection, and traders who came across his ships on their way to the New Hebrides understood Boki to say that he was going to colonize Erromanga and set up a trading post there. At Honolulu it was known only that Boki had said he would never come back until "a certain chief" (obviously Kaahumanu) was dead.

Six months went by; then in June 1830, the brigantine *Dhaulle* put in at Honolulu with news that Boki's ship had never reached Erromanga. The *Dhaulle* had heard reports in the New Hebrides that a severe gale was blowing when the *Kamehameha* left the island of Rotuma for Erromanga, and that pieces of wreckage had been sighted later on the open sea. In

July a schooner up from the south confirmed this, adding the information that the *Becket* was returning alone.

On the afternoon of August 3, 1830, the *Becket* dropped anchor at Honolulu. She had only twenty men aboard—twelve natives and eight foreigners. All the rest were dead. The *Becket* had arrived at Erromanga ahead of the *Kamehameha,* and Manuia had settled down to wait. Boki's ship did not appear. Instead word came that charred flotsam had been seen at sea. Manuia sent a boat to circle the island. It found nothing. Manuia stayed five weeks, but his Hawaiian sandalwood searchers and the helpers they had picked up on the sland of Rotuma could not do much. The Erromangans were hostile, the Hawaiians were nervous; the two parties clashed and blood was shed. Then sickness descended on the *Becket*—an intermittent fever, possibly malaria. One hundred and eighty men died before the ship made Rotuma again, and another twenty were landed there sick. Manuia was among the dead. His body, stitched into a tarpaulin, was brought home to be buried at Honolulu.

Boki was never heard of again. The Protestant missionaries were sure that God had passed judgment on a hardened sinner. Boki had formed his expedition for unworthy purposes and had profaned the Sabbath with his hasty loading. It was easy to conclude that the further sin of smoking in the gunpowder-filled hold brought about Boki's violent death. For the Christians the account was closed, but the response of the commoners of Honolulu was different—they wailed day and night for a long time.

The affair had a strange aftermath. In 1831 a native from Boki's old territory at Waianae hurried into Honolulu shouting, "Boki is at Waianae! Boki is at Waianae with a warship!" "The people were in an uproar, some frightened, some pleased," wrote a native historian. "The red dust rose in clouds from the plain . . . as natives and foreigners started out on horseback for Waianae. The church party who had declared Boki a stinking spirit became like a blunted needle." But it was all a hallucination. The man had dreamed it, and he was whipped through the town for causing a disturbance. Reality had dealt Boki false to the last.

The Moral Wars

Boki left his wife Liliha in charge of Oahu. She mourned his death, but the Christians could not persuade her to look for consolation at Kawaiahao, and when she slipped back into the old loose life she liked so well the chiefs decided to take the governorship away from her. They laid their plans while they were on a tour of the windward islands with the king. Liliha had her own ideas on the subject; she had no intention of giving up without a fight.

She called together her followers, most of them from Boki's lands at Waianae. Her lover of the moment, the chief Paki, bought muskets, powder, and shot from the Honolulu merchants, who were watching events with interest. Toward the end of February 1831, so Levi Chamberlain heard, Liliha had five hundred men, then a thousand, under arms at the Honolulu fort and the battery on top of Punchbowl hill behind the town. The Christian chiefs sent Liliha's father, Governor Hoapili of Maui, to talk with his daughter. It was the story of Bingham and Boki all over again. Hoapili dissolved the rebellion with words. Meekly, Liliha resigned the government of Oahu, surrendered her arms, and went with her father to Lahaina.

Once the safety of the town was guaranteed the chiefs brought the king back to Honolulu. On April 1 Kauikeaouli announced that he had sequestered the lands and forts of Honolulu and given them to Kaahumanu. She in turn said that the government's policy in future would be enforced on Oahu by her brother Kuakini, who was already Governor of Hawaii.

Kuakini was an enormous man, well over three hundred pounds in weight, a chief of great authority whose word had always been law among the common natives. Now he was a Christian, and he was in a position to lay down the moral law to foreigners. He began by forbidding gambling, the retailing of liquor, and the sale of liquor licenses at Honolulu. His policemen, led by a native called Big Ben, patrolled the town incessantly, taking wine from dinner tables in private homes, breaking up billiards and bowling games, and putting a stop to Sunday music-making, dancing, carousing, and even horseback riding.

At the height of the Sunday storms, natives used to gather in the streets of Honolulu to watch the show as foreigners armed with clubs rode out in defiance of the law and Big Ben's constables pursued them on foot and dragged them from their saddles. The foreigners made aggrieved protests about these "encroachments" on their "Liberties, Religion and harmless amusements." The Christian chiefs held fast, but in demanding "universal silence" on Sundays they condemned themselves to noisy argument all week long. Hiram Bingham, at the center of the commotion, became convinced that some of the foreigners were plotting to take his life. Written charges and denials flew back and forth between Kawaiahao and the town, and the air was poisoned for a long time.

The chiefs who removed Liliha from office and cleared the foreigners from the streets on Sundays decided at the same time that Catholicism should be extirpated. Several members of the French colony at Honolulu had already gone home. Two priests and a handful of lay workers and catechists remained. They had managed, while Boki was governor, to gather several score natives about them, but once Boki was gone their position became precarious. Natives who attended Mass were jailed or set to hard labor, and the priests were told to leave. They refused to go voluntarily, and in the end the chiefs put a government schooner, the *Waverly,* under the command of a resident of Honolulu named William Sumner, and instructed him to land the priests on the coast of California, where presumably a Catholic community would take them in. Father Alexis Bachelot and Father Patrick Short were drummed to the waterfront and put aboard the *Waverly* on December 24, 1831, while salutes were fired from the fort and the battery on Punchbowl. Only the lay workers remained at Honolulu with the baptized natives, fewer than two hundred in all, most of them children.

The chiefs hardly thought their action needed justifying. To them one kii, or idol, was very like another; heathen or Catholic, it made no difference. Idolatry had been outlawed ·when the kapus were overthrown. Not Catholicism itself but idolatry caused trouble, and idolatry was at the same time insubordination. The priests were guilty, so they were expelled.

The expulsion had at least the tacit approval of the Protestant missionaries and their patrons at the American Board Rooms in Boston, all of whom distrusted "Jesuits" deeply. Hiram Bingham, for one, thought the presence of Catholics in the islands was a disaster. The archipelago simply was not big enough for two religions. The Congregationalists had priority; the Papists were interlopers. Bingham and his colleagues made their views clear in sermons and in other ways. Levi Chamberlain of the mission depository, a gentle Calvinist, believed that force was not justified by Scripture and would not serve any good purpose, but even he came down against the priests and hoped that "the Lord would open the way for their removal." In any case, the missionaries said, the matter was entirely out of their hands: the chiefs had the sole right to grant or deny residence to outsiders.

To foreign residents all this shuffling of responsibility was self-serving. As they saw it, the persecution of native Catholics and the expulsion of the priests stemmed from the inspiration if not the direct instruction of Protestant missionaries. A case could easily be made along these lines. Bingham was with the chiefs when they decided to remove the priests. The 1831 general meeting of the Sandwich Islands Mission did not disapprove of the decision. The chiefs were cautioned against persecution for conscience's sake, but at the same time they were urged to be "decided and energetic" in their policies. On the very day King Kauikeaouli signed William Sumner's commission as captain of the *Waverly,* the Protestant missionaries fasted and prayed that divine guidance might aid the chiefs, and Bingham remained in close contact with Kaahumanu until the priests were gone. To the foreigners all this added up to something more than guilt by association. Whatever the rights and wrongs of the case, the chiefs had their way. Catholicism was completely broken up—the priests banished, the remaining lay workers helpless, the most ardent native converts in jail.

Kaahumanu and Bingham, the architects of the Protestant victory, could be well pleased with themselves. The churches were crowded, even though the reward of church membership was withheld from all but a very few. A temperance society on Oahu attracted more than a thousand Hawaiians (and exactly six foreigners). On Maui several hundred natives pledged themselves to give up smoking. The common school system, a shaky structure staffed by natives in various stages of enlightenment, was working as well as could be expected. By the early thirties about fifty thousand pupils, most of them adults, were enrolled in about eleven hundred common schools, and this meant that four out of every ten Hawaiians were learning to read from Christian text books in their own language.

Education, in fact, was booming. The quarterly hoikes, or school examinations, were approached so enthusiastically that all work would come to a halt for a week or ten days as natives crowded around the mission stations, waiting their turn to demonstrate their accomplishments. The Hawaiians managed somehow to graft onto these occasions their talent for display, for decoration, for jollity, for public performance, for enjoyable communal experience. Even within the confines of literacy and piety echoes of the great hula gatherings of the early twenties could be heard.

"The shell horn [has been] blowing early for examination of the schools in the meeting house," wrote the newly arrived missionary Reuben Tinker at Honolulu in 1831. "About 2000 scholars present, some wrapped in large quantity of native cloth, with wreaths of evergreen about their heads & hanging toward their feet—others drest in calico & silk with large necklaces of braided hair and wreaths of red & yellow & green feathers very beautiful & expensive.

"It was a pleasant occasion in which they seemed interested & happy, and it answers for them in place of our . . . commencements, & cattle shows and election &c., with less exposure of health & morals for the gentlemen drank no rum, & the ladies were not severely clad. The king & chiefs were present, and examined among the rest. They read in various books, and 450 in 4 rows wrote the same sentence at the same time on slates. They perform with some ceremony. In this exercise, one of the teachers cried out with as much importance as an orderly sergeant . . . & immediately the whole company began to sit up straight.—At the next order, they stood on their feet at the next they *'handled'* slates or 'presented'—i.e. they held them resting on the left arm as a musician would place his fiddle—at the next order, they brought their pencils to bear upon the broad sides of their slates ready for action. Mr. Bingham then put into the crier's ear the sentence to be written, which he proclaimed with all his might and, a movement of the 450 pencils commenced which from their creaking was like the music of machinery lacking oil. Their sentences were then examined & found generally correct."

Bird Feathers

Kaahumanu was growing old. She entered the seventh decade of her life and her seventh year as a baptized Christian in 1832. A few months earlier she had made the latest of her many tours on behalf of the Gospel, traveling through rural Oahu and exhorting the natives to worship the true God. In the spring of 1832 she greeted with tears of joy a new contingent of Protestant missionaries, the fifth sent by the American Board since 1820. This was almost her last public act. She had been ill and weak for some time, and now she withdrew from Honolulu to her country house in the cool green valley of Manoa. Her servants carried her there on a bedstead, and she never went back to the town. By the summer of 1832 she was measuring her life in days. Commoners from all over Oahu gathered in a great silent circle about her house. She asked to see her missionary friends and they came to stand among the chiefs at her bedside, bringing with them a final gift, a morocco-bound copy of the New Testament in Hawaiian, just completed at the mission press. Before dawn on June 5 she died, calling for Bingham and whispering the words of a Congregationalist hymn: "Lo, here am I, O Jesus, Grant me thy gracious smile."

As the missionaries were well aware, the death of their powerful patron might put the gains of the past year in jeopardy. The whim of ruling chiefs still passed for policy in the islands, and no one could be sure how King Kauikeaouli would behave now that the regency had come to an end. It was soon announced that the king would rule as well as reign in future, but that he would be advised in state matters by a new kuhina nui—the female chief Kinau, who was a daughter of Kamehameha the Great, one of the widows of Liholiho, and a half-sister of Kauikeaouli.

Kinau, a communicant at the mission church, might become another Kaahumanu; Kauikeaouli, a willful eighteen year old, was hardly a church goer, much less a church member. He was showing signs of turning into another Liholiho. He had spent a good part of his childhood cultivating a taste for low life in the company of Governor Boki and British Consul Charlton. By the time he was fourteen or fifteen he was a tavern keeper and billiard room owner. And he was a practiced seducer, a cool invoker of royal sexual privilege. Susan Jackson, a sixteen year old part-Hawaiian girl, was his lover for several months before she married the American merchant Stephen Reynolds, and even after the wedding she went on keeping assignations with Kauikeaouli, explaining to Reynolds that it was her duty to go to the king's house whenever he called for her. The king had other interests as well. Lahilahi Marin caught his eye; he became enamored of a girl called Kaamanaeile; he pursued the wife of the chief Kahekili; and Kinau, his half-sister, the ostensibly pious kuhina nui, was beaten by her husband for her intimacy with the king. Then, early in 1832, Kauikeaouli chose a new mistress, Kalama, the daughter of a minor chief, and announced that he would marry her (though he did not say when). Kalama was not of the highest rank; from the chiefs' point of view the match was not all that could be desired. To the missionaries it was just another of the king's disgusting entanglements. The church members held a fast day, offering prayers for his salvation. Throughout all this Kauikeaouli remained deeply attached to his sister Nahienaena, so much so that the missionaries thought it only prudent to keep the princess on Maui, away from her brother.

Another special friend of the king was Liliha, Governor Boki's widow. Kauikeaouli spent a great deal of time with her, and with a part-Tahitian commoner named Kaomi, the leading spirit in a group of showy young men who called themselves the Hulumanus, or bird feathers. Kauikeaouli was piqued by the chiefs' efforts to restrain him even after the regency was at an end, and, encouraged by Liliha and Kaomi, he declared a kind of inventive guerrilla war on Christian morality.

The king and the Hulumanus began by drinking thirty-two barrels of spirits in a week, a fairly sizeable affront to the native temperance society. They went out looking for church members and forced them to drink gin, in a parody of the scene at the breaking of the kapus in 1819, when ai noa, free eating, had been used to symbolize freedom from old restrictions; now free drinking meant freedom from the church. They mocked Christian burial by interring in a coffin, with prayers in Hawaiian, the body of a baboon, a short-lived pet given to the king by the commander of a visiting American warship. Kauikeaouli sent a crier through the streets of Honolulu to announce the lifting of penalties for moe kolohe, or adultery, and for all other crimes except theft and murder. A few days later he ordered the prostitutes of Honolulu to pay court—and taxes—to his mistress Kalama. He was becoming a monarch of misrule.

Having done his best to flout the authority of the chiefs, Kauikeaouli announced at a public meeting on March 15, 1833, that he was taking complete control of the government. All the lands conquered by Kamehameha the Great would now be his; the adjudgment of life and death, the determination of right and wrong, rested solely with him. He would rule justly, he said, but neither chiefs nor foreigners were to have any voice in law making. While the shock of all this was still sinking in, the king surprised everyone by partly reversing his stand and confirming Kinau in the post of kuhina nui.

During the next twelve months the Christian chiefs worked hard to resurrect the moral laws, but it was almost impossible. The king's example was catching: commoners all over Oahu went back to the hula and other old pastimes, and schools and churches emptied out with amazing speed. The Hulumanus continued on their riotous way: when one Hulumanu's wife left him for a church member, the rest of the fraternity ordered all the cannon in the town fired in mock salute. The king opened the fort and freed all the sailors imprisoned there; at this Kinau took over the fort and refused to give it up to the king. Kauikeaouli left Honolulu and went roaming about Oahu for several weeks. In his absence the chiefs proclaimed the moral laws again, but in the country districts of Koolau, Waialua, and Puuloa, the king and the Hulumanus passed through quiet villages like a plague of locusts.

All this time the king had been lavishing favors on Kaomi, encouraging him to take land from Christians and parcel it out among the Hulumanus, letting him impose special taxes so that he could pay his debts. Eventually the high chiefs could stand it no longer. They had Kaomi arrested in his sleep, tied up, and locked in the fort. The king asked them to let his friend out, but they would not, and he had to go and free Kaomi himself. This was on March 15, 1834, the anniversary of the day when Kauikeaouli had taken control of the government. Four days later the foreigners of Honolulu, who had been greatly amused at the disintegration of the holy community, formed a procession and rode from a tavern called the Oahu Folly to present the king with a gorgeous uniform made for him in Lima, Peru, at a cost of $850. The king put the outfit on and went back to the Folly with the foreigners, applauded by hundreds lining the streets.

Kauikeaouli's long drawn out revels came to an abrupt end in June, 1834. A sudden call came to the English physician Thomas C. B. Rooke at Honolulu—the king was at Pearl River, a few miles down the coast, and he needed treatment at once. The rumor was that Kauikeaouli had tried to kill himself; as the merchant Stephen Reynolds heard it, he had tried to cut his throat and drown himself. Rooke and all the chiefs set off immediately; so did Hiram Bingham and the medical missionary Gerrit Judd.

Kauikeaouli refused to tell the missionaries what had happened, but the story soon came out. The king's sister Nahienaena had been with him at Pearl River. Apparently Kauikeaouli wanted to go to Maui with her. She refused, out of fear of the Christian governor of the island, Hoapili, and the rejected king, in deep despair, tried to end his life.

Six weeks later Kauikeaouli made another effort to shake off the Christian conventions that rested so uncomfortably on him. He slept with Nahienaena openly and then tried to take her with him to Waianae, Boki's old district, as far away from "teachers" as possible. But the Christian chiefs intervened and sent Nahienaena back to Maui, where heavy church discipline was laid on her.

Early in 1835 Kauikeaouli conceded that the chiefs had won. He approved a new code of laws dealing with murder, theft, adultery, drunkenness, perjury, and other crimes, and he placed law enforcement in the hands of Kinau. From that time on he virtually abandoned the direction of affairs of state. He spent most of his time with foreigners, riding, sailing, bowling, or playing billiards, or sharing with Kaomi an occasional reminiscence of the riotous days of 1833.

Nahienaena was uncontrollable. She was excommunicated from the church on Maui in May, 1835. She took to visiting the king again, and toward the end of the year she became pregnant. The chiefs arranged a marriage for her with the young chief William Pitt Leleiohoku, son of the late prime minister Kalanimoku. Nahienaena's child was born in August 1836. It was a boy, and it lived only a few hours. Nahienaena, obese, debauched, diseased, and guilt-stricken, died on the next to last day of the year. She was not much more than twenty years of age. For years afterward, on the anniversary of her death, Kauikeaouli would go to Lahaina and feast and drink there, close to her tomb, and think his own private thoughts.

Once More the Priests

The old problem of Catholicism became acute again when in September 1836 Father Arsenius Walsh arrived at Honolulu as the representative of the recently organized Vicariate Apostolic of Eastern Oceania. Kinau and the Protestant chiefs told Walsh he must leave at once, and he was saved from expulsion only by the intervention of British Consul Charlton and the coincidental arrival of two ships, HMS *Actaeon* and the French man of war *Bonité*. (Walsh was a member of a French missionary order but a British subject, hence the interest of both nations.) Walsh was warned by the chiefs not to teach Catholic doctrine to anyone, native or foreign, on pain of being sent away from the islands.

The prohibition still stood when in April, 1837, Father Alexis Bachelot and Father Patrick Short, the two priests expelled in 1831, returned to Honolulu. They did not make their presence known, but they were discovered and told to leave. They chose to remain. The ship that brought them, the *Clementine,* was scheduled to sail on May 22, and the chiefs were determined to see the priests aboard. Native constables led Bachelot and Short from the French mission buildings to the waterfront, where a boat was to take them out to the *Clementine*. The priests insisted that the constables should "force" them to enter the boat by laying hands on them, and this was done, though no violence was used.

The *Clementine* was owned by a resident of Honolulu named Jules Dudoit, a man of French extraction who claimed British citizenship. Dudoit was opposed to the expulsion. He refused to have the priests aboard unless they came voluntarily and unless he was paid for their passage. The priests were put on deck over his loud objections. Then Dudoit took the position that the *Clementine* had been seized by the chiefs. He hauled down his British flag and went ashore with his crew, leaving Bachelot and Short on the ship. British Consul Charlton met him in the street and burned the *Clementine*'s colors on the spot.

King Kauikeaouli, who had been visiting Maui, came to Honolulu to hear the claims of Dudoit and others. The king took the public position that the government had not seized the *Clementine* and that the priests were not prisoners, but he would not allow them to land.

Dudoit was supplied with letters of complaint from the British and American consular agents at Honolulu addressed to the commanders of the Pacific fleets at Valparaiso, and he set out for Chile in the schooner *Flibberty Gibbet*. The boat leaked; Dudoit had to turn back. By coincidence two warships put in at Honolulu just then: HMS *Sulphur,* commanded by Captain Edward Belcher, and the French frigate *La Vénus,* commanded by Captain Abel du Petit Thouars.

Belcher and du Petit Thouars tried, singly and in combination, to have the priests released from their floating prison. After two conferences which got nowhere the commanders blockaded the harbor, took possession of the *Clementine,* and put the priests on shore. Belcher hoisted the British flag on the *Clementine;* du Petit Thouars landed three hundred men to protect Bachelot and Short while they made the short walk from the harbor to the French mission buildings.

Kauikeaouli came down again from Lahaina. Finally an agreement was reached with the two naval commanders that the priests might stay ashore until passage was available to some civilized part of the world. Belcher guaranteed in writing that Short would not break the laws of the kingdom; du Petit Thouars guaranteed that Bachelot would not preach.

The men of war sailed without further incident. In September Short left for South America. In November two more priests arrived. Father Columba Murphy was allowed to land only because he did. not tell the chiefs that he was a priest. His companion, Father Louis Maigret, was barred from residence; he sailed quite soon, accompanied by Bachelot. This left only Walsh and Murphy at Honolulu, and they were severely limited in their work by an edict signed by the king on December 18, rejecting the Catholic religion and prohibiting its teaching anywhere in the islands. Catholic teachers landing from ships might be imprisoned until they could be removed; captains might forfeit their vessels and be fined for refusing to carry them away.

So much for the priests. Native Catholics came under harassment as well. Some were put in irons and others were set to cutting and carrying stone, and the most persistent offenders were made to cart excrement away from the fort. After the total ban of December 1837, the chiefs ordered their policemen to search huts at Honolulu, hoping to surprise Catholics at prayer. Some converts left for Boki's old lands at Waianae, where tolerance for Catholicism lingered on under the new head man.

Kinau died in April 1839, and the first act of the new kuhina nui, a female chief named Kekauluohi, was to order the arrest of the Waianae Catholics. Sixty-seven of them were brought back to Honolulu. One man died of exhaustion on the forced march of thirty miles. The rest were interrogated by the chiefs. All but thirteen were released after they promised to obey the law. The recalcitrants were taken to the fort and tied up overnight, some of them with their arms raised and bound over a seven foot partition. They were turned loose after Hiram Bingham and others told the chiefs they were being unnecessarily harsh.

A week later two more women were arrested and questioned at the fort. Then they were shackled, one to a tree and the other to the eaves of a low thatch house, without food or water. Next morning they were found by Jules Dudoit (the owner of the *Clementine* and now the informal consular agent of France). Bingham was called. He and Artemas Bishop, another Protestant missionary, remonstrated with the governor of Oahu, Kekuanaoa, who said he was not responsible for the punishment but agreed that the women were being punished for their religion. In the end the two were freed.

Nine native Catholics remained in jail at Honolulu. Some had been at hard labor since 1836; the others had joined them in 1837 and 1838. The chiefs made no move to release them.

The Great Awakening

By the late eighteen thirties the Protestant missionaries were able to look back with a measure of detachment on the bad days that followed Kaahumanu's death and the outburst of King Kauikeaouli earlier in the decade. Then the Hawaiian churches generally, and especially those on Oahu, had been dragged into depression, and the common school system fell into ruins and had to be reorganized. Bingham and his colleagues wrote embarrassed letters to their patrons in New England, explaining that at the islands appearances were deceiving, that the outward Christianity of the natives was a product of pressure by the chiefs, that often the chiefs themselves were attracted to Christianity for the wrong reasons, and that the bad influence of even one chief, not to mention backsliding kings and princesses, could be disastrous.

Under Kinau's regime the tone of the missionaries' letters brightened. The commoners found their way back to church, and the schools, operating under a somewhat sounder system of instruction and inspection, became fashionable again. The publications of the mission press were once more in demand, and book after book of the Old Testament was being translated, so that by the end of the decade the complete Bible in Hawaiian would be available. Natives everywhere were giving up smoking, conscientiously and repeatedly; temperance societies were enrolling more and more members; and the chiefs were getting ready to make total abstinence a national policy. Taking all this into consideration, the missionaries could regard the hounding of Catholic priests and their converts as simply the dark side of a fine new enthusiasm for Protestantism.

Within the mission itself things had never been better. Between June 1831, and April 1837, five new companies of American Board evangelists arrived in the islands. By the beginning of 1838 nearly ninety workers were in the field, thirty-seven of them ordained ministers, at seventeen stations in the most heavily populated districts of the major islands.

Thousands of natives came to church regularly, yet only a few could be called Christians, at least by Congregationalist definitions. It was a curious situation. Except in the most benighted rural districts the natives no longer suspected the Christians of bringing disease and death by their prayers. Churches were sometimes called luakinis, the old word for state temples, but no one still believed that the missionaries killed people to use their blood for communion wine. In fact a good many Hawaiians had come to accept and even approve of Christianity. They kept the Sabbath well, far better than the average foreigner did. They enjoyed dressing up for church (though admittedly they liked undressing afterwards too). Their ability to memorize long passages of Scripture was amazing. They had an appetite for oratory that amounted almost to an addiction, and they enjoyed a good sermon immensely—the longer the better, so it seemed.

The natives understood that their old gods had abdicated in favor of a single new god with a new set of kapus. They knew that this Christian God watched them, and that he wanted them to do right; and they knew that they had all done wrong at some time or other. They had any number of good examples to follow—Opukahaia, whose story could reduce entire classes at the mission schools to tears no matter how many times it was told; the female chief Kapiolani, who had proved her faith by defying the volcano goddess Pele in the crater of Kilauea; Puaaiki, a deformed and sightless court buffoon who had become a powerful witness for Christ under the new name of Blind Bartimeus; and, of course, the great Kaahumanu herself. And they had bad examples to contemplate as well—the unfortunate Liholiho; the renegade George Kaumualii; the wastrel Boki; the doomed Nahienaena. The missionaries never neglected a chance to improve the occasion of a significant death by talking about rewards and punishments, and the natives had been told often enough that each individual would have to make for himself the choice between heaven and hell.

A missionary could easily spend his whole day listening to horror stories from the heathen past, told with every appearance of sorrowful candor, and the natives made a habit of accosting their pastors after church or rousing them at some outlandish hour of the night to discuss their manao, their thought, on troubling points of doctrine. But appearances were not everything, as the missionaries had found out just a few years earlier. They knew from their own personal experiences, too, that genuine conversion was usually accompanied by sharp anguish. They prided themselves on being able to detect the most cleverly concealed of doubtful motives, and very few natives managed to convince them that their sense of guilt was really satisfactory. Among the more experienced missionaries it became almost a matter of honor to go slowly in admitting Hawaiians to church membership. So after seventeen years the list of native Christians was still short: less than twelve hundred names. One out of every two Hawaiians attended church, but not one in a hundred had been granted the privilege of communion with Christ.

This disproportion seemed particularly striking to some of the new arrivals among the missionaries. The older brethren had never given up their dream of the holy community, but after years in the field most of them were ready to admit that holiness might be a long time coming.

Their younger colleagues landed at the islands with the fever of their own conversion still on them, ready to do great things.

Several of the newcomers had been converted by the celebrated American revivalist Charles Grandison Finney, who at the height of his powers could bring whole congregations to the ground, groveling in terror, and then raise them up again full of a sense of salvation. Those who had not felt the touch of Finney were at least familiar with his techniques—the massing of audiences in tightly packed crowds for "protracted meetings" that might last several hours or even days, the impassioned sermons that hammered home over and over again the terrors of hell and then held out the blessed promise of heaven, the ready acceptance of shouting and sobbing and even uncontrollable convulsions as signs that God was wrestling with the Devil for the sinner's soul.

It was easy for religious conservatives to scoff at the crudity of Finney's methods, but the force of his preaching was undeniable and the results were astonishing. Not many of the younger missionaries doubted that God blessed Finney's work in the United States. The only question in their minds was whether his way of doing things would have any effect among the odd congregations of the Sandwich Islands.

The answer came from Titus Coan, who began preaching in 1835 on the east coast of the island of Hawaii. When Coan arrived there the church at Hilo, under David Lyman, had about twenty members. Coan set himself the punishing task of talking to every native in the parish, between fifteen and sixteen thousand people spread over a belt of difficult country a hundred miles long. At first Coan found the Hawaiians "hard as a nether millstone." By the middle of 1837 he had about eighty converts, and he was impatient for more. "This people are . . . dead," he wrote, "but God can raise them. Is it not *time for him to work?*" In the fall he noticed a slight stirring at the village of Hilo itself. "State of things interesting here," he wrote to Levi Chamberlain at Honolulu. "Sinners anxious. The Word has power. Pray for us."

Coan was hoping for a clear sign from God. It came with devastating force. "On the 7th of November, 1837, at the hour of evening prayers," he wrote, "we were startled by a heavy thud, and a sudden jar of the earth. The sound was like the fall of some vast body on the beach, and in a few seconds a noise of mingled voices rising for a mile along the shore thrilled us like the wail of doom . . . The sea, moved by an unseen hand, had all of a sudden risen in a gigantic wave, and this wave, rushing in with the speed of a racehorse, had fallen upon the shore, sweeping everything not more than fifteen or twenty feet above high-water mark into indiscriminate ruin. Houses, furniture, calabashes, fuel, timber, canoes, food, clothing, everything floated wild upon the flood . . . The harbor was full of strugglers calling for help, while frantic parents and children, wives and husbands ran to and fro along the beach, calling for their lost ones. As wave after wave came in and retired, the strugglers were brought near the shore, where the more vigorous landed with desperate efforts, and the weaker and exhausted were carried back upon the retreating wave, some to sink and rise no more till the noise of judgment wakes them . . . Had this catastrophe occurred at midnight when all were asleep, hundreds of lives would undoubtedly have been lost. Through the great mercy of God, only thirteen were drowned.

"This event, falling as it did like a bolt of thunder from a clear sky, greatly impressed the people. It was as the voice of God speaking to them out of heaven, 'Be ye also ready.' "

The natives were more than ready to believe that God was speaking to them through Coan. People from all over his district came to listen to him. At times the number encamped around the mission station at Hilo reached ten thousand, and crowds appeared like magic whenever Coan went on a preaching tour. His native assistants would go ahead of him to the meeting house and marshal the congregation in "compact rows as tight as it was possible to crowd them, the men and women being separated, and when the house was thus filled with these compacted ranks, the word was given to them to *sit down,* which they did, a mass of living humanity, such perhaps as was never seen except on Hawaii."

Coan used to watch with excitement this assembling of the "Sacramental host" and the "mustering of the troops of hell in order to bring on a general engagement, and once more to test 'the weapons of our warfare.' " Like the master Charles Grandison Finney, whose convert he was, and like all the other great Protestant evangelists of his century, Coan saw his work as a tremendous struggle. His principal ally was a fighting God, "whose arm is omnipotant, and whose voice is thunder . . . whose eyes are as a flame of fire and whose spear gleams lightning . . . who judges and makes war in righteousness." For Coan it was always "Jehovah's hammer," or "the battle-ax of the Lord," or the "arrows of the Almighty," which "broke sinners down;" and to be brought to the point of repentance was to be "slain of the Lord."

Like Finney too, Coan had the immense satisfaction of seeing the Spirit of God at work before his eyes. It was a common thing for him to reduce hundreds of natives at a time to weeping, shouting, and falling. His hearers came to feel the terrible presence of God so strongly that they quivered in every muscle, or wailed in "tremendous throes" like a "dying giant," or broken down with an "earthquake shock." Sometimes the fallen lay "groaning on the ground for 15 minutes or ½ an hour after the fight was done."

The revival spread outward from Hilo. In the nearby district of

Waimea Coan's colleague, the young missionary Lorenzo Lyons, was soon stirring up his own storms of holy emotion. On Maui, the coastal district of Wailuku had also been struck by the tidal wave, and excitement ran high there. Oahu and Kauai had not been badly affected by the tidal wave itself, but religious enthusiasm was carried all the way along the chain just the same. Coan's revival began at the height of the fall whaling season, when Hawaiians traveled between islands in great numbers, and when women especially left the rural districts for the ports. Far more than the missionaries wanted Him to be, the Hawaiians' God was Love, and native women would have seen nothing strange about selling their bodies to sailors and then giving their souls to Christ. At least their sins would be fresh and well remembered, and they could repent on the spot.

Not all the missionaries were pleased with what Coan had done, and neither were the leaders of the American Board in Boston. After all, Bingham and the others of his generation had been struggling against sin for seventeen years with very little result. They did not exactly accuse Coan of being a charlatan. It was just that the pioneers were accustomed to thinking that the place for religious struggle was in the mind, and they were a little taken aback to find unseemly physical outbursts associated with spiritual surrender. So, with the backing of their masters at Boston, the older missionaries as a group and the conservatives among the new became critics of the revival even while the revival was filling their churches as never before. At Honolulu Kawaiahao Church simply over-flowed, and a second church was formed under Lowell Smith at Kaumuakapili, amid a tangle of grog shops and native huts at the rear of the village. Despite this, Hiram Bingham, regularly involved in scenes of fainting and falling at Kawaiahao, could not bring himself to believe that "convulsions" proved anything one way or another. Dwight Baldwin, a medical missionary at Lahaina, insisted that there was a difference between outward signs and inward feeling. Others talked darkly about "excited minds" and "peculiar views."

Coan did not really care what anybody else thought; he knew who was right and who was wrong. "I have little fear of the noise of praying Christians and wailing sinners, if so be the wailing is confined to time," he wrote. "In eternity it will roll up in fearful and augmenting notes for ever and ever. The most dangerous noise in a revival springs up, not, perhaps, from the devil, nor from scoffers and open opposers, but from false or timid, or dictatorial friends." His colleague Lorenzo Lyons of Waimea agreed; he was privately attracted to the teachings of an American sect known as the Millerites, whose calculations showed that Christ would come again in 1843, and this made him desperately eager to get as many Hawaiians inside the church as possible.

He and Coan did their best. Between November 1837 and May 1838 they admitted more than thirty-two hundred natives to church membership (almost trebling the size of the mission church in the islands), another thirty-two hundred during the next twelve months, and more than seventy-five hundred during the following year. At that point, in 1839-1840, Hilo and Waimea together had three out of every four church members in the islands. On a single extraordinary day in 1838 Coan baptized one thousand seven hundred and five converts, and during the early forties his church had more than six thousand members in good standing. The American Board had never heard of a bigger Protestant congregation anywhere in the world.

If Coan and Lyons were right in admitting natives to the church in such members and with such speed, then the rest of the missionaries had been wrong to keep them out for so long. As it turned out, Lyons could not hold his converts. Within a few years he was excommunicating hundreds and watching thousands more drift away. Conservatives in the islands and at home in New England had a field day at his expense. But Coan lost members only at the same rate as the conservatives did, and there was not much anybody could do but admit, finally, that he was a remarkable man.

Coan's wish was "to die in the field with armor on, with weapons bright." Age dulled the shine of his weapons somewhat, but he had his wish. He lived and preached at Hilo for another forty years, until in 1882, in the midst of a small but satisfying revival, he suffered a paralytic stroke. He died praising God.

The End of the Holy Community

Hiram Bingham, the reluctant revivalist, was just taking the measure of Titus Coan's great awakening when a most unwelcome visitor arrived at Honolulu. On July 9, 1839, the French frigate *L'Artémise,* commanded by Captain C. P. T. Laplace, appeared off the harbor. Laplace was up from Tahiti, where he had been extracting indemnities from the native government for wrongs allegedly inflicted on Frenchmen there, and he was under orders to do the same at the Sandwich Islands. Laplace's presence in the Pacific had been known at Honolulu for some time, and in June King Kauikeaouli, looking somewhat apprehensively toward a visit from *L'Artémise,* gave instructions that Catholics should no longer be persecuted. This was not enough to satisfy Laplace. Without even coming ashore he issued a "manifesto" demanding complete religious freedom for Catholics, a bond of $20,000 from the chiefs to guarantee compliance, and a salute for the French flag.

Laplace gave the chiefs the best of incentives to act quickly: he threatened to bombard Honolulu if his terms were not met. Foreigners were offered asylum aboard *L'Artémise,* but from this asylum Laplace specifically excluded the Protestant missionaries, authors, as he put it, of the insults suffered by France at the hands of the native government. The missionaries were to be regarded as part of the Hawaiian population, facing the unhappy consequences of a war they themselves had provoked. Samuel N. Castle of the mission depository was afraid that the missionaries' wives might be exposed as well to the "unbridled lust" of the French; and Dwight Baldwin of Lahaina, alarmed at a distance and thinking that perhaps his remarks about Catholicism over the past few years had been too forthright, wrote hastily to the American consular agent at Honolulu, asking for a passport in case it was needed.

The king was away on Maui, as he so often was in the years after his sister's death. The chiefs, closer to Laplace's guns, decided to pledge Kauikeaouli in advance to the terms of the French manifesto. With the help of some members of the foreign community the bond money of $20,000 was raised. Kauikeaouli arrived at Honolulu on July 14, and he and his advisers spent the next three days with Laplace, negotiating a treaty of "commerce and friendship," considerations which had never played a large part in dealings between the two countries. One stipulation, Article VI, overturned the national policy of total abstinence by providing that French merchandise, including wines and brandies, should be admitted to Hawaiian ports under duties limited to 5 percent *ad valorem.* Article IV placed trials of French residents accused of "any crime whatever" in the hands of juries to be chosen by the French consul and approved by the Hawaiian government. These two matters were to cause controversy at the islands for more than a generation.

Laplace's visit was enough to take the edge off the great awakening. After two decades of evangelical work the idea of the holy community seemed on the verge of realization, but now in the space of a few days Laplace had come and gone and Catholics were on equal terms with Calvinists, drinkers with teetotallers. In more ways than one it was the end of an era.

As if to emphasize this, Hiram Bingham, who had dominated the missionary enterprise for twenty years, went home to New England in 1840. The native Christians of Kawaiahao, busy building a new and substantial stone church to Bingham's design, did not want their pastor to leave, but the foreigners could hardly wait to see him gone. A few of his countrymen at the islands conceded that he had done some good, though they wished God had called him to do it somewhere else. Among the rest of the white men Bingham inspired a feeling of bottomless and helpless rage. They found him impossible to like, and it was equally impossible just to tolerate his presence or ignore him. Bingham refused to be tolerated, and it was not in him to be ignored. Long before he left his enemies were thinking of him not as a mere man but as an archetypal figure, the "meddling, dogmatical preacher," the Puritan in black coat and tall hat—a plague unfairly visited upon men who hung their conscience on Cape Horn when they sailed to take up residence in the islands.

No other missionary came in for such sustained and violent abuse, but Bingham was never able to see (as his colleagues were) that his troubles stemmed from personality as much as policy. He simply rendered everything to God, and in God's name he was willing to suffer indefinitely. He was a relentless examiner of his own as well as others' motives, but self-scrutiny never led to a self-doubt, and only once to an expression of apparent self-pity. "When I was a boy of fourteen," he wrote toward the end of his ministry at Honolulu, "my teacher told my Mother, that 'Hiram was a peacemaker in the school.' After the test of a college life, I received a similar testimony from my reverend President . . . And I have lived long enough in Honolulu to know whether I can be insulted by friend or foe . . . and yet studiously seek to do good in meekness to those that oppose themselves: but I have not lived in strife long enough to *love* it. Yet 'when I am for peace, they are for war.' And I would fain know how I may in future avoid the stings of these thorns in my side? *When will they cease?"*

Bingham did not really want them to cease. He left the islands only because his wife was seriously ill, and he spent the next several years writing a six hundred page autobiography, more than a quarter of a million words long, in which he fought the old battles over again and won them all.

Bingham never gave up hope of returning to Kawaiahao, but circumstances prevented it, and perhaps this was a kindness in disguise. Within a few years of his departure it became clear that the missionaries would not win the kind of total victory for Puritanism that he and his fellow pioneers had been so sure of.

In the eighteen twenties and thirties the missionary party and the court party had been one and the same, and this was sufficient to shape polite society: those who were not for the Protestants were by definition against them, and against the government too, and so they could be ignored or opposed. The social ideas of the missionaries were best suited to those early times, when the simplest of strategies could make right and wrong seem dramatically distinct. Bingham and his colleagues specialized in purposeful distinctions, and their list was long: the ministry, set apart from other men for holy work; the missionary kingdom, afloat in the

Pacific, that ocean of iniquity; the churches, islands of virtue in sinful villages; within their congregations, a small proportion of communicants; in the mission house lots, fenced yards where Christian children could play unsullied by contact with rude natives and ruder foreigners; in marriage, an ineradicable preference for partners of good, pious New England stock; in death, burial in the separate mission plots of each church yard.

On essential points such as these true missionaries never changed their minds. But the world shifted beneath their feet, and the excluders became the excluded. As early as the eighteen forties the American Board began pressing the missionaries to bring the Protestant churches of the islands forward to independence. The Hawaiian Evangelical Association, organized in 1854, superseded the Sandwich Islands Mission, and in 1863 the Association broadened its membership to include native Hawaiian clergymen. Mormon missionaries came to the islands in the eighteen fifties, and Episcopalians in the sixties, to join the Roman Catholics in diluting the influence of Calvinism. Within the Protestant churches themselves, once the excitement of the great awakening had died down, Christianity became a workaday religion, observed as a matter of convention. Christian chiefs in large numbers backslid and had to be disciplined. Among the commoners temperance societies rose and fell, and groups for social prayer and hymn singing were formed and disbanded, but the statistics for offences against the moral laws remained constantly high. The Hawaiian kingdom was a Christian nation, to be sure, but it was just like other Christian nations. Mark Twain, who visited the islands in the eighteen sixties, concluded that sin no longer flourished there in name, only in reality.

So it might be said, with some truth, that on their own terms the missionaries failed, that the road they marked out for the natives to follow to heaven was paved with good intentions. But they failed worthily, even brilliantly. They were the only foreigners at the islands in the early days who concerned themselves wholeheartedly with the fate of the Hawaiians. Every institution in the young kingdom came to bear their unmistakeable stamp, and it was never quite erased; a century after Bingham left the very word "missionary" was still a shibboleth in the islands. And if the missionaries failed, they did so, after all, in the face of the most implacable of religious truths—the kingdom of God is not of this earth.

CHAPTER FOUR

The Nation

1839—1854

Large and Unfamiliar Fishes

"IF A BIG wave comes in," wrote the Hawaiian scholar David Malo in 1837, "large and unfamiliar fishes will come from the dark ocean, and when they see the small fishes of the shallows they will eat them up." Malo was convinced he could feel a huge swell far more dangerous than any tidal wave building up in the Pacific and bringing to the islands the most predatory big fishes of all. "The white man's ships have arrived with clever men from the big countries," he wrote, "they know our people are few in number and our country is small, they will devour us."

What frightened Malo was, quite simply, the wave of the future. More than a thousand white men were living at the islands when he wrote, and by the early fifties this number had doubled. Foreigners were hard to keep out, and once they were in they were likely to make trouble—not necessarily because they were clever men but because they came from great countries. The average white man who came to the islands had good reason to be modest about his personal background, but no foreigner would allow his national origins to be slighted. A man who had never carried much weight in his home country was lucky to stumble upon an inconsequential place like the Hawaiian kingdom where a mere announcement of nationality could make up the difference. Three great powers were represented in the Pacific—the United States, Great Britain, and France—and annexations were being carried out in Polynesia south of the equator. By the end of the forties New Zealand was British, and Tahiti and the Marquesas Islands were French. No one could tell which power would become paramount at the Hawaiian Islands, or when. Hopes rose and fell as warships of each nation in turn came to show the flag, and disputes between foreigners went on incessantly in the law courts, in the columns of newspapers, on the streets, and in the taverns. But however much they argued among themselves the foreigners were agreed on two points—the Hawaiian population existed to be dominated, and the Hawaiian government existed to be humiliated. And so Honolulu, where most of the white men gathered, became a stage upon which posturing expatriates acted out their public passions and their private pains.

The difficulty was that a self-important foreigner could summon up a warship just by shaking his fist, or so it seemed to the Hawaiians. The council of chiefs was less and less able to hold its own; the day of naïve despotism softened by Christianity was almost over. Toward the end of the eighteen thirties, after almost sixty years of contact with white men and two decades of instruction in the schools of Protestant missionaries who were also American republicans, the chiefs were forced to consider in earnest a fundamental reconstruction of the government of the kingdom.

They began at the beginning. In 1838 William Richards, a missionary at Lahaina since 1823, accepted an appointment as "Chaplain, Teacher and Translator" to King Kauikeaouli and began to instruct the chiefs in "political economy." Almost at once it became clear that the government could not be remade to suit foreigners without bringing in revolutionary changes in the relationship between chiefs and commoners. In 1839 the king announced a national policy of religious toleration and followed it with a declaration of rights for his subjects. In 1840 the government took over the management of the elementary schools. Late in the same year a constitution for the kingdom was drawn up, embodying the principle of representative government, and a national legislature began to meet. Between 1845 and 1847 organic acts were passed, consolidating the existence of a cabinet, a civil service, and an independent judiciary. By the end of the decade the traditional land system, under which tenure was granted at the pleasure of the chiefs who controlled the land, had been superseded by an arrangement that permitted Hawaiian commoners and foreigners alike to buy and sell land. In 1852 a new constitution was framed, giving every adult male subject of the king, native born or naturalized, the right to vote in the election of representatives to the lower house of the national legislature.

Without constant pressure from foreigners this transformation would certainly not have come about so quickly, and of course the chiefs had to have the help of foreigners in accomplishing it. The declaration of rights of 1839 and the constitution of 1840 were drafted by a group of highly intelligent Hawaiians educated for the most part by Protestant missionaries at Lahainaluna Seminary on Maui, among them David Malo and John Ii; but they could not do everything. During the forties more missionaries joined William Richards in the service of the king: the physician Gerrit P. Judd; Lorrin Andrews, former principal of Lahainaluna; Richard Armstrong, who had succeeded Hiram Bingham at Kawaiahao Church; and Edwin O. Hall, a printer and secular agent of the mission at Honolulu. For the rest the chiefs simply had to hope that among the clever men who came from great countries they might find friends as well as enemies.

At the islands it was impossible to predict quite what the tide would bring in. Beached sea captains and sailors could always be hired to work as harbor pilots, road supervisors, constables, jailers, and hangmen, but substantial talent was harder to come by. The government did about as well as could be expected, perhaps a little better. A young New Englander named James Jackson Jarves, unhappy in marriage and incompetent in business but able to write a clear, vigorous, and witty prose, started a weekly newspaper, the *Polynesian,* which in 1844 became the official organ of the government. John Ricord, educated to the law in New York State, came to the islands at the age of thirty-two by way of Louisiana, Texas, Arizona, Florida, and Oregon. His past held a few unanswered questions (had he spent time in jail in the east? picked a pocket in Buffalo? bilked a client in Florida of fourteen thousand dollars?), but he was capable, combative, and fiercely energetic—and, besides, he was the only lawyer in the islands. Less than a fortnight after his arrival early in 1844 he was commissioned as attorney general of the kingdom. Another young lawyer, William Little Lee, a consumptive on his way by ship from New York State to Oregon for his health's sake, came ashore at Honolulu in 1846 and stayed to be named chief justice of the Hawaiian supreme court while he was still in his twenties. Robert Crichton Wyllie, a diminutive middle-aged bachelor who looked like a French dancing master, appeared at Honolulu in 1844 with a fortune he had made in business in South America. Wyllie had vague connections among the minor aristocracy of Scotland, considerable social pretensions, the beginnings of a medical education, a vast appetite for information about practically everything on earth, and a dreadful compulsion to write down what he knew. He expected to stay only a short while, but he became interested in the future of the kingdom, and in 1845 he was offered the portfolio of foreign affairs; he accepted, and served devotedly until his death twenty years later.

By the end of 1844 there were fourteen white men working for the government; by 1851, forty-eight—twenty-five Americans, twenty-one Britishers, one Frenchman, and one German. Each of them, as a condition of his employment, had signed an oath of allegiance to the king. Among the noisy expatriates of the foreign community this was enough to ruin any man's reputation. "Gold, to be sure, has very powerful attractions," wrote one American in disgust, "honor and ambition, many more —but what honor can be obtained by being counsellor and companion of this almost sooty sprig of royalty, I cannot imagine."

No doubt each of the king's foreign advisers had his own definition of honor and his own estimate of what it was worth to compromise his Western citizenship. And no doubt each fish gave thought to the size of the pond he was about to swim in. For a missionary the decision to go into government was an exceptionally difficult one. He would have to break his formal connection with the American Board and suffer as well the open disapproval of many of his brethren. Gerrit Judd spoke for his colleagues in office when he said that he had been advising the chiefs for years at their request, and that he had accepted a post in the cabinet only because it gave him a better chance to be useful to the kingdom. His argument was that a man of strong Protestant principles could serve the country more worthily than a foreigner who did not profess religion. Even though he was no longer a missionary he was still a Puritan, and if anything was needed to convince him he was right it was the violence of the foreign community's objections to his appointment and his policies.

The three most important members of the cabinet, Judd, Ricord, and Wyllie, signed a "Political Creed" that pledged them to support the monarchy as "indispensable" to the preservation of the Hawaiian people. If the islands were subjected to foreign domination, the creed maintained, the native race would disappear. But since the Hawaiians had not arrived at a "pitch of civilization" that would enable them to govern themselves it was the duty of the king to employ foreigners, at least for the time being, though of course properly trained natives would eventually take their place.

Not many Hawaiians were persuaded of the white man's good intentions. While the national legislature was in session at Honolulu in 1845 natives on Maui were holding prayer meetings and collecting thousands of signatures for petitions against foreigners, especially those in government posts. "If this kingdom is to be ours," they asked, "what is the good of filling the land with foreigners?"

The natives of Dwight Baldwin's church at Lahaina were among those who prayed fervently that they might have "no haole rulers," and Baldwin himself was known to be passionately against missionaries who took the oath of allegiance, but he excused himself of responsibility for the unrest. The name of David Malo came up several times, and he was admonished by the legislature. Toward the end of the year the king took the trouble to tour Maui, explaining why the government needed the help of foreigners, but even this did not quiet matters entirely. In 1848, a year of bloody revolution in Europe, the natives of Maui, among whom were some careful students of foreign affairs, began to talk about storming the fort at Lahaina and killing all the white men. Rumors at Honolulu put Malo in the middle of the uproar again: he was supposed to have more than a thousand men in arms, ready to descend on Oahu. Malo, of course, had nothing of the sort in mind. With every year he grew more embittered about foreign influence, but he was a loyal subject of the king. The unrest on Maui, so the Privy Council decided, was "words only;" it would be best if "the matter be laid aside as if it had not been heard of."

Foreigners at the islands had much less to complain about; typically, they complained much more. The privilege of residence, the right of full naturalization, a fair degree of freedom to do business, freedom of speech, freedom of worship, exemption from labor taxes, access to the courts, and the right to trial before a jury approved by a consul—none of this satisfied them. Their presence had forced the government to westernize itself at great cost and in great haste, and then they chose to act as if the government did not exist. When the government reminded them of its existence they wrapped themselves in a foreign flag and claimed immunity. And so, all too often, trivial local happenings were turned into international issues. Consuls and commissioners pushed Hawaiian officials aside roughly, and legal cases in endless procession—property disputes, business failures, sailor riots, rapes, newspaper wars—made their way to the diplomatic level.

Whose law should prevail? The white members of the cabinet did their best to give the government of their adopted country a gravity that would compel the respect of foreigners, but it was next to impossible. Judge baiting, a favorite sport of foreigners brought before the Hawaiian courts, was encouraged by the fact that the highest court in the land met, as William Lee observed, "in an old grass house, floored with mats, without benches, seats or comforts of any kind, with one corner partitioned off with calico, for judge's office, clerk's office, police court, and jury room." Attorney General Ricord reminded the foreigners that the courts of the kingdom took their authority from God Almighty; the foreigners claimed he said the courts *were* God Almighty, and renewed their attacks. Foreign Minister Wyllie, ransacking the law of nations for precedents that would help preserve the independence of the kingdom, was ridiculed too: even as a medical student he had amazed people, so the foreigners said, by his ability to split a single hair into enough material for a whole wig. Gerrit Judd, successively President of the Treasury Board, Recorder and Interpreter, Minister of Foreign Affairs, Minister of the Interior, and Minister of Finance, wore gold crowns on his coat, sat in the royal pew at church, rode about town in a gilded and brocaded coach, and announced his comings and goings with seventeen-gun salutes. This made the foreigners laugh when it did not make them cry.

As far as dignity and a sense of proportion were concerned the foreigners themselves did not have a flawless touch. When the kingdom adopted the Code of Etiquette of the Congress of Vienna to settle questions of precedence in the official community a great hoot of scorn went up among the diplomats, but then they spent the next few years arguing bitterly about who should stand first in line. Once the code was adopted the king began to hold receptions at court, and at one of these early social functions, which was attended by all the diplomats in full dress, the British Consul General took to Attorney General Ricord with his fists. And the United States Commissioner, who regarded Kauikeaouli's domains as a toy kingdom beneath contempt, still found it necessary to send home to Washington a manuscript list of foreigners' grievances two hundred and eight feet long—twelve inches of handwritten grievance for every eight whites in the kingdom, men, women, and children.

Obscured by all this solemn buffoonery, and struggling to get into the light, were some serious questions. Was Kauikeaouli a real king or just a savage in a dress suit given false importance by a clique of puffed up sycophants who had sold their birthright for a red sash and a feathered hat? Was the Hawaiian kingdom a sovereign nation like other nations? Did the kingdom have a right to remain independent if it could not meet the demands of civilized powers? And if not, who should control the islands?

Because the government was weak local questions had a way of escaping to the outside world. And because the kingdom's treaty relations with the great powers were disadvantageous the outside world had a way of pressing very hard on the government. Several times in the reign of King Kauikeaouli Honolulu lay under the guns of foreign warships, and each year seemed to make it less likely that the kingdom could survive. "Such has always been the case with large countries," wrote David Malo, "the small ones have been eaten up."

Evil, said Malo, was at the door, ready to "come in and bite us." The defenses of the government were simply inadequate. For practical purposes the white cabinet members *were* the government: Ricord was the law, Wyllie was the foreign office, and Judd was everything else. Three men could not contain the whirl of crisis stirred up by foreigners. Ricord left the islands in 1847, bequeathing the insoluble problem of the courts to William Lee. Wyllie was forced to carry on an interminable and vexing correspondence with Washington, London, and Paris. He was temperamentally incapable of using one word where a thousand would do, and he covered hundreds of pages of official stationery each week with his spiky and indecipherable handwriting. His papers became a kind of personal seismograph of national upheaval, and eventually he wrote and minuted and docketed himself into a state of hallucinatory exhaustion. At the same time Judd's tightly knit personality began to unravel under the strain of office, and he made so many enemies in the foreign community and in the cabinet that at last, in 1853, he was forced out of office. King Kauikeaouli did very little to hold things together. He did not much want to be king—at one point he was heard to say he would rather be the captain of a clipper ship—and as the scale of events grew larger he shrank more and more from responsibility. His health failed completely in 1854, and most people, waiting for him to die, thought the kingdom would die with him.

Their Finest Hour

The harbinger of trouble as the eighteen forties opened was, not surprisingly, British Consul Richard Charlton. The immediate matter at issue was land. Ever since 1826 Charlton had held possession of a sizeable piece of ground not far from the waterfront at Honolulu and a small plot in the rear of the town at a place called Beretania (a Hawaiian rendering of the word "Britain"). The land was a gift from the chiefs, in gratitude for sympathy shown by the British government on the death of King Liholiho and Queen Kamamalu in London in 1824; it was to be used for official purposes by the incumbent consul. The legality of Charlton's tenure as Britain's representative was never questioned. Nor was there any controversy about the boundary dividing Charlton's downtown lot from the one next to it, a place named Pulaholaho that covered more than an acre of land at the beach front. Then in April 1840, Charlton presented to Governor Kekuanaoa of Oahu a document purporting to be a lease of Pulaholaho, dated 1826, signed by Boki as Governor of Oahu and Kalanimoku as regent of the kingdom, and good for two hundred and ninety-nine years.

The difficulties were obvious. A signed lease was a most formal instrument from a period in which land matters were handled verbally and boundaries were defined by custom. Pulaholaho had been occupied continuously by natives—at times as many as fifteen buildings stood there— and not once had Charlton protested or asked for rent. Boki and Kalanimoku were long dead; no living chief had ever heard of the lease; and no one at Honolulu, native or foreign, had ever seen the document before Charlton presented it and demanded to be put in possession of Pulaholaho.

The government developed two lines of thought. First, the lease document might be a forgery. Second, the lease would be invalid even if the signatures of Boki and Kalanimoku were genuine. They were mere administrators; in 1826 Kaahumanu was sole regent, and she alone had the right to deed or lease land.

King Kauikeaouli told Charlton the lease was worthless, but Charlton would not be put off. He said that if his claim was not honored the government would be in far worse trouble than at the time of the *Clementine* episode. At the same time Charlton himself found it hard to stay out of trouble. His wandering cattle continued to trespass on others' lands. He was fined five dollars when his dog bit a foreign woman. He got into a violent argument with James Jackson Jarves, editor of the *Polynesian,* and hit him with a horsewhip. A friend of Jarves threw Charlton to the floor. The consul suffered a broken finger and badly bruised hip, and was fined six dollars for assault. He wrote to the Foreign Office in London, asking for a man of war to protect British interests at the islands.

Eighteen months went by and no ship came. Neither did the government make any move to put Charlton in possession of Pulaholaho. Charlton brooded over this, and over several legal cases which had gone against Britishers in the courts. Then in September 1842, without any announcement beyond a single curt note to King Kauikeaouli, Charlton left the islands, bound for London, avowedly to secure "justice" for British subjects and at the same time to stop the rise of American influence at Honolulu. The personal insults he had suffered at the hands of the government, he added, would not go unredressed.

Charlton left as his deputy a young Englishman named Alexander Simpson, a relative of Sir George Simpson, Governor of the Hudson's Bay Company in North America. Sir George had visited Honolulu earlier in 1842 and had become interested in the question of the Hawaiian kingdom's independence. At his suggestion a diplomatic mission (consisting of William Richards, the chiefs' adviser, and Timothy Haalilio, a capable young chief who had been private secretary to King Kauikeaouli) was dispatched to try to get equitable treaties and a recognition of independence from the United States, Great Britain, and France. Alexander Simpson, by contrast, was a strong imperialist. From the moment of his arrival at Honolulu he began to plot the annexation of the islands by Great Britain.

The younger Simpson's views were common knowledge. The Hawaiian government refused to recognize him as consul. Publicly Simpson objected; privately he described the king as a "cypher," and Gerrit Judd as the source of his troubles, a man of bad character and anti-British prejudices.

Soon after his "appointment" Simpson found himself defending the absent Charlton. Charlton owed a business firm in Valparaiso a considerable amount of money, and he was sued for it in the Honolulu courts, where he was found liable for almost ten thousand dollars. Simpson argued, as almost all foreigners did automatically, that the local courts had no jurisdiction in the case, but the government went ahead and attached Charlton's property on behalf of his creditors. Thereupon Simpson wrote to the commander of the British fleet in the Pacific, asking him as a matter of urgency to send a man of war to Honolulu to exact full recompense for past injuries, and to stay as long as British interests were in need of protection. The message reached Admiral Sir Richard Thomas at San Blas, Mexico. He dispatched the frigate *Carysfort,* commanded by Lord George Paulet, under instructions to guard British interests and to restore Charlton's property, by force if necessary, should the situation be as Simpson described it.

Just a few days after Richard Charlton sailed for London with his case book of grievances, the British Foreign Office issued a policy statement setting out its views on the Pacific islands. More frequent visits by naval commanders should be made, and real grievances ought certainly to be redressed, but native governments should be treated with "great forbearance and courtesy," and their laws and customs should be respected. The object was "rather to strengthen those authorities and to give them a sense of their own independence, by leaving the administration of justice in their own hands, than to make them feel their dependence on Foreign Powers, by interfering unnecessarily in every matter in which a foreign subject is concerned, and to compel those rulers by peremptory menace, or a show of physical force, to render to foreign subjects that measure of justice which may appear to the aggrieved person, or to the officer who steps forward in his behalf, to be his due." Neither Richard Charlton, nor Alexander Simpson, nor Admiral Thomas, nor Lord George Paulet, nor any of King Kauikeaouli's advisers knew of this statement of policy when, on February 10, 1843, the *Carysfort* anchored at Honolulu.

Paulet would not deal with anybody but the king. He sent a list of grievances to Kauikeaouli, adding an ultimatum—if matters were not settled, "immediate coercive steps" would be taken. He was sure that one shot from the *Carysfort* would frighten off any number of Hawaiian troops assembled to prevent a landing. An American man of war, USS *Boston,* was at Honolulu, but its commander, John C. Long, was quite without instructions to cover a cannonade; he could do nothing but watch. On the morning of February 18 a brig was towed into the harbor so that Britishers could be safe from the threatened attack. All over town foreigners piled money, papers, clothes, and household goods on carts and sent them down to the waterfront to be put on board. Early in the afternoon news came that the king had given in, and salutes were fired to mark the agreement.

Alexander Simpson was to be recognized as consul, and King Kauikeaouli was to confer with him directly in settling grievances. Charlton's attached property was to be returned. In several commercial cases involving Britishers new court hearings were to be held. Britishers could be confined in irons at the Honolulu fort only on felony charges, defined according to British law, and their trials must be heard by juries approved by the British consul.

British honor had been vindicated by British naval strength. Alexander Simpson, however, had still bigger things in view, and Paulet backed him up. As sailors from the *Carysfort* brawled with natives along the waterfront, Simpson and Paulet went on to extort further concessions from the government. Britishers dissatisfied with court verdicts filed claims for indemnities amounting to more than a hundred thousand dollars, and Kauikeaouli was forced to sign a clearance for Charlton's lease of Pulaholaho.

The demands became so pressing that Kauikeaouli and his advisers concluded that Paulet was aiming at the annexation of the islands. On February 23 the king met privately with French Consul Jules Dudoit, Acting United States Commercial Agent William Hooper, Gerrit Judd, and Commander Long of the *Boston,* to discuss the possibility of ceding the islands to France and the United States jointly, thus forestalling a cession to Great Britain on Paulet's terms. Papers were prepared, but on the morning of February 24 Judd changed his mind and would not support the king's decision to sign. Kauikeaouli was desperate. He could see the British were out to ruin him; he had made up his mind not to go on, so his advisers reported. Various abysmal alternatives were considered, but there was nothing to be done. On February 25 Kauikeaouli relinquished his kingdom at last to Paulet, with the stipulation that the Hawaiian government would make every effort to get back its sovereignty.

The formal cession was carried out at the Honolulu fort. British marines and Hawaiian soldiers formed a hollow square on the parade ground, and Paulet and his officers took their places with the king and the chiefs on the veranda of one of the fort houses. Kauikeaouli made a short speech in Hawaiian and Gerrit Judd translated it into English: "Hear ye! I make known to you that I am in perplexity by reason of difficulties into which I have been brought without cause; therefore, I have given away the life of the land, hear ye! But my rule over you, my people, and your privileges, will continue, for I have hope that the life of the land will be restored when my conduct is justified." The deed of cession was read, the Hawaiian flag was hauled down, and the British flag was raised. Paulet's ship exchanged salutes with the fort, and the *Carysfort's* band played "God Save The Queen," and then, with "refined cruelty," "Isle Of Beauty, Fare Thee Well."

Under the terms of the new government the king and his advisers continued to administer the affairs of the native population. To handle business affecting foreigners a commission was to be created, consisting of the king or his deputy, Paulet, and two officers from the *Carysfort*. After some hesitation Gerrit Judd agreed to serve as the Hawaiian representative.

In theory the king had the right to protest the seizure of the islands, but in practice Paulet made every effort to stop him from doing so. The British version of events was to be carried to London by Alexander Simpson in the government schooner *Hooikaika,* confiscated and renamed *Albert.* Kauikeaouli asked Gerrit Judd to find someone who would put the government's case. At a dance aboard the *Boston* Judd talked privately to a twenty-four-year-old American merchant, James F. B. Marshall, who agreed to undertake the mission.

Judd prepared Marshall's credentials, working by night in the royal tomb on the palace grounds, and using as a desk the coffin of Kaahumanu. When the documents were ready a canoe brought the king down from Maui to sign them. In darkness at Waikiki Kauikeaouli penned his name and left, while Paulet sat at dinner a few miles away at Honolulu. The *Albert* sailed on March 11 with Simpson aboard, and also Marshall, who for public purposes was said to be traveling on business for the Honolulu firm of Ladd & Co. A few Americans at Honolulu knew what was happening, but Paulet suspected nothing.

As soon as the commission government began its work it became clear that Paulet had no intention of confining himself to the affairs of foreigners. New taxes were imposed on the natives; the liquor laws of Honolulu were relaxed, and the laws against fornication were repealed. A new constabulary was recruited, and a native regiment called The Queen's Own was organized, and Judd was ordered to use treasury funds to pay the wages of the turncoats.

On behalf of the king and the national legislature Judd protested. Paulet would not restore the old laws. Judd continued to object, Paulet became abusive, and Judd resigned from the commission on May 11. Now Paulet could not claim to have even the semblance of cooperation on the part of the Hawaiian government. The king asked Paulet to reinstate Judd. Paulet would not. Judd continued, of course, to hold office in the cabinet, and he used his post at the treasury to harass Paulet. He began by withholding funds from The Queen's Own regiment, and only the appearance of an officer from the *Carysfort* in full uniform with side arms made him hand over the money. Then Judd went even further: he took all the government's papers to the royal tomb and conducted his official business alone there at night, leaving Paulet stranded in his efforts to review cases involving foreigners.

While Judd was fighting Paulet to a standstill at Honolulu the British government's policy statement on the Pacific islands was making its way to Admiral Sir Richard Thomas on the west coast of South America.

Paulet's actions were wildly outside the scope of these instructions. As soon as Thomas read the message from the Foreign Office he sailed for Honolulu aboard his flag ship, HMS *Dublin*. He arrived on July 26, conferred with Paulet, had an audience with the king, framed some articles of agreement providing that in future British subjects at the islands would have parity of treatment with other foreigners, and then announced that the independence of the kingdom would be restored immediately.

On July 31 the whole town assembled on the plains east of Honolulu to watch the ceremonies. Paulet was there too, looking sour. As the king appeared, escorted by his royal guard, the crowd cheered, a Hawaiian flag was broken out, and cannon were fired on the plains, at the fort, in the harbor, and at the battery on Punchbowl. British marines passed in review and then fought a mock battle. The martial observances ended about noon. In the afternoon Kauikeaouli walked in procession with his chiefs to the stone church at Kawaiahao. There Gerrit Judd read in Hawaiian Admiral Thomas' declaration returning sovereignty to the king. Kauikeaouli's speech was short. The life of the land, he said, is preserved in righteousness—"Ua mau ke ea o ka aina i ka pono."

To mark the restoration all the prisoners in the fort were released. Labor taxes were remitted for ten days. The Queen's Own regiment was disbanded, and its members were pardoned for having sworn allegiance to a foreign ruler. All over Honolulu there were official dinners, private dances, and drunken brawls. At a great temperance feast held in Nuuanu valley the newly written Restoration Anthem was sung, to the tune of "God Save The Queen:"

> *Hail to the worthy name!*
> *Worthy his country's fame!*
> Thomas, *the brave!*
> *Long shall thy virtues be*
> *Shrined in our memory*
> *Who came to set us free*
> *Quick o'er the wave!*

Then the dignitaries lowered themselves to mats spread on the ground under a canopy of Hawaiian flags and addressed themselves to quantities of cooked pig, fish, turkey, and poi. Only the Britishers of Honolulu did not attend.

On August 23 the *Carysfort* hoisted sail, but to everybody's disappointment there was no wind. Two days later she made her way out of the harbor. In September news came that the British government had disavowed the seizure of the islands. Admiral Thomas remained at Honolulu until March 1844, suffering as best he could through more temperance dinners, dispensing dignified benevolence, and doing a great deal to salve the wounds inflicted by Paulet. Later in the year the *Carysfort* came back to Honolulu in the course of a Pacific cruise. Salutes were exchanged between ship and shore, but the king refused Paulet's request for a conciliatory audience, and in a fit of pique Paulet ordered his gunners to fire random volleys of blanks in the middle of the night, waking and alarming the town. The Hawaiians had the last word, just the same. Paulet's final communication with the government, a letter written from Hilo, Hawaii, before he left for the northern Pacific, complained that a native laundry man had stolen some of his clothes.

All this time the independence mission of William Richards and Timothy Haalilio had been overseas. The two envoys spent the month of December 1842, at Washington, trying to convince Daniel Webster, secretary of state in the administration of President John Tyler, that American interests in the Pacific would be endangered if the Hawaiian Islands should fall into the hands of a European power. Webster was unresponsive, and he remained so until Richards let it be known that if independence was not guaranteed he would place the islands in the hands of Great Britain. As a matter of fact he was empowered to do anything he wanted: he was carrying papers signed and sealed by King Kauikeaouli but otherwise completely blank. By the turn of the year the administration was ready to make its views known. No nation should seek exclusive commercial privileges at the islands, much less tamper with the independence of the kingdom. The United States, whose interest was paramount there, would regard with dissatisfaction any attempt by another power to take possession of the islands. President Tyler, without saying so directly, was applying the Monroe Doctrine in the Pacific Ocean.

Richards and Haalilio reached London to find that Richard Charlton had got there ahead of them, but Charlton's arguments in favor of a British annexation of the islands lost whatever force they might have had when news came of the Tyler administration's pronouncement on Hawaiian independence. At the beginning of April 1843, the Earl of Aberdeen, head of the foreign office, told Richards and Haalilio that Britain was ready to recognize King Kauikeaouli's sovereignty as an independent monarch.

The Hawaiian envoys were in France when word of Paulet's seizure of the kingdom reached Europe. The British government disavowed Paulet's action and announced that the occupation would be ended as soon as the grievances of Britishers were adjusted. François Guizot, the French minister of foreign affairs, suggested a three-power declaration of support for Hawaiian independence. The United States, keeping up its traditional policy of avoiding entangling alliances, declined to be a partner in any joint statement. Britain and France went ahead and signed a dual agreement, dated November 28, 1843, engaging "reciprocally to consider the Sandwich Islands an independent state." Hawaiian independence seemed well established, at least for the moment.

Richards and Haalilio had done as well as they could reasonably have hoped. They had not, however, succeeded in getting the great powers to put their treaty relations with the Hawaiian government on an equitable basis. The United States would not make any treaty at all. France seemed ready to negotiate a new agreement of some sort, but in the meantime the treaty forced upon King Kauikeaouli by Laplace in 1839 still held. Britain drafted a new treaty, but without consulting the Hawaiian government; the document was simply sent to the islands for signature. Full membership in the family of nations was obviously a long way off.

For one happy moment, but only for a moment, it seemed as if the last had been heard of Richard Charlton. He was removed from the office of consul to the islands, and the alleged grievances he had brought to London were left to the Hawaiian government for disposition—all except one, and that one was Charlton's claim to the lease of Pulaholaho. Charlton's successor, Consul General William Miller, was told to make sure Charlton's lease was genuine and then to put him in possession of his land. Reams of evidence were collected at Honolulu to prove that Charlton could not possibly have a real claim, but Miller, supported by his home government, went ahead and measured the lot for Charlton. His original instructions specified that Charlton should receive only those parts of Pulaholaho that had not been appropriated by others, but Miller's boundary lines surrounded twenty-three houses with more than one hundred and fifty occupants and cut through a stone house belonging to King Kauikeaouli.

Pulaholaho was worth about fifteen thousand dollars. Charlton returned to the islands in May 1844, with great expectations, only to run up against more legal difficulties. In 1842, when he was being dunned for his commercial debts, he had refused to pay, and he had added to his refusal a public statement, repeated several times, that George Pelly, the Honolulu agent of the firm that was pressing him, was a sodomite. When Charlton appeared at Honolulu again Pelly took him to court for slander and won a substantial judgment. Pelly paid his attorney and gave the rest of the damages—$3,450—to Mrs. Charlton. Charlton said that if Pelly was not a sodomite the jurymen who convicted him certainly were, and he narrowly avoided another set of slander suits.

Charlton sold his properties at Honolulu and left the islands for the last time in 1846, but litigation concerning his lands and leases continued to pass through the courts and government offices for the rest of the decade. In particular, a prolonged and bad tempered argument sprang up between Minister of Finance Judd, Minister of Foreign Affairs Wyllie, and

Consul General Miller over the leasehold and rents of Charlton's former premises at Beretania, now occupied by Miller. The three dignitaries managed to quarrel for months about the value of a few shade trees Miller had chopped down. In 1851 Wyllie expressed a fervent wish that the grave might "close over Charlton and his mysteries, for ever, without any further question as to his motives or his doings." Charlton died in England at the end of 1852.

Ladd & Co.

While Richard Charlton was turning the kingdom upside down over an acre of land at Honolulu three young Americans were planning to float a great company that would sell all the uncultivated land in the islands to capitalists in the United States and Europe. Peter Brinsmade, William Hooper, and William Ladd were the principals of Ladd & Co. All were New Englanders, and Brinsmade had been a student at Yale Theological Seminary. These were useful recommendations. The missionaries supported Brinsmade's appointment as United States Commercial Agent, succeeding John Coffin Jones; and when Brinsmade was away from Honolulu William Hooper acted as his deputy.

The three partners, then, had the blessing of forces for good in the community. But, as it happened, their connection with the mission, and the mission's influence with the chiefs, brought into existence one of the most spectacular of the many financial bubbles in Hawaiian history.

Ladd, Brinsmade, and Hooper opened their store at Honolulu in 1833, at a time when the natives of the rural districts were flocking to the port towns in large numbers. Among the missionaries this caused great concern. In their view Honolulu and Lahaina were cities of the plain, places where Hawaiians would lose their souls. The best hope for the future was a civilized, Christianized, sturdy native yeomanry. If the Hawaiians would only go back to the virgin land of the countryside and cultivate the soil they could be saved, and the nation would be saved too.

Ladd, Brinsmade, and Hooper, putting all these notions together, thought they could see a way to make an honest profit out of good works. The affair began soundly enough. In 1835, with the permission of the chiefs, the partners leased a tract of land at Koloa, Kauai, and for several years they ran a sugar plantation and mill there, sharing the modest profits with their native laborers. In 1837 they put forward a more ambitious scheme involving the lease of a whole district, and when that came to nothing they went further.

Using William Richards as a go between, they negotiated a secret contract with King Kauikeaouli in November 1841, under which Ladd & Co. was given the right to arrange for the cultivation of all unoccupied and unimproved lands in the kingdom. Sites must be selected within twelve months and operations must begin within five years; the agreement would run for a century. A joint stock company would be formed. The king was to have unlimited subscription rights, and capitalists of any nation could buy into the scheme.

At the end of 1841 the continued independence of the nation was by no means certain. Accordingly Ladd & Co. stipulated that if independence was forfeited the contract should lapse. An agreement was made authorizing Peter Brinsmade to go overseas as an informal agent of the kingdom, promoting independence at the same time as he disposed of the exclusive rights of Ladd & Co. under the November contract.

Brinsmade visited the United States, Britain, and France in turn, without finding any takers for his uncultivated lands. Belgium seemed to offer better prospects, and he was looking into the situation there when he heard that his helpful friend William Richards had come to Europe to obtain assurances from the great powers on the matter of Hawaiian independence. Brinsmade had been making representations on behalf of independence; now Richards' independence mission could be set to work for Ladd & Co. Richards carried a power of attorney from his king; Brinsmade had the power of persuasiveness. Seduced by the promise of a directorship in the great colonization company to be formed, Richards signed, on behalf of King Kauikeaouli, the "Belgian Contract" of May 1843, under which Ladd & Co. transferred its assets to the Belgian Company of Colonization, which in turn agreed to set up a subsidiary called the Royal Community of the Sandwich Islands, with a capital of several hundred thousand dollars. For this transfer Ladd & Co. would receive $200,000, together with additional cash in lieu of shares. The Royal Community would send out settlers as soon as the independence of the kingdom was secured.

At Brussels, then, things looked good for Ladd & Co. But at Honolulu Brinsmade's partners were in trouble. The firm had always been short of working capital—indeed, that was why the partners decided to sell their assets. (It developed later, as a matter of fact, that they had quietly sold a half interest in the plantation at Koloa to a New York businessman in 1840, before they sold the whole plantation over again to the Royal Community.) By the end of 1843 Hooper and Ladd were badly in need of the promised $200,000 from Belgium. Until it arrived they would have to borrow, and interest rates at Honolulu were ruinous—3 percent per month.

To add to their woes Paulet's seizure of the islands and the complications that followed delayed the recognition of the kingdom's independence. Brinsmade's letters from Europe grew gloomier and gloomier. The Royal Community made no move to sell stock. William Richards reconsidered his early enthusiasm; he would give "no small sum," he told Brinsmade, to have his name off the contract papers. The house of cards was about to collapse. Brinsmade tried to prop it up. He stayed on in Europe as long as he could, looking for new investors. Nothing worked. Penniless, he left for home, and arrived at Honolulu early in 1846 on an unpaid ticket.

He came back to a bankrupt firm. Ladd & Co. had failed in November 1844. The firm owed the government about fourteen thousand dollars, and its debts in Honolulu totalled more than a hundred thousand dollars. Ladd and Hooper closed their doors and proceeded to allow the government, which represented the lesser of two evils, to recover its money.

The government allowed a decent period of waiting, but by March 1845, it was clear that the Belgian Contract would never come to anything. Gerrit Judd, who in William Richards' absence had become the confidant of the chiefs, was a great Hawaiian nationalist, and he had never approved of Ladd & Co.'s plan to flood the islands with foreign capital and foreign settlers, especially Belgian Catholics. Now he could take exemplary action against the partners as interlopers, and defaulting interlopers at that. William Ladd used a familiar defense. He claimed that the Hawaiian courts did not have jurisdiction in the case. When he was overruled he and his partners took the position that the government could not sell any property held by Ladd & Co. because all the firm's assets had been transferred to the Royal Community. Next they tried to regain the right to select lands under the original contract with King Kauikeaouli, dated November 1841. The government argued that once the firm transferred its assets to the Royal Community the partners lost their contractual rights; they were trying to get back a cake that had already been eaten. In November 1845, the contract of 1841 expired by limitation. The only possibility left open to the firm was to sue for damages. Peter Brinsmade sued James Jackson Jarves of the *Polynesian* for $50,000, on the ground that Jarves had published articles which damaged Brinsmade's chances of attracting investors in Europe. He lost. Then Ladd & Co. sued the government for breach of contract. The value they placed on their damaged rights was $378,000.

On his way home from Europe Brinsmade had tried without success to interest the United States government in his firm's case. The Polk administration's lack of sympathy did not inhibit the newly appointed United States Commissioner to the islands, Anthony Ten Eyck, from coming out strongly in support of Ladd & Co. Ten Eyck, in fact, became the firm's principal counsel, and he argued the case at great length and with great heat against Attorney General Ricord.

The stakes were very high. Almost every merchant at Honolulu had a financial interest in the outcome of the case, and the town broke up into factions. Brinsmade and his supporters started a newspaper, the *Sandwich Islands News,* in opposition to the *Polynesian,* and week by week torrents of invective were poured over the heads of the government's advisers. Gerrit Judd retaliated by setting native policemen to watch William Ladd's house, and he gave Police Prefect Arthur Brickwood a Treasury office spy glass to keep track of people going in and out of Brinsmade's house. Ten Eyck and the *Sandwich Islands News* defined the battle as one of right reason and humanity against the callous and encrusted powers of the state monster; Ricord and the *Polynesian* appealed to order and properly constituted authority against anarchy. Ten Eyck made William Richards look alternately venal, foolish, and incredibly naïve (the last was without doubt closest to the truth). Ricord made the partners of Ladd & Co. seem like practiced rogues who used political intrigue to get themselves out of financial difficulties.

A panel of arbitrators heard Ladd & Co. give evidence which covered more than five hundred closely printed pages. Then, quite abruptly, the firm withdrew its suit, claiming that the government had used ruinous procrastination, allowing extravagant expenses to pile up to the point where it was financially impossible for the partners to go on with the case.

The villain, so they said, was Gerrit Judd. He had used his cabinet office to harass them beyond endurance, and in addition he had obtained separate judgments against them, attaching their property and entering their homes to seize articles of the most trifling value, down to family Bibles. None of this had anything to do with the firm's suit against the government, the partners said. Judd was pursuing his private interests, trying to collect rental money on a wharf he had leased to Ladd & Co. Under the arbitration compact the partners were supposed to be protected against sacrifice and alienation of property. Rather than put up with browbeating they abandoned the arbitration, gave up their claim to damages, and assigned their assets to a committee of their creditors.

Even then the affair would not die. It was a complex business, and it bred new law suits and new feuds at every turn, filling the town with "bitterness and revenge," according to the wife of the missionary Richard Armstrong. "We all rejoiced," she wrote, "to have pious, principled men come here as merchants, but O their example has been infinitely worse than the infidel, because they have disgraced our cause." The businessmen of Honolulu, no friends of the missionaries, were not upset at that—

indeed they took a grim pleasure at the fall of the pious partners—but they were extremely unhappy to be left holding Ladd & Co.'s worthless paper. Several divisions of the firm's assets were tried, all of them painful, none of them satisfactory. William Ladd decided to stay at Honolulu to try to pay off his debts, and Gerrit Judd, determined to collect his rental money, continued to make periodic raids on Ladd's property.

Peter Brinsmade, for his part, felt betrayed and abandoned after what he regarded as an honorable attempt to gather merit along with money. In a series of articles in the *Sandwich Islands News* he ran the gamut from rage to pain and then elegiac calm as he took inventory of the wreckage of his business and his private life. At the end of it all he was left with nothing but a tiny plot of land on Kauai; and to obtain title even to that he had to petition the government, begging the cabinet's indulgence so that his dead wife might remain buried there, secure from the legal storms that shortened her life.

The Great Mahele

Not many foreigners at the islands wanted Ladd & Co. to win their case, but most of them would have agreed that the traditional Hawaiian land system was due for an overhaul. Almost from the very beginning the interests of the chiefs and the interests of white men had been in conflict. The issue grew more acute each year. It would have to be resolved, and if the islands were ever to live up to their potential as an outpost of civilization in the Pacific it would have to be resolved the white man's way. As for the Hawaiian commoners, very few foreigners paid any attention to them, but those who did—the missionaries, for example—had no doubt that a revolution in landholding could only benefit the natives.

The chiefs were not so sure. They were perfectly pleased with things as they stood. The old dispensation gave them control of the land, and land was power because it was the source of life. The basic unit was the ahupuaa, in theory a wedge with its point in the mountains and its base at sea outside the reef. As Curtis Lyons, a surveyor and son of the missionary Lorenzo Lyons, described it, all the necessities of life were available within the ahupuaa, "from uka, mountain, whence came wood, kapa, for clothing, olona, for fish-line, ti-leaf for wrapping paper, ie for ratan lashing, wild birds for food, to the kai, sea, whence came ia, fish, and all connected therewith." Commoners were not serfs; they were free to move from one ahupuaa to another, from the train of one chief to another. But they had no rights in the land. They paid heavily in produce and labor for the privilege of cultivating the soil. Even white men who wanted to do business at the islands held property only at the pleasure of the chiefs. What could be more satisfactory?

Any changes, then, would be made at the expense of the chiefs. Still, by the forties there was evidence that the chiefs would have to come to terms with change in this as in so many other matters. The look of the whole Pacific was changing, especially along the west coast of northern America. The Oregon Territory was being opened up to settlement, California was on the verge of great things, and the islands would surely be drawn into the American orbit. The foreign community, growing rapidly, now included substantial businessmen as well as beached sailors. These men had important interests to protect and they were calling on their home governments for support. At the same time the missionaries kept talking about the need to promote industry and thrift and all the other Calvinist virtues among the common people, and in their mind the best way to do this was to encourage the commoners to become small land-owners.

The first formal statement of the idea that commoners had rights of ownership in the lands of the kingdom appeared in the constitution of 1840. Then in 1841 the national legislature empowered the governors of the various islands to lease land to white men for as long as fifty years, and directed foreigners to register their leases in writing so that there should be no misunderstandings about terms and rents. This was meant to be an improvement over the vague and indeterminate verbal leases of the past, but the foreigners, perversely, chose to regard it as an imposition, and their consuls protested to King Kauikeaouli and Governor Kekuanaoa of Oahu.

After this the land question was held in abeyance while the question of the kingdom's independence was fought out on the diplomatic level. By 1844 King Kauikeaouli appeared safe on his throne, and the issue of property rights for foreigners and commoners was brought up again. The chiefs, pushed along by Gerrit Judd and some of their other advisers, agreed to a serious examination of the problem. "This measure," wrote Robert Wyllie soon after his arrival at Honolulu, "will do much credit to the government; it will set for ever at rest many complaints arising from a misconception of the nature and permanency of land-donations made by the chiefs, as a mark of personal esteem, or in payment of presents made or services rendered to them; it will fix property on a secure basis, facilitate advances of money to proprietors, encourage population and the improvement of land, and prevent further disputes about titles and their limits."

That was a tall order, of course, and as it turned out the government was wildly optimistic about the time it would take. A Board of Land Commissioners, appointed in 1846, was given two years to register claims and settle disputes. The Board remained in existence for almost ten years, and when it disbanded in 1855 it left undone enough work to keep a good many civil servants busy for the rest of the century.

The land division, which came to be known as the Great Mahele, was complicated. The king gave up his rights to all the lands of the kingdom, except for certain estates which in time became known as the crown lands, reserved to the reigning monarch. The chiefs were given the chance to take out fee simple titles to land they had previously held in fief as retainers of the king. Commoners were allowed to buy small lots, or kuleanas, in fee simple. Chiefs and commoners alike had to have their lands surveyed and pay a commutation fee in order to perfect their titles. For the most part chiefs paid their fees in land, and this became government or public land. Aliens were allowed to lease land for as long as fifty years, and in 1850 legislation was passed allowing them to purchase property on the same terms as subjects of the kingdom.

White men did not need to be told more than once about the benefits of a secure title. Businessmen and missionaries came before the Board of Commissioners one after another, and so did the heirs of the beached foreigners of past decades, ready to claim compensation for services rendered long ago. The humblest of men made their claims and paid their fees: Bob the Tailor Kilday, who cut cloth for King Liholiho in the era of the first Hawaiian dandies and was rewarded with a lot in Nuuanu valley, which he held stubbornly in the face of the chiefs' efforts to remove him; Louis Gravier, a French sailmaker who outfitted one of the ships Boki took on his fatal sandalwood expedition; Dutch Harry Zupplien, a tavern keeper who since 1810 had been burying his hard-earned money in his back yard; Yankee Jem Vowles, a notorious barroom brawler; Black George Hyatt, a negro musician who played the clarinet for three Hawaiian kings and led the orchestra at Honolulu's first cotillion; Long Tom Gandall, the chiefs' gunpowder expert; John Gowan, citizen of Boston, who was Kaumualii's linguist on Kauai; Portuguese Jo; Charles the Lascar; and dozens of others. Some of the claims were more substantial. Alexander Adams, once Kamehameha's pilot and now the lusty patriarch of a large part-Hawaiian family, claimed and was awarded a town lot at Honolulu, about four acres of land at Waikiki, nearly three hundred acres of taro land and upland in Kalihi valley to the west of Honolulu proper, and an estate of twenty-five-hundred acres at Niu, a sunny valley a few miles east of Diamond Head. William Sumner, who had taken the French priests away from the islands in 1831, claimed and was awarded an estate of seven thousand acres at Moanalua, west of Honolulu.

The natives, chiefs and commoners alike, were slower to make their claims. It took two years to get the chiefs to agree to a division between themselves and the king. Gerrit Judd was the intermediary. "You can never know," he wrote to Robert Wyllie, "what obstacles had to be encountered; whose feelings were hurt, whose rights, in his or her estimation, were disregarded . . ." Once the division was made the chiefs were supposed to pay their commutation fees and take out their titles, but a good many of them did not do it, and laws had to be passed in 1854, 1860, and again in 1892 to give them enough time.

The commoners were just as dilatory, and even those who knew what a fee simple title was often got lost in a maze of claims, hearings, and commutations. In the end something like ten thousand kuleana claims were awarded to commoners, for about thirty thousand acres of good agricultural land, as compared with chiefs' lands of a million and a half acres, government lands of about the same extent, and crown lands of not quite a million acres.

No one knew quite how to define a kuleana. One government land agent might simply mark off a spot of ground planted in taro. Another, understanding that taro land had to lie fallow for two or three years, might look at the area under cultivation and multiply it by two or three. Another might be working in a district where the resident missionary had the interests of the commoners very much at heart (and in some cases missionaries themselves worked as agents and surveyors), and there the kuleana might be as much as fifteen, thirty, or even forty acres.

The surveyors, according to Curtis Lyons, used every possible method of measurement and every conceivable scale, and their meridians pointed everywhere. No district was surveyed by one man; at Waikiki as many as a dozen men had a hand in operations, and they produced overlaps and interlayers by the score. The surveyors' native helpers were enthusiastic but muddled. The poles and flags reminded them of the makahiki, and the folded tripod of the measuring instruments looked to them like the bundled bones of their ancestors. They thought the chain being dragged along the ground marked the boundary, and the compass was a mystery to them. A systematic government survey was not set up until 1870, and it took a generation after that to reduce confusion about boundaries to a minimum.

Long before then, however, the outlines of a nation committed to Western property practices became visible. Over fish ponds, taro patches, heiau sites, lokus or game playing areas, and kapu places of bygone days, the amateur surveyors and draftsmen laid their measurements. Boundaries in valleys, once defined by the direction taken by a rolling stone, were fixed by triangulations. Traditional landmarks—streams, trees, prominent rocks, and heaps of stones—gave way to markings on maps. The old konohiki system, under which a chief appointed an agent or steward to manage his lands and collect his taxes, was replaced by a stystem under which each owner determined for himself the best use to which his land might be put, being free to cultivate, lease, or sell at will.

It was a genuine revolution, and the white men who saw it through had no doubt that it was all for the best. For the foreigners, certainly, it was the beginning of a new era; but for the Hawaiian commoners it was the beginning of the end. In their first exercise of free choice they chose to uproot themselves. They were liberated at last from the burdensome tax payments to the chiefs that had kept them tied to the land, and most of them found more interesting things to do than grow taro, which required a long time and a lot of hard work. The idea of the kuleana, the small freehold lot cultivated as an independent family farm, never took hold. In the old days the taro patch and the family had flourished together; a single word, ohana, served to describe both a cluster of taro roots and a family group. The Great Mahele, the great division, cut the connection, because once the commoner was free to buy land he was also free to sell it, and that was a freedom he understood. So the great division became the great dispossession. By the end of the nineteenth century white men owned four acres of land for every one owned by a native, and this included chiefs' lands. The commoners had had their moment, and it had passed by. They were left with not much more than a terrible sense of deprivation.

Who Is the Despotic Dr. Judd?

Of all the white men in the Hawaiian government no one did more for the chiefs than Gerrit Judd. In formal processions at Honolulu he always marched closest to the king, and no matter how much this upset the other cabinet ministers the chiefs never begrudged him his place of honor. He had their unreserved confidence. He spoke their language fluently, looked after them when they were ill, translated state papers for them, and defended with all his considerable strength the right of the Hawaiian kingdom to be recognized as a sovereign nation.

Under King Kauikeaouli Judd held several posts in turn. In 1842, as president of the Treasury Board, he brought a kind of rough order to the tangled finances of the kingdom. In 1843, as unofficial minister of foreign affairs, he carried on a running battle against Alexander Simpson and Lord George Paulet. From then on, whatever his formal title, he handled all sorts of governmental business, from the minutest matters concerning markets, wharves, roads, and rents, to the most involved diplomacy. He never saw much point in confining himself to the stated responsibilities of a single department; good policy in one place was good policy in another, and he would be the judge of what was good policy.

So wherever the foreign residents looked they saw Judd. They did not like what they saw. Judd's cool assumption that he knew what was best annoyed them. It brought back memories of another man who knew what was best for everyone. "I am at present," wrote Judd to an acquaintance in 1845, "the King Bingham of the Sandwich Islands." Judd liked to use the oath of allegiance as the test of a white man's intentions. If a foreigner would not sign it Judd would have nothing to do with him, and the foreigner might then find the government deaf to his requests, whatever they concerned. Not surprisingly, consuls and diplomats began to write home about Judd in uncomplimentary terms, and soon even the British foreign office was asking, "Who is the despotic Dr. Judd?"

Judd would not have cared for the word "despotic," but all the same he liked power and he knew its uses. He kept an unbreakable hold on the government's finances, and he was almost the sole source of patronage. His intimacy with the chiefs was firmly rooted. It never occurred to Judd that some day he might have to bend with the wind. He was growing into a knotty tree with hard bark, the biggest one in the forest, and it would take a lot of chopping to bring him down.

His enemies began sharpening their axes in earnest as early as 1845. During one of the many disputed commercial cases being heard in the Honolulu courts the government published a pamphlet setting out its views, and the American merchant Charles Brewer took offense at some things that were said about him in print. He cancelled his paid advertisements in the *Polynesian,* the government's newspaper, and gave his business to the *Friend,* a monthly published by Samuel C. Damon, chaplain of the Seamen's Friend Society at Honolulu. Judd, who was Minister of Foreign Affairs at the time, set about to make Damon raise his advertising rates. He told Brewer not to "war with the government," threatening that if he did the government would war with him "by all lawful means." Brewer took his case to United States Commissioner George Brown, and Brown demanded the impeachment of Judd on the ground that he was an instrument of arbitrary and oppressive government.

Judd survived the challenge effortlessly. King Kauikeaouli appointed three men to the investigating committee—Attorney General John Ricord, who was indebted to Judd for his employment; Minister of the Interior

Keoni Ana, son of old John Young and the only Hawaiian member of cabinet during the reign of Kauikeaouli, who was indebted to Judd for whatever efficiency his department had; and John Ii, a reliable Christian Hawaiian. Testimony favorable to Judd was well received; very little of any other kind was heard. The outcome was a foregone conclusion.

Commissioner Brown was not satisfied. The tone of his official letters to the king became abusive. Brown was distinguished for chronic bad temper and overbearing Americanism, and the government had had to put up with him for two years already. It seemed long enough. He was informed that no more of his communications would be received, and until his departure from the islands a year later he remained in a kind of diplomatic limbo. For most men this would have ended matters, but Judd was never one to leave loose ends dangling. As a last step he had Charles Brewer removed from his nominal post as Peruvian consul to the kingdom.

As fast as Judd got rid of one set of enemies another appeared. In 1848 he faced impeachment again. This time George M. Robertson, a clerk in the Department of the Interior, brought sixteen charges against him, with one hundred and seventy-five specifications. Judd was portrayed as "unmatched" in selfishness, vindictiveness, arrogance, hardheadedness, partiality, and vile hypocrisy. Robertson alleged that Judd interfered with the administration of other state offices; used his friendship with William Paty, harbor master and customs commissioner at Honolulu, to trade in imported goods without a license; deprived residents of property by illegal methods; set spies among the foreigners of Honolulu; appropriated public money and property to his own use; misdirected funds, spending excessively on roads in Nuuanu valley (where his home was) and starving other parts of Honolulu; and was generally incompetent.

With his situation rather more serious than it had been during the impeachment proceedings of 1845 Judd took an extraordinary step, one that cost him some valuable support in the official community. Ever since the Ladd & Co. case the *Sandwich Islands News,* under a succession of editors, had been hammering away at the government. Among its best efforts was a series of burlesques, the Tongataboo Letters, describing an imaginary archipelago governed by a group of dreadful clowns, among them a character easily identifiable as Judd. The *News* also took up the question of Attorney General Ricord's departure from the islands in 1847, asserting that the government had juggled truths in allowing Ricord to relinquish his allegiance to the kingdom and take up American citizenship again. Judd wanted to find out who was responsible for these scurrilities. He talked privately to a government employee named William Rogers and gave him $300 to spend on information. Rogers bribed Charles Peacock, a printer at the *News,* to steal the manuscripts of the offending articles.

The handwriting on one set of sheets was that of Anthony Ten Eyck, George Brown's successor as United States Commissioner, a passionate defender of Ladd & Co., and an open enemy of the cabinet.

Honolulu burst into uproar. Ten Eyck was pinned to the wall, exposed as an anonymous subverter of the government to which he had presented his diplomatic credentials. He claimed that he was not the author of some of the manuscripts, but just a copier. This helped him not at all. King Kauikeaouli closed correspondence with him and began proceedings to have him removed from office.

But what about Judd's Machiavellian methods? Minister of the Interior Keoni Ana was upset. Minister of Public Instruction Richard Armstrong did not know what to think. Judd's brother-in-law Asher Bates, the government's legal adviser, reassured Armstrong: in civilized countries, he said, spies were regarded as odious, but not those who paid spies. Foreign Minister Wyllie was not so easily convinced. In his opinion Judd had not acted like a gentleman, and for Wyllie that was a serious matter. "I would wash my hands, at once, from such a Government," he wrote to Armstrong, "were it not that the King is wholly blameless, & that on such trying emergencies, when danger & disgrace unjustly threaten the *Throne*, it becomes *trebly* the duty of every Minister, not to abandon it." The larcenous printer Peacock, for his part, said he had done the deed for patriotic reasons (he was an allegiance man), and that the $300 would get him out of the country ahead of the retribution of Ten Eyck's friends (in fact he did not leave until 1850, and then just ahead of his creditors). Judd was unrepentant. It was a dirty business, he agreed; but, as he put it, when a man was hunting a fox and the animal ran into a hole it had to be tracked.

The cabinet declared that Judd's act had no official sanction. Then Asher Bates and Supreme Court Justice William Lee published an opinion to the effect that the stolen papers could not be regarded as property because they had no monetary value—hence their removal from the *News* office was not larceny. The Privy Council even voted to reimburse Judd for the $300 he had laid out.

With this out of the way the attention of the community returned to the matter of Judd's impeachment. The investigating commission met more than forty times, heard testimony that filled an entire volume of the Privy Council Record, reduced the number of charges from sixteen to six, and finally ruled in favor of Judd. Judd appeared once again as the grey eminence of government, a man capable of reaching far beyond the statutory bounds of his office to raise up and pull down men of all sorts, often, so it seemed, for purely personal reasons. But at the end of it all he remained Minister of Finance, with the confidence of the king.

Treaties

What Foreign Minister Wyllie wanted more than anything in the world, so he often said, was to see the treaty arrangements of the Hawaiian kingdom put on an equitable basis. It was a lifetime's work for him and more. In the forties and fifties a handful of lesser European powers having very little to do with the Hawaiian Islands—Denmark, Norway and Sweden, and some of the German states—agreed to treaties that were fair in every respect, and two great powers—Britain and the United States—were prodded into relaxing their discriminatory attitudes. But France refused to make any real concessions, and this meant that Wyllie could never complete his "grand design," a series of identical treaties with all nations on an equal footing. The existing treaties contained most favored nation clauses, so that a weakness at any one point meant weakness everywhere.

There were a good many questions unresolved between the Hawaiian kingdom and France. Were Catholic schools at the islands really being treated fairly by Protestant ministers of public instruction? Should French be an official language at the Honolulu customshouse together with English and Hawaiian? Did a Frenchman charged with a misdemeanor (the French word "délit") as distinct from a serious crime have the right to trial before a jury approved by his consul? Did the kingdom have autonomy in setting tariffs, or could France demand to have wines and spirits passed through the customshouse at special rates?

Laplace's treaty of 1839 had been revised in 1846. When a new French consul commissioner, Guillaume Patrice Dillon, arrived at Honolulu to see to the ratification of the new text, it was hoped that these questions would be settled once and for all. But to Wyllie's dismay Dillon turned out to be a Gallic version of Richard Charlton. The tone of his instructions was temperate enough ("moderation makes secure what boldness has obtained"), but Dillon himself was far from temperate. Wyllie, under protest, signed a treaty that left the Hawaiian kingdom still at a disadvantage. Dillon stayed on at Honolulu, pressing absurd claims incessantly, writing voluminously for the *Sandwich Islands News,* abusing the king, and trying to stir up trouble among the members of the cabinet.

King Kauikeaouli, it seemed, was cursed with obnoxious men of this kind. Richard Charlton, John Coffin Jones, George Brown, Anthony Ten Eyck, Guillaume Dillon—one after another they became unbearable, and in 1849 Kauikeaouli set about for the fifth time to have the official representative of a foreign power removed from office. James Jackson Jarves, who had left the islands in 1848 and was living on the American mainland, was commissioned to put the matter of Dillon before the French government in the course of a review of treaties in the United States and Europe.

Just then, as it happened, the commander of the French fleet in the Pacific, Rear Admiral Legoarant de Tromelin, was planning a visit to the islands. Since the time of Laplace in 1839 there had been very little bombast from French naval commanders. In 1842 Captain S. Mallet of *L'Embuscade* had accepted the assurances of the Hawaiian government that Laplace's treaty was being discussed at Paris by William Richards and Timothy Haalilio, and in 1846 Admiral Ferdinand-Alphonse Hamelin of *La Virginie* had returned the $20,000 bond posted by the chiefs at Laplace's insistence. De Tromelin himself had left a good impression on Robert Wyllie during an earlier visit, and when his flag ship *La Poursuivante* anchored again at Honolulu in August 1849, Wyllie invited him to stay at Rosebank, his pleasant house in Nuuanu valley. De Tromelin declined the invitation and took up residence instead with Consul Dillon.

Dillon promptly told de Tromelin his troubles, and with Dillon no story ever lost in the telling. De Tromelin was quick to agree that the impertinent Hawaiians must be rebuked; French honor was at stake. On August 22 he issued an ultimatum that brought back the days of Laplace and Paulet. Unless his demands were met, he said, he would use "all the means at his disposal" to obtain redress. Wyllie played for time. There were no issues, he said, that could not be resolved once James Jackson Jarves reached Paris. De Tromelin repeated his ultimatum. Wyllie replied that any violence would be on the conscience of the French.

On August 24 de Tromelin posted circulars in Honolulu, announcing that he would order an attack on the town next day. The foreign residents secured their property as best they could; at Kawaiahao Church $45,000 in gold and silver was left with the Protestant missionaries for safe keeping. At sunrise on August 25 a crier went through the streets warning natives to stay indoors. Consul Dillon left his house, striking his flag and declaring that the Hawaiian government would be responsible for any damage his property suffered. Early in the afternoon boatloads of French sailors came ashore. Over the protests of British Consul General William Miller and United States Consul Joel Turrill, they proceeded to wreck the fort.

They turned all the prisoners loose, spiked the ancient cannon on the battlements, broke swords, muskets, and bayonets, and threw hundreds of kegs of gunpowder into the harbor, blackening the water for days. They ransacked Governor Kekuanaoa's house, smashed everything including his clock, and scrawled obscenities and self-congratulatory phrases ("Les Braves Poursuivantes") on the walls in charcoal. They broke calabashes and dropped the pieces into a well, and they dragged away camphor wood chests containing mementoes of Kekuanaoa's dead wife Kinau. They placed guards at the fort, the powder magazine, the government offices, and one or two other buildings, and then retired to the harbor, where they seized the king's yacht, the *Kamehameha III*. The government calculated the damage at more than a hundred thousand dollars, or about a year's revenue for the kingdom.

In the harbor the American man-of-war *Glyn*, on her way back from a voyage to the western Pacific, lay with springs on her cables, ready to turn broadside and engage *La Poursuivante* and her companion ship *Le Gassendi* if they opened fire on the town. They did not, and the excitement of the day subsided—a little too fast, in fact, to suit some of the foreign residents. Later in the week some Americans drinking in a waterfront grogshop concocted a scheme to fool the French into thinking that the foreigners were about to make a sally on the fort. Their efforts were rewarded on the night of August 30, when the French doubled their guards and marched them about importantly with torches and drumbeats till a late hour, chasing shadows.

There was no diplomatic settlement. De Tromelin left on September 5, taking with him Consul Dillon, who was bound for France (and, though he did not know it, for reprimand and dismissal). The royal yacht *Kamehameha III*, manned by a French crew, had already sailed for Tahiti; she was never returned to the king.

In the wake of these outrages Gerrit Judd was commissioned to take the treaty problems of the kingdom to the United States and Europe, where he and James Jackson Jarves, singly or jointly, would try to arrange a settlement. His instructions, like those of William Richards earlier in the decade, were broad indeed. In the event of a drastic emergency he was empowered to place the islands under the protection of a foreign nation, or even to sell them, subject to the agreement of the Hawaiian legislature.

With Judd went Prince Alexander Liholiho, the future Kamehameha IV, and his brother Prince Lot, the future Kamehameha V. Alexander Liholiho was fifteen years old, Lot eighteen. It was an interesting trip for them, though Judd kept them on an uncomfortably tight rein. They saw the gold fields of California, the jungles of the isthmus of Panama, the city and the harbor of New York, the House of Commons and Madame Tussaud's waxworks in London, and the Louvre, the Bibliothèque Nationale, and the opera in Paris (and the Bois de Boulogne, teeming with *petites horizontales,* a scene that reminded Lot of Nuuanu Street in Honolulu).

Judd kept his eye on serious matters. At San Francisco he met Charles Eames, who was on his way to the islands to replace Anthony Ten Eyck as United States Commissioner. Eames was empowered to negotiate a treaty. Judd wanted to include a clause guaranteeing the independence of the islands, but Eames did not think this lay within the scope of his instructions. Eventually they agreed on a draft that left the question of independence open.

Judd went on to Panama and New York; the treaty went ahead of him to Washington. There, James Jackson Jarves had already negotiated a treaty with John M. Clayton, secretary of state in the administration of President Zachary Taylor. Jarves had been well received. The news of de Tromelin's visit to Honolulu was still fresh in the United States, and Taylor's administration was ready to take a strong stand on the subject of Hawaiian independence. Jarves and Clayton drafted and signed a treaty that gave the kingdom substantial equality in its relations with the United States. Just at that point the text of Judd's treaty arrived from San Francisco, and Jarves and Clayton sat down to make a composite of the two versions. The end result was a somewhat diluted version of Jarves' original accomplishment, but all the same it was satisfactory. Judd used it later as the model for a new treaty with Great Britain.

In France Judd had no luck at all. The agents deputed to talk with him were instructed to hold to the existing treaty and to reject as well any demands for indemnities arising out of de Tromelin's depredations at Honolulu. Judd spent two and a half miserable months at Paris before his patience ran out. He left with nothing accomplished, convinced that he would have had to stay six months before a decision was reached, and that even then the decision would go against him.

Trouble followed Judd and the young princes home from France, as it was bound to do. In December 1850, the war ship *Sérieuse* arrived at Honolulu, carrying a new French consul, Emile Perrin. Perrin gave himself a few months to get settled and then produced a set of demands that echoed those of Dillon in 1849. He announced that he had "extraordinary" powers to enforce them if necessary. Actually Perrin was bluffing, but King Kauikeaouli and his advisers had no way of knowing that, and the continued presence of the *Sérieuse* was ominous.

The king sent a memorandum to British Consul General Miller, asking if he would guarantee to protect the kingdom against the French. Miller's instructions gave him no such powers. He spoke privately to Perrin, decided that Perrin would not use force, and then advised the king not to put the islands in the hands of any power. The king prepared a document placing his possessions under the protection of the United States until France recognized their independence, and United States

Commissioner Luther Severance accepted the papers in a sealed envelope. Severance conferred with Captain William H. Gardner of USS *Vandalia,* which was in Honolulu harbor, and Gardner agreed to fire on the *Sérieuse* if the French used violence.

Perrin got wind of these plans, as surely he was meant to do. He adopted a more moderate tone, and then left for France in May 1851, to get new instructions. He came back in January 1853, empowered to make a treaty but enjoined against threatening the kingdom. "You will declare openly, Monsieur," his instructions read, "that we have never had, nor will we ever have, any thought of establishing over the Sandwich Islands a protectorate either direct or indirect, or of exercising there any exclusive influence, religious, political, or commercial."

France's real involvement at the islands was, and always had been, miniscule. At the time of de Tromelin's visit in 1849 a foreign resident reviewed the record. There were, he wrote, only twelve Frenchmen in the kingdom, apart from priests. Honolulu had only one French merchant, who did one thousandth part of the islands' business; the same was true of Honolulu's only French tavern keeper. In all of Honolulu's history only one complete cargo of French goods had passed through the customs-house. During the past five years not one French merchant vessel had arrived. Between one hundred and fifty and five hundred American whale ships visited the islands each year, compared with fewer than ten French whale ships. Almost all the liquor in the islands was imported and drunk by Britishers and Americans. There were more Chinese than Frenchmen in the kingdom, doing six times the amount of business without complaining that they suffered because Chinese was not an official language of the government.

Perrin and Wyllie had years of dispute behind them, and years of bickering lay ahead. In 1858 they brought yet another unsatisfactory treaty to the point of ratification, but when Perrin died at Honolulu in 1862 relations between France and the Hawaiian kingdom were still not on an equal footing. After 1853, however, the two men argued behind closed doors, without drawing the whole kingdom into their quarrels, and as far as the security of the islands was concerned the French difficulty slowly subsided to proportions that reflected reality—that is to say, insignificance.

When the Bough Breaks

Gold was discovered in California in 1847, and British Consul General Miller predicted immediately that trouble would follow for the Hawaiian kingdom. Migrants were moving westward across the American continent in great numbers, and Miller was sure that some of the flow would spill over into the Pacific. This, he thought, could only be bad. There were too many Americans at the islands already for his liking; they were notorious law breakers, and any sudden increase in the size of the crowd might very well make them uncontrollable.

Miller was not the most impartial of witnesses; on matters American he always spoke like a good Britisher. But it was true that filibustering was in the air. Rumors kept coming out of San Francisco in the late forties to the effect that shadowy groups there were plotting the overthrow of the Hawaiian kingdom. Then in October 1851, the San Francisco newspapers published reports that more than one hundred and fifty "restless young bloods" were about to set sail for the islands with the purpose of "revolutionizing the government of his Kanaka Majesty." This news reached Honolulu just ahead of the clipper *Game Cock,* which entered the harbor on November 15 carrying a party headed by the well-known goldfields capitalist and vigilante Sam Brannan.

Wyllie convinced himself that the kingdom was in imminent danger. The Privy Council voted to increase the number of foreign policemen at Honolulu, and Wyllie, who was "Secretary at War and of the Navy" as well as Minister of Foreign Relations, drew up an elaborate (and totally unworkable) scheme for the defense of the islands, calling for thousands of native "pikemen" and "cavalry," and white militiamen pledged to take the marauders without killing them, since for "every one dead 100 stout yankees would take his place."

What were the *Game Cock* men really up to? They were a motley group, mostly goldfields opportunists with a sprinkling of revolutionary exiles from Europe, and among them was at least one who would take a bribe. This man said Brannan had heard that King Kauikeaouli was tired of being harassed by the European powers and would gladly give up his throne and retire on an annuity. Brannan planned to set up a new government, and the *Game Cock* men had been picked for key posts—collector of the port, commander of the armed forces, governor of this or that island, and so on.

If this was what Brannan had in mind he needed only to consult the policy statements of the great powers on the subject of Hawaiian independence in order to find out how absurdly unrealistic his ideas were. In any case he did not come at all close to putting his scheme into practice. He tried to get an audience with the king at Lahaina, but Kauikeaouli would not see him, even after Brannan and his party politely sent in their calling cards. Rumors of violence were heard, but no shiploads of desperadoes landed on the outer islands and no pirate ship appeared to cut off the king's yacht between Maui and Oahu.

Brannan went back to San Francisco, having done nothing more than inquire into business opportunities, and most of his men followed him, after one or two clashes with the Honolulu police over heavy drinking and reckless riding. A few who stayed were arrested and convicted, on evidence supplied by a disgruntled confederate, of rifling the *Game Cock*'s mailbags on the voyage out and destroying letters warning of the filibuster.

Brannan and his men, who perhaps were really only advance scouts, reported unfavorably on the chances offering at the islands, and the filibuster movement in California died away for the time being. Secretary at War Wyllie wanted to keep up a strong standing army, but soon taxpayers began to complain that great numbers of troops at the ready put a strain on the treasury, and at the end of March 1852, the Privy Council moved to discharge all but a skeleton force.

The next disturbers of the peace were not filibusterers but rioting sailors. The fall whaling season of 1852 was a great success; Honolulu harbor was jammed, and several thousand seamen were taking their usual boisterous liberty in the grogshops along the waterfront. On the night of November 8 a sailor named Henry Burns from the whaler *Emerald* was put in the fort with several other men for drunkenness and disorderly conduct. Burns tore some bricks from the floor of his cell and threw them at the door. Jailer George Sherman went into the pitch black cell and flailed about with his club; he hit Burns on the head and injured him fatally.

Next morning, before a coroner's jury could meet, a lynch mob of sailors marched on the fort to find Sherman, and Governor Kekuanaoa had to put all his policemen and soldiers under arms to keep them out. Burns was buried at the seamen's cemetery in Nuuanu valley on November 10, and that night a mob formed again, brandishing clubs, waving guns, and threatening to set fire to the town. Some of them went to the fort a second time. Others surrounded the police station at the waterfront, drove the constables out, broke up the furniture, piled it up, and set fire to it. When the fire companies arrived the sailors cut their hoses, and the police station and several other buildings burned down.

One whaling ship in the harbor caught fire. The wind that night was a light breeze from the south. If the regular northeast trades had been blowing, from the town to the sea, the whole fleet, densely packed in the harbor and loaded with whale oil, might have been set ablaze.

Some of the rioting sailors were sobered by this near disaster, but the rest, in whom the fire had raised a thirst, went on to invade the waterfront taverns and drank them dry in succession. By eleven at night they were very drunk, and they got the idea of attacking the homes of Minister of Public Instruction Richard Armstrong and Minister of Finance Gerrit Judd. The night was dark and the going was hard for drinkers who had left all sense of direction in the grogshops. Those who went looking for Armstrong never found him, and the others who set off to climb the hill to Judd's house in Nuuanu valley got very tired indeed. Only a few of them reached the gate, and they were turned away at pistol point by Judd, his son Charles, and some family friends.

On the morning of March 12 Marshal of the Kingdom William C. Parke finally issued a writ of martial law, and the native constabulary, reinforced by two hundred and fifty hurriedly drilled volunteer militiamen, went out to clear the streets. That night the town was quiet. Forty or fifty sailors were in the fort, many of them cut and bruised by stones and clubs, but no shots had been fired. The riot was over.

Several of the ringleaders were given prison terms, and they were still in jail at Honolulu in 1853 when a much greater disaster overtook the town and the kingdom—smallpox. "There were six out of the number convicted who had had smallpox," wrote Marshal Parke, "and in the great epidemic . . . they did a work for which no money could compensate them."

On February 10, 1853, the American merchant ship *Charles Mallory* out of San Francisco appeared off Honolulu flying a yellow flag, the signal of serious disease aboard. A passenger was suffering from smallpox. He was isolated on a reef at Kalihi, west of the harbor. The others who came ashore were vaccinated and quarantined at Waikiki.

Richard Armstrong was put in charge of an improvised vaccination program, and the Privy Council directed Gerrit Judd, the former missionary doctor, to pick sites for a quarantine station and a pest hospital. By the end of March the quarantine period was over and no new cases had appeared, the sick man at Kalihi was better, and the *Charles Mallory* had sailed. Honolulu settled down to wait out the slack period of the late spring and summer. In the fall the whaling fleet would come again; in the meantime merchant ships continued to arrive from the west coast of America, where smallpox was rampant.

In May the disease appeared once more. Two Hawaiian women fell sick at their homes on Maunakea Street in downtown Honolulu. As soon as the diagnosis was confirmed their yards and the adjoining lots were fenced off so that contaminated clothing and grass houses could be burned. Three Royal Commissioners of Health were appointed—Gerrit Judd, Marshal William Parke, and the English physician Thomas C. B.

Rooke. They made plans calling for a general vaccination, the opening of hospitals, a system of warning and inspection for ships entering the harbor, and the establishment of a network of sub-commissioners on the outer islands.

The physicians of Honolulu worked as fast as they could to get vaccine matter ready, and the drugstores were besieged by people asking for vaccination, but the disease spread as if nothing were being done. Soon almost every district of Honolulu was reporting cases. A day of national humiliation, fasting, and prayer was called for June 15. Protestant ministers set up vaccination and food stations. Catholic priests tended the sick and baptized the dying, and some newly arrived Mormon elders labored to expel the disease by laying on hands and anointing with oil. By June 18, 41 natives were dead and 114 were sick; in the next week the figures doubled. July and August were terrible months. On Oahu more than four thousand cases and fifteen hundred deaths were reported, most of them at Honolulu. By October the town was safe, but the rural districts of Oahu continued to suffer. On the outer islands isolation, lucky experience with the unreliable vaccine matter, and strict attention to quarantine saved Niihau, Molokai, and Lanai, but not even the most desperate efforts could keep the disease away from Kauai, Maui, and Hawaii—the three islands between them lost at least four hundred and fifty dead.

By the end of January 1854, when for the first time no new cases or deaths were recorded, the islands had reported a total of 6,405 cases and 2,485 deaths. Richard Armstrong, who was in charge of the kingdom's census, thought these figures were far too low. He believed that for every death the government heard about, two or three went unreported. In his opinion the toll was probably as high as five or six thousand.

Only a handful of white men were among that number, even though everybody was exposed to the disease. The Hawaiians had never given much attention to Western ideas about medical treatment, and in this instance they paid a terrible price. At Honolulu many natives were vaccinated or inoculated, and if they were lucky the vaccine took. Thousands of others refused to be helped. Some scratched their arms, simulating vaccination marks, rather than submit to the white physicians and their volunteer helpers. Others went to native medical kahunas for aid. The dreadful consequences were plain. Hawaiians fell sick everywhere. Some were abandoned and died alone; their bodies were left to rot. Others were buried where they lay, without coffins, in graves so shallow that wandering pigs and dogs could unearth them. Some native families nursed their sick at home, devotedly and uselessly, and carefully laid the dead under the dirt floors of their thatch huts or in their house yards, following their old burial practices and condemning themselves to follow the dead into the grave.

At Honolulu life fell apart. The produce markets emptied out; fresh beef could not be found anywhere; no one trusted pork or chicken from native farms; and fish and vegetables were served only with great trepidation. Workers and domestic servants disappeared. Hawaiians left the town by hundreds, the healthy to get away from the loathsome disease, the sick to escape they knew not what. They went into the hills and the country districts to wait out their time—and to spread infection without knowing it—or they took to boats and canoes in defiance of the Health Commissioners' orders and headed for the outer islands.

For those who stayed at Honolulu death was all around. Yellow flags hung in doorways on every street, and the legal columns of the *Polynesian* were filled to overflowing with attorneys' announcements winding up the estates of Hawaiians who had committed their property but not their person to Western ways, who had bought title to their lands and made their wills but had not been vaccinated.

Teams of wagon drivers patrolled the town, picking up the sick and the dead. Among these workers were six seamen jailed after the riot of 1852. They and their fellow wagoners became so hardened to death that they were able to stop at a tavern for a drink, leaving their load of corpses outside. But at the big pest hospital at Kakaako, just seaward of Kawaiahao Church, another of the freed prisoners, Peter Jordon, began to see ghosts; and as for the Hawaiians who were confined there, they were sure they would die—or be killed. White doctors were carrying out autopsies, and the natives fell into a panic when they heard that a man's throat had been cut and his body mutilated. At the height of the epidemic forty or fifty bodies were buried each day at Kakaako, and before the worst was over more than a thousand corpses were packed into the ground there, many of them laid on their sides to save space, in graves just wide enough to admit a body and only three feet deep.

It was a terrible time, and just when things were at their most desperate, politics became infected as well. In mid-July a letter signed by "A Physician" appeared in the *Polynesian* criticizing "government apathy." Marshal Parke and his wagon drivers had done good work, the writer conceded, but there should be fifty more like him. Why would not the government act more efficiently? Was it waiting for aid from the foreign residents? If so, they would help. Action was needed because the fall whaling season was at hand and if Honolulu was not ready to receive the fleet the town would be ruined.

Public meetings were held a few days later, and seven resolutions were forwarded to the Privy Council, calling for the burning of contaminated houses, improved vaccination, and the appointment of volunteer leaders to take charge of preventive measures in each district of Honolulu. From then on the government based its work on these resolutions.

The meetings did not stop there. George Lathrop, the physician who had diagnosed the first smallpox cases on Maunakea Street in May, read a "pungent" series of resolutions attacking Gerrit Judd and Richard Armstrong for "negligence" in the early stages of the epidemic, and at yet another meeting a resolution was passed calling for their dismissal. A Committee of Thirteen was appointed to circulate petitions.

Among the thirteen were George Lathrop; Dr. Wesley Newcomb; William Ladd of the ruined firm of Ladd & Co.; J. D. Blair, an obscure lawyer; and a dentist named John Mott Smith. They and their supporters, most of them Americans, claimed that Judd and Armstrong were great peddlers of influence in the government, but that they had not used their powers to stop smallpox from entering the kingdom at Honolulu and spreading to the outer islands. Armstrong's plan for vaccination after the first case appeared on the *Charles Mallory* was useless, so they said (this was a harsh judgment). The Health Commissioners should never have allowed amateurs to vaccinate natives (it was true that many vaccinations did not take, but the thing at fault was the quality of the vaccine, and it was made up by physicians). Judd had rejected a better vaccination plan put before him by Honolulu's physicians (this was never proven); in fact he had been paid $2000 (by whom not specified) to let the *Charles Mallory* enter the harbor.

While these half truths and outright lies were being flung about, the Committee of Thirteen was collecting signatures for its petitions. The white signatories described themselves as loyal citizens and denizens who identified themselves unhesitatingly with the fate of the kingdom. But, they warned, history showed that monarchs surrounded by "pernicious councillors" could never make their people happy. Judd and Armstrong must go—the living, and the dead too, clamored for their dismissal: "Their inefficiency and misdeeds may be artfully conceal'd from your Majesty, but their selfish cupidity, political imbecility, and malfeasance in office are well known, and grievously felt by your people."

What the dead really thought no one could tell, of course; and the clamor of the living was confusing, to say the least. Of the more than two hundred and fifty loyal white men, 189 turned out not to be subjects of the king, but aliens, and a good many names on the petitions seemed to have no owners at all. As for the eleven thousand five hundred natives who endorsed the petitions, most of them made their mark, and some did not even do that—their crosses were penned by the same hand that wrote in their names. On the other side three thousand native names were signed to petitions supporting Judd and Armstrong. A committee of the Privy Council considered all the evidence and concluded that even if all the petitions against the two ministers were genuine there were no real grounds for dismissal.

This was only a recommendation; the final decision would be taken by the Privy Council proper. The question was considered on August 17. Nine councillors spoke; the rest remained silent. Robert Wyllie's view was that the principle of cabinet responsibility was at stake. He would not take part in a move that might lead to some members recommending the dismissal of others. Keoni Ana followed Wyllie's lead. Judd and Armstrong were of course disqualified from voting on their own future. Asher Bates was absent when the vote was taken. The chiefs were divided, four against four. The deciding vote rested with Honorary Privy Councillor Charles Gordon Hopkins, an Englishman, a naturalized Hawaiian, and a protégé of Wyllie. He voted to dismiss Judd and Armstrong.

Judd resigned from the Royal Commission of Health on August 22, but he did not surrender his post as Minister of Finance. The king sent Prince Alexander Liholiho to receive Judd's ministerial papers. Judd would not hand them over. For another week he clung to his portfolio. Finally the king directed all his ministers to resign. Judd was the last to return his commission. On September 5 Kauikeaouli reappointed every minister except Judd. Richard Armstrong retained the portfolio of Public Instruction, and Judd was succeeded as Minister of Finance by a former United States Consul at Honolulu, Elisha H. Allen.

At the Honolulu courthouse, where the first hostile public meetings were held, the Committee of Thirteen and its supporters gathered in triumph on September 8. Dr. Wesley Newcomb was in the chair. Great applause greeted resolutions from George Lathrop, John Mott Smith, and J. D. Blair, celebrating the end of the "malignant tyranny" of Judd and calling for manifestations of public joy at the birth of the "delightful influences of liberty, free conscience and independent action."

Accordingly on the night of Saturday, September 10, a torchlight procession with bands and banners made its way through the town to the king's residence, as all manner of guns were fired and street corner orators declaimed before excited crowds. To mark the great occasion the opposition newspaper changed its name from the *Weekly Argus* to the *New Era*. Judd, thoroughly shaken and embittered, announced his return to private practice as a physician.

For the rest of his life Judd remained convinced that he had been cut down by a clique of dishonorable men acting solely from personal spite. In his eyes they were simply the last in a long line of enemies who had been plotting his destruction ever since he came to power—Lord George Paulet, George Brown, Charles Brewer, the partners of Ladd & Co., Anthony Ten Eyck, George Robertson, and now, finally, the Committee of Thirteen.

This was part of the truth, to be sure. The leaders of the Committee were George Lathrop and Wesley Newcomb, and Judd had crossed swords with them both. In 1851 Judd and two other referees ruled against

Lathrop in a law suit concerning the lease of a sugar plantation. Soon afterward Lathrop applied for a loan from the government, only to be refused by the same Privy Council that had just lent $3,000 to Judd's prospective son-in-law Aaron B. Howe. In 1852, when the tariff was lowered on liquor imported for medicinal purposes, Lathrop expected to enjoy the benefit of the reduction, but Judd had him barred on the ground that he sold liquor by the glass to customers at his drugstore. Lathrop appealed. The evidence showed that his use of "medicinal liquor" was far greater than that of any other doctor at Honolulu, and his petition was denied. As for Wesley Newcomb, Judd and he began to bicker at the time of the first smallpox scare, and hardly stopped after that. They disagreed over the best way to prepare vaccine matter, then over quarantine measures, then over the right of doctors to enter quarantined areas. Finally, one day, the exasperated Judd ordered Newcomb out of his office. Newcomb left, telling Judd, as Judd's son Charles reported, that he would "kick *his Ass* for him the next time he met him."

At the same time Judd was fighting battles on several fronts. He was a vehement and aggressive total abstinence man (though he chewed tobacco, to the scandal of some of the missionaries), and he took every opportunity to harass the publicans and drinkers of Honolulu. Then too, he had incurred a great deal of enmity at the time of the land division, when he had invoked the oath of allegiance to keep foreigners from getting title to property. Other ghosts returned to haunt him as well. William Ladd appeared in 1853 as a member of the Committee of Thirteen; and George Robertson, who had brought the impeachment charges of 1848, became Speaker of the House of Representatives in 1852 and engaged Judd in a running argument over his administration of the treasury.

None of this would have mattered very much if Judd had not been making enemies in the inner circles of government. Almost every white man of importance in the official community had been his protégé to begin with, but one by one they broke with him. James Jackson Jarves resigned from the editorship of the *Polynesian* and left the islands largely because of what he regarded as shabby treatment from Judd. John Ricord, whose temper matched Judd's, had the same bad experience, and to complicate matters Ricord became hopelessly infatuated with Judd's fifteen-year-old daughter Elizabeth and was desperately hurt when she turned down his proposal of marriage.

Next to Judd himself Robert Wyllie was the most influential member of cabinet, and in a situation where lines of responsibility were not clear there was hardly room enough for two great pretenders, especially two men so different in style and substance. Judd, an inconsistent political theorist, served a king and tried to turn the kingdom into an American republic, with himself as unofficial ruler; Wyllie was devoted to the idea of monarchy and a hierarchical society. Judd was a common man who had muddied his boots somewhat on his way to a position of power; Wyllie the aristocrat was above all that, flicking at specks of political dust with his handkerchief and speaking always and only of honor. Judd was a spare Calvinist; Wyllie was an Anglican. Judd was a teetotaler; Wyllie was a convivial drinker. Judd was the solidest of family men, with several children; Wyllie was a perpetual bachelor, eternally patting little children on the head and pressing coins into their hands, inviting groups of older girls to his home for meetings of what he coyly called his Tea and Twaddle Society, appearing at children's fancy dress balls dressed as Little Bobby Wyllie in kilt and sporran, dancing elaborate and delicately safe attendance on the respectable married ladies of Honolulu, making mystifying references to a vague, hopeless, heart breaking romance (with a Chilean nun?) that had completely unmanned him years before he came to the islands, and never, never mentioning marriage. Judd was abrupt to the point of rudeness; Wyllie was long-windedly polite to the point of absurdity. Judd was a compulsive saver of money, Wyllie was a prodigal spender; neither could afford to be anything else.

It was over money that their latent enmity became open. In 1847 Wyllie blocked Judd's claim to $1,000 for services rendered during the Ladd & Co. law suit. Judd was annoyed, and he expressed his annoyance by refusing to translate for Wyllie during meetings of the Privy Council (Judd understood Hawaiian perfectly, Wyllie did not understand it at all). Wyllie retaliated by casting aspersions on Judd's competence as Minister of Finance. Wyllie was further upset by Judd's use of bribes to get information against Anthony Ten Eyck in 1848, and when Judd was impeached in that year Wyllie spoke against him at some length. He had established to his own satisfaction that Judd was no gentleman.

When Judd was named to go to Europe in 1849 Wyllie, most uncharacteristically for a man who made so much of integrity, sabotaged the mission by leaking Judd's secret instructions to British Consul General Miller. (As it happened Judd did not have to invoke the clauses that authorized him to sell the islands, but all the same there is no doubt that Wyllie meant to stab him in the back.) When Judd came home again Wyllie ridiculed his efforts as a diplomat and provoked him to a terrible outburst of temper. By 1850 the two were not on speaking terms, and their letters for the next ten years were alternately excessively impersonal and excessively personal.

On the very brink of the smallpox upheaval Judd unwisely withheld a treasury payment to Wyllie. The sum at issue was $9.06½. Wyllie, who had served the Hawaiian government without salary for some time, was enraged. He dashed off a thirty page letter to Judd, calling him an uncivil, wretched quibbler, and reminding him that the expenses of the diplomatic mission of 1849, amounting to thousands of dollars, had been approved unhesitatingly by Wyllie. When the final reckoning for Judd came in the Privy Council Wyllie stood aloof and let him be voted out of office.

Judd regretted his loss of office deeply, but not the course of action that brought him to the brink of dismissal. He was sure he had done well; few generals, he said, ever came off from so long a campaign with fewer scars or less injury to their uniforms. There were many who would have disagreed, arguing that Judd's interest and that of the kingdom were not always the same, and that Judd was not always careful of the difference. Apart from the general question of whether one man's version of Puritanism was a satisfactory state policy for the kingdom, there was the matter of money. Before and after Judd's dismissal his handling of the kingdom's finances was criticized. No one denied that he performed a great service in the early forties as President of the Treasury Board, but later on, it sometimes seemed to his colleagues as well as his enemies that he was heating his own irons at the government's fires. Did he really deserve $1,000 for his part in the Ladd & Co. suit, and if so did his services include dunning William Ladd for private purposes? When he fired the government's auditor, William Jarrett, and pursued him through the courts on charges of embezzlement and eventually ruined him, was he accurate enough in his own accounting to know for certain that he himself was not responsible for the alleged deficiences? Was it wise of Judd to appoint his own seventeen-year-old son Charles to succeed Jarrett? And was it wise of the two Judds then to auction the government's herd of horses on Kauai to themselves? When the government foreclosed on the sugar plantation of Aaron Howe on Maui, who set the price of sale and took possession of the crop and the agricultural machinery—Judd the Minister of Finance on behalf of the government, or Judd the private citizen? All these matters were argued at length in private and in public, and some were never really laid to rest.

"The disposition to accumulate is human," wrote Judd in 1852, "it is American and more; properly guarded and for right ends it is Bible." Judd was human, he was an American, and he was sure he lived by the Bible. He left office by no means a rich man. Many white men, in and out of government, did far better than he (Richard Armstrong and William Lee, to name only two). The opportunities were there for the taking, and Judd had his share of chances. In 1843, for example, one of the chiefs offered him the whole of Manoa valley near Honolulu. If he had accepted the gift it would have made him extremely wealthy. He turned it down. When he died in 1873 after fourteen years in missionary work, eleven years in government office, and twenty years in business, he was worth only about fifty thousand dollars. He could well afford to stand amazed at his own moderation.

Thirteen Men on a Dead Man's Chest

Far more important than the question of Judd's dismissal from the king's ministry was the issue of the kingdom's continued independence. The warships of the French and the filibuster party of Sam Brannan had come and gone, leaving Kauikeaouli's sovereignty intact for the time being. Then, during the political upheaval of 1853, the possibility that the islands might be annexed by the United States became a topic of consuming interest.

A good many Americans in the kingdom were Manifest Destiny men, rabid nationalists, their minds inflamed by the election to the American presidency of the expansionist Democrat Franklin Pierce, who took office in 1853. Others, less extreme, saw annexation to the United States as a fine alternative to engulfment by France or Great Britain. And it was clear to everyone that the Hawaiian economy would benefit if the islands could find a place within the tariff structure of the United States.

One of the strongest annexationists in 1853 was, of all people, Gerrit Judd. The fierce protectiveness he had once shown toward the kingdom had changed to a willingness to bargain away the throne of the Kamehamehas. Like everything else about Judd this conversion was complex. When he set out for Europe in 1849 he was the undisputed master of governmental policy—indeed the very fact that he rather than Foreign Minister Wyllie went on a diplomatic mission demonstrated this. But it was not always a good idea for a man of influence to leave the islands. William Richards, for example, went overseas in 1842 and came home to find Judd in his place. Now the same thing happened to Judd. He returned to find new groupings confronting him in the cabinet, organized by Wyllie, who made it a point never to leave the islands. In his last years of office Judd had his own way less and less often, and this did not set well with him. By 1853, apparently, he was ready to pull the temple down around him.

In the course of his travels abroad Judd had met a good many American expansionists, among them United States Senator William Henry Seward, who later became secretary of state in Abraham Lincoln's cabinet. Judd also struck up an acquaintanceship with Alfred G. Benson, a New York shipping millionaire, who was ready to gamble heavily against the survival of the kingdom. Judd, in fact, was the keeper of a spectacular secret: he was Benson's agent in a plan to buy the islands outright for five million dollars. Judd presented the offer to King Kauikeaouli just before he was dismissed from office, and without any doubt the discovery that Judd was willing to have the islands sold out from under the feet of the Hawaiians made the chiefs more receptive to the idea that he should no longer be a minister of the crown.

The Committee of Thirteen, which led the agitation against Judd, had its political ambitions too, but those ambitions were not altogether clear. George Lathrop for one had nothing but contempt for the Hawaiian monarchy. To him one Kamehameha was very like another—"a nigger." Several of his fellow committee members shared this view. But they disagreed, or at least changed their collective mind a number of times, about the best disposition of the kingdom. Sometimes they seemed to favor simple annexation by the United States. At other times they were said to be getting ready to mount a filibuster, followed by the establishment of a revolutionary republic, and then, possibly, a sale at profit to the United States.

The worst fears of David Malo were coming true. Whichever way things went the days of the kingdom were numbered, so it seemed. Malo died in October 1853, with the noise of filibuster rumors and annexationist petitions loud in his ears, and he asked to be buried high up on the steep slopes of Mount Ball behind Lahainaluna, above the rising tide of the foreign invasion.

King Kauikeaouli himself was coming to despair of the future. At a cabinet meeting early in February 1854, he instructed Foreign Minister Wyllie to find out, secretly, the terms on which the United States might consider annexing the islands. Wyllie was strongly opposed to annexation, but at the king's behest he consulted David Gregg, the newly arrived United States Commissioner. Gregg, who was not empowered to make a treaty, was more than ready to negotiate *ad referendum* while waiting for word from Washington.

Wyllie and Gregg began their secret meetings in February. At the same time the Committee of Thirteen started posting handbills and calling meetings. Gregg heard that George Lathrop and the Committee currently favored revolution rather than annexation. If the islands entered the Union as a state, Lathrop said, then Hawaiians would become American citizens, and the Committee was against equal rights for kanakas in a white man's country. So the Committee was planning a coup for the summer of 1854, when there would be no American man of war at Honolulu and no whalers in town. Californian filibusterers would be recruited, five hundred stand of muskets and two howitzers would be imported, and King Kauikeaouli, Prince Alexander Liholiho, and Governor Kekuanaoa of Oahu would be taken into custody and held until an independent republican government was formed.

Late in February the Privy Council placed $5,000 at the disposal of

Secretary at War Wyllie, and he recruited native soldiers and hired drill masters. Lathrop watched them at work and was not impressed; his opinion was that sixteen good men could whip the king's army.

David Gregg grew uneasy. Every vessel from the west coast, he noted, was bringing down passengers, "able-bodied and hearty men, who have no business, but are in constant association with the 'Committee of Thirteen' & their adherents." Early in March one of these hearties, a "General" O'Hinton, was overheard telling people in Lathrop's drugstore that a republic would be established within a few weeks. Gregg concluded that filibusterers were being recruited gradually, to avoid all risk from the neutrality laws of the United States. At the first opportunity a blow would be struck.

The town was very tense, and for a few hours one night it seemed as if the time had come. A ship was seen standing off and on outside the harbor. It was supposed to be carrying filibusterers, men who would land at a signal from their fellow conspirators ashore and put the natives' houses to the torch. The alarm was sounded and troops took up defensive positions along the beach. In the morning it was discovered that the ship was an innocent merchantman waiting for good weather to come inside. Everybody laughed, said Gregg, except the government, whose troops kept drilling six days a week.

In mid-March the orthodox annexationists made their bid for the support of the natives. Over the noisy objections of the Committee of Thirteen (and the protests of British Consul General Miller and French Commissioner Perrin) a clerk in Richard Armstrong's Department of Public Instruction began circulating a Hawaiian language newspaper, the *Nu Hou*, filled with articles favoring annexation. A meeting was called at Kawaiahao Church so that the natives could discuss matters. When John Ii spoke in favor of independence the crowd applauded loudly; when Gerrit Judd spoke for annexation he was hissed into silence. Judd could not let the matter rest. He followed Ii home, and became so heated that Ii had to ask him to leave.

Lathrop and his fellow conspirator, the lawyer J. D. Blair, continued to be bumptious. They attended the king's birthday levee in mid-March, an act which David Gregg found impertinent in men who were planning the overthrow of the kingdom. Lathrop found a good deal to criticize about the affair. The supper was bad, he told Gregg, the dancing was bad, everything was bad. The natives were ignorant. Not one of them knew his own age, not even the king; Wyllie fixed the date of the royal birthday. Lathrop and Blair had a great many things to say about "niggers," and Lathrop told Gregg he could "never endure" being ruled by a king who was not white.

Gregg was not impressed by the leaders of the Committee. Blair he considered a poor lawyer, almost a simpleton, "wise in his own conceit however, and professing all the elements of a great man. He is for revolution and a Republic, in order to find a suitable theatre for his immense abilities!" Lathrop was a good physician, "no doubt," but he thought himself a statesman; the shoemaker ought to stick to his last. As for Wesley Newcomb, "he is tolerably learned in Conchology, but otherwise is not remarkably gifted with sense or discretion. A more violent excitable little & unscrupulous partisan cannot be found on the face of the globe." The Committee men altogether were "foolish conspirators, without anything but the desperation which pertained to the character of Catiline & his associates."

All this time Gregg and Wyllie had been carrying on their secret negotiations. Gregg was finding the Hawaiian way of doing business dilatory and timid, and the Hawaiian government was finding the pressure of events at Honolulu unsettling. The town, in both official and private circles, was notorious for leakages of confidential information. Late in May Gregg heard that Gerrit Judd, who was no longer a minister of cabinet, knew all about the annexation treaty. British Consul General Miller also learned enough to know that something was afoot, and before the summer was over he had all the important facts.

One of the most difficult questions Gregg and Wyllie had to settle was the status of native Hawaiians under American rule, and Miller, who had always maintained that Americans to a man were racists and slave holders, seized on this to embarrass Gregg. If Hawaiians signed away their sovereignty, Miller said repeatedly, they would be delivering themselves to a country which practiced race hatred, slavery, vigilantism, and lynch law, which was filled with crime and corruption, and which had a congenital hatred of aristocracy. Prince Alexander Liholiho and his brother Lot did not need secondhand warnings about these things. While they were in the United States with Gerrit Judd in 1850 they were mistaken for negroes more than once, and for Hawaiians of royal blood this was a humiliating experience. Both the princes set themselves against annexation.

Americans at Honolulu always celebrated July the Fourth with a maximum of flourish. The year 1854 was a particularly hopeful one for them; perhaps by 1855 the kingdom would be under the American flag. As the holiday approached annexationists and Committee men maneuvered for control of the celebrations. Gregg considered the question of the public observances very important. He and Wyllie had just placed a draft of their treaty of annexation before Alexander Liholiho, and it was most necessary that the prince be kept in a good mood. If the Committee of Thirteen got hold of the July 4 celebrations there was no telling what they might do or say, and just one extravagant speech could very easily kill any chances of annexation. Gregg was relieved when the organizing meeting rejected J. D. Blair as orator of the day and chose him instead.

The traditional July the Fourth parade was full of splendid symbolism for those who had eyes to see. "A car, decorated with evergreens, in which were seated thirty-two girls of American parentage, dressed in white, wreathed in flowers, each bearing the name of a State on her sash, in large gold letters, was drawn by a power unseen," wrote Mrs. Gerrit Judd. "Next followed 'Young America,' a company of very young men in uniform, with another triumphal chariot, on which was placed a beautiful boy, the very personification of health, strength, and beauty. 'Young Hawaii' was in tow, and represented by a boat gaily trimmed, in which were eight young native lads, fancifully dressed, and carelessly eating sugar-cane."

Gregg worked hard over his oration. He did not expect the British and French residents to like it, but he thought nonetheless that he was justified in trying to arouse a strong feeling of nationalism among his countrymen. In his opinion there had been too much subserviency to British arrogance; besides, he hoped to counteract Consul General Miller's "insidious and unfair" prejudicing of native minds on the subject of annexation.

The speech, heard by a large crowd and reported fully in the press, did not change a single native's mind. All it did was to goad Miller to new heights of rage. The old Britisher had been very ill earlier in the year. Robert Wyllie, who had practiced medicine in his youth, thought Miller might be suffering from softening of the brain. Miller kept pressing the antiannexationist cause, with all the urgency and sincerity of the slightly insane.

Gregg went on with his treaty negotiations, hoping to get a satisfactory draft to the Hawaiian legislature before the end of the 1854 session. Miller arranged for native members of the House of Representatives to submit opposing motions. Gerrit Judd went about the town soliciting signatures in favor of annexation. John Ii and the high chief Paki spoke for independence. King Kauikeaouli, who for months had been in a state of chronic drunkenness and ill health, drank on. A new memorial favoring annexation reached the government. Late in July J. D. Blair and George Lathrop left on a mysterious trip to California, and soon afterward yet another self-styled west coast "Colonel" arrived at Honolulu and began to make political pronouncements to anyone who would listen.

At the customshouse early in September a box of pistols was discovered among some goods being unloaded from a ship. This was enough to bring the native troops out again. All these alarums and excursions were very frustrating to Gregg, who was hoping for a provisional transfer of sovereignty as soon as possible. This would cut off any attempt at a filibuster, and then Americans would migrate to the islands in great numbers, making the place safe from Britain and France. But there was always a delay. Now it was King Kauikeaouli; he would have to be consulted, and he could not be consulted because he was in a "peculiar condition."

After months of strain and uncertainty Gregg pushed the issue to a crisis in November. He told Wyllie that the number of Californians at Honolulu had increased dangerously. Hundreds more were poised ready to leave the west coast for the islands, and hundreds of foreign residents would join them when they arrived. If the government resisted, Honolulu might be set on fire. Gregg and Captain Dornin of USS *Portsmouth,* one of several warships in port at the time, advised Wyllie on November 12 that an instant surrender of sovereignty to the United States was the only way to escape violence.

Wyllie was sure that Gregg and Dornin were practicing straight-faced political blackmail. Now he saw a chance to get the government out of its predicament. He wrote hasty notes to the representatives of all three great powers—Miller, Perrin, and Gregg—asking for guarantees of protection if a filibuster broke out. The *Portsmouth* had a companion ship at Honolulu, but HMS *Trincomalee* was there too and so was the French warship *L'Artémise.* Gregg and Dornin had no choice but to honor Wyllie's request.

Once he secured his tripartite guarantee of protection Wyllie returned enthusiastically to his favorite notion of a yeoman Hawaiian army. He summoned up a local force, infantry, "Artillery" and natives "armed with short Axes, cutlasses, swords & spears . . . for close fighting." Clothed in military might, Wyllie halted all treaty negotiations until they could be "honorably resumed, after every trace of coercion had been removed."

Negotiations were never resumed. Honolulu remained in virtual suspended animation until December 8, when the Cabinet Council met and composed a proclamation to be signed by the king. It was announced that, in the face of threats to the kingdom, aid had been requested from Great Britain, France, and the United States. As a result, Hawaiian independence was "more firmly established than ever before."

Of all the actors in this unresolved drama the two most important were off stage a good deal of the time—Chief Justice William Lee and Prince Alexander Liholiho, both of whom were absent from Honolulu for months on end in 1854. During the prolonged negotiations Lee was traveling among the outer islands, ostensibly on judicial business. All drafts of the treaty were sent to him, and he took his time about sending them back. Lee was strongly against annexation, just as Wyllie was, and he hoped that if the treaty could be delayed long enough the need for it would go away. As long as there was a possibility of annexation the United States would not permit a filibuster. At the same time Lee wanted to make sure that the treaty, if it ever got to Washington, would be unacceptable. So he arranged for a clause to be included guaranteeing that the islands would enter the Union as a state, not a territory, and that native Hawaiians would have all the rights and privileges of American citizens. This would never pass the United States Senate; it was a century ahead of its time and Lee knew it. A filibuster, then, would be impossible as long as the United States had a treaty in view, and the United States would never ratify a treaty that contained a statehood clause. With any luck the kingdom would be safe once more, its independence guaranteed by the great powers, and the future of the Hawaiian people would be secure, at least for a time.

Prince Alexander Liholiho cooperated willingly with Lee. He did not like Americans at all, and he wanted to be king. So he stayed away from Honolulu as much as he could, knowing that no decision would be made without his consent, and therefore making his consent all but impossible to achieve. Wyllie, in the thick of things at Honolulu, was ready to let Lee direct the action from behind the scenes. In the end Lee succeeded as completely as he could have wished.

King Kauikeaouli put his name to the proclamation of December 8 in an infirm, shaky, disconnected hand. It was probably the last time he signed an official paper. He died at Honolulu on December 15, 1854. Wyllie hastened to have Alexander Liholiho proclaimed king as Kamehameha IV. Within an hour of Kauikeaouli's death Governor Kekuanaoa took a company of soldiers to the principal street corners of the town, and while minute guns were fired on Punchbowl the death of the old king and the accession of the new were announced.

Annexationism went into eclipse. The Committee of Thirteen, too, lost its spirit. Several of its members left the islands, and those who remained began to reconstrue the history of their organization into a chronicle of serious-minded, well-intentioned, mild, orthodox American patriotism. The young Kamehameha IV quickly created a new focus of power in the government and a new style of life at court, and cabinet members, foreign residents, and natives alike turned, as David Gregg said, "with deference to the rising sun."

CHAPTER FIVE

A New Society, A New Economy

1855—1876

The Dance of Life

WITH WARSHIPS hull down over the horizon and diplomats reduced to silence for the time being, life was quite agreeable. Once it became clear that the kingdom was not about to be swallowed up by one or another of the great powers, foreigners were able to turn their attention to the pleasures of private life again, and when they did a good number of them found, rather to their surprise, that they were beginning to take root at the islands. "Like the pandanus tree, which lets long fibrous cables into the earth to anchor," wrote the editor of the *Polynesian,* "it is also so with man."

This was something new. As the *Polynesian* remarked, the "ambiguous traders of twenty and thirty years ago" had no intention of becoming permanent residents. Their past was "bright with the morning sheen of boyhood and home," and the future, "like an untried whaling ground, was supposed to contain fish of miraculous proportions, monsters that would turn you in your two hundred barrels of domestic bliss." In the early days white men at the islands looked back or they looked forward; they hardly lived in the present at all.

But by Alexander Liholiho's time some of them at least were ready to let their cables into the earth and accept the kingdom, with all its faults, as home. No longer were merchants satisfied with a trundle bed in an attic above a store. "They marry at once," said the *Polynesian,* "and live in villas . . . Piano-fortes, harps, guitars, and two-decker accordeons from Houndsditch, give an air to their parlors. French and Spanish novels lay strewn upon their sofas and centre tables; their gardens are sweet with roses . . . and the canary bird in its golden-barred pagoda, shares the open window with a passion flower. Their children grow up with the shade trees to which the kids, their playmates, are piqueted, and share with the ducks the delight of being bespattered by the fountain. Where is the man who, seeing these things, will persist in thrusting Dr. JOHNSON down our throats, and any longer pretend that to enjoy the present is to demoralize the mind?"

For all the *Polynesian*'s tongue-in-cheek rhapsodizing, the serenity of the times was not totally undisturbed. It was still possible for a man invited to a friendly dinner at the British Club to end the evening locked in argument about the rights and wrongs of imperialism, and some die-hard Americans were supposed to be starting a new club that would be more political than social. But at least invitations were being tendered and accepted across the walls of nationality that used to block off one part of the foreign community from the next. Even at Honolulu, a place notorious for its feuds, a concern for manners was stirring. Diplomats no longer attacked members of the Hawaiian government at official gatherings, and the royal court became what it should always have been—the scene of polite expressions of good will among nations. There were some who thought things were rather overdone, considering what the Hawaiian kingdom was; a visiting Japanese diplomat, for example, put the king down as "more or less the headman of a village of fishermen." But the resident diplomats seemed to be taking ritual politeness as seriously as they had once taken doctrinaire obnoxiousness. Under Alexander Liholiho, as David Gregg remarked, the most likely way for a minister or a consul to die was of a "fit of etiquette."

When a contretemps did occur at the highest levels of society it was likely to be a scandal rather than an international incident, and Honolulu's scandals ran the gamut from melodrama to bedroom farce. The leading man in the first performance was M. Marion Landais, chancellor of the French consulate at Honolulu. Landais was something of a lady killer, and he was not a man to keep his conquests quiet. He was cutting a public and indiscriminate swath among the young and not-so-young ladies of Honolulu when his eye fell upon Mrs. Charles Brewer, the wife of one of the leading American merchants of the town. Soon Mrs. Brewer could be seen making her way through the taro patches of Nuuanu two or three times a week to visit Landais at his home, where the blinds always seemed to be drawn.

One night in December 1855, French Commissioner Emile Perrin was strolling about town. He happened to go by the Brewers' house, and there he saw Landais on the sidewalk blowing kisses to a figure in the window. Perrin crossed to the other side of the street. Landais challenged him, saying that a French diplomat had come to a pretty pass when he "condescended to play the spy." Perrin replied that Landais was "handsomely engaged," but that this was perhaps not very strange for a "Mulâtre Dominique," and then Landais took to Perrin with his sword cane.

By chance Marshal William Parke was out walking too. Perrin, bruised and bleeding, got him to take Landais into custody. Landais applied for a writ of habeas corpus, but the courts ruled that the affair was a matter for the French government and that Perrin, as Landais' superior, was within his rights in having a junior officer confined temporarily.

Perrin and the Hawaiian authorities agreed that no good purpose would be served by trying Landais at Honolulu for assault and battery; a court case would only drag the compromised lady and her husband through the mud. Landais and his sword cane were sent back to France. (When Marshal Parke first saw the weapon it was stuck in its sheath so tightly that it took two men to get it out, but Perrin had the blade cleaned, sharpened, and oiled before he shipped it back to France as incriminating evidence.) Mrs. Brewer left for the United States with her husband. Perrin stayed on at Honolulu, spreading the story that Landais had committed incest with his daughter some years before, that his wife had found out about it and left him, and that this was why Landais had decided to come to Honolulu in the first place.

The second great scandal of Alexander Liholiho's reign involved the Princess Victoria Kamamalu, daughter of Governor Kekuanaoa of Oahu, heiress of Kaahumanu, sister of the king and Prince Lot, and the intended bride of the high chief David Kalakaua. One night in January 1857, Prince Lot had as his dinner guest at the palace a Honolulu auctioneer named Marcus Monsarrat, British born, a naturalized Hawaiian subject, and a married man. Monsarrat took his leave late in the evening, but later still Lot, alerted by a servant, found him in Victoria's room with his clothes in some disarray. Lot told Monsarrat that if he stayed at Honolulu it would be at the risk of his life. Monsarrat sailed hastily for San Francisco, leaving his wife and family behind.

Monsarrat pushed his luck and came back to Honolulu in May. Alexander Liholiho commanded him to leave forever. Monsarrat said he would never go voluntarily. The king had him arrested and locked up in the palace. There were rumors that some of the town's foreigners would try to rescue him, but nothing happened, and next morning Monsarrat was marched down to the harbor and put on board a ship bound for the west coast.

Monsarrat's banishment for life was the sole responsibility of Alexander Liholiho. There were legal arguments that might have been made against his course of action, but nobody advanced them. The vindication of royal honor was all important.

The urbane Robert Wyllie was inclined to look at the whole affair simply as a lapse in taste. In his opinion Victoria Kamamalu's missionary teachers at the Chiefs' Children's School had made the mistake of bringing her up like any common school girl. If she had been taught to know her dignity as a princess, Wyllie said, no mere auctioneer would ever have been able to find access to her person.

Alexander Liholiho was less detached. According to David Gregg, he said that the befouler of his sister's virtue should have been shot down like a dog. Later on, however, the king, happy in his own marriage with the charming young Queen Emma, yielded to the pleas of Monsarrat's wife and reduced his term of banishment. Just a few months after he made this generous gesture the king shot and seriously wounded his own private secretary, an American named Henry A. Neilson, in what he believed to be a defense of Emma's honor.

Alexander Liholiho in his mid-twenties was a handsome man with a flashing intelligence, but less than robust and given to occasional black moods. He suffered from asthma, and for this and other reasons of health he made it a habit to get away from Honolulu as often as affairs of state allowed. He liked to travel between islands with a convivial group of friends, and many of his happiest days were spent relaxing at Kailua on Hawaii and Lahaina on Maui, playgrounds of the chiefs for generations. In September 1859, the king was at Lahaina. As usual the royal suite occupied a number of houses, and there was a good deal of informal visiting back and forth. The diversions available were mild enough, perhaps even boring. Somehow a suggestion arose (it was never made clear just how) that Henry Neilson was trespassing on royal prerogative with Queen Emma. The king, mortified, loaded a small boat with liquor, went out to sea for two days, came back at night, picked up a brace of pistols, walked to Neilson's house, found him on the veranda in his night clothes ready to retire, and shot him in the chest at close range.

The wound was not fatal, but it was serious enough. Within a day or two Alexander Liholiho, stricken by conscience and alcoholic remorse, had satisfied himself that Neilson and Emma were guiltless. This, of course, did not restore Neilson's health; he remained an invalid. The king was distraught. With great difficulty his advisers dissuaded him from abdicating. His moods went up and down with the doctors' reports on Neilson's condition, and his own health suffered under the strain. Neilson died in 1862 of consumption and related ailments. Without any doubt the chest wound contributed to his early death.

There was no suggestion that Alexander Liholiho should stand trial; legal proceedings were never discussed, much less initiated. The king turned to religion for solace. Not, however, to the religion of his youth; as Gerrit Judd put it, Alexander Liholiho, "educated by the Mission, most of all things dislikes the Mission." Judd went on to say, unkindly, that the king, having been compelled to be good as a boy, was "determined *not* to be good as a man. Driven out to morning prayer meeting, Wednesday evening meeting, monthly concert, Sabbath school, long sermons, and daily exhortations, his heart is hardened to a degree unknown to the heathen." This might have been a fair description of the king before his marriage to Emma and before the shooting of Neilson, but Judd was writing in 1861, and by that time the chastened Alexander Liholiho was hard at work bringing the Episcopal church to Honolulu.

Alexander Liholiho had attended Episcopal services in London during his trip abroad with Prince Lot and Gerrit Judd, and he had come to the decision that the established religion of Great Britain was much more suitable to a monarchy than the cold and spare Protestantism of New England. The constitution of the kingdom placed all creeds on an equal footing, so Episcopalianism was not established as a state religion, and no appropriation from government revenues could be made for the new church. But the king and queen, like other citizens, were free under this same constitutional provision to support any religious faith they chose. Alexander Liholiho offered to donate a site for an Episcopal church at Honolulu, together with $1,000 a year for a clergyman.

The Hawaiian consul at London, Manley Hopkins (brother of Wyllie's friend at Honolulu, Charles Gordon Hopkins), enlisted the aid of several prominent English churchmen, and at their suggestion a missionary bishopric was formed. The Reverend Thomas Nettleship Staley was picked to lead the mission.

Alexander Liholiho and Emma awaited his arrival eagerly. The bishop was to baptize their four-year-old son, Prince Albert, a sturdy, good-tempered little boy, the apple of their eye and the darling of the natives. Since Kamehameha I no reigning Hawaiian monarch had produced an heir who survived to maturity, and so the hopes of the dynasty were locked up in the life of the young prince, Ka Haku O Hawaii, as the natives called him. Queen Victoria had consented to act as godmother by proxy, and a silver christening cup was sent to Honolulu in care of a newly appointed British Commissioner, William Webb Follett Synge.

Synge arrived at Honolulu some months ahead of Bishop Staley, to find Prince Albert fatally ill. Not long before, Alexander Liholiho, irritated at something the prince had done, doused the little boy with cold water. Whether or not this had anything to do with it, Prince Albert came down with a mysterious disease. Some thought it was sunstroke, others "brain fever." The king's physicians could not save him. He was given a hurried baptism according to the rites of the Church of England, performed by the Reverend Ephraim W. Clark of Kawaiahao Church. On August 27, 1862, the prince died, leaving his father and mother heartbroken and the native community in desolation.

Bishop Staley arrived to take up his work in October, before the general grief had subsided. Emma was baptized within two weeks of his landing, and at the end of November the royal couple were confirmed as members of the newly chartered Hawaiian Reformed Catholic Church. Robert Wyllie joined them two days later, together with Attorney General Charles Coffin Harris and Supreme Court Justice George M. Robertson. In December the high chief David Kalakaua was confirmed, and he took a seat on the first synod with Governor Kekuanaoa of Oahu. A few years later Staley was made a member of the Privy Council, and at one point there was a move to have him appointed President of the national Board of Education.

All this upset the Protestant missionaries. They had not objected to the idea of an Episcopal church when it was first mentioned because they assumed it would be a simple affair, conducted by a low church clergyman. Now they were challenged by a bishop on territory they had come to regard as their own, and by the highest of high church bishops at that, a Reformed Catholic, a "pervert to Popery," as the phrase went.

For the time being Staley could afford to ignore the complaints of the Protestants. The official community supported him, and the Hawaiian translation of the Book of Common Prayer was done by the king himself. Staley took an interest in the commoners as well, and he was not as critical as the Protestant missionaries had been. Not long after he arrived he went to watch a hula at Waikiki, and he encouraged a revival of traditional dancing and chanting at the funerals of chiefs. The Hawaiians, for their part, liked the theatricality of the Reformed Catholic service, the chanted liturgy, the rich vestments, and the pictures on the walls of the church. Native Protestants might ridicule the whole business (one told his pastor that the bishop looked like a pupule, a crazy man, with an auction flag on his back), but Staley managed to fill his church three times each Sunday.

Staley's patron, King Alexander Liholiho, died on November 30, 1863, at the age of twenty-nine. For days the palace grounds were filled with weeping natives, and memorial dances and chants were performed while the body lay in state. Staley arranged the order of the funeral procession, and he relegated the Protestant missionaries to a place they found insulting. The result was that only one Congregationalist minister attended the service. This was Ephraim Clark of Kawaiahao, and he went, so he said, mostly because he wanted to look at the Reformed Catholic church building, which he had never visited. He reported that "nothing could be more popish" than the rites observed by Staley; the display of the bishop's crozier and "all the other flummery" was "not a little disgusting."

The Protestants were humiliated again when Princess Victoria Kamamalu died in 1866. Once more the palace grounds were crowded with mourners, and this time the native chants were as Hawaiian as anyone could have wished; some of them celebrated the sexual prowess of the princess. Victoria Kamamalu had been a member of Kawaiahao Church, and services were conducted at the palace by the Reverend Henry Parker, son of the missionary Benjamin Parker. But Staley claimed the right to bury all members of the royal family, whether they were Reformed Catholics or not. He insisted that the royal cemetery in Nuuanu valley was consecrated ground, and Parker was forbidden to pray at the grave side.

It was not only good American Protestants who were offended by Staley. The Roman Catholics of the town, under Bishop Louis Maigret, regarded Reformed Catholicism as nothing but a dangerous heresy. And American patriots generally suspected the Reformed Catholic priests of being tools of British imperial policy. This was hardly accurate. But it was transparently clear that Alexander Liholiho cultivated the English and had no time for most Americans. (One of his first acts on becoming king was to subscribe to the London *Times*. He also took the *Illustrated News,* the *Quarterly Review*, the *Edinburgh Review, Blackwood's Magazine*, the *Westminster Review*, and *Punch*, and read them all. American periodicals he was likely to throw out the window half read.) After he died the widowed Emma paid a visit to Europe and spent some time in England as a guest of Queen Victoria, and this only strengthened the fears of the Americans. Alexander Liholiho's brother Lot, who became Kamehameha V, was quite open about the British connection. "We thought," he wrote, "get England to be interested in *us* by means of her Church, and let the Englishmen contribute their wealth Clergymen & laymen to ornament and sustain this Church, she will begin to learn more of us and take more interest in us which well fostered will ripen into a great friendship, not only between the rulers of the Countries but the friendship of the people of England. This fact was underlying the whole Church History from the beginning . . ."

In the end Staley did not manage to make a permanent place for himself at Honolulu, mostly because he ran into difficulties with the white members of his own congregation. He was a High Churchman and a good many of his parishioners, as it happened, were Low Church. The pastor and his flock quarreled on points of doctrine and practice. While Staley was away on a visit to England a petition was circulated among his congregation at Honolulu to have him removed. He resigned in May 1870.

His superiors in England gave some thought to turning the mission over to American Episcopalians. The dowager queen Emma was furious at the idea that her church might be passed from hand to hand. The English affiliation was saved, but not much else could be salvaged.

Bishop Alfred Willis, who arrived in 1872 to take charge of the renamed Anglican Church in Hawaii, stayed for thirty years, but at the end of that time his church was still a minor denomination in the islands.

The Protestants did not try to hide their pleasure at Staley's discomfiture. It came at a particularly flattering time for them. In 1870, the year of Staley's resignation, the fiftieth anniversary of the arrival of the first American Board missionaries was celebrated by almost fifteen thousand Hawaiians, about a fourth of the total population of the kingdom, organized into fifty-eight churches, thirty-nine of which had native ordained ministers.

This, of course, was evidence of a considerable achievement, a success that was not matched in any other group of islands in the Pacific at such an early date. But, as the missionaries themselves were forced to admit, the great days of Puritanism were already in the past. By the time Alexander Liholiho came to the throne the Calvinist missionaries had lost their position as sole arbiters of right and wrong in the kingdom. It was not simply that the Sandwich Islands Mission had been disbanded with three quarters of the population still outside the Protestant church, nor that other religious groups were competing for the souls of Hawaiians; but rather that in the white community Englishmen, Europeans, and non-Puritan Americans were taking it upon themselves to decide what might or might not be regarded as acceptable behavior.

The missionary virtues, to put it bluntly, were becoming unfashionable. Mark Twain, who visited the islands in the eighteen sixties, spoke for a good many residents when he called the missionaries "pious; hard-working; hard-praying; self-sacrificing; hospitable; devoted to the well-being of this people and the interests of Protestantism; bigoted; puritanical; slow; ignorant of all white human nature and natural ways of men, except the remnants of these things that are left in their own class or profession; old fogy—fifty years behind the age . . ." The missionaries had only a simple past to draw upon in trying to make the future secure for their faith, and they did not know how to cope with a complex present in which the enemies of holiness were much more subtle, devious, and disarming than they had been in the old days. Among some of the natives of the rural districts praise-god bare-bones morality still had an appeal, but in the towns, and especially at Honolulu, the only town that really mattered so far as the world was concerned, the messengers of God were regarded more and more as eccentric disturbers of the social peace.

One of the mission's most determined efforts to control the future was made in the field of education, and the results showed clearly the extent and limitations of their success. Punahou School, opened at Honolulu in 1841 for the benefit of the children of the missionaries, was intended to re-create small town New England in the tropics, as far as that was possible, and it had fair success in its first generation. Lahainaluna Seminary on Maui, established in 1831 with the idea that it would produce a steady flow of native Christian scholars, had a more checkered career.

Perhaps the most important academy of all was the Chiefs' Children's School at Honolulu. Every future Hawaiian monarch after Kamehameha III, and a good many other high chiefs, went to school there between 1839 and 1850. Like the students of Punahou they got a New England education in the English language. Parts of it took. In later life Alexander Liholiho and Emma worked as hard as any New England philanthropists, trying to halt the ravages of depopulation among their people. William Lunalilo, who reigned briefly as king in the eighteen seventies, bequeathed part of his estate to the care of elderly and infirm Hawaiians; and Bernice Pauahi Bishop, the last descendant of Kamehameha the Great, left the income from her vast lands to be used for the education of native Hawaiians.

The missionaries could congratulate themselves on these counts, but there was another side to the story. Alexander Liholiho, educated by Amos Starr Cooke and his wife Juliette, two rather spartan American missionary teachers with republican leanings, became an Episcopalian and planned to send his own son to school at Eton or Rugby. His brother Lot grew into a taciturn, uncompromising nativist. William Lunalilo, a devastating dinner table wit who could score at will off Western diplomats and naval commanders, was a charming wastrel and a drunkard, in the care of financial trustees all his life. As for David Kalakaua, who came to the throne after Lunalilo, he was a king extravagant in the use of royal prerogatives sexual, financial, and political, totally improvident, alternately a client and a racial enemy of Americans. His reign was the very negation of missionary teaching. Kalakaua's sister Liliuokalani inherited the kingdom only to lose it.

Long before that happened the holy community had been dismantled, piece by piece. When amateur theater came to Honolulu the missionaries, to whom actors were just one step above hula dancers in depravity, encouraged their followers to call the theater "Hale Diabolo," house of the devil. But every Hawaiian monarch after Kamehameha II attended the theater, and Alexander Liholiho and Emma themselves took part in amateur theatricals. Drinking at the royal court became an open issue in the reign of King Kaukeaouli, and the missionaries lost their battle against it. With drinking went dancing, and with dancing went other nuances of polite behavior. By the late fifties most holidays were being celebrated with dances in the evening, including the solemn national days which used to be marked by temperance feasts or periods of fasting and humiliation. As early as 1850 necklines on evening gowns were low enough to make fan play an interesting provocation rather than a tropical necessity, and propriety soon encompassed whispered compliments over iced drinks and midnight carriage rides after the dance.

By the sixties the missionaries were in full retreat. One of the most lavish events of King Alexander Liholiho's reign was a gigantic fancy dress ball given by Robert Wyllie, a fanatic for the social graces and a tireless dancer. It was attended by every person of any importance outside the Protestant mission community (even Bishop Louis Maigret of the Roman Catholic mission, dressed of course as himself). Wyllie appeared in the costume of a highland chief, and so did the venerable Governor Kekuanaoa of Oahu. There was a Titania, an Undine, and a Beau Brummel; and Queen Emma came as the goddess Cybele—a *very* non-Protestant religious figure.

By the end of the sixties the retreat of the missionaries had turned into a rout. Their own children, confined to calisthenics ("Presbyterian dancing") at Punahou, were quick to take up real dancing once they left school. Public dances were so crowded that two bands were needed and the gallopade was a positive danger. At the opening of a skating rink at Honolulu Queen Emma sat in the royal box and watched the lancers, the quadrille, and the grand march performed—all on skates. Within a year or two of the mission's fiftieth anniversary the native members of the choir at Kawaiahao Church were organizing mid-summer dances; the elderly wife of the Reverend Lowell Smith of Kaumakapili Church was seen swimming at Waikiki on a Sunday; and the children of missionaries were "dancing themselves silly" at weekend parties in the country.

The Dance of Death

Among the beautiful girls who graced the court of Alexander Liholiho and Emma were several young people of good family part-white and part-native. Emma herself had some white blood, from her grandfather John Young, the friend of Kamehameha the Great, and she was brought up in the house of her adoptive father, the English physician Thomas C. B. Rooke. Far more than any other Hawaiian queen (except perhaps the imperious Kaahumanu) Emma was a leader of fashion, and she chose to surround herself with a bevy of pretty, wellborn young ladies-in-waiting, native, part-native, and white. In her day it would have been impossible for a guest to wind his way through a court cotillion without finding on his arm a girl or two of part-Hawaiian ancestry.

Young people of mixed blood had had a harder time only a decade or two earlier. In the first place there was the constant presumption and the usual fact of illegitimacy. Then too, the missionaries had never liked the idea of mixing the races, even under the most proper circumstances. When the chiefs suggested that missionaries' daughters would make good wives for the young princes Alexander Liholiho and Lot, the proposal got a cold reception. And when the bachelor missionary Samuel G. Dwight married a Hawaiian girl he was suspended from the mission by the vote of his brethren.

Some of the missionaries were even against educating part-white children in the English language. As Gerrit Judd said, a boy might possibly get an honest job as a businessman's clerk, but the girls would, "if we may judge from past experience, become mistresses for 'Gentlemen.'"

This was true enough, as the experience of Hannah Holmes had shown. In the twenties and thirties she had been the archetypal part-white beauty of Honolulu, pursued and won by any number of "Gentlemen." She took it upon herself to give the daughters of other gentlemen the benefit of her experience. With the help of the American merchant Stephen Reynolds she started a dancing school, and Reynolds kept it up for years, teaching his pupils all they would need to know in polite society should polite society ever recognize their existence. Polite society kept its back turned.

The daughters of Stephen Reynolds' girls were luckier. But even so they had problems, not so much of race alone as of race and class together. The nation was, after all, a monarchy, a graded society, and no matter what the constitution of the kingdom said there was still an enormous distance between chief and commoner. For the common-born native wife of an established white businessman there might be a kind of tolerance, but for the single Hawaiian girl of ordinary origins there was none. Some of the white bachelors of Honolulu were able to divide their time between the drawing rooms of the valleys and the dance halls of the waterfront, and certainly the princes of the kingdom never saw the need for too much class consciousness on their own part, at least after dark; but it was a brave or insensitive girl who tested the boundaries between the demi-monde and the fashionable world.

At Honolulu, if nowhere else in the kingdom, the boundaries were quite clear. Respectability drained away along the lower reaches of Nuuanu stream and disappeared altogether where its waters flowed into the harbor. The main road that ran inland from the waterfront was known to sailors as Fid Street, for its barrooms and brothels. With the land reforms of the late forties its name was formally changed to Nuuanu Street, but a change in name did not alter its character. A sizeable section of the waterfront around Nuuanu Street and Maunakea Street was given over to euphemistically named "boarding houses," taverns, coffee shops, and other places of assignation. On the assumption that the natural area of vice ought to have a legal definition, the government passed an ordinance in 1848 limiting the issue of liquor licenses to this area. It was generally understood that the harbor was no place for a lady.

The lower classes—natives, common born part-whites, and white workingmen and sailors—liked the waterfront just the same, even if by definition no ladies were to be found there. At least there were bright lights and entertainments: a night at the variety theater or the circus, conversations in the coffee shops, promenades on the crowded streets, and dancing. During the reign of King Alexander Liholiho Christmas Day in downtown Honolulu was celebrated with an elegant supper, toasts to all and sundry, and "the most intricate quadrilles, foreign waltzes, polkas, mazurkas, redowas, etc." The "Working Man" who recorded the scene was amazed to find among the "humble orders" of the native population so much "grace and elegance."

The lower classes were only imitating their betters. But what was grace and elegance to a workingman struck others as nothing more than swinishness. Marshal of the Kingdom William Parke, who held the view that in matters of morals what was good for New England would be good for the Hawaiian kingdom, thought the dance halls of Honolulu were a disgrace, the great scene and indeed the primary cause of a vast incidence of fornication and adultery. He wanted the vile places suppressed; otherwise, he warned, the rising generation of Hawaiians, "from whom so much is expected, and for whom so much has been done, must irretrievably fall, and be consigned to infamy and shame."

In 1856 two well-known tavern keepers, Joe Booth of the National Hotel and Joseph Dawson of Liberty Hall, both Englishmen, were sentenced under the common nuisance laws for allowing native women to assemble for "lewd purposes" at their dance halls. Booth appealed his conviction to the supreme court, where a foreign jury acquitted him. The verdict produced a spate of shocked letters in the *Pacific Commercial Advertiser,* edited by Henry M. Whitney, son of the pioneer missionary Samuel Whitney; and there was some hand wringing by the Hawaiian language *Hae Hawaii,* which had missionary affiliations. The editor of the *Polynesian,* the bohemian Englishman Charles Gordon Hopkins, served on the jury, and his paper ran a long letter from a juryman explaining why he voted against convicting Booth.

The prosecution's argument, said the juryman, was that dancing with prostitutes corrupted public morals. His own view was that the words "strumpet" and "prostitute" connoted a class of women, socially degraded, who sold themselves for money—women clearly separate from the rest of society. In the Hawaiian kingdom no such distinction existed. The dance

hall women might be "better looking, some more bold, some more mer-
cenary than the general run of females throughout the islands, but it is a
fact which we are all well aware of, that after singling out an insignificant
fraction of the well educated and the well looked after, the remainder—
the vast majority of native women—are all one class; one in habits, one in
feeling, one in morals, one in their associations. There is no proscribed
class as in other countries . . ." How, then, could the native women
be prevented from gathering where they wished? They *were* the public;
their morals were public morals. Could the whole female population be
declared a nuisance? "It is much to be feared that there exists here some of
the Anglo-Saxon race with the selfish, unsympathising, over-bearing
natures, only too characteristic of it, who, in their anxiety to establish a
cordon sanitaire around the pure morality of their own sons, or their own
brothers, would hardly hesitate to return even this verdict." He himself could
not agree with it, and that was why he voted to overturn the conviction.

So Joe Booth was to be freed because all, rather than a few, Hawaiian women were immoral. This was a sweeping judgment, on the face of
things. But it was true that native women had never been able to take very
seriously the laws against adultery, moe kolohe (literally, "sleeping mis-
chievously"). And it was true that dance halls and other waterfront dives
were busiest in the whaling season, when the ports filled up with sailors
and women flocked to help them spend their money.

Whether or not this seasonal pastime deserved the name of prostitution it was certainly a big business. All through the whaling era the Hawaiian kingdom suffered from an adverse balance of trade, and prostitution
was a useful corrective. If Marshal Parke and the other moralists had been
able to find a way to kill the dance halls they might have struck a blow for
purity, but far more certainly they would have struck a blow against
prosperity.

In the first two decades of the whaling trade Honolulu was the only
port that satisfied both shipmasters and common seamen, because it
offered good facilities for picking up supplies and transshipping cargoes
and at the same time it was the one place in the kingdom where sailors
could be sure of finding liquor and women. At Lahaina on Maui, where
supplies were plentiful and an open roadstead provided reasonably good
anchorage, the government's policy was to forbid the issue of liquor
licenses, and so only staunch Christian whaling captains made Lahaina
their automatic first choice. Then in the forties two things happened to
change the situation. First, the white potato began to be grown in quantity
on Maui, and sailors liked it much better than the sweet potato of Oahu.
Second, Governor Hoapili of Maui died. He was one of the most devoted
Christian chiefs of his generation, and he had taken great pains to keep

down grogshops and brothels. The governors who followed him were interested more in money than in morals. Vice had always flourished on Oahu, but now Maui sported both the white potato and the prostitute, and the combination was irresistible. Lahaina became Gomorrah to Honolulu's Sodom. By the mid-forties twice as many whaling ships were putting in at Lahaina as at Honolulu.

When the potato boom died away in the mid-fifties Honolulu came into its own again, and common sailors found they could still do very well for themselves there. During the early months of 1860, while the last whaling ships of the fall season of 1859 were still in port, a Japanese diplomatic mission to the United States, the first of its kind to visit a Western nation, stopped at Honolulu for a few days on its way to the Californian coast, and a shore party did some sight-seeing in the town. "After we had walked about half a mile we saw a large house," wrote Yanagawa Masakiyo. "There were many musical instruments in it. Several people were playing the Hawaiian guitar, violin and castanet. We stood outside and listened because it was most interesting. One westerner came and led us upstairs. There we saw several hundred men and women in a large room which was about 100 feet by 50 feet." A game of billiards was under way. "When the ball went into the hole a music box played automatically. This was a signal that the game had been won, so the players drank wine and became very merry.

"We went upstairs and turned to the left, where we entered another long hall in which the light was very dim because of the scarcity of the lamps. In this part of the building were about forty bedrooms. We thought this very strange and upon inquiry found it a house of ill fame. After the evening entertainment many of the guests retired to these rooms for which they paid $1.50 each."

Those were 1860 prices. A decade or so earlier the *Sandwich Islands News* published some figures on the economics of prostitution. On the average a sailor would spend about ten dollars in his few weeks ashore. In a flush season at least twelve thousand seamen would take liberty at Honolulu alone, leaving $120,000 in the town. Most of this money passed through the hands of prostitutes. Thus native women at Honolulu could put into the hands of merchants something like $100,000 a season (a sum equal to the annual revenue of the government during the forties). Most retailers did not even bother to build up their stocks until the whaling season, since it was only then that their customers had money. Retailers paid wholesalers, and wholesalers paid customs duties to the government, and so the wheels of commerce turned.

Nothing the moralists could say or do would stop this. As long as native women wanted bright clothes, as long as their husbands, fathers, and families were short of money to buy horses or pay taxes, and as long as sailors spent their season's earnings in port, there would be prostitution in the kingdom.

Hawaiians were more than willing to endanger their immortal souls at the ports, so it seemed. And to make matters worse they were putting their bodies in jeopardy as well, because Honolulu and Lahaina were notoriously the places where disease entered the kingdom—influenza and measles (sometimes fatal, because Hawaiians had no immunity against them), typhoid, and eventually smallpox.

An epidemic of some sort was always a danger; infection from venereal disease was a dreadful actuality. Ever since the time of Captain Cook it had been taking its toll, and now the whaling ships brought diseased sailors by the hundred to the islands twice a year. Apothecaries did about two-thirds of their business in medications for venereal disease among the Hawaiians, but of course the disease persisted, and after a season at the port, women would return home, gaudily dressed, to spread infection in the rural districts.

As late as 1860 the Protestants of Honolulu were still talking about the wages of sin, but others were thinking in more practical terms. Alexander Liholiho, deeply concerned with the fate of his people, worked hard to establish Queen's Hospital at Honolulu, and soon after the hospital opened the legislature passed an act ordering prostitutes to register and submit to medical inspection. This did something to relieve the situation, but not enough. Venereal disease, the "great waster" of the nation, was eating into the native population on a large scale, together with the rest of the long list of diseases the Hawaiians could not withstand.

The ports kept growing, and so did the white community, but the total population of the kingdom declined tragically. At the turn of the nineteenth century only a few hundred natives lived at Honolulu and Lahaina, and the total native population of the kingdom was more than a quarter of a million. By 1840 the proportion was about eleven thousand natives at the ports in a total population of one hundred thousand; by 1860 about eighteen thousand in less than seventy thousand; and by the early seventies about eighteen thousand in less than sixty thousand.

Those with a taste for statistical oddities might have noted that these figures made the Hawaiian kingdom one of the most highly urbanized nations in the world, even though its biggest town had only fifteen thousand inhabitants. Those with the beginnings of a conscience were faced with the fact that the Hawaiian people seemed to be on the way to extinction. "It can scarcely be said," wrote George Kenway of Waimea on the island of Hawaii, which was particularly hard hit, "that there is any Native population at all. The hill sides and the banks of watercourses show for miles the ruins of the 'olden time'—Stone walls half sunk in the ground, broken down and covered with grass.—large broken squares of trees and imperfect embankments.—remains of old taro patches and water runs now dried up and useless, and many other such tokens that like old coins—old Castles and old books, impress one with a melancholy curiosity about a people that cannot now be found."

Whales

Whatever the kingdom's situation was, whaling had made it so. Since the beginning of the eighteen twenties whaling ships had been putting in at Honolulu, Lahaina, and lesser ports such as Hilo and Kealakekua on Hawaii and Waimea and Koloa on Kauai. More than a hundred of them made use of Hawaiian ports in 1824, more than a hundred and seventy in 1829. During the next twenty years the Pacific whaling fleet doubled in size and then almost doubled again, and as the whole industry moved northward from the equatorial hunting grounds on the equator to the Japan Sea and finally to the Arctic the Hawaiian Islands became the center of a booming trade. Eight times before 1860 the annual total of ship arrivals at Hawaiian ports was more than five hundred, and in the record year of 1846 the figure reached almost six hundred.

All this meant money in hand, and not only for Hawaiian women. It became a commonplace to say that no one could do business at the islands without the whalers. The wages of native seamen, profits on the sale of supplies, commissions on the transshipment of oil and bone from the islands to the United States, speculation in bills of exchange, and returns on all sorts of services from ship chandlering to boardinghouse keeping made whaling indispensable.

In one or two other specialized ways the whaling industry was a money-maker. The native constables of Honolulu, for example, did well out of it. Until the end of the eighteen fifties they were paid a percentage of fines imposed by the police courts. They would wait for a whaling ship to come in, watch the liberty party hire horses, and then, as the seamen set off at a gallop, bring them up short for "furious riding." The offense was a Honolulu specialty, and it was so profitable that seamen called the fort "The Mint."

Getting whalermen out of the fort was a consul's responsibility, and so was practically everything else that affected a seaman once his ship entered Hawaiian waters. American whaling ships and merchantmen far outnumbered all others at the islands—in fact, of all ports in the world Honolulu and Lahaina were the most frequently visited by American ships in the forties and fifties—and so the United States consulates were busy places.

At the height of the whaling era Hawaiian posts were the most eagerly contested in the whole of the American consular corps, and the reason was simple—at the islands a man might make his fortune in the service of his country. Consular expenses covered the care and repatriation of sick, disabled, and abandoned sailors, and consuls quickly found ways to doctor their accounts. They recruited "patients" among the riffraff of the ports and kept them on the hospital books as long as they could, charging their "treatment," keep, and clothing to the United States government. Under the consuls' secret system of competitive bids among physicians and businessmen for services to the hospitals, costs were two or three times as high as the going rate elsewhere in the kingdom, and prices there were normally twice as high as in the United States.

Toward the end of the eighteen fifties it was discovered at Washington that "relief of seamen" in the Hawaiian Islands was costing more than $150,000 a year—more than half the sum appropriated for the relief of American sailors all over the world. Special commissioners were sent to the islands aboard the American war ship *Levant*. The criminality of the consuls was established without a doubt, and the *Levant* set off on her return voyage with a full report. She was never heard of again. The consuls went back to falsifying their accounts, and they kept it up until the decline of the whaling industry took the profit out of it.

If the profit went out of the consular hospitals it would go out of everything. The mere thought that the whaling industry might collapse some day was enough to give nightmares to the calmest businessman at the islands. The government was well aware that pinchpenny New England firms, upon whose patronage the kingdom's solvency rested, would direct their ships to ports where costs were lowest, and so duties and charges at Honolulu and Lahaina were kept as light as possible. But the whaling industry was unstable by its very nature. Each season as the first ships arrived from the north with advance news, the chances of profit or loss were calculated in haste along the waterfront, and the slightest fall in the size of the fleet, the average catch, or the price of oil and bone, sent tremors through the countinghouses.

The merchants had to learn to live with uncertainty, contenting themselves with the hope that if one year was bad the next might be better. But they could do nothing more than hope, because the things that made for good and bad years were out of their hands. Between the mid-forties and the mid-seventies at least one year in five was disastrous, and each bad year raised the grim possibility that the industry might fail altogether. Everybody knew what that would mean for the kingdom. As early as 1844 Robert Wyllie had put it into words: without the whaling fleet the Hawaiian Islands would relapse into "primitive insignificance."

Between 1845 and 1855 the whaling fleets of the North Pacific and the Arctic were at their largest and prices for oil and bone were high. Then in the late fifties the industry entered a long and irreversible decline.

The symptoms had been evident for some time. As one whaling ground after another was exhausted, ships had to go farther and farther afield, until at last the distant and difficult Arctic fisheries became the most important. In the fifties ships were likely to leave a New England port and not return for as long as four years. To begin with, this trend toward lengthy voyages was useful to businessmen at Honolulu and Lahaina, because ships that did not go back to their home port for several seasons were forced to make a good many stops at the islands to pick up supplies and transship cargoes; and whether a voyage was a success or a failure the middleman on shore had to be paid for his services. But extended voyages were costly, profit margins fell, ship owners reconsidered their commitments, the number of ships in the fleet was reduced, and middlemen at the islands began to suffer along with entrepreneurs in New England.

Misery did not love company. The New Englanders complained that rapacious businessmen at Honolulu were "fleecing and shaving" honest whaling captains, and to keep money out of the reach of the "grasping" Honolulans some of the New London and New Bedford houses began sending their own merchant ships to the islands, where their agents distributed supplies and loaded return cargoes of oil and bone. Indignant noises were heard at Honolulu when the first of these ships arrived, but by the late fifties the general opinion was that the New Englanders had outmaneuvered themselves. In their efforts to beat the Hawaiian businessmen they were shipping supplies such as beef, flour, sugar, and molasses, all of which were produced at the islands and could be bought at Honolulu and Lahaina more cheaply than the same goods shipped around Cape Horn or picked up on the Californian coast.

One way to strike back at the New Englanders was to start a local whaling fleet. As the newspapers said, a single ship based on Honolulu was worth four owned in New England. By 1858, nineteen ships registered in the kingdom were combing the offshore grounds of the islands or going north to hunt in the Arctic. But even this was no solution. The Hawaiian fleet and the Pacific fleet were tied together in their troubles. In 1859 an oil well was brought into successful production in Pennsylvania, and from then on a new kind of oil lamp lit up the writing on the wall for the whaling industry.

The Civil War all but ruined the New England fleet. A good many whalers were converted into merchantmen, and others were sold and the proceeds reinvested in some more reliable industry. The Union government bought a number of them and sank them to block the harbor entrances at Charleston, South Carolina, and other ports.

Enough still sailed the Pacific, however, to interest the Confederates. The raider *Shenandoah*, commanded by Captain James Waddell, pursued Union whalers and merchantmen as far north as the Arctic and as far west as the Marianas Islands, seizing cargoes and burning ships. Many Hawaiian seamen were aboard ships that came under Waddell's guns. Abandoned at ports all around the North Pacific, they made their way home distressed and destitute. Eventually the Hawaiian government declared the depredations of the *Shenandoah* a public disaster and voted money to meet the expenses of repatriation.

Waddell overstepped himself in 1865 when he attacked the merchantman *Harvest,* which was not an American ship at all: she was owned by the Honolulu firm of H. Hackfeld & Co., she flew the Hawaiian flag, and she was manned by native seamen. Waddell came upon the *Harvest* at Ascension Island in the Marianas, ordered her crew ashore, and burned her to the waterline.

The Hawaiian kingdom had announced its neutrality, but most American businessmen at the ports were northerners, strongly pro-Union. Waddell became the greatest villain on earth to them. After the sinking of the *Harvest* the Hawaiian government demanded the surrender of the *Shenandoah* as a pirate ship, and businessmen threatened Waddell with the "blubber room" if he ever showed his face at the islands.

Before the indignation over Waddell had died away another disaster overtook the whaling fleet. In the fall of 1871, thirty-three ships, including some of Hawaiian registry, were trapped in the ice floes north of Bering Strait in the Arctic. The crews escaped, but the ships and their cargoes were ground to pieces. Rescue ships brought five hundred native Hawaiian seamen back, penniless and exhausted. By the end of October the consular hospital at Honolulu had 541 American sailors on its books, and another hundred were billeted in the town.

While they waited to be sent home the Americans sat about the streets, passing the time with songs:

> *Do your best for one another,*
> *Making life a pleasant dream,*
> *Help a worn and weary brother,*
> *Pulling hard against the stream.*

Some preferred to help themselves. A few went in for larceny; others sold the clothes the American consul had doled out to them. It was small recompense for a lost livelihood. The Arctic disaster probably cost the Hawaiian Islands two hundred thousand dollars and the industry at large ten times as much. And there was no recompense for this, either, then or later; it was a virtual death blow.

Sugar

Each time the whaling fleet betrayed the islands by its absence, voices were heard arguing that the kingdom should look for ways to take wealth from the soil instead of the sea. If agricultural products could be developed and marketed the instability of the whaling industry would no longer be a problem; and, as a side benefit, the people of the ports would not have to go on thinking of themselves as whoremasters to whalermen.

The idea of agriculture looked especially attractive during the late forties, when the California gold rush suddenly brought into being a new market for Hawaiian produce. The timing was excellent. The whaling season of 1847-1848 had not been a success, and many businessmen at Honolulu and Lahaina were badly overstocked. But by the end of 1848 the stores had been stripped of everything that might be useful at the gold fields, from pickaxes, shovels, and lamps to Bibles and playing cards. The floating population of white men at the ports had disappeared, and hundreds of natives were gone too.

Those who chose to stay at the islands on fixed incomes found they had made an expensive choice. Prices for goods and services rose to dizzy heights. But businessmen, once they reconciled themselves to the sudden disappearance of debtors and got used to extravagant demands from their remaining employees, discovered to their delight that they could not help making money. Everything they sent to the diggings turned to gold, so it seemed.

Under these happy circumstances restraint was difficult. Men of common sense who had refused to take a chance on the lottery of life in California caught gold fever at a distance. They used their trading profits to gamble in real estate at the islands. Opportunity knocked in 1848 and again in 1849, and the noise compelled attention. In 1850 the Hawaiian government passed laws permitting aliens to buy land in fee simple. Investors went heavily into debt to buy property, betting in effect that the gold rush would never end. Some covered their bets mentally by reasoning that even if the gold gave out they would not be stranded; the United States was committed to westward expansion, and sooner or later the islands would fall into American hands. In the short run landowners could supply the goldfields with high priced meat, vegetables, and sugar, and later their fee simple titles would guarantee them wealth under the American flag. One way or another the future was theirs.

The reckoning came sooner than they hoped. By the end of 1851 surface gold in California was mined out. The west coast market collapsed, the tide of trade and travel turned and set in the direction of Australia, where a new rush was starting, and the Hawaiian kingdom found itself in the midst of a depression. Real estate speculators—those who had used their newly bought lands to supply the Californian market and those who had planned simply to hold their property for resale at a profit—were trapped, unable to meet their loan and mortgage payments. And by the end of 1854 it was obvious that annexation would not save them.

Among those who had overextended themselves were the sugar planters. Sugarcane grew wild in the islands, and many attempts were made in the early nineteenth century to turn it into a cash crop. Refining techniques were primitive to begin with, but even so Hawaiian sugar could be sold on the American west coast. Land, machinery, and labor were expensive at the islands, but the potential rewards were enormous. Scores of thousands of dollars, borrowed at perilous rates of interest, were poured into the plantations. When the Californian market failed, disaster followed immediately.

The procession of bankruptcies was mournful in the extreme, and many planters were shaken out of the business altogether. Still, the Royal Hawaiian Agricultural Society did not think the darkness was unrelieved. In 1852, when things were at their worse, the Society's poet laureate composed an ode for the annual meeting:

> *Then on! bear on, the plough is ready,*
> *With which to turn the waiting soil;*
> *The torch of science now burns steady,*
> *To light you on your chosen toil;*
> *Then swerve not from the path before you,*
> *But onward with unfaltering tread;*
> *Success shall wave her banner o'er you,*
> *And Hawaii rise as from the dead.*

Exhortation was all very well, but what the planters really needed was money. By borrowing from the government at twelve percent per annum a few of them managed to scrape together enough to weather the bad years. But by the end of the decade, with the end of whaling close at hand, capital once tied up at the ports was freed for reinvestment. The west coast market recovered as Oregon and California gained population. By 1860, although commerce at the islands was generally depressed, the number of plantations had risen to twelve. All of them were busy, and sugar prices were rising.

The Civil War, which crippled whaling in the Pacific, made the Hawaiian sugar industry. Southern sugar disappeared from the market in the northern states of the Union, and prices climbed so high that planters in the islands could make good profits even after paying heavy tariffs at American ports of entry. By 1866 there were thirty-two plantations and mill companies at the islands compared with twelve in 1860. Fewer than a million and a half pounds of sugar were exported in 1860; in 1866 the figure was about seventeen and three-quarter million pounds.

It seemed clear as never before that sugar was the staple the kingdom needed. At one time or another beef, wool, dairy goods, cotton, vegetables, silk, and rice had been produced in quantity, but none of them had solved the pressing economic problem of the balance of trade. The kingdom stayed alive by offering services to shipping and by handling the transshipment and re-export of goods. Now the soil was beginning to yield a crop for which it was well suited, and for which there was a growing demand.

It was still possible, of course, to lose money on a spectacular scale in the sugar business. Robert Wyllie was one who did. He had dreams of retiring from the Ministry of Foreign Affairs and taking up life as the bountiful Scots laird of a model community of Hawaiian plantation workers (whose language he did not speak). In the fifties he sank thousands of dollars in a coffee plantation at Hanalei on Kauai. In 1860 he changed the name of his estate to Princeville, in honor of the son of Alexander Liholiho and Emma, and began to cultivate sugar. Wyllie was a great dreamer, and his "rules of conduct" for laborers at Princeville read like a combination of the Sermon on the Mount, the kingdom's Masters and Servants Act, and certain pastoral passages from the novels of Sir Walter Scott. It was a brave vision, but Princeville ruined him. Once he had been worth about a quarter of a million dollars, but he was almost bankrupt when he died in 1865. His nephew, Robert Cochran Wyllie, who inherited the estate, came out to the islands to count his money, took up residence at Princeville, examined the plantation's books for the first time, and cut his throat.

Princeville plantation was an "independent," and by the time of Wyllie's death a good many planters had come to see that independence might be costly. There was a case to be made for sharing financial risks with an agency at Honolulu that could arrange loans, import machinery, and handle the shipping and sale of sugar. H. Hackfeld & Co. had taken over the management of the ill-fated Koloa plantation of Ladd & Co. in the forties, and by the end of the fifties some of the other big mercantile houses—most notably Castle & Cooke (a firm started by two former missionaries) and C. Brewer—were withdrawing their money from whaling and investing in plantation agencies.

The biggest of the agencies was Walker, Allen & Co., an American firm which by 1866 had an interest in twelve plantations and mills.

Walker, Allen & Co. led the Hawaiian sugar industry through the booming years of the Civil War, only to find that once the war was over the nightmare of 1851 returned. The American market contracted, prices dropped, and investments at Honolulu foundered. Walker, Allen & Co. had assets of $700,000 and liabilities of $600,000, but most of the assets were in the form of uncollectable debts owed by plantations caught in the slump. In January 1867, the firm filed bankruptcy papers, and in the debacle that followed, eight plantations went under the hammer and the Honolulu Sugar Refinery had to be closed for refinancing. Creditors realized less than thirty cents on the dollar.

The crisis had come at a moment when the planters and their agents at Honolulu were struggling to find a permanent place for themselves in the market at San Francisco. At the heart of the matter were the twin problems of quality and quantity. In the language of the business, most sugar sent from Honolulu to San Francisco before about 1863 was of low grade, below "No. 12, Dutch Standard." Refiners at San Francisco used this low-grade sugar (and similar grades from the Philippines and China) to produce white sugar. After 1863, because of technical improvements in milling at the islands, increasing amounts of sugar came from Honolulu at "No. 12 Dutch Standard" or above. More than half the Hawaiian crop was now "grocery grade," needing no further refining before it was sold at retail. This meant that Hawaiian sugar was in direct competition with "coffee sugars" turned out by the San Francisco refineries.

In 1865 the Hawaiian planters were invited to subscribe to a proposal put before them by San Francisco & Pacific Refineries. They were asked to process half or more of their sugar at grades lower than "No. 12 Dutch Standard." This would ease competition in the San Francisco market. In return San Francisco & Pacific would import less raw sugar from other places, and would pay Hawaiian producers for their low-grade sugar at a rate 15 percent above the price listed in Manila.

Essentially it was a quota system. Samuel N. Castle of Castle & Cooke supported the idea strongly. He was a former business agent of the Protestant mission at Honolulu who commented frequently on commercial matters, and his biblical style gave his pronouncements a magisterial, almost prophetic, quality. For the moment, however, he was without honor, and he was, after all, an agent and not a planter. Most planters calculated that demand for sugar on the American mainland was rising fast enough to absorb any increase in production at the islands. They would do best, they thought, to go on producing high grades even if the average price fell somewhat.

Castle was right and they were wrong. When the Hawaiian planters refused to sign contracts San Francisco & Pacific Refineries placed heavy orders at Manila for raw sugar. This was made into high-grade sugar, which was sold in competition with high grade sugar from Honolulu. The market was flooded, prices dropped, and planters, agents, and refiners all suffered.

Somewhat chastened, and sobered even more by the failure of Walker, Allen & Co. in January 1867, the men of the Hawaiian sugar industry listened more attentively when Mr. R. Feuerstein of San Francisco & Pacific came to Honolulu and re-opened the matter of contracts and quotas. A good many planters went on arguing in favor of independence. Those who had mortgage payments to meet needed the extra profits from high grades; only those who owned their land could make money from low-grades, and not many Hawaiian planters owned their land. The market at San Francisco appeared to be rising; why sign contracts at all? And if contracts must be signed, why with only one San Francisco house? Too many eggs would be in one basket. Against this, Samuel Castle and those who had been converted to his views spoke for safe and sane growing, milling, and marketing. Under a contract system the buyer would come to the door. Planters and agents would not have to depend on a capricious market thousands of miles away. The sensible course was to sign. Some of the wealthier planters took the lead, and Feuerstein went back to San Francisco with contracts for more than half the crop of 1867.

Most planters on contract did well, but this encouraged them to think that they might do better as independents. When Feuerstein came back to negotiate contracts for the crop of 1868 he found he had to offer inducements: a price increase, and a bonus for those who would sell all their crop to San Francisco & Pacific. Planters on contract did better in 1868 than they had the year before, and again this only led them to try their luck in the open market. Refinery contracts were abandoned halfway through the season. From then on price levels were set by supply and demand, and uncertainty ruled for the next few years.

All the same it was uncertainty of a new order. Between the mid-fifties and the mid-seventies the value of goods exported from the Hawaiian Islands increased from less than three hundred thousand dollars to a million and a half dollars. In 1869 a landmark was reached: for the first time exports of all kinds exceeded imports in value. Two years later, in 1871, exports of domestic goods alone were worth more than imports, and from then on the kingdom had a favorable balance of trade. The transformation had been brought about by the growth and consolidation of the sugar industry.

During the fat years of the gold rush the planters realized for the first time that the sugar industry had a serious labor problem. Making phrases about it was easy, especially for missionaries who were just beginning to take a serious interest in the agricultural prospects of the kingdom: the harvest was ready, they said, but the laborers were few. Finding a remedy was harder.

Because there was nowhere else to turn the planters looked to the native population, but they were not pleased with what they saw. A good many Hawaiians worked on the plantations—about one in every two able-bodied men by the early seventies—and though some said they did as well as anybody could, others said that one white man was worth three or four natives. Others again compared Hawaiian plantations unfavorably with those in the Caribbean—not, they hastened to add, because they wanted slavery in the Hawaiian kingdom, but because they wanted to show what might be done with a disciplined work force.

Discipline was certainly a touchy point. Among the Hawaiians some curious attitudes toward work had developed in the years since the breaking of the kapus. The land reforms of the late forties had given them the chance to become independent small farmers, cultivating their kuleanas, but even this did not turn them into enthusiastic workers, and the royal brothers Alexander Liholiho and Lot had some severe things to say about kuleana holders who preferred sleepy subsistence to profitable labor.

Then there were those who did not seem to want to work at all. They would rather follow their women to Honolulu or Lāhaina, or find a relative in town who had a job, and settle down comfortably in his house, eating his fish and poi, smoking his tobacco, wearing out his playing cards, and sleeping on his mats. To be sure, work was available in stores and factories; an educated man could always find a job as a clerk, and a skilled native tradesman could make good money. Some occupations, like the piloting of coastal schooners, were largely in the hands of the Hawaiians, but the most noticeable thing about the towns, in the eyes of jaundiced white men, was the number of natives visible, idle, and unproductive: hordes of children swimming naked in the harbor at Honolulu; boat-boys asleep under the wharves when they were not pestering visitors, brawling outside taverns, or silently stripping the copper sheathing from ships' hulls and jetty piles; grown men flying kites or playing marbles; courthouse and post office loafers; coffee shop loungers; and droves of flashily dressed horseback riders, men and women, who passed along the main streets enveloped in dust and clamor.

The sharpest criticism of the Hawaiians was that they had no "ambition," that they were not willing to invest time to make money. And yet that was not entirely fair. During the gold rush, while planters were crying out for workers who would be satisfied with a modest wage, hundreds of Hawaiians were going into business for themselves on Maui, growing potatoes and hauling them to the ports where they were snapped up by the shipload and sent to San Francisco. Natives called the potato fields "Nu Kaleponi" or New California, because in those days potatoes were gold and a man could dig a fortune out of the ground.

Of course the potato boom did not last very long, and when prices dropped the Hawaiians lost interest, even though they might still have made a modest profit. Then it was said that they had no stamina, that they were prodigal spenders of time, investing everything in projects that promised them dividends of excitement, without any thought for the future. As a matter of fact the Hawaiians did not share the white man's view of time. Even after they were taught how to count and how to use a Western calendar they preferred to call the days, weeks, and months of the year by the old native names. They liked to celebrate western holidays—the more the better—but they did not see the point of reckoning the year in four financial periods with a settling day at the end of each quarter.

White men gave a great deal of thought to the question of these attitudes, arguing over whether they were inherited or acquired. But no amount of theorizing would produce more Hawaiians, and even if every living native went to work on the plantations there still might not be enough to go around. The industry would have to look elsewhere for a labor supply.

As early as 1850 the question of bringing immigrant laborers to the islands was taken up by the newly formed Royal Hawaiian Agricultural Society. In preparation for the plantation era the national legislature passed an act "For the Government of Masters and Servants," and under its terms a shipload of Chinese "coolies" was brought to Honolulu in January 1852, and the workers were distributed among planters.

These were by no means the first Chinese in the islands. Vancouver saw one in 1794, and by the end of the eighteenth century there were several. A Chinese living on Lanai in 1802 was supposed to have been the first man in the kingdom to boil sugar, and during the next half century a few Chinese started one-man sugar plantations and mills on the outer islands.

In 1852, the year the first coolies came, seventy-one Chinese were living at Honolulu and thirty-one of them were in trade of one sort or another. Their "customs" were regarded either as mysterious or laughable and their doings were reported facetiously in the newspapers when they were mentioned at all, but it was conceded that most Chinese businessmen were honest and industrious. They did their best to keep their reputation good. In 1856 they gave a grand ball for the newly married king and queen, Alexander Liholiho and Emma. The hosts spent about four thousand dollars on food and decorations, and they practiced quadrilles so that they could join in the dancing. Since the intricacies of directing a ball were "practically above the comprehension of a Chinaman," as the *Pacific*

Commercial Advertiser put it, four white men did the job, dressed in Mandarin costume complete with fan—Edward "Weong Chong" Hoffman, Barnum "Chong Fong" Field, Gustav "Ming Ching" Reiners, and D. C. "Weong Kong" Waterman. The "celestial evening" was a great success, and the social position of the Chinese merchants was defined: decorum, deference, and an occasional happy public gesture would assure them an amused tolerance.

Coolies were not merchants, however, and planters did not find them amusing. Within a year of the arrival of the first immigrant workers in 1852 the penal clauses of the Masters and Servants Act were being invoked, and recalcitrant coolies found themselves in the fort at Honolulu on bread and water for refusing to work. A few planters took to using a whip, and one shot a coolie in the leg.

The trouble makers were in a minority, but even good workers made trouble in another way. As soon as their five year contracts were up in 1857 (just a few months after the Chinese merchants' ball) they left the plantations and settled in the towns, most of them at Honolulu. Objections were heard immediately. Unemployed coolies stole, gambled, set fire to buildings, and made nuisances of themselves in general with their "filthy habits." Seventy white businessmen petitioned the government to invoke the vagrancy laws, and Marshal William Parke was directed to arrest offenders.

More coolies were brought in from time to time, and they followed the same path to the towns. By the end of the fifties white men at Honolulu had had enough. The *Pacific Commercial Advertiser* was complaining that nothing but "insecurity to life and property" resulted from the presence of the Chinese in town, "some of the vilest coolies that ever escaped hanging in their own countries. The thoughtless importation of coolies, a few years ago, because they were cheap labor, is now producing some lamentable fruit in the shape of burglary and murder." The *Polynesian* agreed: "A murder one Sunday, an arson the next, by Coolie hands, is . . . rather strong upon the weak nerves of our community . . . In February next the last of the Coolie contracts expires, and we may then expect a still further increase of liberated laborers from the plantations of the other islands, to swell the crowd of Chinamen already prowling about Honolulu without any apparent means of livelihood. We fear that the next Legislature will be obliged to take their case under consideration, the constitution to the contrary notwithstanding."

But what was the alternative? The native population of the islands continued to decline; attempts to recruit plantation workers from the South Pacific failed (some islanders were brought in, but they were surely the most melancholy plantation workers who ever lived); and it was generally conceded that imported European labor would be too expensive. In 1864 a Planters' Society was organized and in the same year the government established a Bureau of Immigration. At one time or another Malaysia, India, and Japan were considered as sources of supply. The first two yielded nothing. A single shipload of Japanese, the Gannen Mono or first-year people, arrived in 1868, but it was almost twenty years before any more came. The Chinese, at least, were available. Between 1852 and 1876 several thousand were imported. By the middle of the eighteen sixties there were more Chinese men than white men at the islands. Not all of them went home when their contracts expired, and a good many of those who stayed came to the towns when their stint on the plantations was over. Willingly or unwillingly the white men and the natives of the kingdom had to make room for them.

The kingdom had begun to import laborers at a time when the recruitment of plantation workers was under attack in many parts of the world. The British government was casting an anxious eye at blackbirding in the Pacific. Concurrently the United States Congress passed an act in 1862 prohibiting American citizens from carrying on the coolie trade in American ships, and in January 1867, resolutions were added to the act, describing the trade as "inhuman, immoral, and abhorrent."

The word coolie had more than one meaning. Sometimes it referred to men kidnapped or forced into service. At other times it was used to describe any kind of bonded or indentured or contract laborer of any color other than white, though usually Oriental. The second meaning was the one that met the case in the Hawaiian kingdom. Slavery proper was prohibited in the constitution. But the fundamental morality of the contract labor system was debated at length, and as the years went by the debate grew noisier and noisier.

The plantation managers who had to make the system work lived mostly on the outer islands, and their critics lived mostly at Honolulu. Some of the members of the disbanded Sandwich Islands Mission and some of their sons went into the sugar business, and they could see nothing much wrong with a contract that contained penal clauses, but other members of the old missionary family who did not have a vested interest in sugar began to talk about coolie labor and slave labor in the same breath. It did not matter to them that conditions for coolies were demonstrably better in the Hawaiian kingdom than at any other place around the rim of the Pacific, including China itself. They were transplanted abolitionists, and one kind of servitude looked like another as far as they were concerned.

Henry M. Whitney, editor of the *Pacific Commercial Advertiser*, did not like Chinese very much, but he liked the contract labor system even less. He forced himself to admit that the plantations had to have workers, but beyond that he would not go. Free migration, he thought, would meet the needs of the industry, bring a better type of coolie to the islands, and do away with the iniquities of the system.

The planters regarded Whitney as a considerable nuisance, and by 1870 they were holding meetings on the outer islands to see what they could do about stopping his paper from circulating. Whitney sold the *Advertiser* to some journalists who were better disposed toward the Masters and Servants Act, and went on attacking contract labor in his Hawaiian language paper, *Kuokoa*.

More intransigent still were Curtis Lyons, son of the evangelist Lorenzo Lyons, Luther Gulick, son of the missionary Peter Gulick, and Sanford B. Dole, son of the missionary Daniel Dole. They harassed the Planters' Society and the government's Bureau of Immigration at every turn, attacking the penal clauses of contracts and the practice of assigning contracts from one employer to another without the consent of the worker, as if a man were a chattel. When, after a series of turbulent meetings at Honolulu in 1869, the government decided to go ahead with the importation of more coolies, Lyons took his fight to the floor of the legislature, where he tried to have the repugnant penal clauses of the Masters and Servants Act repealed. The effort failed, just as all attempts were to fail until American law superseded Hawaiian law after the annexation of the islands at the turn of the century.

A Warning Voice

Laborers for the plantations might have to be brought from China; sugar would have to be sold in the United States. During the whaling era it was New England whose ties with the Hawaiian kingdom were closest; now it was California. East coast, west coast, or both—it made not much difference to Americans at the islands. Any tie was better than none. And if an economic tie could be developed into a political tie, so much the better again. To most American residents (though of course not to Englishmen, Frenchmen, Germans, and other foreigners) the benefits of an American connection were obvious. In their minds the question was merely one of arrangements: would a treaty of commercial reciprocity be enough to hold the two nations together for the time being, or would it be best if the United States annexed the kingdom?

Alexander Liholiho the anglophile and Lot the nativist were unlikely to agree voluntarily to annexation. On the other hand neither one was against a reciprocity treaty on principle. If Hawaiian sugar could be sold free of duty on the American market the prosperity of the kingdom would be guaranteed, and a prosperous kingdom was likely to remain independent politically.

No matter what Americans at the islands proposed, the decisions that counted would be made at Washington, and of course American statesmen had more on their minds than the fate of the Hawaiian kingdom and its sugar plantations. It was difficult to predict how things might go. The only way to find out was to press the issue, and when this was done the results were disappointing. In 1855, the first year of Alexander Liholiho's reign, William Lee was commissioned to negotiate a reciprocity treaty at Washington with William L. Marcy, secretary of state in the Democratic administration of Franklin Pierce. The kingdom approved the draft immediately but in the United States Senate it lingered for almost two years and then died for lack of interest. The news of the treaty's final defeat did not reach the islands until the middle of 1857, and by then the United States was getting ready to fight a terrible civil war. It was another ten years before reciprocity came under serious consideration again at Washington.

Americans at the islands did not let distance diminish their sense of allegiance to the land of their birth, and the Civil War made them more demonstrative than ever. Honolulu, the capital city of a neutral kingdom, was decked out in bunting; American women wrapped bandages for the gallant wounded lying in hospitals thousands of miles away; and news of every important battle was greeted with torchlight parades, fireworks, flag hoistings, speeches, champagne toasts, and patriotic singing.

All this fervor was directed to the support of the Union. Abraham Lincoln did better in mock elections at Honolulu in 1860 and 1864 than he did in most of the United States. A southern lady rash enough to fly the Stars and Bars from her veranda had the flag pulled down and torn to pieces by her neighbor's daughter. Henry Whitney advertised "Union Must Be Preserved" envelopes in red, white, and blue for sale at his book store, along with copies of *Uncle Tom's Cabin*. Thomas Spencer, a merchant at Hilo, Hawaii, organized a company of native militiamen—"Spencer's Invincibles"—and wrote President Lincoln a letter offering their services to the Union; when he was told that he was violating the neutrality laws of the Hawaiian kingdom he burst into tears.

What all these transplanted readers of *Uncle Tom's Cabin* really thought of the South's peculiar institution and its relation to life at the islands was hard to determine. Among Americans in the kingdom generally abolitionism was strong, among the old Protestant missionaries it was stronger still and among some of their children it was strongest of all. Henry Whitney, Luther Gulick, Curtis Lyons, and Sanford Dole unhesitatingly applied New England principles to Hawaiian practices in the debates over contract labor, and a good many young men of American parentage went to war for the Union, including several missionary children, who were Hawaiian subjects by virtue of their birth in the kingdom. But men who had invested in the sugar industry saw no contradiction between the southern aspect of their livelihood and the northern aspect of their American ties. And in the Hawaiian kingdom as in the northern United States there were strong Unionists who were strenuous racists. The all-American Alexander J. Cartwright, pioneer of baseball, leader of July the Fourth parades, and organizer of a Union fund raising drive at Honolulu, spoke publicly and habitually of "damned black kanakas" and worse, by which he meant all Hawaiians from the royal family down and white men who paid the crown polite attention as well.

Americans who chose to stay at the islands during the Civil War could not do their fighting in the Union army. Instead they spread turmoil in Hawaiian politics. The trouble started in earnest when Lot came to the throne as Kamehameha V in December 1863. He inherited a constitution framed largely under the direction of William Lee, who combined a strong interest in the kingdom's independence with a strong wish to make its institutions as republican as possible. The outcome was a surprisingly American document: Article 78 of the constitution of 1852, for example, provided for universal male suffrage in elections for the House of Representatives. Robert Wyllie, who took his own constitutional views from Victorian Great Britain, objected to Lee's work as "too Republican." He thought it could be "less so, & still free." Wyllie and a good many other monarchists, Hawaiian and white, offered amendments to the constitution at every session of the national legislature during the reign of Alexander Liholiho. At the heart of their hostility was the matter of the vote. On the eve of the Civil War, Wyllie wrote that "establishing Universal Suffrage, virtually hands over the power of governing this Kingdom to its *ignorance* & its *poverty*—a principle which, I believe, will soon, unless corrected, destroy the United States' Great Confederation & will eventually destroy every Country where it becomes the fundamental law."

King Lot could not have agreed more. He took his place on the throne without swearing an oath to uphold the constitution, and a few months later he made it clear that he had substantial changes in mind. "I believe," he told the cabinet in March 1864, "that universal suffrage is a right altogether beyond the political capacity of this people as it exists to-day. To jump by one bound from feudalism which involves unquestioning obedience to the will of a superior, who ruled and thought for those under Him, to the very extreme of political influence, is an ordeal which the wisest of people could hardly be equal to . . . As a general rule prosperity and the accumulation of property follow intelligence and as a test of intelligence prosperity might be accepted as an index of the capabilities of the individual. Equally necessary is it that the system under which a people lives should be adapted to its genius and that its habitual habits of thought and traditional methods of reasoning should be regarded in every system of Government intended for their adoption . . . As a principle I think the prerogatives of the Crown ought to be more carefully protected in the various articles of the Constitution, and that the influence of the Crown ought to be seen pervading every function of the Government for which the Constitution provides. I am not convinced that in the instrument of 1852 the first Estate of the Realm enjoys a weight proportionate to that of either the Second or Third Estates."

Early in May the king issued a proclamation calling for a constitutional convention, and he and Robert Wyllie made a tour of the islands to speak in favor of a stronger monarchy. Under the old constitution native Hawaiians usually had a majority in the lower house of the legislature (though of course they were heavily influenced by the appointed Nobles of the upper house and by the cabinet). Lot was asking his people to disenfranchise themselves. They seemed willing enough to do so. As for white men, most of them could meet the modest property qualifications that Lot and Wyllie were proposing. But the Americans in particular were not willing to give up the principle of universal suffrage and legislative supremacy, even though they had no respect for natives as voters.

After more than a month of heated discussion the convention found itself deadlocked over the question of property qualifications for voters, and the *Pacific Commercial Advertiser* used the occasion to remind its readers that in Europe kings who opposed liberal constitutions were likely to lose their thrones—not, of course, that there were any revolutionary "fiery spirits" in the Hawaiian kingdom. King Lot broke the deadlock by dissolving the convention. "As we do not agree," he said in his closing speech, "it is useless to prolong the session, and as at the time His Majesty King Kamehameha III gave the Constitution of the year 1852, He reserved to himself the power of taking it away if it was not for the interest of his Government and people, and as it is clear that that King left the revision of the Constitution to my predecessor and myself therefore as I sit in His seat, on the part of the Sovereignty of the Hawaiian Islands I make known today that the Constitution of 1852 is abrogated. I will give you a Constitution."

In Lot's new constitution, proclaimed on August 20, 1864, very little of the constitution of 1852 survived. Voters and candidates for election now had to pass a property test. Elected representatives were to meet in the legislature together with the king's appointed Nobles, which meant that the independence of the legislature was compromised. The power of the crown and of the king's personally appointed cabinet ministers was strengthened. It had taken a *coup d'état* to do it, but the king had got what he wanted.

Lot meant to be a real king, and he did not much care what white men thought of him. White men in turn, and especially Americans, did not much care for Lot. A gap was opening up between the races, and it made the national legislature a strange place, filled with white members who refused to learn Hawaiian and native members who refused to speak English.

The fact that anything at all got done there was due mostly to the special genius of the parliamentary interpreter, a young man named William Ragsdale, half-white, half-Hawaiian. There were any number of young men of mixed blood in the kingdom, but there was only one Ragsdale. Mark Twain saw him at work and was fascinated. "Bill Ragsdale," he wrote, "stands up in front of the Speaker's pulpit, with his back against it, and fastens his quick black eye upon any member who rises, lets him say half a dozen sentences and then interrupts him, and repeats his speech in a loud, rapid voice, turning every Kanaka speech into English and every English speech into Kanaka, with a readiness and felicity of language that are remarkable—waits for another installment of talk from the member's lips and goes on with his translation as before. His tongue is in constant motion from eleven in the forenoon till four in the afternoon, and why it does not wear out is the affair of Providence, not mine. There is a spice of deviltry in the fellow's nature, and it crops out every now and then when he is translating the speeches of slow old Kanakas who do not understand English. Without departing from the spirit of a member's remarks, he will, with apparent unconsciousness, drop in a little voluntary contribution occasionally in the way of a word or two that will make the gravest speech utterly ridiculous. He is careful not to venture upon such experiments, though, with the remarks of persons able to detect him. I noticed when he translated for His Excellency David Kalakaua, who is an accomplished English scholar, he asked, 'Did I translate you correctly, your Excellency?' or something to that effect. The rascal."

Poor Ragsdale did not hold his job for long. He was not the first man of mixed blood who found it hard to keep his balance. He was in and out of jail and the insane asylum at Honolulu more than once (and when he was away from the legislature the interpreting was done without correctness and courtesy, so the newspapers said); and he ended his days a leper.

But while he lived he loved politics. He never missed an election day at Honolulu if he could help it. He was always on the spot, curveting and caracoling through the streets on a big grey horse, bawling out his political preferences (always for the king's party), and whipping voters into line.

White men looked askance at the political style of Ragsdale and his friends. Most of the king's candidates were on the government's payroll, and so were a good many of the voters who turned in ballots supporting the ministry. The *Pacific Commercial Advertiser* alleged that a captain in the Royal Household Troops threatened tenants of government lands with eviction if they voted for American candidates, and in 1868 a contributor to the *Advertiser* observed that when the Household Troops themselves came down to the polls they "did not vote as they usually carry their muskets, one one way, another the other, but they voted as one man and all one way, holding their ballots over their heads . . . This was a detachment of the Light Guards. Next came a body of the Blackguards . . ." Henry Whitney had a name for men who voted by the numbers, in or out of the legislature. He called them hoopilimeaai, a term which the king's ministers chose to translate as "lick-spittles" when they debated whether to prosecute Whitney to make him mend his manners.

With all this bad feeling in the air, and a good deal of it finding expression in strong words, it was not surprising that Hawaiians came to connect Americanism with racism. The issue was simple. Were Americans really trying to take control of the kingdom? And if they were, was there anything the natives could do about it? By the middle of the eighteen sixties the situation was begining to look ugly. On the floor of the legislature in 1866 a fist fight broke out between white and Hawaiian members, and it ended with the Hawaiians shouting a warrior chant from the time of Kamehameha the Great. This was only one straw in the wind. During the election campaign of 1868 a document entitled "Ka Makamae Hawaii" (The Loyal Hawaiian) appeared at Honolulu, couched in old style language and predicting dire things if the "American" party was returned to office. The "Warning Voice" who signed it said that a vote for such foreigners was a vote for men who would high-handedly snatch the kingdom away; they had been conspiring for decades and they were still conspiring.

On the face of things the Warning Voice had a point. At the time Ka Makamae Hawaii appeared the American man-of-war *Lackawanna* was in Honolulu harbor, and she had been around the islands for a year. After the Civil War the United States deployed a good many ships in the Pacific, and several of these, making up the North Pacific squadron, visited Honolulu in rotation. So there was nothing unusual in the presence of an American warship. But the *Lackawanna* was assigned to Honolulu for an "indefinite period," and her commander, Captain William Reynolds, was well known as a loud and persistent advocate of a prompt annexation of the kingdom by the United States. Reynolds had been stationed at a naval store in the islands during the fifties and early sixties, and at the height of the annexationist crisis of 1853-1854 his wife had made a handsome embroidered silk American flag with the idea that it would soon be raised over the kingdom. Now Reynolds was back, and he was still talking about annexation. All things considered, the Hawaiian government found it hard to give him a warm welcome. Actually the *Lackawanna* had been sent to

Honolulu because a brief and belated flare-up of trouble between France and the Hawaiian kingdom seemed to be threatening worse things to come, and the United States wanted to keep an eye on developments. But this was never made clear, and at Honolulu it was widely believed that the Hawaiian government rather than France was under surveillance. King Lot was ill. He was a bachelor and he had not named an heir; if he should die a political crisis might follow. To Lot the *Lackawanna* might very well have looked like a bird of ill omen, and to others she was an offensive intruder into domestic politics.

Complicating matters even further was the fact that the government had before it a new reciprocity treaty, drafted by Minister of Finance Charles C. Harris and United States Minister Edward M. McCook. The two had met to do their work at San Francisco in May 1867, and Harris had taken his copy of the treaty to Washington while McCook brought his to Honolulu. King Lot told McCook that nothing would be done with it as long as the *Lackawanna* was in Hawaiian waters. At the end of July, about six months after she first put in at Honolulu, the *Lackawanna* left, under orders to sail to Middlebrook Island (now called Midway) and take possession of it for the United States. On September 30, while she was still away, the Hawaiian legislature ratified the treaty. Two days later Reynolds was back, and he stayed another eight months.

Before he left again another enigmatic American appeared. Zephaniah S. Spalding arrived in Honolulu in December 1867, allegedly carrying dispatches for United States Minister McCook. He stayed on, asking naïve questions about the possibility of starting a cotton plantation, and secretly writing annexationist letters to his father, a member of Congress, who passed them on to the Department of State at Washington. Spalding spent a lot of time with Reynolds, and this in itself made him suspect. Acting Attorney General Stephen Phillips bribed a clerk from the *Lackawanna* to get copies of Spalding's letters. The clerk was found out, tried, and convicted aboard ship, but by then the Hawaiian government knew as much as it needed to know about Spalding—enough, certainly to object when he was assigned to the United States consulate at Honolulu. The government was forced to suffer his presence until he was replaced in the fall of 1869.

In the meantime the restlessness of the Hawaiians was growing. A native named Kaona, a graduate of Lahainaluna school, a member of the house of representatives in the early fifties and a district judge at Honolulu a few years later, began to have visions that led him to believe the end of the world was at hand. He had good enough reasons for thinking so: the volcanoes on the island of Hawaii were erupting, and there were earth tremors for months, the worst in living memory. Kaona and his followers gathered at South Kona on Hawaii, where they attended the Protestant church of the missionary J. D. Paris. Kaona was allowed to preach, but he insisted on introducing his own forms of worship into the service, and finally Paris locked him out of the church. Kaona distributed Bibles among his people and set up his own church. His followers gave up their belongings, dressed themselves in white robes, and prepared for the end. In March 1868, Kaona, who had been making himself obnoxious to Paris and other white men, was arrested, taken to Honolulu, and pronounced insane. He spent only a few months in the asylum, and while he was there the volcanoes continued to erupt. As soon as he got back to South Kona he began to hear divine voices again. This time they told him that the volcanoes would engulf the whole island, leaving only his part of the coast untouched. In October he sent one of his followers to Honolulu to lease the land at South Kona where his people were encamped, so that their title to the future would be good. The owner of the land would not lease it to Kaona, but neither would Kaona and his two hundred followers go away. The sheriff of the district, R. B. Neville, took a large posse to eject them. Neville was tactless; he fired a pistol shot or two; there was a scuffle that turned into a brawl. One of Neville's constables was dragged from his horse with a lasso, and on Kaona's orders his head was split open with an ax. Neville himself was knocked off his horse, badly bruised. He was tied up and left for some hours, and then Kaona ordered him killed, and one of his followers took a club and beat Neville's brains out, cut off his head, and stuck it on a pole.

Governor John O. Dominis was sent to South Kona with two hundred men, but before he arrived Sheriff J. H. Coney of Hawaii put together a large force of natives and whites and surrounded Kaona's camp. Two hundred of the Kaonaites were arrested, most of them while they were kneeling in their open church, clothed in their white robes and turbans, with their Bibles in their hands. They did not make any real resistance. Their Jehovah banners were torn down, their houses were burned, and they were handcuffed and led away. Several months later Kaona was tried and convicted of manslaughter. He conducted his own defense and made a powerful impression on the natives who packed the courthouse at Hilo, but the jury found him guilty, and he was sentenced to ten years at hard labor.

Kaona was one of a long line of native prophets in the Pacific who came to the realization that time was running out for their people, and whose revelations made it clear to them that nothing but a universal convulsion could bring back a world without white men. To the authorities of the Hawaiian kingdom Kaona looked only like a dangerous madman, and the fact that he took his inspiration from the Bible (with the addition of a few sorcerer's devices) made him all the more reprehensible. So he was sent to jail. But for years afterward his scattered followers met and prayed here and there, and once or twice they even elected a representative to the national legislature.

After Kaona was put out of the way, and Zephaniah Spalding was exposed as a spy, and William Reynolds and the *Lackawanna* finally departed—after all this the kingdom still did not have a treaty of reciprocity. The United States Senate debated the matter in desultory fashion, picking it up and laying it down again several times. In June 1870, the treaty drafted by Harris and McCook in 1867 was rejected at Washington. It was a conclusive rebuff, so it seemed, and it led a good many people at the islands, including some Americans, to give up the reciprocity movement as a bad job.

But where to turn? In the early seventies something of a market for Hawaiian sugar was established in Canada and the British colonies of Australasia, and by 1873 one third of the export crop was going in these directions. From time to time a closer connection with the British colonies was mentioned, but it was a political shadow without substance, and nothing ever came of it. The attraction of the American market was irresistible.

Whisky Bill

King Lot, the last of the Kamehamehas, had been in bad health for several years. He died on December 11, 1872, his fortieth birthday. He had always been famous for keeping his own counsel on important matters, but to be strong and silent about naming a successor was hardly a virtue in a bachelor king. On his deathbed he listened while several names were suggested to him: the dowager queen Emma, widow of Alexander Liholiho; Princess Ruth Keelikolani, a mountainous chiefess who was governor of Hawaii; Princess Bernice Pauahi, the wife of a successful American banker named Charles R. Bishop; William Charles Lunalilo, descended from a half-brother of Kamehameha the Great; and David Kalakaua, an ambitious chief of another family line. The matter was still not settled when Lot died.

Under the constitution of 1864 the legislature would choose a new king. Only two candidates campaigned seriously—David Kalakaua and William Lunalilo, "Whisky Bill." Lunalilo was a great favorite of the Hawaiian commoners, and the fact that he was a chronic drunkard diminished his charm not at all. No one except the most strenuous of teetotallers had a harsh word to say about him. David Kalakaua made dark remarks about the American influence behind Lunalilo's campaign, and his "Skillful Genealogists" cast professional aspersions on Lunalilo's ancestry, but in an informal popular vote held on January 1, 1873, Lunalilo won an overwhelming victory.

A week later the legislature met, and as crowds of natives watched, the members of the assembly voted one by one to confirm Lunalilo as king. The British commissioner and the United States minister, afraid of disturbances, had called for warships, but there was not the slightest sign of violence. Amid tremendous enthusiasm Lunalilo took the oath of office at Kawaiahao Church on January 12, and entered upon his duties the next day.

Three of Lunalilo's four cabinet ministers were Americans, and the portfolio of foreign affairs was held by Bernice Pauahi's husband Charles Bishop, a supporter of reciprocity. It was no surprise, then, when the subject of a treaty with the United States was raised. There were good reasons for looking toward the American market again. Some Hawaiian sugar was being sold in the British colonies, but the connection depended on a struggling steamship line that might go out of business at any moment. The planters had had a bad year in 1872, and the prospects for 1873 did not look much better.

A way out of the difficulty was suggested by Henry Whitney. He had infuriated the planters a few years earlier with his criticism of labor contracts, but he was strongly in favor of reciprocity, and now he proposed something new: the government should lease Pearl Harbor to the United States for fifty years in return for duty free access to the American sugar market.

When Whitney made his suggestion two American military officers were at Honolulu, ostensibly on vacation, but actually on secret business, "ascertaining the defensive capabilities of the various ports and their commercial facilities." Major General John M. Schofield and Brevet Brigadier General B. S. Alexander agreed with everybody who had ever seen Pearl Harbor; it was the largest protected natural anchorage in the Pacific, and once the coral maze that blocked the entrance was cleared it would be a port of the greatest strategic value.

Neither Whitney's proposal nor the conclusion of the two generals was supposed to be public, but by the middle of 1873 the question of reciprocity and the question of Pearl Harbor were being discussed as if they were the same thing. In June Foreign Minister Bishop put a proposal to United States Minister Henry A. Peirce. The kingdom would be agreeable to a treaty of reciprocity based on the document drawn up in 1867 by Charles Harris and Edward McCook, with the stipulation that Hawaiian sugar up to No. 16 Dutch Standard (as against the 1867 figure of No. 12) would be admitted free of duty to the United States. It was to be understood as well that Pearl Harbor might be ceded if agreement could be reached on conditions.

At the very mention of a cession of Hawaiian soil the native population of Honolulu burst into uproar. Crowds met on the streets and in the two big native churches of the town, Kawaiahao and Kaumakapili, to spill out their bitterness. The Hawaiians knew about the alleged commercial benefits of reciprocity, but it was not in them to be analytical about anything like a cession; it was enough for them to know that the life of the land was in danger again. Walter Murray Gibson, an American and a political maverick, started a bilingual paper called the *Nuhou* at Honolulu, with the sole purpose, so he said, of defeating the cession of Pearl Harbor. The *Nuhou* became the public voice of the Hawaiians, putting the issue in terms any native could understand:

> *I am a messenger sent to you;*
> *I ascend the mountain heights;*
> *I descend into the deep vales;*
> *I sweep o'er the stormy main.*
> *The burning heat of the day does not stay me.*
> *I am the comrade of the winds,*
> *And the companion of the rain;*
> *I am a shield against the cold*
> *And darkness cannot dwell with me.*
> *I am a messenger forbidding you*
> *To give away Puuloa [Pearl Harbor],*
> *Be not deceived by the merchants,*
> *They are only enticing you,*
> *Making fair their faces, they are evil within;*
> *Truly desiring annexation,*
> *Greatly desiring their own good;*
> *They have no thought of good for you,*
> *A presuming set only are they,*
> *A proud and haughty set,*
> *Ever soliciting, at the same time flattering,*
> *Desiring that you should all die,*
> *That the kingdom may become theirs.*

King Lunalilo was in the eye of the hurricane. Much against his better judgment he had let himself be persuaded to endorse the cession, and now he was swamped by hostile petitions and resolutions from the very natives who had voted for him so joyfully only six months earlier.

Lunalilo's health had never been sound. If whisky did not kill him tuberculosis would. By the late summer of 1873 he was almost at the end of his strength and his political resources; the brilliant flame was burning itself out. After a last wild round of parties (at one of them he made the band play "God Save The King" seven times on end) he left Honolulu and went to his beach house at Waikiki to rest. But there was no rest to be found. As if the question of Pearl Harbor was not worrisome enough, the standing army of the kingdom, the Royal Household Troops, mutinied and threw the capital into confusion for a week.

White men were not used to the threat of violence from Hawaiians. They were accustomed to thinking of the natives in crowds—the water-front gapers of the early days, the hula dancers of the twenties, the chanting temperance marchers and revival converts of the thirties, the smallpox victims of the fifties, and the aimless drifters and lockstep voters of the sixties, even the agitated political crowds of the moment—but the thought of an armed Hawaiian mob was strange and frightening to them. After all, Sheriff Neville was only five years dead, killed by crazed natives.

The mutiny started as comedy and quickly became something else. On the night of Saturday, September 6, 1873, the Hungarian drill master of the Household Troops, Captain Joseph Jajczay, discovered that four native guards on duty at the treasury had left their posts. He found them carousing downtown and took them back to Iolani Barracks on Palace Walk opposite the royal residence, where they were locked up in a single room with four other delinquent enlisted men. Next morning, while Jajczay was away at church, the prisoners broke down the door with a ball and chain and took off their irons. Jajczay came back and ordered them locked up again, but no one would obey him, and when Jajczay hit one man with the flat of his saber the prisoners knocked him to the ground. Governor of Oahu John Dominis and Adjutant General Charles Judd were summoned. On their orders a handful of reluctant enlisted men made a halfhearted effort to seize the prisoners. Judd stepped forward, the soldiers stepped back, and the prisoners knocked Judd down.

So eight native soldiers had defied their drill master, their adjutant general, and the governor of Oahu, all white men; and no native officer or noncommissioned officer had done anything to restore order. That night the mutineers crossed the street to the palace grounds and brought back three six-pounder cannon. By Monday afternoon the cannon were in place, covering the courtyard of the barracks, and the number of mutineers had grown to forty. Fourteen loyalists left the barracks, but the rest of the troops told Judd and Dominis they would not obey orders until Jajczay was dismissed. On their own initiative, oddly enough, the mutineers continued to mount guard in the regular way at the treasury and the prisons.

On Tuesday the high chief David Kalakaua, Lunalilo's unsuccessful opponent in the royal election and an honorary colonel in the Hawaiian army, went to the barracks to hear the mutineers' complaints. These were simple enough: there was not enough food and there was too much discipline. Meanwhile the king, lying seriously ill at Waikiki, had signed an order commanding the troops to return to their duties. Governor Dominis, who was authorized to carry out the order by force if necessary, read the document at the barracks on Tuesday afternoon. The entire Royal Hawaiian Band and about a dozen soldiers left the barracks with him, but the rest refused either to return to duty or be discharged. They wanted Jajczay dismissed, and Judd too.

Military discipline had collapsed completely, and the mutineers paid no attention to civil authority either. Warrants were sworn out for their arrest at the Honolulu police court, but they declined to be taken into custody by Marshal Parke.

Something would have to be done. The hard core of mutineers numbered less than thirty, but they were obstreperous, and they had cannon as well as ammunition. White families living around Palace Walk evacuated their homes, and the streets near the barracks were filled with natives shouting disparagement of all haoles and applauding as orators harangued them.

On Tuesday afternoon volunteer militia men of the Honolulu Rifles (mostly haoles with a few half-whites) and the Hawaiian Cavalry (including some natives) were marched to the barracks. The town's superintendent of waterworks, an elderly retired sea captain, was sent to disconnect the branch water pipe supplying the barracks. He took an hour to dig his way to the cock, and when he reached it he found he had brought a wrench that was too small. In the meantime soldiers from the barracks were walking back and forth to fill buckets with water from a storehouse outside the walls.

This was impudent enough, but after all only a handful of militia men had answered the call to duty. There were less than two dozen of the Honolulu Rifles on the Palace Walk side of the barracks, posted (as they were painfully aware) only thirty or forty yards from the mouths of the stolen cannon; and on the Beretania Street side the native members of the Hawaiian Cavalry had dismounted to join the mutineers in a fish and poi supper. In the courtyard the red-shirted soldiers, some of them drunk, fired their chassepot rifles into the air and went through the motions of loading and firing their cannon, and on the barracks wall a soldier in an old three-cornered hat stood singing a rude improvised song in the style of the old Hawaiian chants while natives applauded him from the street.

That night the Rifles and the Cavalry were withdrawn, much to the relief of the native and part-native members, who could see no point in fighting their countrymen, and to the greater relief of the haole militiamen, whose experience of war before the mutiny had been confined to marching, maneuvers, inaccurate target shooting, weekend bivouacs under canvas at Waikiki, and dress uniform banquets and dances with their ladies' auxiliaries. Once the militia was gone the mutineers crossed again to Iolani Palace and carried back more ammunition and powder; friends brought food; and a native policeman attached a hose to a tap in the king's stables and filled the soldiers' water buckets for them.

In the hope that reason might prevail if the rebels could talk to the king, a committee of three from the barracks was given safe conduct to visit Lunalilo at Waikiki. The king offered the mutineers clemency if they would obey orders. On Wednesday night they stacked their arms, but they would not leave the barracks. On Thursday a second delegation went to talk to the king. At the same time Governor Dominis organized a squad from the barracks and marched them up to Punchbowl to fire a salute for the birthday of Czar Alexander of Russia in honor of a Russian warship lying in the harbor. The saluting squad stole part of the powder from each charge and took it back to the barracks. On Thursday night more natives joined the rebels inside the walls, bringing their number to sixty or seventy.

Early on Friday morning a letter from the king was delivered to the mutineers, repeating the offer of clemency if they would retire peacefully from the barracks. The rebels set conditions: the Secretary at War must countersign the king's letter; the letter must be printed in the Honolulu newspapers; the loyalist soldiers who had deserted the barracks must bring their equipment back; and all warrants for the arrest of the mutineers must be destroyed. The conditions were met, and at about half past ten the mutineers moved out, taking with them uniforms and other belongings returned by the loyalists. By noon on Friday the barracks was empty, and the king signed an order disbanding the Household Troops.

Within the space of six days the government had been embarrassed, then humiliated, then held to ransom. Clearly it was in everyone's best interest to forget that the mutiny had ever happened. The loyalists were allowed to draw pay for the month of September; the mutineers were given dishonorable discharges and forbidden to work as policemen or prison guards, but none was prosecuted; the chassepot rifles were stripped down and locked away in the barracks; an augmented police force took over guard duties on the streets; and a white man was put in charge of the powder magazine on Punchbowl. Only the ragged remnant of the loyalists, roaming the streets and begging for food and clothing, reminded people of the uprising.

The rebels had dispersed, but the reciprocity treaty and the cession of Pearl Harbor would not go away. Lunalilo's cabinet ministers continued to urge him on, and less than three weeks after the last mutineer left the barracks Chief Justice Elisha H. Allen was commissioned minister plenipotentiary to negotiate a treaty with the United States. For the next six weeks Lunalilo tried to make up his mind about Pearl Harbor. After several partial commitments he announced that he could not give his hearty support to the cession and that it should therefore be withdrawn from consideration.

Immediately afterward the king left Honolulu for Kailua on the island of Hawaii in the vain hope of mending his health. At Waikiki one night he had caught a bad cold while sleeping outside in his armchair. He had a painful cough, and the cold was turning into something worse. He could not eat solid food and he was losing strength steadily, and people who saw him thought he looked hopelessly ill. Hawaiian kahunas were predicting an early death, and so were the royal physicians.

This raised the question of the succession once more. Like King Lot, Lunalilo was a bachelor, and like Lot he had persistently refused to name a successor. While the members of the Cabinet Council tried to reason with the king two chiefs, David Kalakaua and the dowager queen Emma, began campaigning quietly for the throne. Emma had no doubt that she would win. Her line of descent was impeccable; surely Lunalilo would nominate her to follow him, or perhaps even marry her. In Emma's eyes Kalakaua was nothing but an arrogant pretender, using paid genealogists to give substance to his flawed pedigree. The royal election of 1873 showed that as long as Lunalilo was alive no one wanted Kalakaua to be king, and Emma could not believe that the people would choose Kalakaua over a former queen. But the critical months went by and Lunalilo said nothing, and his silence gave Kalakaua a chance to improve his position by vigorous campaigning.

Squabbles over bloodlines concerned white men very little, but for their own reasons foreigners, and especially Americans, saw bad times ahead no matter who won. Neither candidate appeared to have any idea of how important the reciprocity treaty was. Emma was infatuated with the British; Kalakaua was a special enemy of the United States, so it seemed. Kalakaua was widely suspected of having written or at least sponsored the savage campaign document of 1868, Ka Makamae Hawaii. During the mutiny of the household troops he had done nothing to end the rebellion; some people, in fact, thought the uprising was Kalakaua's doing, and this made it easy to believe that he enjoyed watching white men squirm. Now he was busy among the natives of Honolulu, publishing the reports of his Skillful Genealogists, speaking against Americans, and drilling his own small army, the Young Hawaiians, a company drawn from among his tenants and followers. Some people thought he had only eighty men, but others were sure they could count four hundred. Was Young Hawaii just a political machine or might it be a revolutionary force? No one could tell. Perhaps Kalakaua did not intend to let the question of the kingship come to a vote; perhaps he would try to seize the throne. Emma hated him just enough to use violence whether she won or lost, and violence might easily become racial war. The future looked dark, and the diplomats at Honolulu called for warships to protect lives and property.

The question was whether the warships could reach the islands in time. Lunalilo was dying. The government's steamer *Kilauea* had to interrupt her regular sailings to carry the king's physicians back and forth between Hawaii and Oahu. Dr. George Trousseau examined Lunalilo at Kailua on January 16, 1874, and he was convinced that the king could live only a short time. Lunalilo, cheerful but sadly weak, was brought back to Honolulu, and there careful nursing kept him alive until his thirty-ninth birthday, January 31.

If Lunalilo died without naming a successor the question would go to the national legislature for decision. But which legislature? The legislature of 1872, elected under the constitution of 1864, was still in existence. A new legislature, elected by universal male suffrage (reintroduced at the insistence of Lunalilo), would be chosen on February 2, and the house would convene in April. So which set of legislators should vote? The Cabinet Council heard conflicting opinions and decided that the right to choose a new king rested with the incoming legislature of 1874.

Lunalilo survived the day of the national election, but he seemed only hours from death. Someone gave a premature and tactless order to begin draping the palace in black. Almost before the natives could protest this unseemly hastening of the inevitable Lunalilo died, at about half past eight on the evening of February 3, 1874.

A Burning Torch

The foreign community at Honolulu had more or less made up its mind that Kalakaua would win the royal election in the legislature, and the English language newspapers were straining to find reasons why his accession would not be altogether a bad thing. Emma's people were working hard just the same, distributing printed handbills by the hundred, and a commotion broke out when a partisan of Kalakaua added a few words to one of Emma's posters on a bulletin board: "Aole makou makemake e ike i ka palekoki e hookomo ana i ka lolewawae"—we do not wish to see the petticoat putting on breeches. Curtis Lyons, who was something of a gentleman and something of an Emma-ite, smashed the glass and scratched out the offending words, and within minutes a crowd gathered and rival orators went to work.

At her home in Nuuanu valley Emma, so Marshal William Parke heard, was promising "if elected to take no salary repeal the horse tax roads tax and any other tax they want. and the great unwashed are whooping and yelling." Parke heard too that Emma had promised to free all prisoners in the Honolulu jail if she were elected, and he ordered that no convicts were to be released on election day.

So the time went by until all the newly elected representatives, most of them natives and part-whites, were gathered at Honolulu. On the great day, Thursday, February 12, they assembled in the legislative chambers at the courthouse in downtown Honolulu. Emma's followers marched down from Nuuanu valley to the sound of a fife and drum band and surrounded the courthouse while speakers for both parties, standing on high platforms, shouted above the noise. Inside the legislators cast their votes before a packed gallery. Kalakaua's supporters had ballots decorated with a printed heart, and these could easily be seen as they were presented one by one. At about two in the afternoon the voting came to an end, the "exquisite dignity" of the occasion marred, according to Curtis Lyons, only by the last voter, a member from Kauai, who was too drunk to see where he should deposit his ballot. At a quarter to three the ballots were counted—thirty-nine for Kalakaua, six for Emma.

A carriage waited outside to take the news to the new monarch, but before the legislature's committee of five could tell the driver to make for Kalakaua's house the chagrin of the Emma-ites overflowed. They tore the carriage apart, seized lengths of wood from the debris, picked up rocks, branches of trees, and pieces of a garden trellis, and then fought their way inside to get at the native members who had voted for Kalakaua. Marshal Parke had brought eighty native policemen to control the crowd, but once the first blows were struck the constables threw away their badges and fought according to their political convictions. Parke, Charles Harris, Sanford Dole, and other white men tried in vain to quell the uproar. Major William Moehonua, a staunch supporter of Kalakaua, was badly wounded, and so were several others. One representative was thrown from a second story window; he died of his injuries. Parke stood in front of his own office with a pistol, holding off the mob. He saved his records, but he was lucky. "The court house is a perfect wreck," he wrote later, "not a window sash table chair or bench is left . . . rooms are gutted not a book or paper but what was torn into shreds . . ."

Once Parke's policemen disappeared in the crowd the government was all but helpless. The standing army of the kingdom had been dissolved after the mutiny in the barracks. Honolulu's militia companies were still in existence, and if anything they were somewhat less feeble than they had been in 1873, but all the new recruits were white, and no one wanted to risk turning them and their unwilling part-white comrades loose on a rioting native crowd. In the harbor lay three warships—USS *Portsmouth,* USS *Tuscarora,* and HMS *Tenedos.* Kalakaua, Minister of Foreign Affairs Charles Bishop, and Governor of Oahu John Dominis asked United States Minister Peirce and British Commissioner James Hay Wodehouse to send armed troops ashore. One hundred and fifty men were marched into town from the *Portsmouth* and the *Tuscarora,* and seventy or eighty from the *Tenedos.* The Americans cleared the courthouse and posted guards there, and at the armory, the treasury, the prison, and the station house as well. The Britishers headed up Nuuanu valley to Emma's house, drove off her supporters, and came back to mount guard at the palace and the barracks. By sundown some of the rioters were under arrest, and the town was quiet that night except for a few random gunshots and the sound of windows being smashed by Emma-ites who had followed native representatives to their homes. By the next morning it was all over.

Emma had accomplished nothing. On February 13 Kalakaua took the oath of office, and the diplomatic corps recognized him as king. Emma was urged to acknowledge the legality of the election, forswear violence, and offer her support to Kalakaua. Guards from the warships stayed on the streets until February 20, but there was nothing for them to do.

Emma's campaign was a clumsy one. She had pinned her hopes on rank, but very few Hawaiians of any standing responded to this appeal (though it is not clear whether they failed to do so because of their genealogical convictions or because Kalakaua paid more for support). All the same, as the courthouse riot showed, if Emma did not have followers enough to win the throne she had enough to embarrass the government badly; and even after fifty of her people were tried and forty were jailed a hard core of malcontents continued to meet at her house.

Kalakaua lost no time in securing his dynasty by naming his brother William Pitt Leleiohoku as successor to the throne. He showed his face to his subjects in a triumphal procession throughout the islands, and enthusiastic and affectionate crowds greeted him when he came back to Honolulu. He seemed safe enough on the throne, but he did not trust Emma, and she did not trust him, and after one very strained meeting they avoided each other. Emma was warned by one of her supporters that it would not be prudent for her to eat the king's food at public receptions. When the legislature of 1874 was prorogued crowds gathered again at Emma's house, and Kalakaua ordered some of them arrested for using "seditious language." A little later a Hawaiian named J. P. Zephyrin Kahoalii circulated a petition claiming that Lunalilo had named Emma his successor in a verbal "will" and that Kalakaua was elected by fraud. Kahoalii was arrested, and in the first treason trial since the establishment of constitutional government in the kingdom he was condemned to death. (His sentence was later commuted to ten years in jail.)

Until the day of her defeat in the royal election Emma had placed her hopes for the throne in the hands of an Episcopalian Christian Divine Providence. When Providence failed her she turned to other sources of aid. Her loyal cousin, Peter Young Kaeo, confined to the leper settlement on Molokai, had come to know two practicing kahunas, and his letters to Emma were full of stories about encouraging omens—propitious dreams, and signs in the sky. Before the election Emma was inclined to rebuke Peter for his interest in the kahunas, but later on she was willing to combine Christianity and sorcery. On the advice of an old woman, she told Peter in 1875, she was about to "pray that God would please place me on the Hawaiian Throne, and on coming Monday at noon, December 20th, we should have a little feast. A young lamb should be eaten with it at noon, and three drops of its heart's blood with three drops of its gaul should be mixed in a glass of brandy, which I am to drink before eating at noon. This represents the heart's blood of the natives and the [gall is to represent the moving of the times], and on that day the heavens will be cloudless and some wonderful sign will happen . . . She says that the tree with all its roots, branches, etc., will be cut off, meaning the D. K.s [Kalakaua's dynasty] will all die off . . . they are all going to die soon and Queen Emma will reign supreme, living to a good old age over these Islands."

Very few white men knew or cared about the quiet war of nerves going on between Kalakaua and Emma, but for their own reasons they distrusted the king. United States Minister Peirce, who had been in business at Honolulu a long time ago and had returned in the seventies to take up a diplomatic post, and who therefore had many years of experience in Hawaiian affairs, was gloomier than most. He had predicted that if Kalakaua was elected, a reign of "Saturnalia" would commence, causing "the sun of national prosperity to set in clouds of darkness."

At the time this sounded ridiculous. Kalakaua had chosen for his dynastic emblem a burning torch, and he had no intention of letting the torch go out. "The increase of the people; the advancement of agriculture and commerce," he said, "these are the objects which my Government will mainly strive to accomplish." As a candidate for the throne Kalakaua had sometimes sounded like a Hawaiian racist, but if the foreigners had taken the trouble to think back they might also have recalled that he had said often enough that he was not against foreigners, and that there was room in the kingdom for all.

If the foreigners remembered that, they did not believe it. As soon as Kalakaua came to the throne eighty merchants and others petitioned Minister Peirce for protection, and on Peirce's recommendation the United

States Navy assigned the war ships *Tuscarora, Benicia, Lackawanna, Portsmouth,* and *Pensacola* to visit Honolulu in strict rotation.

Peirce professed to think that Hawaiians were mild and amiable "to a certain degree," beyond which they were "human tigers," fit for any kind of violence. This was nonsense. White men were as safe at the islands as anywhere in the world. In fact, when violence threatened it was usually instigated by white men rather than natives, and Hawaiians faced with violence were unusually forbearing. To be sure, feeling against foreigners was strong and growing stronger, as Kaona had shown, and this was not surprising among a native people in danger of losing life and land. Yet the barracks mutiny passed without a shot being fired in earnest. The rioters at the courthouse on election day, unarmed to begin with, had carefully set aside the white men they encountered in their hunt for native legislators, and they had dispersed within minutes after troops were landed. The trials of the rioters went ahead quietly, as they would have done in any Western country, and native jurors correctly found native rioters guilty. William L. Green, a wealthy English merchant who became Kalakaua's first foreign minister, had a much more temperate opinion of Hawaiians than Henry Peirce did. Green thought that despite the momentary outbreak at the courthouse Hawaiians deserved their reputation as a law-abiding people. Indeed the Emma-ites had done nothing worse than election rioters did in England, where people might have been expected to know better.

Whether or not white men liked Kalakaua he was the man they would have to deal with, and the first item of business was still a treaty of reciprocity. Not long after Kalakaua became king, United States Secretary of State Hamilton Fish advised Minister Peirce that both houses of Congress were against reciprocity for the moment. Kalakaua, who had always opposed the cession of Pearl Harbor, hoped that a treaty would be possible without it, and almost from the day of his election he worked to get negotiations under way.

Petitions kept coming to him from planters and businessmen, and the signatures showed that the reciprocity movement at the islands could no longer be regarded, even by its enemies, as an American conspiracy of some sort. Among those who were convinced that "serious disaster" would overtake the islands without a commercial treaty were Theophilus H. Davies, Archibald S. Cleghorn, and Henry Waterhouse, all of British background; the German firms of H. Hackfeld & Co. and F. A. Schaefer & Co.; and the Chinese houses of Chulan & Co. and Afong & Achuck.

Kalakaua decided in August 1874, that he himself would make a trip to the United States, partly for pleasure and partly to bring his royal influence to bear at Washington on the question of the treaty. In October the advance guard left—Elisha H. Allen and Henry A. P. Carter, commissioned as special agents with power to negotiate a treaty. The royal party followed a month later on USS *Benicia*—Kalakaua, Governor John Dominis, Colonel J. M. Kapena, and United States Minister Peirce.

Kalakaua was the first reigning Hawaiian monarch to leave the islands since Liholiho went to London fifty years before, and the first monarch of any country to visit the United States. At the waterfront natives by the hundred crowded around him, some crying, some chanting meles or songs, some wanting just to shake his hand or kiss him. His trip across the American continent and his stay on the east coast aroused great interest. The royal party spent eleven days at Washington. On December 15 Kalakaua was introduced to President Ulysses S. Grant, and three days later he was received by the houses of Congress in joint session. The same evening a brilliant state ball was given in his honor. In New York the showman P. T. Barnum induced the royal party to visit the Hippodrome, and there the circus band played "King Of The Cannibal Isles" while Kalakaua was inspected by the same crowds that delighted in animal acts and freak shows.

Meanwhile the kingdom's special commissioners, Elisha Allen and Henry Carter, were deep in discussion with Secretary of State Hamilton Fish, as they had been since November 18. Their instructions were based on the uncompleted treaty of 1867, with some additions. They were to try to have Hawaiian sugars up to No. 16 Dutch Standard admitted free of duty; they were to see if wool and rice could be included on the schedule; and they were not to discuss the cession of Pearl Harbor. During the first month of their talks the Hawaiian envoys were faced with the same objections that had defeated reciprocity in the past—among them the arguments that proposals for reciprocity with Canada had failed, and that the United States House of Representatives, regarding reciprocity treaties as revenue measures, would want to discuss the matter first.

No doubt King Kalakaua's visit did something to attract the attention of congressmen; certainly Minister Peirce's insistence had its effect upon President Grant's administration. When Carter presented a draft treaty on January 4, 1875, Fish agreed to show it to the cabinet next day. From then until the end of January the negotiators argued not over principle but over the wording of the treaty. A long list of articles to be exempted from duty was agreed upon readily (including Hawaiian rice but not wool). The most difficult question, and the one on which the value of the treaty depended, was that of sugar. On January 30 it was agreed to admit to the United States free of duty all grades of "muscovado, brown, and all other unrefined" Hawaiian sugar commonly referred to in the markets of San Francisco and Portland as "Sandwich Island sugar."

This was the hopeful state of affairs when Kalakaua arrived home in Honolulu on the morning of February 15, 1875. The marine telegraph at

Diamond Head announced the approach of USS *Pensacola,* which was flying the royal standard; the signal guns on Punchbowl fired a salute; and crowds flocked to the waterfront. Between ten and twelve thousand spectators lined the streets as Kalakaua rode to the palace beneath decorated arches inscribed "God Save The King," "Aloha Kalakaua," and "Hawaii-America."

The commercial clauses of the treaty were those of immediate importance to the sugar interests of the islands, faced as they were with "serious disaster." To the United States government commercial considerations were important but secondary: indeed it was more than likely that the reciprocity treaty would cost America money. The clause in the convention that eventually made further discussion possible at Washington was Article IV, perfected in the Senate Committee on Foreign Relations and on the Senate floor. Article IV compensated the United States to some degree for the kingdom's refusal to cede Pearl Harbor. It bound the Hawaiian government not to alienate any territory to foreign powers during the term of the treaty, and not to allow any nation other than America the privileges of reciprocity. With Article IV allowed by the Hawaiian negotiators as a condition of the treaty's chance of success, the document continued on its laborious way through the United States Senate, that graveyard of treaties.

The debate was heated. A constitutional issue was raised—was it within the Senate's province to bind the United States by treaty in matters that affected the nation's revenue? Economic argument followed—no doubt the treaty would cost America something; how much would it cost, and was it worthwhile? Supporters said that it was worth anything if it secured the islands to America politically and strategically; without a treaty the Hawaiian kingdom might look for a British benefactor. Opponents said the islands were bound to America already; money forgone in the reciprocity treaty was money wasted, and the only ones who would benefit were the west coast sugar refiners.

On March 18, 1875, the Senate voted, and the required two-thirds majority was secured. Three weeks later the news reached Honolulu on the mail steamer *McGregor,* which appeared off Diamond Head with its flags flying a coded message of success. Kalakaua ratified the treaty on April 18. Land values in the islands were already up 25 percent, even though President Grant still had to ratify the treaty and Congress had to pass enabling legislation.

The Hawaiian version of the treaty was taken back to Washington, where ratifications were exchanged on June 3, but the United States House of Representatives would not meet again until December, and in the meantime the sugar refiners of San Francisco mounted an attack. The arguments of the sixties were revived: the refiners feared that increased production of sugar in Hawaii would flood the market on the west coast, depress the refinery business there, and cause nationwide distress in the sugar industry. These complaints were countered by the San Francisco Chamber of Commerce, which predicted a general expansion of trade between Hawaii and the American west coast, to the benefit of all. The refiners were silenced in the end by the plantation agencies of Honolulu. J. C. Pfluger of Hackfeld & Co. went to San Francisco in the fall of 1875 to discuss the sale of a large part of the Hawaiian sugar crop of 1876, and he made it clear to the refiners that planters in the islands would not sell to people who opposed the treaty. Hawaiian sugar made up about one-fifth of the market on the west coast. Pfluger and his fellow agents had a good point; the refiners saw it, and after that they either supported the treaty or kept quiet.

Elisha Allen went to Washington in November 1875, to do what he could to speed matters along at the capital, but matters would not be speeded. (Later, Allen referred to this period as the most strenuous time of his life.) The treaty did not reach the floor of the House of Representatives until February 1876, and when it did extended debates took place on topics already argued in the Senate. Week after week the mail ships coming from San Francisco to Honolulu reported no progress. At last on May 26, 1876, the bark *Mary Belle Roberts* arrived decked in bunting. She fired a twenty-one gun salute, and the news was brought ashore that the House had voted in favor of the treaty on May 8.

This was still not the end; the Senate had to concur in the House's implementation. For a third time all the old issues were raised. Representatives of the Louisiana sugar and rice industries appeared before the Senate Committee on Foreign Relations, claiming that the treaty would injure them. When the bill got out of committee at the end of June its opponents managed to have it referred to the Committee on Finance, and it stuck there for more than a month.

The Hawaiian government was busy making the necessary moves to see that the treaty would go into effect immediately the United States Senate wound up its work. A proclamation by King Kalakaua was published; an act admitting the scheduled American goods duty free was passed on July 18 and published on August 16. All this time passed without an encouraging word from Washington, but the mood at Honolulu remained optimistic, at least as late as July 4, when the biggest Independence Day celebration ever was held at Honolulu: 1876 was the centennial year of the United States, and it was also the year of a great step forward in Hawaiian-American relations—or it would be if only the Senate would hurry.

But as the mail ships brought little news, and bad news at that, the mood of the islands changed. At Honolulu business was temporarily depressed; ships lay idle, unable to secure freight; the Hawaiian legislature, which had been in session since April 29, had long since exhausted important topics and was occupying its time with trivialities. Tempers were frayed; everybody was on the "ragged edge of uncertainty." On August 23 the *Hawaiian Gazette* remarked that it seemed almost impossible that the Senate would act before the close of the session. The waiting ended the very next day. The Pacific Mail Steamship Company's *City of San Francisco,* commanded, ironically enough, by Captain James Waddell of *Shenandoah* fame, arrived with unofficial news that the Senate had voted favorably. As she came around Diamond Head dressed in a "rainbow of bunting" the word spread like wildfire in the town, and crowds gathered at the waterfront with "hearts too full for utterance."

The silence was broken soon enough. The *Hawaiian Gazette* for August 30 carried an ecstatic headline: "Hurrah! For America and Hawaii! The Glorious News at Last! Hurrah! Our Luck Still 'Consistent!' Arrival of the PMSS City of San Francisco Bringing the News of the Passage of the Bill rendering operative the Treaty of Reciprocity ! ! ! The Treaty goes into effect as soon as the bill is signed by the President! President Grant signed the bill on Tuesday of last week, August 15th. Hip! Hip! Hurrah ! ! ! With a Tiger."

Kalakaua and his ministers decided to delay any great public demonstrations until official word came from Washington. The next steamer to arrive, the *City of New York,* brought news that President Grant had named September 9 as the day on which the treaty would go into effect. Kalakaua announced the date of the great occasion, and in the wake of an all night torchlight procession and fireworks display the Hawaiian kingdom moved forward into a new era.

For twenty-five years the American merchants of Honolulu had been urging reciprocity. During the last twelve months, however, the business community had known the worst kind of uncertainty, and possible losses as well as benefits began to be discussed, especially by Englishmen whose British connections were excluded from the treaty's provisions by Article IV and who were afraid that tariff revisions might drive them from the Hawaiian market altogether. Ever since the election of 1874 the Emmaites and their British friends at Honolulu had been developing a propaganda against reciprocity. This became the focus of an embryonic political party which did well in the 1876 elections, returning two out of four candidates in Honolulu and several elsewhere. Just before the treaty went into effect a small group of dissidents in the legislature, led by the anti-American Englishman Godfrey Rhodes, mounted an inconclusive general attack on the whole idea of reciprocity.

Whether or not these diversions had an influence it seemed that in the crucial weeks some of Honolulu's businessmen were looking the wrong way. Aboard the *City of San Francisco* was the west coast sugar refiner Claus Spreckels, one of those enemies of reciprocity whose minds were changed by the Honolulu sugar agents in 1875. Taking the first available ship to the islands after news was telegraphed from Washington that the treaty was safe, Spreckels landed quietly at Honolulu and bought half the sugar crop of 1877 before the price responded to the passage of the treaty. Still, there was more than enough of everything to go around. The treaty would run for eight years, and with any luck it would be renewed. The treaty years would surely be the fattest in Hawaii's history. In December, Peter Cushman Jones of C. Brewer & Co. struck a most satisfactory balance for his firm and wrote in his account book: "So ends the year 1876, Praise God."

CHAPTER SIX

$$Out\ in\ the$$

$$Noonday\ Sun$$

1876—1887

The Philosophy of the Planters

AMONG THE WEALTHY PLANTERS of the kingdom were a few who prided themselves more on knowing how to live than on making money, and James Makee of Rose Ranch on Maui was one who took the matter very seriously in a lighthearted sort of way. Over the years he put about a million dollars into his plantation at Ulupalakua on the slopes of the volcanic mountain of Haleakala, and the thousand acres he kept under crop yielded him eight hundred tons of sugar in a good year. At the same time he cultivated the good life on a grand scale. His rambling plantation house was ringed with guest cottages, and he liked to keep the cottages filled and the guests content. He bought a piano for his parlor and an organ for his chapel, and outside he built a billiard room, a tennis court, and a bowling alley with one small kanaka boy to tend each pin. His gardens were a riot of bright flowers, and when at last a visitor got tired of watching the roses grow he could take a saddle horse for a canter among the thousands of shade trees Makee had brought in to give the landscape some variety, along with birds to sing in them. All this lavishness was placed at the disposal of guests without ceremony, and though Makee knew when and how to put on a show (for a royal visitor he would call out a welcoming party of scores of torch bearers) he handled most social occasions with an understated grace. Once, while the common seamen of a touring warship were enjoying barbecued beef at Makee's private landing, Makee himself was serving fowl to the officers in the dining hall of the plantation house. After the main course the admiral, full of good food and good cheer, remarked that his host was fit to carve a peacock at a Roman feast, and Makee replied nonchalantly, "Gentlemen, the birds you have just eaten—were peacocks!"

In his last years Makee expanded his holdings at Ulupalakua, started a second plantation on West Maui, and went into partnership with King Kalakaua in another estate on Kauai. After he died the new owners of Ulupalakua turned Rose Ranch into a cattle range. But very few other plantations went out of the sugar business in the quarter century the reciprocity treaty was in force; in fact the acreage under cane in the islands increased 1,000 percent, reaching a total of one hundred and twenty-five thousand acres in 1898. In 1879 the total value of the kingdom's sugar estates was less than ten million dollars; by the end of the century the plantations were capitalized at something like forty million dollars. Between 1875 and 1890 the export crop increased from twenty-five million pounds a year to two hundred and fifty million. By 1897 the figure was five hundred million pounds, and at the end of the century Hawaiian sugar accounted for ten pounds in every hundred sold on the American market.

One set of figures showed a steady decline during the reciprocity period, and there was a good reason for it. In 1882 almost ninety planters and millers were in the business; by 1900 the figure had fallen below sixty. It took money to make money, and large plantations, many of them incorporated as joint stock companies, were more efficient than small ones.

This handful of planters depended heavily in turn on an even smaller group of businessmen—their agents at Honolulu, the heads of mercantile houses that imported laborers, machinery, and all sorts of supplies for the plantations and then negotiated the sale of crops on the American market. The arrangement had its drawbacks, as the planters saw things. "It would be a God-send to the planters," wrote one critic in 1884, "if the agency system was done away with, unless it is done in a more legitimate manner. This paying for shrinkage, cooperage, cartage, polarizing, large interest, expense of telegram to learn Cuban basis, exchange when against, but no credit for exchange when in favor and not receiving the back commission paid to agent in San Francisco, is enough to make any planter hail with joy any change in the handling of sugar that might bring down expenses from over twenty percent to where they should be. The planters are paying for too many fine residences in Honolulu to be entirely satisfied with present arrangements."

But the leading sugar factors—H. Hackfeld & Co.; W. G. Irwin & Co.; Theo H. Davies & Co.; C. Brewer & Co.; E. A. Schaefer & Co.; Castle & Cooke; J. T. Waterhouse; and M. S. Grinbaum & Co.—argued that though anyone could make money out of sugar in good times, it was the agencies' influence with the banks and the government that kept planters solvent in bad times. A healthy commission, or even a share in the ownership of a plantation, was not too high a price to pay for such a service, and if everybody, agent and planter alike, could afford a fine residence or at least look forward to owning one, who was being harmed?

Of course not everyone who worked in the sugar industry had a fine house. Beyond the guest cottages at Ulupalakua, and at every other plantation, stood the laborers' quarters, and life there was less than elegant. Men might be housed six to a hut or forty to a barracks. The buildings were supposed to stand eighteen inches above well-drained ground; the law allowed three hundred cubic feet of air space for each inhabitant; and the tenements were to be kept in good repair and whitewashed regularly. The law was observed about as well as most laws.

Housing was free, and so were some other services, but still there was not much left over for luxuries. Nine hours a day in the fields, twenty-six days a month, would earn a man between ten and eighteen dollars a month depending on his job and his nationality. And a worker might find that his master had something to say about the way he spent his money. He was strongly discouraged, for example, from drinking rum or smoking opium at the end of a hard day's work. As one planter put it, if anyone injured his horse he lost the benefit of the animal's labor. So with men who drank rum or smoked opium (or even men who got sick)—they did not do all the work their masters paid for, and a man had a right to ask for his money's worth. The courts were sympathetic to this line of thought.

The great problem for the planters was to keep the laborers' quarters full. Even before the reciprocity treaty went into effect it was clear that Hawaiian workers could never supply the needs of the sugar industry, and by the early eighteen eighties the native population of the islands had fallen to such a low point that the Hawaiians could not muster more than about five thousand able bodied men for work on the plantations.

To add to the Hawaiians' miseries a new and appalling scourge was at work amongst them—leprosy. The natives called it mai pake, Chinese disease, though no one really knew who brought it to the islands. It had been observed in the kingdom as early as 1830. By 1865 there was so much of it about that the legislature passed an act "to prevent the spread of leprosy," and in 1866 the government schooner *Warwick* began transporting lepers to a settlement on an isolated peninsula on the north coast of Molokai.

The Norwegian scientist Armauer Hansen identified the *bacillus leprae* in 1868, but very little was known about the way leprosy was transmitted from person to person. A good many white men at the islands shared the widespread belief that leprosy was associated with venereal disease, perhaps even a form of it. It was not surprising to them that leprosy found most of its victims among the natives. Hawaiians were physically promiscuous; they lived and slept in common far more freely than white men could bring themselves to do. Leprosy, then, seemed like a judgment as much as a disease. So bestial were the appetites of the Hawaiians, said the *Pacific Commercial Advertiser,* that it was difficult to summon up on their behalf "that pity we are ready to feel for all unfortunates."

Among the unfortunates who went voluntarily to Molokai was William Ragsdale, the parliamentary interpreter. He found a kind of sad enjoyment in putting his political skills at the service of the administration of the settlement, and he lived out his last three years with the title, self-bestowed, of Governor. Other lepers had to be taken by force, and one man, a native of Kauai named Koolau, refused to be taken. He fled with his family and a small group of diseased Hawaiians into the almost inaccessible valley of Kalalau, and for months he stood off the law with his rifle. He killed several deputies and outlasted the sheriffs' posses, and he died a free man, but still a leper, and because he was a leper, a murderer.

If Koolau was desperate he had every reason to be. There was no cure for leprosy. The Hawaiian government did its best to find one. Inquiries were made all over the world, and all kinds of doctors were encouraged to try their skills and their exclusive remedies—Mohabeer the Indian; Sang Ki and Akana, two Chinese; a Japanese named Goto; Kainokalani, a Hawaiian kahuna; Americans who mixed their own patent medicines; and the German bacteriologist Eduard Arning, who got permission from Kalakaua's government to make the deadly experiment of implanting leprous tissue in the flesh of a living subject, a condemned native murderer named Keanu.

Nothing worked. By the end of the eighteen seventies more than a thousand lepers had been sent to Molokai. The lucky ones had a kokua, a helper, a wife or husband or friend to look after them; the rest looked after themselves. The government housed them, and Christian ministers, Protestant, Mormon, and Catholic, helped them down the rotting road to the grave. In 1873 a young and earnest Belgian priest went to Molokai— Father Damien Joseph de Veuster, a member of the Hawaiian mission of the Sacred Hearts. For the next sixteen years he lived among the lepers. He shared their life utterly without fear—and without discretion or even common sense, so his critics said. In 1883 it became clear that he had contracted leprosy, and after that he was an outcast even from his own church; his fellow priests would not celebrate the Mass with the chalice and vestments he used, and the missionary sisters would not receive communion from his hands. Damien the Leper died in 1889.

Hundreds of natives followed him in death at the leper settlement, and once again the possibility had to be considered that the Hawaiian people might die out altogether. The kingdom needed population as desperately as the plantations needed labor. In the period of the reciprocity treaty the government spent more than a million dollars encouraging immigration, and the planters and their agents added a good deal more on their own account. Sometimes the two imperatives—population and labor—seemed to complement each other fairly well; more often they were in conflict.

The planters wanted immigrants to be servile laborers. A man should work out his contract and then if he would not sign up again he should go home, preferably at his own expense, to be replaced by a laborer just like him. It would be good if single men came to the islands; families would cause extra expense, at least until the children were old enough to go to work. Workers did well, the planters found, under overseers or lunas of a different race. This helped prevent "collusion." The best arrangement of all was to put white lunas in charge of work gangs. Beyond that, there was not much agreement among planters about the most useful racial mixture. Native Hawaiians would work cheaply, but they did not work very hard, and in any case there were not enough of them. Portuguese from Madeira and the Azores were industrious, but they asked for too much money and they were impatient to buy land of their own. As long as Japanese were few in number at the islands they were fairly highly regarded, even though they were obsessed with bathing and their taste in food was strange. Whatever the defects of the Chinese, they had the virtue of availability; they arrived with or without contracts, in good times or bad, more and more each year, until by the middle eighteen eighties there were too many of them even for the planters, and steps were taken to limit their entry.

The government wanted to be able to regard immigrants as people, not just as units of labor. The kingdom's population had to be replenished, and ideally a laborer should be considered as a potential citizen. Portuguese, Norwegians, Swedes, and Germans were welcome, but of course they had Western views on matters such as wages, and this made them unacceptable to the planters. If the native Hawaiians could not replenish themselves then some similar people would have to be brought in—a "cognate race," as the phrase went in the seventies and eighties. All sorts of possibilities were explored—Hindus, Malays, Pacific islanders. In the end the choice was narrowed down to Chinese and Japanese, again because they were available.

Over the years a good many Chinese men married Hawaiian women, and it was hard to complain about the quality and quantity of the offspring (the merchant Chun Afong, for example, had twelve daughters and four sons). But most Chinese could not find Hawaiian wives, or did not want to, and the popular opinion was that in any case a Chinese would remain a Chinese no matter what was done for him or to him at the islands; he would never assimilate, and however useful he might be on a plantation he was a menace once he left for the towns, because he would work for next to nothing and drive white and native tradesmen out of jobs.

Some influential men thought the Japanese offered better prospects. One went so far as to say that the Japanese could not really be regarded as "Asiatics:" at home they were Westernizing themselves as fast as they could, and at the islands they would surely do the same. But once the Japanese made their presence felt in great numbers they seemed to relapse into the worst kind of oriental stubbornness, and by the end of the century they were being talked about as a yellow peril more insidious even than the Chinese, threatening the very existence of Western civilization at the islands.

So as the years of the reciprocity treaty ran their course it began to appear that the planters had got their way at considerable expense. They could bring in their crops cheaply and the reciprocity treaty guaranteed them good profits. But were they fobbing off other kinds of costs onto society at large? What was the future of a country whose population was so wildly mixed in origins and attitudes?

Samuel Chenery Damon, chaplain of the Seamen's Friend Society at Honolulu for forty years, saw something fine in the thought that there might be a real meeting of mankind at the islands. Anglo-Saxons might have special virtues, he conceded, and of course they enjoyed the priceless benefits of Christianity, but just the same white men should not be allowed to push other races aside in the interests of trade. "Now, away with all these race antagonisms," wrote Damon. "There is not a sufficiently large population so that those of any one race can stand aside and aloof, forming a clan; all races must come into contact . . . There may be some rubbing and attrition [but] there will come a happy blending of races into one truly Christian brotherhood."

Damon was a good and useful man, and no one had an unkind word to say about him, but he was regarded as an eccentric on the subject of race. And even he had no doubt that the Anglo-Saxon version of civilization deserved to triumph. He simply wanted its triumph to be a gentle one.

The Anglo-Saxon planters and their Anglo-Saxon friends at the islands, Americans, Britishers, and Germans, had no doubt either that the future was theirs, and they were not gentle men. Occasionally they would make the effort to speak as if no conflicts of interest beset the kingdom, and as if race was not a political issue. They talked about the sugar industry as being good for everybody, and about fitness to govern as being the only consideration that should prevail in politics. But to them it was unthinkable that immigrant laborers from the Orient should ever share political power. And although the Hawaiian could not be denied his place in the kingdom it seemed to the planters, looking about them, that the native was unfit to govern himself.

The conclusion was inescapable. "The word in the beginning seems to have been spoken to the white man," wrote one planter, "when he was commanded to 'subdue the earth and have dominion over it.' Europe was given to the white man, America to the red man, Asia to the yellow man and Africa to the black man. And with slight exceptions the white man is the only one that has ventured beyond the 'bounds of his habitations.' He has over run Europe, and crossing the Atlantic westward has taken possession of America, and is 'monarch of all he surveys' from Cape Horn to Behring's [sic] Strait. He has stepped across the Pacific Ocean, leaving the imprint of his enterprising foot upon the various islands of the sea; he has taken possession of Australia and India, with their countless thousands; he has gone to Africa, and this time to stay, you bet—this time, it will not be a Mungo Park, a Livingstone, a Baker or a Stanley, as a traveler or explorer. The coming of the white man to Africa means government, enterprise, agriculture, commerce, churches, schools, law and order. It will be better for the colored man to have the white man rule. It is better for the colored man of India and Australia that the white man rules, and it is better here that the white man should rule, not that he should hold the offices and be King, but he must do a large share towards making the laws and then seeing that they are obeyed by the King and people."

The Conscience of the King

So race was the issue after all. King Kalakaua understood that as well as he understood anything. His people had been dispossessed of their lands and they were being steadily disenfranchised by death, but while they lived they could vote, and if they all voted together they could make sure that Hawaiians sat in high places. Election days at Honolulu, so a visitor observed early in Kalakaua's reign, were highly charged occasions; the streets were full, there was "an epidemic of gabble and gesture," and the king's men "in their red Garibaldi shirts ran through the dark crowd like sparks over the backlog of an open wood-fire."

As far as the planters were concerned it was bad enough that the fire was alight, and worse that the king and his native followers warmed their hands by it. Kalakaua, for his part, saw no reason why he should cramp his Hawaiian royal style, and he played politics to clear an area of freedom for himself. A luau for native voters during election week, the gift of a shirt or a pair of trousers, the friendly loan of a few dollars so that a man could identify himself at the polls with a valid tax receipt, a dipper full of gin served on the way to the ballot box, even the fatherly presence of the king to watch over the voters as they deposited their ballots—these small encouragements were enough to ensure that the House of Representatives was packed with native members. And as time went by more and more native politicians turned up on the government's payroll between legislative sessions.

The king did not stop there. Under the constitution of 1864, which was still in force, the appointment of Nobles to sit in the legislature was a royal prerogative. So was the choice of cabinet ministers. The king could appoint and dismiss ministers at will, and Kalakaua did precisely that. Before he was finally curbed he made thirty-seven ministerial appointments—more than all the kings before him had made among them—and eleven of those went to men with Hawaiian blood.

For white men this meant that the times were badly out of joint. Not every white man with a financial interest in the islands was a Hawaiain citizen, and not every white man with a grievance against the king felt compelled to take out naturalization papers, but even if the white community had been able to vote as a bloc Hawaiians would have outnumbered them at the polls. And a white cabinet minister, whatever his talents, could never be sure of his tenure.

Most of the productive land of the islands was in the hands of white men, and the sugar industry was virtually the sole support of the kingdom, and yet good business sense did not seem to be able to get a hearing at the royal court. The planters and businessmen kept reminding Kalakaua how much he owed them, but most of the time he did not seem to be listening.

The king served notice early in his reign that he was a man who wanted his way, when he began to agitate for a new palace that would match his personal eminence. Since the mid-eighteen forties a modest house called Iolani, not far from Kawaiahao Church at the east end of Honolulu, had been the home of the Hawaiian monarchs. But Iolani and its surrounding apartments were not grand enough for Kalakaua. "The life of my noble wife and myself," he wrote in 1876, "is not so pleasant in this place, the houses are filthy and in poor condition, and it is only with great effort to hide our humiliation that we live here. And it would be well that the citizens feel humiliated also regarding this thing." After much elaborate planning, construction of a second Iolani Palace was started in 1879. It took the best part of four years to build, and it cost more than three hundred thousand dollars, with its "American Florentine" galleries and towers, its red velvet draperies, its wall mirrors framed in gold, and its seven-foot marble royal bath.

To see so much money committed to a wanton frippery like the palace upset the planters and businessmen greatly, and they were distressed even more when Kalakaua embarked upon another potentially expensive misadventure. In November 1879, a plausible Italian named Celso Caesar Moreno arrived at Honolulu aboard the *Ho Chung,* a coolie ship owned by the China Merchants' Steam Navigation Company. Moreno had friends among the China Merchants, who wanted to increase their share of the labor trade. They had plans as well to start a steamer service between China and the United States, and for this purpose a subsidy from the Hawaiian government would be helpful. On his own account Moreno was interested in a project to lay a cable across the Pacific, and he carried with him a copy of an act passed by the United States Congress in 1876 awarding him a franchise. It was an impressive looking document, signed and sealed by the Secretary of State, and only those who actually read it would notice that Moreno's franchise was not exclusive, and that in any case it had already expired.

Moreno spoke more than a dozen languages, and one of them was the language of confidential flattery. He had himself introduced to Kalakaua, and before long the king was telling United States Minister James M. Comly that Moreno "had shown himself to be a very entertaining companion, a man of large and novel views in political and state affairs," and that he was frequently surprised to find "how exactly Mr. Moreno's views coincided with his own."

That was the best of recommendations. Moreno's plans for a steamship subsidy and a cable bill went before the legislature of 1880 with the king's blessings. Moreno added another bill of his own, an opium-licensing plan of large and novel proportions. He was prepared to spend money on votes: an average of fifty dollars for a run of the mill legislator, three hundred for a man of principle. Perhaps he should have gone higher. The steamship subsidy passed but was never implemented, the opium act passed in amended form and was vetoed by the king, and the cable bill failed.

The planters and businessmen had been watching Moreno. "The indignation of the public at the part played by a certain impecunious adventurer in the case is great," said the *Pacific Commercial Advertiser.* "His boasted power to oust the Ministry, and his assumption of prescience in regard to Regal acts may satisfy his own egotism, but will never enhance the brilliance of his fame, or add one tittle to his influence. He has been measured by a discriminating community, and their estimate of him is small, notwithstanding his alleged connection with distinguished people of other lands; and the public will be heartily glad at the opportunity to bid him an everlasting farewell." Kalakaua did not want his new friend to leave. He prorogued the legislature at noon on August 14, and an hour later his cabinet ministers were asked to resign. In a new cabinet named that day Moreno was given the portfolio of foreign affairs. His Hawaiian naturalization papers bore the same date as his ministerial commission.

This was too much. The diplomatic corps at Honolulu refused to do business with Moreno, and an agitated public meeting petitioned Kalakaua to have the adventurer removed from office. "The abdication of the King, the crowning of Queen Emma, annexation to the United States, the lynching of Moreno were as openly discussed on the streets as the claims of the Presidential candidates are in Washington," wrote United States Minister Comly. Kalakaua held out for five days and then asked Moreno to resign. The king made a point of saying he was acting of his own royal free will, and he followed this up by writing to the home governments of Minister Comly, British Commissioner James Hay Wodehouse, and French Commissioner J. L. Ratard, and asking for *their* removal.

Moreno departed from Honolulu on August 30, leaving behind him, so the *Hawaiian Gazette* said, an Augean stable of corruption, mismanagement, and fraud—a rather overwrought estimate of the effect of his few days in office. Kalakaua gave his friend, as a farewell gift, secret powers to negotiate treaties of neutrality for the Hawaiian kingdom in the United States and Europe. With Moreno went three part-Hawaiian youths, James K. Booth, Robert Boyd, and Robert W. Wilcox, to be educated under his benevolent supervision in Italy.

Perhaps because the widely traveled Moreno had filled his mind with stories of the great world beyond the islands, Kalakaua decided that it was time for him to make a royal tour. He had enjoyed his visit to the United States some years before, and now he planned a more extensive itinerary: he would become the first reigning monarch in history to travel around the world. The kingdom's treasury, the repository of the planters' taxes, would pay for the journey; he could look into the question of immigration while he was away; he would certainly learn more about the art of being a king. He could see no reason why he should not go.

The king's suite consisted of only two official persons—Royal Commissioner of Immigration and Minister of State William N. Armstrong, and Charles H. Judd, Kalakaua's chamberlain—both of them, as it happened, sons of Protestant missionaries who had held cabinet posts under King Kauikeaouli. The plan was for Kalakaua to travel incognito, but the royal valet Robert, a drunken German of mysterious origins who had arrived at Honolulu as a ship's cook but who insisted on signing himself Baron von Oehlhoffen, broke out the royal standard at the first opportunity, and that was that.

At San Francisco, where the party took ship for the Far East, Kalakaua was wined and dined by the sugar refiner Claus Spreckels. In Japan Emperor Mutsuhito offered his visitors the use of a moated palace, exquisitely furnished, and the services of innumerable attendants and entertainers, including geisha. Kalakaua was most impressed. On his own initiative he invited the Emperor to join him in creating a Union and Confederation of Asiatic Nations and Sovereigns, and he suggested as a good beginning the arrangement of a marriage between his niece Princess Kaiulani (who was then five years old) and a young Japanese prince. The Emperor did not want to involve himself in a confederation, and the marriage was an impossibility too, as the young prince explained: "I am very reluctantly compelled to decline your distinguished proposal for the reason that I am already betrothed to my future companion in life; so I sincerely trust that your Majesty will not be disappointed at what duty compels me to do."

This was a disappointment, to be sure, and so was the refusal of the Japanese government to send migrants to the islands, at least for the moment. But the rest of Kalakaua's time in the East was, by and large, well spent. He had a rather enigmatic but interesting meeting with a viceroy of the Chinese Empire; dinner with the Governor of Hong Kong; a few days in the unearthly splendor of the court of the King of Siam; then the royal party went on to Singapore, Burma, India, and finally Egypt, where the Khedive entertained Kalakaua between excursions to the Sphinx and the pyramids.

Things took a brief turn for the worse when Kalakaua reached Europe. The expansive Celso Caesar Moreno met him at Naples and carried him off from the official party. Armstrong and Judd were annoyed. They made sure that Moreno was not allowed to trade any further on his friendship with the king. His commission to negotiate treaties was revoked, and the education of his three young protégés, Boyd, Booth, and Wilcox, was put in the hands of the Hawaiian consul at Bremen. While all this was being attended to, Kalakaua visited King Umberto of Italy and had an audience with Pope Leo XIII.

From Italy Kalakaua went to England. He stayed sixteen days in London, and there he met Queen Victoria, the Prince of Wales, Prime Minister William Ewart Gladstone, and dozens of other great men and women who were in town for the season. Kalakaua spoke English well and he had a commanding physical presence; he made an excellent impression. The only embarrassments he encountered were minor ones, and not altogether to his discredit; when the Prince of Wales invited him to a private dance, for example, Kalakaua had trouble finding knee breeches and stockings that would admit his powerful legs.

Kalakaua paid brief visits to Belgium, Germany, Austria, France, Spain, and Portugal, and then returned to England and left by steamer from Liverpool for New York. President Chester A. Arthur met him at Washington, and on the other side of the continent he was the guest of Claus Spreckels again. The royal party reached Honolulu on October 29, 1881, after an absence of ten months. All over the kingdom, natives celebrated Kalakaua's return with feasting and dancing.

The trip had been a great experience. Kalakaua had stood where Alexander the Great had stood, and Julius Caesar, and Napoleon; and the foremost rulers of his own day had welcomed him with cannon salutes and guards of honor. Pomp and circumstance agreed with Kalakaua. He came home more convinced than ever that a king should rule as well as reign.

On the way around the world William Armstrong had tried to take advantage of long days at sea to instruct Kalakaua in the intricacies of constitutional government and the theory of ministerial and parliamentary responsibility. The king was not a good pupil. "My explanations of the evolution of the British Constitution confused him," wrote Armstrong. "I said to him . . . while describing the growth of the English government, 'the British nation has a prehensile tail,' as an essayist, Emerson, says: 'it clings to traditions and old forms, but it improves their substance.' 'Then,' said the King, 'it is a monkey government, is it? I don't want anything of that kind in my country.'"

Tradition, form, substance—what did the words count for in the Hawaiian kingdom? Planters and businessmen, who prided themselves on being men of substance, thought Hawaiian traditions were the most arrant nonsense. But for Kalakaua tradition and form were the very things that gave substance to life, and whenever he ran the three words together it generally meant that he had found a new way of using the planters' substance to support his notions of tradition and form.

The completion of the new Iolani Palace late in 1882 gave the king a chance to make a grand gesture. On the ninth anniversary of his accession to the throne, February 12, 1883, he staged a coronation ceremony for himself. It had not seemed an important matter in 1874, but his world tour showed him how things were ordered elsewhere, and he did not want to be remiss. A pavilion for participants and a large covered amphitheater for spectators were built in the palace ground, and on the great day Kalakaua was invested with royal regalia—the feather cloak of Kamehameha I, a palaoa or whale tooth pendant of the kind worn by the ancient chiefs, and a puloulou, or kapu stick. The king then took his gold crown, raised it, and placed it on his own head. All the cannon of the town and the guns of warships in the harbor were fired in salute, the royal torch blazed high, and a choir sang a Christian anthem composed for the occasion, "Cry Out O Isles, With Joy!"

For two weeks the celebrations went on. A statue of Kamehameha the Great was unveiled opposite the palace; there was a coronation ball, and a fireworks display, and a regatta, and an afternoon of horse racing in Kapiolani Park at Waikiki.

The natives enjoyed it all to the full, but the *Planters' Monthly* talked about folly and extravagance, "directly damaging to the property interests and welfare of the country," and the *Hawaiian Gazette* was full of pointed criticisms. Invitations were sent to all the courts of the world, the very ones Kalakaua had visited at such expense in 1881, and no ruler or statesman of any consequence thought a visit to Honolulu worth the risk of seasickness. Only a few hundred of the king's subjects bothered to march in procession—office holders mostly, and people who wanted to show off their finery; and all they got for their pains was mud on their boots, because money that should have gone for street improvements was being frittered away on the coronation. The pavilion and the amphitheater looked as cheap and tawdry as stables, so the *Gazette* thought. The marshal's proclamation of Kalakaua's style and title was ridiculous, and the king bungled the act of crowning himself—instead of holding the crown with both hands he picked it up by the small button on top and lowered it comically onto his head. No one cheered. The reception after the ceremony fell flat, and the guests left, "many thinking how uneasy must rest the head with such a crown."

Kalakaua had gone to a good deal of trouble over the arrangements for the coronation ceremonies, and if the official events were a sometimes uneasy mixture of Hawaiian and European tradition he wanted to make the popular celebrations as Hawaiian as possible. His hula dancers, who had been rehearsing for months, performed in public all one afternoon and into the night. The *Gazette* was shocked. One or two dances were acceptable, a "skillful and pleasing calisthenic exercise," but most were simply vicious. "Truth compels us to declare that *here* we stand face to face with that which reminds us of, we had almost said which is the same as that monstrous incarnation of brutishness, the benighted, *phallic* worship, whose leprous visage was so horrid that even the Senate of pagan Rome found it necessary to interdict it as an intolerable nuisance. No 'cleanly wantonness' this, but a deliberate attempt to exalt and glorify that which every pure mind must hold as the type of what is to be kept out of sight, and out of mind as the representative of all that is animal and gross, the very apotheosis of grossness."

So much for Hawaiian traditions and forms. William R. Castle, a practicing attorney and the son of the missionary turned businessman Samuel N. Castle, looked at his printed hula program, asked for translations of some of the Hawaiian words, and decided that it was an obscene publication. He brought charges against William Auld, one of Kalakaua's aides, and the printer of the program, Robert Grieve, who put out, of all papers, the *Hawaiian Gazette* itself. Grieve claimed complete ignorance of the Hawaiian language; he had taken the king's program on good faith, he said, and he had no idea of what he was printing (though clearly the *Gazette*'s reporter at the hula had some idea of what he was watching and listening to). Witnesses at the hearing made the point that certain kinds of native meles or chants were traditionally sung in honor of parts of the body; others testified that Hawaiian was a very ambiguous language; the judge ordered the court cleared while definitions of words were discussed. Grieve and Auld were fined as common nuisances. Grieve appealed and a higher court reversed his conviction.

The king was not at all abashed when white men attacked his sponsorship of Hawaiian traditions and forms. They could have no way of knowing what they were talking about, and depravity was surely in the eye of the beholder. Kalakaua continued to encourage his official genealogists in their reconstruction of the family lines of the old ruling chiefs; he collected and stored the stripped bones and feather cloaks of great men of the distant past; he supported legislation to permit Hawaiian kahunas to practice their version of medicine legally; he had the Hawaiian creation chant, the Kumulipo, recorded in writing for the first time; and he formed a secret society, Hale Naua, whose object, according to its constitution, was "the revival of Ancient Sciences of Hawaii in combination with the promotion and advancement of Modern Sciences, Art, Literature, and Philanthropy."

Because Hale Naua was a secret society it invited speculation. It was Kalakaua's idea, and its membership was limited to men with Hawaiian blood, and so the king's critics concluded that it was an evil invention. "Its by-laws are a travesty of Masonry, mingled with pagan rites," wrote William D. Alexander, son of a missionary, brother of a planter, and a frequent spokesman on behalf of forces for good in the community. "So far as the secret proceedings and objects of the society have transpired, it appears to have been intended partly as an agency for the revival of heathenism, partly to pander to vice, and indirectly to serve as a political machine." Kalakaua saw no need to justify his secret purposes, whatever they were.

The Shepherd Saint

If the fires of racial strife burned hot, so the planters and businessmen said, it was because the king's most devoted supporter, Walter Murray Gibson, a white man and an American, kept blowing on the flames.

Gibson was that most unsettling of political figures, a traitor to his class. The Americans at the islands had to put up with him for twenty-five years, and they never forgave him his treason.

Gibson's betrayal of his racial origins would have been enough to damn him, but there was more. The planters and businessmen liked a man to stand up and be counted, not hide behind a smoke screen of words. There were men of great vision among them—Henry P. Baldwin, Samuel G. Wilder, James Campbell, Benjamin F. Dillingham—who saw a kind of rugged poetry in the laying of railroad tracks and the blasting of tunnels and the drilling of artesian wells, but they usually translated that poetry into the prose of technical reports and balance sheets and customshouse summaries, letting figures for the current year and forecasts for the unlimited future speak for themselves. Gibson knew as well as anyone how to put dollars to use, and if he had been simply a manipulator of money the planters would at least have understood him, no matter how much they disapproved of him. But Gibson refused to make himself accountable to the businessmen in their own terms, and for this they hated him.

From the beginning no one knew quite what to think of Gibson. He had appeared at Honolulu in 1861, traveling, so he said, for "scientific purposes" connected with the ethnology of the Malaysian and Polynesian races. He gave some well-attended public lectures on his adventurous life and his racial theories, but he did not leave for the East Indies when he said he would, and the longer he stayed at the islands the more it appeared he was up to no good.

For one thing he was a Southerner, and he made a public remark indicating that he did not care much for the Union, and this was an unpardonable thing to say at Honolulu during the Civil War. Then some people heard that he was on Maui, outfitting a privateer to be used against Union ships. Nothing came of this. Next it emerged that he had some connection or other with the Mormon church (a fact he had not mentioned), and that he was trying to persuade the native Mormons of the kingdom to emigrate and set up a new community under his leadership, perhaps somewhere in Malaya, perhaps in New Guinea.

The Mormon church at the islands was in disarray. When the first missionaries arrived at Honolulu in 1850 they found the government reluctant to recognize their faith as a true religion, despite the constitution's guarantee of toleration to all creeds. In the face of considerable opposition from the white community the elders began work among the Hawaiians, and in a short time they were able to organize a native City of Joseph on the island of Lanai. Then in 1857 the president of the mother church in Utah, Brigham Young, ordered the missionaries to return home for the duration of the war the Mormons were fighting against the government of the United States. Native elders kept the Hawaiian church going in a desultory way for the next few years, and Gibson, who had been converted to Mormonism in Utah in 1860, picked up the work in 1861.

His title, so he told the natives, was "Chief President of the Islands of the Sea and of the Hawaiian Islands," for the Church of Jesus Christ of Latter Day Saints, and his task was to put new life into the settlement of the Saints on Lanai. Contributions would be accepted, and a zealous man would be allowed to purchase a high position in the church. With good luck and good management the Hawaiian Mormons would be able to buy the valley of Palawai, and their church would have a permanent home.

"There are 10,000 acres of land in this valley, which could probably be bought for twenty five cents an acre or $2,500.00," wrote Gibson. "I hope to influence the government to let us have all of this valley, and most of the island to develop and then we will dig, and tunnell and build and plant and make a waste place a home for rejoicing thousands . . . I would make millions of fruits where one was never thot of. I would fill this lovely crater with corn and wine and oil and babies and love and health and brotherly rejoicing and sisterly kisses and the memory of me for evermore."

The native Mormons worked willingly, even harnessing themselves to the plough, but their enthusiasm waned when they discovered a worm in the fruit: the land they thought they owned at Palawai turned out to be registered not in the name of the church but in the name of Walter Murray Gibson. A committee from Utah arrived in 1864 to make an investigation. They had Gibson excommunicated, but they could not make him give up Palawai. Most of the natives left Lanai for a new settlement at Laie on Oahu, and there the Church of the Latter Day Saints flourished. By the end of the eighteen seventies one Hawaiian in ten was a Mormon.

Before the excommunication, while things were still going well, Gibson was lyrically happy at Palawai. "My heart leaps as I look upon it from the mountain tops," he confided to his diary. "Blessed art thou Lanai among the isles of the sea, thou art my refuge and my sweet hope. Thy grassy slopes are a sweet prospect. Thy balmy air fills my frame with pleasurable wellness. I am sure I hear the voice of God in these hills, and it would be fitting for His footsteps in the valley. I am born again here. I have sloughed off my old world worn sense of being. I am sure that I look with virgin eyes upon a new world and a new life full, of purpose and pleasant toil, without any shame and cowardice. Who or what shall I fear where I am king—and I shall keep within my kingdom. Though it is but an ark on the waves now. It is but a foothold, and even a doubtful foothold upon a poor bare island. But in my tremendous faith and hope there is a domain and a dominion. I am King; not of Oceanica, not of Malaysia, not of Hawaii nei, not of Lanai, but of Palawai on this day of grace. But this is but the baby of my kingdom, sweet grassy slopes of Lanai. Smile sweet valley, thy baby smile, thou hast no ruggedness nor evils of manhood. No type of man's sins are here, no angry beast to tear, no deceitful serpent to sting, no thieving eagle nor mean scavenger vulture hovers over thee, no annoying insect teases, there is nothing to fear or shun. Thou art naked yet smiling. The upturned face of the valley ever smiles its baby smile. Oh smiling Palawai, thou infant hope of my glorious kingdom. Blessed is Lanai among the isles of the sea."

The notions of birth and new beginnings were full of ambiguity for Gibson, who told several stories about his own origins. The most elaborate version was that he was one of two children born aboard ship during a storm at sea, and that somehow the babies were exchanged and given to the wrong mothers. Gibson was brought up in the humblest of circumstances in the southern United States, and his "parents" died while he was still a boy, leaving him nothing. This did not matter. The real story would come out one day: his true father was an English nobleman, and in time he would have his father's estate.

Gibson had the unconscious wisdom not to follow up his claim in England, but he never relinquished the fixed idea that he had been cheated of his rightful inheritance. In the Pacific, luckily, he found a place where he could be a king nonetheless, a Prospero whose Caliban was the Hawaiian, for whom also the question of a vanished birthright was full of poignancy. Gibson admitted to himself that his domain on Lanai was small and his subjects were mere brown men, hardly more than backward children. But he was a man of vast if uncertain ambition, and he did not really mean it when he told himself that he would keep within his baby kingdom. The way ahead from Palawai might be cloudy, but Gibson would surely know what he was looking for when it came into view. "Lines of power, of influence shall radiate from this shining crater," he wrote. "I set up my standard and it goes hence to the islands of the sea. Lanai shall be famous in Malaysia, in Oceania."

As a matter of fact Gibson had tried his hand more than once before at controlling the lines of power among the islands of the sea. He had been a gunrunner in the Caribbean during the early eighteen fifties, and then he had sailed for the Dutch East Indies with the idea of creating a kingdom for himself there, like James Brooke, the White Rajah of Sarawak. Gibson was no Brooke; he wound up in the Dutch colonial prison of Weltevreden under sentence of death. He escaped and returned to the United States, and his claims for damages against his persecutors brought the American and Dutch governments closer to war than they wanted to be. Gibson's petitions were rejected after a congressional investigation showed he had brought his troubles on himself, but he was sure that he had been on the brink of great things, and the journey to the Hawaiian Islands gave him a chance to start over, to be born again, as he put it.

Gibson was obviously a man who could change the focus of his political vision at will without any sense of strain. He congratulated himself on finding a refuge at Palawai, but at the same time he took steps to find out if perhaps his inheritance lay in the kingdom at large rather than within the narrow confines of Lanai. While he was still "Chief President" of the Mormons he made it known to the government that his "followers" on Oahu, Maui, and Hawaii were asking him for advice on how to vote in the elections of 1862. He was looking, he said, for ways to wield his "little influence" in the best interests of the country, and he mentioned in passing that he could bring in twenty-five hundred votes.

If this was not quite true at the time it became so later on. Gibson got to know the Hawaiians better than any other white man of his day. He commanded their language to perfection, and he worked hard to establish himself as their champion against the businessmen of Honolulu and the planters of the outer islands. He was willing to cooperate with anyone in making plans to replenish the population of the kingdom by health measures or by immigration, but beyond that he set himself apart from his fellow Americans.

In 1878 he declared himself a candidate for the national legislature, and the native voters of Lahaina on Maui returned him with a good majority. Opinions varied on his usefulness in the Assembly. The *Pacific Commercial Advertiser* found him sincere, frank, courteous, earnest, and indefatigable. The *Hawaiian Gazette* was less impressed: "He got up more special committees, made more reports, and by his officiousness and vanity kept the legislature in a continual ferment of excitement, merely to enable him to air his inordinate ambition to shine as a leader of the Assembly; and par excellence, the special friend and protector-general of the remnant of the Hawaiian race."

The *Gazette* might not have appreciated Gibson, but the voters did. In 1880 he was returned by a large majority, as one of only three white men in the House of Representatives. To make sure that his policies were kept before the nation, he bought the *Advertiser* and the Hawaiian language newspaper *Elele Poakolu*.

The *Elele Poakolu* did well from the beginning, even though the businessmen would not advertise in it, and this new success only confirmed the view of the white community that Gibson was a dangerous racist and a demagogue. When he announced his intention to run for a seat in the legislature again in 1882, the *Saturday Press,* the whitest of the white men's newspapers, published a pamphlet entitled *The Shepherd Saint Of Lanai,* raking over Gibson's Mormon past and his purchase of Palawai with the money of the native Saints. Gibson did not come out of the story well, but the pamphlet was useless as a political weapon; it was written in English, and most of the voters in the kingdom read only Hawaiian, if they read anything.

Gibson was far too good a politician to make such elementary mistakes of strategy and tactics. This time he was running for office from Honolulu, and he arranged to have his name placed on fifteen electoral tickets. The valid votes cast totalled 1,451; Gibson got 1,153. The message was clear, so the *Advertiser* said. "The stupid and cowardly spirit of slander" had received a "signal rebuke from a free, generous, and independent people."

Halfway through the legislative session of 1882 there was a crisis of confidence in the ministry. Gibson was approached by a group of white men with the offer of a minor cabinet post. He turned them down. Then Kalakaua offered him the premiership and the portfolio of foreign affairs. Gibson's moment had come; to the surprise of no one at all he accepted.

Gibson was fifty-eight when he was sworn in as premier. It had taken him a long time to reach this new turn in the road. He was a distinguished-looking man, but somehow he made people uneasy still. The American visitor David Graham Adee found him a "tall, thin old gentleman," with "white hair and beard, a mild, cold blue eye, a fine patrician nose, and a tolerably port-wine complexion, which probably once was fair. The general effect is that of a portrait of the Duke of Wellington in later life in parliamentary attire. The Premier's voice is soft and low, and confidential to a rare extent. He is an unquestionably eminent-looking veteran, of smooth address, silky manners, and a somewhat fascinating mode of speech, in the estimation of the susceptible and sympathetic—a fine old fellow, I should say; wise as a serpent, but hardly as harmless as a dove. That he has a proclivity for primacy, a faculty for public affairs, is evident; and that his ambition decidedly tends in the direction of state-craft, even if his artillery falls somewhat short of its aim, none can doubt . . ." Whatever his aim, Gibson was in a position to call the shots in the kingdom. He proclaimed a New Departure in national policy.

His Royal Saccharinity

Gibson and Kalakaua were well met. They had made their way to lofty positions and they liked the view from the top. Between 1882 and 1887 Kalakaua kept changing cabinets, but Gibson stayed on. He held every ministerial post in turn and many appointments of lower rank, often several at the same time. He was a consummate political strategist, Kalakaua's Minister of Everything. Just the same there was something to the criticism that Gibson was all sail and no ballast. He talked about economy in government, but it was fatally easy to find extravagance in his operations. He was always ready to encourage Kalakaua's expensive flights of fancy, and even when he turned his attention to solid projects such as improvements in roads or steam transport between the islands, there was a dangerous leakage in the government's accounts. The kingdom had never been so prosperous, and yet the national debt kept growing. The subject of a huge loan cropped up again and again—two million dollars, four, ten.

Fairly clearly the government needed the good offices of someone who had a sober respect for money. In the cabinets of Kalakaua's early years there were several such men—Samuel G. Wilder, the owner of a steamship line; William Lowthian Green, a wealthy merchant; Henry A. Peirce, who had made a fortune at the islands in the early days—but the king dismissed them one after another. In the end the finances of the kingdom fell into the hands of Claus Spreckels, the San Francisco sugar refiner. Spreckels was not a Hawaiian citizen, and he never held an official post in the government. He did not need to: he was a law unto himself.

As soon as the passage of the reciprocity treaty was confirmed in 1876 Spreckels hurried from San Francisco to the islands to get a grip on as much of the sugar crop of 1877 as he could, and he left everybody standing. "Let us be wide awake and meet Fortune half-way," said the *Hawaiian Gazette,* welcoming the treaty, "for we may rest assured that Fortune will not come more than half-way to meet us." Spreckels did not need to be lectured on Fortune. Long before the *Gazette*'s homily was on the streets he had come and gone and was back in San Francisco with promises of more than seven thousand tons of sugar for his refinery in 1877, and his son John had bought a part interest in a plantation on Maui.

Spreckels got himself fairly started in the sugar planting business in 1878. He chose to open up the dry central plain of Maui, "a dreary expanse of sand and shifting sandhills, with a dismal growth in some places of thornless thistles and indigo," as the traveler Isabella Bird Bishop described it. Two other enterprising planters on Maui, Samuel T. Alexander and Henry P. Baldwin, Hawaiian-born sons of Protestant missionaries, were already building an irrigation channel seventeen miles long, the Hamakua Ditch, to water their plantation at Haiku. Spreckels took a leaf from their book. He bought a half interest in sixteen thousand acres of dry land on the Waikapu Commons, leased from the government another twenty-four thousand acres at Wailuku Commons, and then petitioned the cabinet for water rights.

The cabinet was willing to give the matter serious study, but Spreckels wanted quick action. If the ministers could not make up their minds then Kalakaua should ask them to step aside in favor of men of decision. On the night of July 1, just a week after Spreckels first broached the matter, Chief Justice Charles Harris was working on a draft of the lease and Spreckels and his irrigation engineer Hermann Schussler were sharing a bottle or several of champagne with Kalakaua at their hotel. At two in the morning Kalakaua had his cabinet ministers wakened so that they could submit their resignations.

Harris put it to Spreckels and Schussler that they were responsible. "Schutzler & Spreckles replied to me." he wrote, "we are only defending our own interests, I said & it is the first time money has been used in this country to procure official favors, and now with the King. You have injured our pride & done damage to those who are doing good to you, and who have spent an immensity of time & trouble bringing your plan into shape, & who didn't want, & couldn't be induced to take a dollar of your money. They denied that they had used pecuniary considerations.

"I replied to them, gentlemen, will you undertake to deny me that you have promised the King a gift of $10,000 & a loan of $40,000 at 7% —holding out in my hand a Note of the King's in which he said that Mr. S had offered to lend him $40,000 to pay some Notes which were then running at 12%. Of course there was nothing that could be said. The $10,000 has since arrived and been received by the King . . ."

Spreckels got his lease. It was dated July 8, 1878, and on the same day the king's chamberlain copied an entry into his cash book: "Bills payable Amt 4 Notes dated July 8th 1878 given by His Majesty favor of Claus Spreckels for $10,000 each at 2, 3, 4, & 5 years with int. at 7 per cent per annum payable semiannually and secured by net receipts of Crown lands 40,000."

Spreckels was given six years to build his ditch and thirty years to enjoy the benefit of the water rights, to be followed by another thirty if the government agreed to extend his lease. Samuel Alexander and Henry Baldwin were given a new reason to finish the Hamakua Ditch quickly—if they failed their work would revert to the government, and now the government had signed over the water rights in the Hamakua district to Spreckels, subject to prior rights. Alexander and Baldwin beat their deadline by a whisker. While they were still celebrating, Spreckels was getting his own project under way. Within a year he had contracted to spend half a million dollars on a water course thirty miles long that would carry sixty million gallons a day along ditches, through tunnels, across valleys on trestles, to a reservoir at his plantation. Spreckels took off his first irrigated crops in 1880. From then on, as long as he owned land in the kingdom, he kept looking for ways to increase the productivity of his plantations. He expanded his acreage, drilled wells, cut more ditches, tried new varieties of cane, and pioneered in the use of advanced harvesting and milling techniques. Spreckelsville on Maui was a model plantation. And its owner never stopped cultivating his political interests.

One weak point in Spreckels' arrangements was that he held twenty-four thousand acres of land on Maui only by a lease from the government. It would be foolish to allow elaborate improvements to fall into the hands of the government at the end of his thirty year tenancy. A lease had been good enough to start with, but considering the investment of millions of dollars he was making in the sugar industry a fee simple title would be much more satisfactory in the long run.

Spreckels worked out an ingenious strategy to get what he wanted. In 1880 he approached the high chiefess Princess Ruth Keelikolani, half-sister of Alexander Liholiho and Lot Kamehameha, and offered to buy out her claim to a part interest in the crown lands of the kingdom. Ruth's claim was doubtful. For one thing her close blood relationship with the Kamehamehas was not accepted universally; under one interpretation of the genealogical evidence she was not entitled to call herself the heiress of the dynasty. Then again her claim rested on the assumption that the crown lands were the private property of the Kamehamehas, and a statute meant to dispose of that idea had been on the books since 1865. But Ruth asserted all the same that she was entitled to half the crown lands, or about half a million acres. Now, for ten thousand dollars, she sold her interest to Spreckels. If she really believed her claim was good this was an odd thing to do, since she was signing away her right to lands worth three quarters of a million dollars. Some people at Honolulu thought it was an inept piece of work on Spreckels' side, too.

But Spreckels had at least three strong legal opinions in his favor, one of them prepared by the lawyer Edward Preston just two months before Preston became attorney general in the cabinet of Walter Murray Gibson. Another member of that cabinet was Minister of the Interior Simon Kaai, steward of Princess Ruth's estates, who had managed Spreckels' payment of ten thousand dollars to Ruth.

When the legislature of 1882 met, Spreckels made the government an offer. If he could get a fee simple title for his twenty-four-thousand acres of lease land on Maui he would not press his claim to the half-million acres of crown land. Suddenly his ten thousand dollars looked like a good investment.

Minister of Foreign Affairs Gibson drew up a bill to fit the case, Attorney General Preston introduced it, and Minister of the Interior Kaai moved to have it considered immediately. A spirited debate followed. Among the members of the legislature were a few Hawaiians who were independent of the king's party. One of them was George Washington

Pilipo, a man who always spoke his mind. "There is something strange about this," said Pilipo, opening his attack on the bill. "The Minister of Foreign Affairs gave notice a few days ago of his intention of introducing the Bill, and now another Minister brings it in. Who is the cause of this? The person who is agent for a high chiefess of this kingdom. What are we to think of such a native Hawaiian, the same color as myself, whose duty is to watch over and protect the interests of the country? And who says, 'We shall protect you in this.' The Attorney-General and the Minister of Foreign Affairs . . . a man whose mouth is full of *aloha* for Hawaiians, but whose actions are not. We must consider what a man does, and not what he says . . . I think that taking crown lands away from the crown and giving them to another person is a step toward destroying the independence of the country . . . The Ministers are frightened. If they cannot protect the dignity of the throne, they had best leave their seats. It makes me ashamed to see a Ministry who are afraid. Where is the danger? Is it from Great Britain, from Germany or the United States? No! It is from one man—a merchant."

Pilipo and his native friends were outnumbered. The bill passed its third reading on July 20, 1882, and the king signed it into law the next day. On August 11 Spreckels made out a quit claim giving up his interest in the crown lands, and he received in return a royal patent in fee simple for his lease land on Maui from the commissioners of crown lands, Charles H. Judd, Edward Preston, and Walter Murray Gibson.

When Spreckelsville Plantation was founded in 1878 its sugar was marketed through W. G. Irwin and Company, a leading sugar factoring house at Honolulu. In 1880 Spreckels bought a partnership in Irwin and Company, and within two years he and William Irwin controlled almost the entire Hawaiian sugar crop. Irwin did not mind the use of the word "monopoly;" his firm's preeminence, he said, was a matter of "business, of pure, competitive dealing." The credit, in his judgment, belonged to Spreckels, "one of the smartest businessmen in America today. He has been identical with the sugar interests of the Hawaiian islands for many years, and has built up his present enormous business by his superior business ability. As I told you, our firm directly controls one-third of the sugar crop of the islands. The other two-thirds we purchase of the other planters paying them cash for what we get, or its equivalent, and as much as any one else can afford to give them. Any one else can go in and buy from them, and if any responsible firm or man would offer them a fraction more per pound for their sugar than we could give they would surely take it . . ."

Other men in the sugar industry would admit, grudgingly, that Spreckels was a formidably efficient businessman. Spreckelsville could get its crops off more cheaply than any other plantation and still command high prices for its sugar; Spreckels' Oceanic Steamship Company, subsidized by the government, carried Hawaiian sugar to Spreckels' refinery at San Francisco. But the general opinion was that Spreckels had far too much influence. In less than ten years Ona Miliona, the owner of a million, as the natives called him, had put a stranglehold on the sugar industry, and for a short time in the eighteen eighties it seemed as if he might squeeze everyone else to death. He could do almost anything he chose with King Kalakaua and Premier Gibson, both of whom owed him money, and this meant that the government was practically in his hands. It looked, indeed, as if nothing could stop Spreckels, Herr Von Boss, His Royal Saccharinity. "Mr. Spreckels," said William Irwin deprecatingly, "naturally has something to say in the government of so small a country, where he has so much invested."

In 1883 Spreckels turned his attention to the matter of the Hawaiian coinage. The existing system had little to recommend it. United States gold coins were legal tender for any amount, and United States silver coins could be used to pay debts up to fifty dollars. All sorts of other coins—Mexican, Chinese, Danish, Swedish, English—passed from hand to hand and were discounted at various rates.

Spreckels and Gibson worked out a scheme by which Spreckels would supply the kingdom with a million dollars worth of silver coins, taking payment in government gold bonds bearing an interest rate of six per cent. Kalakaua was willing: all the best kings had their heads on coins. The minting could very well have been carried out by direct negotiation between the Hawaiian government and the United States treasury, and there was no need for a private agent, but Spreckels had his way. Amid dire predictions from the merchants of Honolulu that a million dollars in silver coin would dislocate the economy of the kingdom, he went on to have the coins struck. He stood to make good money from the transaction. A silver piece with a face value of one dollar would cost him about eighty-five cents; a million dollars' worth would net him a profit of one hundred and fifty thousand dollars.

As soon as the first Kalakaua coins appeared at Honolulu three of Spreckels' opponents, William R. Castle, Sanford B. Dole, and W. O. Smith, went to law with the idea of preventing Spreckels from exchanging the silver coins for the government's gold bonds. Kalakaua, Spreckels, and Gibson arranged some changes in the membership of the cabinet, and when the court's decision failed to clear a path for the issue of the bonds to Spreckels the Privy Council went ahead and approved the payment just the same.

At the moment when the Kalakaua silver coins began circulating, Spreckels and his partner William Irwin opened a bank at Honolulu. Until then the only banking firm in the kingdom was Bishop & Co., a most conservative house. Spreckels and Irwin conducted their business modestly enough to begin with—sugar was selling at depressed prices for the time being—but soon they raised their sights. Spreckels began talking about a national bank with power to issue a circulating paper currency.

A banking bill, launched by the usual champagne parties for king and legislators, went before the Assembly of 1884 in May. The opposition was appalled. If the bill passed, Spreckels would control the internal commerce of the islands as well as the shipping and refining of the sugar crop. The whole kingdom would exist at his pleasure. "Shall we then," asked the *Hawaiian Gazette,* "sit tamely down and folding our hands meekly wait till the thief eases us of our purses, wait till the wolf tears out our entrails, wait till the snake is coiled completely round our limbs, and with glittering beady eyes fascinating ours, gives the final constriction and breaks every bone, leaving us a pulpy mass to do with as he will?"

The Honolulu Chamber of Commerce petitioned the legislature against the bill; a Citizens' Committee For Mutual Protection called a series of meetings. Not one of the speakers had a good word to say for Spreckels' national bank. The founders, said Clarence W. Ashford, "do not carry their arguments in their heads, but in canvas bags, and we all know the result when the contents of those bags are spread before the legislators." Ashford finished his speech amid cheers and the noise of stamping feet.

The legislators were frightened off. A committee report being discussed at the same time showed all sorts of discrepancies in the accounts of the Gibson ministry, and in the general uneasiness the bank bill was defeated by a vote of 35 to 2. A substitute act, passed later in the session, was a much more limited document. William Castle and Sanford Dole, who had led the fight against Spreckels, introduced a motion of no confidence in Gibson's ministry. It was defeated, 21 to 25, but the margin was significant: all four members of the cabinet had to vote to save themselves. In the aftermath of the argument over the coinage, the legislature passed a Gold Law reaffirming the business community's preference for hard money. By the end of the session it was clear that for the first time since 1876 Spreckels had taken the losing side in a major campaign. The opposition looked forward to more of the same.

Spreckels, of course, was not a man to brood over a temporary setback. Even if the bank bill had to be written off as a total loss he still had substantial political assets. He held more than half the national debt of the kingdom. He was also the holder of a mortgage on Premier Gibson's lands at Palawai. King Kalakaua had been in debt to him since 1878, and if he persisted in playing cards with Spreckels he would never get out.

As late as the middle of 1886 the working alliance between Spreckels, Kalakaua, and Gibson seemed to be intact. But some serious tensions were developing. People were referring openly to Spreckels as King Claus, and in the legislature some members of the opposition kept asking pointedly who was in charge of the kingdom, His Majesty Spreckels or His Majesty Kalakaua.

This was intolerable to Kalakaua. He was more than willing to run himself and his country in debt to Spreckels, and he acknowledged the debt by allowing Spreckels to suggest the names of useful men for posts in the cabinet—"this little shuffle of the knaves in the pack," as the *Hawaiian Gazette* put it. But for Kalakaua the real stakes were higher than that, and he had no intention of letting Spreckels outbid the monarchy.

Early in the twentieth century, when Spreckels, Kalakaua, Gibson, and the Hawaiian monarchy itself were dead, a story found its way into print concerning the end of the alliance. It may not have been literally accurate, but it had a ring about it that made it truer than truth. One day in 1886 Kalakaua, Spreckels, and two visiting admirals, a Britisher and an American, were deep in a game of euchre. Spreckels drew a hand that had three kings, one ace, and one low card. "If this were poker," he said jokingly, "I have the winning hand here." One of the admirals said he was ready to bet, and showed his hand—three aces. "My four kings would still win over your aces," said Spreckels. Kalakaua asked, "Where is the fourth king?" Spreckels said, "I am the fourth king." Kalakaua got up angrily and left. The Royal Hawaiian Band, which had been providing background music for the card game, played "God Save the King," and Spreckels bowed to the band master.

The two great men had come to a parting of the ways, and now Kalakaua got ready to throw Spreckels himself into the discard. To do this it would be necessary to buy Spreckels off, to loosen his hold on the national debt, without embarrassing the kingdom. The question of a new loan came before the legislature of 1886, as it had done before every legislature of Kalakaua's reign. Kalakaua spoke of "enterprises of an exceptional and important character," and Gibson introduced a bill calling for a loan of two million dollars, more than enough to pay Spreckels in full. But Spreckels, who had reached the point of wanting the crown and the government to cut down on spending, argued for economy. Gibson was discomfited. He might owe mortgage payments to Spreckels, but he owed his cabinet post to the king, and Kalakaua wanted to go on living like a king even if this meant bigger and bigger debts. Spreckels got a reluctant promise from Gibson that no loan would be made, put matters in the hands of his two nominees in the cabinet, Robert J. Creighton and John T. Dare (sweepings from the floor of his refinery, as the *Gazette* called them), and left for San Francisco.

For the second time in two years Spreckels had made a tactical blunder. A new benefactor for the kingdom appeared almost immediately.

Henry R. Armstrong, representing a British financial syndicate, arrived at Honolulu on August 7, and Kalakaua greeted him enthusiastically. Again Premier Gibson was in the middle: he had promised Spreckels that no loan bill would be passed, but here was the king wining and dining Henry Armstrong. Toward the end of August Armstrong went back to San Francisco, where he could be in touch with his principals in London by cable, and the legislature met to argue the merits of a loan. On September 1 an act calling for a loan of two million dollars was passed. It was understood that at least part of the money would be raised in London, presumably by Armstrong's syndicate.

George Macfarlane, Kalakaua's chamberlain, a member of the House of Nobles and a friend of Henry Armstrong, took the news to Spreckels in San Francisco. Spreckels, as always, was quick to appreciate a change in circumstances. He had opposed the loan, but if there was to be one he wanted part of it. He made arrangements with Armstrong to invest in the new bonds, on condition that the Hawaiian government paid off the old bonds he held. An amended version of the loan act, framed to meet Spreckels' specifications, came back from San Francisco to Honolulu for consideration by the legislature.

Before the Assembly had time to act Spreckels himself appeared again at the islands. He had changed his mind. Now he wanted all the loan. If the London syndicate became the government's principal creditor, Spreckels' voice would no longer carry much weight in Hawaiian politics. Kalakaua knew this as well as Spreckels did; that was precisely why the king wanted the loan to go to London. Gibson was still in the middle.

Spreckels watched proceedings in the legislature from a seat in the visitors' gallery as Attorney General Dare moved an amendment to the already amended loan bill. Dare proposed that Spreckels should at least be paid off before any new debts were incurred. The debate was spirited, and it turned on the question of Spreckels' influence, past, present, and future. If Dare's amendment passed, Spreckels would still be in the game; if it failed, Spreckels would be forced to leave the table. It failed, and a good many people thought Spreckels had brought the debacle on himself. "Mr. Spreckels," wrote Gibson, "on one or two occasions, and especially at my residence on Ocb^r 13th ventured to express himself in such a dictatorial manner to His Majesty in the presence of several members of the Assembly—saying that his views must be carried out or he would '*fight*,' and exclaiming that this meant a withholding of financial accommodation and an immediate demand for what was owing to him—that he aroused then & there a determination on the part of the native members present to resist the dictation of 'ona miliona' (Mr Spreckels), and as they themselves avowed, to see whether their chief Kalakaua or Mr Spreckels were king. This occurred during the noon recess of the Legislature and at

2 P. M. of the same day the opposition to the proposed amendment of the Loan Act was open and manifest. This amendment devised and insisted upon by Mr Spreckels was voted down by a large majority. It will be claimed that there were other influences at work especially that of parties representing London Capitalists. The influence existed and had been brought to bear to some extent on the Government, yet I can say positively that this influence had ceased to command attention, that His Majesty and His Ministers had distinctly decided to accept Mr Spreckels' amended Loan Act as transmitted from San Francisco by him, and that they had agreed to permit the loan to be floated by his agency . . . it was through Mr Spreckels' offensive dictatorial manner arousing the sensitive native members to indignation, that these arrangements were thrown aside at the last moment."

Spreckels gave back the royal decorations Kalakaua had pressed upon him earlier and left for San Francisco, where he made some caustic remarks about his former friend the king. Kalakaua, he said, was a man who could not be reached by calm reason, but who was easily approached at the drinking or gaming table. The gin bottle was his divinity. He had been led for a long time by gin-drinking adventurers, men with everything to gain and nothing to lose by encouraging his escapades. They filled his head with chimerical schemes for spending money, with the result that the king had become "crazy upon the subject of loans."

Kalakaua and his government went ahead and bought their freedom from the choleric Spreckels. The cabinet was reorganized—only Gibson retained his portfolio—and Spreckels was paid off with part of the London loan. It seemed a great success: the first issue, a million dollars worth of bonds, had been oversubscribed within a few weeks and was selling at a premium in London. But once the technicalities of the new arrangement came under scrutiny it appeared that freedom was costly. Administrative expenses were high. The bonds were sold at a discount of 2 percent, and Henry Armstrong's syndicate had taken a commission of 5 percent. Over and above this a sum of seventy-five thousand dollars seemed to be missing; it was never recovered, and eventually it had to be written off as a loss. Then there were other costs, unsuspected when the loan act was framed. In the end it appeared that the kingdom had paid about a quarter of a million dollars to raise one million dollars—and this did not include interest charges. It might have been cheaper to put up with Spreckels, but of course by the end of 1886 Kalakaua was not about to weigh pennies in the balance of power and prestige.

The Empire of the Calabash

The planters and businessmen, who might have been expected to appreciate Kalakaua's victory over Spreckels, examined the freedom their king had bought and decided it did not suit them. "While former Cabinets were piloting and steering the ship of State, with Mr. Spreckels behind the curtain as prompter, we felt safe, although things were not quite to our liking," wrote one man with a conveniently short memory, "but now I feel that we are drifting—drifting upon an unknown sea, with neither compass, chart nor rudder, and where we will fetch up nobody knows." Spreckels in retrospect, then, was not as bad as Kalakaua and Gibson in actuality.

As a matter of fact the king and his premier did seem to be setting a new and dangerous course on the wide Pacific Ocean, with nothing to guide them except Gibson's compelling but misty vision of the lines of power and influence among the islands. To be sure, Gibson was not the first to think of broadening the political interests of the kingdom. Years before, Robert Crichton Wyllie had corresponded at length with an enthusiast named Charles St. Julian, of Sydney, Australia, who wanted to see the Hawaiian kingdom become the "guide the guardian and the National head of a system of small sovereignties" in the Pacific. Nothing ever came of St. Julian's plans, but his ideas had not been forgotten entirely when Kalakaua came to the throne.

Kalakaua enjoyed thinking of himself as a man of importance in the Pacific. Gibson encouraged him, and so did Celso Caesar Moreno. During the legislative session of 1880 Gibson introduced a resolution that spoke of the kingdom's "Primacy in the family of Polynesian States," and called for the appointment of a royal commissioner who would travel among the islands of the Pacific, representing the "enlightened, humane and hospitable spirit" of the Hawaiian government. By this time Kalakaua's imagination, according to United States Minister James Comly, was "inflamed with the idea of gathering all the cognate races of the Islands of the Pacific into a great Polynesian Confederacy, over which he will reign."

Gibson kept playing with the idea of primacy after he became head of the cabinet in 1882, and in 1883 he raised the enterprise to the diplomatic level when he framed a resolution opposing any new annexations by the great powers in the Pacific. This "Hawaiian Protest" was delivered to twenty-six governments. Very few of them were directly concerned with the Pacific; fewer still answered, and their answers were barely polite.

Gibson was not conscious of any rebuff. In 1885 he sent another sheaf of documents to the great powers; again his letters were received with impassivity. Late in the same year the Hawaiian minister to the United States, Henry A. P. Carter, the kingdom's most experienced diplomat, was commissioned to make what Gibson called a political reconnaissance. The idea was to have the Hawaiian kingdom recognized as a leader in a "more complete political organization" of the Pacific islands. Carter was well received at the chancelleries of the great powers but somehow he always seemed to have arrived just too late: annexations had only recently been made here, there, and everywhere, and could not be rescinded. Nothing but self-denial would change things, and the imperial nations were not in a self-denying mood.

So far the stones Gibson had thrown in the Pacific at Honolulu were making very few ripples elsewhere in the ocean. The thing was to imitate the masters, and use bigger stones. Kalakaua's Board of Genealogy made the convenient discovery that in ancient times the Hawaiian kingdom had included within its borders Ocean Island, a tiny dot on the map far to the north west of the Hawaiian archipelago, and all the intervening atolls and reefs. In September 1886, Kalakaua and Gibson arranged to have them annexed. Gibson put it to the United States that Midway Island, American since 1867, was a natural link in this chain of islands and should be given up, but Secretary of State Thomas F. Bayard could not bring himself to agree.

This was not much more than a gesture, but at the same time Gibson was planning greater things. He had begun to interest himself in the question of the Samoan Islands, one of the few remaining independent archipelagoes in the Pacific. Gibson was not the only one whose attention was on Samoa. Two rival chiefs, Malietoa and Tamasese, claimed the title of king, but if something called sovereignty really existed it was hard to tell who embodied it. Civil war was always a possibility among the natives, and three great powers, Germany, Britain, and the United States, each made special claims in that quarter of the Pacific. Germany pushed hard to control affairs, and Britain and the United States were alternately afraid to involve themselves too heavily and afraid to leave things to the Germans, who obviously wanted to annex the whole Samoan group.

Into these troubled waters Kalakaua and Gibson boldly despatched a Hawaiian embassy. On December 23, 1886, John E. Bush, a part-Hawaiian who had been a member of cabinet earlier in Kalakaua's reign, was commissioned as the king's "Envoy Extraordinary and Minister Plenipotentiary near His Majesty the King of Samoa," and, for good measure, near the King of Tonga and the chiefs and peoples of Polynesia generally. Bush took with him his family, a secretary named Henry F. Poor, and an artist, J. D. Strong, who was to paint views of Polynesian places and people. Bush was instructed to present himself to Malietoa, who at that point was recognized as king by Britain and the United States and by at least a part of the Samoan population, though his rival Tamasese had a following and was supported by the Germans. If Malietoa showed any interest at all in a confederation with the Hawaiian kingdom Bush was to invite him to speak his mind privately. If a working alliance came into being perhaps Tonga could be encouraged to join, and then the Cook Islands.

Bush promised Malietoa the Grand Cross of the Royal Order of the Star of Oceania (one of Kalakaua's inspirations), wined and dined the Samoan court, broached the idea of a confederation, and got a good response. "My wits, this evening, was ready at hand," Bush wrote to Kalakaua, "and, I manage to satisfy the King, it was for his benefit as well as for his country . . ." Malietoa consulted his parliamentary advisers, and on February 17, 1887, he signed an agreement with Bush. Celebrations began immediately and went on all night.

The great powers were much less enthusiastic. When news of the projected confederation became public, the United States warned Kalakaua and Gibson in a friendly way that they were out of their depth; Germany refused to take the alliance seriously, but thought there were indications that Bush was a stalking horse for the Americans, who might suddenly annex Samoa; and Great Britain interpreted Gibson's plans for Hawaiian primacy as an attempt to sow "anarchy and disorder." Gibson expressed astonishment and indignation at these agitated responses to "the friendly greeting which King Kalakaua sends to his brother Polynesian monarch."

At the same time he was working to give added weight to the Hawaiian program of primacy. Not long after Bush left for Samoa the Cabinet Council authorized the purchase of a gunboat for the kingdom. Nothing so formidable was ever bought, but Gibson did bring into existence a new Hawaiian Navy—one ship, the *Kaimiloa,* a guano trader converted at great expense into a training vessel, equipped with four brass cannon and two Gatling guns, commanded by a chronic drunkard named George E. Gresley Jackson, a former lieutenant in the British Navy, and manned by a crew of sixty-three, twenty-four of them boys from the Honolulu Reformatory School, where Jackson had been principal.

Gibson's critics had great fun with the *Kaimiloa.* The newly designed naval ensign, a flag showing a yellow shield decorated with a kapu stick and two kahilis, topped by a gold crown, all on a white field, looked to the *Hawaiian Gazette* like a "drumstick on a crown, on a shield, two dustbrushes, the whole on a field changeable with an impenetrable haze." The Hawaiian ambassadors, lurching from lagoon to lagoon in the South Seas under their new colors, could think

> *How prospered the alliance grand*
> *Among the Chiefs of Isles of sand*
> *By the eternal trade winds fanned;*
> *How there amid the breaker's dash*
> *Is planted, now with armed clash*
> *The Empire of the Calabash!*

Gibson tried to explain that the influence of the *Kaimiloa* would be primarily moral, whatever that meant. Moral or martial, her influence would not be felt at Samoa for some time; under a full head of steam, and burning four to six tons of coal a day, she could make five or six knots. The *Kaimiloa* left Honolulu in the middle of May 1887. For the first eleven days of the voyage Captain Jackson was too drunk to navigate with any precision; when he recovered he found his chronometers were not working properly; and the *Kaimiloa* made her Samoan landfall on June 14, 1887, more than one degree of longitude off her intended course.

Samoa was becoming a crowded and busy place, but the Pacific was a big ocean, and reliable information about the activities of the Hawaiian embassy and the existence of a Hawaiian Navy took a long time to reach the capital cities of the great Pacific powers, the more so since Gibson, for his own inscrutable reasons, had not been candid with Kalakaua's representatives at Washington, London, and Berlin. Great Britain, Germany, and the United States were getting ready to meet at Washington to discuss the Samoan question, and they made it clear that the Hawaiian government was not entitled to a seat at the conference, and that whatever Kalakaua and Gibson were up to, it was an impertinence that should cease at once.

The members of the Samoan embassy knew nothing about this. They had been hoping the *Kaimiloa* would be commissioned as a man of war, and they were disappointed to find that she was not to be used as a fighting ship. "I think," wrote Henry Poor to the Hawaiian ministry of foreign affairs, "you should have given us discretionary powers with regard to Samoa and let us have the key to one of the padlocks which hold your 'dogs of war' It might not be necessary to fire a shot but it would be foolish to bluff Tamasese without we knew we could fall back on powder and shot. I believe his reconciliation could be promptly secured if he realised we would show our teeth."

Some people in Samoa were already convinced that the Hawaiian kingdom was showing a tooth or two. By making a treaty with Malietoa, Kalakaua was indicating that he did not regard Tamasese as a legitimate claimant for the title of king; and Tamasese was the Germans' favorite. Everywhere Bush and his men went they were followed by Germans.

When the *Kaimiloa* arrived and began making short trips between islands she was shadowed by the German corvette *Adler;* and the German consul called for an attack squadron to support the *Adler.* The impossible was on the verge of becoming possible: the German Empire might be about to declare war on the Hawaiian kingdom.

But even a short experience with Ambassador Bush and Captain Jackson of the *Kaimiloa* made it hard for anyone to think of them as serious imperialists. Less than a month after Malietoa signed the articles of confederation his assistant secretary of state wrote to Gibson about Bush's "disreputable" conduct and his "intemperate" habits. "He is the most dissipated man who had held a high position at this place for many years. His associates here are mostly of the lowest kind of half castes and whites." And less than a month after the *Kaimiloa* arrived some of her crew mutinied and had to be forcibly restrained by the captain of the *Adler* from blowing up the powder magazine of their own ship.

Expressions of annoyance and veiled warnings from the great powers were accumulating at Honolulu even before the *Kaimiloa* sailed, and not long after she left, Gibson began to have serious doubts about what he had done. Germany might go to war against the Hawaiian kingdom; probably the best thing to do was to follow the advice of Britain and the United States and recall Bush and Jackson from Samoa. A year before, Gibson had told the legislature that the great powers had a high regard for the Hawaiian kingdom, and that the future was full of hope. "What was Prussia but a one-horse State a few years ago, and others that can be mentioned? What was Rome but a one-horse State at its beginning? . . . What are we in the midst of the broad Pacific that great nations should send their captains and officers to do honor to us . . . The Great Powers never think of us as a one-horse State." But quite obviously they did. The embarrassing truth was that Gibson had made a serious miscalculation about the lines of force and influence among the islands of the ocean, and on June 10 he wrote a letter recalling the Samoan embassy, "to avoid any possible appearance of any indiscretion or precipitancy," so that the great powers would not have "the slightest grounds of apprehension as to our conduct." It was late in the day for that. Gibson wrote, as a matter of fact, before the *Kaimiloa* even reached Samoa, but his letter went astray and was not delivered for more than a month, and this last bungle gave Bush and Jackson more than enough time to be as indiscreet and precipitate as their worst enemies could have wished. For all practical purposes, however, the short and melancholy life of the Empire of the Calabash was at an end. Gibson would have to think again about the nature of his elusive inheritance.

A Cloud on the Sun

Ever since Kalakaua came to the throne the planters and business-men had been telling him, through their newspapers at Honolulu, that it was a wise ruler who paid attention to well-meant advice from the influential inhabitants of his kingdom. Some of the king's native admirers took an opposite view. White men who criticized the Hawaiian monarchy were overstepping themselves, especially those who had never bothered to take out naturalization papers, and the others who, though born at the islands, reserved their ultimate loyalty for the land of their fathers and saved their scorn for the land of their childhood.

Premier Gibson was magnanimous in the face of criticism. The monarchy, he was fond of saying, was willing to give anyone a hearing. If a man had a grievance the constitution offered him any number of means of redress. Let him petition the king, or publish a newspaper, or go to law, or, if he really meant what he said about his interest in the kingdom, let him become a citizen and vote or run for office.

Gibson was at his most irritating when he spoke like this. It was clear to his opponents that he and Kalakaua had run roughshod over the constitution: they had subverted the legislature, purged the civil service of all but sycophants, and they were planning to pack the supreme court; and to top it all off they were on their way to bankrupting the kingdom.

This last point alone would have been enough to outrage some of the planters. To them, money was sacred and politicians and civil servants ought to approach it with reverence. Economical government, attentive to the needs of commerce, was what was needed. "Mr. Gibson can govern till doomsday," said the *Planters' Monthly* in a moment of desperate expansiveness, "provided the government is good." But to others—businessmen and professional men at Honolulu for the most part—a balanced budget was not enough. It should be the reflection of a balanced national life, and Gibson could not guarantee that. A good government should spend money conservatively, to be sure, and keep reliable books, but it was more important still that looseness and excess of any kind, political or moral, should not be allowed to flourish in ruling circles.

By these strict standards Kalakaua and Gibson governed badly, and their critics took pains to point out to them what might happen if bad government went on too long. News of revolution in Europe was played up in the English language papers, and whenever some hapless monarch was dethroned or exiled or assassinated a spate of editorials drew attention to the need for a good understanding between king and people.

But understanding was hard to come by between a willful Hawaiian king and a headstrong white opposition, and in the end a number of white men concluded that a capacity for good government was determined genetically. A congregation of American Protestants listening to Sereno E. Bishop, son of a Protestant missionary, preach a Thanksgiving Day sermon at Fort Street Church in Honolulu, heard him give thanks that he was white; the mass of the non-Teutonic, non-English-speaking population of the kingdom, he said, was "low in mental culture," and nothing could be expected of such inferior people. Others spoke of the "rottenness" of Kalakaua's regime, and the *Hawaiian Gazette* talked of Premier Gibson's government as a boil that should be halved and quartered, probed and squeezed.

Beneficial surgery was needed, then, but until 1887 the instrument was not at hand. Mass meetings were good only for emotional bloodletting; petitions, however strongly they were worded, seemed to make no impression on Kalakaua; and attempts to build a strong political party of opposition ran into the dismal fact that Kalakaua and Gibson controlled too many votes. In 1880 a slate of Independents was drawn up, but after six years Reform had not got very far. The king still dominated the legislature. Almost every one of the twenty-eight royal candidates in the election of 1886 was on the government's payroll; all of them were natives, except one, and the sole white man was Premier Gibson's son-in-law, Fred H. Hayselden.

This in itself was a demonstration that the Hawaiian was not altogether unteachable politically; he had grasped at least certain elements of Western government. But, said the political correspondent of the *Planters' Monthly,* "he does not yet realize that to all this power there are necessarily some bounds and limits fixed, as well as the moral and personal obligations attending it . . . The white man has organized for the native a Government, placed the ballot in his hands, and set him up as a lawmaker and a ruler; but the placing of these powers in his hands before he knows how to use them, is like placing sharp knives, pointed instruments and dangerous tools in the hands of infants."

So the Hawaiian must be disarmed and saved from himself—again. Just as the Protestant missionaries, seventy years before, had come to save the natives from pagan debauchery, now another tiny band of righteous men would save them once more, this time from self-government. It was a matter of moral duty for those who loved the Hawaiian people and their islands (though the natives would have said that white men loved only those parts of the islands they owned). It was a matter of racial right for those who believed in the destiny of the white man. It was, finally, a matter of self-interest. When these arguments were set out it was hard for white men to find reasons why things should be allowed to go on as they were.

Of all the haoles in the kingdom none took his duties and rights and self-interest more to heart than Lorrin A. Thurston, grandson of the pioneer Protestant missionary Asa Thurston. Young Thurston was a student at Punahou School when Kalakaua was elected king in 1874, and when the followers of Queen Emma rioted at the Honolulu courthouse he and some of his friends played truant to watch. This minor delinquency was the last Thurston ever admitted to, but as a fledgling lawyer with a strong sense of right and wrong, he saw delinquency, political and moral, all around him during Kalakaua's reign—the stuffing of ballot boxes and the selling of offices, the drinking of too much gin, the dancing of the hula, the smuggling and smoking of opium.

With the encouragement of Sanford Dole, another missionary boy, Thurston went into reform politics in the eighties. He wrote some of the *Hawaiian Gazette*'s most sarcastic political columns; he edited the *Daily Bulletin,* another opposition journal, for several months; and in 1886 he ran for office as an Independent candidate for the combined districts of Molokai and Lanai. The government sent fifty special constables to look after the king's interests at the polls; Thurston and his friends hired fifty strong young men at five dollars a day to keep an eye on the constables. Thurston was elected, and one of his first acts in the legislature was to demand and carry out an investigation of Premier Gibson's influence on the balloting on Lanai.

Thurston and Sanford Dole emerged as leaders of a small but hostile opposition party in the Assembly of 1886. They were tireless and fearless debaters, and they were on their feet a great deal. Thurston in particular never missed an opportunity to embarrass the king's party. Early in the session a bill was introduced to control the sale of liquor. One clause barred habitual drunkards from buying alcoholic drinks. Minister of Finance John M. Kapena rose, drunk, to argue against the bill on the grounds that no one could tell who was a habitual drunkard and who was not. Thurston thought it could be done—he could see one before him. He moved that "Ministers of the Crown" be included in the provisions of the bill. By a vote of the Assembly he was ordered to apologize. He spoke at length, but his speech was hardly an apology, as the journal of the legislature showed.

"I consider," said Thurston, talking about Kapena, "that the presence of a member of the House in such a state, be he a Representative, Noble or Minister, is an insult to this Assembly and disgrace to this nation, and it would be perfectly in order to move that he should be removed from the House by the Sergeant-at-Arms and ordered to apologize to the Assembly. (Sensation) If a man can lead a dissolute drunken life, to the neglect of his duties, and at the same time occupy one of the highest offices in trust in the gift of a nation—

The Minister of Foreign Affairs (excitedly) 'Silence sir! Stop!'

The Minister of the Interior (in union) 'Order! Mr. President!'

The Minister of Foreign Affairs. 'Mr. President, this is too bad! disgraceful!'

Representative Thurston (continuing and speaking rapidly)—unchecked and unrebuked, he becomes a moral plague spot and a debauching influence on the whole civil service and the entire community."

Thurston was the perfect Independent. It was obvious that he lived and breathed Reform. One of the native members of the Assembly noticed that when Sanford Dole got up to speak he did not shake his fists at the members of the cabinet; but Thurston "talked very loud and gesticulated violently." Perhaps it was "a peculiarity of the hon. member, that he could not speak in any other way. The clenching of his fists was very significant."

Other people thought so too. Toward the end of 1886 Thurston had a conversation about clenched fists and Reform with one of his friends, a physician named S. G. Tucker. As Thurston recalled the occasion in his memoirs, he was standing at his front gate when Tucker drew up in his buggy and said: "Thurston, how long are we going to stand this kind of thing?" "What kind of thing?" asked Thurston. "The running away with the community by Kalakaua," said Tucker, "his interference with elections, and running the Legislature for his own benefit, and all that." "Well," said Thurston, "what can we do about it?" "I suggest," said Tucker, "that we form an organization, including all nationalities, which shall force him to be decent, and reign, not rule, or take the consequences."

Thurston talked things over with a number of trustworthy men—his friend William A. Kinney; Sanford Dole, William R. Castle, Nathaniel B. Emerson, and W. E. Rowell, all of them descended from Protestant missionaries; Peter Cushman Jones of C. Brewer and Co.; Clarence W. Ashford, a Canadian-born lawyer; Alatau T. Atkinson, a schoolteacher and opposition journalist; and several others. They all agreed that Tucker's idea was a sound one, and in January 1887, the first meetings of the Hawaiian League were held. Thurston drew up a constitution, and the founders memorized it and then destroyed the written version; it was too dangerous to keep, so they thought. As Thurston recollected the wording, the League was described as a voluntary organization, to secure "efficient, decent and honest government in Hawaii," and its members pledged their lives, property, and "sacred honor" to this purpose. They also swore to keep the existence of the League secret.

The secret was not kept perfectly. Thurston and William Kinney administered the oath to new members in their law office, and their partner, William O. Smith, could not help hearing what was going on. Other people, as well, guessed what was afoot. By the middle of 1887 the League had more than four hundred members. Dr. Tucker had spoken of admitting "all nationalities." What he meant was white men of all nationalities. No Orientals need apply, and no Hawaiian names appeared on the list Thurston kept in a notebook; a handful of part-Hawaiians with Western names did join, but they were far outnumbered by Americans, Britishers, Germans and Portuguese.

The question of how to deal with Kalakaua was discussed at length. Should he be allowed to keep the throne as a figurehead in a constitutional monarchy? Should he be made to abdicate in favor of a republic? And if so, then what—independence or annexation to the United States? Clarence Ashford's brother and legal partner Volney, who had the wildest and spikiest military mustache in the kingdom and a mind to match, wanted to kill the king and have done with it, then fill government offices with members of the League. This was far too strong even for Lorrin Thurston's tastes, and Sanford Dole and Peter Jones, two solid members of the executive Committee of Thirteen, resigned when it appeared as if the radicals might get hold of the organization.

Volney Ashford's political ideas were frightening, but his martial skills were an asset. Early in 1887 he took command of the Honolulu Rifles, an all-white volunteer militia company, drilled them into a high state of efficiency, and put them at the service of the League. Ashford started with a single company and soon added three more, one of them composed of Portuguese. About a hundred Germans, optimistically calling themselves the Drei Hundert or Three Hundred, attached themselves to Ashford as well. Consignments of arms and ammunition kept arriving at Honolulu addressed to Castle & Cooke, E. O. Hall & Son, and to the surprising shop of Mrs. Thomas Lack, who advertised threads and silks, corsets, dress patterns, sewing machines, sporting goods, shotguns, and rifles. By June, Colonel Ashford had more than two hundred men under arms.

It would be convenient for the League to be able to say that Kalakaua and Gibson brought their downfall on themselves, and in a sense they did. The reputation of the regime had sunk very low during the legislative session of 1886, and nothing happened in 1887 to improve matters—the London loan turned out to be expensive, in fact the next thing to a confidence trick; the Samoan embassy departed for the South Pacific, followed by the *Kaimiloa,* trailing black smoke and gin fumes; and then a splendid scandal, just what the League wanted, burst about the head of the king.

One of the measures passed by the Assembly of 1886 changed the law regulating the use of opium in the kingdom. Opium had come to the islands with the first Chinese coolies, and the traffic grew by leaps and bounds. Beginning in 1860 licenses to sell the drug were auctioned by the government, and by 1874 a monopoly cost the successful bidder more than forty-five thousand dollars. Then a law was passed prohibiting the use of opium altogether. But great quantities were smuggled into the kingdom; by 1884 fourteen hundred cases of illegal possession and sale had come before the courts. Two acts to re-open the traffic under license were vetoed by the king in the early eighties. In 1886 he changed his mind and signed a licensing act into law, over the loud protests of Thurston and the other Independents.

A rice planter named Tong Kee, usually known as Aki, wanted the license, which was supposed to be priced at no less than thirty thousand dollars. The government's registrar of conveyances, Junius Kaae, told Aki the king might be able to help. Following Kaae's instructions, Aki took Kalakaua thirty thousand dollars in gold and certificates of deposit, for which he got no receipt. Then he was told that it was not enough, that a second bidder had come on the scene. Aki raised another thirty thousand dollars, and then eleven thousand more. He visited the king's bungalow in the palace grounds, always by night, carrying his tribute in a basket, and bringing as well a small baked pig as a ceremonial gift. After all this Aki did not get the opium license; the cabinet awarded it to the merchant Chun Lung for eighty thousand dollars. Aki thought that at the very least he ought to get his money back, but Kalakaua told him it was all gone, used up in paying the royal debts. Aki swore out an affidavit, got others to do the same, and took the documents to the *Hawaiian Gazette*.

"These are incontrovertable facts," said the *Gazette*. "They are backed up by sixty odd pages of sworn affidavits, by fourteen persons, establishing them beyond a possibility of doubt. The only question is whether Kaae got any of the money, or whether the King kept it all. Both admit that the money was paid, but each points his thumb over his shoulder at the other and says 'he did it.'" This was not quite true. Kalakaua said nothing at all. But that in itself was damaging enough.

The opium scandal broke at the end of May 1887, while Premier Gibson was trying to get out from under the wreckage of his program for the primacy of the Pacific. This combination of troubles abroad and at home was enough to create a crisis for the government, and the Hawaiian League and the Honolulu Rifles were more than ready to take advantage of it.

One of the constant complaints of the opposition had been that Kalakaua, Generalissimo of the armed forces of the kingdom, spent too much money on military flourishes. Now the efficiency of the king's army and navy was about to be tested. No one could call the *Kaimiloa* a threat of any kind, except perhaps to the reputation of the kingdom, and Kalakaua was uncomfortably aware that the only well-organized military company was the Honolulu Rifles, whose members at that moment were drawing a bead on his crown. A few months earlier Kalakaua had attended an exhibition drill and dance staged by the Rifles, and he had presented Colonel Volney Ashford with a Hawaiian flag. Ashford accepted the flag, "this beautiful emblem," as he called it, "of the unity of many peoples who, blended together on a benignant basis of political and race equality, combine to form the Kingdom of Hawaii, of which Your Majesty is the honored Sovereign." Kalakaua said he confided in the patriotism of the Rifles. A strange occasion—Kalakaua must have known that Ashford and a good many other members of the Rifles were also members of the Hawaiian League, and Ashford must have known that the king knew. Now it was June, and the League and the Rifles had made up their minds that political and racial equality were not worth talking about any more, and that Kalakaua was a king without honor.

Gibson, whose whole life had been one long storm at sea, was an expert at gauging the strength of political turbulence, and he thought the situation was serious. "The tempest," he wrote in his diary, "seems to be rushing to climax." The staff at the Honolulu customhouse was ordered to report on any unusually large consignments of arms and ammunition. Iolani Palace was barricaded, the royal guard was doubled, cannon emplacements were dug in the grounds, and a new invention, electric light, was installed so the whole area could be lit at night.

Did this mean, the *Hawaiian Gazette* wanted to know, that Gibson and Kalakaua proposed to continue their course of "plunder and defiance," and were they ready to "shoot down the citizens of this community who may have the termerity to object? If this is what it means, we warn the King and the Government that they are treading on dangerous ground." It was difficult to tell from this kind of utterance where sovereignty lay—the *Gazette* made it sound as if white men were the only "citizens of the country" who mattered, and the king emerged as the prime subverter of public order. The League, in fact, was moving toward revolution.

The diplomats at Honolulu all received petitions from their nationals asking for help in establishing good government, and the opposition newspapers called for a public meeting. On June 27 United States Minister George W. Merrill visited Kalakaua at Iolani Palace, and the king asked him what could be done. Merrill said there was unanimity among the "tax payers" on several points. Gibson must go; the new cabinet must be made up of men who had the confidence of the community; and Kalakaua must stop meddling in governmental business.

The only course left open to Kalakaua at this stage was to decide who should be thrown to the wolves first. The choice, not surprisingly, fell upon Gibson. During the night he and the other cabinet ministers were asked to resign, and next morning the news was on the streets in special editions of the English language newspapers.

The supporters of the League wanted to see this change for the better made permanent, and notices were posted calling for a public meeting on June 30. On the morning of the meeting Kalakaua and the acting governor of Oahu ordered troops into the streets to keep the peace and protect government buildings against possible violence. The only militia company up to the assignment was the Honolulu Rifles, and as Sanford Dole said, "while the troops were patrolling the streets under nominal orders of the government, they were actually under orders of the league." The revolution was over before it started.

Business came to a halt for the public meeting, which was held at the armory of the Honolulu Rifles. Outside, the Rifles, those who were not on duty elsewhere in the town, were lined up in uniform. Inside, Peter Jones was chosen chairman, and he called on Lorrin Thurston to read a number of resolutions. Thurston stood up to speak dressed in his Rifles uniform. First, he said, a new cabinet must be named by the king. Second, Gibson must be dismissed from every post he held. Third, the king should pay back the money he had taken from Aki. Fourth, Junius Kaae must be removed from office. Fifth, the king must promise to reign, not rule— no more interfering in elections, influencing legislators, coercing cabinet members, or using his official position for private purposes.

Kalakaua had already met the first two conditions by dismissing Gibson's cabinet and asking the merchant William Lowthian Green to form a new ministry. This was made known to the meeting by the banker Charles R. Bishop. Thurston spoke again, to great applause. The king's reorganization of the cabinet, he said, reminded him of a story. "I remember reading somewhere of a man who was going to shoot a coon, and the coon said: 'Don't shoot; I'll come down.' The King is the coon and this meeting is the gun." Two dozen speeches were heard altogether, some inflammatory, some less so. The consensus of the meeting was that a new constitution should be framed at once. A Committee of Thirteen waited on the king, and he promised them an early answer. Even then, apparently, Kalakaua had hopes of finding a way out. He asked the diplomats if they would take charge of the government. They advised him to make his peace with the League and the Rifles. He could do no other. He drew up a letter, indicating his "gratification" that his people had taken the "usual constitutional step in presenting their grievances," and surrendered his authority on every disputed point. As for the opium bribe, he said, he did not admit the truth of the accusations, but he was ready to let the new cabinet settle the matter. The Committee of Thirteen got a copy of this letter on the afternoon of July 1, and on the same day the new cabinet took office—William Green, Premier and Minister of Finance; Godfrey Brown, British by birth and Hawaiian by citizenship, Minister of Foreign Affairs; Lorrin Thurston, Minister of the Interior; and Clarence Ashford, Attorney General. All of them were members of the Hawaiian League. Without any question Reform was in the saddle.

Volney Ashford's Rifles had been on the streets since the time of the mass meeting, and when a rumor was heard that Gibson was planning to leave quietly for San Francisco his house was put under surveillance. While the king was preparing his letter of capitulation another rumor swept the town—a big consignment of guns had arrived at the customs-house, and they had not been ordered by the League or the Rifles. The Rifles impounded them, but Ashford did not stop there; he thought the time had come to make an example. Gibson and his son-in-law Fred Hayselden were marched down to the waterfront, and there Ashford got ready to hang Gibson from the yardarm of a sailing ship in the harbor. Lorrin Thurston and some other members of the League's Committee of Thirteen asked Ashford what he thought he was doing, and Ashford said he wanted to strike terror into the community. The Committee had less terrible plans for Gibson and Hayselden. They were charged with "high crimes and misdemeanors," specifically embezzlement, and bound over for trial.

Lorrin Thurston and the other constitution makers had a draft ready to show the king on July 6. "The cabinet," recalled Clarence Ashford, "proceeded in a body to the Blue Room of the Palace for the purpose of submitting it to the King and of requiring his signature and oath thereto." Kalakaua kept them waiting for a period "commensurate with regal dignity in the premises," and when he came in and bowed to the cabinet ministers there was "a thundercloud on his brow, that bespoke no pleasant prospect ahead. The document was read to His Majesty, who listened in sullen, and somewhat appalling silence. And then came a general silence, followed by an inquiry from Mr. Green, whether His Majesty approved and would sign the document. This was the signal for the opening of argument, which proceeded until about sundown of that long summer day. The King argued, protested, inquired as to the effect of certain phases of the changes made by the new, in the former Constitution, and for considerable periods appeared to be gazing into space and weighing the probabilities of success in the event of a refusal . . . I have spoken of the thundercloud which rested upon his brow throughout the greater period of that long interview, and of the sullen and forbidding countenance which he then presented. But, at the end, all those sinister signs and symbols dissolved into a smile, as sweet as seraphs wear, as, with apparent alacrity, the King reached for a pen and attached his signature to that instrument whereby he was reduced from the status of an autocrat to that of a constitutional Sovereign."

Gibson and Hayselden had been arraigned on charges of embezzlement in police court on the morning of the same day. After years of accusations about their personal corruption the hearing was anticlimactic. Their books and papers were examined. Attorney General Ashford concluded that there was no evidence to substantiate the charges against them, and they were freed.

Gibson left for San Francisco on July 12, traveling, he said, for his health. This was not the usual face-saving remark; Gibson was, in fact, dying of tuberculosis. He gave some even-tempered interviews to the San Francisco newspapers and then went straight to the hospital.

His tormentors at Honolulu would not let him be, even at a distance of several thousand miles. Late in 1887 he was sued in his absence for breach of promise of marriage by Mrs. Flora Howard St. Clair, a traveling book agent who had called on him at Honolulu. Gibson, said Mrs. St. Clair, bought some of her etchings, talked about his lonely life, assured her that he was white of hair but green of heart, and proposed marriage. Gibson, in San Francisco, told the newspapers that Mrs. St. Clair had shown him sample copies of her etchings, "French art" of the "nudity order," and that she had compared her own beauty favorably with that of the etched Venus she was offering for sale. Gibson said he had been a widower for forty years, and it was unlikely that at his age he would propose marriage to a book agent, the widow of a gambler. He put the whole thing down as a conspiracy. Mrs. St. Clair, he said, was in the pay of his political enemies. Her attorneys, by no coincidence at all, were Lorrin Thurston, William Kinney, and William Smith.

Mrs. St. Clair had the best of it. The jury was out for an hour, and when they came back they awarded her damages of ten thousand dollars. Fred Hayselden settled for eight thousand on Gibson's behalf. The verdict was regarded as an excellent joke at Gibson's expense, and a minstrel song about "Pa Gibby's Wooin'" was sung to loud laughter at Honolulu:

> *Poor Gibsy's in a hospital, or was at last reportin',*
> *A prey to ills of flesh and mind, and sick of Widder courtin';*
> *He'd only hugged and kissed her twice, and didn't muss no collars,*
> *But, jest for dat, he had to pay a cool eight thousand dollars!*

Gibson was past caring. His disease was in the last stage. He died on January 21, 1888. He had always wanted a funeral in the islands, and his body was brought back to Honolulu for burial. It was placed on view in Arion Hall, close to the courthouse and the palace. Now that Gibson could not bother the reformers any more, the *Daily Bulletin* was ready to lay him to rest gently. "Thus we have seen the last on earth of a remarkable man, a man of varied attainments and diversified experiences. He had his friends, and he had his enemies. Let us speak kindly of the dead, if our profession of Christianity is anything more than a hollow pretence."

Lorrin Thurston had some business at the courthouse on the day Gibson's body was put on view. Sanford Dole was there with his brother George, and he suggested that they all go to see "old Gibson" for the last time. "So," Thurston recalled, "we joined the line moving past the bier. When I got to a place where I could look down into the coffin, I was shocked to see that an embalming fluid, with which the body had been treated, had turned it coal-black. Against that color, the snow-white hair and beard presented a startling contrast. While we went into the street, we were silent for some minutes. Then Sanford asked: 'What do you think of it?' After a pause, George Dole said deliberately: 'Well, I think his complexion is approximating the color of his soul.'"

CHAPTER SEVEN

Aloha Oe

1887—1900

Bulwarks of Liberty

THE CONSTITUTION makers of 1887 were the most conservative of revolutionaries. In the heat of the military moment, when they were getting ready to fire the shot that would be heard around the island of Oahu, a few of them compared themselves with the framers of the American Declaration of Independence, striking off freedom's fetters; but the document their leaders presented to Kalakaua showed a positive reverence for restraint. Having curbed an irresponsible native king, the reformers were not about to turn the country over to a masterless rabble of mixed origins. "I have," said one politically minded planter a few months before the crisis, "an exalted idea of the destiny of the white man and of his power to control and govern both men and elements." The constitution of 1887 was meant to perfect that power. Its provisions, according to its supporters, were "bulwarks of liberty." Of course, by definition a bulwark, a powerful safeguard or defense, would put walls between men; and if only those within the walls enjoyed the full benefit of the constitution, and others, in fact most people, were left outside, where was liberty?

The reformers were the first to admit that discrimination existed— they used the word themselves—but they believed that walls between people were necessary. "Advocates of universal suffrage may put forward what specious arguments of human equality they please," said the *Hawaiian Gazette,* "but it stands to reason the necessity of government lies as much in property rights as in anything else. Life and property are the two principal wards of organized government, as they are the only stakes men have to pledge in defense of established order." So discrimination, properly defined, was founded not on race but on "condition." Hawaiian natives who had been able to vote in elections for the House of Representatives could still do so, provided they paid their taxes and swore an oath to uphold the constitution of 1887; and now that the upper house of the legislature was elective rather than appointive they could vote for Nobles as well, provided they could meet the qualification—an income of six hundred dollars a year or taxable property worth three thousand dollars. If this qualification excluded two Hawaiian voters out of three, as it did, it was not aimed at them as a people; it simply offered them an incentive to better their condition as individuals and thus earn the right to take a responsible part in politics.

The new constitution said nothing about Hawaiian citizenship as a basis for voting. After a short period of residence in the islands a man could vote, and his oath to uphold the constitution did not affect his citizenship in the country of his birth. Here, however, discrimination became openly a matter of race. "Residents" of American or European parentage could vote; Orientals could not (except for those born in the kingdom, who could not very well be excluded from the franchise). It was the intention of the reformers to bar Oriental immigrants and even naturalized Chinese and Japanese from the polls, and the supreme court upheld this reading of the constitution. Once these bulwarks of liberty had been moved into place the Reform party was ready to go the polls. A special election in September 1887 gave Reform a handsome victory, demonstrating the proposition that foreign voters knew what was best for the country.

Immediately the question of the treaty of commercial reciprocity between the Hawaiian kingdom and the United States was taken up. Its original term had expired in 1883, and since then it had been renewed for twelve months at a time. The Hawaiian sugar industry depended for its prosperity on a privileged place in the American market, and whenever a reduction in the tariff or an abrogation of the treaty was suggested in the United States Congress there was great uneasiness at Honolulu.

In July 1887, the Hawaiian minister at Washington, Henry A. P. Carter, was in the middle of a series of talks with Thomas F. Bayard, Secretary of State in the Democratic administration of Grover Cleveland. Opinion in Congress was hardening in favor of a renewal of the treaty only on condition that the United States should be given exclusive use of Pearl Harbor as a naval station. This had been suggested in the eighteen seventies when the first reciprocity treaty was being negotiated, and Kalakaua had been strongly against the idea then. He was still against it.

Bayard kept telling Carter that the cession of Pearl Harbor would do the kingdom no harm: it would not mean any loss of independence, and things could be arranged so that the navy would vacate the harbor whenever the treaty was allowed to expire. Carter was persuaded; he suggested to his government that the longer the discussions were allowed to drag on the less chance there was of getting a renewal of the treaty, even with a cession of the harbor. Kalakaua was not moved. He told British Commissioner Wodehouse that he would "never ratify that Treaty," and that all native Hawaiians would oppose it.

The Reform cabinet felt no such qualms. Two weeks after the special election of September 1887, the cabinet council recommended that the treaty be renewed on the terms arranged by Bayard and Carter, and Kalakaua, who could no longer depend on support from the legislature, gave his reluctant approval. A "supplementary convention" containing the Pearl Harbor amendment was proclaimed at Honolulu on November 29, 1887.

With this out of the way the reformers could turn their attention to matters closer to home. In the special legislative session of 1887 and the regular session of 1888 they set themselves to remove every trace of Kalakaua's influence in the running of the kingdom. Under the new constitution no officer of government could be elected to the legislature, and no member of the legislature could be appointed to any civil office (except a ministerial post). This opened the way for a wholesale purge of the government service. After a long debate on the eve of the revolution the members of the Hawaiian League had decided against a spoils system; it would not go well with their announced principles of purity and honesty in government. So Kalakaua's appointees were to be dismissed only on grounds of incompetence, corruption, or "political offensiveness," and League members were to be preferred for jobs on the government's payroll only if "all other things were equal." Often enough, of course, the reformers and their friends turned out to be more equal than anyone else. On the floor of the assembly at the same time Kalakaua's favorite programs were being voted down one by one—the board of genealogists and the native Hawaiian board of health were abolished; the opium license law was repealed; the control of the kingdom's armed forces was taken from the royal Generalissimo and given to the minister of foreign affairs, and the Hawaiian Navy was abolished; the last members of the unfortunate Samoan embassy were recalled; the young Hawaiians being educated in Europe were ordered home.

The effect of all this was to knock Kalakaua over and bind him hand and foot. Worse still, the reformers seemed to enjoy kicking the king while he was down. They ordered an investigation of his part in the opium license scandal of 1886. Kalakaua admitted taking the money offered him by Aki, but he said the seventy-one thousand dollars was meant as a "gift." He was told to pay it back, and when he said, accurately, that he could not—he was about a quarter of a million dollars in debt—his financial affairs were put in the hands of trustees. At the same time another embarrassing case was making its way through the courts. During the elections of 1886 Kalakaua had used his royal exemption from customs duties to free fourteen thousand dollars worth of liquor from the bonded warehouse at Honolulu, and he spread it lavishly among the ten thousand native voters of the kingdom. Now his letters to the staff of the customshouse were read in open court, and the *Hawaiian Gazette* published them word for word. Kalakaua took this as a "personal affront" aimed at him by the Reform cabinet, and he felt the wound so deeply that he asked his ministers to resign. But once again his hands were tied: under the new constitution the king could appoint ministers, but only a vote of no confidence in the legislature could remove them from office.

The reformers obviously hoped the king would give up the struggle and resign himself to life as a ceremonial monarch, but Kalakaua kept looking for ways to make his presence felt. The constitution gave him one possible opening—the use of the royal veto. Under the old constitution the king's veto had been absolute; now it could be overridden by a two-thirds vote in the legislature. The reformers took it for granted that Kalakaua would not exercise the veto without the advice of his ministers, but Kalakaua was in no mood to take advice from a cabinet whose most headstrong members, Lorrin Thurston and Clarence Ashford, were using every opportunity to humiliate him. He saw his ministers as little as possible, and he would not talk to Ashford at all.

In the special session of 1887 five bills sent to Kalakaua to be signed into law were returned to the legislature, and they had to be passed again with a two-thirds majority. The question of the king's independent veto was put before the supreme court, and to the reformers' surprise the court decided in favor of Kalakaua. Attorney General Ashford was disgusted, but for the moment nothing could be done; cabinet and legislature would have to put up with the noise of Kalakaua rattling his constitutional chains.

Lorrin Thurston was half convinced that the king might try something desperate to free himself. Once, Thurston recalled, he paid an official visit to Kalakaua at the Bungalow, a building in the grounds of Iolani Palace, and while he was sitting with his back to a door that opened onto a hallway he heard a shuffling of feet and some whispering outside. "Any persons there," he thought, "easily could have opened the door and attacked me from behind." Thurston remembered that King Alexander Liholiho, thirty years before, had shot his private secretary and had escaped indictment because he was held to be above the law. "In the light of Kalakaua's very obvious dislike of me, I did not propose to subject myself to any such treatment by him, directly or indirectly, without means of defense. Therefore, and thenceforth, during the entire three years of my cabinet incumbency, I carried a loaded six-shooter in my coat pocket whenever I had to go to the Palace alone. If the King made any attempt to take advantage of his official immunity for assault on me, I should be in a position to counter, without waiting for an official indictment." Thurston never had to use his revolver.

Red Shirts

Before 1887 Kalakaua behaved as if he were convinced he could do no wrong; after the revolution people acted as if he could do nothing right—except perhaps abdicate. Kalakaua was childless, and his younger brother, William Pitt Leleiohoku, named to succeed him, had died in 1877. Next in line for the throne was his sister Liliuokalani. Toward the end of 1887 two members of the Reform legislature, William R. Castle and James I. Dowsett, Jr., asked Liliuokalani privately if she would consider taking the throne, and she did not reject the idea out of hand.

Castle and Dowsett wanted to get rid of Kalakaua because he was obstreperous; others at Honolulu thought he was craven, and that a stronger monarch was needed. Early in 1888 Liliuokalani was approached by a group of native Hawaiians, and she sent them to Kalakaua to suggest, using "only respectful words and no threats," that he might give way to her. Kalakaua answered that everyone should "wait a while."

One man did not see much virtue in waiting. This was Robert W. Wilcox, born on Maui in 1855 of a Hawaiian mother and an American father. Wilcox served his apprenticeship in Hawaiian politics under Walter Murray Gibson, and in 1880 he was chosen to go with Celso Caesar Moreno to be educated in Italy. After the Reform cabinet cut off his support he came home, bringing with him a "fair knowledge" of engineering and military tactics, a splendid officer's uniform, an aristocratic Italian wife, and an infatuation with military flourishes and political intrigue.

Wilcox saw himself as a kind of Hawaiian Garibaldi, but there was no place at Honolulu for his exotic talents. The reformers were busy redistributing patronage in the civil service, and any friend of Gibson's was no friend of theirs. Wilcox finally got a job as a surveyor at the waterworks; but, as he pointed out peevishly, this was hardly suitable employment for a man of his education—he had been taught to calculate by the metric system, and all the pipes and ditches at Honolulu were in feet and inches.

Wilcox could not keep his elegant wife on the pittance he brought home from the waterworks, and he saw no future in dragging a surveyor's chain for a salary "which would not keep a cat alive." Liliuokalani helped pay his passage to San Francisco so that he could look for a better job there. While he was on the west coast his wife left him and went home to Italy. Wilcox nursed his various grievances for a year and then made his way back to Honolulu.

He set up shop as a surveyor and went to work in a half-hearted way, but his mind was on more exciting things. Liliuokalani gave him the use of a house she owned at Palama, on the west side of Honolulu, and there, in June 1889, Wilcox began holding secret meetings with a handful of men who called themselves the Liberal Patriotic Association, a raggle taggle of part-Hawaiians who thought they had been badly used by the reformers, and a few down-at-heel foreigners—Italians, Germans, and one Belgian. When Wilcox got to the stage of buying guns and ammunition he raised the money from some sympathetic Chinese, men who had no affection for the reformers and their exclusive ideas about who might or might not vote.

By day Wilcox drew up engineering plans; by night he drew up constitutions; and in his spare time he took charge of the exercises of the Kamehameha Rifle Association. He was plotting the overthrow of the Reform constitution. What he had in mind after that was not clear. Perhaps he would allow Kalakaua to stay on as king; perhaps he would invite Liliuokalani to take the throne. At least the political ins would be out and the outs would be in, and Wilcox would have made his mark.

By the middle of July the king, the cabinet, and the resident diplomats at Honolulu all knew that Wilcox was up to something, but no move was made to arrest him. An American warship, USS *Adams,* was in port; a British man of war was expected shortly; the marshal of the kingdom, John H. Soper, had thirty special constables on call; this seemed enough.

Wilcox had been recruiting among the native Hawaiians of Honolulu. By the end of July he had about eighty men, all of them supplied with red Garibaldi shirts, about a third of them armed with rifles, and the rest carrying pistols and bird guns. At three o'clock in the morning of July 30 Wilcox led his revolutionary army from Liliuokalani's house at Palama through the streets of Honolulu to the palace. He was wearing his Italian officer's uniform and he was carrying a constitution for Kalakaua to sign. If he really meant to overthrow the Reform government he might have done better to take the police station and the army barracks and then arrest the cabinet ministers in their beds, but this did not occur to him.

Wilcox picked up some more volunteers along the way to the palace, but when he got there he found that the king was not at home. Kalakaua was spending the night at the private residence of his wife, Queen Kapiolani, and as soon as he heard what was happening he left for his boathouse on the harbor with an escort of royal guardsmen. Wilcox sent him a message, then another, and another, asking him to come back to the palace and sign the new constitution, but Kalakaua stayed where he was.

Lieutenant Robert Waipa Parker of the royal guard would not let Wilcox into the palace, and so the Patriots took up positions in the grounds and in the government office buildings across King Street. Early in the morning the volunteer militia companies of the kingdom were called out. Their commander borrowed ten thousand rounds of ammunition from USS *Adams*, and his men were sent to occupy buildings that looked down into the palace grounds—the Opera House and Kawaiahao Church.

Wilcox's messengers went back and forth to the king's boathouse; the morning dragged on and nothing much seemed to be happening, inside the palace grounds or out; but then someone fired a shot and all at once everybody fired. Wilcox's men had four small cannon in the palace yard and they scored a few hits on the Opera House, but the government's rifle men soon drove the gunners away. At about midday the militiamen rushed the government office building and forced the Patriots out. Across the street Wilcox and his followers, still unable to get into the palace, took refuge in the Bungalow, the biggest outbuilding in the grounds. There was nowhere else for them to go, but it was an uncomfortable place to be. The government troops poured rifle fire down on them from the Opera House, and in the afternoon two young men, Hay Wodehouse and Arthur Turton, who pitched for a local baseball club, began lobbing sticks of dynamite over the palace walls onto the roof of the Bungalow.

The dynamite tore the roof and the second story to pieces, and the noise was appalling. After a little while one of Wilcox's men came out with a white sheet tied to a pole; the others followed, and it was all over. Wilcox surrendered his sword to Colonel Volney Ashford of the volunteers. A detachment of armed men from USS *Adams* came ashore to patrol the streets for the night, but all the fight was gone from the Patriots and their friends and the town was quiet.

Seven of Wilcox's men had been killed and a dozen or so wounded. About seventy more were arrested, but only three were brought to trial on serious charges. Albert Loomens, a Belgian, became the first foreigner in the kingdom's history to be convicted of treason. He was sentenced to death by hanging, but the sentence was commuted to one year in jail, to be followed by banishment. Ho Fon, a Chinese journalist, was convicted of conspiracy and fined two hundred and fifty dollars. Wilcox himself was charged with treason (though he insisted that he had Kalakaua's authority for what he did). Several of his fellow Patriots turned state's evidence and testified against him, but it was obvious that no jury composed of native Hawaiians would ever convict him of a capital offense. In the end he was tried for conspiracy. The evidence against him was overwhelming, but the native jurors could not be made to appreciate that. One of them, a well-known political comedian called Bipikane who took his name, Beef Man or Ox Man, from his habit of roaring like a bull on the floor of the legislature and announcing that he would gore his opponents' arguments to death, kept interrupting the prosecution's case, and finally he was ejected and charged with contempt of court. Wilcox was found not guilty by a vote of nine to three, and he emerged with a greater following among the natives than he had had before. Two books celebrating his exploits were published: *Ka Buke Moolelo O Hon. Robert William Wilikoki* (The History Of The Honorable Robert William Wilcox), and *Duke Hao O Hawaii A Me Na Moolelo Pakui* (The Iron Duke Of Hawaii And Other Stories). The first sold three hundred copies at two dollars; the second came out as a pamphlet for seventy-five cents and swept the market.

Chief Justice Albert Francis Judd, in his charge to the jury which convicted Albert Loomens, made the point that unsuccessful rebellion was always treason, and treason was the most serious of crimes against the state. True enough; but after Robert Wilcox was acquitted Sereno E. Bishop, editor of the *Friend,* a Protestant clergyman, and a member of the Hawaiian League, had the grace to concede that "if the Revolution of June 30, 1887, had come to issue of battle, and had failed, and its leaders had been tried for treason by a white jury, that they would have been similarly acquitted, in the face of all law and evidence, and this amid general applause."

Some of the natives insisted that the wrong men had been tried. "Who are the murderers?" asked John E. Bush in his Hawaiian language paper *Ka Leo O Ka Lahui.* "Who shot these native Hawaiians all to death? Who gave the authority and by what right can a number of whites seize guns and go out to shoot natives without the proclamation of martial law? Whose hands are stained with the race-loving country loving blood of these true hearted Hawaiians. What church was turned into a blood flowing fort . . . ?"

The accused murderers in power paid no attention to Bush. They disbanded one of the native volunteer militia companies because some of its members had refused to fight against Wilcox and others had joined the insurrection; they had the fence around the palace grounds lowered from eight feet to three and a half feet; they told Kalakaua to put the arms in the palace under the control of the cabinet; and then they took up the regular business of government again.

The Torch Is Quenched

Wilcox and the Liberal Patriotic Association had changed nothing. Kalakaua was still king, and he was still bound by the constitution of 1887. Not long after the uprising at the palace his cabinet ministers got a new and satisfactory opinion from the supreme court, one that virtually compelled the king to approve measures put to him in cabinet council, but even with this next to last area of independence closed off Kalakaua still managed to find ways of obstructing the work of the Reform ministry. A division was opening up between Attorney General Ashford and his colleagues, and as often as not a vote of three to one in favor of a given plan was the best the cabinet could muster. Kalakaua did not like Ashford any more than he liked the other reformers, and he had a special hatred for the attorney general's brother, the ferocious Volney Ashford, who during the revolution of 1887 had extorted five thousand dollars from Kalakaua and his family—"despoiling the enemy," as he called it. But now Kalakaua found a use for Clarence Ashford. He took the position that if his ministers expected him to agree with them they ought first to agree among themselves, and he found a malicious satisfaction in withholding his signature from measures presented to him by the divided cabinet.

The cabinet was having trouble outside the council rooms as well. The reciprocity treaty had been renewed in 1887 at the cost of conceding the use of Pearl Harbor to the United States Navy, but since then some ominous changes had occurred on the American political scene. A Republican president, Benjamin Harrison, had come to power in the national election of 1888, and there was talk at Washington of lowering the tariff on sugar or even removing it altogether in favor of a bounty to be paid to American producers. Where would the Hawaiian kingdom stand if that happened? Its privileged place in the American market would be lost, the country would be plunged into depression, and the cession of Pearl Harbor would have been for nothing.

Two or three options seemed worth investigating. Perhaps another buyer for Hawaiian sugar could be found. Clarence Ashford, Canadian by birth, favored a treaty of reciprocity with his home country. The other members of cabinet thought Canada might be considered as a port in a storm, but they hoped the storm would not break. With any luck the United States could be persuaded to make a special exception for Hawaiian sugar, so that American interests at the islands would not be threatened. "If it should become necessary to seek markets outside of the United States for our products," wrote Minister of Foreign Affairs Jonathan Austin, "intimate associations with foreign purchasers would naturally tend to the alienation of our feelings for the United States, and sympathies would naturally prevail for the interests of those with whom we were in close commercial relations . . ." The ideal solution, of course, would be a continuation of reciprocity with the United States, and Henry A. P. Carter, the Hawaiian minister at Washington, was urged to keep this thought before the Harrison administration.

Carter and James G. Blaine, Harrison's secretary of state, worked out a tentative arrangement under which reciprocity would be maintained and the United States would guarantee the independence of the kingdom, even landing troops for this purpose if necessary. Kalakaua thought this amounted to a virtual protectorate, and the merest suggestion that it might become official policy was enough to enrage the native population of Honolulu. The usual round of mass meetings was held, the usual harangues were made, the usual petitions were forwarded to the king. The cabinet made its usual response: prosperity and independence were its aims, and the new treaty would guarantee both.

Minister Carter did not like the idea of foreign troops on Hawaiian soil, but he thought that on balance the price was worth paying. "I have always been opposed to their landing, even for drilling," he wrote to Kalakaua, "but they have been allowed to so long that they would probably do it whether we wished or not, and it rests with every naval commander to do as he pleases and help which side he pleases . . . If a revolution was started against the throne to establish a republic or for any other purpose, they might land and prevent the defence of the throne, all this I think is wrong. I do not think we can get them to agree not to land . . . but I would try and get them to agree never to land except when the Government was in danger and then only to sustain the Government which is a monarchy . . ."

Kalakaua felt that this was cutting too close to the bone. When Minister of Foreign Affairs Austin drew up a commission empowering Carter to negotiate with Blaine the king refused to sign it. The Reform cabinet had driven him into a corner, but there he stood. The constitution directed him to obey the wishes of the cabinet, the supreme court had told him it was his duty, and he had conceded this a few months earlier—but still he would not sign. His agreement, he said, applied only to matters affecting the internal affairs of the kingdom. Treaties were something else again. Besides, Attorney General Ashford happened to be out of the kingdom, the cabinet was incomplete, and the ministers knew his views on that subject.

Minister of the Interior Lorrin Thurston could hardly contain himself. He observed that this was not the first time Kalakaua had refused to comply with the advice of his ministers. The experience of the cabinet had been one long struggle to get him to do his duty. The history of such actions on the part of sovereigns in the past had had the uniform result of bringing disaster upon sovereign and country. Kalakaua heard him out and said simply: "I am willing, Let it come."

Neither Thurston nor Kalakaua could tell how soon disaster would come, or if indeed it would come at all, and in the meantime the cabinet ministers had to try to find a way of going on with the treaty negotiations. In April 1890, they concluded that the clause about the landing of American troops had better be left out, and a modified commission was drafted for Minister Carter. On the advice of Attorney General Ashford Kalakaua refused to sign this document too, and before a new strategy could be put into action the worst happened: United States President Benjamin Harrison signed into law the McKinley Act, which removed the tariff on raw sugar entering the United States and in the process all but wrecked the reciprocity treaty with the Hawaiian kingdom. Sugar from foreign countries would be admitted free to the United States, and the price of domestic sugar would be supported by a bounty of two cents a pound paid to producers. The act would go into effect on April 1, 1891, and this meant that Hawaiian planters and those who depended on them had nothing to look forward to except disaster. Henry N. Castle, editor of the *Pacific Commercial Advertiser,* wrote that people were "plunged into the depths of despair." One or two plantations might be able to make money, he thought, but "most of them would collapse if such a state of things continued long. Well, we will hope for the best, and try to make money in something else if sugar busts."

More than sugar was about to bust. While the United States Congress was considering the McKinley Act the Reform cabinet at Honolulu was entering its last days. Between the special election of September 1887, and the regular election of February 1890, opposition to Reform had been growing, and by the time the election campaign of 1890 got fairly under way a new organization, the National Reform party, was in the field. It was a curious hybrid, made up of two factions that came together for the special purpose of beating the Reform party: Hui Kalaiaina (the Hawaiian Political Association) and the Mechanics' and Workingmen's Political Protective Association. The Hawaiian kingdom should remain independent and prosperous, and Asiatics should not be allowed to ruin the country—on this Reformers and National Reformers could agree. They disagreed on the single crucial question of the right to rule. Robert W. Wilcox was an active member of Hui Kalaiaina, and he did not mince words: "We don't want these white men who are wandering about and coming here; they are a good for nothing lot, all they want is money, and when they get it they get up and go away. It is only the real natives of the country who have any feeling of love for their own land." This kind of talk, however, did not sit well with the Mechanics and Workingmen, most of whom were white men. If the National Reformers wanted to cut down the exclusive Reformers, they would have to sink their racial differences, at least for the time being. The National Reform platform asked quietly for "a liberal modification" of the "property and income qualifications now required of electors for Nobles, in order to include in that voting privilege a worthy class of natives, small land-owners and mechanics, who are now unjustly debarred."

The answer of the Reformers was the same as it had always been. The white man had civilization behind him, and civilization was almighty. The progress of society, the logic of events, was too strong for those who wanted to turn the clock back. If a poor white man worked hard he could improve himself, and so could a native. The Hawaiians should join hands with the best foreign element and press forward into the future. Do that, and the property qualification would drop away by itself.

Natives in the National Reform party knew better than to pay attention to exhortations from white men. They had a more immediate problem; they had to put their political plans and promises before an electorate limited by the Reform constitution. Robert Wilcox had an answer for this, too: native voters should disregard the election law and lie about their wealth. As matters turned out, nothing so drastic was necessary. The election went off in orderly fashion, and the result was a legislature almost equally divided between Reform and National Reform. Without any doubt the position of the Reform cabinet was weakened, and very likely the march of progress would be slowed down.

Everyone knew that Robert Wilcox was the man who had brought in the solid native note; he was the hero of the moment among the National Reformers. His friend and fellow partisan John E. Bush, the one time ambassador to Samoa, drew the obvious conclusion: "the voice of the People demands that the Roman patriot and Garibaldian pupil should have a seat in the incoming Cabinet."

The legislature would meet in May, but once again Wilcox seemed to find it difficult to wait. In April, Marshal of the Kingdom John H. Soper reported that Wilcox was planning another insurrection, this time with the help of Volney Ashford, who had gone sour on Reform. They were going to recruit revolutionaries and seize the police station. The Attorney General wanted to dismiss Soper for insubordination, but he was voted down.

Wilcox and Volney Ashford never did attack the police station, but the legislative session of 1890 opened in an uneasy atmosphere just the same. The National Reformers might very well be strong enough to control the assembly, and the Reform cabinet was divided within itself—the attorney general against the rest.

Most of the early meetings of the legislature were devoted to the concerns of the cabinet—treaty negotiations with the United States, and squabbles between Clarence Ashford and his colleagues. "If anyone wants to know what it is to be in hell without waiting for eternity," said the overwrought Thurston early in June, "let him be in a divided Cabinet, knowing that every word and act is being reported and misconstrued by a traitor—with the knowledge that a man is among you who you cannot trust, and the possibility of another 30th of July hanging over your head."

Thurston did not have to wait long for release. On June 13, after a long debate on a motion of no confidence in the ministry, he and the other two majority members of cabinet submitted their resignations, and Ashford followed.

Four days later Kalakaua announced the appointment of a new ministry, led by his good friend John A. Cummins, an affable part-Hawaiian. The cabinet looked "safe," if nothing else, and moderates on both sides of the assembly were relieved. Robert Wilcox and his friend John Bush were not nearly so pleased. The radical wing of the National Reform party had been insulted, in their view, and the Roman patriot and Garibaldian pupil was still without a position befitting his talents.

Wilcox and Bush and other natives began talking about a new constitution, by which they meant a constitution like the old one of 1864, guaranteeing the supremacy of the king. Questions were raised on the floor of the assembly, mass meetings of natives were held at Honolulu, and by the middle of August a petition was ready for presentation to the king. Forty-three native constitutionalists in dress suits, top hats, and white gloves marched to the palace with their petition, accompanied by the Royal Hawaiian Band, and asked the king to put the need for a convention before the legislature.

Kalakaua was willing, but worried men in and out of the legislature were certain that if the Reform constitution were rewritten trouble would follow. Two of the resident diplomats at Honolulu agreed. British Commissioner Wodehouse and United States Minister John L. Stevens took it upon themselves, as a matter of "duty" to their own governments, to tell Kalakaua that disaster would be the result if he tried to force a law calling for a constitutional convention through the legislature.

Robert Wilcox said disaster would come if a constitutional convention was *not* held. "People say there will be no trouble," he told the legislature, "but I say that if the people are not granted their rights the streets will be sticky with blood. We will have another 30th of June. Buildings will be blown up, many people killed, and I myself will take a hand if the people are not granted their rights."

If the constitution was revised it would be another monarch who would benefit. Kalakaua's health had been bad, and when the legislature was prorogued in November (without having called a constitutional convention) he decided that he would take a vacation trip. His sister Liliuokalani was appointed regent, and on November 25 Kalakaua sailed for San Francisco. He enjoyed himself in California, but his health did not improve. Early in January 1891, he suffered a stroke, and later in the month his doctors discovered that he had Bright's disease. Kalakaua spoke to his people for the last time from San Francisco, using an Edison recording machine; on January 18 he lapsed into unconsciousness, and two days later he died, at the age of fifty-four. His body was brought back to Honolulu on USS *Charleston,* and the festivities planned for his return gave way to mourning among his native subjects. In his funeral procession marched the Hawaiian societies, among them the members of Hale Naua, "very heathenish in looks and howling," as Sereno Bishop noted in his diary, with the high priest of the secret society carrying a feather helmet, a kapu stick, and a sacred gourd. Kalakaua was buried at the royal mausoleum in Nuuanu valley. "The torch that burns at midday," wrote a sympathetic journalist, "has been quenched."

Liliuokalani

The new monarch, Liliuokalani, was a complicated woman, and a good many people found it hard to fit the pieces of her personality together. She was a conscientious Christian, with a pew at Kawaiahao Church and a long and worthy list of charitable interests; and yet her closest friend in private and in public, Charles B. Wilson, part English, part Tahitian, whom she made marshal of the kingdom and defended against all sorts of attacks, had the blithest of attitudes toward orthodox Protestant morality, saying that things such as drunkenness, gambling, and opium smoking were crimes only because the statute books made them so. On coming to the throne at the age of fifty-two Liliuokalani was sure that she knew her own mind; and yet in the most difficult days of her reign, when she would have done well to listen to responsible advice, she let herself be guided by the prognostications of a medium, a German woman, Fraülein Wolf, who had the run of the palace. Like her brother Kalakaua and the other members of her family, Liliuokalani had a talent for music, and she wrote some of the most beautiful and delicate songs in the Hawaiian language, including "Aloha Oe," that soft farewell with a dying fall; and yet she had a strong streak of unfeminine toughness, almost coarseness, that surprised those who ran up against it in conversation.

On one matter Liliuokalani would hear no argument at all. She had sworn an oath to uphold the constitution of 1887, but she did not take this to mean that she could not rule the country. While Kalakaua was king Liliuokalani had some uncomplimentary things to say about his waverings (though, to be sure, in the eyes of his political opponents Kalakaua looked stubborn enough, especially after 1887). Now that she was queen Liliuokalani proposed to make it clear where sovereign power lay in the kingdom.

To her this issue at least was a simple one, and so it might have been in simpler times. But Liliuokalani was faced with a political situation that matched and exceeded her own personal complexity. It was hard to tell exactly what was happening in the kingdom, because many things were going on beneath the surface and the surface itself was agitated. Lorrin Thurston talked about the scene as "kaleidoscopic," and the metaphor was irresistible. Unstable political patterns kept forming and reforming, and the slightest jolt shifted them. Of course, as Thurston might well have gone on to say, a powerful enough jolt might break the whole apparatus and scatter the fragments so that they could never be pieced together again.

The McKinley Act was compounding all the other uncertainties. It had gone into effect on April 1, 1891, and it was crippling the Hawaiian sugar industry. At Washington Minister Carter tried his best to get a better arrangement, and after he died late in 1891 the new minister, John Mott Smith, took up the struggle, but he found it heavy going; the Harrison administration was unsympathetic, and nothing was accomplished.

When the sugar industry was in trouble the whole kingdom was in trouble. The Reformers of 1887 had asserted that their solid property rights gave them the right to rule, but now the ground seemed to be opening up beneath their feet, and good government might disappear down a crack in the earth. Politicians had to find somewhere to stand. For conservative Hawaiians there was no problem; they stood where they had always stood. A group called the Native Sons of Hawaii spoke for them, advocating a return of governing powers to the monarch. Robert Wilcox and John Bush, experts at changing position, took new ground altogether. They had been monarchists for as long as it appeared that there might be something in it for them, but now Kalakaua was dead and Liliuokalani had abandoned them. Wilcox could not even get an appointment as royal chamberlain, much less a post in the cabinet. So he and Bush formed a new political group, the Liberal party, and Bush began to talk fiery republicanism in his newspaper. Liliuokalani had to be restrained from sending some of her household troops to smash his presses. The Reformers of 1887, who had not done well in the elections of 1890 and who looked forward to the elections of 1892 with even less optimism, were getting ready to make the great leap to the solid ground of the United States. They saw an unreasonable queen on one side and irresponsible agitators such as Wilcox and Bush on the other, and they concluded that the only course that offered any hope at all for the future was annexation to the United States. A man who had not talked to Lorrin Thurston for some time came across him in mid-1891 and was surprised to find that Thurston's "patriotic enthusiasm" for the kingdom had turned into "a sort of hopelessness." Thurston said that "with the large majority of 14,000 voters blind enough to be beguiled by Wilcox and Bush, whom neither monarch nor ministers could suppress, he did not see much future for Hawaiian independence, which he thought, depended much upon the commercial credit of the country."

One day early in 1892 Thurston was outside his office in downtown Honolulu when Henry E. Cooper, an American attorney recently arrived from California, came up to him to talk politics (people were always coming up to Thurston to talk politics). Cooper thought Liliuokalani was a dangerous woman; at any moment she might make a move against the constitution of 1887. In that case, Cooper asked, what would Thurston do? Thurston said he would oppose her. Cooper wanted to know who else shared Thurston's views. The leaders of the community generally, Thurston said. "But," said Cooper, "do you know exactly the men who think with you, upon whom you could put your hand at a moment's notice, if action was called for?" Thurston said he did not. "Well," said Cooper, "I think that you should know in advance who can be depended on, and what you propose, should action become necessary." In Cooper's opinion the only way out of an intolerable situation was annexation to the United States. Thurston agreed. Soon afterward a dozen or so men met at Thurston's office to form an Annexation Club. The members decided that the club should be small and that it should be secret—a necessary precaution, because what they were proposing was treason.

As it happened, Thurston was about to leave for the United States on business, and he stayed away long enough to visit Washington and see what the statesmen there thought about taking the Hawaiian Islands. James H. Blount, chairman of the House committee on foreign relations, was cool. He put Thurston down as a "pretty uppish sort of person," and thought no more about the matter. But Blount was a Democrat, and the administration was Republican. Secretary of State James Blaine was cordial, and Secretary of the Navy Benjamin Tracy passed on to Thurston some encouraging words from President Harrison—that "if conditions in Hawaii compel you to act as you have indicated, and you come to Washington with an annexation proposition, you will find an exceedingly sympathetic administration here."

On his way home from Washington Thurston took time to put his views on paper for Blaine. Thurston thought he could distinguish several groups of people at the islands who had an interest one way or another in annexation—foreigners with a financial investment in the country; permanent settlers; the native leaders of the Liberal party; the common natives; and the queen and her faction. The first three groups, by and large, were for annexation; the common natives were undecided; and the queen's party was against the idea. The sugar industry was in such bad condition that any change would be welcomed; the planters would be willing to give up cheap contract labor and abide by the labor laws of the United States if this meant that they could get a bounty like the one enjoyed by American producers. The Liberal leaders, snubbed by the queen, were ready to put their faith in universal suffrage under the American flag; this would give them control of the legislature, and they would also control patronage—and "loaves and fishes" were important to them.

The most compelling reason for annexation, Thurston said, was that good government was impossible without it. Under the constitution of 1887 there was racial unrest, caused by the exclusion of natives and Orientals from the franchise and by the diversity of nationalities within the foreign community. The constant possibility of insurrection was frightening away capital, and the development of the islands was being delayed. Only union with a powerful country could stabilize the situation.

The annexationists' natural choice as a senior partner was the United States. To make the islands into a state of the Union would be too dangerous, given the backward nature of the electorate, but a territorial form of government would be suitable. The queen could be retired on a pension, and the common natives could be brought to realize that prosperity was more in their interest than independence. If they were stubborn about it, then a *coup d'état* and the establishment of a provisional government might be a necessary prelude to annexation, though Thurston thought this unlikely; or so he said.

While Thurston was making his way back to Honolulu the factions he had listed for Blaine came to grips in the legislature. The elections of 1892 produced a strange assembly, in which no party had a majority. The Liberals of Bush and Wilcox, the remnant of the Reform party of 1887, the rump of the National Reform party of 1890, and a number of unattached members were all looking for allies, dropping old friends, and picking up new ones.

Robert Wilcox, as usual, was ready to shake the kaleidoscope harder than anyone else. His Liberals had not done as well in the elections as they expected, and Liliuokalani's studied neglect was galling. Bush and Wilcox held some public meetings to make their contempt for queen and constitution obvious, and then Wilcox went underground and organized yet another insurrectionary group, the Hawaiian Patriotic League, with the idea of overthrowing the government and setting up a new regime, this time, presumably, a republic.

He was no luckier than he had been before. Marshal of the Kingdom Charles Wilson, Liliuokalani's favorite and the target of the noisiest speeches of Bush and Wilcox, heard about the League and managed to plant some spies at its meetings. They brought back reports of revolutionary talk, and on the eve of the opening of the legislature Wilcox and his friends, among them Volney Ashford and the bellowing Bipikane, were arrested. Preliminary evidence was taken, but no one was actually brought to trial. The queen's advisers thought it best to let the matter drop, since Wilcox would have to be tried before a native jury and he would almost certainly be acquitted again. Ashford was told in plain terms to leave the kingdom, and he did; Wilcox was freed to take his seat in the legislature, a month late.

The legislative session of 1892 was the longest in the kingdom's history, and the constitutional questions before it would determine whether the kingdom would live or die. Some members of the assembly wanted a constitutional convention. What if they succeeded in having one called? Where would the convention locate sovereignty? Liliuokalani simply wanted her cabinet ministers to obey her; if they refused she might proclaim a new constitution that suited her better. For Thurston and the other annexationists the constitutional question was paramount, too: would they be able to maneuver into office a cabinet favoring annexation and get an annexation resolution through the legislature, or would they have to wait until Liliuokalani gave them an opening for revolution by trying to promulgate a new constitution in some unconstitutional way?

More than seven months went by before answers to these questions were found. Between May 1892, and January 1893, seven motions of no confidence in cabinet ministries were introduced, and four succeeded. Each time a new cabinet was proposed a struggle for power took place, but no faction ever won a convincing victory, and this meant that a further shakeup was inevitable.

It also meant that some of the basic business of the legislature was not given proper attention. For one thing, the appropriation bill was held up badly, at a time when financial policy needed careful attention. The depression caused by the McKinley Act was at its lowest point. New sources of revenue would be welcome, but where could they be found?

Early in the session an inflationary banking bill was discussed unenthusiastically, and then in July Liliuokalani's medium, Fraülein Wolf, came up with an inspired solution. She read in her cards that a man would visit the queen with a plan which would bring money flowing into the country. And so it turned out. A Mr. T. E. E., never fully identified, paid a call on Liliuokalani at the palace and put before her a scheme to introduce a national lottery. Fraülein Wolf thought this was a good idea. "She says I must have the House accept it," wrote Liliuokalani in her diary; "it would bring 1,000,000." One million and more, so it seemed: Mr. T. E. E. promised the kingdom twelve and a half million dollars over twenty-five years, to pay for railroads, harbors, bridges, wharves, roads, an oceanic cable, and other good works.

Liliuokalani could see several splendid points in favor of the lottery. The kingdom would prosper again; the government, meaning herself, would have sources of revenue outside the control of the monarchy's opponents in the legislature; and annexationist talk would lose its force. So the lottery became a hotly disputed political issue.

"No plan," wrote Mr. T. E. E. and his friends in their public prospectus, *The Golden Era,* "has ever been proposed for the improvement of a country that has not been bitterly opposed. In this case the bill is opposed by those who have ample means, but who do not want to see any other influence in this country that will interfere with their control and direction of men and affairs.

"It is this class who have brought the country to the present chaotic state. It has been said on the floor of the House that the nation will be bankrupt within thirty days if material assistance is not at hand.

"This same class is responsible for this state of affairs and yet they oppose the only means of rescue.

"It is said that certain parties are forcing bankruptcy on the country so that they can bring forward schemes for annexation. They would ruin the country and then give away the wreck."

Another bold scheme to raise revenues was in the air at the same time. Marshal Wilson was known to think that the opium traffic in the islands should be licensed (by his enemies he was accused of taking part in the smuggling of opium). Over the opposition of the moralists both a lottery bill and an opium licensing bill were introduced in the legislature. The opium bill passed its third reading on December 31, 1892. As for the lottery bill, the queen's man in charge, a part-Hawaiian named William White, waited until it had a good chance of passage; finally, on January 10, 1893, when several of its opponents were absent, he brought the bill out of committee and pushed it through its second and third readings.

The queen had suggested January 14 as the day for the prorogation of the legislature. There was one other piece of business she wanted to attend to before then: her most recent ministry had opposed both the lottery and the opium licensing bill—it would have to go. A vote of no confidence in the ministers was moved by a native member on January 12, and then for an hour other native members one by one spoke in favor of the motion. The question at issue was simple, said Representative G. P. Kamauoha. Would the ministers do "what the Queen and the Hawaiian people wanted in regard to the Lottery, the Constitutional Convention, etc. Would they do as the Queen wanted them to?"

So in the last days of the legislature the questions of the lottery, the opium license, and the fight over the constitution all ran together. The cabinet was voted out of office; Liliuokalani appointed four new ministers, none of them distinguished for anything beyond personal amiability; then she signed into law the lottery act and the opium license act, and exactly at noon on January 14 she declared the legislative session at an end.

The very mention of the word "constitution" so close to the end of the session was enough to convince Lorrin Thurston and the other members of the Annexation Club that the day they were waiting for was just around the corner. They were sure that Liliuokalani was about to take the constitution into her own hands; and once she did so, they believed, they would be justified in attacking the monarchy and petitioning for annexation to the United States.

Who would follow them? It was hard to tell, but one thing was certain: Lorrin Thurston was overoptimistic about the number of people in the kingdom who wanted annexation. A newspaper editor from San Francisco had spent several weeks at Honolulu in October and November trying to collect accurate figures. He found only ten members of the legislature openly in favor of annexation and more than thirty against it; and of course the nature of the franchise made it likely that annexationists would be overrepresented in elective politics. So it was safe to say that annexationists were a tiny minority.

But among the annexationists of 1893 were a good many of the men who had framed the constitution of 1887, and mere numbers were not important to them; indeed, like their arch enemy Robert Wilcox, they seemed to have their own method of calculation. Sereno Bishop, a convinced annexationist by the end of 1892, could disregard the political arithmetic of the editor from San Francisco. Bishop wrote that he thought of himself as one of a "multitude," and that among the multitude were "very many of the best citizens of Hawaii." Perhaps he meant to say that one of the "best citizens," or even one of the best resident aliens, was worth ten of the lesser sort of men at the islands. In any case, he insisted, it was wrong to speak of such fine men in terms of "disloyalty." The best men had chosen a higher loyalty, that was all. "They felt it their duty to Hawaii, and to all her people, to seriously entertain the prospect of what they believe to be the coming change, and to be duly prepared for it." The "manifest tendency of events," wrote Bishop, "has latterly created an irresistible pressure upon my mind to admit that they are in the right." It was never hard for a good man like Bishop to admit that he was right, and if enough good men admitted that they were right they could attempt revolution.

Royalists and Republicans

After Liliuokalani prorogued the legislature she walked back to Iolani Palace to prepare for another ceremony, the most important one of her life. The household troops were lined up in front of the palace and the

Royal Hawaiian Band was playing when, early in the afternoon, a procession of native Hawaiians dressed in evening suits and top hats filed up the steps into the throne room. One man carried a covered package, and in it was the text of a new constitution. Liliuokalani was about to restore the liberties of the Hawaiian monarchy and the Hawaiian people. The procession symbolized the wish of her loyal subjects for a new constitution, but the document itself was her own; she had been working on it secretly for months. In future only true Hawaiians would be allowed to vote, and they would not have to be rich men to cast a ballot or run for office. The queen's people would elect their Representatives, and the queen herself would appoint Nobles to sit with them. Official acts of the sovereign would no longer need the advice and consent of the cabinet, and ministers would serve during the queen's pleasure. When Liliuokalani read her proclamation, as she proposed to do, first in the throne room and then from the balcony outside so that the crowd in the palace grounds could hear her, the bondage of 1887 would be at an end.

Earlier that day the queen had told her cabinet ministers what she was planning, and they went into a quiet panic. They had been in office less than a week, and whatever they thought about the need for a new constitution they did not think that their promises to Liliuokalani included standing beside her while she pulled the kingdom down over her head. The ministers knew enough about the temper of the queen's opponents to realize that they would welcome the chance to challenge her, and no minister of the crown could look forward with pleasure to that confrontation.

While the legislature was in its last hours Minister of the Interior John F. Colburn and Attorney General Arthur P. Peterson went downtown to find someone to advise them. They found the right people—Lorrin Thurston and William O. Smith. The advice they got was predictable: they should not follow the queen, but they should not resign either, because if they handed in their commissions the queen would only appoint a new set of ministers who would do what she said.

So Colburn and Peterson went back to the palace after the end of the legislative session to try to stop the queen from bringing on a revolution, which would surely be the outcome of any attempt on her part to proclaim a new constitution. Liliuokalani took the position that her cabinet was obliged to support her, but eventually the ministers convinced her that she should at least postpone the proclamation, if not abandon it altogether. When Liliuokalani appeared on the balcony and announced that the day of freedom had not yet come there was a stir among the natives in the crowd, but they were persuaded to go away quietly. "O, ye people who love the Chiefs," said the queen, "I hereby say unto you, I am now ready to proclaim the new constitution for my Kingdom, thinking that it would be successful, but behold obstacles have arisen! Therefore I say unto you, loving people, go with good hope and do not be disturbed or troubled in your minds. Because, within the next few days now coming, I will proclaim the new constitution."

Or did she really say "within the next few days?" She spoke in Hawaiian, and the words she used were "ua keia mau la," which might mean "in a short time," or simply "sometime." Whatever she meant, Lorrin Thurston and the members of the Annexation Club believed that the time had come for them to act.

They and several dozen supporters met in the law office of William O. Smith. A Committee of Safety was formed (Thurston was thinking back to 1887, when his law partner William Kinney showed him some books about the French Revolution and the Jacobin Committee of Public Safety that ruled during the Terror). All except one of the thirteen committeemen were members of the Annexation Club. They stayed in session that afternoon, and in the evening they resolved to take steps to form and proclaim a provisional government. The queen herself, they said, had committed a revolutionary act when she proposed to alter the constitution, and this justified the "intelligent part of the community" in taking things into their own hands to establish law and order.

One man went to interview Captain G. C. Wiltse of USS *Boston,* which was in port at the time, and Wiltse seemed to approve what the Committee planned. Lorrin Thurston and two others talked to United States Minister John L. Stevens, and he put no impediment in their path; according to Thurston he said that the queen, by her revolutionary act, had put herself outside his protection, and that if a provisional government could show *de facto* control of affairs he would recognize it. Wiltse and Stevens agreed that American troops would be landed to protect American lives and property if the situation seemed to warrant it.

Late that night at Thurston's home the business of drafting papers for the provisional government was begun, and the next morning, Sunday, January 15, Thurston went to talk to Minister of the Interior Colburn and Attorney General Peterson. He told them that the Committee of Safety could not let matters rest. Colburn and Peterson went off to confer with some white businessmen who supported the crown, and they decided that the best thing to do was to issue a proclamation saying that no new constitution would be invoked. This was done, but it did not stop the Committee of Safety.

The queen could not get any assurance from United States Minister Stevens that he would support the monarchy against armed insurrection. Some of Liliuokalani's supporters were in favor of declaring martial law immediately and arresting the Committee of Safety, but the general opinion was that this would be the signal for armed conflict, which was to be avoided at all costs. The royalists knew that the Committee was planning a mass meeting for the next day, Monday, January 16, and the cabinet made plans for a simultaneous meeting in support of the queen.

On Monday morning the Committee of Safety, six of them Hawaiian citizens by birth or naturalization, five of them Americans, one an Englishman, and one a German, sent a letter to United States Minister Stevens. They wanted assurances that Stevens would support them, but for the moment they wanted Stevens to hold their letter without acting on it. "We, the undersigned," they wrote, "citizens and residents of Honolulu, respectfully represent that, in view of the recent events in this Kingdom, culminating in the revolutionary acts of Liliuokalani on Saturday last, the public safety is menaced and lives and property are in peril, and we appeal to you and the United States forces at your command for assistance.

"The Queen, with the aid of armed forces, and accompanied by threats of violence and bloodshed from those with whom she was acting, attempted to proclaim a new constitution; and while prevented for the time from accomplishing her object declared publicly that she would only defer her action.

"This conduct and action was upon an occasion and under circumstances which have created general alarm and terror.

"We are unable to protect ourselves without aid and, therefore, pray for the protection of the United States forces."

In the afternoon several hundred supporters of the queen met at Palace Square. It was a subdued gathering. Liliuokalani's advisers hoped that if they left the crisis alone it might go away by itself, and they did not want to take chances with inflammatory speeches. Among the orators were Robert Wilcox and John Bush, whose infatuation with republicanism had come to an abrupt end; but even they spoke reasonably quietly, and the only outcome of the meeting was a resolution accepting the queen's word that she would not try to alter the constitution by unconstitutional means.

At the Honolulu armory things were noisier. About fifteen hundred people gathered to hear what the Committee of Safety had to say. Lorrin Thurston explained what had been happening, and asked the meeting to empower the Committee to "consider the situation and devise ways and means for the maintenance of the public peace and the protection of life and property." The queen had promised to maintain the constitution, he said, but her word was worth nothing. "Last Saturday the sun rose on a peaceful and smiling city; to-day it is otherwise. Whose fault is it—Queen Liliuokalani's. It is not her fault that the streets have not run red with blood . . . She wants us to sleep on a slumbering volcano, which will one morning spew out blood and destroy us all. The Constitution gives us the right to assemble peacefully and express our grievances. We are here doing that to-day without arms. The man who has not the spirit to rise after the menaces to our liberties has no right to keep them. Has the tropic sun cooled and thinned our blood, or have we flowing in our veins the warm, rich blood which loves liberty and dies for it?"

No one mentioned dethroning the queen or bringing the monarchy to an end, but everyone understood that this was what would happen. Only one man, the sugar planter Henry P. Baldwin, suggested using constitutional means to get what was needed, and he was howled down.

On the order of Captain Wiltse troops from the *Boston,* four boatloads of them, came ashore during Monday afternoon. A few were posted at the United States Consulate near the waterfront, another detachment marched up Nuuanu Street to Minister Stevens' office, and the rest were finally billeted at Arion Hall, not far from the palace. The queen's ministers did not want them in the town. Minister of the Interior Colburn and Minister of Foreign Affairs Samuel Parker went to Stevens, and he told them to put their protests in writing. They did, but Stevens took his time about replying, and his answer, dated Tuesday, January 17, did not say what Colburn and Parker wanted to hear. The troops stayed on.

The bluejackets from the *Boston* came ashore too soon for the Committee of Safety as well. Thurston and the others had not sent word to Stevens that the American troops were needed. After the mass meeting they decided that they needed more time to prepare for the provisional government, but Stevens and Wiltse went ahead anyway.

Revolution was an exhausting business. Minister Stevens was confined to bed all Monday, and that night Lorrin Thurston and two other members of the Committee, William R. Castle and William C. Wilder, fell ill. The work of laying the ground for the provisional government went on without them. An executive council and an advisory council were chosen, and a "finance committee" was set to collecting guns and ammunition.

The Committee of Safety, casting about for a president, asked Thurston if he would take the job. He said it would not be a good idea. He had business interests that might keep him away from the islands, and in any case he was known as such a "radical mover" that he would be a hindrance rather than a help in such a public position. The choice then fell on Sanford Dole. So far he had taken no part in the revolution beyond helping with the drafting of a constitution. Dole was never a man who looked for power; power came looking for him. He took all Monday night to make up his mind. Then on Tuesday morning he wrote out his resignation as a member of the queen's supreme court and went to tell the Committee that he would accept the presidency.

Thurston, still sick in bed, was busy composing a proclamation announcing the end of the monarchy. By about two on Tuesday afternoon it was ready—a long document, surveying the constitutional history of the kingdom and drawing attention to the fact that while the Kalakaua dynasty ruled instability reigned. "The constitutional evolution indicated has slowly and steadily, though reluctantly, and regretfully, convinced an overwhelming majority of the conservative and responsible members of the community that independent, constitutional, representative and responsible government, able to protect itself from revolutionary uprisings and royal aggression is no longer possible in Hawaii under the existing system of government.

"Five uprisings or conspiracies against the government have occurred within five years and seven months. It is firmly believed that the culminating revolutionary attempt of last Saturday will, unless radical measures are taken, wreck our already damaged credit abroad and precipitate to final ruin our already overstrained financial condition; and the guarantees of protection to life, liberty and property will steadily decrease and the political situation rapidly grow worse." So the monarchy would have to go, and a provisional government would take its place, "to exist until terms of union with the United States of America have been negotiated and agreed upon." Annexationism was out in the open at last.

The next thing was to get the recognition of Minister Stevens and Captain Wiltse, and this involved doing what Stevens said: taking possession of the government buildings and controlling the town in general. The annexationists had a volunteer armed force at their disposal, the old Honolulu Rifles, whose members had supported the revolution of 1887. When the Reform cabinet fell from power in 1890 the legislature dissolved the Rifles, but the militiamen continued to meet informally and they still had their guns and their uniforms. Now they assembled at the armory, and one of their officers went to look over the government buildings and see if the queen's troops were on guard there.

The queen's cabinet ministers had called a conference of the resident diplomats, and they got some disappointing advice: Liliuokalani was urged not to use force in resisting the revolution. Minister Stevens was not at the conference: he sent a note saying that he was ill and could not come. Arthur Peterson and Samuel Parker visited him at the American legation. Stevens, lying on a couch, gave no help at all and promised none. He would not even put his reasons in writing. Peterson and Parker left him and went to set up headquarters for the rest of the day at the police station in downtown Honolulu.

Just before Sanford Dole and the members of the Committee of Safety set out to take possession of the government building and proclaim the existence of the new regime, John Good, who had been collecting arms for the annexationists under the eyes of the native police, came out of a store on King Street and headed toward the armory with a wagonload of guns and ammunition. A policeman grabbed at the reins and another tried to climb onto the wagon. Good shot one of them in the shoulder. The noise attracted a big crowd, and while people were running to see what had happened, Sanford Dole and the committee walked to the government building and took possession. The queen's cabinet ministers were still at the police station, drafting a plaintive note to Stevens, asking yet again for his protection.

Did possession of the government building mean control of the town? Captain Wiltse of the *Boston* thought not. The queen had not surrendered, and she still had several hundred men under arms, probably twice as many as the annexationists, though so far the royal troops had not come out to fight. Dole and his followers would have to do better. They did, and they were rewarded by a letter from Stevens recognizing their regime.

Liliuokalani had not yet given up and her cabinet ministers were still at the police station, where Marshal of the Kingdom Charles Wilson was refusing to hand over his powers to the annexationists. But there was not much the queen could do, and not long after sunset she gave up. She surrendered, so she said, not to the revolutionaries but to the "superior force of the United States of America, whose minister plenipotentiary, His Excellency John L. Stevens, has caused United States troops to be landed at Honolulu and declared that he would support the said provisional government." She surrendered, moreover, under protest, expecting confidently that once the United States government learned the facts she would be reinstated. Marshal Wilson handed over the police station, and two hundred and seventy Hawaiian soldiers at the barracks stacked their arms. The Hawaiian monarchy was no more.

The provisional government's writ of martial law had been announced earlier; volunteers and bluejackets from the *Boston* were on the streets. That night the executive and advisory councils of the provisional government met and concluded, to no one's surprise, that their next step should be to seek a treaty of union with the United States. Lorrin Thurston, William R. Castle, and William C. Wilder, the three invalids of the revolution, were chosen to make the journey to Washington, and others joined them along the way.

So good government triumphed, and the "overwhelming majority of the conservative and responsible members of the community" could breathe easy. But not quite, because the "overwhelming majority" amounted in reality only to a few hundred men; in fact it would better be described as a determined and rather lucky minority. Not since the days of Kamehameha the Great had the Hawaiians distinguished themselves as a fighting people, and even the wildest of Hawaiian insurrectionaries, Robert Wilcox, was more likely to assail his enemies with words than with bullets. Just the same, the revolution would hardly have gone so well without the presence of the *Boston*'s bluejackets, and even after the queen lowered her royal standard and retired from the palace the *Boston* stayed on at Honolulu. Minister Stevens had recognized the provisional government with what some people would have called undue haste, and his recognition implied that the new regime was capable of looking after itself. But evidently it was not. "Disquieting rumors" were heard around town; Dole and his wife, as well as some of the other annexationists, did not think it was safe to sleep at home. On January 31 the advisory council asked Minister Stevens to raise the Stars and Stripes. Stevens had assured United States Secretary of State John W. Foster that the provisional government was gaining power and respect, that everything was quiet, and that annexationist sentiment was increasing; but at the same time, he wrote, renegade whites, hoodlum foreigners, vicious natives, and evil-disposed persons in general were looking for ways to stir up the forty thousand Orientals in the kingdom, and so the American flag should be hoisted. It was, and William D. Alexander, seeing the "ensign of Freedom" raised over the government building for the first time, thought he could see the price of government bonds and plantation stocks going up too.

When Lorrin Thurston visited Washington in 1892 the Harrison administration assured him of a warm welcome if ever the annexationists' plans matured. Now in 1893 Thurston and the other commissioners were on their way to the American capital with a treaty of annexation in their hands, and Harrison was there to receive them. But it was a curious welcome. The American national elections of November 1892, returned the Democratic Party to power, and in March 1893, Grover Cleveland would replace Harrison as president. The Hawaiian revolution had come too soon or too late, and much as Harrison sympathized with its aims there was little he could do for Thurston and his colleagues.

He did what he could. The annexation commissioners were asking for territorial status within the governmental system of the United States. Statehood was out of the question, and everybody understood why—the islands had an embarrassingly mixed population, with white men of whatever nationality outnumbered ten to one. Then too, the islands had special needs for contract labor, and if United States law was applied in all its strictness the sugar industry might suffer. Secretary of State John Foster was cooperative, though some of the more extreme requests of the commissioners had to be turned down. President Harrison sent the draft of an annexation treaty to the Senate on February 14, and neither the arrival of the queen's representatives at Washington nor the pleas made on behalf of the heir to the throne, the school girl Princess Kaiulani, made much impression on the Republicans in power.

The treaty marked time during the last days of Harrison's administration, and when President Cleveland took office he withdrew it. The new Secretary of State, Walter Q. Gresham, told Thurston and William Castle that the treaty had been "precipitated upon the administration" at short notice, and that nothing could be done until more was known about it. What did this mean? Did Cleveland and Gresham doubt the good faith of the overwhelming majority of the conservative and responsible members of the community of the Hawaiian Islands? Evidently so. On March 11 James H. Blount, the former chairman of the House committee on foreign relations, the same man who had such a cool conversation with Thurston in 1892, was given secret instructions to proceed to Honolulu, examine the situation there, find out why the revolution had taken place and appraise the part played by Minister Stevens, and see how the Hawaiian people regarded the provisional government.

Blount kept his instructions to himself, and all that Thurston and the others could discover was that his word would be "paramount" in all matters concerning the United States at the islands. "Paramount Blount," as he was known from the moment he arrived at Honolulu, was certainly worth getting to know, and annexationists and royalists alike prepared to offer him hospitality. Blount was cordial but neutral, and he was infuriatingly close-mouthed about what he was doing. He and his wife settled down in a cottage on the grounds of the Hawaiian Hotel (owned by a royalist, as it happened), and a stream of suppliants visited them there (including representatives of a new and different annexation club, one of whose committee members was Robert Wilcox, who had given up his royalist allegiance again); but so little information came out of Blount's rooms that he acquired a second nickname, "Minister Reticent."

His published report was a bombshell. Secretary of State Gresham told Cleveland that Minister Stevens, an accredited representative of the United States, had helped to overthrow the Hawaiian monarchy. Gresham advised Cleveland not to put the treaty of annexation before the United States Senate again, and suggested that in the name of justice the monarchy ought to be restored.

Who could handle the return of sovereignty to the queen? Cleveland, for one reason or another, had trouble filling the post of Minister to Hawaii. The man who finally took the job, Albert S. Willis, was instructed to deplore the reprehensible conduct of Stevens, and to offer the queen her throne again on condition that she in turn offer amnesty to the revolutionaries. Cleveland and Gresham were taking high moral ground, higher even than that of the revolutionaries themselves, who had so persistently announced that they had the clearest possible vision of what was right and good. There had been no genuine revolution, wrote Gresham. The queen had been overawed by Minister Stevens and the troops from the *Boston*. "Her submission was thus coerced. The affair was discreditable to all who engaged in it. It would lower our national standard to endorse a selfish and dishonorable scheme of a lot of adventurers."

These were harsh words. But, as Albert Willis found, Liliuokalani was in a harsh mood too. He understood her to say that she would not grant an amnesty to the people who had tried to overthrow her government; they should be beheaded. Whether she used the term "beheaded" was not clear; it was not the customary form of capital punishment at the islands, and her own version of the conversation merely mentioned the death penalty in general, or at the very least banishment. Whatever happened, she did not want the revolutionaries free to foment another revolution. They had rebelled in 1887 and again in 1893, and the next time, she said, the case was likely to be even more serious. Willis, taken aback, said he would have to ask his government for new instructions.

Liliuokalani did not relent until the middle of December, and by that time Cleveland had referred the whole question of the Hawaiian revolution and its aftermath to the "extended powers and wide discretion" of Congress. Willis, unaware of this, took Cleveland's original request to President Dole and his provisional government: would they restore the monarchy?

They would not, and their reasons covered eighteen typewritten pages, handed to Willis by Dole at midnight on December 23. The provisional government did not recognize the right of President Cleveland to settle its domestic affairs. Recognition by the United States and the other great powers was a fact, and nothing could alter that. If American troops had acted illegally in helping the provisional government to establish itself, that was a matter for the American conscience alone. "We have done your government no wrong," the document concluded; "no charge of discourtesy is or can be brought again us. Our only issue with your people has been that, because we revered its institutions of civil liberty, we have desired to have them extended to our distracted country, and because we honor its flag and deeming that its beneficent and authoritative presence would be for the best interests of all of our people, we have stood ready to add our country, a new star, to its glory, and to consummate a union which we believed would be as much for the benefit of your country as ours. If this is an offense, we plead guilty to it."

Just four days after Dole and his colleagues refused to surrender their authority, the United States Senate began its own hearings on the revolution. Senator John T. Morgan of Alabama, chairman of the committee on foreign relations, presided, and he was as much an annexationist as Blount had proved a royalist. Blount had taken his evidence at Honolulu, but he had not interviewed members of the Committee of Safety. Morgan called witnesses at Washington and accepted affidavits where he could find them. The provisional government got a very good press in the Morgan Report. No one was to blame for the revolution, said Morgan in his final statement, except the queen. Some of his committee members did not quite agree with him, but even so they did not recommend any further action on any of the questions raised. There would be no restoration of the monarchy, and no annexation of the islands either, at least for the moment. Neither would there be any interference in the political affairs of Hawaii by other powers. Resolutions passed in both House and Senate warned that intervention would be regarded as an act unfriendly to the United States.

Farewell to Thee

So the revolution was incomplete. Liliuokalani was inexperienced at being a queen, and her inexperience cost her the throne; the United States was inexperienced at annexing territory overseas, and this meant that the provisional government had to find ways of keeping the possibility open until the United States was ready to act. The answer, obviously, was to establish a republic along American lines.

The well-intentioned revolutionaries of 1893, so Sanford Dole said, had been moved by admiration for American civil liberties. But a glaring problem confronted them, the same one that had vexed the revolutionaries of 1887. If American civil liberties were granted to every man at the islands, then the very men who admired liberty most would be swamped at the polls by a rabble of brown men and yellow men who could have no real idea of what liberty meant. "These Islands are totally unfit for an ideal Republic," wrote Attorney General William O. Smith. "In general terms the problem to be solved is, how to combine an oligarchy with a representative form of government so as to meet the case."

As always, Lorrin Thurston was full of ideas. He agreed with William Smith that democracy would have to wait. American liberties should be given only to those who appreciated them, and in this connection he drew attention to the constitutional arrangements of the state of Mississippi, where government was carried on successfully even though a large part of the population was politically incompetent. What applied in Mississippi applied in Hawaii: the will of the majority could not be trusted; unlimited free speech would be dangerous; trial by jury, expecially by native jury, would open the way to contempt for law.

Thurston was still too much of a "radical mover." Other members of the provisional government did not want to suppress freedom totally—just sufficiently. They wrote into their draft constitution most of the clauses of the Bill of Rights of the American constitution, but then when they got ready to submit the constitution to a convention they stipulated that any man wanting to vote in the election of delegates would have to sign an oath declaring his allegiance to the new regime and swearing that he would oppose any attempt to restore the monarchy. This caused a good deal of hard feeling. Many white men at the islands were not citizens of Hawaii, and they did not want to take the chance that the oath might cost them their original citizenship. Many natives, royalists at heart, could not bring themselves to sign the oath either. So balloting for the convention was very light.

The government made doubly sure of keeping the convention safe by arranging that elected delegates should be in a minority. Eighteen men chosen by ballot sat with nineteen appointed by the government. The republican constitution that emerged was satisfactory to all but the most extreme oligarchs. Voters would have to swear allegiance to the republic. Candidates for office and voters in elections for the upper house (to be called the Senate) would have to meet high property qualifications. The right to vote might be extended to foreigners who had turned out for the annexationists in the revolution; otherwise only citizens by birth or naturalization could vote. And to be naturalized a man would have to come from a country that had a naturalization treaty with Hawaii. This was meant to exclude Japanese and Chinese from the franchise, and as an extra precaution the constitution contained a clause to the effect that voters should be able to speak, read, and write in English, and explain the constitution in English as well.

In the opinion of the provisional government even those few thousand voters who had elected the delegates who had approved the constitution could not be trusted to endorse it, and so the constitution became law not by plebiscite but by proclamation. Liliuokalani had lost her throne for trying to alter the constitution by fiat, and now, circumstances having altered cases, the revolutionaries of 1893 invoked the name of liberty and did substantially the same thing.

Sanford Dole announced the inauguration of the republic and proclaimed himself president on July 4, 1894. This bow in the direction of the United States was rewarded when President Cleveland sent a letter of recognition to the new regime. Queen Victoria followed suit later in the year, just after the republic's first elections under the new constitution returned to office the newly formed American Union party, whose policy could be summed up in one word—annexation.

Recognition by the great powers was all very well, but a good many natives and part-Hawaiians, and even a few royalist white men, were not ready to give up hope for the monarchy. Liliuokalani's agents spent some time at Washington in 1894, trying to get positive assurances from President Cleveland and Secretary of State Gresham that the monarchy would not be left alone to die, but they had no luck. When this became known at the islands the royalists, encouraged by Liliuokalani, began gathering arms for a strike against the republic.

Late in 1894 a shipload of contraband arms from San Francisco was transferred to a coastal steamer off windward Oahu, and the guns were brought ashore at Waikiki under cover of darkness. Bombs were made in downtown Honolulu, and caches of guns were planted in various places around the city, some of them at the home of the royalist newspaper editor John Bush, and more in Liliuokalani's flower garden. The government got wind of the royalists' plans, and in December Bush and several others were arrested and charged with conspiracy, but after that nothing much happened until the turn of the new year.

The royalists meant to launch their attack on Monday, January 7. But on the night of January 6 a squad of policemen and volunteers sent to Waikiki to look for hidden guns was fired on near a hut belonging to Henry F. Bertelmann, a part-Hawaiian royalist. Charles L. Carter, a member of the annexation commission sent to Washington in 1893 and a member of the republican legislature elected in 1894, was fatally wounded.

The government called out several companies of regulars and volunteers belonging to the Sharpshooters and the Citizens' Guard. The royalists retreated to the slopes of Diamond Head and then to the valleys behind Honolulu—Palolo, Manoa, Pauoa, and Nuuanu. It took about ten days to flush the rebels out of the dense scrub. The government troops enjoyed the chase, but the royalists, in the field for days without food or water except what they could scavenge, got less and less enthusiastic. A good many of them surrendered in batches, and eventually their leaders were captured.

They were a mixed group. Like the insect to the window pane, Robert Wilcox returned to revolution, this time on the side of the queen he had repudiated two years before. Another instinctive insurrectionary, Volney Ashford, who had been banished from the kingdom in 1892, came back after the revolution of 1893, and was picked up in 1895 fighting for Liliuokalani—or, rather, fighting against the republic. Three or four other white men appeared to be involved in the planning if not the fighting, and most of the rest of the leaders were part-Hawaiians, retainers of Liliuokalani or staunch traditionalists.

The biggest catch of all was Liliuokalani herself. Ever since the uprising began the Executive Council of the republic had been trying to make up its mind what to do with her, and finally on the morning of January 16, while the last of the royalists were still at large, Liliuokalani was arrested and confined in one of the apartments of Iolani Palace (which had been renamed the Executive Building by the republicans). The grounds of her home at Washington Place were searched, and in the garden the searchers found what they were looking for—a regular ammunition dump: twenty-one bombs, some of them made with coconut shells; more than thirty rifles; thirty-eight cartridge belts and about a thousand rounds of ammunition; and some pistols and swords.

The republican press wanted vengeance. The hottest of the hotheads were for hunting the rebels down and killing them, and then sentencing any captured leaders to death under martial law. Very few royalists were killed in combat, but one hundred and ninety-one were brought to trial before a military commission. The commission sat for thirty-six days. Five men, including Robert Wilcox and Henry Bertelmann, were sentenced to death. Several others got twenty to thirty years' imprisonment and heavy fines; and the natives who were convicted generally got a few months or a few years at hard labor.

Liliuokalani, before the first of the trials began, had signed a document announcing her abdication from the throne. She described it as a "forced abdication," and said she agreed to it only because she hoped it might save some of her followers from suffering the death penalty. Attorney General Smith told her that she was in no position to abdicate: she had ceased to be queen on January 14, 1893, when she tried to abrogate the constitution. Smith added that she should not expect her letter of "abdication" to free her from standing trial for treason. She was brought before the military commission under her married name of Liliuokalani Dominis (her husband, the American John O. Dominis, had died in 1891 not long after she came to the throne). She denied knowledge of the bombs in her garden, but admitted that she had planned to establish a new cabinet at the time of the uprising. The military commission sentenced her to five years at hard labor and fined her five thousand dollars.

In the end no one died for royalist principles at the hands of a republican hangman. The five men under sentence of death had their sentences commuted to long terms of imprisonment. Then on July 4, 1895, they and all the other royalists in jail were told that their sentences had been reduced. Another reduction was announced in November, on Thanksgiving Day, and the prisoners, all but one, were freed on New Year's Day, 1896.

The uprising left a few small difficulties in its wake. Some of the men tried before the military commission claimed American citizenship. Clearly they should be punished, but what if this alienated the United States? A sensible compromise was reached: American prisoners were encouraged to leave the islands, and most of them did. The same thing applied to British citizens, and among those who chose exile were Volney Ashford and his brother Clarence.

Then the question of the royalists' arms had to be considered. Guns had been shipped to the islands from San Francisco, and apparently the

United States government had done nothing to prevent it. Surely this was a violation of international law, and if it was then Secretary of State Gresham was ultimately responsible. Lorrin Thurston, the Hawaiian minister at Washington, had an angry interview with Gresham. The matter of the neutrality laws was never explored fully because Gresham got so annoyed with Thurston that he asked for his recall. Thurston arrived home in May 1895, announcing that Gresham had "repeatedly gone out of his way in what has appeared to be an attempt to pick a quarrel with me, to such an extent that the hostile spirit which he envinces is more or less personal to myself." A fair enough judgment, considering that Thurston embodied the Hawaiian revolution and Gresham had long since set his mind against the revolutionaries.

The last of the royalist prisoners to be freed was Liliuokalani. She had been put under house arrest at first; later she was paroled, and then set at liberty. In November 1896, she was given full citizenship and freedom of movement again, and her first act was to go to Washington to plead the case of the monarchy. She was almost four years too late. Ever since the revolution of 1893 the Hawaiian republicans had been campaigning systematically to discredit her on the American mainland. If the revolutionaries were right to overthrow the monarchy then, necessarily, the queen had been wrong, and it would be helpful if she could be proved wrong in every respect. One of the most enthusiastic blackeners of Liliuokalani's character was the Reverend Sereno Bishop, who was the Hawaiian correspondent of United Press and a frequent writer of articles for newspapers and periodicals on the American east coast. When Liliuokalani came to the throne in 1891 Bishop described her as a pious Christian lady. But within a year or two Bishop convinced himself of the righteousness of the annexationists' cause, and this meant that he had also to convince himself of the queen's essential wickedness. He shone the white light of his pure intentions on the ruins of the Hawaiian royal house and caught glimpses of appalling things scuttling about in the shadows— or perhaps just on the edges of his own mind. The queen was under the influence of kahunas, heathen sorcerers, so Bishop said; she encouraged the dancing of the lascivious hula; she made sacrifices to the volcano goddess, Pele; and, horror of horrors, her blackness was physical as well as moral—she and her brother Kalakaua were notoriously the children of a female chief of the second rank and her paramour, a negro bootblack named John Blossom. If this kind of talk would not discredit the queen nothing could, and Bishop could be sure, as he needed to be, that his motives were of the best.

Liliuokalani's people were no better than she was, according to Bishop. Two out of three native Hawaiians could read, and most of them called themselves Christians, but this could not be taken to mean that they were responsible citizens. They were shiftless, drunken, untrustworthy, with no idea of the value of work. In fact the great majority of them earned whatever money they had by selling their women as prostitutes to Chinese and Japanese laborers. Once again, of course, Bishop was arguing against the monarchy and for the republic, but it was just possible that he was digging a pit for his own annexationist hopes. Why would the United States want to annex such a sink of depravity?

Manifest Destiny

During the eighteen nineties the question of Oriental immigration became more acute than ever at the islands. The influx of Chinese in the eighties had led the Hawaiian government to limit their entry and then exclude them for a time, and beginning in 1886 Japanese were admitted in great numbers as a counterbalance. In 1894 the United States Congress finally repealed the McKinley Act; the bounty on sugar produced in the United States was removed, and the Wilson-Gorman tariff, in conjunction with the reciprocity agreement, restored Hawaiian sugar to its privileged place in the American market. This brought on a new demand for immigrant labor, and the Japanese were ready to supply the need. Immediately the old paradox returned: Hawaii was bound to the American market; to supply that market Hawaii had to import Oriental immigrants; and too many Orientals, this time Japanese rather than Chinese, would endanger Americanism at the islands. The Hawaiian Republic had some new problems to consider as well: the prospect of annexation to the United States, and the growing influence of Japan in the Pacific.

As early as 1892 United States Minister John Stevens had seen the kind of tension that might be built up if Hawaii was subjected to strain from both sides of the ocean. "Hawaii," he wrote, "has reached the parting of the ways. She must now take the road which leads to Asia, or the other, which outlets her in America, gives her an American civilization and binds her to the care of American destiny. The nonaction of the American government here will make Hawaii a Singapore, or a Hongkong, which could be governed as a British colony but would be unfit to be an American territory or an American state under our constitutional system. If the American flag floats here at no distant date, the Asiatic tendencies can be arrested and controlled without retarding the material development of the islands."

The American flag was not yet flying, but the Hawaiian government had to do something. The old plan of encouraging white laborers to come to the islands showed no more prospects of success than it ever had. The only solution to the political and social problem seemed to be to cut off the flow of Japanese. In 1897, by which time there were more than twenty thousand Japanese in Hawaii, three shiploads of new immigrants were held up at Honolulu, and the laborers were forbidden to land. The reaction of the Japanese government was prompt. Japan was working to put herself on an equal footing with the great powers of the world, and she was in no mood to allow a small and insignificant country like Hawaii to discriminate against subjects of the emperor. On the other hand Japan was unlikely to carry matters so far as to antagonize the United States, and in the end the question of the immigrants was put before arbitrators. Just the same the people of Honolulu would have felt easier if the Japanese war ship *Naniwa* had not turned up to lend point to the Japanese arbitrators' wishes.

One development in the United States gave the annexationists new heart. In the national elections of November 1896, the Democrats were defeated; in March 1897, just at the time of the Japanese protest, the unhelpful Grover Cleveland departed from office and the Republican William McKinley was inaugurated as president. McKinley was not yet a convinced annexationist, but he was no Cleveland either. Henry Cooper of the Hawaiian annexation commission saw him not long after the inauguration. McKinley received him warmly, and the commissioners were delighted. "The difference between the attitude of the present administration and the last one," wrote William O. Smith, "is like that of the difference between daylight and darkness."

So it seemed indeed. The Hawaiian delegation met frequently with senior men in the Department of State, and by the middle of June they had a treaty ready for the Senate to consider. Its terms were very like those of the uncompleted treaty of 1893, and McKinley urged favorable action. Annexation, he said, was "no new scheme." For three-quarters of a century the United States and Hawaii had steadfastly maintained their relationship. Union, "despite successive denials and postponements, has been merely a question of time. While its failure in 1893 may not be a cause of congratulations, it is certainly a proof of the disinterestedness of the United States, the delay of four years having abundantly sufficed to establish the right and the ability of the Republic of Hawaii to enter, as a sovereign contractant, upon a conventional union with the United States . . . *Under such circumstances annexation is not a change. It is a consummation.*"

The *Hawaiian Star* thought so too: "Hawaii may be regarded as a bride whose marriage day is not yet definitely fixed, but who is prepared to go through the ceremony whenever the signal is given." But when would the signal be given? One party was willing; the Hawaiian Senate ratified the treaty on September 9. The other party dragged its heels. Two groups of congressmen, one favorable to the match, the other against it, traveled to Honolulu in the fall to look the bride over before Congress met. They returned to Washington for the opening of the legislative session, and to the disappointment of the annexationists at the islands the Senate did not approve the match immediately but settled down to debate all kinds of objections. Perhaps the good offices of President Dole of the Republic would help. The Hawaiian legislature voted him ten thousand dollars to defray expenses, and sent him off to Washington at the turn of 1898 to lobby for the treaty in his dignified way.

The Senate chose to discuss the treaty in secret. The House of Representatives had no constitutional authority over the passage of the treaty, but it debated the issue of annexing Hawaii just the same, and it did so in public. The debate was echoed and amplified and distorted all over the country. The question of Hawaii's fate had become part of the larger question of the position of the United States in the world. The choice confronting the American people was both simple and portentous: they had tamed their great continent, and now that they stood at the ocean's edge on both coasts, they had to decide if the United States was ready to take the risk and the responsibility—and the rewards—of annexing territory overseas.

Everyone had an opinion: politicians, businessmen, clergymen, and every kind of man in the street. And everyone was certain that he was right and his opponents were wrong. People used the same words—duty, responsibility, inevitability, and destiny—and came to opposite conclusions. Annexation of what was called "non-contiguous territory" would either fulfil or pervert America's destiny, strategic, commercial, political, and moral; and it seemed that none of these special destinies could be disentangled from the others. Whatever happened, the United States would never be the same again.

One grand theorist in particular had quite precise plans for fitting Hawaii into his schemes. Captain Alfred Thayer Mahan, a formidable and original naval strategist, was sure that the Pacific Ocean was about to become the theater of a great clash between the powers of the Orient and the Occident. American self-interest was involved, to be sure, but so was the survival of all of Western civilization. Whoever held the Hawaiian Islands would control the whole Pacific, from the isthmus of Central America to the Aleutian Islands and as far west as Asia. The United States should annex Hawaii. This, wrote Mahan, would be "no mere sporadic effort, irrational because disconnected from an adequate motive, but a first-fruit and a token that the nation in its evolution has aroused itself to the necessity of carrying its life—that has been the happiness of those under its influence—beyond the borders which heretofore have sufficed for its activities." A study of comparative religions showed that churches which rejected missionary enterprise were foredoomed to decay. "May it not be so with nations?"

Mahan had any number of disciples in high places, among them the powerful Republican senator Henry Cabot Lodge, Assistant Secretary of the Navy Theodore Roosevelt, and Captain George Dewey of the Far East Squadron of the United States Navy. But there were others who saw certain disaster where Mahan saw certain glory. Carl Schurz, a friend of former Secretary of State Walter Gresham and a strong antiannexationist, had a powerful and forbidding vision of what would happen if the United States went searching for empire overseas. The continental United States was virtually impregnable; distant island possessions could only weaken the country's strategic position. Worse still, to enter the tropics would be to debilitate democracy, and to incorporate the population of Hawaii in the population of the United States would be ruinous. Schurz formulated a kind of political and biological law: bad blood and bad customs would drive out good. A rapid deterioration of the American people and their institutions would follow, and the future would be filled with turbulence, demoralization, and decay.

Mahan and Schurz were at opposite poles, and there was a world of argument between. Lorrin Thurston, working harder than he ever had, assembled all the points of dispute, endorsed the favorable comments and rebutted the rest, and published his argument as *A Handbook On The Annexation Of Hawaii*. If America annexed Hawaii, then the Japanese would be curbed; peace would be served because an item of international dispute had been removed; American shipping and commerce would benefit; and the United States would dominate the Pacific. Looking at the other side of the question for purposes of debate, Thurston listed the most commonly repeated objections. The constitution of the United States said nothing about the annexation of territory; Hawaii was not contiguous with the American mainland; Hawaii's people were different from those of the United States and were unfit to be incorporated; annexation would cause problems with foreign powers; Hawaii would be indefensible in time of war; and so on, and so on. One recurring line of complaint was that the revolution of 1893 and the annexation movement that followed were a put-up job for the benefit of the planters, who wanted the protection of the American tariff. Thurston and others explained, as patiently as they could, that sugar had not much to do with the case. The planters would have to balance the benefit of the tariff against the loss they would incur if cheap contract labor were cut off, as it would be under United States law. Most of them, in fact, would rather keep the tariff advantage they held under the reciprocity treaty and let the political advantages of annexation go. So annexation was no planters' plot; it was a genuine movement for good government.

The prophets of the new order were at a tactical disadvantage against the defenders of the old. There might be twenty good reasons for annexation; but just one good reason against it—or even one bad reason vehemently argued—could hold things up indefinitely. Most people had taken a position on Hawaiian annexation at the time of the revolution in 1893, and not many changed their minds, but the question was so important that everybody had to have his say many times over, as if chants and responses would somehow produce magical results. The secret debates in the Senate at the turn of 1898, however, produced nothing in the way of magic. Some simple counting of heads about February showed that the treaty of annexation commanded a majority, but not a two-thirds majority, and under the rules governing the passage of treaties this meant that it would fail.

That was a blow, but not a fatal one. Republican parliamentary strategists could see another way of accomplishing what they wanted. A joint resolution, passed by a simple majority in both the House and the Senate, had brought Texas into the Union some fifty years before; perhaps it would work again for Hawaii.

On March 16, 1898, the Senate Committee on Foreign Relations reported favorably on a resolution for annexation. On May 17 the House Committee on Foreign Relations did the same, making the passage of the joint resolution a near certainty. The fact which finally made the destiny of the United States manifest in relation to Hawaii was that in April the United States had gone to war against Spain.

This war had been in the making for some time. A brutal and incompetent Spanish colonial administration in Cuba was offensive to Americans concerned with good government close to their own shores, and from 1895 onward the problem of the Caribbean was set beside the problem of the Pacific in the great debate over the future of the United States. When Congress declared war on Spain in April 1898, the war resolutions called only for Cuba to be freed from Spanish control. At the same time, however, the position of Spain in the Pacific Ocean gave Alfred Thayer Mahan and his school of strategists a perfect opportunity to make the destiny of America manifest in another place. Spain had controlled the Philippine Islands since the sixteenth century. On May 1, 1898, weeks before American troops fired their first shots in the Caribbean, American ships under the command of Captain George Dewey sank a Spanish fleet in the harbor of Manila in the Philippines. Within a matter of days a good many Americans persuaded themselves that the holding of the Philippines was essential, and once this was conceded there seemed no reason any longer to oppose the annexation of Hawaii, which could serve as a way station to the western Pacific and the continent of Asia.

The annexationists of the Hawaiian Republic could hardly have been more pleased. The legislature decided against proclaiming neutrality; Hawaii would act as an undeclared ally of the United States against Spain. Troopships carrying American soldiers to the Philippines arrived at Honolulu on June 1, and the men were greeted with enthusiasm.

Meanwhile Congress debated the joint resolution on annexation. The opposition was on its last legs. The stirring events of the war made carefully considered constitutional arguments seem like studied pusillanimity, and fears for the future, held up against the accomplishments of the present, took on the shape of crude caricature. In the House, Representative Champ Clark talked about the indefatigable "jingo bacillus" of imperialism. Annex one island and more would be sure to follow, because an appetite for empire fed upon itself. And Hawaii alone would be more than the United States could stomach in the long run. What if Hawaii became a state? "How can we endure our shame when a Chinese Senator from Hawaii, with his pigtail hanging down his back, with his pagan joss in his hand, shall rise from his curule chair and in pigeon English proceed to chop logic with George Frisbie Hoar or Henry Cabot Lodge? O tempora! O mores!" Clark was clowning, others were more sober; but nothing they said affected the outcome. The resolution was put to the vote on June 15, and it passed by a vote of 209 to 91.

The Senate, as always, took its time. Once more the old arguments were rehearsed, but with the American flag flying or about to fly in the Caribbean and the Philippines an irresistible urge developed to see it fly in Hawaii too, and to keep it flying there. "The party of men who propose to take it down," said Senator Henry M. Teller, "will reckon with the great body of the American people, who believe that it is the best flag and the best Government, better calculated to bring peace and prosperity to men than any other flag and Government under the sky." On July 6 the Senate passed the resolution 42 to 21.

President McKinley signed the resolution on July 7, and a week later to the day the news arrived at Honolulu. The annexationist press of the kingdom was delirious with excitement. The native Hawaiians were desperately gloomy. Liliuokalani, who had been on the American mainland, came home sadly on August 2, ten days before the transfer of sovereignty was to take place. Before then several small administrative obscurities had to be cleared up, and one large and important diplomatic problem had to be resolved. Japan's protest over the refusal of Hawaii to admit free laborers in 1897 was still being considered. At the urging of the United States the Hawaiian Republic paid Japan seventy-five thousand dollars as an indemnity, in return for which Japan was to drop all claims in the matter.

With this out of the way the ceremony of transferring sovereignty could be held. Two American warships were at Honolulu. Detachments of marines came ashore and were met by the Hawaiian National Guard. The troops marched to the Government Building on King Street (Iolani Palace, as the Hawaiians still called it). The senior representative of the United States at the islands, Minister Harold M. Sewall, read the resolution of annexation; President of the Republic Sanford Dole made a short speech in response; the Hawaiian anthem, "Hawaii Ponoi," was played for the last time as the song of an independent nation, and the Hawaiian flag was hauled down. The Stars and Stripes took its place, and the band played "The Star Spangled Banner." "To the Hawaiian born it was pathetic," said the *Pacific Commercial Advertiser*. "As the last strain of Hawaii Ponoi trembled out of hearing, the wind suddenly held itself back. The Hawaiian flag as it left the truck dropped and folded, and descended lifeless." Hawaii was dead, but Hawaii-in-America had taken its first breath. "The American flag climbed slowly on its halyards, and just as it reached the truck, the trade wind breaking from its airy leash, caught it in its arms, and rolled it out to its full measure."

This was the ultimate dispossession. The Hawaiians had lost much of their reason for living long ago, when the kapus were abolished; since then a good many of them had lost their lives through disease; the survivors lost their land; they lost their leaders, because many of the chiefs withdrew from politics in favor of nostalgic self-indulgence; and now at last they lost their independence. Their resistance to all this was feeble. It was almost as if they believed what the white man said about them, that they had only half learned the lessons of civilization. Every so often a firebrand like Robert Wilcox would call them to arms, but the response was always a sorry one. They chose to operate within the conventions laid down by white men, and by doing so they put themselves at a disadvantage. They listened to political harangues and composed chants to fit the political occasion; they drew up petitions, and they read the stirring editorials in the Hawaiian language newspapers; but beyond that they did not go. And so they became Americans.

They were told that this was for the best, but they found it hard to believe. It sounded like more missionary talk, of the kind they had been hearing for decades, and they said so. In fact the word "missionary," used by people like Robert Wilcox, was a horrible epithet. And Wilcox used it generously: in his language anybody who wanted the islands to fall into the hands of the United States was a missionary. Of course it was true that among the revolutionaries of 1887 and 1893 and the annexationists of 1898 there were a good number of descendants of Protestant missionaries

—the "mission boys," as Lorrin Thurston described them. In his own confused way Wilcox was right about the intentions of the mission boys; they were fond of saying that they looked always to the higher good, and by the eighteen nineties the United States had come to embody the higher good. The United States responded in kind; in the mixture of motives that led to the annexation of the Hawaiian Islands a strong strain of Protestant religiosity was present, a desire to do good for unfortunates regardless of what the unfortunates thought about it. The Hawaiians were unable to do much about their political fate, but in good Christian fashion they voted with their consciences. As recently as 1870 one Hawaiian in every four had thought of himself as a Protestant. After it became clear that Protestantism entailed aggressive Americanism the Hawaiians began to drop away from the old missionary church. They did not abandon Christianity altogether, but they changed their allegiance. At the beginning of the eighteen nineties the Roman Catholic church and the Mormon church had more than eighteen thousand members between them, and the Protestant church had fewer than three thousand members.

This was the Hawaiians' judgment on good fortune and bad. The underlying question, of course, was just how unfortunate the Hawaiians really were. King Kalakaua, coming home in 1881 after his world tour, remarked to his traveling companion William Armstrong that with all its faults the Hawaiian kingdom was not a bad place, and that with all their misfortunes the Hawaiian people were not badly off—better off, in fact, than most. They had enough to eat and wear, and they were certainly happier than any people he had ever seen; they were never in debt, because no one trusted them; their kuleanas brought them a living; they enjoyed music and the outdoor life; they never went to bed hungry; no one robbed them; and they had no dyspepsia (which was common in America, as Kalakaua observed). Armstrong said: "Your people are dying out and will soon be extinct." "Well, if they are," said Kalakaua, "I've read lots of times that great races died out, and new ones took their places; my people are like the rest. I think the best thing is to let us be." But the Americans could never bring themselves to let the Hawaiians be.

CHAPTER EIGHT

The Territory

1900—1941

Chiefs and Retainers

TOWARD THE END of his life Lorrin Thurston reviewed the accomplishments of the "mission boys," and he found, unsurprisingly, that they were a "splendid body of men." "Instead of using their vantage ground for their personal aggrandizement, they devoted their efforts and influence to winning for Hawaii the fullest possible participation in control of its own affairs as an integral part of the United States, with all the freedom of that status. Having practically complete control of the terms of annexation, they secured citizenship for citizens of Hawaii, thereby relinquishing political power, and handing over to the native sons of Hawaii the proud position of American citizenship—a status not accorded the people of Porto Rico, the Philippines, Guam, or Samoa, all of which came under the American flag about the same time as Hawaii did."

Thurston painted an edifying picture, but it was not one that many people would have recognized in 1900. After August 12, 1898, Hawaii was part of America, but it was America with a difference, and the people at the islands who had been most enthusiastic about annexation were adamant about the distinction. They had not changed their minds since 1893; to them the American way was still the best way, but too much Americanism would be self-defeating. As Sereno Bishop said, the Hawaiians who opposed annexation were incompetent to judge the situation, and the implication was that they would be politically incompetent still. Others agreed with Bishop. No matter which flag flew at the islands race was the only issue that counted in local politics, and to allow a Hawaiian to vote on equal terms with a responsible white man would be to hand over power to the "hater of things American." Statehood for Hawaii was unthinkable, all the best men agreed, and even territorial status would have to be handled carefully.

Sanford Dole, governor designate of the territory, held this view. Natives should not be allowed to vote "simply because they were grown up." "I believe," said Dole early in 1900, "it is exceedingly necessary to keep out of politics this class of people, irresponsible people I mean." Dole was ready to exclude as well "irresponsible people" such as the Portuguese, even though a good many of them had supported the revolution of 1893. And neither Dole nor any other man in a position to influence Hawaii's political future admitted the possibility that Hawaii's Orientals might someday be responsible citizens. (In this, to be sure, Dole and his friends had the agreement even of the "irresponsibles"—Hawaiians, Portuguese, and everyone else at the islands.) Dole's idea of a good constitution was the one he had helped to frame for the Hawaiian Republic in 1894. When President McKinley made him a member of the commission charged with drafting an organic act for the Territory of Hawaii, Dole did his best to see that the interests of responsible white men were served. His fellow commissioners were congenial men—one of them was the same John T. Morgan who had defended the revolution of 1893 on the floor of the United States Senate—and they recommended that candidates for office and voters in elections for the Hawaiian senate should have to meet a property qualification.

Congress disagreed. There were things about the American political tradition too important to discard because of peculiarities in Hawaii's local condition. Hawaii's organic act, which became law on June 14, 1900, stipulated that citizens of the Republic of Hawaii in 1898 would automatically become citizens of the Territory of Hawaii and thus of the United States. They could vote in all local elections, provided that they were male, of age, and had been resident in Hawaii for the required length of time. Nothing was said about property qualifications, either for voters or for candidates.

Oriental immigrants were excluded from the franchise by the definition of citizenship, but the same definition admitted Hawaiians, and even if the Hawaiians were a dying people they could still command an absolute majority at the polls. When political parties began to organize for the first territorial elections the natives did not support Republicans or Democrats. They gave their votes to a third group which campaigned under the name of the Home Rule Party. The leading spokesman for Home Rule was Robert Wilcox, and his advice to native voters was simple: "Nana i ka ili"—look at the skin; in other words, vote Hawaiian. The Home Rulers won fourteen seats in the territorial House, as against nine for the Republicans and four for the Democrats; they won nine of thirteen seats in the Senate; and they elected Wilcox as Hawaii's delegate to Congress.

The first territorial legislature was worse than anyone thought it could be. The organic act directed the legislators to do their business in English, but the Home Rulers insisted on speaking Hawaiian. They tried to free native prisoners in the jails. They resurrected one of Kalakaua's favorite measures, an act to license kahunas as physicians, and Governor Dole had to use his veto. They wanted to lower the tax on female dogs, because a payment of three dollars a year was a hardship for natives who wanted to eat luau dog. Even their most serious efforts were frivolous. They sent a list of names for political appointments to Dole, expecting him to act favorably on their recommendations, when they knew perfectly well that the governor's right of appointment in most cases was not limited by the legislature. The session lasted two months, and at the end of that time no appropriations had been made. Dole was disgusted. He had to call a special session to get money to keep the government running.

As long as the Home Rulers could elect three out of every four members of the legislature nothing much would be accomplished. When the responsible white men of the territory placed themselves within the American political framework, they gave up the right of revolution. The only thing they could do was to win native voters away from Wilcox and the Home Rulers and thus bring the Republican party to power.

So the Republicans invited Jonah Kuhio Kalanianaole to run against Wilcox for delegate to Congress in 1902. On the face of things this was a curious choice. Prince Kuhio was the adopted son of Kalakaua's wife Kapiolani. He was a favorite of Liliuokalani, who named him and his brother David Kawananakoa heirs to the throne after the young Princess Kaiulani died. Both princes fought for the queen in the uprising of 1895, and both were imprisoned for their pains. In 1900 Kawananakoa became a Democrat, and now Kuhio was asked to become a Republican, the ally of the men who overthrew the monarchy.

Would he be chief or retainer? Whatever the nature of the arrangement, and the mutual services involved, Kuhio was able to draw enough voters away from the Home Rulers to be elected delegate to Congress in 1902 and nine more times after that. His success meant the beginning of the end for Home Rule. By 1912 the party was finished.

Robert Wilcox died not long after his first defeat by Kuhio. During his final illness he ran for the post of sheriff of Honolulu, and his campaign was a summation of all the wild things he had ever said. If he was elected, so he told one crowd of natives, he would suspend all the laws and let the Home Rulers put ropes round the necks of the Republicans and have them dragged through the streets.

Kuhio was not impressed by wild talk. He thought he could see advantages in an alliance with the Republicans. The white man wanted control of the territory's government, and the Hawaiians wanted the loaves and fishes of political patronage. That would do, at least for a beginning. But the Republicans, who did not regard the Hawaiians as equal partners, would try to buy political support as cheaply as they could, in the same way as they bought everything else they needed to run their businesses. So the Hawaiians were likely to get only the crusts of the loaves and the bones of the fishes.

Kuhio was happy enough to serve the interests of Hawaii's businessmen at Washington, but just the same he could hardly forget that he was a Hawaiian chief, and he kept asking more for his people than the white leaders of the Republican party wanted to give. The relationship between the Hawaiian chief and the Republican chieftains was always uneasy.

All political roads in Hawaii led to Honolulu. The territory's administration, like its business arrangements, was centralized, and as long as the appointed governor was friendly to big business the balance of power within the Republican Party would always be with white men, even though it was Kuhio who brought in the votes that gave the Republicans control. One way for Kuhio to change this would be to campaign for a measure of home rule on each island. This would increase the value of each native vote, and it would create more patronage jobs for Hawaiians in the rural districts. Kuhio was able to make county government the leading issue in the territorial election of 1904, and in 1905 a commission began work on a counties act.

This was victory of a sort, a redistribution of loaves and fishes, but over the long run Kuhio found it hard to hold his own with the white leaders of the Republican Party. As Hawaii's delegate to Congress he was inundated by good advice from the Honolulu Chamber of Commerce, the Hawaiian Sugar Planters' Association, and the Merchants' Association. They helped pay the salary of his secretary, and they set up offices of their own at the national capital. They talked directly with Washington on matters such as the choice of a governor for the territory, and on other important topics. Kuhio, "Prince Cupid" as everyone called him, was well known and well liked at Washington, a good host and a good guest, a congenial drinking partner and card player, but his voice was only one of several that powerful people listened to when they were considering what should be done about Hawaii.

Apart from the practical question of whether he and his native followers were getting a large enough return on their political investment in Republicanism, Kuhio had to give some thought to what was happening to the Hawaiian people as a whole. The same cries of dispossession and disaster that were heard all through the nineteenth century could still be heard: the white man had taken the native's land, and Orientals were taking away his employment, on the plantations and in the towns. "If conditions remain as they are today," said Kuhio in 1920, "it will only be a matter of a short space of time when this race of people, my people, renowned for their physique, their courage, their sense of justice, their straight-forwardness, and their hospitality, will be a matter of history."

The Hawaiian had all but ceased to be a person; he was defined as a problem. Other people talked about him in abstract terms, and one of the words most frequently used was "rehabilitation." Everyone had his own ideas about what that might mean, and mainland Americans, misunderstanding the situation at the islands as they almost always did, occasionally used a phrase such as "blanket Indian." No one in Hawaii thought seriously about putting Hawaiians on reservations: still, after much discussion, the conclusion was reached that the Hawaiian could be made a useful member of society again only by removing him from society, by making special, exclusive provisions for his welfare to protect him against the ruinous competition of more aggressive races, white and yellow.

Most people agreed further that rehabilitation somehow involved the land. "This is our land," said one Hawaiian, the better part of a century after it had ceased to be so. "It belongs to us. Strangers have come here from the other side and have fattened on the land . . . Everybody gets rich through the Hawaiians, and we are thrown out." That was the simplest possible statement of the issue, but no matter what else was said the survival of the Hawaiians seemed to depend upon a return to the soil. "We are living on soil that was once their peculiar domain," wrote the editor of the *Hilo Tribune-Herald,* a white man. "We have given them much in the way of better ideals and broader vision, but we have taken much from them. If it were possible to set aside lands which are now idle and give the Hawaiians domicile there it would be a fine thing to do."

Fine things would not come cheap, and so the next subject to be discussed was how much the rehabilitation of the Hawaiian might cost in the way of land and who should pay. Not altogether by coincidence, rehabilitation became a popular topic of conversation at a time when some excellent land was about to be put on the market. This was important. Earlier efforts to get homestead programs under way, not only for deserving Hawaiians but for men of any race who wanted to do some small farming, had run into trouble because most of the good agricultural and pastoral land in the islands was spoken for by wealthy planters and ranchers. But between 1917 and 1921 leases on more than two hundred thousand acres of government land would expire, and along with a great deal of pasturage more than twenty-six thousand acres of developed sugar land would be available for homesteads, if the territorial government would make it available—or, more to the point, if the United States Congress would direct the territorial government to make it available. The sugar planters had seen this coming. They argued that homesteading in Hawaii had failed in the past and was likely to go on failing. So to take good sugar land from those who could make it yield a profit and give it to those who could not was foolish. Not even the Hawaiians would be served, because a bankrupt native on an unworkable small farm would be no better off than an unemployed native in a miserable tenement at Honolulu.

But rehabilitation was a powerful word, and Congress was willing at least to give its advocates a hearing. A territorial legislative commission, the first of its kind from the islands, visited Washington to present evidence to congressional committees. What emerged was the Hawaiian Homes Commission Act of 1920, a masterly blend of shadow and substance.

The supporters of rehabilitation for the Hawaiians never suggested that homesteads should be made available freely to applicants of any race—just Hawaiians. Sugar planters did not want to lose good land to homesteaders of any race, so it was no pain to them to agree that a homesteading act, whatever its other provisions, should benefit only Hawaiians. But what if Hawaiians applied for homesteads in such numbers that they in themselves became a threat to good sugar land? That would be paying too high a price for rehabilitation. A way would have to be found to use other locations for homesteads. Other land might not be fertile, but the point of homesteading was not to make the Hawaiian rich, just to make him work and take pride in his efforts. If the planters' leases were renewed, part of the lease rentals could be used by the territorial government to set Hawaiians up on homestead lots far away from the sugar plantations. Thus the planters could keep their productive lands, and the Hawaiians, making unproductive lands bloom, would have a new reason for living. Or so the perfected argument ran.

"Personally," wrote Governor Charles J. McCarthy in the middle of the deliberations, "I have my doubts as to whether the Act will do all that is claimed, but I am strongly in favor of it and I am willing to give it all the support I can. If it works it will be the best thing that could possibly happen to the Hawaiians and also to the Territory at large. Should it fail the Hawaiian people will have only themselves to blame."

McCarthy was too generous with his praise and blame. The Act gave Hawaiians of more than half native blood the privilege of applying to a commission for a ninety-nine year lease of a small agricultural or pastoral lot (they were not allowed to buy the land, because then they could sell it, and the dispossession of the Great Mahele in the nineteenth century would be repeated). The land they might lease was defined carefully. Forest reserves were excluded, and so was land already being used for cultivating sugar, and land already occupied by homesteaders under previous agreements. What was left was land that no one had ever been able to make productive.

About twenty thousand Hawaiians qualified for homestead lots under the Act. But, as the part-Hawaiian politician John Wilson observed, rather less than two hundred thousand acres of land were made available, and not all at once. If the "average acreage allowed each person was 1,000, the largest number of homes which could be supplied the Hawaiians would be 193. If the estimated average is 500 for each home-seeker, the total number of homes supplied would be 386. Certainly there are more than 386 Hawaiian families in this Territory who should be provided for under any rehabilitation scheme, and how the fathers of this bill intend to satisfy those who are not so provided is a problem the solving of which does not seem to be even on the dim horizon."

Even for Hawaiians who managed to convince the administrators of the Act that they deserved a homestead lot, the horizon was dim indeed. On Molokai, at the Kalanianaole settlement (named for Kuhio who, ironically, supported the planters' requests to have their lands exempted from homesteading), the native farmers had to pump water from a spring that turned salty within a few years. Irrigation was talked about endlessly but nothing was done, and by the end of the twenties the homesteaders, still not rehabilitated, were signing contracts with the pineapple firm of Libby, McNeill & Libby. In the thirties and forties homesteaders on other islands began to ask the Hawaiian Homes Commission not for farm lots but for household lots. (Most Hawaiians, after all, were some generations from the taro patch, and they had not much more than a stylized yearning for the land.) By that time no one was prepared to say much about the prospects for rehabilitation in what amounted to rural tenements.

In one way at least the native Hawaiians were rich in land. When Princess Bernice Pauahi, heir to the estates of the Kamehamehas, died in 1884, she left her lands, amounting to one-ninth of all the land in the islands, to be used for the benefit of the Hawaiian people. Under the terms of her will the income from her estate was to be used to support two schools, giving preference to students of "pure or part aboriginal blood," "one for boys and one for girls, to be known as, and called the Kamehameha Schools." Her hope was that this lavish bequest would work a transformation among young Hawaiians.

Princess Bernice's husband, the banker Charles R. Bishop, was chairman of the first board of trustees of Bishop Estate. His colleagues were the attorney William O. Smith; the businessman Charles Montague Cooke, son of the missionary who taught Princess Bernice at the Chiefs' Children's School and then went on to found the firm of Castle & Cooke; the Reverend Charles McEwen Hyde, an eminent Protestant clergyman; and Samuel Mills Damon, son of the first seamen's chaplain at Honolulu and a member of the banking firm of Bishop & Co. No Hawaiian was appointed to the board. So once again the well-intentioned white man had control of the natives' land and was setting out to teach the Hawaiian how to be a Hawaiian.

The trustees, meeting in 1885, two years before the first class was enrolled at the boys' school, eight years before the revolution of 1893, thirteen years before Hawaiian independence was extinguished, and thirty-five years before the Hawaiian Homes Commission Act was passed, could still talk about a future in which Hawaiians would "compete with other nationalities in the struggle for national existence." The "beneficent but inexorable law of competition in human society, a fundamental law in all physical life," would have to be recognized. The young Hawaiian would be helped to "hold his own from the first in this honorable rivalry, so that he shall work out his own future under the conditions most favorable for his success."

Well, perhaps. The first principal of the boys' school, a New Englander named William Brewster Oleson, was a member of the revolutionary committee that imposed the bayonet constitution of 1887 on King Kalakaua; he helped put down the insurrection of Robert Wilcox in 1889; and he took part in the revolution of 1893. Trustee Smith was a revolutionary too, and both he and Trustee Damon held cabinet posts under the provisional government and the Hawaiian Republic. So the young Hawaiian would work out his future under political conditions laid down for him by others.

According to the will of their benefactor the boys and girls of Kamehameha Schools were to get "first and chiefly a good education in the common English branches, and also instruction in morals and in such useful knowledge as may tend to make good and industrious men and women." Instruction in "the higher branches" was to be "subsidiary to the foregoing objects." The "good" was easy to take care of, at least on paper: teachers were "forever" to be "persons of the Protestant religion." In practice, of course, the good did not triumph immediately; one principal of the boys' school early in the twentieth century complained that he found no "general conception of honor, of speaking the truth, or of the sacredness of property rights such as we find in American boys." The basis of industry was even harder to define. What should a Hawaiian expect for himself in the early days of the Territory? Not a great deal, evidently; and certainly not a job of any substance at Castle & Cooke or Bishop & Co. "The object of the Manual School," wrote the members of the education committee of the boys' school in 1911, "is to turn out tradesmen from the shops and from the agriculture department boys who will know how to work on the farm. Sufficient academic work should be given to make the best tradesmen and the best farmers. All idea of preparing at Kamehameha for the High Schools or at Oahu College should be discouraged." This was making the "higher branches" subsidiary with a vengeance; it was also a literal reading of Princess Bernice's will.

Charles Bishop, who was in favor of preparing the boys for a life on the land, noted one difficulty early in the school's existence. The soil of the boys' campus, west of Honolulu, was arid and rocky, badly suited for training in agriculture. As Bishop said, it was not "such as a man would choose with the expectation of making a profit off of it," and so it "would not afford a good practical lesson for an industrious man without capital to use or to waste." On the other hand, as some Hawaiians found, it provided perfect preparation for farming the land made available to them under the Hawaiian Homes Commission Act.

After the Kamehameha Schools had been in existence for more than a generation some members of the Alumni Association made a comment on their education. A good many of them had managed to go on to high school and to college, and what they saw there brought them to the unhappy conclusion that Princess Bernice's endowment was being misused. Despite all the money spent, the public schools of the territory offered a better education than Kamehameha Schools. For a Hawaiian to be good and industrious was no longer enough, if it ever had been, and the trustees of Bishop Estate should think again about what they were doing. "The assumption is made by the school authorities that the mind of the Hawaiian boy is capable of developing up to a certain stage only and no further," the alumni wrote in 1916. "The man who takes that position is entirely wrong . . . We represent the body of men who are today suffering the lack of this education and we ask of you to raise the standard for the sake of the young people of the land who are to be men and women of the future. The school authorities are making every effort to strengthen the industrial work of the pupils; that is very commendable; but the training of the hand must be accompanied by the proper training and development of the head."

The alumni were saying in the clearest of voices that they did not think they had much reason to be grateful to the white trustees of Kamehameha Schools for the gift of a second-rate education. But not every Hawaiian would have agreed with their criticisms. Many natives were happy to have a white benefactor, in or out of Kamehameha Schools. Even among Hawaiians who wanted their countrymen to rehabilitate themselves there were those who accepted as a matter of course the dominance of white men, the new chiefs—as important as the old chiefs now that the kingdom was a thing of the past, perhaps even more important. The "old families"—Castles, Cookes, and the rest—would always help the Hawaiian if he proved himself "deserving," in the words of the Hawaiian Protective Association, and the Hawaiian would do well to look up to the old families, "for they will always have kindly feelings for him." That was true enough; the old families' list of benefactions, public and private, was endless. The only point at issue was whether native Hawaiians, free citizens of the United States under the organic act, would ever be anything but objects of charity in their home islands.

The Rising Sun

For the Orientals of Honolulu the twentieth century opened tragically. In December 1899, a case of bubonic plague was discovered in Chinatown, where seven thousand Chinese, Japanese, and Hawaiians lived cooped up in less than fifty acres of space close to the waterfront. Armed guards were posted to see that no one went in or out of Chinatown without permission from the Board of Health. Before the turn of the new year another dozen cases of plague were reported, and more were expected. A sanitary commission appointed to investigate living conditions among the Orientals brought back horror stories of shops, restaurants, stables, chicken coops, and privies huddled together without light or ventilation or drainage; houses and stores built directly over cess pools; gutters full of filth; lice, fleas, cockroaches, flies, and rats everywhere. The government decided that if an epidemic was to be avoided the worst parts of the quarter would have to be burned, even if this meant that landlords such as the Bishop Estate would lose their rents and hundreds of Orientals would lose their homes and their livelihood. The first "sanitary fire" was lit on December 31, and from then on plague spots were burned systematically and the dispossessed Orientals and Hawaiians were sent to quarantine camps on the outskirts of town.

On January 20 a fire was started near the corner of Beretania Street and Nuuanu Avenue, where five deaths from plague had occurred within a few days. Four fire engines were at the ready, and every fireman in Honolulu was on the scene, but this was not enough to prevent disaster. The condemned buildings had been burning for about an hour when the wind freshened and scattered sparks along the roof tops where the firemen could not reach them. Kaumakapili Church, with its high twin towers, burst into flame. The fire crossed Beretania Street; by midday it was out of control, and during the afternoon it burned its way almost to the waterfront. People in the path of the flames rushed to escape from Chinatown and were turned back by the guards stationed at the boundaries of the plague area, and as the smoke rose over the city Orientals who had already been evacuated to the quarantine camps came running back to try to save the belongings they had left behind. The guards stopped them at the entrance to Chinatown and they could do nothing but watch as their homes and stores burned.

Thirty-eight acres of Chinatown were destroyed, and about seven thousand Chinese, Japanese, and Hawaiians were confined to the quarantine camps for several months before they were allowed to go back and pick over the rubble of their homes. Oriental businessmen had to wait even longer for the government to hear their claims for damages. They asked for more than three million dollars; they were awarded about a million and a half.

Some of the Orientals felt put upon. They appreciated the food and clothing they were given by generous white men and women at the camps, but this expression of kindness was after the event, and they were not at all sure that the fire was accidental to begin with. It seemed too much of a coincidence that only the homes of Orientals were destroyed and only the businessess of Orientals were burned. The fact of the matter was that the wind had changed, and no one could have predicted that. But the *Pacific Commercial Advertiser* did not ease the situation by suggesting, while the ashes of Chinatown were still warm, that the fire would give the white man's business district room to expand. Downtown Honolulu was crowded already. The Orientals would be just as well off if they moved across Nuuanu stream to the west, and in any case the *Advertiser* would rather see "Asiatics pressed back than the owners of Honolulu's most beautiful and stately homes." The *Advertiser* was saying what had been said for years at the islands—that the Oriental must be kept in his place.

If bubonic plague was a terrible disease at least fire would cure it; the festering sore of Chinatown could be cauterized. But the Oriental remained, and there was no indication that he would ever go away. By comparison the problem of the native Hawaiian was insignificant. If a white man could not summon sympathy for the suffering Hawaiian he could at least pretend that the natives were dying out, and that pangs of conscience were irrelevant. But this kind of reasoning could not be used to dispose of the Orientals. They were in Hawaii to stay, and they showed every sign of perpetuating themselves in great numbers.

The first Chinese coolies brought to the islands in 1852 were expected to do their work on the plantations and no more. No one wanted them to enjoy the same range of opportunities as white men, or even natives. When they moved to the towns they were criticized as relentless invaders, unfair competitors, subverters of the established order. The Japanese who came to the islands in the eighteen eighties were supposed to do what the Chinese would not do—solve the labor problem without creating a social problem. But Japanese, like Chinese, went to the towns, and proceeded to compete with white men and natives in the same way. By the end of the nineteenth century the Oriental problem was largely a Japanese problem, not because the Chinese problem had disappeared but because the size of the Japanese problem put it in a different perspective. When Hawaii was annexed to the United States in 1898 America's Chinese Exclusion Act, passed in 1882, went into force at the islands. The sugar planters, needing more laborers, brought in more Japanese; between 1896 and 1900 the Japanese population of the islands rose from less than twenty-five thousand to more than sixty thousand. In the first seven years of the new century another forty thousand were brought in, and even after the "Gentlemen's Agreement" of 1907 stopped the flow of Japanese workers to the United States, Japanese women—"picture brides"—kept coming to Hawaii until 1924, when the United States Congress passed a definitive Japanese Exclusion Act.

Ever since annexation, when the contract labor laws of Hawaii were superseded by the labor laws of the United States, the Japanese had been trying out the strike as an economic weapon. In 1909 five thousand of them went on strike for higher wages. The Japanese were getting eighteen dollars a month for twenty-one days' work; Portuguese and Puerto Ricans were getting twenty-two or twenty-three dollars for the same work.

The planters' policy had always been to adjust wages to racial background, and the Japanese could not help but feel the slight, but even the most outspoken of their newspapers, the *Nippu Jiji,* tried to reduce the argument to economic terms. "If a laborer comes from Japan, and he performs same quantity of work of same quality within the same period of time as those who hail from opposite side of the world, what good reason is there to discriminate one as against the other. It is not the color of the skin or hair, or the language that he speaks, or manner or custom, that grow cane in the field. It is labor that grows cane, and the more efficient the labor the better the crop the cane field will bring. We demand of higher wages of planters in the full confidence of the efficiency of our labor, and, also, in the equally full confidence in the planters' sense of justice and equity in all things that pertains to human affairs, especially in the delicate relation between capital and labor."

The planters did not share this view of justice and equity. Strike-breakers were hired to cut cane on Oahu at a dollar and a half a day, twice what the Japanese had been earning. The strikers' families were evicted from their company homes, and Yasutaro Soga, editor of the *Nippu Jiji,* was arrested for conspiracy, along with the leaders of the Japanese Higher Wage Association. The strikers did not have much money; they could not hold out, and when they went back to work it was at the old wage.

The planters had to have Japanese labor, but they wanted to be able to keep the Japanese under control, and the best way to do that was to make sure other labor was available when it was needed. So they encouraged migrants from many places to come to the islands. Russians, Spaniards, and Germans were imported at great cost; most took one look at conditions on the plantations and left for the American mainland. More Portuguese arrived early in the twentieth century; several hundred American Negroes were brought in; and some Puerto Ricans and Koreans were recruited. Then another source was tapped—the Philippine Islands, which had the advantage of being an American dependency. By 1932 more than a hundred thousand Filipinos had been brought to the islands. But during the early years of the twentieth century the Japanese were still the biggest single group of plantation workers.

They struck again for higher wages in 1920. Living costs rose sharply during World War I, but an ordinary field hand was still making only seventy-seven cents a day and the planters were not willing to make up the entire difference with bonuses. The Japanese on Oahu bargained with the Hawaiian Sugar Planters' Association, got nowhere, and decided to strike.

This time the planters made a purely racial issue of the dispute. They talked about a deliberate attempt on the part of conspirators to "Japanize" the islands. If agitators could control the plantation laborers, said the *Star Bulletin,* they would be "as completely the masters of Hawaii's destiny as if they held title to the land and the growing cane. They would be the autocratic dictators of Hawaii's industrialism . . . Hawaii would be as thoroughly Japanized, so far as its industrial life is concerned, as if the Mikado had the power to name our governor and direct our political destiny . . . Never lose sight of the real issue: Is Hawaii to remain American or become Japanese? A compromise of any nature or any degree with the alien agitators would be a victory for them and an indirect but nonetheless deadly invasion of American sovereignty in Hawaii. The American citizen who advocates anything less than resistance to the bitter end against the arrogant ambition of the Japanese agitators is a traitor to his own people."

The volatile organizer of the Filipino Federation of Labor, Pablo Manlapit, led his workers out on strike even before the Japanese, but then he began to act strangely, calling off the strike because the Japanese, so he said, were conspiring to take over the industry, and then calling the strike on again without further explanation. Under pressure from the planters the Filipino labor organization shook itself to pieces.

With Manlapit out of the way for the time being the planters could turn to the Japanese. They told the workers who lived in plantation camps to leave their homes. Four thousand found shelter in the country districts of Oahu; the rest came with their families to be billeted at Honolulu in

Buddhist temples and Japanese sake breweries—about six thousand people in all.

The strikers carried pictures of Abraham Lincoln in their parades and demonstrations, but somehow the Oriental paintbrush made even Lincoln look Japanese, and as the strike went on week after week the race war predicted by the *Star Bulletin* seemed more and more likely. It was fatally easy for people to talk in terms of irreconcilable opposites; it was harder to find a middle ground where antagonists might meet in good faith.

At the height of the strike the Reverend Albert W. Palmer of Central Union Church at Honolulu, where many of the city's Protestant businessmen worshipped, put forward a plan of conciliation. Palmer and his friends thought the Japanese were wrong to present their economic demands as a national group. They should call off the strike, disband the Japanese Labor Federation, and allow an interracial sugar workers' organization to take its place. As for the planters, they should welcome the Japanese back to work and then let the laborers choose representatives by secret ballot to meet with management and settle disputes in conference.

The Japanese accepted Palmer's proposal; the planters rejected it out of hand. They had insured their crops, and their plantations were being worked by strikebreakers—Hawaiians, Portuguese, Puerto Ricans, Chinese, and Koreans. They were in a position to outstay the Japanese, just as they had done in 1909. At the end of June the Japanese surrendered. They talked about the "magnanimity" of the planters and the "sincerity" of the laborers, and about an "unreserved understanding" between the two parties. What this meant was that the laborers went back to work on the same old terms, hoping that the planters would make improvements in wages and conditions.

Again the planters tried to find a way out of their difficulties by importing other kinds of labor. A commission was sent to Washington to put the case for an exemption from the labor laws of the United States. If Chinese could be brought to the islands for five years at a time and then shipped home after their stint of work on the plantations, the sugar industry would be saved and Americanism would triumph. With any luck so many Japanese would be put out of work that they would be forced to go home to Japan, and the conspiracy would be foiled. Congress was not persuaded that the Oriental menace in Hawaii would be put down by adding more Orientals, of whatever kind, to the population. No special laws were passed.

Once again, then, Americans from the islands were not able to convince their countrymen that things were different in Hawaii. Yet no special insight was needed to see where the trouble lay. The planters' dilemma had been discussed a thousand times; it was as old as the sugar industry, and it was something the planters had brought upon themselves and upon the islands at large. Sugar required cheap labor, and one way to make sure that labor stayed cheap was to bring in as many laborers as possible. No white man would work in the fields for the wages the planters offered. By the same token, immigrants who would take low wages were not likely to make good citizens—or, at least, good American citizens. So, as the United States Commissioner General of Immigration observed, either the planters were "insincere in their declared desire to Americanize the islands or else their efforts are at crosspurposes with their ambitions." As long as the sugar plantations of the islands were worked by Orientals Hawaii would not approach "the actual standard of an American Territory."

Paradoxically, the Japanese did not lack a capacity for loyalty; in fact they were overendowed with patriotism. But in them this prime virtue looked like a vice, because they directed their loyalties homeward, or at least they did in the beginning. "We are subjects of Dai Nippon," wrote the editor of the *Yamato* in 1895. As far as most white men in Hawaii could see nothing had changed in the twentieth century.

So what was the future of Hawaii? "Supposing, for the sake of an example," said the wealthy businessman Walter F. Dillingham in 1920, "that the Japanese on one of her mandated islands in the Pacific should develop the island by bringing in a great number of American citizens, and finally they had a situation where 110,000 red-blooded Americans were on the island where there were 18,000 pure-blooded Japanese. How would I feel having a college classmate visit me, to usher him from the boat to the house, kick off sandals and toss a kimona and say, 'This is my home. My wife and I came here from America fifteen years ago, and we have made our home here and have entered into the spirit of the life. I want you to meet my boy.' In comes a fine, upstanding boy, fifteen years of age. I say, 'He is going to the University of Japan. He reads, writes, and speaks Japanese better than he does English, and if we ever have a rumpus with Uncle Sam that boy is true blue; he is going to fight for the Empire.'

"Now just imagine pointing with pride to your son and saying that, and you realize what you're asking of the Japanese in Hawaii."

Under United States law an immigrant of Japanese ancestry could not become a naturalized American citizen—not even if he served in the United States armed forces, as some of Hawaii's Japanese found after World War One. So as long as the first generation of Japanese migrants, the issei, survived at the islands Hawaii would have a large alien population. But what about the second generation, the nisei, young people born in Hawaii of Japanese parents? They were American citizens by birth, and when they grew up they would have the vote as a matter of right. Even if the older Japanese could not be made to conform to the American tradition the younger Japanese must be made to assimilate, because they were Americans whether anyone wanted them to be or not.

What was an American? For one thing he ought to be a Christian, and he certainly ought not to be a Buddhist. "As an ethical system," observed the *Friend* not long after Japanese migration to Hawaii began in earnest, "Buddhism is far superior to heathen Hinduism, although it has totally failed to elevate the Japanese people anywhere near to the current morality and decency of Christian peoples."

Missionaries, Christian and Buddhist, began work among the plantation laborers during the eighteen nineties. Oddly enough, some of the planters encouraged Buddhist priests to visit the laborers' camps. Some of the Japanese of the early years were unruly, even violent, and if the teachings of the Buddha would curb their temper without spoiling their capacity for work, well and good. In this as in other cases the planters' reasoning did not run in a straight line toward Americanization, but others saw the difficulty. When the Honpa Hongwanji mission, the most important Buddhist group in the islands, applied in 1906 for a charter of incorporation as a religious organization, Governor George R. Carter rejected the application on the ground that it was not compatible "with the best future interests of this Territory." The Buddhists had to wait another year, and then a new governor, Walter F. Frear, signed their charter.

The Christian missionaries did poorly. In 1916 there were more than a hundred thousand Japanese in Hawaii, and only seventeen hundred of them were Christians. The Buddhists did much better, but the planters were no longer pleased. Somewhere along the way meekness got lost, and by 1920 several of the Buddhist priests were encouraging strikers. The planters understood this to mean that Buddhist missionaries were apostles of arrogant Japanese nationalism, and the priests took their place alongside newspaper editors such as Yasutaro Soga of the *Nippu Jiji* and Fred Makino of the *Hawaii Hochi* as devil figures in the Japanese conspiracy.

Other conspirators were identified as well, and a good many of them turned out to be teachers at Japanese language schools attached to Buddhist temples. The first language schools, established at the turn of the twentieth century, made no secret of their intention to give young Japanese a good schooling in preparation for their life as subjects of the Emperor. No one would have begrudged the Japanese that, as long as they went home to Japan to live. But if they stayed in Hawaii how could a double allegiance be defended? At first the leader of the Honpa Hongwanji mission, Yemyo Imamura, paid no attention to criticism of his schools, but as more and more nisei boys and girls enrolled in the public schools of the territory and came to language school after hours he had to reconsider what his teachers were doing. By the time World War One was over the Buddhist language schools were committed to preparing their students for life as American citizens and not as Japanese subjects, but the extent of their commitment did not satisfy ardent Americanizers, particularly in the years just after World War One, when immigrants everywhere in the United States were being told to cut their ties with the past and look to a one hundred percent American future.

The Daughters of the American Revolution, Aloha Chapter, spoke for all the Americanizers in Hawaii when they announced that they were "unequivocally opposed to all practices within the borders of the United States of America subversive to the peace and order of our Nation and the undivided allegiance of our people, and unalterably opposed to all foreign-language schools of whatever nationality . . ." The members took a "firm stand for Americanism in its truest and loftiest form, and for one language—that of our heroic Revolutionary ancestors who gave their fortunes and their lives that the United States might live and prosper, and one flag—'Old Glory'!"

This did not leave much room for the Japanese language schools. How could they claim to be teaching loyalty to the United States, asked one good American, when the fifteen petaled imperial chrysanthemum was displayed on all their school buildings? Why did classes meet on Thanksgiving Day, one of the most sacred and cherished of all American holidays? And how could the schools justify flying the Japanese flag above the Stars and Stripes on New Year's Day?

If that was the sort of thing they were doing they should be stopped, so the Americanizers thought. The question came before the territorial legislature at the worst possible time for the Japanese—during the sugar workers' strike of 1920. Some leaders in the Japanese community argued for the integrity of the schools. Others thought compromise was essential; if the Japanese stood up too strongly for their rights they might lose the schools altogether. In the end the Japanese cooperated with the legislature in framing new regulations. Beginning in 1921 the schools were licensed by the territorial Department of Public Instruction. Teachers had to demonstrate a grasp of the English language, American history, and the ideals of democracy, and they had to pledge themselves to teach their students loyalty to the United States.

The Americanizers regarded this victory as only the opening shot in a long campaign. They reviewed the curriculum and the textbooks of the language schools in 1921, and then they went on to insist that the kindergarten and the first two years of the schools should be abolished. The Japanese objected, but they were told that if they did not agree the legislature would simply pass a law over their heads.

Hawaii, said Governor Wallace R. Farrington, had a "time-honored reputation for friendliness toward every race and nationality." Law-abiding aliens would not be ostracized and penalized, but "radical and insulting" aliens would be dealt with severely. At the same time opportunities should "forever remain open especially for the American youth of alien ancestry, and he should be encouraged in every way to join the American ranks and cooperate in the advancement of our American commonwealth." If the Japanese wanted to assimilate, then, the door of opportunity was wide open before them, so Farrington said.

But just as surely the language school regulations would close some other doors behind them. The Japanese had to decide whether one set of open doors was enough. Several of the language schools went to court and got temporary injunctions against the regulations. The territorial legislature of 1923 passed a new and more severe act regulating the schools, and more of the schools put their case before the courts. In 1925 the legislature moved to prevent the schools from taking out injunctions, and during the next two years the contest went from court to court in the territory and then to the appellate courts of the United States, where the petitions of the Japanese were upheld. The territory appealed to the United States Supreme Court, without success. On February 21, 1927, Associate Justice James G. C. McReynolds read a decision in favor of the language schools. The territory's attempt to deny the owners and patrons of the schools "reasonable choice and discretion in respect of teachers, curriculum and text books" amounted to a "deliberate plan to bring foreign language schools under a strict governmental control for which the record discloses no adequate reason." Most of the parents whose children went to the language schools were aliens, but the Constitution protected them just as it protected American citizens.

Alien, citizen—for the Japanese these words were loaded with meaning, because they divided father and son. How much did a young Japanese born in Hawaii owe to his father, and how much did he owe to the United States? Could he be a Japanese in private and an American in public, Japanese in one part of his mind and American in another? Even if he changed his allegiance altogether he could not change the color of his skin, and some people in Hawaii thought matters began and ended there. "The Oriental races," wrote Edward P. Irwin in the Honolulu monthly *Paradise of The Pacific* in 1924, "are practically all of small stature, yellow or brown color and, in the case of the Japanese, characterized by flat features, protruding teeth and short legs. We have a right to ask ourselves if we want to incorporate such characteristics in the American body."

Crude racism aside, a usable definition of Americanism was hard to come by. One of the most wholehearted Americanizers in the Japanese community was the Reverend Takie Okumura, a Protestant evangelist who had been at work among his countrymen in the islands since the eighteen nineties, preaching, writing, and organizing Christian language schools in opposition to the Buddhists. For him as for the white Americanizers Christianity and Americanism were inseparable, but in some ways he was more Japanese than the most conservative Buddhist. He wanted the Japanese, young and old, to show their acceptance of their new country by accepting what they were offered in Hawaii. This would mean making filial loyalty into an economic and political principle, and some of the younger Japanese were not sure just how American that might be. The native Hawaiians had made an uneasy conditional peace with the white fathers of the Republican Party who administered the Hawaiian Homes Commission Act and the Kamehameha Schools, but for the sons of Japanese immigrants the white fathers were the plantation managers who offered a dollar a day for work in the fields when times were good, and the lunas, the field foremen, who cracked a black snake whip when times were worse. If Japanese were to be Americans, then surely life should offer more than that. How could a Japanese become an American if he could not think of himself as a man?

A Quota of Sweetness and Light

For all their troubles with the Japanese the planters did well. Between 1896 and 1932 the number of plantations in the territory dropped from fifty-six to forty-two, but the acreage under sugar increased, the labor force doubled in size, from twenty-five thousand workers to fifty thousand, and the production of sugar quadrupled, from a quarter of a million tons a year to more than a million.

Decade by decade the industry became more efficient. The Hawaiian Sugar Planters' Association established an Experiment Station in 1895, and its scientists and engineers quickly developed sophisticated approaches to the problems of crossbreeding cane, eradicating insect pests, fertilizing soil, conserving water, and perfecting machinery for the fields and the mills.

At the same time the business managers of the industry were learning efficiency. In 1898 two of the leading sugar agencies, Castle & Cooke and Alexander & Baldwin, took on the Spreckels plantation interests in a stock battle and emerged in control of Spreckelsville on Maui. In 1905 the members of the Hawaiian Sugar Planters' Association combined to buy their own refinery at Crockett in California, thus taking the Hawaiian crop out of the hands of west coast refiners and returning a greater share of profits to the islands. In 1910 Claus Spreckels' old partner William Irwin merged his interests with C. Brewer & Co. and gave Brewer & Co. control of the Oceanic Steamship Line. At the end of World War One, while the properties of the German-owned agency of Hackfeld & Co. were still frozen at Honolulu, a new firm, financed largely by men who already had interests in sugar agencies, arranged with the United States Alien Properties Administration to take over Hackfeld's assets. The new company, patriotically named American Factors, took its place in the sugar industry as one of the Big Five, along with Castle & Cooke; Alexander & Baldwin; Theo. Davies & Co.; and C. Brewer & Co. By 1932 the agencies were strong enough to make some alterations in the management of the pineapple industry, which began as a straggling supplement to sugar late in the nineteenth century and developed into a highly promising second staple for the islands, supplying three-quarters of the world market. James D. Dole, head of the Hawaiian Pineapple Company, bought the entire island of Lanai in 1922 for something more than a million dollars, and his firm led the industry. But Dole found himself short of funds in the depression of the late twenties and early thirties, and in 1932 the sugar agencies took control of Hawaiian Pineapple.

The Big Five controlled 75 percent of the sugar crop by 1910, and 96 percent by 1933. By a kind of inevitable extension they came to control as well every business associated with sugar: banking; insurance; utilities; wholesale and retail merchandising; railroad transportation in the islands; shipping between islands and between the islands and California. The agencies, established in the nineteenth century to serve the plantations, had become the tail that wagged the dog.

"These companies," wrote a federal labor investigator in 1906, "take a profit on nearly all the freight that passes the plantation boundaries in either direction. Their commissions, which are very liberal, are collected in bad as well as in good years. Moreover, they are the plantations' bankers, and have the pickings of their financial transactions. In addition to the plantation agencies, there are transportation companies, both land and marine, and irrigation companies, all living off the plantations and taking their profits in lean years as well as in fat ones. The stock of all these companies is owned by the men who are most heavily interested in plantation stocks. These inside investors are therefore often making a comfortable income out of the sugar industry during years when the outside investor is receiving no return on his capital. They can afford to have their sugar dividends passed so long as the dividends upon their railway, steamship, or agency stock continue to come in regularly. Thus the compensation that capital receives from the industry is greater than appears on the surface. Probably there is never a year when the plantations do not pay the running expenses of the people of the Territory."

Economic power meant political power, and so the same handful of men ran the government of Hawaii. "There is a government in this Territory which is centralized to an extent unknown in the United States, and probably almost as much centralized as it was in France under Louis XIV," said the Attorney General of Hawaii in 1903. He was in a position to know. His name was Edward P. Dole, and by no coincidence he was related to Sanford B. Dole, first governor of the territory—as, indeed, were four other important men in Dole's administration. Those outside the magic circle in the early days of the territory talked enviously or bitterly or resignedly of "the family compact." They could very well have used the same phrase as late as the nineteen thirties, and it was amazing how often, even at that late date, the names that turned up on boards of directors and public commissions were those of the missionary family of the nineteenth century. Every one of the Big Five had at least one direct descendant of a missionary on its board, and Alexander & Baldwin had six—William Alexander, Henry A. Baldwin, F. F. Baldwin, William O. Smith, A. C. Castle, and J. P. Cooke. Those names and others from the missionary family—Judd, Wilcox, Dole, Damon, Thurston, Hall, and Chamberlain—appeared on the boards of almost every important firm that did business at Honolulu: Inter Island Steam Ships; Matson Navigation; Oahu Railroad and Land; Honolulu Rapid Transit; Honolulu Gas; Hawaiian Electric; Mutual Telephone; Waterhouse Trust; Hawaiian Trust; Bishop Trust; International Trust; Allen & Robinson; Lewers & Cooke; Bishop Bank. Relatives by marriage—Athertons, Frears, Tenneys, Galts, Waterhouses, and others—served with the "mission boys." Even the "Big Sixth," Walter F. Dillingham, the aggressive, imaginative, faintly piratical land developer, probably the single most powerful businessman in Hawaii in the nineteen twenties and thirties, was related to the missionary family through his mother. A member of the United States Attorney General's staff drew a diagram of interlocking directorates in 1932, and the result was a picture of lines of power and influence such as Walter Murray Gibson, Claus Spreckels, and King Kalakaua would never have dreamed of in their most extravagant moments.

Every appointed governor of the territory was beholden in some way or other to one or another of the Big Five, and the agencies were well represented on governmental boards that dealt with tax appraisals, land leases, and other items of interest. As far as candidates for elective office were concerned, money could always be found to support a worthy Republican—sometimes an excess of money, as federal investigators learned when they looked into the allotment of campaign funds at the islands. But the money was well spent. Between 1900 and 1940 eight out of every ten men elected to the territorial legislature were Republicans, and the legislators could hardly help being considerate of their benefactors. At the islands there was a place for everybody, and everybody was in his place—and the place of the Big Five was at the center of affairs. The unkind were tempted to call the arrangement a spider's web, but the officers of the Big Five and the directors of the Hawaiian Sugar Planters' Association saw nothing wrong in having a table of organization that covered their industry and their islands efficiently.

No responsible member of a Big Five firm minded being accused of paternalism. Plantation workers' wages in Hawaii were higher than anywhere else in the world, and if laborers' living conditions were bad before the big strikes of 1909 and 1920 they were better afterward, because by then management was ready to concede the point that a happy worker was less likely to strike than a disgruntled one.

The sugar agencies, of course, had to balance the happiness of their workers against the profits of the plantations, and sometimes the balance was struck unhandily, at least in words. For every statement about the need to treat workers as human beings there was another that cast doubt on the humanity of the managers. "Up to the present time," said one observer at the turn of the century, "the Asiatic has had only an economic value in the social equation. His presence is no more felt than is that of the cattle on the ranges." Two decades later the planters were ready to speak more generously about at least one kind of Asiatic. By 1920, apparently, the Chinese had become "trustworthy, upright and honored . . . law-abiding, law-respecting, thrifty, industrious, and respectable." But this was when the planters were importuning Congress for permission to kill the Japanese conspiracy at the islands by bringing in Chinese, and at exactly the same time the Japanese were being described as subhuman in morality and superhuman in ingenuity. Ten years later again, in 1930, Richard A. Cooke, president of C. Brewer & Co. and a trustee of the Planters' Association, could still say that in strict ethical terms he could see "little difference between the importation of foreign laborers and the importation of jute bags from India."

Words such as these might or might not mean anything, particularly if, like Cooke's, they were not meant to be repeated in public. The real test for paternalism was whether it worked in practice. It worked reasonably well although, not surprisingly, it tended to wear thin when it went unappreciated. In 1924 Pablo Manlapit, at the head of a new Filipino Higher Wages Movement, took three thousand sugar workers out on strike, and when some of his followers at Makaweli on Kauai armed themselves and captured two strike breakers (also Filipinos), a riot broke out and sixteen strikers and four policemen were killed. Governor Wallace R. Farrington sent National Guardsmen to Makaweli with machine guns and rifles, and more than a hundred Filipinos were arrested; sixty were sent to jail, and Manlapit himself was paroled only after he promised to leave Hawaii.

Manlapit's strike was the last of any consequence for more than a decade, and the dominance of the Big Five persisted undisturbed into the nineteen thirties. On the plantations the racial balance among workers in the sugar and pineapple industries shifted in favor of Filipinos against Japanese, with contingents of other nationalities filling the ranks. But the more things changed in the fields the more they seemed to remain the same. By and large each worker knew what he could expect from life. For a Filipino or a Korean it was simple—field work on an hourly or daily basis, or if he was interested a contract that gave him a small incentive for doing his work well; for a Japanese, if he was willing and lucky, a job involving supervision of other workers at a low level; for a Portuguese, a job as a luna, but nothing more. The plantation manager and his immediate subordinates would always be white men, haoles, and in the islands the Portuguese, even though they were Europeans by name, were never counted as haoles. The top jobs went to Americans, Englishmen, Scots, and Germans, men who understood the white man's heritage of command. On his own plantation the manager's word was law, and if he in turn had to obey the higher law handed down from the agency at Honolulu there were compensations: a good manager in a good year could make about as much money as the governor of the territory, and life at the plantation house was comfortable.

Very likely, then, things would not change drastically on the plantations. But the towns were changing at a fast rate. The Chinese had almost disappeared from the plantations; most of them were living at Honolulu, and a surprising number of them had gone into business for themselves. On the streets of Chinatown, rebuilt after the fire of 1900, Chinese was still spoken, but more and more Chinese were choosing to live away from Chinatown in the suburbs of Honolulu, and there they were beginning to live like Americans. The Filipinos, still close to the peasant life of their home islands, did not seem to be ready to make the journey from the fields to the town, but the Japanese were well on the way. Between 1902 and 1932 the number of Japanese on the plantations dropped from more than thirty thousand to less than ten thousand, which meant that more than a hundred thousand were living in towns or on land of their own.

The Japanese had a high birthrate, and a high birthrate meant more and more American citizens of Japanese ancestry. That prospect was enough to frighten a good many men who had a vested interest in keeping things as they were. Alien Japanese were manageable—they could be prevented from taking out homesteads; they could be prohibited from working on territorial and federal construction projects; they could be barred from traveling to the American mainland; their language schools and their newspapers could be harassed; and their laborers' organizations could be beaten in any long strike. But what about the nisei, who might be on the verge of taking the advice of the Americanizers, and who would have the law behind them if they did? In 1920 only three voters in every hundred at the islands were Japanese; in 1926 it was eight in every hundred, and in 1936 it was one in every four.

Was there any way to head off this apparently inexorable movement? Perhaps the Japanese could be encouraged to return to the plantations. But as the planters said, what they needed was a man who thought of the cultivation of cane and pineapple as his mission in life, and not many plantation workers' sons had this sense of mission. They were going to public school, and they were being taught that in America not every immigrant's son was a field worker.

Once again, then, too much Americanism appeared subversive. "We are fond of saying that the children of America, of whatever parentage, are entitled to all the education we can give them," wrote Edward Irwin (the same man who found the flat features and short legs of the Japanese repulsive). "They're not, of course; they're entitled to only such an amount as we think is best for them." On the face of things Irwin did not have much to worry about. A federal commission sent to investigate Hawaii's schools in 1920 was not impressed; the tax system of the territory was weighted so strongly in favor of property owners that the public schools were starved (though private schools thrived). Even so, some of the leaders of the business community thought the education being offered to public school students was excessive. John Hind, president of the Hawaiian Sugar Planters' Association, called progressive teachers "visionary high-brows;" education, in his opinion, should be "looked on more in the light of a business matter." Why, he asked in 1925, should the territory "blindly continue a system that keeps a boy or girl in school at the taxpayers' expense long after they have mastered more than sufficient learning for all ordinary purposes, simply to enlighten them on subjects of questionable value; subjects on which they could as well enlighten themselves (if by any chance their inclinations tended in that direction) and at the same time, by entering some field of employment will, besides earning wages, be gaining experience and efficiency, and above all learn to appreciate the value of a dollar by working for it. . . . The solution as I see it, is that the taxpayer be relieved of further responsibility after the pupil has mastered the sixth grade, or the eighth grade in a modified form."

The important thing was to prevent the Japanese from "taking over," whatever that might mean. The situation was variously described, but all the descriptions seemed to threaten evil. In 1920 the Japanese had to be controlled on the plantations; by the nineteen thirties they were loose in society at large, and that was a more formidable problem. If Americanization did not take hold among the nisei the islands might become an extension of the Japanese political system in the Pacific, and that was unthinkable. But if Americanization through education was successful, the Japanese—once Hawaii became a state—might vote together and elect a governor of their race, and that would be insupportable.

The Honolulu Martyrdom

In all the careful social calculations being made at the islands during the twenties and thirties one large group of men was usually discounted: the members of the United States armed forces who manned the naval base at Pearl Harbor and the army posts strung out from Fort Ruger at Diamond Head to Schofield Barracks on the central plain of Oahu. The servicemen could not be ignored altogether—there were too many of them for that. But neither could they be assimilated—again, there were too many of them. So they were tolerated, but only just.

Pearl Harbor became the home of the Pacific fleet, and Schofield Barracks was the biggest army post in the United States. Even in the years of disarmament after World War One between fifteen and twenty thousand men were stationed in Hawaii. These figures made the armed services big business in the islands, and especially at Honolulu. The building of a dry dock at Pearl Harbor alone involved a payroll of sixty thousand dollars a month for almost ten years (a period that included a fresh start after the first pourings of concrete collapsed). Walter Dillingham's Honolulu Dredging and Construction Company and his Oahu Railroad and Land Company did well out of the development of the harbor, an undertaking second in cost only to the Panama Canal, according to one estimate; and all sorts of smaller businessmen—taxi operators, barbers, tattoo artists, night club owners, and brothel keepers—made a killing whenever the fleet came back from maneuvers or the enlisted men of Schofield came into town with their pay.

For the most part, however, the serviceman's money was more welcome than the serviceman himself. A surprising number of soldiers and sailors married local girls in Hawaii—thousands of them over the years— and this showed acceptance of a sort, but a feeling of estrangement between the two communities, military and civilian, persisted just the same. The question resolved itself into a matter of in groups and out groups, and the dividing line between servicemen and residents could not have been more clearly marked.

This game of ingroups and outgroups had been played for a long time at the islands, and a man's perception of the game depended upon his place in it. On the plantations—and in the armed services, for that matter —everything was in the open, with rank and occupation displayed for all to see. But there were other versions of the game in which definitions were more subtle, so much so, in fact, that they might escape an uninstructed observer. Someone unfamiliar with Chinatown, for example, might miss the point that more than one dialect of Chinese was spoken there, that the two main groups of Chinese immigrants, the Punti and the Hakka, had not much time for each other, and that community organizations such as the United Chinese Society papered over differences among other groupings based on family, clan, village, district, and provincial loyalties—all jealously preserved, and set aside only for compelling reasons. Someone unfamiliar with the Japanese might not understand that most of them came from the southern prefectures of Japan, and that they wanted themselves distinguished at all costs from the minority of migrants who came from the Ryukyu Islands, the Okinawans. A Korean did not want to be mistaken either for a Chinese or a Japanese, and his country's unhappy history made his point for him, if anybody took the trouble to find out about it. Chinese, Japanese, and Koreans alike took their various positions seriously, especially in relation to those late arrivals, the Filipinos, among whom, in turn, there were divisions—between Tagalog, Visayan, and Ilocano.

People who lived in Hawaii for any length of time could not help becoming aware of what the local game involved, and with practice they became skillful players. For most the skill was purely mechanical, simply a matter of carrying in the mind not one stereotype but several. But even these people developed a talent for manipulating stereotypes that very few mainland Americans had. This was demonstrated every day, in conversation. Out of the welter of languages and dialects spoken at the islands an expressive pidgin emerged, and a conscientious island dweller made a point of using the correct version whenever he spoke to someone who looked different from himself. Even white men and women took it up, because it got better results than the historic expedient of raising the voice and speaking slowly and clearly in perfect English on the assumption that not even the stupidest alien could fail to understand.

The serviceman, and especially the career officer, was a different case. An enlisted man from Pearl Harbor or Schofield, using up his liberty passes at the brothels of Hell's Half Acre or Tin Can Alley on the west side of Honolulu, might gradually come to appreciate the subtle differences between one kind of local girl and another, but his superior was likely to take a simpler and sterner view of the social situation in Hawaii. An officer who was also a Southerner, for example, would have his own sense of rank and station and his own sense of the fitness of things, and he might be unable to see Hawaiians as anything but exotic Negroes, Orientals as little brown men indistinguishable one from the other, and "local boys," especially those of mixed blood, as the embodiment of all that was worst in human nature.

So in actuality many different games were being played at the islands. White residents—most of them, anyway—observed local conventions without any intention of committing themselves to localism, but even this small concession was likely to be beyond a naval officer in whose considered view a local boy had broken the rules just by being born.

Once in a great while the rules were shattered, and then terrible things happened. In 1928 a deranged Japanese youth named Myles Fukunaga kidnapped the ten-year-old son of F. W. Jamieson, a white businessman, because Jamieson's firm, Hawaiian Trust, was about to evict Fukunaga's parents and their seven children from their rented home at Honolulu. Fukunaga demanded ransom, got it, and then strangled the boy. For a moment Honolulu seemed to be on the brink either of lynch law or racial war. The moment passed almost before it was perceived. Fukunaga was tried, convicted, and hanged not as a representative of his race, but as a sad and solitary criminal.

Fukunaga's crime was unsettling enough, but one way or another it could be put out of sight. This was impossible when, three years later, Thalia Massie, the twenty-year-old-wife of Thomas Hedges Massie, a submarine lieutenant stationed at Pearl Harbor, told a story which—if it was true—meant that every rule of life at the islands had been broken. And once her story became known the polite conventions and limited agreements that made it possible for men of different races to live together more or less comfortably were rendered meaningless.

On the night of Saturday, September 12, 1931, Mrs. Massie and her husband went with some of their friends to the Ala Wai Inn, a restaurant overlooking the drainage canal that marked the boundary of Waikiki. The Inn was done up like a Japanese tea house with a dance floor downstairs. It was popular with the junior officers of Pearl Harbor; they liked to take a table on Saturday nights, do some talking and dancing, and have a drink or two (usually of okolehao, Hawaii's potent answer to Prohibition, a liquor distilled from mashed ti root, sold illegally and drunk openly everywhere at the islands). Thalia Massie was at the Ala Wai Inn under protest. After four years as a Navy wife she still did not like dancing or drinking, she did not like crowds, and she did not like most of her husband's submariner friends. Late in the evening she had an argument with one of them and slapped his face, and then she went outside, by herself.

The Hawaiian orchestra usually packed up for the night at twelve o'clock, but this time someone paid for another hour of music. Lieutenant

Massie looked here and there at the Inn for his wife between midnight and one o'clock, but the dance came to an end and she was still missing. She had wandered away from the Inn, down John Ena Road toward Ala Moana, a road which ran along the water from Waikiki past a shantytown toward Honolulu. At about one o'clock she staggered out onto Ala Moana and hailed a car driven by a man named Eustace Bellinger. Her jaw was broken, her face was bruised, her lips were swollen, and she could hardly make herself understood. She asked Bellinger if he and his friends were white, and then she told them that she had been beaten up by five or six Hawaiian boys. She did not want to call the police, and Bellinger drove her home to Manoa valley.

Lieutenant Massie left the Ala Wai Inn when it closed. He thought that perhaps his wife had gone home with some Navy people who lived in Manoa, and he tried their place. Mrs. Massie was not there, so he used their telephone to call his own house. His wife answered. "Come home at once," she said. "Something awful has happened." Massie found her crying, and it was some time before she could tell him what had happened— the Hawaiians who forced her into their car on John Ena Road had beaten her, taken her to Ala Moana, raped her, so she said, and left her there. Massie called the police just before two o'clock.

The police were already looking for a carload of local boys. Between midnight and one o'clock a Hawaiian woman named Agnes Peeples and her husband, a white man, were driving through the intersection of King Street and Liliha Street, some miles away from the Ala Wai Inn on the other side of Honolulu, when another car came through the intersection and nearly collided with them. Both cars stopped; Mrs. Peeples got out, and one of the passengers in the other car, a Hawaiian named Joseph Kahahawai, got out too. They exchanged words, and then they exchanged blows. Mrs. Peeples took the number of the other car and went straight to the police. A radio description was being broadcast when Lieutenant Massie telephoned to say that his wife had been assaulted.

Massie took his wife to the emergency hospital to find out if she was badly injured. While they were there a police car with its radio turned up loud broadcast the details of the fight between Agnes Peeples and Joe Kahahawai. The number of the car, 58-895, and its make, a Ford phaeton with a cloth top, were mentioned several times, and then some added information came over the air: the driver of the car, a young Japanese named Horace Ida, had been picked up for questioning. After Mrs. Massie was examined she went to the police station to tell her story once again, in detail, and this time she was able to give the police a description of the car in which she had been abducted. It was a Ford tourer, she said, and its number was 58-805. Horace Ida was brought into the room, and she asked him some questions. He did not say much. Later he told the police the names of the others who had been in the car with him: Joe Kahahawai, the Hawaiian who hit Agnes Peeples; Henry Chang, a Chinese-Hawaiian; David Takai, a Japanese; and Benny Ahakuelo, a Hawaiian. The police arrested all but Ahakuelo on Sunday morning and took them to the Massies' house in Manoa. Mrs. Massie was sure Chang had assaulted her, but she could not identify any of the others with certainty. Benny Ahakuelo was arrested later the same day. By that time Mrs. Massie was in Queen's Hospital under the care of her own doctor, and Ahakuelo, Chang, and Takai were brought there. She said she could not identify Ahakuelo. The five young men, telling their stories to the police separately, said they had been driving around in Ida's car the night before. They had spent some time at a dance in Waikiki, and some time at a party in Nuuanu valley. They had nothing to do with the attack on Mrs. Massie.

The English language newspapers at Honolulu were sure the police had the right men. The *Advertiser* called them "fiends" who had kidnapped and maltreated a "white woman of refinement and culture," a "young married woman of the highest character." (The *Advertiser,* as a matter of fact, gave its readers their choice of sexual shocks on the day the first news of the assault on Mrs. Massie was released. Its front page carried wire service stories about the evangelist Aimee McPherson, who had eloped with her voice teacher; a "society love tangle" on the American mainland; a duel over a "German beauty;" a kidnapping that turned out to be a "love hoax;" and the adventures of a "white queen of the jungle.")

Mrs. Massie's name was not printed, but within a few days the five suspects were identified in the press. The two Japanese, Horace Ida and David Takai, had never been in trouble with the police, but the other three had. Joe Kahahawai had been jailed earlier in 1931 for assault and battery. Henry Chang and Benny Ahakuelo were convicted in 1929 of attempted rape, and they served some months in prison before they were paroled. This clinched the case against them, so a good many people thought.

While the prosecutor's office was preparing its case the suspects were tried in the newspapers; in fact "local boys" as a group were tried. Every stock character in the drama of outraged sexual morality made an appearance in the letters-to-the-editor column—"Indignant Citizen," "Vigilante," "Mother Of Three Daughters," and all the rest. Every imaginable act of lust was discussed and every imaginable punishment was considered—whipping, sterilization, emasculation. As the *Advertiser* said, the "gangsters" of Hawaii deserved nothing less; they were beasts at once primitive and degenerate, less civilized than the aboriginal blacks of Australia or New Guinea.

Mrs. Massie's mother, Grace Hubbard Bell Fortescue, arrived at

Honolulu before the trial began. Lieutenant Massie had sent her a hasty telegram, and she took the first ship to the islands. As soon as Mrs. Fortescue heard her overwrought daughter's story she began to worry that Thalia might be pregnant—a terrible prospect. Mrs. Fortescue arranged for an examination and an operation. The results showed no sign of pregnancy.

Among the interested parties in the case was Rear Admiral Yates Stirling, Commandant of the Fourteenth Naval District, which included Pearl Harbor. Stirling was an officer, a gentleman, and a Southerner. He had spent part of his career fighting revolutionaries in the Philippines and Chinese warlords on the Yangtze River, and he found little to impress him in the East. Hawaii, where not only Filipinos and Chinese but Japanese and native Hawaiians lived in what seemed to him disgusting closeness to white men and women, impressed him even less. He had nothing but scorn for "enthusiastic priests of the melting-pot cult," and even on the most beautiful Hawaiian day he could not get the "sordid people" of the islands out of his mind for more than a few minutes at a time. Now that the local boys had shown their true sexual colors Stirling was caught between two duties: his responsibility as an officer serving the United States government, and his responsibility to his private code of honor. His first inclination, as he said, was to "seize the brutes and string them up on trees." But he realized that the law must take its course, "slow and exasperating" though it was bound to be.

When the case finally came to trial in November 1931, the selection of a jury took two days. The difficulties were obvious. White jurors, haoles, might find the defendants guilty because of their race; Oriental or Hawaiian jurors might do the opposite. The Navy had a special interest in the verdict, too, and the Navy was one of the best customers of Honolulu's businessmen. If a juror worked for a firm that did business with the Navy, how would he vote? In the end a jury was chosen consisting of six white men, one Portuguese, two Japanese, two Chinese, and one Hawaiian.

The case for the prosecution was shaky, to say the least. The defendants had undergone a thorough physical examination when they were arrested, and their bodies and the clothes they were wearing that night showed no sign that they had had sexual intercourse. Neither, for that matter, did Mrs. Massie's body or her clothes show that she had been raped. That she had been beaten was clear; but beyond that very little was clear, even though her story of what happened after she left the Ala Wai Inn got more and more detailed the more often she told it. In court she identified four of the five defendants, more than she had managed to do before, but of course they were the only suspects she was ever shown, and she had never been asked to identify them in a line up. She also got four of the five digits in the number of Ida's car correct, but again she had the help of the police in this. Her beads and cigarettes and other belongings were found in a clearing off the Ala Moana, and tire marks from Ida's car were found there too, but this did not mean much either, because some of the detectives assigned to the case had driven Ida's car to the spot to conduct their searches. The defense leaned heavily on the element of time. It was unlikely that five men could have raped Mrs. Massie a total of six times, as she said they did, *when* she said they did, and then driven to the other side of town in time to get into a near collision at the corner of King and Liliha Streets when this was known to have happened. To be sure, no other suspects had come to light, but then the police were not looking for other suspects.

The jury stayed out from the afternoon of Wednesday, December 2, until the afternoon of Saturday, December 5, when sounds of fighting were heard in the jury room. The foreman came out to say that they could not agree. Judge Alva E. Steadman told them to try again, but at ten o'clock on Sunday night the foreman sent out a note saying that the jury found it impossible to reach a verdict. Steadman declared a mistrial. A new trial would have to be arranged, and in the meantime Ida, Kahahawai, Chang, Ahakuelo, and Takai were freed on bail.

As Admiral Stirling heard it, "The vote of the jury began and remained to the end, seven for not guilty and five for guilty, the exact proportion of yellow and brown to whites on the jury." In Stirling's view the mistrial was a plain miscarriage of justice. The defendants were not men "who might be given the benefit of a reasonable doubt." Stirling was sure he spoke for most good Navy men. They were under discipline, but all the same the admiral "half suspected" that he would hear any day that one or more of the defendants had been found "swinging from trees by the neck" in Nuuanu valley. Stirling was half right in his half suspicions. Six days after the court case ended some men from the submarine base found Horace Ida in downtown Honolulu, bundled him into their car, drove over the Nuuanu Pali to windward Oahu, took their leather belts, and beat and kicked him unconscious.

Mrs. Fortescue was brooding over the unsatisfactory verdict too. She had rented a house in Manoa valley, and Thalia was living with her while Lieutenant Massie was on sea duty. The Navy assigned a guard to watch the house at night: Machinist's Mate Albert O. Jones, whose job at the submarine base was to train the boxing team. Jones had two pistols, a .45 service automatic and a .32 automatic he bought himself. Mrs. Fortescue also bought a gun, a .32 revolver. All over town, in fact, white women, and especially Navy wives, were taking out licenses for pistols. Mrs. Fortescue, however, had something special in mind when she armed herself. She wanted to get a confession from one of the beasts who—she was sure—had raped her daughter.

She did not take long to work out a plan. The five defendants still had to report each day to the Judiciary Building in downtown Honolulu. Mrs. Fortescue spent a morning there, watching them come and go one by one. She took her son-in-law into her confidence, and then told Jones what she proposed to do. Jones got a member of his boxing team, Fireman First Class Edward J. Lord, to join in the plot. Mrs. Fortescue made up a document meant to look like a summons. Part of it was handwritten, the rest was clipped arbitrarily from a newspaper headline: "Life Is A Mysterious And Exciting Affair, And Anything Can Be A Thrill If You Know How To Look For It And What To Do With Opportunity When It Comes." That night Mrs. Fortescue studied a photograph of Joseph Kahahawai's "brutal, repulsive black face," so that she would recognize him instantly when she saw him.

The next morning, Friday, January 8, 1932, Lieutenant Massie and Edward Lord drove to the Judiciary Building, in a rented Buick; Mrs. Fortescue and Albert Jones followed in Massie's Durant roadster. When Kahahawai came out of the courthouse Jones waved the summons at him, pushed him into the Buick, and climbed in after him. Massie drove back to Manoa valley, with Mrs. Fortescue and Lord following in the other car. At Mrs. Fortescue's house Jones and Massie threatened Kahahawai with terrible things if he did not admit that he was a rapist. Massie, as good a southern gentleman as Admiral Stirling, had been sexually humiliated, and Mrs. Fortescue, herself a southern gentlewoman, was proud to see her son-in-law, "small, erect, dominating," striking terror into the heart of the dark-skinned Kahahawai. She looked away for a second (so she said later), and while her back was turned a pistol went off. She looked again to see Kahahawai on the floor, shot through the chest. Within a few minutes he was dead. The men stripped the bloodied body and put it in the bathtub, and tried to think what to do next.

Kahahawai's cousin, Edward Ulii, had been at the Judiciary Building when Kahahawai was taken away in Massie's Buick. Ulii heard something about a summons, but he noticed that the car did not go in the direction of the police station. Ulii went to the police himself, and a radio call was put out for the Buick. Less than half an hour later Detective George Harbottle (who had worked on the Massie case), saw the car heading along Waialae Avenue to the east of Honolulu, with Mrs. Fortescue at the wheel and the rear window shade pulled down. Harbottle went after it. Some miles out of town he passed the Buick, got out of his car, and signaled Mrs. Fortescue to stop. She would not. Harbottle fired two shots and gave chase again. Not far from Hanauma Bay he forced the Buick to the side of the road. He put Mrs. Fortescue, Massie, and Lord under arrest, opened the back door of their car, and saw a white bundle tied with rope. A human leg was sticking out from under the covering, and it was cold. Kahahawai was on his way to being thrown in the sea.

The three were taken back to Honolulu in a police wagon, with the body of Kahahawai in a wicker basket at their feet, still tied in its covering of canvas and bed sheets. Albert Jones was found at the Massies' house, drunk, with the fake summons and a spent .32 shell in his pocket. He was arrested, and all four of the conspirators were charged with first-degree murder. Mrs. Fortescue was aghast. "But it wasn't murder!" she wrote later in a magazine article entitled "The Honolulu Martyrdom," which cast herself and her family in the role of martyrs. "We had not broken the law. We were trying to aid the law. Without a confession we knew there was no chance of clearing the slime deliberately smeared on a girl's character." Perhaps; but Kahahawai had not confessed, and now he was dead. And if his body had been thrown in the sea nothing would have been known about the cause of his death, and that was a question the law was bound to be interested in.

"People who take the law into their own hands always make a mess of it," said the *Honolulu Star Bulletin*. Mrs. Fortescue could only agree. "Now, of course," she told a reporter not long after the killing, "I realize we bungled dreadfully, although at the time I thought we were being careful." But what about the unwritten law? Would that excuse Mrs. Fortescue and Thomas Massie their lack of expertise? They could argue that without the rape case there would have been no killing, and even though there was no conviction in the rape case surely there was incitement enough—after all, as Admiral Stirling said, Americans, and especially Southerners, could not be expected to take the violation of their women lightly.

Griffith Wight of the prosecutor's office was in a difficult position. When he was pressing the case against Kahahawai and his friends for the rape of Thalia Massie he had the support of a good part of the white community. Now he had to convince a grand jury that the respectable white killers of Kahahawai should be brought to trial for kidnapping and murder, and he knew it was asking too much to expect the people who had demanded justice a few weeks earlier to speak in the same firm voice this time. At first the twenty-one grand jurors, most of them white men, reported against indictment. Judge Albert M. Cristy refused to accept their report and sent them back to reconsider their responsibilities. Their next report contained an indictment for second-degree murder.

Mrs. Fortescue, looking for the best attorney possible, settled on Clarence Darrow, easily the most celebrated criminal lawyer in the United States. Darrow was seventy-five years old, in poor health, and long past his best as an advocate; but the weight of his reputation was impressive, and in the limited legal circles of the territory it might be decisive. Darrow looked into the case, professed himself interested in the psychology of a "crime that was not a crime," agreed to defend all four of the accused, and took ship for the islands in March.

Darrow's adversary, John C. Kelley of the prosecutor's office, was a tough and energetic man in his early forties, not easily overawed by reputation; indeed he had something of a name in the territory as a local Darrow. The selection of a jury began on April 4, and as the two men and their juniors went through the ritual of challenges it began to look as if local experience might mean more than a little. Of the twenty-six venire men only nine were white, and the twelve who survived the attorneys' challenges made up the usual mixed bag of haoles, Chinese, Portuguese, and Hawaiians.

Once the hearing of evidence got under way lines formed overnight outside the courthouse, and a place in line near the door was worth fifty dollars in the morning. The best people were willing to pay the price. Their presence gave the proceedings a kind of grisly chic, and the social reporters of the English language newspapers were careful to note who sat where. Almost to a woman the best people were for Mrs. Fortescue; the rest, the locals, were less committed to the idea that an "honor killing" was no crime.

Massie, as the aggrieved husband, took the responsibility for the killing (although Admiral Stirling liked to think Mrs. Fortescue pulled the trigger out of mother love, and years later Albert Jones said he fired the shot). Massie testified that he was able to remember everything except what happened just before and after the pistol went off. Then, to show why Kahahawai was kidnapped in the first place, Darrow had Thalia Massie tell, all over again, what happened on the night of September 12. Putting the two stories together, Darrow argued that Massie killed Kahahawai in a temporary fit of insanity.

From the first it was clear that Darrow was uneasy with jurors whose faces he could not fathom. No one could play on a jury's emotions better than he—his towering reputation had been made that way—but a Honolulu jury was an unfamiliar instrument. Would Hawaiians and Orientals be able to understand that a white man tortured by strain might crack and commit a crime and then have no knowledge of it? The case for the defense hung on that single point.

Darrow retained two psychiatrists, "alienists" as they were called then, to testify that Massie was insane when the shot was fired. One talked about ambulatory automatisms caused by psychological strain; the other talked about changes in the function of the suprarenal glands that might bring on chemical or shock insanity. Kelley also had two specialists, and they said—in their own technical language—that Massie was sane. Most people in the courtroom, and probably the twelve men in the jury box, simply let the big words go by.

Darrow's summation took almost four and a half hours. It was a classic performance (and, as it happened, Darrow's last—he never took another courtroom case). "At times," wrote a reporter, his voice was "as soft as a woman's. At others, it was like thunder that could be heard a block away. He was eloquent. He was dramatic. He was impressive in his rages, as his 225-pound body crouched and bent and his long, lean arms thrashed through the air. Now and then he brushed away a tear when dwelling upon some tragic part of the evidence." Darrow had never been unwilling to subordinate strict legalism to the higher law of humanity, and in the past he had often carried juries with him. But this time as he rang the changes on passion and pain, base lust and mother love, he found it hard going. "When I gazed into those dark faces," he said later, "I could see the deep mysteries of the Orient were there. My ideas and words were not registering." Mrs. Fortescue saw the same thing. "The stoical Oriental faces betrayed no emotion. Ethnologically and traditionally, white and yellow and brown are races apart. How could such a plea appeal to the six men to whom the white man's code is a mystery?"

Kelley talked about love too. He observed that the dead man's parents were in the courtroom. Had Mrs. Fortescue lost a son, or Thalia Massie a husband? No. "But where," asked Kelley, "is Joseph Kahahawai?" Then he talked about law—which, he said, Darrow had neglected to do. The "code of the white man," whatever that was, should not be allowed to usurp the place of the law. The four defendants conspired to kidnap Kahahawai. Kidnapping was a felony. Kahahawai was killed as a result of the kidnapping, and the law called that felony murder.

Judge Charles S. Davis gave his charge to the jury on April 27, the eighteenth day of the trial. They reached their verdict after forty-eight hours. All four defendants were found guilty of manslaughter, and leniency was recommended. On May 4 they were sentenced to ten years at hard labor in Oahu Prison.

They did not go to jail. Under the protection of the high sheriff they left the courtroom and walked across King Street to Iolani Palace, where the governor of the territory, Lawrence M. Judd, had his offices. Darrow went inside with them. Ten minutes later Judd announced that he had commuted the sentences from ten years to one hour, to be served in the custody of the high sheriff.

Ultimate Loyalty

Hawaii, for all its plantations and its scores of thousands of inhabitants uninstructed in the white man's code, was not the South. Assaults on white women were rare and lynch law killings were all but unheard of. So it was not surprising that the beating of Thalia Massie and the death of Joseph Kahahawai did terrible things to peoples' minds. And yet nobody was prepared to say that the nightmarish business was entirely unexpected. It was as if someone walking down a warm and sunlit path had accidentally kicked aside a stone and discovered, with a shock all the more frightening because it was unconsciously anticipated, a hidden world of crawling obscenity. Whether the obscenity was really there or not mattered very little; people were sure they could see it, and until they had their fill of looking they would never let the stone be put back in place.

The local people of the islands saw not so much obscenity as ugliness of a familiar kind. Just a few years earlier Myles Fukunaga, a Japanese of poor family, acting under great strain, had kidnapped and murdered a white child of good family, and Governor Judd had refused to grant him executive clemency. Now Thomas Massie, a white man of good family, acting under great strain, had kidnapped and killed a Hawaiian of poor family, and he and his fellow defendants were freed by Judd. Joseph Kahahawai had not been found guilty of rape, and yet he was dead, killed by people who took the law into their own hands. The crime of Thomas Massie and the others was real—the jury that said so was properly constituted, even if some of its members were not white men—and yet their punishment was negligible. For local people the lesson was not a new one, and it was all the more galling for that: there was still one law for the favored few and another for the rest, and white men would always have the best of the bargain. Governor Judd was aware of the complaints, and he knew that whatever he did would seem the height of injustice to someone or other. He could only follow his best judgment, and his judgment told him that if Massie and the others went to jail it might mean the end of Hawaii as a territory of the United States.

Judd was probably right. The language of the organic act that set out the relationship between Hawaii and the rest of the Union was prosaic enough, but still it was easy for mainland Americans to think of the islands as distant and mysterious, and from there it was only one step to thinking of the people of the islands as sinister. If Hawaii was unsafe for one white woman it must be unsafe for all white women. Thus, for example, the editorial staff of William Randolph Hearst's *New York American* could tell without even looking that the obscenity under the stone was real. "The situation in Hawaii is deplorable. Outside the cities or small towns the roads go through jungles and in these remote places bands of degenerates lie in wait for white women driving by." Such a place obviously did not deserve to go on governing itself under the American flag. In ordinary times, perhaps, this would have sounded merely ludicrous, but these were not ordinary times, and the Hearst papers were calling for the sternest of official measures to curb degeneracy.

Somehow the figure of forty rape cases got fixed in the minds of journalists on the American mainland. Sometimes it was published as the number of rapes committed every year in Hawaii, sometimes as the number committed on white women alone, sometimes as the number of unsolved or unpunished cases. Even after calculations showed that the number of convictions for sex crimes at Honolulu in any one year was about the same as in other American cities of the same size, the feeling of outrage did not diminish: if this was the story the statistics told then the statistics must be at fault.

That was always a possibility, of course, and a close look at the workings of the Honolulu police showed that it was more than a possibility. Seth Richardson of the United States Attorney General's office, reporting to the Senate after an investigation of law enforcement in Hawaii in 1932, found the police force riddled with politics, "impotent, undisciplined, neglectful, and unintelligent." The best way to become a policeman was to have some Hawaiian blood, and for most patrolmen and detectives no other qualification was needed; only two in ten had even the beginnings of a high school education. Richardson was not the first visitor to speak of the friendly, openhearted, generous character of the Hawaiians, but he pointed out that by the same token a Hawaiian in a policeman's uniform might not give strict attention to the letter of the law.

The city and county attorney of Honolulu at the time of the Massie case was a popular political figure, elected by an overwhelming majority, but he tried no cases, Richardson found, partly because he did not know how and partly because he was deaf. And to complete the picture, the administration of Oahu Prison was a sorry joke. Most of the guards, like most of the prisoners, were Hawaiians, and a Hawaiian jail was like no other. A prisoner who had urgent business on the outside could always make arrangements for a short leave of absence, and some did not bother even with that small formality. Three weeks after the mistrial in the Massie rape case, two convicts set out to get okolehao for the prison's New Year party, and they decided not to come back. One was a burglar, the other was a murderer, and before they were caught there was more rape on the record. That was hardly a joke, considering the state of affairs at Honolulu just then.

Governor Judd was aware that he had problems. He had appointed a crime commission in 1930, and the territorial legislature of 1931 passed some laws in accordance with the commission's recommendations. After the Massie case showed that these improvements were not sufficient the governor, urged on by Walter Dillingham and the "Law Enforcement Committee" of the Honolulu Chamber of Commerce, called a special session of the legislature in 1932. The legislators considered a bill to punish rape by death on the unsupported testimony of the complaining witness, and another providing for the sterilization of sex criminals, and then they took up once again the matter of getting politics out of police work.

Their efforts did not satisfy Seth Richardson. Under the organic act the territory's federal, circuit, and district court judges were all appointed by the President with the advice and consent of the United States Senate. Richardson suggested that the chief of police and the county attorneys as well should be appointed by the President.

The Hearst papers saw no reason to stop there; they advocated martial law for the islands, and the ultimate suggestion along those lines was that Hawaii should be stripped of its territorial status and placed under a commission appointed by the President, the theory being the familiar one that a population of dark-skinned rapists had no claim on the rights and privileges enjoyed by good Americans under the Constitution. So the sexual argument became a matter of national policy.

To the great dismay of the defenders of territorial government some members of Congress seemed to be taking these extreme proposals seriously. At one time or another three congressional committees held hearings on Hawaii, and bills were introduced attacking the integrity of the territory's institutions. One would have enabled the President to name as governor of the territory a mainlander, a "carpetbagger," someone who had never lived at the islands. Another, forced on Senator Hiram Bingham of Connecticut (a direct descendant of the pioneer missionary) by some of his colleagues in the Committee on Territories, called for commission government. Debate and discussion, in and out of Congress, went on for months. In the end none of the bills became law. But it had been a close thing, and no one really believed the issue was dead.

One man who wanted to keep it alive was Admiral Stirling. In his mind nothing was random; there was no such thing as an isolated incident; and so what began with a problematical rape and a controverted killing ended in a total indictment of the islands, a world-wide calamity. "The result of the miscarriage of justice in Hawaii," he wrote, "has lessened the prestige of white peoples the world over, wherever they are in contact with the darker skinned people." And the likelihood was that things at the islands would get worse rather than better, because of the "intermixture of races" there. "Scientists have stated that these intermixtures tend to produce types of a lower moral and mental caliber than the pure-blooded types of each race, and this intermixture is increasing to an extent that will tend to make each generation of mixed bloods, with the continual introduction of a greater proportion of oriental blood, contain a majority of individuals of lower intellect and increasing degeneracy." Such people, "bred for centuries" in alien ways, were unfit for self-government. For Stirling the only value of the islands was strategic, and if self-government diminished that value then self-government must go. In Hawaii of all places the United States could not afford to take chances. "It is true that ours is a democratic government under a constitution, and it is also true that one of our basic principles of government is against legislation without representation. But we do apply this axiom of government to our ships of war and to our military reservations?" Obviously not. So Stirling advocated "control . . . inception, promulgation, and enforcement" of law by the national government, and administration by men "primarily of the Caucasian race, specially selected," men "not imbued too deeply with the peculiar atmosphere of the islands," men "without preconceived notions of the value and success of the melting pot." And because Hawaii was primarily a fortress, the commission should include officers of the armed forces.

Territorial status had its disadvantages, to be sure, as the uproar over the Massie case demonstrated, but it was preferable to colonial status, and under a commission government Hawaii would be no better off than those other depressed holdings of the United States in the Pacific—American Samoa, Guam, and the Philippines. Stirling did not have his way, and for this the people of the territory could give thanks.

But there were more troubles in store for Hawaii. Only two years after the Massie case Congress made a new attempt to alter Hawaii's status. This time the attack was an economic one, aimed at the sugar industry. Ever since 1876 the industry had depended for survival upon its place in the American market. The reciprocity treaty carried the industry until 1900, and after that the protection of the tariff laws of the United States was extended in its entirety to the islands. This was a satisfactory arrangement, and the Hawaiian Sugar Planters' Association saw no reason to think the situation would ever change. Almost every business deal, buying or selling, involved the mainland states; in fact the mainland had few better customers in the world than Hawaii. And yet, even with this substantial tie in existence, there was evidence that Hawaii's economic place in the Union was not secure. As the organic act of 1900 was interpreted at Washington, Hawaii, which paid taxes like a state, was not necessarily entitled to all the federal benefits enjoyed by the states. Granted, a great deal of federal money was spent on-military and naval installations, and this was a welcome contribution to the economy, but Hawaii's delegates to Congress had to fight an unceasing battle to get the territory its fair share of federal money for things like conservation and improvements to roads and harbors. In 1923 the territorial legislature found it necessary to draw up a "Bill of Rights" for Hawaii and circulate it at Washington to draw attention to the matter.

Even with the evidence of economic discrimination before them the territory's businessmen could hardly bring themselves to believe that Congress might legislate against Hawaiian sugar. And yet it happened. In 1934 the Jones-Costigan Act was passed, establishing quotas for each sugar-producing area in the American national market. The effect was to raise the share of the market open to mainland producers at the expense of "offshore" and foreign producers. Hawaii lost between 8 and 10 percent of its previous market, and to add insult to injury the islands were classified with Puerto Rico and the Philippines as "foreign" places where future cuts in the quotas might be made if necessary.

This had all the earmarks of a new disaster. The lobbyists of the Hawaiian Sugar Planters' Association at Washington did their best to convince congressmen that they were making a mistake, and when this did not work the planters took their case to court. The supreme court of the District of Columbia found against the islands: Hawaii was defined as a properly incorporated territory, but the power of Congress to legislate for the territory was confirmed, and this implied the power of Congress to discriminate in matters such as the sugar quota. Eventually the Department of Agriculture was persuaded to alter its percentages, and the sting went out of the Jones-Costigan Act as far as the islands were concerned. But the judicial principle stood: Hawaii was still the creature of Congress.

The objectionable nature of the territorial arrangement had never been brought home so clearly. Before the nineteen thirties very few of the territory's business leaders wanted a change in Hawaii's political status. But so ominous was the Jones-Costigan Act that they were led to consider striking a new and complicated balance concerning the future of the basic industry of the islands. In some ways it suited the sugar planters (and the pineapple growers too) to insist that Hawaii deserved special treatment. For example, when immigration from the Philippines to the United States was cut off by congressional action in the thirties, the Hawaiian Sugar Planters' Association claimed that this would work a hardship at the islands, where a steady flow of plantation labor was needed. Congress was urged to make provision for Hawaii's needs. But if Congress could discriminate in favor of Hawaii, why not against Hawaii? The Jones-Costigan Act and the judicial decision that followed were painful reminders that swords had two edges. So the leaders of industry and commerce, meaning the Big Five, had to decide where the greatest measure of security for their long-term interests could be found. Either they could persevere with the territory, maintaining a powerful lobby at Washington for special purposes, or they could press for complete equality in the partnership between Hawaii and the rest of the Union. This meant advocating statehood for Hawaii.

Almost every territorial legislature since 1903 had passed resolutions endorsing statehood. But in the early years the fact that the Big Five were against statehood cast doubt on the significance of the votes. No one could tell whether a politician was supporting the resolutions because he genuinely wanted something done, or because he knew that nothing would be done.

Prince Jonah Kuhio Kalanianaole, Hawaii's delegate to Congress, introduced the first statehood bill in the House of Representatives in 1919, and the second in the next session. Neither came back from committee. At the opening of the nineteen thirties Delegate Victor S. K. Houston, himself a convinced believer in statehood long before it was fashionable, introduced a statehood bill. His timing could not have been worse. He spoke before the House of Representatives on December 9, 1931, three days after the mistrial in the Massie rape case and a month before Joseph Kahahawai was kidnapped and killed, and the question then became not whether Hawaii was ready for statehood but whether the islands were fit to remain a territory.

In January 1935, the month in which the Jones-Costigan Act took effect, Delegate Samuel Wilder King introduced a new version of a bill to enable Hawaii to frame a state constitution, and this time the response of Congress was more cordial. A sub-committee of the House Committee on Territories visited the islands and held public hearings.

The congressmen appeared to like the islands, and they seemed more than ready to let the advocates of statehood have their say. Not surprisingly, one or two of the committee members learned enough about Hawaii to know that enthusiasm for statehood was a new thing among the territory's big businessmen, and they wanted to find out more about this sudden conversion. The Jones-Costigan Act was mentioned fourteen times by different witnesses, and they all agreed that it represented a crisis in the conversion process. Then, asked the committee's chairman, Eugene B. Crowe, was the statehood movement just a matter of more money for big business? Yes and no, said Charles R. Hemenway of Alexander & Baldwin, stepping delicately around the edges of the question. "Those who have felt that the time has not yet arrived, I believe, were thoroughly sincere in their belief that a further period of probation was proper; the purse-string idea did not influence their opinions. As to whether or not the industries would be better off with statehood, we face the possibility of discriminatory action as compared with other business carried on by our fellow citizens on the mainland, which we think is unfair."

For businessmen who—perhaps with some misgivings—had brought themselves to look statehood in the face at last, it was disconcerting to hear ill-disposed witnesses testify that big business, the Big Five, the new apostles of statehood, would be the ruination of the islands if Hawaii became a state. "The plantations and allied interests," said Fred W. Beckley, "the Bishop Estate, a landed octopus, fiduciary companies, the bar association, and inter-island transport facilities are all more or less subject to the whims and dictation of King Sugar and his son Pineapple, as well as his nephew, Island Cattle Ranches, and their high-priced beef, and so forth. They are but tentacles of the 'Big Five' octopus of King Sugar's oligarchy."

Beckley and the others who thought as he did were arguing that as long as Hawaii did not have complete self-determination in its local politics the Big Five would at least have restraints imposed upon them by Washington. But if Hawaii became a state the voice of the state would be the voice of the Big Five, and no other voices would be audible. To which no response was possible except to say that things were not nearly as bad as Beckley made them sound, and that, in any case, big business was known to flourish in a good many states on the mainland, places where statehood seemed to work.

The other side of the argument concerned the labor force whose presence at the islands was the responsibility of the Big Five. As long ago as 1920 the most strenuous Americanizers in the territory had been able to find some good in at least one kind of Oriental, the Chinese, who was described (admittedly for special purposes) as a model of deportment by contrast with the turbulent and unassimilable Japanese. Now, in 1935, if statehood was to be considered seriously at Washington, a way would have to be found to convince the visiting congressmen that the Japanese had changed their ways.

Very few senior representatives of the Big Five made an appearance before the committee; those who did maintained a discreet silence about the Japanese. This did not mean that the subject went undiscussed, but it did mean that the witnesses who presented themselves as spokesmen for the community were of a different kind. Social workers, teachers, university professors—the enthusiastic priests of the melting pot so despised by Admiral Stirling—testified one after another that the Japanese problem, which once seemed so alarming, could now be seen in its true light, as five parts pure imagination and five parts misunderstanding. The optimists used the homeliest of illustrations to make their point: Japanese children enjoying the story of George Washington and the cherry tree (filial piety and a traditional Japanese symbol turned American); Japanese children reciting the Gettysburg Address and feeling no sense of strangeness about the words "our fathers"; Japanese parents choosing American first names for their children. Did it matter that almost nine out of ten Japanese children still went to language school? Evidently not as much as it once did. Perhaps the language school, imparting American ideals in the mother tongue of the Japanese, was the best means of weaning children of alien parentage away from their alien background without breaking family ties. Perhaps the alien parents themselves had something to teach Americans about family closeness and its value to society—at least young Japanese, Admiral Stirling to the contrary, turned up in criminal court far less often than their numbers warranted.

One of the most persuasive witnesses was Romanzo Adams, a professor of sociology at the University of Hawaii. He carried in his head an overwhelming amount of statistical information about all the racial groups of Hawaii, and he could say with authority, if anyone could, whether. or not the behavior of the territory's Orientals was irredeemably alien. Adams was also a sensitive observer of people who did not know they were being observed. He spoke of his experiences with Orientals on the American mainland and in Hawaii, and his conclusions were interesting. Every so often at a college football game on the mainland, he said, he would see "one or two or three students of oriental birth looking dignified and not expressing any particular emotion of one sort or another, just looking on and not doing anything to create criticism. I didn't see them express human emotions at all; but when I came to Hawaii I found it very different. There was a contest down at the track in which white young men, Chinese, Japanese, part Hawaiian, and maybe a few pure-blood Hawaiians all took part together; they all seemed to belong as though in one society. That was the important thing . . ." Adams believed he was watching them being made over into Americans. "It takes place in a favorable way and they hardly know it themselves."

David L. Crawford, president of the University of Hawaii and chairman of the bipartisan Citizens' Committee on Statehood, brought together all the sanguine testimony. Hawaii's period of tutelage had been long enough, he said. The citizens of the territory, including the nisei, had conducted themselves responsibly by the best American standards. The islands met the traditional requirements for statehood in such matters as population, area, and resources. Most people in Hawaii were for statehood because they knew the islands would benefit, but the United States would benefit too, and that should not be forgotten.

Crawford made another point, one that took on a new significance in the years just ahead. "We place national safety above local welfare, and in advocating the admission of Hawaii to statehood we believe that we are not in the slightest degree endangering the safety of the Nation. The United States maintains certain defense structures and services in Hawaii in the development of which this Territory has been glad to cooperate; no instance can be pointed to, we believe, wherein our local government has failed to cooperate. This would continue to be true under statehood, for a very large majority of Hawaii's citizenry would insist upon such cooperation regardless of racial ancestry."

The Committee considered carefully everything it had heard, conceded the weight of testimony favoring statehood, and concluded that the time was not yet ripe. The whole subject needed "further study."

In 1937 a joint committee of Congress—twenty-five members in all, representing both houses—arrived at the islands for two weeks of public hearings. From the beginning it was clear that none of the old issues of debate had been exhausted. The Big Five came in for unusually bold criticism (which was entertaining for the New Deal Democrats on the committee); and the question of the Japanese returned to dominate the hearings.

Since 1935 full scale war in the Pacific between Japan and the United States had moved a step closer, and now the open-hearted testimony of the educators seemed to ring a little hollow. The congressmen demanded answers to any number of pointed questions. Was it true that the Japanese government claimed rights over Japanese at the islands, even the nisei born under the American flag? What sort of rights? How many of the Japanese in Hawaii were aliens?

These were blunt inquiries, but no simple answers were possible, because the situation was complex. Until 1924 Japan, like most countries, held that Japanese born overseas were automatically subjects of the emperor. In 1924 the imperial government passed a law loosening this tie: from then on a Japanese born overseas would have Japanese citizenship only if his parents registered his name at a Japanese consulate within fourteen days of his birth. Japanese born overseas before 1924 were also allowed to expatriate themselves; the process was cumbersome, and it took a good deal of time and money, but at least it existed, and that was something.

Once the congressmen got this clear (and some never did get it quite clear) they went on to ask how many Japanese born at the islands before 1924 had expatriated themselves, and how many born after 1924 had been registered for dual citizenship by their parents. In other words, if war broke out between Japan and the United States, how many Japanese of military age living in Hawaii would owe some sort of duty, however formal, to the Emperor?

Wilfred C. Tsukiyama undertook to answer the question. He put himself before the committee as a representative case. He was a nisei; his wife was an expatriate by marriage; he had four children, none of whom were registered at the Japanese consulate—all were American citizens free and clear. As for the larger issue, Tsukiyama said what most people knew—that accurate statistics were hard to come by. There were about one hundred and fifty thousand Japanese in the territory. About one hundred and thirteen thousand were citizens, and of these about sixty thousand were born after 1924. Only about one in every ten young children was registered at the consulate. Granted, a good many nisei born before 1924 had not gone through the process of expatriation, but they did not feel any less loyal to the United States because they lacked an expensive and meaningless piece of paper.

This did not satisfy some of the congressmen. By their arithmetic about thirty thousand of Hawaii's Japanese had dual citizenship, and this was unsettling. It was all very well to be assured that young Japanese were joining the Boy Scouts and the Young Men's Christian Association, but did that mean anything? The visible evidence was that they did not care enough about loyalty to make a simple move that would relieve them of criticism instantly.

Tsukiyama and others in his position resented that line of talk. They wanted to be judged by their life day to day; just because the loyalty of the heart was not visible did not mean that it was a fraud, so they said.

As in 1935, most of the witnesses urged statehood, but here and there, like a specter at a wedding feast, the old story of the Japanese conspiracy reared its head. Oddly enough, the great theorist of conspiracy was not an American citizen by birth. John F. G. Stokes came to Hawaii from Australia in 1899 (a good year for Americanism at the islands), and he took out citizenship papers in 1904. He did not consider that his immigrant origins disqualified him from speaking as a true American; he was American by choice, so he said, and this gave him a better title than any nisei, whose citizenship was a mere "incident of birth."

Once his credentials were established to his own satisfaction, Stokes took up matters of substance. A good many people still had silent reservations about the Japanese; Stokes voiced every objection, systematically arranged and presented. He had tried to warn the committee of 1935 about the Japanese conspiracy, without success. (His well meant comments, made while others were testifying, did not endear him to the chairman, and somehow it was always five minutes before adjournment time when he was recognized.) Now he refused to be thwarted. He came to the 1937 hearings armed with the fruits of years of research, ready to quote from Japanese religion and Japanese folklore, from Japanese newspaper stories, and even from meaningful inscriptions on Japanese wrapping paper.

Like Admiral Stirling before him, Stokes could not believe in the randomness of life, and he could not let himself think that one Japanese might act differently from another. So every Japanese at the islands, issei or nisei, was a knowing instrument of imperial policy. Everything they did was part of a pattern, in this case a conspiratorial pattern, and if good Americans could not see what was going on then that was proof that the conspiracy was brilliantly conceived and carried out. The Japanese Empire was using Hawaii as a stepping stone to world domination, and the conspiracy was half way to success already. The melting pot was working, said Stokes, but it was a Japanese melting pot and American culture was being melted. White people at the islands were becoming "Japan-minded" as a result of subtle pressures exerted in typically silent, ingratiating, and calculating Japanese fashion. Even the Big Five had been subverted. The imperial government had arranged for "highly educated and intelligent" Japanese to be placed in the homes of important people as servants. By the exercise of the "gentle divine spirit" of Shinto thought these infiltrators reached positions of trust, and then when questions arose concerning the Japanese they could have a "powerful though unconscious influence."

The committee heard Stokes out, but at the end of the discussions they announced that they were more interested in patterns of another kind. They wanted the territory to hold a plebiscite on statehood. This was done in 1940, as the circling sounds of war grew louder and more people came to share the bad dreams of John Stokes. The vote was two to one in favor of statehood, but what did that mean? How many Japanese voted yes, and for what purpose? Why, asked Stokes, who believed in commission government, should Americans turn the islands over to men whose loyalty was unproved, men tied by birth and indoctrination to an aggressive power which might at any minute declare war on the United States?

CHAPTER NINE

Now We Are All Haoles

1941–1959

Tora, Tora, Tora

ONE OF THE most outspoken witnesses at the statehood hearings in 1937 was a thirty-year-old nisei named Shigeo Yoshida. He had nothing in common with the theorists of conspiracy except a belief that only a world crisis could resolve the burning issue of the loyalty of the heart. "As much as we would hate to see a war between the United States and Japan," he said, "and as much as we would hate to see the day come when we would have to participate in such a conflict, it would be much easier, for us I think, if such an emergency should come, to face the enemy than to stand some of the suspicion and criticism, unjust in most cases, leveled against us. It is extremely difficult to bear up under the gaff of suspicion and expressions of doubt which have been leveled at us. It would be easier for me to pack a gun and face the enemy."

That was being arranged. By December of 1941 no one doubted that Japan and the United States were on the brink of open conflict in the Pacific. The fighting might start anywhere at any time—it was assumed that Japan would strike first and very likely without warning—and war would certainly bring on the test that Shigeo Yoshida half dreaded and half demanded.

So in his own strange way John Stokes, sniffing the winds that blew over Hawaii and smelling conspiracy, was right, or anyway half right: there was a conspiracy, and the Japanese government was at the center of it. Stokes was wildly wrong in thinking that Hawaii's Japanese were also conspirators, but after all he spoke in 1937 and he had not much more to go on than his own limited perceptions. Four years later, men in a position to discover the workings of the real conspiracy—men, in fact, with so much information at their disposal that it was an embarrassment—were just as wrong in their way as Stokes had been in his.

The American government knew an amazing amount about the activities and intentions of the Japanese militarists. Observers in the Far East sent regular reports to Washington describing the movements of Japanese troops on the Chinese mainland. Radio operators monitored Japanese naval transmissions all around the Pacific, and analysis of these signals made it possible to plot the position of the Japanese fleet—most of the time, at least. In September 1940, Japan's most secret diplomatic code was broken, and from then on a few highly placed intelligence officers at Washington had access to messages being passed between Tokyo and Japanese embassies everywhere in the world. All indications pointed to war late in 1941. A series of secret radio dispatches from Tokyo containing the words "East Wind Rain" was intercepted, and it was believed that this meant Japan was planning to break diplomatic relations with the United States. The Japanese had a secret deadline for the end of negotiations. This was known. At Japanese consulates from Paris to Honolulu documents were being burned. This was known. In the first week of December the best estimate was that Japan would launch a massive attack, probably within the next few days, almost certainly somewhere in Southeast Asia.

Intelligence officers at Washington told senior army and navy officers what they thought of the situation, and in Hawaii Admiral Husband E. Kimmel and General Walter C. Short acted accordingly, just as officers in command at other places in the Pacific were doing on much the same information. The naval base at Pearl Harbor and the army posts on Oahu were as ready as they would ever be. Several times since 1936 war games and drills had shown that it would be difficult to attack the islands successfully, and in recent months both the Army and the Navy had stepped up their training programs for the men who would have to fight the Japanese in the Pacific. But where in the Pacific?

At the beginning of December some Japanese aircraft carriers and their supporting ships disappeared from the radio traffic analysts' charts. This was nothing new for the North Pacific—it had happened several times already in 1941—and it might mean only that the ships were in Japanese home waters, where they used a radio frequency that could not be picked up by American listening posts. There was no further sign of the carriers' presence in the North Pacific until the morning of Sunday, December 7, and when the sign came it was not immediately understood, because people seeing and hearing peace turn into war could not quite comprehend what was happening.

At about a quarter to four on Sunday morning the watch officer

on the mine sweeper *Condor,* at work just outside the entrance to Pearl
Harbor, sighted something that looked like the periscope of a submarine.
The *Condor* signalled to the destroyer *Ward,* and the commander of the
Ward, Lieutenant William W. Outerbridge, new to the ship and new
to the patrol (it was his first night on the job), sounded general quarters.
The *Ward* patrolled for two and three-quarter hours without sighting
anything, and then in the early light of day the conning tower of a submarine was spotted astern of the supply ship *Antares,* close to the entrance
of the harbor. Outerbridge took the *Ward* right up to the submarine at
full speed. His gunners hit the conning tower at a range of about fifty
yards, and the *Ward* let go her depth charges almost on top of the submarine. Outerbridge watched the submarine sink and then sent two coded
radio messages to Fourteenth Naval District Headquarters, doing his best
to make it clear that what he had attacked was really a submarine and not
a piece of flotsam or a whale (the Navy had sunk several whales around
the islands). The lieutenant on duty at the Harbor Control Office of
Headquarters was alone. He began telephoning his senior officers. This took
some time, perhaps longer than it would have done on any other day of
the week. Seven o'clock on Sunday morning was the low point of the
Hawaiian weekend.

At Opana on the other side of the island the Army had a radar
tracking station, one of several mobile units. Radar was in an early stage
of development; the sets were not altogether reliable, but they were the
best the Army had, and General Short ordered them to be in use every day
between four and seven o'clock in the morning, the hours he considered
most dangerous. On this Sunday morning Private Joseph L. Lockard was
operating the set at Opana and Private George E. Elliott was plotting the
sightings. It was an unusually quiet three hours, and the only reason the
two men stayed on after seven o'clock was that Elliott, who was new to
the work, wanted some more practice with the oscilloscope. He and
Lockard could not have gone anywhere in any case; the truck that was to
take them to breakfast was late. At two minutes after seven Elliott got a
reading, and he called Lockard over to help him with it. Lockard thought
at first that something was wrong with the oscilloscope, that it was giving
out two main pulses instead of one. But then it became clear that something big was appearing on the set—the largest group of planes Lockard
had ever seen. He and Elliott decided to plot it, because it would be a
good technical problem for them. The sighting was at a distance of one
hundred and thirty-six or seven miles; at one hundred and thirty-two miles
they decided they would call their information center at Fort Shafter near
Honolulu and report what they were doing. The enlisted man at the
switchboard there could not find an officer immediately. Seven o'clock was
breakfast time at Fort Shafter too. The only officer in the building was

Lieutenant Kermit A. Tyler, and he was not a permanent staff member. He was a pilot in the Air Corps, and his only reason for being at the information center was that his commanding officer thought all pilots should learn something about the general radar system. Tyler knew that the aircraft carriers from Pearl Harbor were out at sea, probably running maneuvers with their planes, and he knew some B-17 bombers were coming in from the mainland that day. Very likely the radar set at Opana had picked up one or the other. "I don't know," he said later, "but it seemed to me that there was still nothing irregular, that they probably might be friendly craft. So I thought about it for a moment and said, 'Well, don't worry about it,' and went back awaiting the hour and time until the next relief." At Opana, Lockard and Elliott went on tracking the incoming planes. At twenty-five past seven they were sixty-two miles out; at twenty-one minutes to eight they were only twenty-two miles away. Then the sighting disappeared from the oscilloscope; the planes were in a dead zone, screened by the hills between Opana and Pearl Harbor.

Lieutenant Tyler's duty at the information center was to end at eight o'clock. At five minutes before the hour he heard the sound of explosions down by the sea and walked outside to see what was happening.

The Japanese planes came through the cloud cover over Oahu to find what they had hoped to find: Pearl Harbor was full of ships, and along Battleship Row off Ford Island within the harbor eight of the biggest were at anchor. The carriers were missing, and that was a disappointment, but there was opportunity enough, and if the battleships and cruisers could be knocked out the American fleet in the Pacific would be crippled. There was nothing to stop the Japanese. At the air bases on Oahu, from Ford Island itself and Hickam nearby to Wheeler, Ewa, Bellows, and Kaneohe farther away, fighters and bombers were lined up wing tip to wing tip on the ground, as a safeguard against sabotage. The leader of the attack force, Mitsuo Fuchida, knew he could not fail. At seven minutes to eight, without bothering to wait for the first bombs to be released, he sent a radio message to the Japanese aircraft carriers two hundred miles to the north, repeating the code word for success: "Tora, tora, tora,"—tiger, tiger, tiger.

On Battleship Row the morning watches were getting ready as usual to hoist the colors at eight o'clock, when the first wave of dive bombers attacked the grounded planes at Ford Island naval air base just a few hundred yards away. The band on the *Nevada,* at the head of the row, was actually several bars into "The Star-Spangled Banner" as the torpedo bombers started their run down Southeast Loch, coming in broadside onto the battleships and letting go their torpedoes only fifty or a hundred feet above the water. The ships moored in the exposed outboard position took the first shock, but not even an inboard anchorage gave protection. All over the harbor antiaircraft guns and machine guns opened up, but any kind of organized defense was beyond them. The sky was full of Japanese planes. By the time the high bombers moved in thirty minutes after the attack started, Battleship Row was a shambles. Doomed ships were spewing burning oil everywhere, and black smoke billowed hundreds of feet into the air. The *Oklahoma* took several torpedoes and turned over, trapping scores of men inside. The *West Virginia* and the *California* sank; the *Tennessee* and the *Maryland* were seriously damaged; the flagship *Pennsylvania,* caught in dry dock on the other side of the channel, lurched onto one side; and the *Arizona,* devastated by bombs and torpedoes, blew up and sank, taking more than eleven hundred of her crew with her. The *Nevada* was the only battleship that managed to raise the colors, and the only one able to get under way. Badly damaged, harassed by a swarm of dive bombers, she steamed erratically down South Channel, but she could not make the open ocean and had to be run aground on a sand bank.

At the air bases the picture was just as grim. The Army and the Navy had four hundred and two planes on Oahu altogether; the Japanese attacked with only three hundred and sixty. But the attackers were armed and in the air and the defenders were on the ground, their crews on a four-hour alert. Very few American planes got aloft, and the Japanese bombed and strafed the rest at will.

About ten o'clock the attack force regrouped and withdrew. The radar unit at Opana that tracked the planes in to Pearl Harbor tracked them out again to the northwest, but no pursuit was possible and no systematic search was made for the waiting Japanese carriers. By early afternoon the jubilant pilots were aboard again and the big ships were on their way back into the empty North Pacific.

The first appalling inventory of death and destruction on Oahu was begun while the smoke still hung over Pearl Harbor, but a long time passed before the statistics of carnage were complete. After the war a board of inquiry made its report. "Military and naval forces of the United States suffered 3,435 casualties; Japan, less than 100. We lost outright 188 planes; Japan, 29. We suffered severe damage to or loss of 8 battleships, 3 light cruisers, 3 destroyers, and 4 miscellaneous vessels; Japan lost 5 midget submarines. The astoundingly disproportionate extent of losses marks the greatest military and naval disaster in our Nation's history."

War

The governor of Hawaii, seventy-two-year-old Joseph B. Poindexter, was at his official residence, Washington Place, near Iolani Palace in Honolulu, when the first bombs fell at Pearl Harbor. Before he left for his office there was an explosion near his driveway, and not long after he reached his suite another rocked the palace grounds. These were not Japanese bombs; the attackers left the city alone. But Navy antiaircraft shells, loaded in haste and badly fused or not fused at all, fell in dozens of places in Honolulu and exploded on impact. The governor was one of hundreds of civilians who found out about the war at first hand that way.

Poindexter went from the palace to radio station KGU and broadcast in a trembling voice a proclamation that the Hawaii Defense Act was in force. This measure, passed by the territorial legislature in October, gave the executive full emergency powers in time of war, but Poindexter discovered that he did not even have the power to make his announcement without interruption. The Army called KGU to get the governor off the air: the Japanese might be coming back, and if they were they could home in on the radio transmission.

At midday General Walter Short came to the palace and told Poindexter that the territory should be placed under martial law. The Japanese might be planning to land troops the next day, and Short considered it likely that the local Japanese would help them by sabotage. Poindexter asked Short to wait while he called President Franklin Delano Roosevelt in Washington. A Navy censor was already installed at the Honolulu switchboard, and the operator took an infuriatingly long time establishing Poindexter's credentials and the purpose of his call, but the call itself was brief: Roosevelt supported martial law.

General Short's proclamation wasted few words. The people of the territory, citizens, residents, and aliens alike, were warned against giving aid or comfort to the enemies of the United States. Any disorder or rebellion would be put down by force. Ordinances would be published to control the showing of lights, meetings, censorship, possession of firearms, ammunition, and explosives, "and other subjects." "In order to assist in repelling the threatened invasion of our home," wrote Short, "good citizens will cheerfully obey this proclamation and the ordinances to be published; others will be required to do so. Offenders will be severely punished by military tribunals or will be held in custody until such time as the civil courts are able to function."

Nothing like this had been known on American soil since the Civil War, and then only in rebellious or captured southern states. Once again the people of Hawaii had the strictest of definitions of good behavior imposed upon them. Governor Poindexter told Secretary of the Territory Charles M. Hite that he "never hated doing anything so much" in all his life. He asked General Short how long the military government would last. The general thought that if the attack on Pearl Harbor turned out not to be the prelude to an invasion then martial law could be lifted in a "reasonably short time."

While Poindexter and Short were arranging the transfer of authority to the Army, a strange version of the war in miniature was being fought a hundred and fifty miles away to the northwest of Honolulu on the island of Niihau. If Hawaii was like no other place in the United States, Niihau was like no other place in Hawaii. Since 1864 the island had been privately owned, and the Robinson family, which held title to the land, also held the view that their two or three hundred Hawaiian tenants would be best served if the outside world was kept at a distance. The rest of Hawaii had long since come to terms with the twentieth century, but Niihau had not. There were, for example, no radios on the island, and even if there had been, very few of the Niihauans spoke any English. Once a week the Robinsons crossed the channel from Kauai in their motor sampan. Otherwise the Niihauans were on their own, and for the most part they liked it that way.

The war came to Niihau when a Japanese pilot, unable to get back to his carrier, landed his damaged plane on a plowed field. A Hawaiian named Hawila Kaleohano took the flyer's papers, and everybody settled down to wait for the Robinson's sampan, which was due the next day. But the week went by, and on Friday the sampan still had not come—the Army had forbidden Aylmer Robinson to make the trip. Two Japanese, one an alien and the other an American citizen, lived on Niihau. The flyer appealed to their patriotism and asked them to get him a gun. The alien, wanting nothing to do with the scheme, went into hiding. The citizen, Yoshio Harada, produced a shotgun, and he and the pilot went back to the plane and worked its machine guns loose. With this formidable armament they could control the island, but the machine guns did them no good; a resourceful Niihauan named Benehakaka Kanahele stole the ammunition on Friday night.

The pilot wanted his papers back, but Hawila Kaleohano was nowhere to be found. The flyer did the next best thing: he burned Kaleohano's house. Early on Saturday morning he and Harada captured Benehakaka Kanahele and his wife, and Kanahele was sent to look for Kaleohano while his wife was kept hostage. Kanahele came back alone, and the pilot got angry. He was going to shoot the two Hawaiians, and rather than have that happen Kanahele decided to jump the gun. He was fifty-one years old, but his stamina was good. He took three bullets in the stomach without faltering, picked the pilot up, and brained him against a stone wall. Harada turned his shotgun on himself. The fighting war on Niihau was over.

On the other islands the problem was not one Japanese pilot in the service of the Emperor, but one hundred and sixty thousand Japanese civilians, issei and nisei, alien and citizen, a third of the population of the territory, with loyalties still unproved. To many people it seemed inconceivable that the attack on Pearl Harbor could have succeeded without the help of the local Japanese. On December 7 the army and the navy did not see what was before them until too late; for a week or two after that everybody was sure he had seen things that later turned out not to have been there at all. So it was known with absolute certainty, but on the basis of no evidence at all, that the local Japanese put advertisements in the newspapers, outwardly innocent but secretly helpful to the attackers (although how the *Advertiser* and the *Star-Bulletin* would be delivered to the rendezvous of the Japanese fleet in the North Pacific was not made clear); they set fires in the cane fields and cut huge arrows in the cane to guide the incoming planes toward Pearl Harbor; they blocked traffic deliberately on Sunday morning; they fired at American troops from ambush; they signalled to ships bringing saboteurs ashore under cover of darkness (SABOTEURS LAND HERE, said the *Advertiser* in its biggest type on December 8); they poisoned the water supply; in fact they poisoned the air by their very existence.

There were spies in Honolulu, of course. It could not have been otherwise, with Pearl Harbor the primary target of a secret attack. Yet for such an important assignment the espionage arrangements of the Japanese were modest in the extreme, involving very few serious agents at the islands and not much expense. It was an excellent investment, and what made it so worthwhile was the work of one remarkable man, Takeo Yoshikawa, a twenty-eight-year-old ensign in the Japanese naval reserve, assigned to the Japanese consulate at Honolulu in March 1941, as "Vice Consul Tadashi Morimura." Yoshikawa was the classic inconspicuous observer, practicing what was called "open espionage"—collecting information available to anyone who took the trouble to keep his eyes peeled. Yoshikawa spent as much time as he could in conscientious tourism on Oahu. He went for long walks and car trips and catamaran rides and jaunts in private planes, always carrying a cheap camera which he never used. He looked at every military and naval installation, always from a respectable distance, never asking a question and never lingering in any one place more than a few minutes, but coming back again and again as often as he thought it necessary. There was one spot on Aiea Heights overlooking Pearl Harbor that he visited thirty times in two months. His reports to Tokyo sharpened the Japanese navy's knowledge immensely—about ship movements, harbor routines, and the strange workings of that well-established institution, the American weekend, with special reference to Saturday night and Sunday morning.

A handful of other men attached to the Japanese consulate also went in for open espionage, and the consul himself found a way to get copies of interesting telegrams sent out by the commercial wire companies at Honolulu. The consul also cultivated a wide range of acquaintances in the community, and this was what concerned the Honolulu office of the Federal Bureau of Investigation. The FBI kept a card file on local Japanese whose loyalty to the United States was suspect. Within half an hour of the attack on Pearl Harbor the Japanese consulate in Nuuanu valley behind Honolulu was under guard, and the usefulness of Yoshikawa and the others came to an end. By nightfall more than a hundred local Japanese had been arrested—tuna fishermen whose radio-equipped sampans always seemed to be at Pearl Harbor when the fleet was coming in or going out; language school teachers; Buddhist and Shinto priests; and a number of kibei, young Japanese born at the islands but educated in Japan. Several hundred more were put under observation, and thousands more still were questioned by loyalty boards set up on each island. Eventually the number under arrest rose to more than fourteen hundred, mostly Japanese, but also some Italians and Germans, including in particular a German alien named Bernard Julius Otto Kühn, a spy as melodramatic as Ensign Yoshikawa was matter of fact, who had been on the FBI's list for some years. Kühn was the only person convicted of espionage in Hawaii during the war. Yoshikawa left no trail at all, and his story did not become known until long afterward.

There was not much disagreement about what to do with the Japanese under arrest. They would have to be interned. Some were put in camps at the islands, and others were sent to the mainland. But what about the rest of the one hundred and sixty thousand Japanese in the territory? The aliens among them were told to move if they lived near an army or navy base, and they all had to turn in cameras, guns, and anything else that might be useful for espionage or sabotage. But was this enough? Would it be best to intern them all, aliens and citizens both? Then where? And more to the point, exactly how?

They could hardly be sent to the mainland to be put behind barbed wire with the California Japanese—ships simply were not available; and they could hardly be interned at the islands, not even by segregating them all on one island, as someone suggested. In fact, to intern one-third of the population was impossible. If nothing else, it would mean the end of a good many essential industries at the islands, because the skilled trades were filled with Japanese and had been for years. So the idea of a mass evacuation was dropped.

Every effort was made to convince the local Japanese that their best interest lay with the United States, and, to be sure, the great majority needed no convincing, as they had been saying all along. If it was necessary to give visible proof of loyalty, then it should be done—kimonos and Japanese sandals were put away, Japanese clubs and societies of all kinds were closed down, English language classes for old people overflowed. Just in case all this was not enough, the military government ordered the Japanese language newspapers and radio stations censored. It was inconvenient, but far more painful things were happening just then in California, where every Japanese, young or old, issei or nisei, was deprived of his property and herded into what were called relocation camps, but which looked, from inside the barbed wire, very like concentration camps.

Hawaii had a long history of intemperate talk followed by action that was not too disastrously intemperate, and so it turned out this time as it had turned out many times before. Logistics prohibited the internment of the whole Japanese population, but beyond that the good sense of the Japanese community itself, the support of a number of sympathetic and level-headed haoles, and in particular the restraint of Army and Navy intelligence officers and FBI agents, made Hawaii a better place for a Japanese to be than California, where aliens exchanged a peacetime ghetto for a much harsher wartime one.

So much for Japanese civilians at the islands. But what about local Japanese in uniform? On December 7 the Territorial Guard was called out, and the first unit to assemble was the Reserve Officer Training Corps of the University of Hawaii. Most of the cadet officers were nisei. For six weeks they did duty with the rest of the Guard, standing watch under Army orders wherever they were needed. Then on January 21, 1942, Delos C. Emmons, who had succeeded Walter Short as commanding general of the Hawaiian War Department and military governor of the territory, ordered the Japanese guardsmen dismissed—all three hundred and seventeen of them. As if to rub salt in the racial wound, Emmons approved the formation of a Businessmen's Military Training Corps, a haole and part Hawaiian group organized to "watch the local Japanese."

Once again the loyalty of the heart had to be shown in day to day life. A hundred and fifty of the dismissed guardsmen, almost all of them university students or graduates, went to work as laborers for the United States Army Corps of Engineers. They called themselves the Varsity Victory Volunteers, and for ninety dollars a month they helped to dig ditches, lay roads, and string barbed wire. In peacetime this work would have been beneath a nisei university graduate—it was exactly the sort of thing the Japanese wanted to leave behind on the plantation—but the volunteers had to make their own racial point, that race and loyalty were separate things. They and other young Japanese began talking of themselves not as nisei, but as Americans of Japanese ancestry, AJA's.

The Volunteers were not the only AJA's on General Emmons' mind. In March the War Department ordered the induction and enlistment of all nisei stopped, but there were already about fourteen hundred in Hawaii's two National Guard battalions. Farther west in the Pacific the battle of Midway was looming. If it was lost Hawaii would be under the threat of invasion again, and if the enemy landed at the islands there would be Japanese in uniform on both sides of the line. One side at a time was enough, as everybody agreed. The nisei in the National Guard could not very well be discharged: the Army was too short of men for that racial luxury. But all kinds of embarrassment would be avoided if the AJA's were shipped somewhere else.

So the Hawaiian Provisional Infantry Battalion was formed. It was like no other unit in the Army. Its fourteen hundred members were almost all nisei; most of them had gone to Japanese language school when they were younger; and about one in every three had dual citizenship, that bane of the Americanizers. The Army Chief of Staff's office wanted the enlisted men to know that they were not being culled out for internment, but even so the orders were that the battalion was to be shipped to the mainland as quickly as possible, without publicity—and without guns.

The AJA's themselves were not sure about the Army's intentions, understandably enough. They sailed from Honolulu under naval escort early in June 1942, during the battle of Midway; they landed at Oakland, California, and were split into three groups for a five day train ride to the Midwest; and on the final day of the trip one of the trains stopped at a siding flanked by the iron and barbed wire fences and watch towers of an internment camp. Nobody spoke; and nothing happened for half an hour. Then the train backed out of the siding, switched tracks, and rolled on a little farther. The next and final stop was the Army's Camp McCoy, Wisconsin.

At McCoy the AJA's got a new official title: the 100th Infantry Battalion (Separate). They did not need the added word in parentheses to remind them of what they were. There was one order they did not know about, but they saw its workings just the same; AJA's could be commissioned as officers, but no Japanese was to have command of a rifle company. So their leaders were white men. For six months the AJA's trained at McCoy with the internment camp in the corner of one eye, and when they were transferred in January 1943, it was to Camp Shelby, Mississippi, where they ran up against another kind of separateness. In Wisconsin the weather was frigid, but the people of Sparta, the town nearest McCoy, were surprisingly warm. A weekend on leave in Hattiesburg, Mississippi, was something else again.

While the 100th Battalion was at Shelby some hard thinking was going on at Washington and Honolulu about the rest of the AJA's of military age. There were still people in Hawaii who believed that the local Japanese were a menace, and one of them, the businessman John Balch, kept urging mass evacuation as late as 1943. Balch believed he was only saying what other people thought, and he put his words on paper and distributed them as widely as he could. But for all his energy Balch was being left behind. General Delos Emmons, who in January 1942 ordered all AJA's discharged from the Territorial Guard, had a change of heart, and his senior intelligence officer, Colonel Kendall Fielder, needed no change of heart: he had always thought the local Japanese would be loyal and that young AJA's would make good combat soldiers, given any kind of chance.

If the AJA's were to go into combat a decision would have to be made about spreading them around in existing units or bunching them together as a team. Units recruited on a racial or national basis already existed; there were Austrian and Norwegian battalions and Filipino regiments. And in fact a Japanese unit might be more useful than any of these, as a memorandum to Army Chief of Staff General George C. Marshall pointed out. It might have "a profound propaganda effect on certain other peoples who, at present, are more or less unfriendly to the cause of the United Nations, due to the Japanese allegation that this is a racial war. Considering the fighting qualities which enemy Japanese have demonstrated there is no reason to believe that combat units of a high degree of effectiveness could not be developed from loyal personnel of this class. In furtherance of this belief it is reasonable to assume that a particularly high degree of esprit and combativeness could be developed in such an organization due to the desire of the individuals therein to demonstrate their loyalty to the United States and to repudiate the ideologies of Japan." AJA's, then, were Japanese enough to fight like Japanese, and American enough to want to fight well so that they would not seem like Japanese. No AJA would have liked the first part of that line of reasoning very well, but the second part would suit them perfectly.

General Emmons called for volunteers in January 1943. The role of the AJA's had not been an easy one since the war broke out, he said. "Open to distrust because of their racial origin, and discriminated against in certain fields of the defense effort, they nevertheless have borne their burdens without complaint and have added materially to the strength of the Hawaiian area." They behaved well; they bought war bonds in great quantities; and their labor assisted the common defense. Now they were to be allowed to fight, and the "manner of response and the record these men establish as fighting soldiers will be one of the best answers to those who question the loyalty of Americans of Japanese ancestry in Hawaii."

Emmons asked for fifteen hundred volunteers. Within a week he had four thousand, within a month more than nine thousand, or four out of every ten AJA's of military age in Hawaii.

From this group fewer than three thousand were chosen for service. They arrived at Camp Shelby in April 1943, and went into training as the 442nd Infantry Regiment. In July the 100th Battalion got its departure orders, and in August the AJA's sailed for North Africa. Ten months later, on June 5, 1944, two years to the very day after the men of the Hawaiian Provisional Infantry Battalion left Honolulu for Camp McCoy, the 100th Battalion was in Rome. On June 11, at Civitavecchia, forty miles north of Rome, the 442nd Regimental Combat Team, just in from the United States, arrived to join them. The order keeping AJA's out of command positions had fallen by the wayside, and under a combination of white and Japanese officers the 442nd, which absorbed the 100th, fought in Italy, France, and Italy again, where, on the day the war ended, they led the parade of Allied forces.

Few regiments were better known than the 442nd. The Army, for its own good reasons, made a point of publicizing the exploits of the AJA's, and there was no lack of material. Thirty-six officers and six hundred and fourteen enlisted men were killed; forty-five hundred wounded, a casualty rate more than three times as high as the average throughout the United States Army. Between them the 100th and the 442nd won seven presidential unit citations and almost six thousand individual awards.

By the end of the war AJA's were being inducted into the armed forces through regular selective service procedures, and that was a small victory in itself. But the larger question, the future of AJA's in the nation as a whole and at home in Hawaii, presented itself long before that. The men of the 100th and the 442nd saw a good deal of the United States— including the South, which appalled them and gave them a different perspective on life in Hawaii; they met nisei from California, men who had enlisted, some of them, direct from relocation camps, men very like Hawaii's Japanese and yet unlike them; they saw a good deal of the world, and they saw more death than anyone could have wanted. What was it for? Katsumi Kometani, who had been with the 100th since its first days, put the matter formally, talking about these self-evident truths which somehow never seemed to strike all Americans with the same force. "The highest aspiration of our boys in uniform," he said, "is to return to a Hawaii where a citizen irrespective of ancestry will share and share equally in the rights as well as the responsibilities of citizenship. We have helped win the war on the battlefront but we have not yet won the war on the homefront. We shall have won only when we attain those things for which our country is dedicated, namely, equality of opportunity and the dignity of man."

A Commanding General Is Never Wrong

The AJA's of the 100th and the 442nd were not the only men from Hawaii who went to war, just the best known—too well known, in the opinion of a good many people, who pointed out that more than thirty thousand islanders altogether joined the armed services: Hawaiians and part Hawaiians, Chinese, Portuguese, Filipinos, Koreans, and haoles, as well as Japanese. All of these had a chance to ponder the perplexity of seeing self-evident truths about equal opportunity and dignity through the sights of a rifle. At the same time the civilians of the territory found themselves in a situation where freedom and order made conflicting claims, and they chose order without, perhaps, giving the matter enough thought. Martial law had a long life in Hawaii.

General Walter Short, the first military governor, was relieved of command on December 17, 1941, along with Admiral Kimmel of Pearl Harbor, but martial law stayed on after they left. Short's successor, Delos Emmons, who brought himself to believe in the loyalty of AJA's in uniform, could not bring himself to trust the civilians of the territory, and neither could the third military govenor, General Robert C. Richardson, Jr. Governor Poindexter's term of office came to an end and he stepped down not long after the battle of Midway in 1942. His successor, Ingram M. Stainback, watched the war in the Pacific disappear to the west—hundreds, then thousands of miles away. After Midway there was no real chance that the islands would be invaded, and in other parts of the world —Britain, for example, and the hard-pressed islands of Malta and Ceylon —civil government survived even under desperate conditions. But as late as mid-1944 Hawaii still had a blackout, and the war was over in Europe and peace in the Pacific was only a few weeks away before the military curfew in the islands was lifted.

The reason for all this was simple. The Army, as always, was better at taking command than giving it up. On December 8, 1941, Lieutenant Colonel Thomas H. Green, chief executive officer of the military government, moved his staff into the offices of the attorney general of Hawaii at Iolani Palace, and there he stayed for more than a year. Green drew up a table of organization for the territory, an elaborate document that gave the civil government little or nothing to do, and from the offices of the military government came an endless flow of General Orders with the force of law. As Governor Stainback's attorney general, J. Garner Anthony, observed, the orders covered the entire sweep of government except for taxation: "regulation of traffic, firearms, gasoline, liquor, foodstuffs, radios, the regulation and censorship of the press, wireless, cable and wireless telephone, the freezing of wages and employment, the regulation of hours of work, the possession of currency, the collection of garbage, blackout and curfew, rent control, regulation of restaurants, places of amusement, bars, establishment of one-way streets, the removal of keys from parked cars, interisland travel, speed limits, regulation of nationals of foreign countries, registration of females over sixteen, chlorination of water, regulation of bowling alleys, penalties for false statements to military authorities, registration of solicitors including union representatives."

It was an impressive display of energy on the part of Colonel Green's office, but, in the opinion of Garner Anthony and a few others, almost completely unnecessary. The military establishment, not the civil government, had been thrown into confusion on December 7, and Anthony thought the military would be better off giving their whole attention to the conduct of war, leaving civilians to govern themselves.

The three military governors in turn—Short, Emmons, and Richardson—thought otherwise, and so did Colonel Green and his staff. The existence of a General Order was its own justification. But what if the military governor was wrong? asked a former circuit court judge of the territory. "A commanding general is never wrong," replied one of Colonel Green's assistants.

That was how things worked in practice, to be sure, but Garner Anthony had his doubts about the principle. Late in 1942 he put his version of the state of things on paper for Governor Stainback. The beginnings of martial law were easily understood, said Anthony; there was a military and naval disaster, and Governor Poindexter was not strong enough to resist the demands of General Short. But why did the people of the territory acquiesce so long in "a reign that is contrary to every tradition of America"? Anthony thought he saw several reasons. The first was fear. The ordinary citizen did not like martial law at all (and of course the alien was not in a position to have an opinion). People were afraid to speak up; they might be branded as unpatriotic, and they might lay themselves open to punishment. Then again, it was hard for ordinary people to find out what was happening. The press was censored, and there was a blackout on information about public affairs. On top of that, a good many civilians in the territory worked for the military governor either directly or indirectly, and they had a financial interest in keeping things as they were. And the last, but not the least important reason, according to Anthony, was "the existence of a small number of fascist-minded businessmen. They are influential with the 'Office of the Military Governor.' This group, I regret to say, favor the military regime with all its stringent controls of labor, severe and arbitrary penalties for infractions of orders.

To be sure, they want to win the war, but they are also interested in profits and find it extremely convenient to obtain whatsoever they desire in the form of an order from the military authorities. They are not hampered either by democratic processes, such as legislation, or by territorial civil servants who, as a rule, are far more able to deal with the shrewd man of business than the average army officer."

Whether Anthony was right or wrong about the motives of the businessmen, he was right about the fact of their support of the military government. The businessmen, in turn, wanted it thought that they spoke for the majority. "I think," said the magisterial Walter Dillingham in 1944, "that this little community was solidly behind whatever was necessary in the judgment of our military leaders to be done. Just as if they were all in uniform and drilled to support them . . ." Dillingham thought that in the circumstances people felt "a darned sight safer as American citizens under that kind of military control, when the fear of immediate punishment was facing the violator of military law, as against cases dragged along in the courts . . ." It was the fear of punishment, "the teeth in the military control," that made people feel comfortable, so he believed.

The only exception, Dillingham said, was a feeling "among some of our legal fraternity and colleagues that we ought to say, 'By God, we ought to maintain the rights of American citizens,' and all that sort of hooey that nobody cared a damn about." He was right: it was precisely the teeth in the military control that made some of the legal fraternity feel uncomfortable. The writ of habeas corpus was suspended when martial law was declared on December 7, and General Order No. 4, issued the same day, set up military commissions to try serious offenses and provost courts for lesser offenses. The military tribunals for civilians followed the procedures of courts martial, and the officers in charge, who wore their pistols to work, had wide discretion.

There was a general order for everything, or so it seemed, and violations, knowing or unknowing, were bound to be frequent. The officers in charge were busy men. They did their work briskly, and with the understanding that what they were doing was right, and so most people were found guilty as charged, usually in thirty minutes or less. During 1942, about twenty-two thousand people were brought before one provost court in Honolulu. Not many of them were represented by lawyers, and only three hundred and fifty-nine were found innocent. The provost courts collected more than a million dollars in fines, and one or two new ways to make the courts serve the war effort were introduced: a prisoner might be ordered to buy war bonds instead of paying a fine, or he might be ordered to work off part of his sentence by giving a pint of blood to the blood bank.

Some of the legal fraternity, Garner Anthony included, found this sort of thing distasteful, even medieval, but the *Advertiser* did not. Hawaii, so the editorials said, followed the dictates of its military rulers obligingly, proud to have the opportunity to serve in a humble fashion, as a "test tube and a guinea pig." For those who had lost a pint of blood to a provost court this was putting matters rather too literally, but of course the *Advertiser* did not mean it that way.

Governor Stainback had begun his term of office with an effort to reduce the severity of martial law. He was only partially successful, but he and Attorney General Anthony and some of the more uncomfortable members of the legal fraternity continued to harass the military governor as best they could. It was guerrilla war of a curious kind. The objective was simple—to restore civil government—but the military governor was dug in behind the apparently impregnable defenses of his General Orders, and the civil government had to snipe at him whenever an opening presented itself.

Attorney General Anthony won a small skirmish when he persuaded the military governor and his staff to move out of Iolani Palace so that Anthony could move in himself and occupy the rooms that had always been reserved for the territorial attorney general. It was not much of a victory. It took three months to accomplish, and even then the governor remained in the palace grounds, in a temporary building that became known as "the little White House." But it was something, if only in terms of face.

Late in 1942 Stainback and Anthony flew to Washington to enlist the aid of Secretary of the Interior Harold Ickes in their battle. Ickes' own jurisdiction over the territory had been invaded by the militarists in Hawaii, and so he was defending his own frontiers when he supported the civil authorities. He was a big gun, and he made a lot of noise. In February 1943 one hundred and eighty-one General Orders issued by the military governor's office were rescinded, and the civil authorities regained control of a good many areas of government. In particular, trial by jury was restored for violations of territorial and federal law, though the military courts remained to punish violations of military orders.

From then on the battleground shifted to the courts. A case was already on record to show how the military governor's office would conduct its legal strategy. Hans Zimmerman, German-born but a naturalized citizen of the United States, had been interned in Hawaii on December 8, 1941, by the order of a loyalty board. His attorneys asked for a writ of habeas corpus. This was denied in District Court at Honolulu. Federal Judge Delbert E. Metzger ruled that as long as General Order No. 57 was in force he could not issue a writ of habeas corpus, but he made his own position clear, saying that he considered his court to be under duress and

not capable of carrying out its proper functions. Zimmerman's case went
to the Circuit Court of Appeals in San Francisco, and there the validity of
martial law was upheld. Zimmerman's attorneys were prepared to pursue
the issue as far as the Supreme Court, and when they made their intentions known the military government arranged to have Zimmerman released from custody outside the jurisdiction of the Hawaiian courts, so
that no more action would be taken. It was a useful strategy of delay, one
that could be repeated in case after case, and it ensured that a final contest
between martial and civil law would be postponed as long as possible.

The question of habeas corpus came up again in July 1943, after
Secretary Ickes' strenuous efforts had reduced the perimeter of military
government. Two naturalized Germans, Walter Glockner and Edwin
Seifert, interned on Oahu, petitioned for release. This time the court ruled
in their favor, arguing that under the arrangement of February 1943, the
writ of habeas corpus was restored, and that even though the United States
was still at war the islands were in no danger of invasion.

The military governor, General Robert Richardson, was forced to
take evasive action. He did not want to accept the writs and he did not
want to produce Glockner and Seifert. A United States marshal took the
writs to "the little White House" in the grounds of Iolani Palace, announced his business, and was told that General Richardson would be in
conference all morning. He said he would wait. A military policeman tried
to make him wait elsewhere, and while the two were scuffling General
Richardson ran down the steps of the palace and was driven away in a
staff car.

Judge Metzger was outraged; he ordered the general fined five thousand
dollars for contempt of court. Then Richardson counterattacked using a new
General Order No, 31. No more writs of habeas corpus were to be issued,
and anyone who dared to disobey would be fined five thousand dollars or
imprisoned for five years, or both. Judge Delbert Metzger discontinued his
hearings in the case of Glockner and Seifert, and once again the military
government arranged to have the two men set free outside the jurisdiction of
the court. This left the matter of Richardson's fine of five thousand dollars
at the hands of Judge Metzger to be settled. Metzger reduced the amount to
one hundred dollars, and payment was not pressed.

The case which eventually brought the undecided issue of the validity
of martial law to a conclusion concerned Lloyd C. Duncan, a civilian
worker at Pearl Harbor, sentenced to six months in jail by a provost court
on a charge of assault. In March 1944, Duncan petitioned Judge Metzger's District Court for a writ of habeas corpus. The military government
opposed his petition, arguing that Hawaii was still in danger of imminent
attack, and that the provost courts were needed if the war was to be won.
Metzger did not think so. In his opinion there had been no severe military

emergency for more than two years, and the civil government was quite capable of handling cases such as Duncan's. The conclusion was that martial law had no legal existence, and the writ was granted.

The military government appealed the case, and once again Metzger was overruled at San Francisco. The appeals judges there continued to regard the situation in Hawaii as dangerous enough to justify the use of summary punishment as a deterrent. Their decision was handed down in July 1944. Three months later, on October 24, President Roosevelt proclaimed martial law at an end in the territory. This might have been expected to bring the legal battle to a close, but the opponents of martial law wanted to have the last word. They were looking for a legal decision which would establish not only that military courts were unnecessary, but that conviction of civilians in military courts was unconstitutional.

The test case, that of Lloyd Duncan, was heard together with a similar case before the Supreme Court, beginning on December 7, 1945, four years to the very day after Pearl Harbor. The military government's stand was presented for the last time: civil courts in the territory were subject to political influence; they did not offer swift justice; a military commander needed his own tribunal; and the population of Hawaii was untrustworthy. What the Supreme Court would have made of these contentions while the war was on is not certain, but the war was over, and the military government's case rang hollow.

Most of Hawaii's soldiers were on their way home to the islands by the time the court announced its decision. Justice Hugo L. Black spoke for the majority. Responsible military and civil officers, he said, always paid attention to the boundaries between military and civil power. Martial law, as defined for the territory, authorized the military to act vigorously for the defense of the islands against the threat of invasion, but the civil courts should not have been supplanted by military tribunals. In other words, the commanding generals were wrong, and had been from the beginning.

Labor Pains

The big businessmen of Hawaii had always been averse to turbulence. They wanted good conservative calm, and before the war they were able, more often than not, to get their money's worth, bought and paid for. Industrial peace in particular was a costly commodity, but even during the depression of the nineteen-thirties the territory's plantations returned excellent profits, and if the Big Five had to buy the cooperation of labor with perquisites and benefits, at least stockholders did not feel the pinch. The planters never tired of reminding their employees of their good fortune, and certainly it was better on most counts to be a plantation laborer in Hawaii than an agricultural worker on the west coast or anywhere in the South. Still, malcontents were always ready to argue that a gap existed between things as they were on the plantations and as they ought to be, and the most determined were likely to try to form themselves into labor unions—exactly what the planters were doing their best to discourage.

By the mid-thirties two out of every three plantation workers were Filipinos. Their union, Vibora Luviminda, organized by Antonio Fagel on the basis of the natural tie of blood, had some success in 1937, when about thirty five hundred sugar workers on the island of Maui struck for higher wages. In the course of the strike Fagel and several of his countrymen were charged with kidnapping a laborer who did not want to leave his job, and they were sentenced to jail. Despite this, Vibora Luviminda won its point. The Hawaiian Sugar Planters' Association approved pay raises of about 15 percent for workers on the struck plantations.

Vibora Luviminda did better than any other organization of its kind, but for all practical purposes "blood unionism" had had its day. In 1935 the United States Congress passed the National Labor Relations Act, and when this part of the New Deal came into effect at the islands it would mean the end of all talk about union organizers as "criminal syndicalists," punishable under laws enacted by the territorial legislature after the Japanese strike of 1920.

As it happened, the National Labor Relations Act was not applied immediately. Its constitutionality was challenged, and as long as the issue remained in doubt, the biggest firms in the territory kept up their active opposition to unions. A new employers' group, the Industrial Association of Hawaii, led by former governor Lawrence Judd, took the hardest of hard lines. On the plantations and along the waterfront, union workers talked angrily about the use of spies and blacklists, intimidation and violence, and it was widely believed that the Honolulu police and the United States Army intelligence service contributed to the Association's dossiers. Then in 1937 the United States Supreme Court ruled that the National Labor Relations Act was constitutional, and almost immediately examiners appointed under the act arrived at the islands. Before the year was out, Castle & Cooke, one of the Big Five, was charged with violating the labor law, and not long afterward the Industrial Association was disbanded.

So now under federal law the way was clear for workers to organize and press their claims against management through collective bargaining. On the plantations skilled organizers were few—management had been careful to weed them out of the work force. But on the waterfront at

Honolulu the picture was different. After the passage of the National Labor Relations Act, a good many members of west coast maritime unions found it worth their while to spend time at the islands, and a number of them decided to stay permanently. They were veterans of union battles on the San Francisco docks, and the best of them were formidably tough, capable men. To these Californians labor unions based on race or nationality were worthless. The idea might succeed in isolated instances on remote plantations, but that was the limit of its possible effectiveness, and because blood unionism could easily set one group of laborers against another, it finally played into the hands of management. There was a better way to organize, one that cut across racial lines. The new slogan was simplicity itself: Know your class and be loyal to it.

A practical test of the new loyalty came in the spring of 1938, when a strike was called against the Inter-Island Steamship Company. It was a grim confrontation. Inter-Island Steamships had the financial backing of Castle & Cooke and the Matson Navigation Company. The unions about to test their strength were all in their infancy in the territory: the Honolulu Waterfront Workers' Association; the International Longshoremen's and Warehousemen's Union (ILWU); the Inland Boatmen's Union; and the Metal Trades Council.

The strike began harshly enough, and it quickly grew worse. Attempts at conciliation got nowhere. The strikers were stubborn, and when the company brought in strikebreakers to take a ship to the island of Hawaii, several hundred union pickets, many of them carrying sticks and clubs, were at the Hilo docks on August 1 to meet it. So were forty armed policemen. As the strikers marched down to the pier, the police turned fire hoses on them, and then tear gas bombs. Some of the pickets broke and ran, but most of them, determined not to be beaten off, sat down where they were. A few kept coming, and when the police saw this, they opened fire with shotguns.

"They shot us down like a herd of sheep," said Harry Kamoku, one of the leaders of the ILWU at Hilo. "We didn't have a chance. The firing kept up for about five minutes. They just kept pumping buckshot bullets into our bodies. They shot men in the back as they ran. They ripped their bodies with bayonets. They shot men who were trying to help wounded comrades and women. It was just plain slaughter, brother."

It was something less than that. No one was killed, and the leading newspapers, conservatively inclined, referred to the affair as an "incident." But it was bad enough, in all conscience. "The cops say in the papers that they shot low for the legs," said Harry Kamoku. "But we were sitting down. How could they shoot us in the legs? Our boys are in the hospital with wounds in the face—in the groin—in the arms—in the head." Fifty of the picketers, men and women, were wounded, several critically, and Bert Nakano, an active union organizer, was left a cripple. The workers remembered it all as the "Hilo Massacre."

The attorney general of the territory made an inquiry, and a grand jury met, but no one, policeman or picket, was indicted. The strike went on, but the unions were coming to the end of their resources, and in September they gave up and went back to work.

So the new union leaders lost their first major battle, and two years later they lost another. For ten months, beginning in July, 1940, waterfront workers at two ports on Kauai refused to load or unload cargoes, but once again management was able to outwait the longshoremen, and the strike collapsed.

Clearly management could still win battles. But the whole campaign was going in favor of the unions. Their membership was increasing steadily, month by month, and in mid-1941 a new balance of power was reached on the waterfront. The ILWU, on behalf of longshoremen working at Honolulu for Castle & Cooke Terminals, Ltd., signed a contract with management, the first of its kind in the industry at the islands. In the few months remaining before the outbreak of World War II, the ILWU negotiated contracts at ports on Kauai and Hawaii. By the end of 1941 the organization of the waterfront was on the way to success.

The ILWU, in fact, was doing remarkably well for itself. Its locals in the territory were building up close connections with the powerful parent union on the west coast, and cargoes at both ends of the run between San Francisco and Hawaii were loaded and unloaded by ILWU men. The well-being of the islands depended absolutely on the free flow of goods by sea, and serious thought would have to be given to something unthinkable only ten years earlier: a single labor union was in a position to turn the tap of prosperity on or off at will.

The ILWU succeeded in Hawaii where several other short-lived industrial unions failed, and the reward was affiliation with the nationwide Council of Industrial Organizations. Away from the waterfront, craft unions, most of them affiliated with the American Federation of Labor, flourished even more vigorously in the years just before the war. A good many of the AFL's recruits were recent arrivals, defense workers brought in from the mainland as the needs of the armed services grew more pressing. By 1941 the AFL could claim something like eight thousand members as against the CIO's twenty-five hundred. The newcomers had some adjustments to make. The AFL was noted for its coolness to workers whose skins were not white, but of course if the color line was maintained at the islands, the Federation would be denying itself access to a source of strength. Then again, the AFL had an interest in another kind of exclusiveness: the skills of its craft workers had to be protected. At the islands most workers in industry—and agriculture—were unskilled. So the Federation's leaders in the territory had to weigh the usefulness of the AFL's traditions against the facts of the local situation. In 1937 they came to an adventurous decision and tried to found an all-inclusive Hawaiian Islands Federation of Labor, bringing together organized workers regardless of race or occupation. The attempt failed, and this left the way open for the CIO unions to move into organization on an industry-wide basis. The great prize at the islands would be the organization of the sugar and pineapple plantations, and the ILWU, making its appeal on the basis of class rather than craft, was well suited to the task. Once the union's beachhead at the ports was established, its leaders turned to look with a calculating eye at the green fields of the plantations.

The war stopped the ILWU's advance in this direction almost before it started. Labor agreements already negotiated were superseded by general orders issued from the military government's headquarters. Workers were frozen in their jobs, and wages were frozen too. Permission to change employment was almost impossible to get, and anyone who left his job without permission was likely to wind up in provost court charged with absenteeism, for which the penalty under martial law was a fine of two hundred dollars or two months' imprisonment, or both. The AFL managed to hold its own in the face of the general orders and even increased its total membership, as tradesmen came by the scores of thousands from the mainland to work on defense projects at spectacularly high wages. But the CIO unions, and most of all the ambitious ILWU, suffered acutely. Japanese workmen, who made up an important part of the waterfront union, were barred from the docks by the military governor, and on the plantations mill hands and field hands alike could only look with envy at the big payrolls being earned and spent by luckier men working at the service bases.

Good union members, like all good citizens, were ready to do whatever was necessary to win the war in the Pacific. But, again like a number of other good Americans in the territory, they found martial law intolerable, and they were impatient to get back their freedom of action. A flurry of organizing was bound to follow the restoration of civil law, and employers contemplating this could not make up their mind which would be worse—total war with the Japanese, waged at a distance, or total war with the unions at home. Still, unions were a fact of life, their existence guaranteed by federal legislation, and new times demanded new strategies. In mid-1943 the agencies that made up the Big Five banded together with scores of smaller business houses to found the Hawaii Employers Council, and men experienced in negotiating with labor leaders on the west coast were hired to work out plans for the future.

The Council began by making a bow to the inevitable. The right of employees to form unions was recognized, and their leaders were given a formal invitation to the conference table. The hope of management was for peace, not war. If labor could be persuaded that it was getting a fair deal, then with luck strikes and lockouts could be avoided and industry's profits would be preserved. Behind this strategy was the further hope that the new arrangments would be lasting—that management, having given ground a little, would not have to give ground any more.

With or without the blessing of the Employers Council, of course, the unions were determined to go ahead and organize the plantations. Months before the Council was formed, and almost a year before martial law came to an end, Arthur A. Rutledge of the AFL and Jack H. Kawano of the ILWU met on Hawaii to talk over the possibility of a jointly organized union for the whole sugar industry. The plan came to nothing, and the AFL, trying to go it alone immediately afterward, had no success. The ILWU, however, came back into its own in 1944 and 1945, and the speed of its conquests was amazing. Relying on the machinery of the National Labor Relations Act of 1935, the union sent its representatives to one plantation camp after another and then petitioned to be recognized as the legitimate bargaining agent of industrial workers on the sugar plantations. Election victory after election victory followed.

The Employers Council used delaying tactics, arguing over the distinction between industrial workers on plantations, who were covered by the National Labor Relations Act, and agricultural workers proper, who were not. There was a real point to be defined here, but when the National Labor Relations Board made its decision in January 1945 the ruling favored the ILWU. This useful advantage was consolidated by a political triumph. In its first furious year of renewed activity toward the end of the war, the ILWU was able to bring pressure to bear on the territorial legislature in favor of a law to permit the organizing of agricultural workers. After the Hawaii Employment Relations Act of 1945 was passed, no part of Hawaii's economy was exempt from union influence. By the end of 1946 the ILWU had managed to get industry-wide contracts on behalf of virtually all longshore, sugar, and pineapple workers. The AFL was eclipsed, at least for the time being; smaller competing unions were swallowed whole.

There had not been a strike of any importance in the territory since 1940. Direct action on a large scale was out of the question as long as martial law prevailed, and even after the heavy ban of the general orders was lifted the industry-wide organization of the waterfront and the plantations was carried out reasonably quietly. To be sure, this meant only that a major strike was postponed. Labor continued to regard management as a kind of baleful immovable object, and now the ILWU had ambitions to become an irresistible force. A collision would certainly come, and it would inevitably create turmoil: a prolonged stoppage of work in any part of the ILWU's jurisdiction would do great harm to the economy of the territory. And yet, in a sense, both sides looked forward to a confrontation. How else could they test each other's strength?

The test took the form of a strike in the sugar industry. On September 1, 1946, about twenty-one thousand workers on thirty-three plantations walked off the job. Arguments over the substantive issues began immediately and dragged on for weeks. In private, negotiators talked the technical language of job classifications, the cash value of perquisites, closed versus open shops, and work hours. In public one set of partisans talked about management's determination to smash the union, and the other set talked about the threat of union tyranny over every inhabitant of the territory. Government conciliators worked long hours, and at least one gave up in disgust. Pickets marched endlessly, and several score were arrested for unlawful assembly and riot.

The question of discipline became paramount—on one side the solidarity of the several ILWU locals, and on the other the mutual support of the member firms of the Hawaii Employers Council. Beyond that, however, chance played a great part in the outcome. A good many sugar plantations depended on irrigation, and once their workers struck there was no one to water the fields. If the fall of 1946 had been unusually wet it would not have mattered so much. But at Ewa plantation on Oahu, for example, not a drop of rain fell after the strike began, and eventually the owners, Castle & Cooke, reached a point where they stood to lose more in dollars through ruined crops than they would pay in a reasonable settlement with the union. By October Castle & Cooke were ready to buy their way out of the dilemma, and with varying degrees of reluctance the other major agencies fell into line. After seventy-nine days the strike came to an end. Undeniably the union had won.

It was not a total victory. The ILWU was unable to get a closed shop, with compulsory union membership, and the wage increase they settled for was a compromise. But on one crucial point—the conversion of perquisites into cash—the union came out well ahead. The perquisite system had been in existence since the earliest days of the industry at the islands, and it was one of the strongest reminders of the days of paternalism. The plantation worker lived in a company house (from which he might be evicted if he went on strike); he bought his food with company vouchers at a company store; and in all sorts of other ways he was not his own man, because the company did not let him make his own decisions about where to live and how to spend his earnings. Now he was to have the value of these perquisites in cash, and he was free—or at least much freer than before—to make decisions for himself and his family as he chose. As a matter of fact some of the plantation agencies were not altogether sorry to see the perquisite system go. However useful it had been in controlling workers, it was expensive to maintain, uneconomical in a strict sense. Still, there was no blinking the fact that in getting rid of perquisites the union had won a great triumph.

All in all, the power of the ILWU to mount and win a major strike meant that from now on plantation workers would have to be regarded in a new light. At the urgent request of the plantation agencies six thousand laborers from the Philippines were imported in 1946, the year of the sugar strike, but they were the last of their kind and their presence did not really dilute the strength of the union. With the strike victory to remind workers that class loyalty brought rich rewards, it was becoming impossible for employers to play one racial group against another. By 1947 the ILWU could claim more than thirty thousand members. The age of the immigrant laborer was over.

A single union of that size in a population of only five hundred thousand was certainly a force with which to be reckoned. At the same time it was likely that union membership would fall rather than rise in the years ahead, at least as far as the plantations were concerned. During the war the plantation companies lost a good deal of land and a good many workers to the armed services, and the only way to make up the loss in productivity was through greater efficiency. This meant mechanization, and every year after the war brought more of it. Fewer workers would be needed in future, and in time the ILWU might find itself in a defensive position, trying to save jobs for its members. But for the present labor had the edge, and even if membership on the plantations did decline, the union would still be able to bring the sugar industry to a halt with a strike. Then too the ILWU could look elsewhere for members, especially in the towns, where the pickings were bound to be good, even with the AFL as a competitor.

So much for the simple arithmetic of unionization. Another sort of calculation about the labor movement disclosed something even more important than sheer numbers. By the mid-nineteen forties there were citizens in greater strength than ever before among waterfront and plantation workers. This was a reflection of what was happening in Hawaiian society at large, but in the case of organized labor the shift in political status had a special significance. It meant that laborers could vote as well as strike, and this raised the question of where the unions would stand in relation to the established political parties, Republican and Democratic.

Before the war the Republicans virtually owned the territory. If the Democratic party was not regarded as a joke, it was only because the Republicans took seriously even the most feeble stirrings of opposition. And feeble the Democrats were. In their best years they could not elect much more than a third of the territorial legislature. Twice they managed to elect the territory's delegate to Congress, but William P. Jarrett in the nineteen twenties and Lincoln L. McCandless in the thirties found the going rough at Washington, surrounded as they were by the representatives of the planters and businessmen who kept offices at the national capital, and who always seemed to have money to spend in their own good cause.

To compound the miseries of the local Democrats, Democratic Presidents of the United States somehow appointed territorial governors who in turn seemed to have an unusual tolerance for the Hawaiian version of Republicanism. Woodrow Wilson's first choice, Lucius E. Pinkham, who took office after the election of 1912, had worked for the Hawaiian Sugar Planters' Association, and his successor, Charles J. McCarthy, stepped down after one complaisant term of office to take a job as the agent of the Honolulu Chamber of Commerce at Washington.

A greater opportunity for the Democrats came when Franklin Delano Roosevelt was elected President in 1932, but Roosevelt took office while the Massie case was still being argued, and this threw a dark cloud over the whole system of territorial government. The local Democrats made their own troubles worse by taking sides in a violent factional fight between Lincoln McCandless and the Democratic mayor of Honolulu, John H. Wilson, both of whom wanted the governorship. Neither got it. Roosevelt, after spending more than a year making up his mind, appointed Joseph B. Poindexter, who in turn took another eight months to make his own appointments, leaving more than two-thousand Republicans in patronage jobs in the meantime.

All this was demoralizing enough. Worse still, the struggle between McCandless and Wilson almost killed the party at the islands. On the mainland the Democrats were going from strength to strength, but in Hawaii they were losing whatever grip they had, and on the eve of Roosevelt's third victory in 1940 the territorial legislature had only a handful of Democratic members. Year in and year out, then, the winds of conservatism blew over Hawaii, as steady as the trades, and even a violent storm like the one that brought the New Deal to Washington was likely to lose some of its force on the way to the islands.

Republicans in Hawaii had the best possible reasons for wanting to keep things as they were, and they knew of a good many ways to do just that. The territory's organic act, for example, provided for the reapportionment of the legislature whenever the movement of population justified it, but somehow genuine reapportionment never took place. The city of Honolulu grew bigger each year and less secure for the Republicans, but in practice this meant only that a vote cast on one of the outer islands increased in value, and the men who ran the sugar and pineapple plantations made sure that votes were cast and counted reliably. Before the war it was difficult, even dangerous, for a Democrat to say a word openly on the plantations. Keep your mouth shut and use the pencil at election time, said the Democrats, and under the circumstances it was the only possible advice; but somehow the plantations continued to vote Republican. Over the years a sturdy folklore, based on fact, sprang up about managers who planted political spies among their workers, or who watched the movement of the string attached to the pencil in the voting booth, and then held the marked ballot up to the light before dropping it in the ballot box.

The Republican party was a white man's party, and everyone could understand why this should be so, including the Hawaiians and part Hawaiians who voted Republican. The men who led the Democratic party before the war were haoles too, with the exception of Mayor John Wilson, who had some Polynesian blood. Wilson, better than most, could see the obvious—that all the outs together might be able to unseat the ins. If the Republicans were racially exclusive (using the Hawaiian vote just as a political tool), then the Democrats would have to be racially inclusive. This was the only way to make a political advantage out of the disadvantage of a skin that was not white, and if the political advantage could be used intelligently, then after a time perhaps the racial disadvantage would disappear.

Certainly the figures were on Wilson's side. By the mid-nineteen thirties the Japanese alone had between a quarter and a third of all the potential votes in the territory, and if the votes of the citizen Chinese and Koreans and Filipinos were added—not to mention the Hawaiians and part Hawaiians—the total was even more impressive.

So the principle was easy to grasp. But the Democrats hesitated to apply it, because the practical difficulties were great. In the first place there was no assurance that one kind of Oriental would run willingly in political harness with another. No love was lost between Japanese, Chinese, Koreans, and Filipinos, or between any one group of Orientals and the Hawaiians and Portuguese, or between any of these and the haoles of the territory. Then again, the mere thought of admitting Orientals to full partnership in politics was enough to give pause to most of the leading Democrats. On the mainland the Democratic party was making a good thing, even a fine thing, out of championing the dispossessed. In Hawaii, as always, things were different. It was all very well for idealists to testify at statehood hearings about the Americanization of the Oriental and his healthy appetite for local politics—and indeed Orientals were active in precinct work and eager for patronage (as the Hawaiians had always been). In realistic terms, however, if the Democrats of the territory wanted power they would have to look for it not only on the wrong side of the tracks but also on the far side of the color line. The history of their party in national politics did not offer much precedent for this, and so, understandably, they trod cautiously.

It was the ILWU that forced the issue, by demonstrating what might be done if the issue of race could be subsumed in some common cause. As early as 1938 the union was beginning to dabble in politics on the island of Kauai, and once labor came out of the doldrums of the early war years, its influence was felt all through the territory. The passage of the Hawaii Employment Relations Act in 1945 encouraged the leaders of the ILWU to increase their pressure on the political parties, and in 1946 the union set up a Political Action Committee. About a hundred thousand people would be eligible to vote in the territorial elections of that year. The ILWU's membership was climbing toward thirty thousand. Its alien members would have to be left out of calculations, but even so the union's power at the polls was striking. The lower house of the legislature had thirty seats. Fifteen Democrats were elected, and fourteen of them had the endorsement of the Political Action Committee. It was an impressive accomplishment, and the word was that the union did not intend to call a halt there. The next step would be the outright capture of the Democratic party.

In any sensible long-term view this was an unlikely prospect. Too many things were moving in Hawaiian society just after the war for any such sweeping prediction to be trustworthy. Democratic politics was becoming a heady brew, and it would go on fermenting for years as factions within the party formed, fell apart, and recombined. Labor already had an obvious use for candidates who would accept the endorsement of the ILWU, but at the same time the Democratic party was beginning to attract a wide range of supporters who had no interest in merely being used by the union.

Immediately following the war, however, the only group in Democratic politics able to exert a steady and effective pressure on events was the ILWU, and after the sugar strike of 1946 people began to talk about the One Big Union and the Big Five in the same breath, as if they were evenly matched contestants for power. The ILWU would not have regarded this as any more than its due. The union's leaders had planned and carried out a brilliant attack on the Big Five, and they were confident that they had the best of things already. On the plantations and along the waterfront—at the strategic points in the capitalist network of production, distribution, and exchange—the barricades of radical unionism were erected, and battle was joined. In the view of the union the plantation agencies had brought upon themselves a struggle they were doomed to lose. The Big Five, failing to move with the times, had fallen prisoner to history, and the keys to the future—political as well as economic—were in the hands of the ILWU.

Unquiet Peace

To people with an ear for political rhetoric this overweening confidence in the workings of history had a suspiciously doctrinaire ring. It sounded, indeed, like Marxist dogma adapted to local circumstances; and sure enough, in the spring of 1947 the chief of Army Intelligence in Hawaii and his commanding general came privately to Governor Ingram Stainback to warn him that the ILWU was a nest of Communists and that the infestation was spreading. Governor Stainback, a Democrat of the old persuasion, prided himself on his high regard for civil liberties—his record of opposition to the military government during the war spoke for itself— but he drew the line at harboring Communists, however unwittingly. To be told that he himself had offered governmental appointments to men who carried party cards was a further shock. Stainback did not like to think of himself as naïve, and yet, as he put it later, termites had apparently been boring away all round him for years without his knowledge. He made a public issue of communism at once, and the more he talked about it, the more enraged he became. His choler did not subside as long as he lived.

Late in 1947 some firsthand evidence came to light about the extent of the damage already done when a Japanese named Ichiro Izuka published a pamphlet which he called *The Truth About Communism in Hawaii.* Izuka joined the party before the war, when he was an active union worker on the Kauai waterfront, and mainly for this reason, so he said, he was imprisoned without trial for several months in 1942 by the military government. After the war he became disenchanted with communism, and now, having wrestled with his conscience, he was ready to reveal all he knew. If he did not have total recall he had something close to it, and he set out to tell the story of the party in Hawaii complete with names, dates, and places.

Governor Stainback was eager to cleanse himself and his administration of any Marxist taint. The first employees of the territorial government to be fired for their radical political views were John E. Reinecke and his wife. Their names were among those that cropped up both on the Army's list and in Izuka's confessions. John Reinecke held a doctoral degree in linguistics, and he had taught briefly at the University of Hawaii, but at the time he came to the governor's attention he and his wife were teaching in the public school system. They were suspended without pay while their case was investigated. The inquiry, from start to finish, took almost a year. The newly formed Hawaii Civil Liberties Committee protested the whole affair, but the outcome was that the Reineckes lost their jobs.

This was just the beginning. The decision to fire the Reineckes was made public on October 30, 1948, and on the same day Hugh Butler of Nebraska, a Republican member of the United States Senate Committee on Interior and Insular Affairs, arrived at Honolulu to look into what he called the Communist penetration of the islands. Butler talked confidentially with scores of people, and his conclusions were dire. He convinced himself that there were unbroken lines of influence running all the way from Moscow to the Honolulu waterfront and back. The regional director of the ILWU in Hawaii, John Wayne Hall, did exactly what he was told to do by the president of his union, Harry Renton Bridges, who, from his headquarters in San Francisco, ruled as "the unseen Communist dictator of the Territory." Bridges reported directly to the Communist party of the United States, which in turn obeyed orders from the Kremlin unhesitatingly. Thus, wrote Butler, "by the well-known infiltration tactics of world Communism, a relative handful of Moscow adherents in the islands" were sabotaging the economic life of the territory by "strikes, slow-downs, arbitrary work stoppages, and violent racial agitation." Nor did the power of communism end there. "Every aspect" of life was affected: "business, labor, transportation, agriculture, education, publishing, radio, entertainment, and in lesser degree, even the religious life of the community," Hawaii, in sum, was "one of the central operations bases and a strategic clearinghouse" for the Communist campaign against the entire United States.

Jack Hall, described in Senator Butler's report as an "active Communist," was not in the least abashed by the accusation, and his background made it unlikely in any case that he would change his ways to please a touring senator. In the mid-nineteen thirties, when Hall was a young merchant seaman sailing out of San Francisco, he left his ship at Honolulu to help organize the territory's waterfront workers, and he never went back to sea. More than anyone else he was responsible for the rise of the ILWU at the islands, and he grew in authority with the union. He and a handful of others had been strong enough in the early years to pull the ILWU through bad times, and now, with thirty thousand union brothers to back him up, he felt less vulnerable than ever.

Hall simply dismissed Ichiro Izuka's pamphlet as part of a bosses' plot to break the union. Then, while the political loyalties of his associates the Reineckes were still under investigation, he and the other union leaders went ahead with their plan to take over the Democratic party. At the Democratic territorial convention of 1948 the ILWU and its supporters were so strong that the conservative wing of the party was pushed into a corner, and Governor Stainback complained that everything was falling into the hands of Communists, lock, stock, and barrel. This was hardly true. The ILWU might have been strong enough to control the convention, but it was far from controlling every Democratic vote in the territory, especially now that the issue of communism had been raised. The territorial legislature that met early in 1949, not long after Senator Butler went back to Washington to write his gloomy report, was dominated by the Republican party, and the Democratic opposition was divided fairly evenly—and very acrimoniously—between right, center, and left.

The composition of the legislature made it clear that the ILWU could not look for political advantage there in 1949, and the leaders of the union turned again to direct industrial action. In January the longshoremen's locals asked for a wage increase. From then until the end of April bargaining went on with the assistance of federal mediators, but the strike deadline passed without a settlement, and on May 1 about two thousand dock workers walked off the job.

This handful of longshoremen was in a position to do more damage to the economy than the twenty thousand sugar workers who struck in 1946. The sugar strike was bad enough; the dock strike was catastrophic. The territory had never been subjected to anything like it. Virtually no goods entered or left Hawaii, and businesses of all sorts began to crumple up and die. After a month, and then two months, the parties to the strike were nowhere near agreement, and violence broke out on the picket lines in July when police escorted nonstrikers to their jobs on the wharves past groups of union members armed with clubs and pieces of lead pipe.

By the middle of the summer about thirty-four thousand people were out of work. The territorial legislature, meeting in special session, passed a dock seizure act on August 6, and Governor Stainback signed it into law the same day. Another act followed, aimed at preventing the union from taking out injunctions against the government. The union's lawyers could not allow this, and a second front of battle was opened in the courts. In mid-August the government took over the major stevedoring companies, and after that ships were able to come and go from the east coast of the United States. But of course most of Hawaii's business before the strike was with the west coast, and ILWU workers at San Francisco, Los Angeles, and Seattle refused to embarrass their union brothers in the territory by loading or unloading ships in the Hawaiian trade.

At last, on October 23—after 177 days—a settlement was reached. The longshoremen got a satisfactory wage increase, and the stevedoring companies and the ship owners were left to count the cost of six months of enforced idleness. The expense to the territory at large could only be estimated, in vague and appalling terms, at something like one hundred million dollars.

The overtures that brought the strike to an end came from management, and Jack Hall claimed another great victory for the ILWU. But six months was a long time to presume on the patience of people who had to suffer so that the union might prosper, and signs began to appear that the reputation of the ILWU was undergoing a change for the worse. When Harry Bridges arrived at Honolulu during the strike and took his place on the picket line, he was greeted by a storm of vilification. The depression that settled over the islands brought dark thoughts with it, and the idea that Bridges and Jack Hall had secret and malign purposes—that the dock workers' walkout was in fact part of a Communist campaign—became harder to dismiss.

Senator Hugh Butler, for one, was sure of it. "This," he wrote, "is the familiar pattern of Communist 'softening up' by economic attrition before the big push for the final *coup d'etat*. If the Territory of Hawaii can be prostrated by this system of a slow economic bleeding, it must ultimately become a social bog ripe for the wrecking blow of Communism."

Certainly something was wrecking life at the islands. The *Hilo Tribune-Herald* concluded during the strike that the atmosphere was being poisoned not by communism itself, but by the fact that the *issue* of communism was being used "for purposes revoltingly dishonest." Senator Butler, for whatever reason, was doing his best to convince the nation that Hawaii was an outpost of the Kremlin. The ILWU, dismissing this as irresponsible red baiting, went on with its own equally irresponsible blockade of shipping. And to top it all off, said the *Tribune-Herald*, "certain management groups could hardly be expected not to make the most of the rising outcry against Communism, to the extent that it has become almost a cocktail party pastime to demand signed non-Communist statements from friend and neighbor; the words 'commie' and 'fellow traveler' are bandied arrogantly and carelessly by people who don't know what they are talking about, with tragic damage to some perfectly guiltless names and reputations. . . ."

By now the Cold War was fairly under way, and if it was true that the enemy without had allies within the United States, then very likely some of them were in Hawaii. But how many, and who were they? Lists of names were being waved about, just as they were on the mainland, and the more vigorously they were waved the longer they seemed to grow. If that went on, friend and neighbor would not be able to trust even a signed non-Communist statement. It was time, as the *Tribune-Herald* said, to bring the issue to a head.

The territorial legislature agreed. In the wake of the dock strike an act was passed creating a subversive activities commission, and to set the seal on this expression of sincerity the legislature resolved to ask for a visit from a subcommittee of the United States House of Representatives Committee on Un-American Activities.

The committee had already carried out extremely well-publicized investigations in many places on the mainland. The hearings held at Honolulu in April, 1950, followed a familiar pattern: assurances by the visiting congressmen that the Communist menace could not survive exposure to the righteous anger of a loyal populace; the serving of subpoenas; and then a parade of witnesses, variously cooperative and hostile.

On the mainland the committee was accustomed to call "professionals" to testify about the workings of communism—former party members who had seen the error of their ways and were prepared to do their penance in public, repeatedly and for a fee. Their version of affairs was published in the Honolulu newspapers, and their place at the hearings was taken by Ichiro Izuka, who told his painful story over once more, at his own expense. Several other former members of the party in Hawaii added their quota of confession to the record.

Despite the urging of the committee and its counsel, however, some subpoenaed witnesses would not name names. Stephen Murin, chairman of the Hawaii Civil Liberties Committee, believed it would be un-American to do so, even though a refusal might land him in trouble. "I could go ahead and do it," he said, "but I feel that I would be betraying those people who in the long run, who in the historic past had made America what it is. It is not because I want to get you gentlemen angry, because I enjoy the job of sitting here and have the people say, 'That dirty this and that.' It is not because of that. I think that in the long run history will bear me out, those of us who are standing up today and having the guts, if you want to call it that, having the guts to say, 'No agent of the Government can tell me that it is wrong for me to associate with John Doe, or wrong for you to read that book,' we are serving the American people."

Most of the others did not want to have to explain themselves at all. They simply invoked the Constitution of the United States. One after another they were sworn and identified, and then, after a pointed question, they said what thousands of witnesses all over the United States found themselves saying in similar circumstances. When Jack Hall's turn came he was asked: "Are you now or have you ever been a member of the Communist Party?" Hall said: "On the advice of counsel, I refuse to answer on the ground that it might incriminate me." Thirty-eight others at Honolulu made the same response, and in the process the people of Hawaii found out more about the Fifth Amendment than they thought they would ever have to know.

At the beginning of the hearings the chairman of the subcommittee, Representative Francis E. Walter of Pennsylvania, announced that he would not hesitate to invoke all the powers at his command against witnesses who obstructed proceedings. The Reluctant Thirty-Nine, as they became known, were cited for contempt of Congress. A good many people wanted to see them punished promptly, but of course the House Un-American Activities Committee was only an investigating body; "exposure" was its only weapon, and it could not hold trials and hand down verdicts. The contempt cases did not come before the courts until January 1951, long after Representative Walter and his associates left Hawaii. To the chagrin of conservatives the federal judge who heard the case was Delbert E. Metzger, the same man who had crossed swords with the military government during the war. Where civil liberties were concerned, Metzger was a man for all political seasons. He ruled that even self-admitted Communists, as well as those described as Communists by others in sworn testimony at the committee's hearings, were entitled to take refuge in the Fifth Amendment, just like other Americans. One after another the Reluctant Thirty-Nine were acquitted.

Among them was Jack H. Kawano, former president of an ILWU local at Honolulu, a man almost as important in the union as Jack Hall. Kawano was going through the same sort of personal crisis as Ichiro Izuka, and after his acquittal in the contempt case he decided he had been wrong in refusing to cooperate with the House Un-American Activities Committee. In July 1951, he went to Washington to give testimony, and once he started he could not stop. By the time he left the witness stand the federal government had enough evidence to bring indictments against Jack Hall and six others under the Smith Act.

At dawn on August 28, 1951, they were arrested at their homes by FBI agents and charged with conspiring to teach the overthrow of the United States Government by force and violence. Taken into custody with Hall were John Reinecke; Koji Ariyoshi, editor of the left-wing *Honolulu Record,* and Jack Denichi Kimoto, of the *Record*'s circulation department; Dwight James Freeman, described in testimony before the Un-American Activities Committee as a Communist party organizer; Charles K. Fujimoto, who in 1948 had announced publicly that he was chairman of the party in Hawaii, and his wife Eileen Kee Fujimoto.

Once again Judge Delbert Metzger outraged the conservatives by allowing bail of five thousand dollars for each of the defendants. A sum of seventy-five thousand dollars had been asked, but Metzger reduced it on the grounds that bail should not be used as a punishment. The grand jury duly returned an indictment against the Hawaii Seven, as they were called, and this marked the beginning of a legal battle that was to last for years.

In November 1951, Judge J. Frank McLaughlin, a convinced and vocal anti-Communist, became responsible for the criminal calendar in federal court, and five of the seven filed affidavits asking him to disqualify himself in the Smith Act case on grounds of bias. McLaughlin refused. Then the defense filed motions to have the indictment dismissed. McLaughlin denied the motions without a hearing, and set the date of trial for February 28, 1952. A further set of affidavits was filed before Judge Metzger by the defense, alleging that grand juries in Hawaii were packed with upper-class whites. Metzger agreed with the substance of the affidavits and ordered the federal grand and petit juries dismissed. Mc-Laughlin ordered the jury commissioners to disregard Metzger's instructions to draw up a more representative list. The two judges locked horns angrily, and the community seemed about to line up in factions behind one or the other. But McLaughlin won the argument over the jury lists, and then Metzger was forced to drop the matter altogether when his term of office expired, and he was not reappointed to the federal bench.

So the case wound its way to the point of actual trial. By the time it came to court, well over a year had passed since the arrest of the seven, and between the opening statements of counsel and the bringing in of the verdict another seven and a half months passed. The prosecution made every effort to link the activities of the seven with a nationwide and worldwide conspiracy against the government, and the jury was convinced. On June 19, 1953, the seven were found guilty as charged, and they were fined five thousand dollars each and sentenced to five years in jail. The defense gave notice of appeal, the seven were allowed bail, and attorneys on both sides got ready to resume the struggle.

The issue of communism in Hawaii, then, remained unresolved. It must have seemed at this stage that the wretched business would never come to an end. In 1950 Francis Walter of the House Un-American Activities Committee had expressed his firm conviction that the people of Hawaii would leave no stone unturned in searching out the "hideous conspiracy" in their midst. Certainly a good many stones had been turned since then, some of them more than once, but anyone who could think back twenty years to the Massie case might have remembered that people did not always agree about what appeared when stones were shifted.

If the first upheaval over communism brought to light only a handful of conspirators, did this mean there were no more to be found? If increased effort did not bring markedly better results, did this mean that the conspiracy had been contained, or that it had gone further underground, to reappear in some new and dangerous form later? How many Communists were there in Hawaii anyway? The number seemed to range from fifty to two hundred, depending on who was counting. And what did these approximations signify? Not very much, according to Judge Delbert Metzger. His opinion was that a few score political heretics in a population of more than half a million could hardly be regarded as a clear and present danger. But was Metzger wilfully closing his eyes? The professional anti-Communist Paul Crouch, a frequent testifier for the Un-American Activities Committee and a witness for the prosecution in the trial of the Hawaii Seven, was fond of saying that if Hawaii was an independent country, unable to rely on the military strength of the United States, fifteen Communists could bring on armed insurrection. Hawaii, of course, did have the support of the United States. And, in any case, did Crouch really mean what he said? Or was he exaggerating for effect, using a dubious means to what he regarded as a good end?

It was a worrying state of affairs that cried out for convincing answers to questions of fact and questions of meaning. But, perhaps because the questions were so urgent, passion blurred perception. Not many people could think calmly and see clearly just then. Answers did not appear in sharp focus, and the circle of confusion grew greater all the time. So the people of Hawaii, like people all over the United States, inspected one by one the unlikely items of information that were constantly being thrown up from the political underworld, and tried in vain to put a value on them all. They heard about discussions of Marxism in bookshops on Nuuanu Avenue; schools for Communist recruits from the islands, held in San Francisco; coded lists of party membership and secret bank accounts; clandestine expeditions to bury subversive books and pamphlets, recorded on film by watchful government agents; attempts by FBI officers to suborn Jack Hall before the Smith Act trial, tape-recorded secretly by Hall's friends and then played on an ILWU radio broadcast. And at the same time they were told about a woman who overheard a conversation in an elevator to the effect that bloody revolution was on the way and that the Communists of Hawaii were arming themselves against the day; and they were told about a choir master who was bringing on the forceful and violent overthrow of the government by dragooning his unwilling choristers into singing the music of Prokofiev. If one story was to be taken seriously, should the rest be? Or did one piece of hysterical nonsense invalidate the rest? No one could say. The truth might be on one side or the other, or somewhere in between, or somewhere else altogether.

All this time the territorial Subversive Activities Commission was publishing its reports; civil servants and professors were arguing the merits of loyalty oaths; and a privately financed anti-Communist organization known as Imua (a Hawaiian word meaning "forward") kept insisting that the worst was yet to come. In 1956 James O. Eastland of Mississippi, a Democratic member of the Senate Committee on the Judiciary, brought a subcommittee to Honolulu to look yet again at the old controverted questions. Eastland subpoenaed several of the Reluctant Thirty-Nine of 1950 and found them still reluctant. As for the Hawaii Seven, convicted in the Smith Act trial of 1953, they continued to wait for their appeals to be heard. At last, in January 1958, the United States Circuit Court of Appeals in San Francisco made a ruling. In line with an earlier decision by the United States Supreme Court in a similar case, the seven were acquitted on the grounds that abstract preaching of Communist doctrine, even allied with membership in the party, did not constitute conspiracy to overthrow the government by force and violence, within the meaning of the Smith Act.

There was the usual ritual indignation, but it soon died away. The fact was that by 1958 communism as an issue of public debate had lost its power to hold the attention of most people in the territory. No wholesale purge of suspected radicals had been carried out, and neither had armed revolution occurred. Dark forebodings simply went out of style.

Nothing had really been settled, then, and yet with the passage of time certain things were making themselves clear. For one, the ILWU, having weathered the sharpest of attacks, was still very much alive and likely to remain so. In 1950 the nationwide Council of Industrial Organizations voted to expel the ILWU because of its Communist leanings. But the rank and file continued to follow the leaders who embodied radical policy. While Harry Bridges fought a long and ultimately successful battle to keep out of jail on the mainland, Jack Hall dealt with setbacks and defections in Hawaii. In 1947, trying to mount a strike in the pineapple industry that would match the sugar strike of the previous year, he was badly outmaneuvered. In the same year Robert Mookini, leader of a pineapple local, went over to the AFL; and Ichiro Izuka and another discontented local leader, Amos Ignacio, set up a rival union on Kauai and Hawaii, also with the help of the AFL. Five years later Bert Nakano, the crippled hero of the Hilo Massacre of 1938, left the ILWU and formed the Federation of Hawaiian Workers.

But the new groups did not prosper. The ILWU stood, and Hall himself was unbudgeable. While he was still under sentence in the Smith Act case a public testimonial dinner was held for him at Honolulu, and there was a large and enthusiastic turnout of guests. So the rank and file of the ILWU—and a good many people outside the union as well—tried and acquitted Jack Hall long before the law courts did, using the scales of simple economic justice to weigh the man and his beliefs. If at one time or another Hall carried a party card, so did Ichiro Izuka and Jack Kawano and Bert Nakano; and if Hall was stubborn enough to take the Fifth Amendment, he was also stubborn enough to stay with the union. It was largely his doing that plantation workers in Hawaii were among the best paid in the world, and as well paid as many industrial workers on the American mainland. In the end, it might have been argued, he did more good for the working man than any number of anti-Communist breakaways.

This was rough-and-ready reasoning, but then not many members of the ILWU were political philosophers. On the basis of the facts as they saw them, they were willing to let Hall go ahead with the work to which he had devoted his life. He did so, with as much energy as ever. Well before he was acquitted along with the rest of the Hawaii Seven he had managed to consolidate the various locals of the ILWU, first into major occupational groupings—sugar, pineapple, longshore, and miscellaneous industries—and then into one formidably powerful body, Local 142, which covered the whole territory. With this, Hall had gone about as far as it was possible to go in making the union strong and in making it his own.

Whether employers liked it or not, then, Jack Hall was still the man with whom they had to deal. A good many businessmen did not like it at all, especially when the ILWU staged short strikes protesting the various prosecutions of Hall and Harry Bridges, and when three thousand of Hall's men walked off the job in 1956 as a protest against the arrival of the Eastland committee at Honolulu.

Walkouts such as these could justifiably be called political, and as Benjamin F. Dillingham II complained to Senator Eastland, it was upsetting to find that in American law a convicted Communist could keep his place at the head of a powerful union while his case was being appealed. "Certainly," said Dillingham, "if a man were under question for treason in the armed services, he wouldn't be left in the line to carry on, while he was under questioning. And I feel that a situation like that has got to be dealt with by proper legal and—proper laws being established. If there is a question about a man's loyalty, he should be suspended until that matter is cleared up."

Yet if Dillingham had been able to set aside his misgivings for a moment, he would have seen that on matters of the greatest importance—the negotiation of contracts for the sugar, pineapple, and waterfront industries—Hall seemed to be mellowing slightly. There was a long strike on the pineapple plantations of Lanai in 1951. From then on, however, the record was less disturbed. Ten years after the sugar strike of 1946 another major battle appeared to be looming. But after some warlike remarks, a settlement was reached that showed something like maturity—on both sides. It was perhaps too early to talk about a recognition of common cause on the part of labor and management. The sugar strike that was averted in 1956 took place in 1958, and for four months the old wounds lay open again. But then in 1959 the pineapple industry went through the task of preparing new contracts without a strike; and the worst days of irreconcilability seemed to be over.

A new balance of power was being struck as well between the ILWU and the Democratic party. For a short time in the late nineteen forties the leaders of the union believed themselves to be within reaching distance of one of their major objectives: control of the Democratic party. But they were driven back. By 1950 the decisive moment had passed, and by 1954 it was clear that such a moment was unlikely to come again.

Not surprisingly, the turmoil over communism had something to do with this. At the Democratic territorial convention of 1950 several of the Reluctant Thirty-Nine, awaiting trial for contempt of Congress, presented their credentials as elected delegates. When they were allowed to take their seats a group of conservatives walked out of the convention. Even so the gathering did not fall into the hands of the ILWU, because although the conservatives left, the moderates stayed, and there were enough of them to damp down the influence of the union.

This was a setback, to be sure, and during the next twelve months the estrangement between the left and the center of the Democratic party became even more noticeable. When Jack Kawano unburdened himself before the House Un-American Activities Committee at Washington, he explained that he had been persuaded to break with the Communist party and sever his association with the ILWU by a group of good citizens at Honolulu. It was Kawano's testimony that led to the indictment of the Hawaii Seven under the Smith Act. Obviously, then, these good Americans did not mind seeing painful things happen to Jack Hall. Kawano insisted on reading the names of his new friends into the record, and it turned out that nearly all of them were active Democrats.

Looking back on this period from a distance of several years, Hall was still bitter at what he regarded as a betrayal by the Democrats. Perhaps he was too much inclined to think in simple opposites: black reaction versus radicalism; management versus labor; the Big Five versus the ILWU. However much this habit of thought strengthened Hall's appeal to members of his union in the years just after the war, it did not take account of everything that was happening in the Democratic party. Hall would not have appreciated the notion that the forces of history were working against him, but it was true enough in a way.

With more and more people every year taking an active interest in Democratic politics, a place could be found in the party for anyone who, for whatever reason, wanted to see the Republican establishment shaken. Among them were convinced liberals in the public school system and at the University of Hawaii; political opportunists with no Republican connections; disaffected Hawaiian and part Hawaiian patronage seekers; small businessmen and professional men, haole and Oriental, operating on the frontiers of the Big Five's empire; and last but not least, a group of earnest young Japanese whose political education, begun in the 442nd Regiment, was completed under the GI Bill.

Very few of these rising men considered that they owed any overriding loyalty to Jack Hall. The union's purposes were not necessarily theirs, and it was certainly not in their interest to associate themselves too closely with alleged Communists. Radical politics aside, Hall's way of running things was at once too demanding and too limiting. If the Democrats were ever to capture power in Hawaii they would have to cast their nets wider than Hall was able to do.

And they would need new leaders within the party itself. One by one the old guard were dropping out of the ranks: Lincoln McCandless, John

Wilson, Ingram Stainback. Oren E. Long, who succeeded Stainback as governor during the Presidency of Harry Truman, served only one term, and he was in any case approaching the end of his active career. The task of working out a strategy for the nineteen fifties was difficult, with many interests to be reconciled, and several years passed before one man emerged at the head of the party.

In some ways John A. Burns was an unlikely standard bearer. He had lived most of his life at the islands, and he spent the war years as a police officer attached to the vice squad at Honolulu. When he took up political campaigning in a serious fashion after the war, he was on the verge of middle age—a common man, without money, quite without social pretensions, and without much claim to depth or subtlety of mind. There was nothing facile or even ordinarily fluent about his speechmaking: the best he could manage was a strained, earnest, faintly brooding kind of utterance. And yet this somber awkwardness was a source of strength as much as a limitation. Because he knew no other way to speak, he spoke simply and plainly, and no one could mistake his meaning, or miss the fact that he meant what he said.

Burns spoke repeatedly and at length about the one issue from which everything else flowed after the war. He was a haole, but he had no love for the white men who controlled the politics of the territory through their grasp on the Republican party. The hour was past, he argued, when a well-born haole should be allowed to act as if the color of his skin granted him a special dispensation. Too few men had been running the territory for too long. It was time for a change.

Anyone who looked at the population figures which used to fascinate and frighten Democrats and Republicans alike before the war, could see that a change was coming. Immigrants were taking out citizenship papers in ever increasing numbers, and their sons and daughters were citizens by birth. The party that could harness this force and turn it into votes would carry everything before it. For the Republican party the signs were ominous; for the Democrats the auguries were correspondingly promising. Jack Burns could see victory ahead, and his deepest convictions told him at the same time that the rise of a party able to cross racial lines would bring about a profound and irreversible change for the better in the life of the territory.

A great amount of work remained to be done. The machinery of the new Democratic party had to be put together, tested, and strengthened against attack, whether by Republicans or radical unionists. Party workers had to be found, and audiences had to be found too. Workers had to be groomed as candidates, and audiences had to be turned into supporters, willing to promise votes and money. All this meant making choices continually between discipline and flexibility. The ILWU, run on discipline, had succeeded in industry only to fall short in politics. The old Democratic party failed everywhere because of factionalism. Burns and his supporters steered a middle course as best they could. Burns himself was as rigorous on the issue of race as any of his Republican opponents. But his rigor took the form of demanding fair representation for every major group of the population. The Democrats became the great exponents of the balanced ticket, to the point where the protégés of Burns could have posed for a composite portrait illustrating the social history of the islands in all its complexity.

When all the secondary bargains were sealed, when the Chinese and the Filipinos and the Portuguese and the Hawaiians and part Hawaiians were accounted for, the fact remained that the Japanese were the crucial element. With their support the Democrats could win power; without it they could not. Electoral results from the mid-forties to the mid-fifties told the story in the plainest of terms. Americans of Japanese ancestry, AJAs, had stood down from politics during the war. In 1946 half a dozen were elected to the territorial legislature. In 1952 they won half the seats in the House. In 1954 they commanded one out of every two seats in the legislature, House and Senate alike. And 1954 was the first year in which the Democrats controlled the legislature.

This was a great year for Jack Burns, but he himself was not yet a winner at the polls. In 1948 he had lost resoundingly in the balloting for congressional delegate to Joseph R. Farrington, son of a territorial governor, a rich man, and a liberal Republican (or as liberal as Republicans got in Hawaii). Farrington died before the elections of 1954, and his widow, Elizabeth, took his place on the Republican ticket. Burns ran against her and lost again—but this time by less than a thousand votes. He would have to wait another two years for his reward.

The governorship of the territory also remained in Republican hands. Hawaii, as usual, was out of step with the mainland. The victories of the Democrats came at the same time as Republican victories in the national elections, and President Dwight D. Eisenhower appointed as governor Samuel Wilder King, a Republican with a dash of New England blood and a dash of Hawaiian blood to balance it.

So the political scene was confused, and the Democrats in the territorial legislature found it hard to get the main planks in their platform translated into law as long as King sat in the governor's office. He used the veto seventy-one times in the course of the session. Just the same, the Democrats enjoyed the new and heady experience of occupying the seats of power. At the end of the war Katsumi Kometani of the 100th Battalion had said he was looking for a Hawaii in which a man of any ancestry could share in the rights as well as the responsibilities of citizenship. This Hawaii seemed now to be in the making.

No one would have been so foolish as to say that the Democratic victory canceled out the issue of race in Hawaiian politics. The question was merely redefined. Jack Burns and his supporters were denounced by the Republicans as racists in reverse, and then when the votes were counted in 1954 the Republicans began, just as vigorously, to woo the motley collection of ethnic minorities that made up an electoral majority.

Between election campaigns the old racial stereotypes flourished as strongly as ever in society at large. All the inhabitants of the territory had their own firm and unshakable views about the bad character of their neighbors. Hawaiians were feckless and lazy; Filipinos were flighty and given to violence; Chinese were grasping; Japanese were unreasonably attached to ideas of pride and honor; Koreans were noisy and rough; Portuguese could never make up their minds whether they were haoles or not; and haoles themselves—even Democratic haoles—were arrogant and condescending.

Clearly no man of good sense would set up house near any of these people, much less let his daughter marry one of them. Yet, strange to relate, Hawaii had no ghettoes deserving of the name, and by the mid-fifties about one marriage in every three in the territory crossed some racial or national line. Whatever the people of Hawaii said about each other, the evidence of daily life indicated that they got along better than almost any other mixed community in the world. In time this would have some whimsical effects on established institutions and ways of life. For one thing the national census, with its crude categories of racial definition, would soon become useless as a description of the special qualities of the people of Hawaii; and then what would happen to racial stereotypes? It was worth thinking about.

For the present, however, the people of Hawaii bore another special brand, one which they were coming to regard as an overwhelming disability. In relation to Americans living on the mainland they were second class citizens still. Hawaii had been a territory of the United States since the turn of the century, and statehood seemed as far off as ever. That was worth thinking about too.

Fiftieth Star

The sign and seal of Hawaii's political maturity would be the admission of the territory to the union of states. As matters stood, the governor of Hawaii was named by the President of the United States, but the people of Hawaii could take no part in Presidential elections. The territory's delegate to Congress was elected by popular vote, but he himself had no vote in the House of Representatives. And Congress could alter at will the substance of Hawaii's organic act, even to the point of abolishing the territorial legislature. Hawaii, in sum, was nothing but a creature of the federal government.

This unsatisfactory arrangement had been in effect far too long to suit the most enthusiastic advocates of statehood, by whose reckoning Hawaii had been waiting a hundred years to be made a state. If the annexation treaty of 1854 was taken as a starting point, this was so. But the treaty was abortive, and its failure was due at least in part to the fact that it contained a statehood clause. So an argument based on sheer lapse of time was not well founded. And even if the enthusiasts took their stand at the year of actual annexation, 1898, they were not altogether on firm ground. They might argue that nothing in the Constitution of the United States provided for territory to be acquired and then kept permanently in an inferior condition, and that Hawaii, therefore, must have been annexed with statehood in mind. Yet here, as well, uncomfortable facts had to be faced: The leaders of the Hawaiian Republic handed over the islands on the express understanding that statehood was not being contemplated. And if the enthusiasts then argued that the promise of statehood, though unspoken, was implicit in the whole tendency of the history of the United States, the country's performance since annexation was not reassuring. In the twentieth century no offshore possession, whether in the Caribbean or the Pacific, had been given equal rights with the mainland states.

If the constitutional record was not conclusive, there were statistics that might be brought to bear. It was easily established that Hawaii had waited longer than any other territory for admission to the Union, and that the wait had been expensive. By the early nineteen-fifties Hawaii was paying more federal tax each year than nine of the forty-eight mainland states. Since the turn of the century the people of the territory, who had no voice in setting these taxes, had contributed more than a billion dollars to the treasury; and because of the inequities of the territorial system they were never sure of getting a fair share of federal services and grants for improvements. Hawaii did not necessarily want its money back, but there was a strong case for saying that only statehood could redress the economic balance.

Another set of figures was put forward as significant, and rightly so. In 1900 the population of the territory was about one hundred and fifty thousand, and six out of every ten were aliens. Fifty years later the population was half a million, which meant that Hawaii had more inhabitants than four of the existing states (and more than any state at the time of admission, except Oklahoma). In 1950, furthermore, nine out of every ten people in Hawaii were citizens, nearly all of them born on American soil. Why should they be denied the full rights and responsibilities of citizenship?

The question had been raised seriously before 1941, and it was thought to be settled by 1945. In the opinion of Samuel Wilder King, who resigned in 1942 as the territory's congressional delegate in order to take up a commission in the navy, the war wiped out all possible objections to admitting Hawaii as a state. After all, Pearl Harbor took the first blow; the civilians of the territory suffered the ignominy of martial law with good grace; and the 442nd Regiment and the rest of Hawaii's thirty thousand servicemen met every demand made upon them. What more could conceivably be asked as evidence of good faith? Within a few years, King was sure, Hawaii would be named a state.

But it was not, and J. Garner Anthony, Hawaii's attorney general during the war, had some severe things to say about the interminable delay. "Any argument against statehood," he declared bluntly in the course of a congressional hearing in 1950, "must be bottomed either upon disbelief in democracy, self-interests, or ignorance of American history."

Anthony aimed these strong words principally at opposition within the territory. There were several obvious targets. Walter F. Dillingham, who in the forties had been sure that martial law was what the islands needed, was equally sure in the fifties that statehood would be a grievous error. Perhaps some other time; but for the moment the people of Hawaii were bound to choose badly if they were given the right to elect their own leaders. The appointive powers of the President and the governor, correctly used, were the best guarantee that the proper class of men would occupy positions of authority. Lorrin P. Thurston, part owner of the widely read *Honolulu Advertiser,* was another who dragged his feet for years on the question of statehood. His family had never endorsed democracy wholeheartedly, and in 1948 Mayor John Wilson of Honolulu became so enraged at the *Advertiser*'s captious editorials that he bought space in other newspapers to denounce Thurston as "Public Enemy No. 2," second only to Senator Hugh Butler as a wrecker of the best hopes of the territory. For Alice Kamokila Campbell, an enormously wealthy part-Hawaiian, every year since the fall of the monarchy had been a bad one, and statehood would bury the past even deeper than before. The thought of a local government dominated by Orientals reduced her to something like desperation. Her mind was filled with regrets for the past and fears for the future, and she spoke out continually in favor of keeping things as they were—not that the present satisfied her, but that any change would be for the worse.

How many people in the territory shared these bleak views about statehood? Probably not very many, though it was impossible to find out precisely. In 1940 a plebiscite showed two out of every three voters in favor of statehood. Ten years later, when a convention was called to draft a constitution against the day when Hawaii actually became a state, 85 percent of registered voters turned out to elect delegates, and the finished document was approved by a great majority in a plebiscite. For twenty years the congressional delegates from Hawaii had been advocating statehood, and every governor appointed since the war did the same—Ingram Stainback, Oren Long, Samuel Wilder King, and the bright young Republican chosen in 1957 by President Eisenhower, William F. Quinn. At almost every session of the territorial legislature resolutions were passed calling for statehood. Before the war money was appropriated for an Equal Rights Commission, and its postwar successor, the Hawaii Statehood Commission, was never short of funds. Almost every organized group in the territory, from the Hawaiian Sugar Planters' Association to the ILWU, was on record as favoring statehood. So perhaps Garner Anthony could be pardoned for thinking that only a tiny minority, "a few craven souls," were against it.

Even if Anthony was right, of course, the decision would be taken at Washington. It was just as important, therefore, to know what was happening on the mainland. On the face of things Hawaii's chances seemed to be getting better every year. In January 1940 an opinion poll published in *Fortune* magazine showed that only 55 percent of mainlanders thought the United States should go to the defense of Hawaii if she were attacked, compared with 74 percent in favor of defending Canada—this despite the fact that Hawaii was an American possession and Canada a foreign country. The actual attack on Hawaii changed some minds at least. A poll taken early in 1946 showed six out of ten mainlanders in favor of statehood for Hawaii, and by 1954, after another ten polls, 78 percent were said to be in favor. So if the anonymous man in the street was to be believed, Hawaii would be welcomed as a state. Newspapers on the mainland gave the same impression. By 1954 the Hawaii Statehood Commission had in its carefully kept clipping files something like two thousand editorials from all over the nation favoring statehood and fewer than fifty in opposition.

At the same time some quite important men were lending their names in support of the campaign. By 1954 eleven congressional committees had discussed the subject in public hearings. Only one man officially involved, Senator Hugh Butler, spoke loudly against statehood in the late forties, and he changed his mind eventually. Beginning with Harold Ickes in 1945, Secretaries of the Interior under Roosevelt, Truman, and Eisenhower were in favor of statehood. So, beginning somewhat later, were the Department of State, the Department of Defense, and the Department of Justice. J. Edgar Hoover, head of the Federal Bureau of Investigation, was not against the idea. In 1948 the national Democratic party included immediate statehood for Hawaii in its campaign platform, and in 1952 the Republicans followed suit. President Truman himself was in favor, and so was President Eisenhower. And those who went in for counting heads on Capitol Hill in the early fifties believed that a straight vote in both houses of Congress would show a majority for statehood.

With all this good will to draw upon, Hawaii should surely have been a state long since. Yet the territory's delegates to Congress, who between them introduced statehood resolutions by the dozen in the House, saw their efforts come to nothing one after another. Debates began and then trailed off, committee meetings were convened and adjourned, the published record grew bulkier and bulkier, and Hawaii seemed no farther ahead.

The Hawaii Statehood Commission did its best to keep the territory's qualifications before the notice of Congress, and as Senator Guy Cordon of Oregon said, far more was known about Hawaii than about any territory previously admitted to the union of states. Despite all this, a handful of representatives and senators persisted in talking as if Hawaii was a subject bound to catch even the best informed man unprepared. It was as if the Korean war was never fought, as if Pearl Harbor had never been bombed, as if Hawaii had not been part of the American political, economic, and statcgic system for decades. These men made it sound, in fact, as if the islands had just surfaced in mid-Pacific, complete with a primitive polyglot population shouting rude and incomprehensible appeals for parity across inconceivable wastes of ocean.

So, at the insistence of a handful of congressmen, the tedious annexation debate of 1898 was staged all over again, and all the old arguments against Hawaii were presented as if they were brand new. It was asserted, for example, that American tradition was against having anything to do with noncontiguous territory. What could be said in answer to this, except the obvious? Hawaii was already under the American flag. In terms of miles it was far from the national capital, but in terms of time it was closer than most territories on the mainland had been when they became states. By airplane it was about a day's travel away, by cable and radio only seconds. Pearl Harbor was bombed; Washington declared war immediately. Noncontiguity had lost its meaning. There was no such thing in the world anymore.

Then it was said that America's special qualities would be corrupted if places like Hawaii were admitted as states. What happened to the pristine virtue of the Roman Republic, asked Representative James G. Donovan of New York, when it started to take in "the senator from Scythia, the senator from Mesopotamia, the senator from Egypt, the senator from Spain, the senators from Gaul; yes, even the senators from England?" What happened to "Roman Culture? What happened to

Roman unity? What happened to all the old-fashioned Roman morals and Roman integrity?" Whatever happened, it was bad, and there was a lesson to be learned from it, so Donovan believed.

The Founding Fathers of the American Republic were well aware of the danger, according to Representative Kenneth M. Regan of Texas, who was sure George Washington never meant Hawaii to become a state. "I fear for the future of the country," said Regan, "if we start taking in areas far from our own shores that we will have to protect with our money, our guns, and our men, instead of staying here and looking after the heritage we were left by George Washington, who told us to beware of any foreign entanglements. I think he had this outpost in the Pacific Islands in mind at that time."

Against folk wisdom like this no rational argument could prevail. It could only be said that Washington had been dead for quite some while, and that twentieth-century America, like it or not, was cast in an imperial role. She was a world power, with especially heavy commitments in the Pacific hemisphere, and Hawaii was an indispensable forward base. Perhaps even more to the point, the United States was asserting a kind of moral leadership in the world, and if that claim was to be made good in the eyes of Asian countries, then Hawaii would have to be fairly treated. "Some of her people," wrote Senator Guy Cordon, a friend of the statehood movement, "have their racial backgrounds in that area, giving the Nation a unique medium of communication and understanding with Asiatic peoples." Statehood would bestow dignity and prestige upon Hawaii, and would "dramatize as few other acts could the principle of self-government which the United States is proclaiming to the world."

But even if all this was conceded, would not statehood give Hawaii undue weight in domestic affairs? As Representative John R. Pillion of New York put it, two senators from Hawaii would be the voting equals of two senators from his own state, and this was iniquitous, because Hawaii had only a few hundred thousand inhabitants and New York had many millions. It was a reasonable statistical argument, but of course it applied to small states already within the union as well as to Hawaii. And then again the matter had been resolved already, in the Constitution of the United States. Precisely because some states were big and others were small and each deserved a voice, the Founding Fathers in their wisdom had arranged for a House of Representatives to be filled on the basis of population, and a Senate in which each state would have only two spokesmen.

To keep Hawaii out of the union on these various pretexts would mean amending the Constitution and nullifying the twentieth century, and this was beyond the capacities of the opponents of statehood. Luckily for them another useful weapon of propaganda was ready at hand: the issue of communism in Hawaii. It was troublesome enough as a domestic matter in the territory, and once it got loose in Congress it was sufficient to delay a decision on statehood for a long time.

Senator Hugh Butler created an uproar in the late forties when he came back from a visit to Hawaii announcing that the Communist party wanted statehood, with a state constitution "to be dictated by the tools of Moscow in Honolulu." Butler conceded that "an overwhelming majority" of the people of Hawaii wanted to see communism put down, but his strong opinion was that it would be fatal to grant statehood before the territory had cleansed itself.

Butler's colleague in the Senate Committee on Interior and Insular Affairs, Guy Cordon, had made a trip to the islands a little earlier, and he saw nothing like the desperate situation Butler perceived. In 1950 Francis Walter of the House Un-American Activities Committee made a point of saying that his exposure of communism in Hawaii should not be held against the territory's ambitions for statehood. Three years later Guy Cordon went back to Hawaii. Since his first visit, he observed, Hawaii had been making strenuous efforts to eliminate communism altogether. A subversive activities commission was at work. The state constitution drafted in 1950 included a stringent anti-Communist clause, which the allegedly all-powerful and Communist-riddled ILWU had been unable to prevent. And throughout the Korean war ILWU men at Honolulu worked on ships bound for Asia to fight communism. Then in 1953 a local jury convicted the Hawaii Seven in the Smith Act case. Cordon concluded that the people of Hawaii were sufficiently alert to the Communist menace, that Communist power and influence at the islands had declined strikingly in the past few years, and that communism was no more of a threat there than in any of the existing states.

Hugh Butler, on his own second trip to the islands in 1952, had reached the same conclusion, and he returned to Washington a convert to the idea of immediate statehood. But the enemies of Hawaii in Congress paid no attention to his change of heart, and after Butler died in 1954 they went on talking as if it was still 1948 and the first shocking news about Hawaii was still hot from the government press.

John Pillion, the man who did not want Hawaiian senators sitting in the same chamber with New Yorkers, had ideological as well as statistical reasons for objecting. Statehood, he said, was a Russian plot, and to admit Hawaii to the union would be to "actually invite two Soviet agents to take seats in our U. S. Senate." Imua, the privately financed anti-Communist organization established at Honolulu in 1949, kept sending frightening reports to Pillion and other congressmen who had a use for them, and this led to complaints in Hawaii that Imua was subverting the statehood movement from within. It was not far from the truth. "As long as the boobs furnish us this material," one senator was supposed to have said, "we will use it."

What could the senator mean by such a remark? John Pillion may very well have believed every word he said about Hawaii, but there were others whose motives were perhaps more devious. Over the years it became evident that the same small group of Southern senators kept turning up consistently in opposition to statehood. Were they merely uncritical anti-Communists, believing whatever Imua said because it came wrapped in the Stars and Stripes? If Americanism was the issue, then why not believe their loyal colleagues in the Senate who had actually visited Hawaii and found nothing out of order there? Or was the animus part of the old Southern tradition in which distance lent disenchantment?

Some Southern senators found it hard to tolerate even the Northern states of the Union, so far away and so heavily infiltrated by people of dubious ethnic stock. Hawaii was not only much more distant but also far more compromised by a cosmopolitan population. James O. Eastland of Mississippi, who at least took the trouble to go to Hawaii in person, found it impossible to doubt that the territory was "tinctured with Communism." (His choice of verbs was interesting.) Others found it easy to agree: George A. Smathers of Florida; Allen J. Ellender of Louisiana; Olin D. Johnston of South Carolina; Thomas T. Connally of Texas.

The wheel of argument was brought full circle by J. Strom Thurmond of South Carolina. To him the issue of communism was serious enough; yet in a higher sense it was irrelevant. The clash of values that concerned him was one of much more ancient origin, expressed in culture but rooted in biology. Hawaii could never be incorporated as a truly American state. The national body politic would reject it like some unassimilable alien substance. "There are many shades and mixtures of heritages in the world, but there are only two extremes," said Thurmond. "Our society may well be said to be, for the present, at least, the exemplification of the maximum development of the Western civilization, culture, and heritage. At the opposite extreme exists the Eastern heritage, different in every essential— not necessarily inferior, but different as regards the very thought processes within the individuals who comprise the resultant society. As one of the most competent, and certainly the most eloquent, interpreters of the East to the West, Rudyard Kipling felt the bond of love of one for the other; but at the same time he had the insight to express the impassable difference with the immortal words, 'East is East, and West is West, and never the twain shall meet.'" Here was the old fear of the Chinese senator, with pig tail and joss stick, rising from his seat to chop logic with the great lawmakers of the nation. Thurmond wanted the apparition banished forever.

The obstructionists managed to have their way for a good many years after World War II. Where Hawaii was concerned, Congress was not accustomed to move quickly. In June 1947, for the first time, a statehood bill passed the House only to disappear from view in the Senate. In March 1950, another bill passed the House, then got through committee in the Senate and back onto the floor. But no further action was taken. In March 1953, the House passed yet another bill, and the experts in Hawaii looked forward to success at last. They were quickly disillusioned. The most elaborate roadblock of all was just being constructed.

A new set of troubles arose because Hawaii, at that point, was not the only territory asking for admission to the union. Congress had the case of Alaska to consider as well. Should either be admitted? Or both? Together or one at a time? If one at a time, then in what order?

The question of timing was a pointed one in the Senate, which was evenly divided between Democrats and Republicans. Before the elections of 1954 it was generally assumed that Alaska would send two Democrats to the Senate, Hawaii two Republicans. (And in 1952, once it became certain that the next President would be a Republican, Senator Hugh Butler suddenly ceased to oppose the entry of Hawaii.) But from 1954 onward Hawaii was a Democratic stronghold, and this confused the tangled situation even further. President Eisenhower, despite the implications for his party in the Senate, remained more or less consistently cordial toward Hawaii. The Southern Democrats, concluding in advance that Democratic senators from Hawaii would certainly be liberals on the question of race, were ready to sacrifice a nominal majority for their party in favor of a coalition with conservative Republicans. The possibilities for delay were almost endless, and they were exploited to the full.

The main strategy consisted of tying Alaska and Hawaii together as candidates for admission. This would make it more than doubly hard for any sort of bill to pass. Objections to either territory would sink the chances of both, and some objection or other could always be found. So for five years, from 1953 to 1958, procedural knots were tied, untied, and then tied again. In December 1956 John A. Burns flipped a coin with the Alaskan delegate for the privilege of presenting House Resolution 49 (for the forty-ninth state). He won the toss, but it was the only victory he could report to his constituents. Statehood seemed closer than ever and yet still far away.

In the periods of gloom that overcame the advocates of statehood from time to time, other proposals were considered. Should Hawaii settle for an elected governor and no representation in Congress? Or should the campaign for statehood be abandoned altogether in favor of commonwealth status, which would bring a remission of federal taxes? Were such ideas sensible compromises with the inevitable, or just red herrings? Benjamin F. Dillingham II, once a strong believer in statehood as the best weapon against communism, changed his mind, and found himself, to his surprise, in unlikely agreement with Harry Bridges of the ILWU, who had also given up on statehood and was supporting the idea of a commonwealth (though Jack Hall still wanted statehood). Ingram Stainback, who favored statehood until he found out about communism, opted for a commonwealth. Lorrin P. Thurston finally dropped his opposition to statehood and accepted the chairmanship of the statehood commission. And so it went on, month after month, year after year.

Like most serious and long drawn out political campaigns, this one was accompanied by side shows. When Senator Tom Connally of Texas announced gratuitously that he was a better American than anyone who lived in Hawaii, a big delegation, labeled "The Connally Caravan," left at once to speak severely to him. Connally was unrepentant. Early in 1954 a half-ton roll of newsprint was set up on Bishop Street in Honolulu, and beauty queens and models urged passers-by to sign the Statehood Honor Roll. One hundred and sixteen thousand signatures were collected, and the end product was presented to Vice President Richard M. Nixon. A few months later someone got the idea of sending the entire territorial legislature to Washington to lobby for statehood. Not every legislator went, but a mixed bag of fifty-three people did, and they talked to everyone who would listen. Not long after that, a new subversive plot was discovered at home: the drivers of tourist buses, mostly Hawaiians and part Hawaiians, were filling their passengers full of antistatehood prejudice. The Hawaii Statehood Commission promptly issued an informative pamphlet to combat the insidious threat. Later again, the film star Dorothy Lamour, who made her screen living lounging scantily clad on the beaches of mythical Pacific islands, declared her support for statehood in an article published in a national magazine. Judge J. Frank McLaughlin, of Smith Act fame, began growing a beard which he swore not to shave off until statehood was granted. He did not say how this would help.

The deadlock in Congress was broken at last in 1958. Jack Burns interpreted the mysterious signals passing back and forth on Capitol Hill to mean that if Alaska was allowed into the union first and separately, then Congress would be unable to justify keeping Hawaii out any longer. Burns came in for some abuse at home when he took this tack, and more when he refused to explain himself. But he turned out to be right. In May, 1958, the Alaska bill passed the House, and in June it passed the Senate. Alaska was the forty-ninth state.

Hawaii would certainly be the fiftieth state; but when? Burns did not think 1958 would be the year, and when he came home to campaign for reelection as congressional delegate, he had to be pushed into saying that he considered statehood a certainty for 1959. A last congressional committee visited the islands to examine Hawaii's credentials, and for the last time John Pillion of New York and James Eastland of Mississippi raised their voices in protest. But somehow over the years, in the mysterious way in which such things usually happened, statehood for Hawaii had become palatable to Congress. The arguments against it, which had always been somewhat ragged around the edges, now looked frayed and shabby, if not downright disreputable.

Early in January, 1959, the House began to consider a statehood bill, and the Committee on Interior and Insular Affairs gave it a favorable vote on February 4. The Senate also had a statehood bill before it, and it came out of committee on March 3. In Hawaii a governor's committee began making plans for celebrations: dancing in the streets, music everywhere, and a huge "international statehood bonfire," all to be seen live on television. On March 11, with Governor William Quinn and Delegate Burns on hand, the Senate passed the bill. On the morning of the next day, March 12, 1959, the members of the House cast their votes, and statehood for Hawaii was a reality at last.

The news reached the islands within minutes. It was a pleasant spring morning in Honolulu, and no one felt like working. Offices and stores emptied out, the streets filled up, the bells of all the churches rang, civil defense sirens wailed (a take cover signal, oddly enough), a lot of beer was drunk, and an American flag with fifty stars flew over Hawaii for the first time.

There was still a good deal of business to be got through before Admission Day. Most important of all, the people of Hawaii had to ratify the congressional vote in a plebiscite. The balloting was held on June 27. Hawaii had two hundred and forty electoral precincts. Only one of them rejected statehood—the island of Niihau, populated almost entirely by Hawaiians. Elsewhere the majority for statehood was conclusive: 17 to 1.

The only thing needed to bind the contract irrevocably was the Presidential proclamation. President Eisenhower chose August 21 for his declaration that "the procedural requirements imposed by the Congress on the state of Hawaii to entitle that state to admission into the Union have been complied with in all respects and that admission of the state of Hawaii into the Union on an equal footing with other states of the Union is now accomplished."

This utterance had a fine official weight to it, but it was a little stilted. While the bells were still ringing at Honolulu on March 12, another man said it better. He was sitting in a bar, the perfect image of the local boy, a blend of any number of racial strains. Looking at himself in a wall mirror, he said with some satisfaction: "Now we are all haoles."

Epilogue

It was a nice thought, but of course the issue of race could hardly be expected to fade away with the echo of the statehood bells. In the special elections of 1959, held at the same time as the vote on statehood, both parties gave great care to the matter of a balanced ticket.

The last appointed governor of the territory, William F. Quinn, campaigned to become the first elected governor of the state. His running mate, James Kealoha, was a Hawaiian-Chinese. Jack Burns opposed Quinn, and his running mate, William Richardson, also had some Hawaiian and Chinese blood to go with his haole surname. Nothing in Burns' political life came easily. He was beaten by Quinn, and the Republican governor and lieutenant governor were sworn in by a member of the supreme court bench of Hawaii, Masaji Marumoto.

In the United States Senate elections, one seat went to the aged Democrat Oren Long, former governor of the territory. The other went to a good American type, a self-made Republican millionaire, the son of an immigrant. Only his name was unusual: Hiram Fong. At last the United States had a Chinese senator. Fong took his seat in the chamber across from Strom Thurmond and James Eastland.

To the House of Representatives went another readily recognizable American figure, the war veteran continuing to serve his country in time of peace. Again, however, Hawaii struck a new note. Daniel K. Inouye, who lost an arm fighting with the 442nd Regiment in Europe, became the first American of Japanese ancestry to win a seat in the House.

Inouye, a Democrat, was a protégé of Jack Burns. In his own right he turned out to be an astonishing vote getter, and this encouraged him to run for the Senate after Oren Long's seat fell vacant. He won more than handsomely, defeating Benjamin Dillingham II. So Hawaii, by the mid-sixties, had sent two Orientals to the Senate.

At the same time the growing population of the islands opened up a second seat in the House for Hawaii, and very shortly these two seats as well were occupied by Orientals, both of them Japanese and both of them

Democrats. Spark M. Matsunaga was another veteran of the 442nd Regiment. His colleague, Patsy Takemoto Mink, was in some ways the most remarkable figure on the national political scene. Her election broke every rule of orthodox American politics: she was Japanese, she was a woman, and she was married to a white man, a haole.

At his second attempt Jack Burns managed to win the governorship, and he did well enough to be reelected four years later. William Richardson served one term as lieutenant governor and then left for the state supreme court bench. His successor, Thomas P. Gill, was a haole, a young attorney who spent one term in the House of Representatives early in the sixties and then, having challenged Hiram Fong in a Senate race and lost, went back into local politics. So once again there were two haoles at Iolani Palace.

Governor Burns was not altogether pleased at this turn of events. Gill brought to his work intelligence and acerbity, in large and equal proportions, and Burns reacted badly to the prospect of four years at close quarters with such a prickly presence. In particular, Gill wanted to keep the voters' minds on the essential differences between Democrats and Republicans, whereas Burns, after years of exhausting struggle to raise his party to power, was beginning to talk about harmony and consensus, something that ought to go beyond party labels. What all this might mean for the future of politics in the state was anybody's guess, but for Burns, presumably, it was the ultimate way of saying that at last the people of Hawaii were all haoles.

At the same time the governor liked to think that Hawaii was influential in promoting harmony and consensus on a large scale, between East and West. This idea had been aired during the statehood debates, but its validity was arguable, to say the least. By the mid-sixties there were Peace Corps training camps at the islands, filled with volunteers on their way to Asia; and at the University of Hawaii an elaborate academic center for "cultural and technical interchange" between East and West was built, with federal funds. No one had anything but praise for the generous and optimistic impulse embodied in these institutions, yet no one could have claimed that their influence was decisive. America and Asia came together in the years after the war with the grinding noise of violent collision. If Hawaii was known at all in Asia at large, it was as a staging post for the American armed forces. Governor Burns was fond of saying that the easy relations between men of various races in Hawaii represented the best hope of mankind. Yet men from Hawaii fought Asians in the Pacific, in Korea, and in Vietnam. And if by some chance the fighting should stop, Hawaii itself would suffer, because military spending had come to rank with the sugar and pineapple industries as a prime source of revenue for the state.

These were uncomfortable realities, but a way was found to put a gloss on the harshness of the situation. Hawaii, after almost two centuries of exposure to civilization, was still a beautiful place, and not even the worst political storms in the Pacific could affect the mild and magnificent climate. After World War II the tourist industry began to grow at a faster rate than the military establishment. Early in the nineteenth century it used to take as long as six months to get from the east coast of the United States by sailing ship. In the nineteen sixties, by jet plane, it took about half a day of actual flying time. So Hawaii was not too far away to be accessible, yet far enough away to be interesting. The appeal of the islands was simple: sun, sea, and sand; surcease from the strain of life in crowded and ugly and violent cities on the American mainland; the illusion that the world was clean and harmless. By the mid-sixties visitors looking for pleasure and relaxation far outnumbered soldiers on their way to war. In fact the number of tourists who came to the islands each year was greater than the number of permanent residents.

Tourism, then, was a big business, ranking with sugar, pineapples, and military spending. Obviously it was worth some close attention and hard thought. The Hawaii Visitors Bureau, trying to establish just what was so attractive about the islands, concluded that the word "aloha" was crucial. It was a Hawaiian word, and it could be used as an affectionate greeting, or as an expression of good will or love. It went together with a kiss on the cheek and the gift of a lei, a flower garland. It captivated tourists descending from the skies, grateful for safe passage but still faintly stunned and disoriented after hours of high-speed travel westward in pursuit of the sun. If the tourist industry could really dispense good will, or even a convincing imitation (a plastic lei?), the value of aloha as a business commodity would be incalculable.

Just the same, those with a sense of the past might have been forgiven for suggesting that true aloha, however it was defined, had been notably absent from Hawaii's history. If things had turned out well at the islands, it was probably due to demographic accident. In the nineteenth century Hawaiians died in large numbers, and the haoles and Orientals who took their place came to the islands, most of them, without wives. The Hawaiians, ingenuous as they were, gave away their women along with everything else they had. The haoles, having taken whatever was at hand as a matter of right, were brought only reluctantly to redistribute the spoils. The Orientals had to fight to clear a place for themselves, and their victory owed little enough to good will. If any one thing saved the situation it was the unlikely institution of the mixed marriage. By the turn of the twentieth century no one group could claim an absolute majority of the population, and with every decade that passed the number of people of mixed ancestry increased. In these unusual circumstances, absolute bloody-mindedness on the question of race was hard to sustain. Compromise, however grudging, was a necessity, and out of grudging compromise a spirit of relaxed acceptance might grow in time.

The different groups of people who made up the population of Hawaii selected what they needed from this ambiguous record, and let the rest go. The Hawaiians, those of them who insisted on the name, lived on consoling myths—every man a great singer and dancer, a great swimmer and surfer, a great lover: a natural aristocrat, descended from kings, dispossessed now but regally forgiving. The Orientals, glad to be liberated from the immediate past of the plantation era, pushed history aside (at least for purposes of public display), in favor of something they called "culture," a rather self-conscious blend of traditional arts and crafts and new elements such as beauty contests, run by their chambers of commerce. As for the haoles, people like the descendants of the missionary families found something of value in the past. But most white men did not have such roots in the islands. The newer arrivals, and especially those who came after the war, accepted Hawaii much as they found it, with interest but without deep curiosity.

Some things left over from the past were irritating. Prime among these was the final legacy of the Big Five. Their economic monopoly was invaded after the war by any number of newly established business houses, some of them big mainland firms, others founded at the islands. But the land system which was the basis of the old fortunes remained intact. The big estates dating from the second half of the nineteenth century were not broken up in the twentieth, and this meant that the tax structure of the state badly needed revision.

Other things, just becoming visible, would certainly cause irritation in the future. The islands were small; the population kept growing (half a million just after the war; three quarters of a million by the mid-sixties). Honolulu was already a crowded city, and getting more crowded. Waikiki, once attractive, was ugly with concrete and asphalt; and away to the west of Honolulu a blue haze could be seen on windless days, a haze that might uncharitably be called smog.

But at least the past did not weigh too heavily on the people of the islands, the future seemed open, and the present was enjoyable enough. Such modest good fortune was unimaginable in most parts of the world, and there was a local phrase to acknowledge this: "Lucky come Hawaii."

History came to Hawaii by way of the sea, and traces of the past are still visible in the water as well as on the land. At Lahaina, close to the harbor, skin divers prospecting on the sandy sea bed occasionally turn up anchor chains and oil lamps and square-face gin bottles from whaling ships, coffee cups from Navy submarines and Matson cruise liners, and splintered calabashes and stone adze heads tossed overboard from Hawaiian canoes. The sand shifts with the currents; one day the past is exposed, the next it is all but obscured, and it takes a sharp eye to bring it to light again. Farther out to sea the past repeats itself endlessly. The tides run, the sun sets, the night passes, and in the morning, just at dawn, the islands come into view again as they did for Cook so long ago, a fresher green breast of the new world than ever the old Atlantic sailors saw, and still a place of gentle, beckoning beauty.

Acknowledgments

I HAVE always found Hawaii a pleasant place to live and work, and it is a pleasure in turn to acknowledge the help I have had in preparing this history of the islands. My requests—for help in locating source material, for assistance in checking translations, for permission to read work in progress, for criticism of my own work—have been met with unfailing generosity.

I wish to thank in particular Jacob Adler, Janet Azama, Dorothy Barrere, Janet Bell, Kay Boyum, O. A. Bushnell, Clara Ching, Henry Choy, Sherwin Chu, Sophie Cluff, Agnes Conrad, Jean Dabagh, Reuel Denney, James Foster, Lela Goodell, Richard Greer, Charles H. Hunter, Louise Harris Hunter, Donald D. Johnson, Yasuto Kaihara, Alfons Korn, Albertine Loomis, Herbert F. Margulies, Mary Muraoka, Thomas D. Murphy, Raymond Sato, Gordon Smith, Margaret Titcomb, and Lawrence Windley.

People in other places, as far apart as Philadelphia and Port Moresby, have also been helpful, and among them I thank Margaret Ashenden, J. C. Beaglehole, Ernest Dodge, Kenneth Inglis, H. E. Maude, Charles Peterson, Richard Pierce, and Malcolm Webb.

Responsibility for errors of fact, lapses in style, and failures of intelligence rests, of course, with me.

Parts of this book have appeared, in different form, in *American Heritage;* the *Annual Reports* of the Hawaiian Historical Society; *Hawaii Historical Review; Hawaiian Journal of History; Journal of Pacific History;* and *Journal of the Polynesian Society.*

Bibliography

A Note on Sources

MOST of the research for this book was done in Honolulu. In the Archives of Hawaii (cited in footnotes and bibliography as AH) are documents and publications relating to the official life of the monarchy, the provisional government, the republic, the territory, and the state; and diplomatic correspondence with other countries. Also in AH is the Cook Collection of documents concerning the discovery of the islands. AH also has a photograph collection. The Hawaiian Mission Children's Society library (HMCS) houses the private and official writings of members of the Sandwich Islands Mission (SIM), and has as well an excellent collection of published works in the Hawaiian language. The Hawaiian Historical Society library (HHS) has a good collection of books and periodicals, and a small manuscript collection. The Bernice P. Bishop Museum (BPBM) is the best place for the study of ancient Hawaii; it also has a large collection of photographs. The Sinclair Library of the University of Hawaii (UH) houses a Hawaiian and Pacific Collection; in the Hawaiian Room is the Kuykendall Collection (KCUH), consisting of notes and copies of documents gathered from all over the world by a scholar who devoted his professional life to making the writing of Hawaiian history respectable. In the microfilm collection of UH are copies of documents relating to Hawaii and the Pacific, from the British Foreign Office (FO) and the United States Department of State (USDS). Ships' logs and journals from the Admiralty series (Adm) of the Public Record Office, London (PRO) and the British Museum (BM) are in the UH microfilm collection. Also at UH is the Hawaii War Records Depository (HWRD). The Honolulu Academy of Arts has an excellent collection of paintings, drawings, prints, and photographs.

Guides to the holdings of repositories at Honolulu are not of uniform completeness. The most substantial are the published *Dictionary Catalogues* of BPBM and the Hawaiian collection at UH. The staff of AH is preparing a typescript inventory of the manuscript collection, and typescript guides to some of the principal official files are already available. Also useful are the card indexes of the most important files. No comparable guides exist for the manuscript holdings of HMCS and HHS.

I have found the following reference works helpful: C. H. Hunter, "Check List of Hawaiian Newspapers," mimeo; B. Judd, comp., *Voyages to Hawaii Before 1860;* S. Elbert and M. Pukui, *Hawaiian-English Dictionary* and *English-Hawaiian Dictionary;* "University of Hawaii Theses of Interest to Students of Hawaiian History," *Hawaii Historical Review,* October, 1962; M. Leeson, "Bibliography on Culture Change in the Hawaiian Islands," BA thesis, University of British Columbia, 1959.

Notes on the Bibliography

This list of references does not pretend to comprehensiveness or even formality. Only those sources actually cited in the footnotes are listed, and often their titles appear in the bibliography shortened unceremoniously. For easy reference from the footnotes, primary and secondary sources are listed together in the bibliography, alphabetically by author or issuing agency. In the case of manuscript materials such as journals, letter books, and ships' logs, the location of the original is given; if the repository is outside the Hawaiian Islands, its name is followed by a Honolulu repository where a microfilm or photocopy can be found, thus: Whitman, J., Journal, Ms. Peabody Museum, Salem (HMCS). Unpublished Master of Arts theses and doctoral dissertations are identified by the letters MA and PhD respectively, followed by the name of the institution granting the degree.

[ABCFM]. Correspondence between American Board of Commissioners for Foreign Missions and members of the Sandwich Islands Mission. Ms. Houghton Library, Harvard. (HMCS).

ABCFM. *General Letters to the Sandwich Island Mission, 1831–1860.* 2 vols. (n. d., n. p.).

ABCFM. *Reports.* Boston, 1820–1870.

Adams, A. Journal. Ms. AH.

Adams, R. *Interracial Marriage in Hawaii.* New York, 1937.

Adee, D. "Memories of Honolulu." *United Service*. May, 1884.

Adler, J. *Claus Spreckels: The Sugar King in Hawaii*. Honolulu, 1966.

————. "Hawaiian Navy Under King Kalakaua." HHS *Report*, 73. 1964.

————. *Journal of Prince Alexander Liholiho*. Honolulu, 1967.

Ala Moana Case. Ms. City and County of Honolulu Police Files.

Alexander, M. and Dodge, C. *Punahou, 1841–1941*. Berkeley, 1941.

Alexander, M. *William Patterson Alexander*. Honolulu, 1934.

Alexander, W. D. *Brief Account of the Hawaiian Government Survey*. Honolulu, 1889.

————. *History of Later Years of the Hawaiian Monarchy*. Honolulu, 1896.

————. "Overthrow of the Ancient Tabu System in the Hawaiian Islands." HHS *Report*, 25, 1917.

————. *Review of a Pastoral Address by the Right Rev. T. N. Staley*. Honolulu, 1865.

Allen, E. H. Papers. Library of Congress. (UH).

Allen, G. *Hawaii's War Years*. Honolulu, 1950.

Aller, C. *Labor Relations in the Hawaiian Sugar Industry*. Berkeley, 1957.

Analysis of the Taxation of the Hawaiian Kingdom for the Year 1881. Honolulu, 1882.

Anderson, R. *History of the Sandwich Islands Mission*. Boston, 1870.

————. *Hawaiian Islands: Their Progress and Condition Under Missionary Labors*. Boston, 1864.

Andrade, E., Jr. "Hawaiian Revolution of 1887." MA, UH, 1954.

[Annales], *Annales de l'Association de la Propagation de la Foi*. Vol 16. 1833.

Anthony, J. G. *Hawaii Under Army Rule*. Stanford, 1955.

Armstrong, R. Journal. Ms. HMCS.

Armstrong Papers. AH.

Armstrong, W. *Around the World with a King*. New York, 1904.

Army and Navy (Kingdom of Hawaii). Ms. file, AH.

Ashford, C. "Last Days of the Hawaiian Monarchy." HHS *Report*, 27. 1919.

Attorney General (Kingdom of Hawaii). *Report*. Published at intervals for the legislature.

Attorney General (Kingdom of Hawaii). Letter Book. Ms. AH.

Auna. Journal. Ms. HHS. Also in ABCFM.

Baker, R. *Third Warning Voice*. Honolulu, 1890.

Balch, J. *Shall the Japanese Be Allowed to Dominate Hawaii?* Honolulu, 1942.

Baldwin, A. *Memoir of Henry Perrine Baldwin*. Cleveland, 1915.

Bamford, F., ed. *Journal of Mrs. Arbuthnot, 1820–1832*. Vol 1. London, 1950.

Banana Claims. Ms. file. AH.

Barber, J., Jr. *Hawaii: Restless Rampart*. New York, 1941.

Barnard, C. *Narrative of the Sufferings and Adventures of Capt. Charles Barnard, 1812–1816*. New York, 1829.

Barrere, D. "Summary of Hawaiian History and Culture." Typescript. BPBM.

Bates, G. *Sandwich Island Notes*. New York, 1854.

Beaglehole, J. *Exploration of the Pacific*, 3rd ed. Stanford, 1966.

————, ed. *Journals of Captain James Cook*. 3 vols. Cambridge, 1955–1967.

Beckwith, M., ed. *Kumulipo*. Chicago, 1951.

Bell, E. Journal. Ms. Turnbull Library, New Zealand. (UH).

Bennett's Own. Newspaper. Honolulu.

Bingham Papers. HMCS.

Bingham, H. *Residence of Twenty-One Years in the Sandwich Islands.* Hartford, 1847.

"Birth Year of Kamehameha I From *Post Mortem* Estimates." HHS *Report*, 44. 1935.

Bishop, C. Journal. Ms. Archives of British Columbia. (UH).

[Bishop] Bird, I. *Hawaiian Archipelago.* London, 1875.

Bishop, S. Diary. Ms. Private collection.

————. Letter Book. Ms. HMCS.

————. *Reminiscences of Old Hawaii.* Honolulu, 1916.

[Blount Report]. U. S. Congress. House. *Hawaiian Islands,* Executive Document No. 47. 53 Cong. 2 Sess. Washington, 1893.

Bloxam, A. *Diary of Andrew Bloxam.* BPBM *Special Publication,* 10. Honolulu, 1925.

Blue, G. "Policy of France Toward the Hawaiian Islands from the Earliest Time to the Treaty of 1846." *Official Papers Read at the Captain Cook Sesquicentennial Celebration.* Honolulu, 1928.

————. "Project for a French Settlement in the Hawaiian Islands, 1824–1842." *Pacific Historical Review.* Mar., 1933.

Board of Health. Ms. file. AH.

Bock, M. "Church of Jesus Christ of Latter Day Saints in the Hawaiian Islands." MA, UH, 1941.

Boit, J. Journal. Ms. Massachusetts Historical Society Library. (HHS).

Bouslog, H. *Fear.* Honolulu, 1951.

Bradley, H. *American Frontier in Hawaii: The Pioneers, 1789–1843.* Stanford, 1942.

Briggs, V. *Experiences of a Medical Student in Honolulu.* Boston, 1926.

Brinsmade Papers. AH.

Brooks, P. *Multiple-Industry Unionism in Hawaii.* New York, 1952.

Broughton, W. *Voyage of Discovery to the North Pacific Ocean, 1795–1798.* London, 1804.

Buck, P. *Arts and Crafts of Hawaii.* BPBM *Special Publication,* 45. Honolulu, 1957.

Burney, J. Journal. Ms. Add Ms. 8955. BM. (AH).

————. Journal. Ms. Mitchell Library, Sydney. (BPBM).

Bushnell, O. "Dr. Eduard Arning: The First Microbiologist in Hawaii." *Hawaiian Journal of History.* 1967.

[Butler Hearings, 1954]. U. S. Congress. Senate. Committee on Interior and Insular Affairs. *Statehood for Hawaii. Hearings.* Parts 2 and 3. 83 Cong. 2 Sess. Washington, 1954.

[Butler Report, 1949]. U. S. Congress. Senate. Committee On Interior and Insular Affairs. *Statehood for Hawaii. Communist Penetration of the Hawaiian Islands.* 80 Cong. 2 Sess. Washington, 1949.

[Butler Report, 1950]. U. S. Congress. Senate. Committee on Interior and Insular Affairs. *Statehood for Hawaii. Report.* 81 Cong. 2 Sess. Washington, 1950.

Cabinet Council Minutes (Kingdom of Hawaii). Ms. file. AH.

Campbell, A. *Voyage Around the World, 1806–1812*. Edinburgh, 1816.

Cariaga, R. "Filipinos in Hawaii." MA, UH, 1936.

Carter, G. R. Papers. AH.

Carter, H. A. P. Papers. AH.

Castle, H. *Letters*. London, 1902.

Chamber of Commerce File. Ms. HWRD.

Chamberlain, D. Journal. Ms. Houghton Library, Harvard. (HMCS).

Chamberlain, L. Journal. Ms. HMCS.

Chamberlain Papers. AH.

Chamisso, A. Von. *Werke*. 3 vols. Leipzig, n. d.

Chaney, G. *Alo'ha!* Boston, 1880.

Charlton, W. Journal. Ms. Adm. 51/4557/191–193. PRO. (AH).

Charlton Land Pamphlets. Several pamphlets bound together. AH.

Chief Justice (Kingdom of Hawaii). *Report*. Published at intervals for the legislature.

Chinen, J. *Great Mahele*. Honolulu, 1958.

Choris, L. *Voyage Pittoresque Autour du Monde*. Paris, 1822.

Clark, E. Letter Book. Ms. HMCS.

Cleghorn Collection. AH.

Clerke, C. Journal. Ms. Adm. 51/4561/217. PRO. (AH).

––––––––. Journal. Ms. Adm. 55/22, PRO. (AH).

––––––––. Journal. Ms. Adm. 55/124, PRO. (AH).

Cleveland, R. *Narrative of Voyages and Commercial Enterprises*. 2 vols.
Cambridge, 1842.

Coan Letters. New York Historical Society. (UH).

Coan, L. *Titus Coan: A Memorial*. Chicago, 1884.

Coan, T. *Life in Hawaii*. New York, 1882.

Colcord, J. Journal. Ms. AH.

[Colnett Argonaut Journal]. *Journal of Captain James Colnett Aboard the
Argonaut, 1789–1791*. ed. F. Howay. Toronto, 1940.

Colnett, J. Journal. Ms. Adm. 55/146. PRO. (UH).

Columbian Centinel. Newspaper.

Coman, K. *History of Contract Labor in the Hawaiian Islands*. New York, 1903.

Congdon, C. "Background and History of the 1946 Hawaiian Sugar Strike." MA,
Columbia, 1951.

Congressional Quarterly Fact Sheet. Mar. 6, 1959.

Congressional Record.

Conroy, H. *Japanese Frontier in Hawaii, 1868–1898*. Berkeley, 1953.

Constitution and By-Laws of the Hale Naua. San Francisco, 1890.

Convention. Newspaper. Honolulu.

Cook, J. Journal. Ms. Egerton 2177A. BM. (AH).

––––––––. Journal. Ms. Egerton 2177B. BM. (AH).

Cook, J. and King, J. *Voyage to the Pacific Ocean, 1776–1780*. 3 vols. London,
1784.

Cooke, A. Journal. Ms. HMCS.

Cooke Collection. HMCS.

[Cordon Hearings, 1948]. U. S. Congress. Senate. Committee on Public Lands. *Statehood for Hawaii. Hearings.* 80 Cong. 2 Sess. Washington, 1948.

[Cordon Report, 1948]. U. S. Congress. Senate. Committee on Interior and Insular Affairs. *Statehood for Hawaii. Report.* 80 Cong. 2 Sess. Washington, 1948.

[Cordon Report, 1954]. U. S. Congress. Senate. Committee on Interior and Insular Affairs. *Hawaii Statehood. Report.* 83 Cong. 2 Sess. Washington, 1954.

Corney, P. *Voyages in the Northern Pacific, 1813–1818.* Honolulu, 1896.

Coronation of Their Majesties the King and Queen of the Hawaiian Islands. At Honolulu, Feb. 12th, 1883. Honolulu, 1883.

"Correspondence Relating to the Last Hours of Kamehameha V." HHS *Report,* 6. 1898.

Correspondence Relative to the Sandwich Islands. London, 1844.

Cottez, J. "Jean Baptiste Rives de Bordeaux, Aventurier Hawaien." *Bulletin de la Société d'Études Océaniennes.* Jun.–Sep., 1958.

Cox, R. *Adventures on the Columbia River.* 2 vols. London, 1831.

[Crowe Hearings]. U. S. Congress. House. Committee on Territories. *Statehood for Hawaii.* 74 Cong. 1 Sess. Washington, 1936.

Dahlgren, F. *Were the Hawaiian Islands Visited by the Spaniards Before Their Discovery by Captain Cook in 1778?* Stockholm, 1916.

Daily Bulletin. Newspaper. Honolulu.

Daily Hawaiian Herald. Newspaper. Honolulu.

Damien Institute Monthly Magazine.

Damon, E. *Samuel Chenery Damon.* Honolulu, 1966.

Davenport, W. "Hawaiian Feudalism." *Expedition.* Winter, 1964.

Davies, A. *Clive of Plassey.* New York, 1939.

Davis, D. "Hawaii's Experience with Unequal Treaties." MA, UH, 1936.

Davis, E. and C. *Norwegian Labor in Hawaii.* Honolulu, 1962.

Daws, G. "High Chief Boki." *Journal of the Polynesian Society.* Mar. 1966.

Daws, G. and Head, T. "Niihau: A Shoal of Time." *American Heritage.* Oct., 1963.

Dedication of the Kapiolani Home Devoted to the Care of Girls, the Children of Leprous Parents, Not Yet Confirmed As Lepers, and Others Suspected of the Disease. Honolulu, 1885.

Dedmon, D. "Analysis of the Arguments in the Debate in Congress on the Admission of Hawaii to the Union." PhD, State University of Iowa, 1961.

Delano, A. *Narrative of Voyages and Travels.* Boston, 1817.

Dibble, S. *History of the Sandwich Islands.* Lahainaluna, 1843.

Dimond Papers. AH.

Dinell, T. and others. *Hawaiian Homes Program, 1920–1963.* Honolulu, 1964.

Dixon, G. *Voyage Around the World, 1785–1788.* London, 1789.

Doi, H. and Horwitz, R. *Public Land Policy in Hawaii: Land Reserved for Public Use.* Honolulu, 1965.

Dole Collection. AH.

Dole, S. "Evolution of Hawaiian Land Tenures." *Overland Monthly.* June, 1895.

_____. *Memoirs of the Hawaiian Revolution*. Honolulu, 1936.

Dorita, Sister Mary. "Filipino Immigration to Hawaii." MA, UH, 1954.

Dozer, D. "Opposition to Hawaiian Reciprocity, 1876–1888." *Pacific Historical Review*. June, 1945.

Duke Hao O Hawaii A Me Na Moolelo Pakui. Honolulu, 1890.

Dutton, M. *Succession of King Kamehameha V to Hawaii's Throne*. Honolulu, 1957.

_____. *William L. Lee*. Honolulu, 1953.

[Eastland Hearings]. U. S. Senate. Committee on the Judiciary. *Scope of Soviet Activity in the United States*. Part 39. 84 Cong. 2 Sess. Washington, 1957.

Edgar, T. Log. Ms. Adm. 55/21. PRO. (AH).

_____. Log. Ms. Adm. 55/24. PRO. (AH).

Egerstrom, C. *Berättelse om en Färd, 1852–1857*. Stockholm, 1859.

Elele Poakolu. Newspaper. Honolulu.

Ellis, W. *Authentic Narrative of a Voyage, 1776–1780*. 2 vols. London, 1782.

_____. *Narrative of a Tour*. London, 1826.

_____. *Polynesian Researches*. 4 vols. London, 1831.

Elsbree, O. *Rise of the Missionary Spirit in America, 1790–1815*. Williamsport, 1928.

Emma Collection. AH.

Evening Bulletin. Newspaper. Honolulu.

Farago, L. *Broken Seal*. New York, 1967.

Farrington Papers. AH.

Finney Papers. Oberlin College. (HMCS).

Forbes, C. Journal. Ms. HMCS.

Forbes, D. Iolani Palace: Research material and photographs. Ms. AH.

[FO 58]. British Foreign Office file relating to the Pacific Islands. Ms. PRO. (UH).

|FO & EX]. Foreign Office & Executive (Kingdom of Hawaii). Ms. file. AH.

[FO Ltr Bk]. Foreign Office Letter Books (Kingdom of Hawaii). Ms. AH.

Foreign Awards, Foreign Register, Foreign Testimony. Ms. AH.

Fornander, A. *Account of the Polynesian Race*. 3 vols. London, 1878–1885.

Fortescue, G. "Honolulu Martyrdom." *Liberty*. July 30, Aug. 6, 13, 1932.

Fortune. Periodical. New York.

Franchère, G. *Narrative of a Voyage to the Northwest Coast of America, 1811–1814*. New York, 1854.

Frankenstein, A. "Royal Visitors." *Oregon Historical Quarterly*. Mar., 1963.

Frear Papers. AH.

Freycinet, L. De. *Voyage Autour du Monde, 1817–1819*. 7 vols. Paris, 1823–1844.

Friend. Newspaper. Honolulu.

Fuchs, L. *Hawaii Pono: A Social History*. New York, 1961.

Fukuzawa, Y. *Autobiography*. Tokyo, 1949.

General Orders (Military Government of Hawaii). Typescript. HWRD.

[Gibson Hearings]. U. S. Congress. House. *Report*. No. 307. 34 Cong. 1 Sess. Washington, 1854.

Gibson, W. Diary. Ms. Mormon Church Archives, Salt Lake City. (UH).

————. *He Mau Olelo Au E Pili Awa I Ke Ola Kino O Na Kanaka Hawaii.* Honolulu, 1880.

————. *Prison of Weltevreden.* New York, 1855.

Giffin, D. "Life of William L. Lee." MA, Vanderbilt University, 1956.

Gilbert, G. Journal. Ms. Add Ms. 38530. BM. (UH).

Gilman, G. "Honolulu As It Is—1848." Ms. HHS.

————. Journal. Ms. HHS.

[Girvin, J.]. *Cummins Case: A Reminiscence of 1895.* Honolulu, 1905.

Glick, C. "Chinese Migrant in Hawaii: A Study in Accommodation." PhD, University of Chicago, 1938.

Godfrey, F. *Proceedings of the Hawaiian Legislature, Session of 1886.* Honolulu, 1886.

Golden Era. Honolulu, 1892.

Golovnin, V. *Puteshestvie Vokrug Sveta Na Voennom Schlupe Kamchatke, 1817–1819.* St. Petersburg, 1822.

Golson, J., ed. *Polynesian Navigation, A Symposium on Andrew Sharp's Theory of Accidental Voyages.* Rev. ed. Wellington, 1963.

Gore, J. Log. Ms. Adm. 55/120. PRO. (AH).

Gould, J. "Filibuster of Walter Murray Gibson." *HHS Report,* 68. 1959.

Gould, R. "Some Unpublished Accounts of Cook's Death." *Mariner's Mirror.* Oct., 1928.

Green, J. *Notices of the Life of the Late Bartimeus.* Lahainaluna, 1844.

Greer, R. "Founding of Queen's Hospital." Ms. in possession of author.

————. "Mutiny in the Royal Barracks." *Pacific Historical Review.* Nov., 1962.

————. "Oahu's Ordeal." *Hawaii Historical Review.* July, 1965.

Gregg, D. Diary. Ms. In Gregg Collection, AH.

————. Letter Book. Ms. In Gregg Collection, AH.

Gresham Papers. Library of Congress. (UH).

Harvey, W. Log. Ms. Adm. 55/121. PRO. (AH).

Hasslocher Papers. AH.

Hawaii Employers Council. "Report of First Annual Meeting." Typescript. HWRD.

[*Haw. Gaz.*]. *Hawaiian Gazette.* Newspaper. Honolulu.

Hawaii Hochi. Newspaper. Honolulu.

Hawaii Sentinel. Newspaper. Honolulu.

Hawaii Star. Newspaper. Honolulu.

Hawaii Times. Newspaper. Honolulu.

Hawaiian Annual. Sometimes called *Thrum's Annual.* Honolulu, 1875–

Hawaiian Evangelical Association. *Proceedings.* Honolulu, 1863.

Hawaiian Evangelical Association. *Report.* Honolulu, 1916.

Hawaiian Hansard: A Complete Verbatim Report of the Hawaiian Legislative Assembly of 1886. Honolulu, n. d.

[Hawaiian Investigation]. U. S. Congress. *Report of Subcommittee on Pacific Islands and Puerto Rico on General Conditions in Hawaii.* Washington, 1903.

Hawaiian Reports (Kingdom of Hawaii). Legal judgments of Hawaiian Supreme Court, collated and published at intervals.

Hawaiian Spectator. Periodical. Honolulu.

Hawaiian Star. Newspaper. Honolulu.

Hawaiian Sugar Planters' Association. *Proceedings.* Published annually.

Hawaiian Sugar Planters' Association. *Annual Report.* Honolulu, 1946.

Hawaii's Story By Hawaii's Queen. Boston, 1898.

Hawthorne, N. *Our Old Home.* Boston, 1863.

[HCLC Report]. U. S. Congress. House. Committee on Un-American Activities. *Report on Hawaii Civil Liberties Committee (A Communist Front).* Washington, 1950.

He Hoikehonua: He Mea Ia E Hoakaka'i I Ke Ano O Ka Honua Nei, A Me Na Mea Maluna Iho. Oahu, 1832.

Healy, T. "Origins of the Republican Party in Hawaii." MA, UH, 1963.

Henriques Collection. BPBM.

He Olelo No Ka Kanawai, O Ka Hawaii Nei Pae Aina. Oahu, 1834–1835.

[HHR]. *Hawaii Historical Review.*

Heuck Papers. AH.

Higher Wages Question. Honolulu, 1920.

Hilo Tribune-Herald. Newspaper.

Hines, G. *Wild Life in Oregon.* New York, 1881.

His Majesty's Cash Book (Kingdom of Hawaii, King Kalakaua). Ms. AH.

"History of the Businessmen's Military Training Corps." Typescript. HWRD.

Hitchcock, C. *Hawaii and Its Volcanoes.* 2nd ed. Honolulu, 1911.

Hite, C. Diary. Ms. HWRD.

Hobbs, J. *Hawaii: A Pageant of the Soil.* Stanford, 1933.

[*Hon. Adv.*]. *Honolulu Advertiser.* Newspaper.

"Honolulu in 1810." Map. BPBM. Honolulu, 1957.

Honolulu Record. Newspaper.

Honolulu Republican. Newspaper.

Hörmann, B. "Germans in Hawaii." MA, UH, 1931.

Horn, J. "Primacy of the Pacific Under the Hawaiian Kingdom." MA, UH, 1951.

Horwitz, R. *Public Land Policy in Hawaii: Land Exchanges.* Honolulu, 1964.

Horwitz, R. and Finn, J. *Public Land Policy in Hawaii: Major Landowners.* Honolulu, 1967.

Houston Papers. AH.

Howay, F., ed. *Zimmerman's Captain Cook.* Toronto, 1930.

Hoyt, H. "Theatre in Hawaii, 1778–1840." HHS *Report,* 69. 1961.

[HSB]. *Honolulu Star-Bulletin.* Newspaper.

Hudson, L. "History of the Kamehameha Schools." MA, UH, 1935.

Humphrey, S. *Four Memorable Years at Hilo.* Wilmington, 1875.

Hunnewell Papers. Houghton Library, Harvard (KCUH).

Hunter, C. H. "Congress and Statehood for Hawaii." *World Affairs Quarterly.* Jan., 1959.

————. "Statehood and the Hawaiian Annexation Treaty of 1893." HHS *Report,* 59. 1951.

Hunter, J. *Historical Journal of Transactions at Port Jackson and Norfolk Island.* London, 1793.

Hunter, L. "Buddhism in Hawaii: Its Impact on a Yankee Community." MA, UH, 1966.

Hutchings' California Magazine. Nov., 1858.

Ii, J. *Fragments of Hawaiian History.* Honolulu, 1963.

Imamura, Y. *Short History of the Hongwanji Buddhist Mission in Hawaii.* Honolulu, 1927.

[Immigration Hearings]. U. S. Congress. Senate. Committee on Immigration and Naturalization. *Immigration into Hawaii.* 67 Cong. 1 Sess. Washington, 1921.

Independent. Newspaper. Honolulu.

Independent. Periodical. New York.

Indices of Awards Made by the Board of Commissioners to Quiet Land Titles in the Hawaiian Islands. Honolulu, 1929.

Ingraham, J. Journal. Ms. Library of Congress. (HHS).

Instructions of the Prudential Committee of the American Board of Commissioners for Foreign Missions to the Sandwich Islands Mission. Lahainaluna, 1838.

[Int. Dept. Ltr. Bk.]. Interior Department Letter Books (Kingdom of Hawaii). Ms. AH.

[Int. Dept. Ltrs. Misc.]. Interior Department Letters Miscellaneous (Kingdom of Hawaii). Ms. file. AH.

Iolani Palace Register. Periodical. Honolulu.

Irwin, E. "Ed Irwin More than Suggests that We Should Not Try to 'Americanize' Orientals in Hawaii, Even If We Can." *Paradise of the Pacific.* Dec., 1924.

Iselin, I. *Journal of a Trading Voyage Around the World, 1805–1808.* New York, n. d.

Iwamoto, L. "Plague and Fire of 1899–1900 in Honolulu." *Hawaii Historical Review.* July, 1967.

Izuka, I. *Truth About Communism in Hawaii.* Honolulu, 1947.

Jackson, F. "Koloa Plantation Under Ladd and Company, 1835–1845." MA, UH, 1958.

"Japs Fail to Interrupt Hawaiian Telephone Service." *Telephony.* Feb. 14, 1942.

Jarves, J. *History of the Sandwich Islands.* London, 1843.

————. *Scenes and Scenery in the Sandwich Islands, 1837–1842.* Boston, 1843.

Johannessen, E. *Hawaiian Labor Movement.* Boston, 1956.

Journal of House of Nobles (Kingdom of Hawaii). Ms. AH.

Journal of Legislative Assembly (Kingdom of Hawaii). Ms. AH.

Journal of Legislature (Territory of Hawaii). Ms. and published versions. AH.

Judd, A. F. "Lunalilo, the Sixth King of Hawaii: Contemporary Letters." HHS *Report,* 44. 1936.

Judd, B., comp. *Voyages to Hawaii Before 1860.* Honolulu, 1929.

Judd, E. Journal. Ms., HMCS.

Judd, G. P., IV. *Dr. Judd: Hawaii's Friend.* Honolulu, 1960.

Judd, H. Papers. AH.

Judd, Laura. *Honolulu, 1828–1861.* New York, 1880.

Judd, Lawrence, Papers, AH.

[*Judd Fragments*]. *Fragments: Family Record, House of Judd.* 6 vols. Honolulu, 1903–1935.

Ka Buke Moolelo O Hon. Robert William Wilikoki. Honolulu, 1890.

Kalakaua Dead: The King Dies on a Foreign Shore. Honolulu, 1891.

Kalanianaole Collection. BPBM.

Kalanianaole Papers. AH.

Ka Leo O Ka Lahui. Newspaper. Honolulu.

Kamakau, S. *Ka Po'e Kahiko.* Honolulu, 1964.

————. *Ruling Chiefs of Hawaii.* Honolulu, 1961.

Ka Nonanona. Newspaper. Honolulu.

Ka Palapala Hemolele A Iehova Ko Kakou Akua. Oahu, 1838. [1839].

Ke Kumu Kanawai, A Me Ke Kanawai Hooponopono Waiwai, No Ko Hawaii Nei Pae Aina. Honolulu, 1840.

Kihara, R. *Hawaii Nihonjin Shi.* Tokyo, 1935.

Kim, B. "Koreans in Hawaii." MA, UH, 1937.

King, J. Journal. Ms. Adm. 55/116. PRO. (AH).

————. Journal. Ms. Adm. 55/122. PRO. (AH).

King, S. Papers. AH.

Kittelson, D. "A Population Table of Hawaii." Ms. UH.

Ko Hawaii Pae Aina. Newspaper. Honolulu.

Kona Church Report. Ms. HMCS.

Korn, A. *Victorian Visitors.* Honolulu, 1958.

Korn, A. and Pukui, M. "News from Molokai." *Pacific Historical Review.* Feb., 1963.

Kotzebue, O. Von. *Voyage of Discovery, 1815–1818.* 3 vols. London, 1821.

Kuhio Papers. AH.

Kuokoa. Newspaper. Honolulu.

Kuykendall, R. "Constitutions of the Hawaiian Kingdom." HHS *Papers,* 21. 1940.

————. *Hawaiian Kingdom.* 3 vols. Honolulu, 1938–1967.

————. "Negotiation of the Hawaiian Annexation Treaty of 1893." HHS *Report,* 51. 1943.

————. "Some Early Commercial Adventurers of Hawaii." HHS *Report,* 37. 1929.

[Labor Hearings]. U. S. Congress. House. Committee on Immigration and Naturalization. *Labor Problems in Hawaii.* 67 Cong. 1 Sess. Washington, 1921.

Lafeber, W. *New Empire.* Cornell, 1963.

Lane, J. "Poindexter Administration." MA, UH, 1966.

Langsdorff, G. Von. *Voyages and Travels, 1803–1807.* 2 vols. London, 1813.

[Larcade Hearings]. U. S. Congress. House. Committee on the Territories. *Statehood for Hawaii. Hearings.* 79 Cong. 2 Sess. Washington, 1946.

Law, J. Journal. Ms. Add Ms. 37327. BM. (AH).

Laws (Kingdom of Hawaii). Honolulu. Published at intervals.

Laws (Territory of Hawaii). Published after each session of the legislature, and collated at intervals.

Lecker, G. "Lahainaluna, 1831–1877." MA, UH, 1938.

Leeson, M. "Bibliography on Culture Change in the Hawaiian Islands." BA, University of British Columbia, 1959.

Leper Settlement, on the Island of Molokai, Visit of His Excellency Walter M. Gibson, President of the Board of Health. Honolulu, 1885.

Leprosy: Report of the President of the Board of Health to the Legislative Assembly of 1886. Honolulu, 1886.

Liliuokalani Collection. AH.

Liliuokalani Diary. BPBM, AH.

Liliuokalani Papers. BPBM.

Lind, A. *Hawaii's Japanese*. Princeton, 1946.

———. *Island Community*. Chicago, 1938.

Lisiansky, U. *Voyage Round the World, 1803–1806*. London, 1814.

[LMS]. Letters between London Missionary Society and Sandwich Islands Mission. London Missionary Society Library. (HHS).

London *Times*.

Loomis, A. "Longest Legislature." HHS *Report,* 71. 1962.

Loomis, E. Journal. Ms. HMCS.

Loomis, M. Journal. Ms. HMCS.

Lord, W. *Day of Infamy*. London, 1957.

Lydecker, R., comp. *Roster, Legislatures of Hawaii, 1841–1918*. Honolulu, 1918.

Lyons Papers. AH.

Lyons, C. "Early Surveying and Land Allotting in Hawaii." Ms. in Lyons Papers. AH.

Lyons, C. *History of the Hawaiian Government Survey with Notes on Land Matters in Hawaii*. Honolulu, 1903.

Mahan, A. *Interest of America in Sea Power, Present and Future*. Cambridge, 1897.

———. *Life of Nelson*. Boston, 1943.

Mahele Book. Ms. AH.

Malo, D. *Hawaiian Antiquities*. 2nd ed. Honolulu, 1951.

Marin, F. Journal. Ms. AH.

Marshal's Letter Book (Kingdom of Hawaii). Ms. AH.

Marshall Mss. Houghton Library, Harvard. (KCUH).

Martin, J. *Account of the Natives of the Tonga Islands*. 2 vols. London, 1817.

Mathison, G. *Narrative of a Visit to Brazil, Chile, Peru, and the Sandwich Islands, 1821–1822*. London, 1825.

Maui News. Newspaper. Wailuku.

McAllister, J. *Archeology of Oahu*. Honolulu, 1933.

McCandless Papers. AH.

McCarthy Papers. AH.

McNamara, R. "Hawaii's Smith Act Case." MA, UH, 1960.

Meares, J. *Voyages Made in 1788–1789*. London, 1790.

Medical Report on the Last Illness and Death of Kalakaua. U. S. Flagship *Charleston*, 1891.

Mellen, K. *An Island Kingdom Passes*. New York, 1958.

Memoirs of Henry Obookiah. New Haven, 1818.

Menzies, A. Journal. Ms. Add Ms. 32641. BM.

Midkiff, F. "Economic Determinants of Education in Hawaii." PhD, Yale University, 1935.

Minister & Envoys (Republic of Hawaii). Ms. file. AH.

Minister of Finance (Kingdom of Hawaii). *Report*. Published at intervals for the legislature.

Minister of Foreign Affairs (Republic of Hawaii). *Report*. Published at intervals for the legislature.

Minister of Foreign Relations (Kingdom of Hawaii). *Report*. Published at intervals for the legislature.

Minister of Interior (Kingdom of Hawaii). *Report*. Published at intervals for the legislature.

Ministerial Conferences (Kingdom of Hawaii). Ms. AH.

Minutes of the Council of State (Republic of Hawaii). Ms. AH.

Minutes of the Executive Council (Republic of Hawaii). Ms. AH.

"Minutes of the Sandwich Islands Mission General Meetings." Ms. HMCS.

Missionary Herald. Periodical. Boston.

Molokai: Description of the Leper Colony on This Island. Honolulu, n. d.

[Morgan Report]. U. S. Congress. Senate. *Hawaiian Islands*. Report 227. 53 Cong. 1 Sess. Washington, 1894.

Morgan, H. *America's Road to Empire*. New York, 1965.

Morgan, T. *Hawaii: A Century of Economic Change, 1778–1876*. Cambridge, 1948.

Morning Post. Newspaper. London.

Mouritz, A. *Path of the Destroyer*. Honolulu, 1916.

Munford, J., ed. *John Ledyard's Journal of Captain Cook's Last Voyage*. Corvallis, 1963.

Murphy, T. *Ambassadors in Arms*. Honolulu, 1954.

Nakahata, Y. and Toyota, R. "Varsity Victory Volunteers: A Social Movement." *Social Process in Hawaii*. Nov., 1943.

Narrative of Five Youths from the Sandwich Islands. New York, 1816.

Neilson Papers. AH.

New York American. Newspaper.

New York Evangelist. Newspaper.

New York Herald. Newspaper.

New York Times. Newspaper.

Nippu Jiji. Newspaper. Honolulu.

Nuhou. Newspaper. Honolulu.

[O'Brien Report]. U. S. Congress. House of Representatives. Committee on Interior and Insular Affairs. *Hawaii Statehood. Report*. 85 Cong. 2 Sess. Washington, 1959.

Official Prospectus—The Kamehameha Schools. Honolulu, 1885.

Okumura, T. *Seventy Years of Divine Blessings*. Tokyo, 1940.

[O'Mahoney Hearings]. U. S. Congress. Senate. Committee on Interior and Insular Affairs. *Hawaii Statehood. Hearings*. 81 Cong. 1 Sess. Washington, 1950.

Order in Council of His Hawaiian Majesty, Prescribing a Code of Etiquette. Honolulu, 1844.

Pa Gibby's Wooin' and De Breach ob Promise Soot! Honolulu, 1887.

Parade. Periodical.

Parke Papers. AH.

Parke, W. *Personal Reminiscences of William Cooper Parke.* Cambridge, 1891.

Patterson, S. *Narrative of Adventures, Sufferings, and Privations.* Providence, 1825.

Paty, W. Journal. Ms. AH.

[*PCA*]. *Pacific Commercial Advertiser.* Newspaper. Honolulu.

[Pearl Harbor Hearings]. U. S. Congress. Senate. Joint Committee. *Investigation of the Pearl Harbor Attack. Hearings.* 39 Parts. 79 Cong. 2 Sess. Washington, 1946.

[Pearl Harbor Report]. U. S. Congress. Senate. Joint Committee. *Investigation of the Pearl Harbor Attack. Report.* 79 Cong. 2 Sess. Washington, 1946.

[Percival Inquiry]. U. S. Navy Dept. Office of Judge Advocate General. Court Martial Records, XXIII, 1830, No. 531. Proceedings of a Court of Inquiry &c., In the Case of Lieut. John Percival. Ms. National Archives, Washington. (HHS).

Pierce, R. *Russia's Hawaiian Adventure, 1815–1817.* Berkeley, 1965.

[Pinkerton Report]. Report of Pinkerton Detective Agency to Governor Lawrence Judd, October, 1932. Typescript. AH.

Pinkham Papers. AH.

Planters' Monthly. Honolulu.

Pleadwell, F. "Voyage to England of King Liholiho and Queen Kamamalu." Typescript. HHS.

Poindexter Papers. AH.

[*Poly*]. *Polynesian.* Newspaper. Honolulu.

Poore, H. Journal. Ms. BPBM.

Portlock, N. *Voyage Around the World, 1785–1788.* London, 1789.

Pratt, J. *America's Colonial Experiment.* New York, 1950.

————. *Expansionists of 1898.* Baltimore, 1936.

Principles Adopted by the Board of Commissioners to Quiet Land Titles. Honolulu, 1847.

Privy Council Record (Kingdom of Hawaii). Ms. AH.

Proceedings of the Executive and Advisory Councils (Provisional Government of Hawaii). Ms. AH.

Proclamation Book (Territory of Hawaii). Ms. AH.

Quimper, M. *Islas de Sandwich.* Madrid, 1822.

Record of Informal Meetings of the Cabinet Council (Kingdom of Hawaii). Ms. AH.

Records of the Church at Lahaina. Ms. HMCS.

[Rehabilitation Hearings]. U. S. Congress. House. Committee on Territories. *Rehabilitation and Colonization of Hawaiians.* 67 Cong. 1 Sess. Washington, 1921.

Reinecke, J. "Language and Dialect in Hawaii." MA, UH, 1935.

Remy Papers AH.

Report of the Case of George Pelly Vs. Richard Charlton, Tried Before His Excellency M. Kekuanaoa, Governor of Oahu. Honolulu, 1844.

Report of the Lahaina Station. Ms. HMCS.

Report of the Proceedings and Evidence in the Arbitration Between the King and Government of the Hawaiian Islands and Messrs Ladd and Co. Honolulu, 1846.

Report of the Waimea Station. Ms. HMCS.

Review of Reviews. Periodical. New York.

Reynolds, S. Journal. Ms. Peabody Museum, Salem, Massachusetts. (HMCS).

Richards, W. Journal. Ms. HMCS.

Richards Papers. AH.

Richardson, J., comp. *Messages and Papers of the Presidents.* Washington, 1896–1898.

[Richardson Report]. U. S. Department of Justice. *Law Enforcement in the Territory of Hawaii.* Washington, 1932.

Rickman, J. *Journal of Captain Cook's Last Voyage, 1776–1779.* London, 1781.

Riou, E. Log. Ms. Adm. 51/4529/43. PRO. (AH).

Rock, J. *Indigenous Trees of the Hawaiian Islands.* Honolulu, 1913.

Roesch, R. "Hawaiian Statehood Plebiscite of 1940." MA, UH, 1952.

Rowland, D. "United States and the Contract Labor Question in Hawaii, 1862–1900." *Pacific Historical Review.* Sept., 1933.

Russ, W. *Hawaiian Republic.* Selinsgrove, Pa., 1961.

————. *Hawaiian Revolution.* Selinsgrove, Pa., 1959.

Ryden, G. *Foreign Policy of the United States in Relation To Samoa.* New Haven, 1933.

Samwell, D. Journal. Ms. Egerton 2591. BM. (AH).

San Francisco *Chronicle.* Newspaper.

San Francisco *Examiner.* Newspaper.

Saturday Press. Newspaper. Honolulu.

Schmitt, R. "Birth and Death Rates in Hawaii, 1848–1962." *Hawaii Historical Review.* Jan., 1964.

————. "Population Characteristics of Hawaii, 1778–1850." *Hawaii Historical Review.* April, 1965.

————. "Population Estimates and Censuses of Hawaii, 1778–1850." *Hawaii Historical Review.* July, 1964.

Schurz, C. "Manifest Destiny." *Harpers New Monthly Magazine* (European edition). Oct., 1893.

Scudder, F. *Thirty Years of Mission Work for the Japanese of Hawaii.* Honolulu, 1917.

Shaler, W. "Journal of a Voyage Between China and the North-Western Coast of America, Made in 1804." *American Register.* 1808.

Sharp, A. *Ancient Voyagers in Polynesia.* Sydney, 1963.

————. *Discovery of the Pacific Islands.* Oxford, 1960.

Shepherd Saint of Lanai. Honolulu, 1882.

[Shoemaker]. U. S. Department of Labor. Bureau of Labor Statistics. Bulletin No. 926. *The Economy of Hawaii in 1947.* Washington, 1948.

[*SIG*]. *Sandwich Island Gazette.* Newspaper. Honolulu.

[*SIM*]. *Sandwich Island Mirror.* Newspaper. Honolulu.

[SIM Journal]. Journal of the Sandwich Islands Mission. Ms. HMCS.

Simpson, A. *Sandwich Islands.* London, 1843.

Simpson, G. *Narrative of a Journey Round the World, 1841–1842.* 2 vols. London, 1847.

[*SIN*]. *Sandwich Islands News.* Newspaper. Honolulu.

Sketch of Recent Events, Being a Short Account of the Events Which Culminated on June 30, 1887. Honolulu, 1887.

Skottsberg, C. *Artemisia, Scaevota, Santalum, and Vaccinium of Hawaii.* Honolulu, 1927.

Smith, B. *Yankees in Paradise.* Philadelphia, 1956.

Snow, E., ed. *Sea, the Ship and the Sailor.* Salem, 1925.

Snow, W. Diary. Ms. HHS.

Snowbarger, W. "Development of Pearl Harbor." PhD, University of California, 1950.

Social Process in Hawaii. Periodical.

"Solid Men of Boston in the Northwest." Ms. Bancroft Library, University of California. (UH).

Sousa, E. "Walter Murray Gibson's Rise to Power in Hawaii." MA, UH, 1942.

Spaulding, T. "Cabinet Government in Hawaii, 1887–1893." UH *Occasional Papers*, 2. Honolulu, 1924.

————. "Constitution of the Hawaiian Republic." UH *Occasional Papers*, 12. Honolulu, 1931.

————. *Crown Lands of Hawaii.* Honolulu, 1923.

————. "Early Years of the Hawaiian Legislature." HHS *Report*, 37. 1929.

Spitz, A. *Land Aspects of the Hawaiian Homes Program.* Honolulu, 1964.

Spotlight. Periodical. Honolulu.

St. John, H. "History, Present Distribution, and Abundance of Sandalwood on Oahu, Hawaiian Islands." *Pacific Science.* 1947.

Stainback Papers. AH.

[Staley, T.]. *Pastoral Address, by the Right Reverend the Bishop of Honolulu.* Honolulu, 1865.

Statute Laws of His Majesty Kamehameha III. Honolulu, 1846.

Steegmuller, F. *Two Lives of James Jackson Jarves.* New Haven, 1951.

Stevens, S. *American Expansion in Hawaii, 1842–1898.* Harrisburg, 1945.

Stewart, C. *Journal of a Residence in the Sandwich Islands, 1823–1825.* London, 1828.

————. *Private Journal of a Voyage to the Pacific Ocean and Residence at the Sandwich Islands, 1822–1825.* New York, 1828.

————. *Visit to the South Seas, 1829–1830.* 2 vols. New York, 1831.

Stirling, Y. *Sea Duty: The Memoirs of a Fighting Admiral.* New York, 1939.

Stoddard, C. *Island of Tranquil Delights.* Boston, 1904.

Stokes, J. "Hawaiian King." HHS *Papers*, 19. Honolulu, 1932.

————. "Honolulu and Some New Speculative Phases of Hawaiian History." HHS *Report*, 42. 1934.

————. "Iron with the Early Hawaiians." HHS *Papers*, 18. Honolulu, 1931.

————. "Kaoleioku: Paternity and Biographical Sketch." HHS *Report*, 43. 1935.

_____. "Origin of the Condemnation of Captain Cook in Hawaii." HHS *Report*, 39. 1931.

Sugar Industry of Hawaii and the Labor Shortage. Honolulu, 1921.

Sullivan, J. *History of C. Brewer and Company, Ltd.* Boston, 1926.

"Summary of Report of Events on the Island of Niihau, in Sequence from 7 December 1941 to 15 December 1941." Microfilm. HWRD.

Suppliment [sic] *To the Sandwich Island Mirror.* Newspaper. Honolulu.

[*Survey of Education*]. U. S. Department of the Interior. Bureau of Education. *A Survey of Education in Hawaii.* Washington, 1920.

Tansill, C. *Diplomatic Relations Between the United States and Hawaii, 1885–1889.* New York, 1940.

Tate, M. "Myth of Hawaii's Swing Toward Australasia and Canada." *Pacific Historical Review.* Aug., 1964.

_____. *United States and the Hawaiian Kingdom: A Political History.* New Haven, 1965.

Taylor, A. P. *Sesquicentennial Celebration of Captain Cook's Discovery of Hawaii.* Honolulu, 1929.

Taylor, E. Papers. AH.

Taylor, W. "Hawaiian Sugar Industry." PhD, University of California, 1935.

Territory V. Ahakuelo et al. Ms. Office of the County Attorney, Honolulu.

Territory V. Grace Fortescue et al. Ms. Office of the County Attorney, Honolulu.

Thomas, B. and Packer, P. *Massie Case.* New York, 1966.

Thompson, A., and others. *Modern Apostles of Missionary Byways.* New York, 1899.

Thrum, T. "Paehumu of Heiaus Non-sacred." HHS *Report,* 35. 1927.

Thurston Papers. AH.

Thurston, L. A. *Handbook on the Annexation of Hawaii.* St. Joseph, 1897.

_____. *Memoirs of the Hawaiian Revolution.* Honolulu, 1936.

Thurston, Lucy. *Life and Times.* Michigan, 1882.

_____. Journal, in *Missionary Herald,* 1821.

Tilton, C. *History of Banking in Hawaii.* UH *Research Publications,* 3. Honolulu, 1927.

Tinker, R. Journal. Ms. HMCS.

Townsend, E. *Extract from the Diary of Ebenezer Townsend, Jr.* HHS *Reprints,* 4. 1921.

Towse, E. *Rebellion of 1895.* 2nd ed. Honolulu, 1895.

Treaties and Conventions Concluded Between the Hawaiian Kingdom and Other Powers, Since 1825. Honolulu, 1887.

Trevenen, J. Notes on Cook and King, *Voyage to Pacific Ocean.* Ms. Archives of British Columbia. (AH).

Turnbull, J. *Voyage Round the World, 1800–1804.* 3 vols. London, 1805.

Turrill Collection. HHS.

Twain, M. [S. L. Clemens]. *Letters from the Sandwich Islands.* San Francisco, 1937.

_____. *Sandwich Islands.* New York, 1920.

Two Weeks of Hawaiian History. Honolulu, 1893.

Tyerman, D. and Bennet, G. *Journal of Voyages and Travels, 1821–1829.* Rev. American ed. 3 vols. Boston, 1832.

"Unpublished Minutes of the Prudential Meetings of the Mission Nov. 19, 1819 to July 22, 1820 and March 14, 1831 to May 18, 1831." Typescript. HMCS.

U. S. Bureau of Census. *Census.* Washington, 1900–1960.

U. S. Bureau of Labor Statistics. *Third Report of the Commissioner of Labor on Hawaii.* Washington, 1906.

U. S. Commissioner of Labor. *Report on Hawaii, 1902.* Washington, 1903.

U. S. Department of Agriculture. *Yearbook.* Washington, 1898.

[USDS]. United States. Department of State. Consular Dispatches, Honolulu; Consular Dispatches, Lahaina; Dispatches, Hawaii; Miscellaneous Letters; Notes From Hawaiian Legation. Ms. National Archives, Washington. (UH).

Vallejo Documents. Ms. Bancroft Library, University of California. (UH).

Vancouver, G. *Voyage of Discovery to the North Pacific Ocean, 1790–1795.* 3 vols. London, 1798.

Van Slingerland, P. *Something Terrible Has Happened.* New York, 1966.

Varigny, C. De. *Quatorze Ans aux Îles Sandwich.* Paris, 1874.

Vause, M. "Hawaiian Homes Commission Act, 1920." MA, UH, 1962.

Victor, P–E. *Man and the Conquest of the Poles.* New York, 1963.

Voice of Labor. Newspaper. Honolulu.

Wakukawa, E. *History of the Japanese People in Hawaii.* Honolulu, 1938.

Wallis, H. "Exploration of the South Sea, 1519 to 1644." PhD, Oxford, 1953.

[Walter Hearings]. U. S. Congress. House. Committee on Un-American Activities. *Hearings Regarding Communist Activities in the Territory of Hawaii.* 81 Cong. 2 Sess. Washington, 1950.

Watts, J. Journal. Ms. Adm. 51/4559/212. PRO. (AH).

Webb, M. "Abolition of the Taboo System in Hawaii." *Journal of the Polynesian Society.* Mar., 1965.

Weekly Argus. Newspaper. Honolulu.

Weigle, R. "Sugar and the Hawaiian Revolution." *Pacific Historical Review.* Feb., 1947.

Weinberg, A. *Manifest Destiny.* Baltimore, 1935.

White, H. "Sugar Industry and Plantation Agencies." *13th New Americans Conference.* Honolulu, 1939.

Whitman, J. Journal. Ms. Peabody Museum, Salem. (HMCS).

Williamson, J. Log. Ms. Adm. 55/117. PRO. (AH).

Williston, S. *William Richards.* Cambridge, 1938.

Wilson Papers. AH.

Wohlstetter, R. *Pearl Harbor: Warning and Decision.* Stanford, 1962.

Wright, T. *Rape in Paradise.* New York, 1966.

Wroth, L. "Early Cartography of the Pacific." Bibliographical Society of America, Papers. 1944.

Yamato Shimbun. Newspaper. Honolulu.

Yanagawa, M. *First Japanese Mission to America.* New York, 1938.

Yates, E. "Reminiscences of Honolulu." Ms. HHS.

Yzendoorn, R. "Bibliography of the Catholic Mission in the Hawaiian Islands."
    Typescript. HMCS.
————. *History of the Catholic Mission in the Hawaiian Islands.* Honolulu,
    1927.

Notes

These footnotes give extremely abbreviated references to sources. Names
of authors, editors, compilers, committee chairmen and other functionaries
appearing in the footnotes may be found in alphabetical order in the bibliography, followed by the title of the work for which they are responsible. If a
work has no identifiable author, the first word or two of its title are used in
the footnotes, and a fuller title is given in the bibliography. In cases where
works or periodicals or collections of documents are referred to in the footnotes only by an identifying tag (for example, *Hon. Adv.*; or HCLC Report;
or FO & Ex) the alphabetical principle still holds good in the bibliography;
the identifying tag appears there, followed by a fuller title.

Prologue

For the background to the discovery of Hawaii, see Beaglehole, *Exploration;*
    Beaglehole, *Journals of Captain Cook,* I, intro., III, intro.; Sharp, *Ancient
    Voyagers;* Sharp, *Discovery;* Golson; Dahlgren; Wallis; Wroth.

Chapter 1: Captain Cook—1778–1779

HIGH ISLANDS AT DAYBREAK pp. 1–8

Contact with Kauai natives, "Their eyes": Cook, Egerton 2177A, Jan. 18–20,
    1778.
Some prayed: King, Adm. 55/116, Jan. 20, 1778.
"Three things": Beaglehole, *Journals of Captain Cook,* II, p. 398.
Cleaver stolen, native killed: Williamson, Jan. 18, 1778.
Tower and burying place: Cook, Egerton 2177A, Jan. 21, 1778.
Iron: Clerke, Adm. 55/22, Jan. 22–23, 1778. See also Stokes, "Iron."
Chief visits *Discovery,* "a drop of Salt Water": Clerke, Adm. 55/22, Jan. 24,
    1778. See also Burney, Add Ms. 8955, Jan. 24, 1778.
"Schemes to deceive": Edgar, Adm. 55/21, Jan. 24, 1778.

"Ye extreme reservedness": Williamson, Jan. 27, 1778. See also Gore, Feb. 1, 1778.

Cook was abstemious: Howay, p. 99; Cook and King, *Voyage to Pacific Ocean*, I, pp. 123–124, II, pp. 196, 215; Cook, Egerton 2177A, Jan. 20, 1778.

Impressions of Hawaiians: Clerke, Adm. 55/22, "Account of these isles;" Cook, Egerton 2177A, [Feb. 2, 1778]; King, Adm. 55/116, Jan. 20, 1778; Edgar, Adm. 55/21, Jan. 24, 1778; Ellis, *Authentic Narrative*, II, pp. 166–187; Cook and King, *Voyage to Pacific Ocean*, II, pp. 221–252.

"A disagreeable mess": Cook and King, *Voyage to Pacific Ocean*, II, p. 235.

KEALAKEKUA BAY pp. 8–11

Maui, "As soon as they got a long side": Cook, Egerton 2177A, Nov. 26, 1778.

Kahekili: Burney Add Ms. 8955, Nov. 27, 1778.

Kalaniopuu's people: Samwell, Nov. 30, 1778; King, Adm. 55/122, Dec. 1, 1778.

Coasting Hawaii: Cook, Egerton 2177A, Dec. 11–31, 1778; Samwell, Dec. 7, 21, 1778; Ellis, *Authentic Narrative*, II, pp. 75–76.

South point, inhabitants "thronged off": Cook, Egerton 2177A, Jan. 5, 1779.

Girls sang and danced: Samwell, Jan. 10, 1779.

A curving bay, "Canoes now began to come off": Cook, Egerton 2177B, Jan. 16, 1779.

Such a crowd: Cook, Egerton 2177B, Jan. 17, 1779; Burney, Add Ms. 8955, Jan. 17, 1779; King, Adm. 55/122, Jan. 17, 1779.

LONO pp. 11–15

Two chiefs: Cook, Egerton 2177B, Jan. 17, 1779; Burney, Add Ms. 8955, Jan. 18, 1779; Edgar, Adm.55/24, Jan. 19, 1779.

"A little old man": King, Adm. 55/122, Jan. 17, 1779.

"We enterd the Area": King, Adm. 55/122, Jan. 17, 1779.

Cook's taste "the coarsest": Trevenen, Notes on Cook and King, *Voyage to Pacific Ocean*, II, p. 457.

A disagreeable amusement: Clerke, Adm. 51/4561/217, "An Account of the Sandwich Islands."

Kapu at observatory: King, Adm. 55/122, Jan. 17, 1779.

Beautiful women: Samwell, Jan. 17–19, 1779.

"In the first Canoe": King, Adm. 55/122, [Jan. 26], 1779.

"These people are so eager after our Iron": Samwell, Jan. 21, 1779.

Stolen knife: King, Adm. 55/122, [Jan. 31], 1779.

Boxing match: Burney, Add Ms. 8955, Feb. 1, 1779; Samwell, Feb. 1–2, 1779.

William Watman died: King, Adm. 55/122, Feb. 1, 1779.

Wooden railing: King, Adm. 55/122, Feb. 1, 1779. See also Thrum, "Paehumu," pp. 56–57.

Kalaniopuu's gift: King, Adm. 55/122, Feb. 3, 1779.

"In all the Islands": King, Adm. 55/122, Feb. 3, 1779.

A BROKEN MAST pp. 16–24

"Afraid of being Abus'd": King, Adm. 55/122, Feb. 7, 1779.

Return to Kealakekua: Burney, Add Ms. 8955, Feb. 11–12, 1779.

Women "trading in their way": Ellis, *Authentic Narrative,* II, p. 102.

"It's impossible": Beaglehole, *Journals of Captain Cook,* II, p. 493.

Firearms: Cook, Egerton 2177B, Jan. 16, 1779; Burney, Add Ms. 8955, Jan. 18, 28, 1779; Edgar, Adm. 55/24, Dec. 23, 1778, Jan. 16, 1779; Law, [Feb. 23], 1779; Howay, pp. 90–91; Riou, Dec. 24, 1778.

Hawaiians "threw away their Stones": King, Adm. 55/122, Feb. 13, 1779.

Theft of tongs: Clerke, Adm. 55/124, Feb. 14, 1779.

Cook threatens to fire: King, Adm. 55/122, Feb. 13, 1779.

Fight with Palea and his people: Edgar, Adm. 55/24, Feb. 14, 1779; Howay, p. 91.

Cook "expressd his sorrow": King, Adm. 55/122, Feb. 13, 1779.

Cutter stolen: Clerke, Adm. 51/4561/217, [Feb. 14], 1779.

"The Captn loading his double Barreld piece": King, Adm. 55/122, Feb. 14, 1779.

"A single Musquet": Burney, Mitchell Library Ms., Feb. 14, 1779.

King went back to the observatory: King, Adm. 55/122, Feb. 14, 1779.

Cook ashore at Kaawaloa: Clerke, Adm. 51/4561/217, [Feb. 14], 1779.

Death of Cook: Almost every journal has an account, and there are several published versions. See Beaglehole, *Journals of Captain Cook,* III, intro. But the only account by a close witness is by Molesworth Phillips, and of course he was fighting for his own life. Phillips' story is in Clerke, Adm. 51/4561/217, [Feb. 14], 1779.

The observatory: King, Adm. 55/122, Feb. 14, 1779.

Their next move: Clerke, Adm. 55/124, [Feb. 14], 1779.

King goes in to parley, a native "had the Insolence": King, Adm. 55/122, Feb. 14, 1779. See also Edgar, Adm. 55/24, Feb. 15, 1779.

"Our horror will be barely conceiv'd": King, Adm. 55/122, Feb. 14, 1779. See also Clerke, Adm. 51/4561/217, Feb. 16, 1779.

Man twirling Cook's hat, four pounders fired: Clerke, Adm. 51/4561/217, Feb. 17, 1779.

Village set afire, natives killed: King, Adm. 55/122, Feb. 14, 1779; Harvey, Feb. 15, 1779; Clerke, Adm. 51/4561/217, Feb. 17, 1779; Watts, Feb. 18, 1779; Edgar, Adm. 55/24, Feb. 18, 1779; Howay, p. 97; Trevenen, Notes on Cook and King, *Voyage to Pacific Ocean,* III, p. 75; Gilbert, pp. 224–259.

Peace party, Koa "minded us so little": King, Adm. 55/122, Feb. 16, 1779.

"On opening it": King, Adm. 55/122, Feb. 16, 1779. See also Clerke, Adm. 51/4561/217, Feb. 20, 21, 1779.

Cook's belongings returned, effects sold: Clerke, Adm. 51/4561/217, Feb. 21, 1779; Edgar, Adm. 55/24, Feb. 16, 1779.

Burial of Cook, "Thus left we Kealakekua Bay": King, Adm. 55/122, Feb. 23, 1779.

THE END OF LONO pp. 24–28

Visitors and sightseers: Dozens of sources mention the site of Cook's death. A few are: Lisiansky, p. 104; E. Loomis, Oct. 19, 1820; Ellis, *Narrative of a Tour*, pp. 110–111; L. Chamberlain, Mar. 19, 1825; Tinker, Aug. 5, 1831; Twain, *Letters from the Sandwich Islands*, pp. 163–164.

Cook monuments: Bloxam, July 15, 1825; *SIG*, Feb. 18, Oct. 28, 1837; *Haw. Gaz.* Nov. 25, 1874; A. P. Taylor, pp. 87–89.

Natives looked back on Cook's death: E. Snow, p. 123; Colnett, Adm. 55/146, Feb. [11], 1788; Vancouver, III, p. 34; Townsend, Aug. 30, 1798; Turnbull, II, p. 84; Golovnin, I, pp. 300–301; E. Loomis, June 12, 1824; Bloxam, June 9, July 15, 1825; Tinker, Aug. 5, 1831; Martin, II, pp. 62–65; Mathison, p. 431; Dibble, pp. 34–39; Egerstrom, pp. 169–170; Varigny, pp. 18–23; S. E. Bishop, *Reminiscences*, p. 26; *PCA*, Jan. 15, 1870.

Missionaries on Cook's death: E. Loomis, June 12, 1824; *Hawaiian Spectator* (1839), pp. 65–66; Bingham, *Residence*, pp. 30–35. See also Stokes, "Origin," pp. 68–104.

Cook's entrails "used to rope off the arena": Kamakau, *Ruling Chiefs*, p. 103.

Celebrations of 1928: A. P. Taylor, generally.

Obscure but menacing change: Burney, Mitchell Ms., Feb. 12, 1779; Munford, p. 141; Gilbert, p. 200.

Williamson: R. Gould, p. 316.

Makahiki festival: Malo, pp. 33, 53, 141–159; Ii, pp. 70–76; Kamakau, *Ruling Chiefs*, p. 52; Colnett, Adm. 55/146, [Jan. 16–17], 1788.

The home of a chief: Kamakau, *Ruling Chiefs*, p. 98.

"Party matters": Clerke, Adm. 55/124, Feb. 16, 1779. See also Charlton, Feb. 16, 1779; Harvey, Feb. 16, 1779; King, Adm. 55/122, Feb. 14, 1779.

Chronically divided authority: Davenport, pp. 15–27.

Luakini heiaus: Malo, pp. 159–187.

Sticks and kapa sheets dismantled: Malo, p. 151.

Ceremony at the beach: Malo, p. 150.

Fighting men: Samwell, Feb. 13, 1779.

Scarred right hand: Beaglehole, *Journals of Captain Cook*, I, p. *cviii*.

Armed marines and shore parties: For examples of Cook's style and tactics see Beaglehole, *Journals of Captain Cook*, I, pp. 87–88, 168–172, 211–212, 234–235, II, pp. 123–124, 254–255, 365–367, 416–417, 433–439, 461, 483; Cook and King, *Voyage to Pacific Ocean*, I, p. 304, II, pp. 85–88, 100–101, 116, 119–120.

Cook shorter of patience: Beaglehole, *Journals of Captain Cook*, III, intro.

His officers might have been right: Law, [Feb. 23], 1779.

Most recent visit to Friendly Islands: Martin, II, pp. 60–61; Cook and King, *Voyage to Pacific Ocean*, I, pp. 292–328.

In the Societies chiefs planned to ambush Cook and Clerke: Cook and King, *Voyage to Pacific Ocean*, II, pp. 118–123.

Clive: Davies, p. 14.

Nelson: Mahan, *Life of Nelson*, p. 11.

La Pérouse: Victor, p. 107.

Gunpowder flask: Beaglehole, *Journals of Captain Cook*, I, p. *cviii*.
"Billious colick": Beaglehole, *Journals of Captain Cook*, II, pp. 333–334·
Gun misfired: Beaglehole, *Journals of Captain Cook*, II, pp. 436–437, 479·
A man "who had Ambition": Beaglehole, *Journals of Captain Cook*, II, p. 323·
Little to do but admire him: J. Hunter, p. 292.

Chapter 2: Kamehameha—1779–1819

ENTER KAMEHAMEHA pp. 29–31

Disposition of his domains: Fornander, II, pp. 200–201; Kamakau, *Ruling Chiefs*, p. 107.
"As savage a looking face": King, Adm. 55/122, Jan. 26, 1779. See also Law, Jan. 27, 1779; Samwell, Feb. 10, 1779.
Kamehameha: Edgar, Adm. 55/24, Feb. 11, 1779; Law, Feb. 11, 1779; Samwell, Feb. 10, 1779; Clerke, Adm. 51/4561/217, Feb. 17, 1779; Ellis, *Authentic Narrative*, II, p. 121; Portlock, pp. 61, 77–78.
Descent: Barrere.
Kamehameha stepped forward: Fornander, II, pp. 202–203; Kamakau, *Ruling Chiefs*, pp. 108–109.
Land division: Fornander, II, pp. 300–308; Kamakau, *Ruling Chiefs*, pp. 118–120.
Kiwalao killed: Fornander, II, pp. 309–310; Kamakau, *Ruling Chiefs*, p. 121.
Kahekili: Kamakau, *Ruling Chiefs*, pp. 128–141, 167, 232–233; Fornander, II, pp. 217–227; McAllister, pp. 95–96.

THE ARTS OF WAR pp. 31–34

Battles along traditional lines: Malo, pp. 53, 58, 65–66, 159–188, 196–197; Buck, pp. 417–464; Barrere; Fornander, II, p. 216; Kamakau, *Ruling Chiefs*, p. 116.
Predatory great chiefs: For their rise see Stokes, "Hawaiian King."
Cook's ships at Kauai: Samwell, Mar. 1–3, 1779; Ellis, *Authentic Narrative*, II, pp. 130–131; King, Adm. 55/122, Mar. 1, 1779; Rickman, p. 331.
Fur trade: The best single account of early Pacific commerce is Bradley, pp. 1–53·
Arms trade, clashes with natives: Dozens of instances, a few are: Portlock, p. 166 ff; Meares, pp. 341, 353–356, 370–372; Dixon, pp. 101, 257; Colnett, Adm. 55/146, Jan. 1–Mar. 20, 1788; Ingraham, Oct. 11, 1791; Letter of Colnett, Apr. 1, 1791, in Quimper; Vancouver, I, pp. 174, 179, 186–187, II, pp. 110, 177, 222, 364–365, III, pp. 29–30, 67–68; Bell, Feb. 14–15, 1793; Menzies, Feb. 24, 1793; Boit, Oct. 16, 1795; Broughton, p. 78; Delano, pp. 388–389·
Women would infect sailors: Lisiansky, p. 103.
Simon and Thomas Metcalfe: Metcalfe to Thomas and others, Mar. 22, 1790, FO & Ex; Ingraham, May 26, 1791; *Columbian Centinel*, Nov. 30, 1791; Vancouver, III, pp. 135–141; *Hawaiian Spectator* (1839), pp. 71–73·
Simon Metcalfe killed: Boit, Oct. 16, 1795·
Young and Davis try to escape: Vancouver, II, pp. 141–142; Bell, Jan. 14, 1794·

THE LORD OF HAWAII pp. 35–37

Kamehameha invades Maui: Kamakau, *Ruling Chiefs*, pp. 148–149.
"Go back": Kamakau, *Ruling Chiefs*, p. 150.
"The rear body": Dibble, p. 66.
A new heiau: Fornander, II, p. 328; Kamakau, *Ruling Chiefs*, pp. 154–155.
"Here I am!": Kamakau, *Ruling Chiefs*, p. 157. See also Fornander, II, pp. 333–334.
"The rain drives down": Kamakau, *Ruling Chiefs*, p. 158.
Pahupu "with eyelids turned inside out": Kamakau, *Ruling Chiefs*, p. 159.
Battle of the red-mouthed gun: Kamakau, *Ruling Chiefs*, pp. 161–162.

THE WAY TO NUUANU pp. 37–41

Honolulu harbor discovered: Circumstances are uncertain—see Stokes, "Honolulu," p. 61 ff.
Kahekili "ceded" Oahu: Bell, Mar. 14, 1793; Stokes, "Honolulu," pp. 61–85.
Kamehameha "ceded" Hawaii: Vancouver, III, pp. 54–57.
"Mingled joy and weeping": Kamakau, *Ruling Chiefs*, p. 168.
Kaeokulani killed: Kamakau, *Ruling Chiefs*, p. 169; Fornander, II, pp. 262–266.
Kendrick and Brown killed: Boit, Oct. 16, 1795; C. Bishop, Sep., 1795; Delano, p. 400; *Friend*, June, 1862; Letter of Lamport and Bonallack to Young and Davis, Jan. 14, 1795, in Bloxam; Dibble, pp. 67–71.
Kaiana's affair with Kaahumanu: Vancouver, III, pp. 6–7.
Battle of Nuuanu: Boit, Oct. 16, 1795; C. Bishop, Feb. 28, 1796; Broughton, p. 41; Kamakau, *Ruling Chiefs*, p. 172; Fornander, II, p. 348; Dibble, p. 71; Jarves, *History of Sandwich Islands*, pp. 164–165.
Footprints of Kaiana: Bingham, *Residence*, p. 47.

REACH AND GRASP pp. 41–44

William Broughton tried to dissuade Kamehameha: Broughton, pp. 41–42.
Kamehameha forced to turn back: Kamakau, *Ruling Chiefs*, p. 173.
Kamehameha sailed for Hawaii. Kamakau, *Ruling Chiefs*, pp. 173–174.
Time for him to perfect a government: Kamakau, *Ruling Chiefs*, pp. 175–186; Turnbull, II, pp. 24–26.
Peleleu canoes: Lisiansky, p. 133; Kamakau, *Ruling Chiefs*, pp. 187–188.
Kaumualii preparing to defend his island: Boit, Oct. 16, 1795; Cleveland, I, p. 232.
"A man-made canoe": Kamakau, *Ruling Chiefs*, pp. 188–189.
Epidemic: The Hawaiians called it mai okuu, probably cholera or typhoid. Martin, I, p. 40; Lisiansky, pp. 111–112; Tyerman and Bennet, I, pp. 423–424.
The diplomatic issue: Kamehameha to George III, Mar. 3, 1810, Apr. 30, 1812, FO & Ex; Broughton, p. 71; Shaler, pp. 137–175; Iselin, p. 78; Campbell, pp. 155–156; Delano, pp. 398–399; Ii, pp. 80–83; "Solid Men of Boston in the Northwest."

THE ARTS OF PEACE pp. 44–49

Ka Mamalahoe Kanawai: Kamakau, *Ka Po'e Kahiko*, pp. 15–16.

Haggling with captains: Dozens of descriptions exist of Kamehameha the trader —a few are: C. Bishop, Feb. 20–21, 1796; Patterson, p. 73; Corney, pp. 84–90, 96; Richards to Wilkes, Mar. 15, 1841, Richards Papers; Barnard, pp. 219–221; Campbell, pp. 211–212; Langsdorff, I, pp. 186–188.

The idea of a fleet of foreign vessels: Bradley, pp. 55–56.

"The husbands and parents": Ii, p. 87.

"Descending a hill": Cox, I, pp. 52–53.

Foreigners on Oahu: Numbers varied greatly—see Campbell, pp. 165–167; Franchère, pp. 69–70.

"It was no uncommon sight": Campbell, p. 166.

John Young: Iselin, p. 74; Freycinet, IV, p. 532; Kotzebue, I, p. 295; L. Judd, p. 44; S. Bishop, *Reminiscences,* p. 24. Young's will is in FO & Ex, 1835.

Isaac Davis: Townsend, Aug. 26, 1798; Campbell, pp. 135–139; Ii, p. 79.

Oliver Holmes: Cox, I, pp. 34–35, 39–40.

Don Francisco de Paula Marin: Mentioned by almost every traveler. Excerpts from his journal are in AH.

"Subjects of a far different nature": Cox, I, p. 36.

Hawaiian apparitions: Corney, pp. 116–117.

Honolulu: "Honolulu In 1810," map.

"There were many": Ii, p. 61.

Hawaiians signing on for voyages: Bradley, pp. 32–33.

Names tattooed: Cox, I, p. 49.

"Scientific amateurs": Cox, I, p. 33.

Rate of change: Campbell, pp. 140–141, 199.

Hawaiians worked harder: Campbell, pp. 162–163.

SCHÄFFER OF SCHÄFFERTHAL pp. 49–53

Sandalwood: Botanists disagree about varieties—see Rock, p. 127 ff; Skottsberg, p. 40–64; St. John, pp. 5–20. Uses—Buck, p. 210.

Early sandalwood trade: Bradley, pp. 26–28.

Davis and the Winships: Document, Dec., 1811, FO & Ex; Marin, Aug. 4, 1812; Bradley, pp. 29–32; Ii, p. 88.

Royal fraternity: Bell, Feb. 15, 1793; Kamehameha to George III, Aug. 6, 1810, FO & Ex; Macquarie to Kamehameha I, Apr. 12, 1816, FO & Ex; Campbell, pp. 148–150; Turnbull, II, pp. 36–37. The Hawaiian flag, designed in Kamehameha I's time, has a Union Jack in one corner.

Russian ships as early as 1804: Kuykendall, *Hawaiian Kingdom,* I, pp. 55–56.

Georg Anton Schäffer: Pierce, pp. 5–33. Pierce prints Schäffer's journal, which is cited below in Pierce's translation and with his pagination.

"He would give her half": Pierce, p. 117.

Fixed bayonets: Pierce, p. 183.

Russian naval expedition: Kotzebue, I, pp. 303–355.

"Did not chase the Russians": Pierce, p. 201.

Schäffer bundled into a boat: Pierce, p. 200.

"It seemed a little early": Pierce, p. 204.

Schäffer hides in his cabin: Pierce, p. 206.

THE KING IS DEAD pp. 53–60

Chiefs might be conspiring: Kotzebue, I, pp. 308, 316, 348–349, 354; Barnard, p. 220.

Kapu system: Davenport, pp. 15–27; Barrere; Malo, pp. 27–30, 53–58; Kamakau, *Ka Po'e Kahiko,* generally.

Jump off a cliff: Townsend, Aug. 26, 1798. See also Martin, I, pp. *xlvii–xlviii.*

Quarterdeck justice: Vancouver, II, pp. 203–211; Iselin, p. 69; Bloxam, July, 1825; Bingham to Anderson, Nov. 14, 1832, ABCFM; *SIG,* Aug. 20, 1836.

Kamehameha dies: Marin, Apr. 20–May 14, 1819; Wyllie to Castle, Apr. 8, 1848, FO Ltr. Bk. 11a; "Birth Year of Kamehameha I," pp. 11–13; Kuykendall, *Hawaiian Kingdom,* I, pp. 429–430.

"The morning star": Kamakau, *Ruling Chiefs,* p. 215.

"In great splendor": Kamakau, *Ruling Chiefs,* p. 220.

"O heavenly one!": Kamakau, *Ruling Chiefs,* p. 220.

Luakini ceremonies political: Vancouver, III, pp. 23, 52–54.

Kaahumanu almost ungovernable: Vancouver, III, pp. 6–7; Campbell, pp. 188, 215; Ii, 50–51.

Kapu overthrown: Adams, Nov. 13, Dec. 1, 1819; Marin, Oct. 4–Nov. 7, 1819; Lucy Thurston Journal, in *Missionary Herald* (1821), p. 176; Bishop to Secretary, Nov. 30, 1826, ABCFM; SIM Journal, Apr. 5, 1820; W. D. Alexander, "Overthrow of Tabu," pp. 37–45; *Hawaiian Spectator* (1839), 334–337.

During Cook's first visit: Samwell, Jan. 29, 1779.

Vancouver found some of them: Vancouver, II, p. 118.

Kapus "generally observed": Campbell, p. 188.

Women put to death, saved: Whitman; Choris, Sandwich Islands section, pp. 11–12.

Kapu and haoles: Vancouver, III, pp. 8–9, 183–184; Campbell, p. 134; Freycinet, IV, p. 543; Whitman; Corney, pp. 36, 47–48, 86–87; Lisiansky, p. 117.

Colnett "took hold of the man": Colnett, Adm. 55/146, Jan. 15, 1788.

Evidence of considerable disarray: An excellent source for this period is Golovnin, Chs. X, XI.

Body floating in the harbor: Choris, Sandwich Islands section, p. 11.

Chiefs at dinner: Kotzebue, I, pp. 329–331.

Chamisso at the heiau: Chamisso, III, pp. 176–177.

"More to feast": Corney, p. 102.

"Sets the wooden gods": Corney, p. 102.

They did not abandon their old faith: Scores of references—a few are: SIM Journal, Mar. 7, 16, 1821; E. Loomis, Mar. 20–21, 1821; Auna, June 4–26, 1822; L. Chamberlain, July 10, 1823, Jan. 2, 1824, Mar. 17, 1825; Richards to Evarts, June 1, 1824, Mar. 31, 1827, ABCFM; Spalding to Parents, Oct. 26, 1832, HMCS.

An incomplete revolution: See Webb, pp. 21–39.
The islands in flames: Tyerman and Bennet, I, p. 473.

Chapter 3: Missionaries and Merchants—1820–1839

GO YE FORTH INTO ALL THE WORLD pp. 61–65

Opukahaia: *Memoirs of Obookiah; Narrative of Five Youths.*
"His form, which at sixteen": *Memoirs of Obookiah,* p. 89.
"The spirit had departed": *Memoirs of Obookiah,* p. 109.
American Protestant missionaries overseas: Elsbree; Anderson, *History of SIM;*
   Smith, generally.
"Fruitful fields and pleasant dwellings": *Instructions of Prudential Committee,*
   p. 27.
The American Board's first mission: SIM Journal contains a narrative account of
   the first mission's organization and voyage out.
"Unrighteousness, fornication": Bingham, *Residence,* p. 23.
"The appearance of destitution": Bingham, *Residence,* p. 81. See also M. Loomis,
   Mar. 31, 1820.
Liholiho and the missionaries: SIM Journal, Apr. 1–15, 1820.
"Toil and privation": Bingham, *Residence,* p. 94.

THE ISLES SHALL WAIT FOR HIS LAW pp. 65–70

The first months were difficult: Whitney to Worcester, July 20, 1820, ABCFM;
   Bingham to Tennooe, July 23, 1820, ABCFM; "Unpublished Minutes of Pru-
   dential Meetings," July 22, 1820.
Hawaiian women thought work "rather a disgrace": M. Loomis, June 21, 1820.
Hula: SIM Journal, Dec. 20, 1820, Jan. 14, Feb. 20, 22, 1821.
Abortion and infanticide: D. Chamberlain, July 20, 1820; E. Loomis, May 7,
   1821.
Four of whom had conceived: SIM Journal, June 19, 1821.
Kahunas: M. Loomis, May 19, 1820; SIM Journal, May 19, 20, 1820.
Kaumualii: E. Loomis, June 28, 1820; M. Loomis, June 28, 1820; SIM Journal,
   Nov. 12, 1820.
Boki: SIM Journal, Sep. 14, 1820.
Kalanimoku: M. Loomis, July 25, 1820.
Kuakini: L. Chamberlain, Feb. 4, 1824; *Poly,* Jan. 4, 1845.
Liholiho: SIM Journal, Dec. 24, 1822; Tyerman and Bennet, I, p. 35; Lucy
   Thurston, *Life And Times,* p. 36.
Liholiho could hardly bear to stay still: Marin, Feb. 3–Mar. 10, 1821; E. Loomis,
   Feb. 3–4, 1821; M. Loomis, Feb. 3–4, 1821; Bingham, *Residence,* p. 145.
Kaumualii put his island at the king's disposal: SIM Journal, July 22–30, 1821;
   E. Loomis, July 23–30, 1821; M. Loomis, July 23–30, 1821.

Kaahumanu married Kaumualii and Kealiiahonui: SIM Journal, Oct. 9, 1821; E. Loomis, Oct. 10, 1821, June 2, 1825; M. Loomis, Oct. 10, 1821.

"The new Kaahumanu": E. Loomis, Dec. 15, 16, 1821; M. Loomis, Dec. 15, 17, 1821; Auna, June 4–26, 1822; L. Chamberlain, Mar. 31, 1824; Bingham, *Residence*, p. 214.

Liholiho refused to be pinned down: SIM Journal, Apr. 4, 1821; Tyerman and Bennet, II, pp. 44, 57–58.

Liholiho drank too much: E. Loomis, Sep. 6, 1820, Mar. 1, 5, 1822; M. Loomis, Mar. 1, 5, 1822; Mathison, pp. 435–436; Bingham, *Residence*, pp. 158–159; Stewart, *Journal of Residence*, pp. 194–195, 198–199.

Sober and in the right mood: Stewart, *Private Journal*, pp. 86, 93, 99, 103, 107–108; Stewart, *Journal of Residence*, pp. 134–139.

Life at the royal court: L. Chamberlain, May 5, 1823; Tyerman and Bennet, II, p. 40; Ellis, *Polynesian Researches*, IV, p. 41; Mathison, pp. 364–365; Stewart, *Journal of Residence*, pp. 99–100.

Liholiho lived in two worlds: SIM Journal, Apr. 15, 1820; E. Loomis, Feb. 5, Mar. 6, Apr. 8, Oct. 18, 1822; Marin, Feb. 26, Oct. 17, 1822; Bingham, *Residence*, p. 180.

Kamamalu was "a conspicuous object": Stewart, *Journal of Residence*, pp. 116–120.

LIHOLIHO IN LONDON pp. 71–75

The bracing morality of New England: Bingham to Evarts, Nov. 21, 1823, ABCFM.

"O Heaven! O earth!": Kamakau, *Ruling Chiefs*, pp. 256–257.

A new moral law: L. Chamberlain, Dec. 21, 1823; M. Loomis, Dec. 21, 1823; Whitney to Evarts, Jan. 4, 1824, ABCFM; Richards to Evarts, Aug. 13, 1824, ABCFM; Bingham, *Residence*, pp. 177–178, 212–214.

George Kaumualii's rebellion: L. Chamberlain, Oct. 12, 1824; E. Loomis, May, 1826; Bingham to Evarts, Sep. 8, 1824, ABCFM; Hoapili to Liholiho, Sep. 13, 1824, FO & Ex; Bingham and others to Evarts, Sep. 17, 1824, ABCFM; Whitney to Evarts, Sep. 30, 1824, ABCFM; Bingham to Parents, Oct. 30, 1824, Bingham Papers; Bingham, *Residence*, p. 239.

They bound a rebel leader: L. Chamberlain, Aug. 10, 1824.

L'Aigle appeared at Portsmouth: *London Times*, May 19, 1824. The London visit is described in Pleadwell; Frankenstein. See also letters of Byng to Granville, May 25–Nov. 19, 1824, PRO 30/29/7.

A "vulgar-looking man": Pleadwell, p. 10.

A "tall, fine, masculine figure": Pleadwell, p. 10.

"The King's name is Dog of Dogs": Bamford, I, pp. 315–316. This was a mistranslation.

That "pair of d – – – – d cannibals": Bamford, I, p. 319.

For the king and queen it was fatal: Documents on their illness and death are in FO & Ex, June–July, 1824.

Discussions with Canning followed: See documents in FO 58/3, July, 1824; *Poly*, Oct. 11, 1851.

Body snatchers: *London Times*, Sep. 2, 1824; *Morning Post*, Sep. 4, 1824.

Valentine Starbuck and Jean Rives: Kekuanaoa to Castle, Oct. 7, 1840, FO & Ex. See also documents in FO 58/3, Aug.–Oct., 1824, *Poly*, Oct. 4, 1851; Cottez, pp. 792–812, 819–844.

Funeral services at Kawaiahao Church: L. Chamberlain, Aug. 23, 1825.

Probation for six months: Bingham, *Residence*, p. 267.

FOREIGNERS AND FRENCH PRIESTS pp. 75–81

Oliver Holmes died: Chamberlain to Evarts, Aug. 27, 1825, ABCFM.

Drinking, gambling, and sleeping: Wildes to Marshall, Mar. 27, 1825, Marshall Mss.

A blast from the pulpit: SIM Journal, July 29, Sep. 29, Oct. 24, Nov. 6, 8, 1821; E. Loomis, Sep. 20, Oct. 23, 1821; L. Chamberlain, Sep. 7, 1823, Dec. 19, 1824.

A dollar a head: L. Chamberlain, Oct. 1, 1823, Feb. 25, 1825; Mathison, p. 437.

William Buckle: L. Chamberlain, Oct. 4, 7, 1825; E. Loomis, Oct. 4, 25, 28, 1825; Richards to Bro. B., Oct. 7, 1825, HMCS; Chamberlain to Ellis, Nov. 3, 1825, LMS.

A noisy public meeting: L. Chamberlain, Dec. 12, 1825; E. Loomis, Dec. 12, 1825.

Ten Commandments in Hawaiian: L. Chamberlain, Dec. 13, 1825.

Richard Charlton: His character may be observed in action in later chapters. A few representative comments are in: L. Chamberlain, Oct. 25, 29, 1827; Reynolds, July 13, 1828, Feb. 25–26, 1836, Oct. 11, 1837; Loomis to Ellis, July 21, 1827, LMS; Bears to Palmerston, Sep. 30, 1836, FO 58/8; Kamehameha III, Nahienaena and others to William IV, Nov., 1836, FO & Ex; Kamehameha III to William IV, 1837, Richards Papers; Statement of Kekauluohi, Kanaina, Kekuanaoa, Oct. 18, 1839, FO & Ex; Documents in FO & Ex, Oct., 1844; Jarves, *History of Sandwich Islands*, pp. 245–247; A. Simpson, pp. 57–58.

A pleasant young man: E. Loomis, May 22, 24, 1821; M. Loomis, May 22, 1821.

"Canting, hypocritical missionaries": Jones to Marshall & Wildes, Dec. 3, 1821, Marshall Mss.

"Nothing but the sound of the church going bell": Jones to Marshall, May 5, 1826, Marshall Mss.; Jones to Cooper, Mar. 7, 1832, Vallejo Documents.

Hannah Holmes shared Jones' bed: Chamberlain to Evarts, Feb. 22, 1827, ABCFM.

"Mad Jack" Percival and the *Dolphin*: E. Loomis, Jan. 27–May 11, 1826; L. Chamberlain, Feb. 19–May 11, 1826; Reynolds, Jan. 14–May 11, 1826; Chamberlain to Evarts, Feb. 7, Sep. 11, 1826, Feb. 22, 1827, Apr. 10, 1828, Aug. 3, 1829, ABCFM. See also Percival Inquiry.

The chiefs' long-standing debts: Kuykendall, *Hawaiian Kingdom*, I, pp. 434–436.

An informal treaty: *Treaties and Conventions*, pp. 1–2.

At their general meeting: "Unpublished Minutes of Prudential Meetings," Sep. 23, 28, 1826.

They published a circular: "To the Friends of Civilization and Christianity," Oct. 3, 1826, FO & Ex; L. Chamberlain, Oct. 27, 1826.

A public meeting on December 8: E. Loomis, Dec. 8, 1826; L. Chamberlain, Dec. 14, 1826; Richards and others to Evarts, Dec. 18, 1826, ABCFM; Ap Catesby Jones to Thurston and others, Jan. 2, 1827, ABCFM.

French Catholic missionaries: Yzendoorn, "Bibliography;" Blue, "Project For A French Settlement," pp. 85–89.

Enough to upset the Protestant missionaries: L. Chamberlain, July 29, Dec. 9, 1830; Bingham and others to Evarts, Jan. 1, 1829, ABCFM; "Unpublished Minutes of Prudential Meetings," Jan. 20, 1830; Bingham, *Residence*, pp. 373, 376, 394–405.

Hawaiian-language geography book: Bingham to Anderson, May 15, 1839, ABCFM; *He Hoikehonua.*

The *John Palmer*, Elisha Clarke, William Buckle, William Richards: Reynolds, Aug. 4–Nov. 26, 1827; L. Chamberlain, Aug. 15–Nov. 29, 1827; Chamberlain to Evarts, Sep. 14, 1827, ABCFM; Hoapili to Kaahumanu, Oct. 24, 1827, ABCFM; Malo to Loomis, Dec. 11, 1827, ABCFM; Richards to Anderson, Dec. 6, 1827, ABCFM.

A fundamental moral law: L. Chamberlain, Dec. 1, 7, 8, 1827; Richards to Anderson, Dec. 6, 1827, ABCFM.

A crowd gathered in a coconut grove: Reynolds, Dec. 8, 1827; L. Chamberlain, Dec. 14, 1827; Bingham to Evarts, Dec. 15, 1827, ABCFM.

THE TROUBLES OF BOKI pp. 82–87

Boki: Daws, "Boki," pp. 65–83.

A calabash of poi: L. Chamberlain, Nov. 13, 1826.

"It is with you": L. Chamberlain, Feb. 13, 1827.

Christian morality: L. Chamberlain, May 19, 23, 1827.

Boki's quiet support: *Annales* (1833), pp. 94–95; *Suppliment* [*sic*] *To The Sandwich Island Mirror* (1840), pp. 11–12; Ii, pp. 154–155.

Hale o Keawe: Clark to Hill, June 20, 1829, ABCFM; Bingham, *Residence*, p. 426.

Rumors: Reynolds, Apr. 1, 8, 9, 1829; L. Chamberlain, Apr. 4, 1829.

"Noisy swine gathered": Kamakau, *Ruling Chiefs*, p. 276.

"The king being desirous": Bingham, *Residence*, p. 343.

"Three native schooners arrived": L. Chamberlain, June 9, 1829.

The king and his sister had slept with each other: E. Loomis, June 28, 1824; L. Chamberlain, Feb. 10, 1826, Aug. 2, Dec. 18, 19, 22, 1828, June, 9, 1829; Reynolds, Dec. 15, 1827, Jan. 10, 1828, June 9, 11, 1829; Ellis, *Polynesian Researches*, IV, pp. 435–436.

"Mutually and strongly attached": Stewart, *Visit To South Seas*, II, pp. 192–202.

Chiefs denied the scandalous talk: Finch to King Kauikeaouli and Chiefs, Nov. 3, 1829, FO & Ex.

Dedication of a new church: L. Chamberlain, July 3, 1829.

A three-cornered menage: Reynolds, Aug. 6, 1827; Clark to Evarts, Dec. 12, 1829, ABCFM; L. Chamberlain, Apr. 2, 1831; Kamehameha III to Jones, Jan. 8, 1839, FO & Ex; Kaahumanu II to Van Buren, Jan. 12, 1839, FO & Ex.

Charlton's cow: L. Chamberlain, Oct. 5, 7, 9, 1829; Cow case and 1829 laws in FO & Ex, Oct. 5, 1829. See also documents in FO 58/5, Oct.–Nov., 1829.

A letter to the chiefs: L. Chamberlain, Mar. 6, 1829; Southard to Kamehameha III, Jan. 20, 1829, FO & Ex; Finch to Kauikeaouli, Nov. 21, 1829, FO & Ex; Stewart, *Visit to South Seas*, II, pp. 255–261.

Sandalwood debts: Acknowledgement by Kauikeaouli and others, Nov. 2, 1829, FO & Ex; Jones to Marshall, Oct. 4, 1830, Marshall Mss.

Boki's business enterprise: Kuykendall, "Some Early Commercial Adventurers."

Boki's sandalwood expedition: Daws, "Boki," pp. 80–81.

"Boki is at Waianae": Kamakau, *Ruling Chiefs*, p. 305; Yzendoorn, *History of Catholic Mission*, p. 52.

THE MORAL WARS pp. 87–91

Liliha's rebellion: Reynolds, Jan. 22, 24, 26, Mar. 7, 12, 15, 16, 1831; L. Chamberlain, Mar. 2, 3, 1831; Chamberlain to Ruggles, Feb. 26, 1831, HMCS; *Annales* (1833), pp. 103, 106; Bingham, *Residence*, p. 407.

The government's policy: Reynolds, Apr. 1, 1831; "The Word of Guidance By the King for the Management of the Kingdom," Apr. 1, 1831, FO & Ex.

Kuakini's policemen: L. Chamberlain, Apr. 1, 2, 1831; *Judd Fragments*, IV, pp. 20–25; Reynolds, Apr. 6, 7, May 1, 7, 1831; Clark to Anderson, Apr. 20, 1831, ABCFM; Bingham to Evarts, Nov. 23, 1831, ABCFM.

"Encroachments": French and others to Kauikeaouli, Apr. 7, 1831, FO & Ex; Clark to Evarts, Sep. 14, 1831, ABCFM.

Written charges and denials: Reynolds, Apr. 7–9, 1831; L. Chamberlain, Apr. 9, 1831; Bingham to Evarts, Nov. 23, 1831, ABCFM; Chamberlain to Evarts, Apr. 20, Dec. 5, 1831, ABCFM.

Catholicism ought to be extirpated: L. Chamberlain, Sep. 20, 21, 25, Oct. 18, 1830, Apr. 2, Sep. 8, 1831, Mar. 19, 1833; Chiefs to Bachelot and Short, Jan. 8, 1831, FO & Ex; Ejection order for priests by Kauikeaouli, Jan. 8, 1831, FO & Ex; Copy of Sumner's Commission, Nov. 5, 1831, FO & Ex; Clark to Anderson, Mar. 30, 1833, ABCFM.

Drummed to the waterfront: Reynolds, Dec. 23, 24, 1831; Bingham Journal, Dec. 24, 1831, ABCFM; L. Chamberlain, Dec. 24, 1831.

Idolatry and insubordination: Kaahumanu II to Elliott, Oct. 1, 1838, FO & Ex; Bingham, *Residence*, p. 394; Yzendoorn, *History Of Catholic Mission*, pp. 44–59.

Tacit approval of Protestant missionaries: L. Chamberlain, Nov. 5, 1831; Bingham to Evarts, Nov. 27, 1831, ABCFM; Clark to Anderson, Sep. 6, 1832, ABCFM.

"The Lord would open the way": Chamberlain to Greene, Nov. 6, 1830, ABCFM.

A case could easily be made: L. Chamberlain, Nov. 5, 1831; "Minutes of SIM General Meetings," Jan. 25, 1830; Anderson to SIM, Nov. 16, 1831, ABCFM, *General Letters;* Bingham to Evarts, Feb. 6, 1832, ABCFM; Clark to Anderson, Mar. 30, 1833, ABCFM.

Temperance society: L. Chamberlain, Sep. 7, 1831.

Smoking: Baldwin to Chamberlain and Judd, Aug. 9, 1832, HMCS; Richards to Chamberlain, Oct. 16, 1832, HMCS; Spaulding to ABCFM, Mar. 16, 1833, ABCFM; Spaulding to Anderson, Dec. 19, 1834, ABCFM.

Fifty thousand pupils: Bradley, pp. 147–149.

"The shell horn has been blowing": Tinker, July 19, 1831.

BIRD FEATHERS pp. 91–94

"Lo, here am I": Bingham, *Residence,* p. 433. See also Chapin to Anderson, May, 1832, ABCFM.

Kauikeaouli would rule: Bingham to Anderson, Mar. 20, 1833, ABCFM; "Proclamations Concerning Our Office," July 5, 1832, FO & Ex.

A tavern keeper: E. Loomis, Nov. 11, 1826; Reynolds, Jan. 6, 1828; Green to Anderson, Dec. 31, 1828, ABCFM; Bingham to Anderson, Aug. 16, 1833, ABCFM; Stewart, *Visit to South Seas,* II, pp. 252–253.

A practiced seducer: Reynolds, July 3, 1826, Feb. 5–8, 17, 18, 1827, July 12–31, Sep. 6–17, 1829, July 11, 17, 1831; L. Chamberlain, Oct. 21, 22, Dec. 31, 1831, Jan. 1–6, 12–17, 1832, Mar. 27, 29, May 23, 1834; Bingham to Evarts, Feb. 6, 1832, ABCFM; Chamberlain to Evarts, Feb. 6, 1832, ABCFM; Chamberlain to Ruggles, Feb. 7, 1832, HMCS; Armstrong to Chapman, Oct. 11, 1847, Armstrong Papers; Bond to ———, Jan, 10, 1848, ABCFM; Bingham, *Residence,* p. 428.

Kaomi and the Hulumanus: L. Chamberlain, Feb. 4, 21, Mar. 9, 12, Apr. 13, Oct. 12, 13, Nov. 7, 1833; Reynolds, July 15, 23, 25, 1833; Chamberlain to Anderson, Mar. 26, 1833, ABCFM.

Complete control of the government: Proclamation of Kauikeaouli, Mar. 14, 1833, FO & Ex; Reynolds, Mar. 15, 16, 1833; Peirce to Hunnewell, Aug. 10, 1833, Hunnewell Papers.

A gorgeous uniform: Reynolds, Mar. 15, 18, 19, 1834; Statement of Charlton and others, Mar. 19, 1834, FO & Ex.

Kauikeaouli had tried to kill himself: Reynolds, June 8–10, 1834; L. Chamberlain, June 11, 1834.

He slept with Nahienaena: L. Chamberlain, June 11, July 22, 1834; Reynolds, July 22, 1834; Tinker, July 29, 1834; Baldwin to Chamberlain, Sep. 16, 1834, HMCS; Chapin to Ruggles, Sep. 30, 1834, HMCS; Records of the Church at Lahaina, July 22, Aug. 7, 1834, HMCS.

A new code of laws: Bingham to Wisner and others, Jan. 6, 1835, ABCFM; *He Olelo No Ka Kanawai.*

Nahienaena was uncontrollable: L. Chamberlain, Apr. 27, July 22, 1834, Jan. 5, May 27, 1835, Dec. 21, 1838; Reynolds, July 3, 1836, Jan. 12, 14, 1837, Dec. 29–31, 1840, Jan. 1, 2, 1841; Andrews to Chamberlain, Jan. 6, 1834, HMCS; Chapin to Ruggles, Sep. 30, 1834, HMCS; Richards to Anderson, Oct. 15, 1834, ABCFM; Green to Anderson, Nov. 12, 1834, ABCFM; Chapin to Chamberlain, Jan. 8, 1835, HMCS; Andrews to Chamberlain, Jan. 19, 1835, HMCS; Andrews to Richards, Jan. 22, 1835, HMCS; Baldwin to Chamberlain, Feb. 2, 1835, HMCS; Richards to Anderson, Feb. 17, 1835, ABCFM; Baldwin to Chamberlain, Mar. 22, 1835, HMCS; Dimond to Dimond, Sep., 1835, Dimond Papers; Armstrong to Anderson, May 5, 1836, ABCFM; Green to

Anderson, July 22, 1836, ABCFM; Baldwin to Chamberlain, Aug. 13, 1836, HMCS; Baldwin to Chamberlain, Apr. 28, 1837, HMCS; Andrews to Chamberlain, Jan. 4, 1840, HMCS; Bishop to Gilman, Jan. 5, 1901, S. Bishop Ltr. Bk.; Records of the Church at Lahaina, Feb. 5, May 25, 1835, HMCS; Report of the Lahaina Station, [June], 1835, HMCS; *SIG*, Sep. 17, 1836, Jan. 7, 14, Feb. 11, Apr. 15, 1837; *Poly*, Dec. 26, 1846; Jarves, *Scenes and Scenery*, pp. 33–38.

ONCE MORE THE PRIESTS pp. 94–96

Walsh was saved from expulsion: L. Chamberlain, Nov. 12, 1836.

The *Clementine:* Reynolds, June 14, 15, 1837; Kamehameha III to Walsh, Dec. 5, 1836, FO & Ex; Bingham to Baldwin, July, 1837, HMCS; Bingham to Judd, July 13, 1837, Bingham Papers. See also documents in FO & Ex, 1837.

Belcher and du Petit-Thouars: See documents in FO & Ex, July 21, 1837.

An edict signed on December 18: See FO & Ex, Dec. 18, 1837.

Native Catholics came under harassment: Anderson to SIM, June 30, 1838, ABCFM, *General Letters*.

Arrest of the Waianae Catholics: *SIG*, June 22, 1839; Yzendoorn, *History Of Catholic Mission*, p. 128.

They were shackled: Reynolds, June 25, 26, 1839.

Nine native Catholics remained in jail: *SIG*, July 6, 1839.

THE GREAT AWAKENING pp. 97–102

Embarrassed letters: Whitney to Anderson, Nov. 23, 1832, ABCFM; Richards to Anderson, Dec. 7, 1832, ABCFM; Bingham to Anderson, Mar. 20, 1833, ABCFM; Chamberlain to Anderson, Mar. 26, 1833, ABCFM; Clark to Anderson, Mar. 30, 1833, ABCFM; Statement of Dibble, June 10, 1833, ABCFM; Judd to Anderson, Oct. 23, 1833, ABCFM; Andrews to Anderson, Dec. 21, 1834, ABCFM.

The complete Bible in Hawaiian: *Ka Palapala Hemolele*.

Smoking: Bingham to Clark, [1832], HMCS; Spaulding to [Anderson], Mar. 16, 1833, ABCFM.

Total abstinence: Spaulding and Richards, "Brief History Of Temperance [1823–1835]," ABCFM; *Hawaiian Spectator* (1838), pp. 335–336.

A curious situation: L. Chamberlain, Feb. 9, 1832; C. Forbes, Sep. 8, 1832; Cooke, Jan. 3, 6, 7, 26, Feb. 3, 18, 22, Apr. 5, 1838; Richards to Evarts, June 1, 1824, ABCFM; Goodrich to Evarts, July 14, 1828, ABCFM; Forbes to Anderson, Nov., 1832, ABCFM; *Poly*, Aug. 8, 1840; Stewart, *Visit to South Seas*, II, pp. 106–108.

Puaaiki: Clark to Anderson, Nov. 1, 1843, HMCS; *Ka Nonanona*, Nov. 14, 1843; Green.

A point of honor to go slowly: Richards to Anderson, May 20, 1828, ABCFM; Bingham to Anderson, Dec. 28, 1828, ABCFM.

Charles Grandison Finney: *Judd Fragments*, IV, pp. 28–29; Tinker, May 11, 18, Oct. 12, 1836, Feb. 22, Mar. 8, 22, 1837; Cooke, Aug. 31, 1837, Oct. 15, Dec. 8, 14, 1839; Letters of Judd to Finneys, 1826–1837, Finney Papers; Cooke to

Brother Charles, Mar. 28, 1837, HMCS; S. Bishop, *Reminiscences,* p. 55.

Titus Coan: Humphrey; Thompson, pp. 31–45.

"Hard as a nether millstone": Coan to Coan, Aug. 29, 1837, Coan Letters.

"On the 7th of November": T. Coan, pp. 51–53.

"Compact rows": T. Coan, pp. 45–46.

"Sacramental host": Coan to Coan, Mar. 16, 1839, Coan Letters.

"Whose arm is omnipotant": Coan to Coan, Mar. 16, 1839, Coan Letters.

Weeping, shouting, and falling: Coan to Coan, Mar. 9, 18, 1838, Mar. 16, 1839, Coan Letters.

Critics of the revival: Forbes to Lyons, Feb. 2, 1838, Nov. 18, 1840, HMCS; Chamberlain to Anderson, Feb. 7, 1839, HMCS; Armstrong to Junkin, July 9, 1840, Oct. 12, 1841, HMCS; Armstrong to Anderson, Sep. 23, 1841, ABCFM.

Hiram Bingham: Smith to Anderson, Nov. 20, 1837, ABCFM; Bingham to Baldwin, Jan. 15, 1838, HMCS; Bingham to Anderson, Mar. 3, Apr. 26, July 30, 1838, Apr. 19, 1839, ABCFM.

Dwight Baldwin: Baldwin to Chamberlain, Jan. 9, Aug. 6, 1838, HMCS.

"Excited minds" and "peculiar views": Dibble, pp. 348–349.

"I have little fear": L. Coan, pp. 43, 49.

Lyons attracted to the Millerites: Bond to Chamberlain, Jan. 24, 1844, HMCS.

Church membership: Anderson, *History Of SIM,* pp. 116–117.

Coan baptized 1705: Coan to Lord, Oct. 21, 1848, HMCS; Bond to Pogue, Nov. 28, 1870, HMCS; T. Coan, p. 57; S. Bishop, *Reminiscences,* pp. 54–55.

Lyons could not hold his converts: Report of the Waimea Station, 1839–1845, HMCS.

"To die in the field": L. Coan, p. 47.

Coan's death: L. Coan, pp. 185, 204.

THE END OF THE HOLY COMMUNITY pp. 103–105

Laplace's manifesto: Laplace to Kamehameha III, July 10, 1839, FO & Ex. See also Reynolds, July 9–Aug. 16, 1839; L. Chamberlain, July 10–Aug. 15, 1839; Cooke, July 10–Aug. 15, 1839; Brinsmade to Citizens of US resident at Sandwich Islands, July 9, 1839, Brinsmade Papers; Ii to Kekuanaoa, July 12, 1839, FO & Ex; American citizens' protest, July 12, 1839, FO & Ex; Kekauluohi and Kekuanaoa to Laplace, July 13, 1839, FO & Ex.

"Unbridled lust": Castle to Anderson, Sep. 16, 1839, ABCFM.

Baldwin's passport: Baldwin to Brinsmade, Nov. 15, 1839, Brinsmade Papers.

Treaty of commerce and friendship: Laplace treaty, July, 1839, FO & Ex; L. Chamberlain, July 9, 10, 13, 19, 1839; Kekuanaoa to Laplace, July 10, 1839, Minister of Foreign Affairs, *Report,* 1851, Appendix, p. 302; Dudoit to Kamehameha III, Aug. 8, 1839, FO & Ex; *SIG,* July 13, 20, 27, 1839.

Meddling, dogmatical preacher: L. Chamberlain, Sep. 5, 1826.

Bingham was never able to see: Cooke, Oct. 25, Nov. 1, 1839; Reynolds, Aug. 3, 1840; Chamberlain to Evarts, Sep. 11, 1826, ABCFM; Bingham to Mother, Apr. 4, 1829, Bingham Papers; Bingham to Cornelius, Apr. 6, 1832, ABCFM; Bingham to Anderson, Mar. 20, 1833, ABCFM; Armstrong to Chapman, Mar. 5, Sep. 27, 1842, July 18, 1844, Armstrong Papers; Armstrong to Chapman, Nov., 1843, Armstrong Papers.

"When I was a boy of fourteen": Bingham to Anderson, Aug. 5, 1835, ABCFM.
A six hundred page autobiography: Bingham, *Residence*.
Forward to independence: Coan and others to ABCFM, June, 1846, ABCFM;
   Poly, Aug. 26, 1854; Hawaiian Evangelical Association, *Proceedings,* 1863,
   pp. 35–54; ABCFM, *Report,* 1870, pp. 82–94; Anderson, *Hawaiian Islands,*
   pp. 307–328.
Unsullied by contact with rude natives: Tinker, Jan. 22, 1838; Blatchely to
   Evarts, —— 15, 1824, ABCFM; Bingham to Evarts, Oct. 15, 1828, ABCFM;
   Chamberlain to Jones, Nov. 18, 1831, HMCS; Chamberlain to Anderson,
   Oct. 16, 1832, ABCFM; Richards to Anderson, Dec. 7, 1832, ABCFM; Good-
   rich to Barnes, May 15, 1833, HMCS; Bingham to Ruggles, Jan. 8, 1834,
   HMCS; Thurston to Goodell, Oct. 23, 1834, ABCFM; Emerson to Anderson,
   Apr. 8, Nov. 19, 1835, ABCFM; Thurston to Anderson, July 2, 1835, ABCFM;
   Goodrich to Bingham, Dec. 11, 1835, HMCS; Chamberlain to Anderson, Oct.
   31, 1836, ABCFM; Tinker to Anderson, Dec. 1, 1836, ABCFM; Chamberlain
   to Children, Dec. 17, 1836, HMCS; Coan to Sister Cooke, Jan., 1839, HMCS;
   Cooke to Brother, Jan. 28, 1840, HMCS; Armstrong to Junkin, July 9, 1840,
   HMCS; Cooke to Mother, July 28, 1841, HMCS; Baldwin to Robinson, Nov.
   19, 20, 1847, HMCS; Cooke to Mother, July 4, 1848, HMCS; Chamberlain to
   Brother and Sister, Sep. 7, 1848, HMCS; Bailey to Mother, Oct. 23, 1849,
   HMCS; "Unpublished Minutes of Prudential Meetings," Sep. 26, Oct. 7, 1826;
   Lucy Thurston, *Life And Times,* pp. 101–102; Jarves, *Scenes and Scenery,*
   pp. 67–68; S. Bishop, *Reminiscences,* pp. 15, 20.
Marriage: Armstrong to Chapman, Apr.–May 3, 1836, Armstrong Papers; Judd to
   Armstrong, Feb. 13, 1853, Armstrong Papers.
Hawaiian Evangelical Association: Hawaiian Evangelical Association, *Proceed-
   ings,* 1863.
Christian chiefs backslid: L. Chamberlain, Apr. 2, 1848; Armstrong to Ander-
   son, Nov. 2, 1846, ABCFM; Coan to Anderson, Feb. 12, 1847, ABCFM;
   Records of the Church at Lahaina, July 21, 1844, HMCS; M. Alexander, p.
   273; Bradley, p. 375.
Offences against the moral laws: Gregg Diary, Aug. 11, 1854; Bishop to Ander-
   son, Oct. 26, 1840, ABCFM. See also Chief Justice, *Report,* 1851–1860.
Sin no longer flourished there: Twain, *Sandwich Islands,* pp. 28–29. See also
   Wyllie to Ten Eyck, Apr. 26, 1850, FO Ltr. Bk. 13; Knudsen to Wyllie,
   Feb. 23, 1865, FO & Ex; Cooke to Amos, May 19, 1865, HMCS; *Haw.
   Gaz.,* Aug. 14, 1867.

Chapter 4: The Nation—1839–1854

LARGE AND UNFAMILIAR FISHES pp. 106–112

"If a big wave comes in": Malo to Kaahumanu II and Mathew, Aug. 18, 1837,
   FO & Ex.
Naive despotism: Cooke, Feb. 7, 1839; Ely to Evarts, Oct. 11, 1824, ABCFM;
   Gulick to Evarts, May 13, 1829, ABCFM; Miller memo, Sep. 25, 1831, FO &

Ex; Emerson to Chamberlain, June 23, 1837, HMCS; Hopu to Kamehameha III, May 21, 1838, Int. Dept. Ltrs. Misc.; Chamberlain to Anderson, Feb. 7, 1839, HMCS; Armstrong to Chapman, Feb. 18, 1840, Armstrong Papers; *Poly,* Oct. 23, 1841.

William Richards: Richards to Chamberlain, July 10, 1838, HMCS.

Religious toleration: *Hawaiian Spectator* (1839), p. 469.

Declaration of rights: *Ke Kumu Kanawai.*

Elementary schools: Kuykendall, *Hawaiian Kingdom,* I, p. 347 ff.

Constitution of 1840: *Poly,* Oct. 16, 1841.

National legislature: Spaulding, "Early Years."

Organic acts: *Statute Laws of His Majesty Kamehameha III.*

Land system: *Indices of Land Commission Awards,* intro.

Constitution of 1852: *Laws,* 1852, pp. 3–17.

James Jackson Jarves: Steegmuller, generally.

John Ricord: Miller to Palmerston, May 10, 1847, FO 58/56; Ricord to Cabinet Council, June 11, 1847, FO & Ex; Cabinet Council Minutes, June 12, 17, 1847; *SIN,* Aug. 31, 1848; Hines, 224–225; Williston, 86–87.

William Little Lee: Giffin, generally.

Robert Crichton Wyllie: Wyllie to Judd, Mar. 21, 1845, FO Ltr. Bk. 5; *Friend,* Nov., 1865.

White men working for government: Armstrong to Chapman, Oct. 11, 1847, Armstrong Papers.

"Gold, to be sure": *Poly,* May 23, 1846. See also Colcord, p. 91.

Missionary decision to go into government: Bond to Chamberlain, Mar. 14, 1843, HMCS; Armstrong to Chapman, Nov., 1843, June 8, 1844, Armstrong Papers; Baldwin to Greene, Sep. 21, 1844, ABCFM; Baldwin to Chamberlain, May 26, 1845, HMCS; Baldwin to Hall, June 3, 1845, HMCS; Alexander to Hall, Sep., 1845, HMCS; Smith to Anderson, Nov. 28, 1846, ABCFM; *SIN,* May 4, 1848.

Political creed: "Political Creed and Principles," June 19, 1845, FO & Ex.

"If this kingdom is to be ours": Petitions in FO & Ex, 1845.

Storming the fort at Lahaina: Reynolds, June 15, 1845; Kaumaea to Kamehameha III, Aug., 1845, FO & Ex; Baldwin to Hall, Nov. 5, 1845, HMCS; Baldwin to Greene, Nov. 8. 1846, ABCFM; Testimony taken by king's commission, June 12, 1845, FO & Ex; Journal of House of Nobles, June 25, 1845; Privy Council Minutes, Oct. 8, 1845, FO & Ex; Deposition of Henry Bennet, July 14, 1848, FO & Ex; Deposition of John Richards, July 16, 1848, FO & Ex; Privy Council Record, Aug. 15, 1848; L. Judd, pp. 137, 139, 145.

"Words only": Privy Council Record, July 14, 1848.

"In an old grass house": Dutton, *William L. Lee,* [8].

The courts were God Almighty: Brown to Calhoun, Jan. 18, 1845, USDS, Disp., Haw.; Statement of Robson and others, Mar. 5, 1845, FO & Ex; Wyllie to Miller, Feb. 2, 1846, FO & Ex; *SIN,* Dec. 9, 1846.

Wyllie's ability to split a single hair: *SIN,* Nov. 18, 1846. See also Gregg to Marcy, Aug. 20, 1856, Gregg Ltr. Bk.

Gerrit Judd: L. Chamberlain, Feb. 8, 1844; Reynolds, Nov. 9, 1844; G. P. Judd, 146.

Code of Etiquette: *Order in Council of His Hawaiian Majesty, Prescribing a Code of Etiquette*; *Poly*, July 20, 1844.

Manuscript list of grievances: Ten Eyck to Buchanan, Dec. 21, 1846, USDS, Disp., Haw.

The kingdom's treaty relations: Davis.

"Such has always been the case": Malo to Kaahumanu II and Mathew, Aug. 18, 1837, FO & Ex.

The captain of a clipper ship: Gregg to Harris, Feb. 3, 1854, Gregg Ltr. Bk.

THEIR FINEST HOUR pp. 112–120

The matter at issue was land: AH has several items bound together under the general title of *Charlton Land Pamphlets*. See also Charlton lease, Dec. 9, 1826, FO & Ex; Interview between Charlton, Kekauluohi and Kekuanaoa, Apr. 16, 1840, FO & Ex; Kamehameha III to Charlton, Apr. 18, Jun. 30, 1840, FO & Ex.

Charlton found it hard to stay out of trouble: L. Chamberlain, Mar. 8, 1841; Kekuanaoa to Charlton, Jan. 16, 1841, Feb. 7, 1842, FO & Ex; *Poly*, Mar. 13, 1841.

A single curt note: Charlton to Kamehameha III, Sep. 26, 1842, FO & Ex.

Sir George Simpson: G. Simpson, II, pp. 171–172.

A diplomatic mission: See documents in FO & Ex, July 9, 1842.

Alexander Simpson was a strong imperialist: A Simpson, generally.

Charlton owed a business firm: *Correspondence Relative to the Sandwich Islands*, generally.

Simpson wrote to the commander: Simpson to Barrow, Nov. 1, 1842, FO & Ex.

"Rather to strengthen those authorities": Canning to Barrow, Oct. 4, 1842, FO 58/13.

"Immediate coercive steps": Paulet to Kamehameha III, Feb. 17, 1843, FO & Ex. Paulet's dealings are collected in FO & Ex as British Commission Documents.

The agreement: Paty, Feb. 18, 1843; Gilman Journal, July, 1843; Cooke to Mother and others, Dec. 15, 1842, HMCS; Cooke to Uncles and others, Dec. 16, 1842, HMCS.

The demands became so pressing: "Dispute with Paulet," Feb. 1843, FO & Ex.

"Hear ye!": Kuykendall, *Hawaiian Kingdom,* I, p. 216.

"Refined cruelty": L. Judd, p. 120.

A commission was to be created: British Commission Documents, 1843, FO & Ex.

James F. B. Marshall's mission: Paty, Mar. 11, 1843; Document at Mar. 2, 1843, FO & Ex.

As soon as the commission government began its work: Kekuanaoa to Haalilio and Richards, Mar. 6, 1843, FO & Ex; Register of land claims in British Commission Documents, FO & Ex.

Judd resigned: Kamehameha III to Judd, June 12, 1843, FO & Ex; *Judd Fragments*, I, pp. 19–20.

The independence of the kingdom would be restored: Thomas to Kekuanaoa, July 26, 1843, FO & Ex.

Restoration ceremonies: British Commission Documents, July 31, 1843, FO & Ex.

"Ua mau ke ea": Kamehameha's words became the official motto of Hawaii.

To mark the restoration: Restoration documents are in FO & Ex, July, 1843; Gilman Journal, July 31, 1843.

"Hail to the worthy name": Restoration Anthem, 1843, HHS.

British government disavowed seizure of islands: Aberdeen to Haalilio and Richards, Nov. 15, 1843, FO & Ex.

Thomas suffered through temperance dinners: L. Chamberlain, Sep. 14, 1843; L. Judd, pp. 125–127.

Paulet ordered his gunners to fire: Judd to Wyllie, Sep. 4, 1844, FO & Ex; *Poly,* Aug. 17, Sep. 7, 1844.

Paulet's clothes stolen: Wyllie to Judd, Oct. 7, 1844, FO & Ex; Wyllie to Paulet, Oct. 8, 1844, FO & Ex.

Independence mission of Richards and Haalilio: Richards Journal, 1842–1845; Kuykendall, *Hawaiian Kingdom*, I, p. 192 ff.

Tyler adminstration's views: Richardson, IV, pp. 211–214.

Britain recognized independence: Aberdeen to Cowley, July 21, 1843, FO 27/663.

Dual agreement of Britain and France: Kuykendall, *Hawaiian Kingdom,* I, pp. 202–203.

Britain drafted a new treaty: *Friend,* Feb., 1844.

Charlton's claim to Pulaholaho: Statement of Facts, FO Ltr. Bk. 8, p. 312 ff; Miller to Judd, Mar. 27, 1844, FO & Ex. See also Depositions of Witnesses, 1845, FO & Ex.

George Pelly was a sodomite: *Report of the Case of George Pelly Vs. Richard Charlton.*

A few shade trees: See letters of Wyllie to Miller, Apr., 1847, FO & Ex.

"Close over Charlton and his mysteries": Wyllie to Miller, Aug. 29, 1851, FO & Ex.

LADD & CO. pp. 120–124

These were useful recommendations: L. Chamberlain, July 27, 1833; Reynolds, July 27, 29, Aug. 8, 1833.

Koloa: Jackson, generally.

A more ambitious scheme: Kuykendall, *Hawaiian Kingdom,* I, p. 178.

Secret contract, November, 1841: Contract in FO & Ex, Nov. 24, 1841.

Belgian Contract, May, 1843: Contract in British Commission Documents, 1843, FO & Ex.

They had sold a half interest in Koloa: Severance to Webster, Jan. 6, 1852, USDS, Disp., Haw.

Interest rates were ruinous: Reynolds, 1844, generally.

"No small sum": Richards to Brinsmade, May 4, 1844, FO & Ex.

A bankrupt firm: Judd to Simpson, Apr. 2, 1845, FO Ltr. Bk. 9; Wyllie to Simpson, Apr. 10, 1845, FO Ltr. Bk. 9; Judd to Ladd & Co., June 12, 1845, Int. Dept. Ltr. Bk. 1.

Ladd used a familiar defense: Protest of Ladd, Aug. 15, 1845, FO & Ex.

Sue for damages: Statement, Jan. 15, 1847, FO & Ex; Brown to Buchanan, May 16, 1846, USDS, Disp., Haw.; *SIN,* Sep. 23, 1846.

Ten Eyck became the firm's principal counsel: *Report of the Proceedings and Evidence in Arbitration Between King and Government and Messrs Ladd & Co;* Ten Eyck to Buchanan, Dec. 20, 1847, USDS, Disp., Haw.

Gerrit Judd retaliated: Privy Council Record, Dec. 26, 1848, Jan. 3, 1849.

The firm withdrew its suit: Privy Council Record, May 17, 1847.

The villain was Gerrit Judd: Wyllie to Judd, Nov. 18, 1847, FO & Ex; *SIN,* Aug. 25, 1847; *Hawaiian Reports,* I, pp. 17–20.

"We all rejoiced": Armstrong to Chapman, Mar. 8, 1848, Armstrong Papers.

A tiny plot of land on Kauai: Lot Kamehameha to Kanoa, Feb. 21, 1857, Int. Dept. Ltr. Bk. 6; Wyllie to Brinsmade, Mar. 27, 1857, FO Ltr. Bk. 26; Cabinet Council Minutes, May 29, 1856.

THE GREAT MAHELE pp. 124–128

"From uka, mountain": Lyons, *History of Hawaiian Government Survey,* p. 24. See also Richards to Wilkes, Mar. 15, 1841, Richards Papers.

Industry and thrift: *Poly,* Feb. 3, 1849.

Rights of ownership: Kamehameha III to William IV, 1836, Richards Papers; Dole, "Evolution."

Lease land to white men: Kekuanaoa to Dudoit, July 7, 1840, FO & Ex; *Poly,* June 19, 1841.

"This measure will do much credit": *Friend,* Oct., 1844.

A Board of Land Commissioners: *Poly,* May 31, 1845, July 29, 1854; *Principles Adopted By Board of Commissioners to Quiet Land Titles.*

The Great Mahele: Lyons, *History of Hawaiian Government Survey,* pp. 4–5, 31; Spaulding, *Crown Lands,* pp. 12, 13; Chinen, generally. AH has the Ms. version of the Mahele Book.

Businessmen and missionaries: Reports to Privy Council, May 25, Aug. 19, 1850, FO & Ex; Minister of Interior, *Report,* 1850, p. 13, 1851, p. 9; *Poly,* July 13, 1850, May 8, 1852; Hobbs, p. 157 ff.

The humblest of men: See Ms. volumes of Foreign Testimony, Register, and Awards, AH.

"You can never know": L. Judd, p. 247.

Kuleana claims, chiefs', government, crown lands: *Poly,* Apr. 29, 1848.

Surveyors: Lyons, "Early Surveying"; Lyons, *History of Hawaiian Government Survey,* pp. 6–15, 35, 38; W. D. Alexander, *Brief Account of Hawaiian Government Survey.*

WHO IS THE DESPOTIC DR. JUDD? pp. 128–131

He handled all sorts of governmental business: Gilman, "Honolulu—1848"; Privy Council Record, Jan. 9, 31, 1849; L. Judd, pp. 239–248.

"I am at present": Judd to Pearce, Jan. 1, 1845, FO & Ex.

The oath of allegiance: Hooper to Citizens of the US Resident at the Sandwich Islands, Aug. 12, 1845, USDS, Disp., Haw.; Wyllie to Seymour, Oct. 10, 1845, FO Ltr. Bk. 5; Miller to Aberdeen, Nov. 1, 1845, FO 58/36.

"Who is the despotic Dr. Judd?": Miller to Foreign Office, Mar. 18, 1846, FO 58/44.

"War with the government": Brown to Calhoun, Dec. 26, 1844, USDS, Disp., Haw.; Judd to Pearce, Jan. 1, 1845, FO & Ex; Statement of Brewer, Feb. 26, 1845, FO & Ex; Statement of Marshall, Feb. 26, 1845, FO & Ex; Brown to Judd, Mar. 7, 1845, FO & Ex; *SIN,* Apr. 21, 1847.

The impeachment of Judd: Depositions at the Palace, Mar. 14–25, 1845, FO & Ex.

A kind of diplomatic limbo: Documents, May 10, 1845, FO & Ex; Wyllie to Brown, Apr. 3, 1845, FO & Ex; Privy Council Record, July 29, 1845.

He had Charles Brewer removed: Wyllie to Secretary of State, Peru, Mar. 31, 1846, FO & Ex.

Robertson brought charges against him: Robertson to Kamehameha III, Oct. 11, 1848, FO & Ex; Privy Council Record, Nov. 30, 1848–Apr. 23, 1849.

The Tongataboo Letters: *SIN,* Sep. 30, Oct. 7, 14, 21, Nov. 18, Dec. 2, 1846.

The handwriting on one set of sheets: Ten Eyck to Wyllie, Dec. 8, 1848, FO & Ex; Documents, Dec. 9, 1848, FO & Ex; Wyllie to Ten Eyck, Dec. 13, 1848, FO Ltr. Bk. 13a; Ten Eyck to Buchanan, Dec. 18, 1848, USDS, Disp., Haw.

Kauikeaouli closed correspondence with him: Wyllie to Ten Eyck, Dec. 13, 1848, FO & Ex; *Poly,* Jan. 19, 1850.

Judd's machiavellian methods: Ana to Kamehameha III, Dec. 10, 1848, Int. Dept. Ltrs. Misc; Armstrong to Kamehameha III, Dec. 11, 1848, FO & Ex.

"I would wash my hands": Wyllie to Armstrong, Dec. 2, 1848, FO Ltr. Bk. 10.

Peacock's patriotic reasons: Privy Council Record, Dec. 27, 1848; Privy Council of Emergency, Dec. 27, 1848, FO & Ex.

It was a dirty business: Ten Eyck to Wyllie, Dec. 8, 1848, FO & Ex.

No monetary value: Lee to Wyllie, Dec. 9, 1848, FO & Ex.

Voted to reimburse Judd: Privy Council Record, Apr. 24, 1849, Jan. 30, 1850.

The grey eminence of government: Wyllie and others to Kamehameha III, Apr. 23, 1849, FO & Ex.

TREATIES pp. 132–136

Wyllie's "grand design": Wyllie to de Medean, Feb. 7, 1857, FO & Ex; *Treaties and Conventions*; Blue, "Policy of France Toward Hawaiian Islands."

Questions unresolved: Heurtel to Kekauluohi, Sep. 20, 1842, FO & Ex.

"Moderation mades secure": Kuykendall, *Hawaiian Kingdom,* I, p. 389.

Dillon stayed on at Honolulu: Minister of Foreign Relations, *Report,* 1848, Appendix, pp. 18–35. See also scores of documents in FO & Ex, 1848, 1849.

Jarves commissioned: Steegmuller, p. 90 ff.

"All the means at his disposal": De Tromelin's letters are with other documents, Aug. 17–Sep. 14, 1849, FO & Ex.

They proceeded to wreck the fort: Turrill to Wyllie, Aug. 25, 1849, FO & Ex; Miller to Tromelin, Aug. 27, 1849, FO & Ex; Armstrong to Chapman, Sep. 5–Oct. 20, 1849, Armstrong Papers; Wyllie to Judd, Sep. 10, 1849, FO Ltr. Bk. 13; Committee report, Sep. 10, 1849, FO & Ex; Statement in Int. Dept. Ltr. Bk. 5, Part 1, pp. 354–355.

A scheme to fool the French: Cooke, Aug. 30, Sep. 4, 1849.

The royal yacht: *Poly,* Nov. 10, 1849.

His instructions were broad indeed: Copies of secret instructions are at Sep. 25, 1849, FO & Ex; Copies of Commission, Sep. 10, 1849, FO & Ex.

Alexander Liholiho and Lot: Adler, *Journal of Alexander Liholiho.*

Judd and Eames negotiate a treaty: A copy is in FO & Ex.

Jarves and Clayton negotiate a treaty: A copy is in FO & Ex.

In France Judd had no luck at all: G. P. Judd, p. 164 ff.

Perrin had "extraordinary" powers: Perrin's correspondence for 1850 and 1851 is in FO & Ex.

Miller advised the king: Miller to Palmerston, Mar. 18, 1851, FO 58/70.

Severance conferred with Gardner: Severance to Webster, Mar. 11–21, 31, 1851, USDS, Disp., Haw.; Wyllie to Miller, Mar. 13, 1851, FO & Ex; Miller to Palmerston, Mar. 18, 27, 1851, FO 58/70; Armstrong to Chapman, Mar. 29, 1851, Armstrong Papers. A very good account of the period is in Kuykendall, *Hawaiian Kingdom,* I, pp. 400–405.

"You will declare openly": Kuykendall, *Hawaiian Kingdom,* I, p. 407.

A foreign resident reviewed the record: *Poly,* Sep. 15, 1849. See also Wyllie to Allen, Sep. 21, 1857, FO Ltr. Bk. 47.

Yet another unsatisfactory treaty: Liholiho to Webster, Oct. 2, 1861, Henriques Collection.

WHEN THE BOUGH BREAKS pp. 137–146

Miller predicted that trouble would follow: Miller to Addington, Sep. 2, 1847, FO 58/56.

"Restless young bloods": R. Armstrong, Oct. 15, 1851; *Poly,* Nov. 8, 1851.

For "every one dead 100 stout yankees": Wyllie to Lee, Nov. 5, 1851, FO & Ex. See also Wyllie to Hopkins, Nov. 20, 1851, FO Ltr. Bk. 15; Privy Council Record, Nov. 10, 1851.

Brannan planned to set up a new government: Parke, pp. 27–31.

Rifling the *Game Cock's* mail bags: *Weekly Argus,* Mar. 10, 1852; *Poly,* Mar. 13, 1852.

Brannan and his men reported unfavorably: Heap to Wyllie, Jan. 16, 1852, FO & Ex.

Sailors' riot of 1852: Armstrong to Armstrong, Oct. 17, 1852, Armstrong Papers; Severance to Webster, Nov. 13, 1852, USDS, Disp., Haw.; Privy Council Record, Nov. 11, 1852; *Poly,* Nov. 13, 20, 1852.

"There were six out of the number": Parke, pp. 35–44.

The *Charles Mallory: Poly,* Feb. 12, 1853.

Royal Commissioners of Health: Greer, *"Oahu's Ordeal,"* deals exhaustively with the epidemic.

National humiliation: Privy Council Record, June 9, 1853; Bishop to Anderson, July 6, 1853, ABCFM; *Poly,* June 11, 1853; Severance to Marcy, July 2, 9, 1853, USDS, Disp., Haw.

Reported cases and deaths: Statistics are collected in Greer, "Oahu's Ordeal."

They paid a terrible price: Cooke, June 17, 24, 28, 1853; Hillebrand to Rooke,

June 14, 1853, Board of Health; Bond to Gentlemen, June 27, 1853, Board of Health.

At Honolulu life fell apart: *Poly*, Aug. 6, 1853.

Wagoners became hardened to death: Damon to Commissioner of Health, July 26, 1853, Board of Health.

Buried at Kakaako: Royal Commissioners of Public Health to Volunteers, Aug. 23, 1853, Board of Health.

Letter by "A Physician": *Poly*, July 16, 1853.

Seven resolutions: *Poly*, July 16, 1853.

A "pungent" series of resolutions: *Weekly Argus*, July 21, 1853; *Poly*, July 23, 1853.

Judd and Armstrong had not used their powers: Removal Letters, 1853, FO & Ex.

"Their inefficiency and misdeeds": Removal Letters, 1853, FO & Ex; *Poly*, Aug. 20, 1853.

Signatures on the petitions: Against Removal, 1853, FO & Ex; Removal Letters, 1853, FO & Ex.

No real grounds for dismissal: Ana to Blair, Aug. 17, 1853, Int. Dept. Ltr. Bk. 6.

The final decision: Cabinet Council Minutes, Aug. 3, 1853; Privy Council Record, Aug. 15, 17, 1853.

Judd resigned from the Royal Commission of Health: Privy Council Record, Aug. 22, 1853.

The king directed all his ministers to resign: Privy Council Record, Sep. 5, 1853.

The end of the "malignant tyranny": *Poly*, Oct. 22, 1853.

A torchlight procession: *Weekly Argus*, Sep. 14, 1853.

A long line of enemies: See Judd's reply to petitions in Against Removal, 1853, FO & Ex.

Judd and Lathrop: Lathrop to Kamehameha III in Council, Nov. 19, 1852, FO & Ex; Reports to Privy Council, Dec. 16, 1852, FO & Ex.

Judd and Newcomb: Cooke, May 21, 1853.

"Kick his Ass": Judd to Armstrong, June 26, 1853, Armstrong Papers.

Total abstinence man: Judd to Ana, Jan. 30, 1845 [?], Remy Papers; Severance to Hammond, Aug. 24, 1853, USDS, Disp., Haw.; G. P. Judd, p. 157.

A running argument over the treasury: G. P. Judd, p. 200.

Jarves' shabby treatment by Judd: Jarves to Wyllie, Aug. 16, Sep. 11, 1848, FO & Ex; Wyllie to Ricord, Mar. 9, 1853, FO & Ex.

John Ricord had the same bad experience: Ricord to Young, May 3, 1847, FO & Ex. See also letters of Ricord to Wyllie, 1853, FO & Ex.

She turned down his proposal: E. Judd, Jan. 6, 1850.

Judd and Wyllie: Lee to Turrill, Oct. 11, 1851, Turrill Collection; Wyllie to Jarves, Apr. 26, 1858, FO Ltr. Bk. 30.

Over money their latent enmity became open: Document, Oct. 5, 1847, FO & Ex; Wyllie to Judd, Nov. 18, 1847, FO & Ex; Document, Dec. 6, 1847, FO & Ex; Wyllie to Ricord, Mar. 9, 1853, FO & Ex; Wyllie to Miller, Sep. 16, 1856, FO Ltr. Bk. 23; Privy Council Record, Oct. 23, Nov. 9, 26, 1847.

Wyllie sabotaged the mission: Miller to Palmerston, Sep. 25, 1849, FO 58/64.

Wyllie ridiculed his efforts as a diplomat: See documents on Judd Mission, FO & Ex; G. P. Judd, p. 193 ff.

An uncivil, wretched quibbler: Wyllie to Judd, July 14, 1854, FO & Ex.

Few generals ever came off: L. Judd, p. 226.

When he fired the government's auditor: Armstrong to Armstrong, Sep. 10, 1851, Armstrong Papers; Goodale to Armstrong, Oct. 16, 1851, Armstrong Papers; Jarrett to House of Nobles, May 30, 1855, FO & Ex; Wyllie to Allen, Aug. 9, 1856, FO Ltr. Bk. 24; Gregg to Jarrett, May 2, 1857, FO & Ex; Documents, May 16, 1859, Int. Dept. Ltrs. Misc.; Minister of Interior, *Report,* 1853, p. 2; *Poly,* May 29, June 19, July 10, 1852, Jan. 15, 1853; *Weekly Argus,* June 9, July 7, 14, 1852.

The government's herd of horses on Kauai: Judd to Young, July 21, 1851, Int. Dept. Ltrs. Misc.; Judd to Armstrong, Oct. 13, 1851, Armstrong Papers; Privy Council Record, July 21, 1851.

The sugar plantation of Aaron Howe: Interior Office to Harris, Feb. 7, 1863, Int. Dept. Ltr. Bk. 7; Harris to Min. of Int., Feb. 23, 1863, Int. Dept. Ltrs. Misc.; Spencer to Judd, Mar. 12, 1863, Int. Dept. Ltr. Bk. 7; Wyllie to Rae, Mar. 16, 1863, FO Ltr. Bk. 37; Interior Office to Harris, Mar. 23, 1863, Int. Dept. Ltr. Bk. 7; Cabinet Council Minutes, Jan. 27, 1864; *Poly,* Feb. 12, 1853.

"The disposition to accumulate": Judd to Anderson, Mar. 22, 1852, ABCFM.

Richard Armstrong: R. Armstrong, Sept. 5, 1853.

William Lee: Wyllie to Ricord, June 21, 1857, FO & Ex.

The whole of Manoa valley: G. P. Judd, p. 120.

He was worth only about fifty thousand dollars: G. P. Judd, p. 239.

THIRTEEN MEN ON A DEAD MAN'S CHEST pp. 147-153

Judd had his own way less: Miller to Addington, Mar. 18, 1851, FO 58/70; Wyllie to Damon, Oct. 12, 1855, FO & Ex.

A plan to buy the islands: G. P. Judd, pp. 208-209.

The Committee of Thirteen: Gregg Diary, Feb. 13, Mar. 30, 1854; Gregg to Marcy, Apr. 13, 1854, USDS, Disp., Haw.

Malo died in October, 1853; *Poly,* Nov. 5, 1853; M. Alexander, pp. 345-346.

United States might consider annexing: Order to Wyllie, Feb. 6, 1854, FO & Ex.

Revolution rather than annexation: Gregg to Marcy, Jan. 5, Feb. 11, 1854, USDS, Disp., Haw.

Native soldiers: Gregg Diary, Feb. 21, 1854; Cabinet Council Minutes, Mar. 4, 1854; Notice in Int. Dept. Ltr. Bk. 5, Part 2, pp. 758-759.

"Able-bodied and hearty men": Gregg Diary, Mar. 4, 1854.

A ship was seen standing off and on: Gregg Diary, Mar. 6, 1854; Gregg to Marcy, Mar. 4, 1854, USDS, Disp., Haw.

Orthodox annexationists made their bid: Gregg Diary, Mar. 22, 1854; Miller to Wodehouse, Mar. 14, 1854, FO 58/79.

Lathrop and Blair at the king's levee: Gregg Diary, Mar. 18, 1854; Gregg to Marcy, July 24, 1855, Gregg Collection.

Gregg was not impressed by the leaders of the Committee: Gregg Diary, Mar. 21, Apr. 27, 1854.

The town was notorious for leakages: Gregg Diary, May 20, 1854.

Miller maintained that Americans were racists: Gregg to Marcy, Mar. 14, 1854, USDS, Disp., Haw.

They were mistaken for Negroes: Miller to Addington, Mar. 18, 1851, FO 58/70; Gregg Diary, May 21, 1855; Adler, *Journal of Alexander Liholiho*, p. 108.

July the Fourth: Gregg Diary, June 11, July 3, 1854.

"A car, decorated with evergreens": L. Judd, p. 227.

Miller kept pressing the anti-annexationist cause: Gregg to Marcy, Aug. 8, 1854, USDS, Disp., Haw.; Wyllie to Barclay, Oct. 12, 1854, FO Ltr. Bk. 18.

Kauikeaouli drank on: Armstrong, Dec. 24, 1854.

A box of pistols: Gregg to Marcy, Aug. 7, 1854 (misdated), USDS, Disp., Haw.

Gregg was hoping for a provisional transfer: Gregg to Marcy, Aug. 7, 1854, USDS, Disp., Haw.

A crisis in November: Parke to Wyllie, Nov. 6, 1854, Kalanianaole Collection, BPBM.

Guarantees of protection: Wyllie to Gregg, Nov. 13, 15, 1854, FO Ltr. Bk. 16; Wyllie to Perrin, Nov. 13, 1854, FO Ltr. Bk. 16; Wyllie to Miller, Nov. 13, 1854, FO Ltr. Bk. 16.

"Artillery": Wyllie to Ricord, Dec. 1, 1854, FO & Ex. See also Wyllie to Remy, Jan. 31, 1856, FO & Ex.

Hawaiian independence "more firmly established": Proclamation, Dec. 8, 1854, FO & Ex.

Lee was strongly against annexation: See Letters between Lee and Alexander, Kalanianaole Collection, BPBM.

Kauikeaouli died: Privy Council Record, Dec. 15, 1854; W. Snow, Jan. 5-10, 1855.

Several of its members left the islands: Reynolds, Mar. 19, 1855; Gregg Diary, Dec. 16, 1855; Lee to Alexander Liholiho, Apr. 23, 1855, Kalanianaole Collection, BPBM; Gregg to Marcy, Feb. 9, 1856, Gregg Ltr. Bk.; Lathrop to Wyllie, Jan. 18, 1858, FO and Ex.

"With deference to the rising sun": Gregg to Marcy, Jan. 24, 1855, USDS, Disp., Haw.

Chapter 5: A New Society, A New Economy—1855–1876

THE DANCE OF LIFE pp. 154–163

"Like the pandanus": *Poly,* June 20, 1856.

"More or less the headman": Fukuzawa, p. 128.

A "fit of etiquette": Gregg to Marcy, Dec. 3, 1856, Gregg Ltr. Bk.

M. Marion Landais: Gregg Diary, Apr. 8–May 30, Aug. 16, Dec. 31, 1855.

Perrin and the Hawaiian authorities agreed: Ministerial Conferences, Jan. 1, 1856; *Hawaiian Reports,* I, p. 353 ff; Perrin to Wyllie, Jan. 1, 1856, FO & Ex.

His clothes in some disarray: Gregg Diary, Jan. 24, 1857; Gregg to Cass, May 20, 1857, Gregg Ltr. Bk.

Monsarrat pushed his luck: Gregg Diary, May 17–22, 1857; Kamehameha IV to Wyllie, May 18, 1857, FO & Ex; Circular, May 18, 1857, FO Ltr. Bk. 23; Banishment decree, May 20, 1857, FO & Ex; Statement of Parke, May 22, 1857, FO & Ex; Gregg to Cass, May 25, 1857, Gregg Ltr. Bk.; *PCA*, May 21, 28, 1857; *Poly*, May 23, 1857.

A lapse in taste: Wyllie to Thierry, June 2, 1857, FO Ltr. Bk. 26.

Shot down like a dog: Gregg Diary, Jan. 27, 1857.

Reduced his term of banishment: Notice, Aug. 29, 1860, FO & Ex; *PCA*, May 26, 1859.

Shot him in the chest: Gregg Diary, Sep. 13, 28, 1859; Neilson to Brother, Oct. 25, 1859, Neilson Papers; Documents, Sep. 21–Oct. 15, 1859, FO & Ex.

Dissuaded him from abdicating: See Ministerial Conferences, and Cabinet Council Minutes, Sep.–Dec., 1859.

"Educated by the Mission": Judd to Anderson, May 1, 1861, ABCFM.

All creeds on an equal footing: Wyllie to Anderson, May 18, 1864, FO Ltr. Bk. 42.

Godmother by proxy: Wyllie to Murray, Feb. 1, 1862, FO Ltr. Bk. 36; Russell to Wyllie, May 12, 1862, FO & Ex.

Doused the little boy: *Hawaii's Story by Hawaii's Queen*, pp. 19–20.

All this upset the Protestant missionaries: Clark to Anderson, Nov. 8, 1862, Clark Ltr. Bk.; Wyllie to Whitney, May 24, 1864, FO Ltr. Bk. 37; Wyllie to Anderson, Dec. 12, 1864, in Cabinet Council Minutes; *PCA*, Dec. 10, 1863, Dec. 10, 1864, Jan. 7, 1865; W. D. Alexander, *Review of Pastoral Address;* Staley, generally.

Staley took an interest in the commoners: Clark to Anderson, Nov. 8, 1862, Clark Ltr. Bk.; Twain, *Letters from Sandwich Islands,* pp. 115–116.

A crazy man: Baldwin to Cooke, Oct. 30, 1862, HMCS.

Alexander Liholiho died: Wyllie to Desnoyers, Feb. 1, 1864, FO Ltr. Bk. 40; *PCA*, Feb. 4, 1864.

"Nothing could well be more popish": Clark to Anderson, Feb. 12, 1864, Clark Ltr. Bk.

Sexual prowess: Kalakaua to Emma, June 2, 1866, Henriques Collection; Twain, *Sandwich Islands,* p. 20.

Parker was forbidden: *Judd Fragments,* II, pp. 233–234.

Alexander Liholiho cultivated the English: Hopkins to Sire, Nov. 3, 1860, Henriques Collection.

A guest of Queen Victoria: Korn, *Victorian Visitors,* pp. 203–255.

"We thought": Kamehameha V to Emma, June 9, 1871, Emma Collection.

A petition was circulated: Harris to Secretary of SPG, Apr. 27, 1869, HHS; Smith and others to Secretary of SPG, Mar. 13, 1869, Emma Collection; *PCA,* Apr. 17, July 10, 1869, Jan. 1, 1870.

Emma was furious: Emma to Kamehameha V, Apr. 7, 1871, Emma Collection.

The fiftieth anniversary: *PCA*, June 4, 11, 18, 1870.

The missionary virtues were becoming unfashionable: Chamberlain to Sister, July 10, 1858, HMCS; *Poly*, Oct. 30, 1858.

"Pious; hard-working": Twain, *Letters from Sandwich Islands,* pp. 101–102.

Punahou School: Alexander and Dodge.

Lahainaluna Seminary: Lecker.

Chiefs' Children's School: See diaries and letters of Amos and Juliette Cooke, HMCS.

Another side to the story: Cooke to Anderson, Feb. 22, 1850, ABCFM.

Amateur theatricals: Hoyt.

Dancing: Reynolds, June 15, 27, 1849; Cooke, May 2, 1848, Apr. 14, 1853; *Poly,* June 23, 1849, Dec. 20, 1856; *PCA,* Nov. 20, Dec. 4, 1856, Mar. 20, 1860.

Fancy dress ball: *Poly,* Dec. 1, 1860.

The retreat had turned into a rout: Castle to Wife, July 21, 1873, HMCS; *Bennett's Own,* Dec. 7, 1869, Jan. 11, 1870; *PCA,* July 22, 1871.

Swimming at Waikiki: Castle to Wife, Aug. 17, 1873, HMCS.

THE DANCE OF DEATH pp. 163–169

Young part whites: *Poly,* Apr. 17, May 1, 1858.

Some white blood: Gregg Diary, June 26, 1856, Mar. 17, 18, 1859.

Mixing the races: Armstrong to Chapman, Apr.–May 3, 1836, Armstrong Papers.

Samuel G. Dwight: See Letters about Mr. Dwight's Case, HMCS.

"If we may judge": Judd to Anderson, Oct. 23, 1833, ABCFM.

A dancing school: Reynolds, Jan. 16, 1849, May 5, 1854.

The natural area of vice: Rooke to Vincent, Sep. 26, 1854, FO & Ex; Privy Council Record, Aug. 28, 1854; *Daily Hawaiian Herald,* Oct. 30, 1866; *PCA,* Aug. 17, 1867.

"The most intricate quadrilles": *Poly,* Dec. 27, 1856.

"From whom so much is expected": Chief Justice, *Report,* 1852, p. 112.

Joe Booth and Joseph Dawson: *PCA,* Nov. 13, Dec. 4, 1856.

"Better looking, some more bold": *Poly,* Jan. 17, 1857.

Honolulu and Lahaina: I thank Lawrence Windley of the Lahaina Restoration Foundation for bringing these circumstances to my attention.

Lahaina became Gomorrah: *SIN,* June 23, 1847; *Poly,* May 3, 1856.

Twice as many whaling ships: Kuykendall, *Hawaiian Kingdom,* I, p. 307.

"After we had walked": Yanagawa, p. 12.

The economics of prostitution: Wyllie to Wheat, Dec. 2, 1855, FO Ltr. Bk. 22; *SIN,* Mar. 10, 17, June 23, 1847.

Medications for venereal disease: *SIN,* June 23, 1847.

Infection in the rural districts: Bond to ——, (undated), ABCFM; Rae to McKibbin, Mar. 4, 1860, Board of Health; Rae to Gulick, Apr. 13, 1870, Board of Health; Saunders to Board of Health, May 9, 1871, Board of Health; *Poly,* July 12, 1862, Apr. 4, 1863, Jan. 2, 1864; Bates, pp. 282–285, 384.

The wages of sin: Spencer to Austin, Oct. 22, 1860, Int. Dept. Ltr. Bk. 7; "To the Committee on the Memorial of Ladies," Kalanianaole Papers, AH; *Poly,* Dec. 29, 1860; *PCA,* Jan. 3, 1861.

Queen's Hospital: Greer, "Founding of Queen's Hospital."

An act ordering prostitutes: *Laws,* 1860, p. 35; Memoranda of Registered Prostitutes, Mar.–Apr., 1868, Board of Health.

Total population: Kittleson; Schmitt, "Population Estimates," "Population Characteristics," "Birth and Death Rates."

"It can scarcely be said": Kenway to Wyllie, June 25, 1848, FO & Ex.

WHALES pp. 169–172

Whaling ships had been putting in: Kuykendall, *Hawaiian Kingdom,* I, p. 309.
"The Mint": *Hutchings' California Magazine* (Nov., 1858), p. 203.
Ways to doctor their accounts: Gregg Diary, Feb. 14, Apr. 21, 1855; Pleasanton
   to Secretary of State, Mar. 24, 1852, USDS, Consular Disp., Lahaina; Baldwin
   to Anderson, Feb. 9, 1853, ABCFM; Gregg to Marcy, Apr. 13, 1855, Originals
   of Official Correspondence, Gregg Collection.
Special commissioners were sent: Borden to Wyllie, Nov. 1, 1859, July 9, 1860,
   FO & Ex; Borden to Gregg, Oct. 11, 1860, FO & Ex; *SIN,* Dec. 2, 1847; *PCA,*
   Feb. 28, 1861; *Poly,* June 15, 1861; *Daily Hawaiian Herald,* Oct. 9, 10, 16, 1866.
"Primitive insignificance": *Friend,* July, 1844.
"Fleecing and shaving": *PCA,* Nov. 11, 1858; *Poly,* Jan. 1, 8, Mar. 5, 1859.
A local whaling fleet: *Poly,* Aug. 30, 1851, May 21, 1853, Dec. 26, 1857; *PCA,*
   Mar. 26, 1857, Apr. 21, 1859; Minister of Finance, *Report,* 1858, p. 4 ff;
   Hawaiian Annual for 1913, pp. 47–50, 63–68.
Oil: *Poly,* Aug. 27, 1859.
The depredations of the *Shenandoah*: Privy Council Record, Jan. 20, 1866;
   Minister of Finance, *Report,* 1866, pp. 2–3.
The *Harvest*: *Harvest* file, 1864, FO & Ex; *Haw. Gaz.,* Aug. 19, Nov. 25, 1865.
The "blubber room": *PCA,* Dec. 9, 1865.
Trapped in the ice: Parke to Hutchison, Oct. 25, 1871, Int. Dept. Ltrs. Misc.;
   PCA, Oct. 28, Nov. 11, 1871; Minister of Finance, *Report,* 1872, p. 5.
"Do your best for one another": *PCA,* Oct. 28, 1871.
Lost livelihood: *PCA,* Oct. 28, 1871.

SUGAR pp. 173–182

Wealth from the soil: *Poly,* Aug. 31, 1850.
Gold rush: Baldwin to Chamberlain and others, Oct. 10, 1848, HMCS; Armstrong
   to Chapman, Nov. 22, 1848, Armstrong Papers.
Land in fee simple: *Poly,* Aug. 18, 1849.
Depression: *Poly,* July 5, Oct. 11, Nov. 15, 1851, Oct. 2, 1852; T. Morgan, pp.
   157–158.
"Then on!": *Poly,* June 5, 1852.
Borrowing from the government: Privy Council Record, Jan. 5, 12, 1852.
The Civil War: T. Morgan, pp. 179–194.
The balance of trade: *PCA,* Oct. 4, 1860.
Princeville: Wyllie to Hitchcock, Nov. 15, 1860, FO Ltr. Bk. 33; Wyllie to Smith
   and others, Apr. 15, 1861, FO Ltr. Bk. 36; Heuck to ———, Sep. 7, 1862, Heuck
   Papers; Wyllie to Peirce, May 26, 1863, FO & Ex; Wyllie to Hopkins, Aug. 12,
   1863, FO & Ex; Wyllie to Peirce, May 20, 1865, FO & Ex.
Cut his throat: Varigny to Hopkins, Feb. 19, 1866, FO & Ex; Korn, *Victorian
   Visitors,* pp. 281–282.
Plantation agencies: White.
Walker, Allen: *Haw. Gaz.,* Jan. 12, 1867.

The market at San Francisco: *PCA*, Supplement, Mar. 2, 1867.

San Francisco & Pacific Refineries: *Haw. Gaz.*, June 24, 1865; *PCA*, July 1, 1865.

Samuel N. Castle supported the idea: *Haw. Gaz.*, Oct. 20, 1866, Feb. 27, 1867.

The market was flooded: *PCA*, Aug. 18, Oct. 13, 20, 1866, Supplement, Mar. 2, 1867.

Contracts and quotas: PCA, Feb. 23, Mar. 2, Apr. 6, 1867; *Haw. Gaz.*, Feb. 27, Mar. 6, 27, 1867.

Uncertainty of a new order: Kuykendall, *Hawaiian Kingdom*, II, p. 163.

Hawaiians worked on the plantations: Wyllie to Rhodes, June 15, 1847, FO Ltr. Bk. 11a; Lot Kamehameha to Wyllie, June 11, 1863, FO & Ex; Wyllie to Lot Kamehameha, June 12, 1863, FO & Ex; *Poly*, Feb. 16, 1850, Oct. 15, 1853; *PCA*, June 28, 1860, Aug. 22, 1861.

Slavery in the Hawaiian kingdom: *Poly*, July 7, 1849.

Some severe things to say: Minister of Interior, *Report*, 1857, pp. 11–13; *Poly*, May 31, 1851, May 24, 1856.

Natives visible, idle, and unproductive: *Poly*, Feb. 2, 1850, Mar. 8, 15, 1856, May 8, 1858, Sep. 12, 1863; *PCA*, Jan. 6, 20, 1872.

The potato fields: *Poly*, Jan. 26, Feb. 2, 1850, Apr. 26, 1851.

View of time: *Poly*, Oct. 15, 1853; *PCA*, Dec. 22, 1866.

"For the Government of Masters and Servants": *Laws*, 1850, pp. 170–176.

A ship load of "coolies": *Poly*, Jan. 10, 1852.

Chinese in the islands: Gilman, "Honolulu—1848"; Glick, p. 7.

"Practically above the comprehension": *PCA*, Nov. 20, 1856. See also Heuck to Albertine, Dec. 7, 1856, Heuck Papers.

The penal clauses: *Poly*, Oct. 9, 1852, Jan. 1, 8, 1853; *Hawaiian Reports*, I, pp. 85–87.

Objections were heard: Robertson to Lot Kamehameha, May 22, 1857, Int. Dept. Ltrs. Misc.; Spencer to Parke, June 4, 1857, Int. Dept. Ltrs. Misc.; Privy Council Petitions, Mar. 5, 1857, FO & Ex; *PCA*, Jan. 28, 1858.

"Insecurity to life and property": *PCA*, Nov. 26, 1859.

"A murder one Sunday": *Poly*, Dec. 3, 1859. See also Chief Justice, *Report*, 1857, p. 13.

But what was the alternative?: Hutchison to Hopkins, Nov. 5, 1872, FO Ltr. Bk. 49; Privy Council Record, Feb. 17, 1865; *PCA*, May 4, 1867, Oct. 30, 1869.

Blackbirding and the coolie trade: McCook to Phillips, July 29, 1868, FO & Ex; Phillips to McCook, Aug. 20, 1868, FO Ltr. Bk. 48.

Henry M. Whitney: *PCA*, June 12, 1869.

Stopping his paper from circulating: *PCA*, Sep. 3, 1870.

Curtis Lyons, Luther Gulick, Sanford B. Dole: *PCA*, Feb. 20, Sep. 11, Oct. 16, Nov. 27, 1869, July 20, 1872.

A WARNING VOICE pp. 182–190

William Lee was commissioned: Correspondence re Mission of William L. Lee, 1855, FO & Ex; Privy Council Record, Sep. 17, 1855.

The Civil War made them more demonstrative: *Poly*, Sep. 25, 1852, Nov. 10, 1860,

June 22, 29, Sep. 21, 1861; *PCA*, June 5, 1862, Jan. 15, 1863, Apr. 29, 1865; *Haw. Gaz.*, Apr. 29, 1865.

The support of the Union: Wyllie to Kamehameha IV, Dec. 1, 1861, FO & Ex; Lot Kamehameha to Brother, Dec. 9, 1861, Kalanianaole Collection, BPBM; Wyllie to Spencer, Dec. 27, 1861, FO Ltr. Bk. 37; *PCA*, Sep. 26, 1861.

Abolitionism: Gregg Diary, Oct. 8, 1856; Wyllie to Wheat, Dec. 2, 1855, FO & Ex.

"Damned black kanakas": Gregg Diary, June 3, Sep. 12, 1857, Jan. 18, Nov. 17–19, 1859; *PCA*, Oct. 30, 1862.

He inherited a constitution: Opinion of C. C. Harris, Dec. 11, 1863, Kalanianaole Collection, BPBM; Dutton, *Succession*.

"Establishing Universal Suffrage": Wyllie to Alexander Liholiho, Sep. 2, 1861, Kalanianaole Collection, BPBM.

"I believe that universal suffrage": Cabinet Council Minutes, Mar. 3, 1864.

"Fiery spirits": *PCA*, July 30, 1864.

"As we do not agree": *Convention*, Aug. 13, 1864.

Lot's new constitution: Privy Council Record, Aug. 20, 1864; *PCA*, July 30, 1864.

"Bill Ragsdale stands up": Twain, *Letters from Sandwich Islands*, p. 85.

Poor Ragsdale: Young to Emma, Oct. 23, 1873, Emma Collection; Privy Council Record, Feb. 15, 1858; Cabinet Council Minutes, Dec. 21, 1863; Documents on Ragsdale, 1873–1876, Board of Health; *Poly*, Apr. 28, 1860; *PCA*, May 12, 1866, Mar. 28, July 4, 1868, May 13, 1871.

He never missed an election: *PCA*, Feb. 15, 1868.

They "did not vote": *PCA*, Feb. 15, 1868.

Hoopilimeaai: *PCA*, Feb. 29, June 13, 1868.

A fist fight: *Haw. Gaz.*, May 15, 1866; *PCA*, June 9, 1866.

"Ka Makamae Hawaii": *Haw. Gaz.*, Feb. 19, 1868.

The *Lackawanna*: Harris Mission to Washington, Mar.–Dec., 1867, FO & Ex; Varigny to Odell, Apr. 19, 1867, FO & Ex; *PCA*, Feb. 9, 1867, May 9, 1868.

Captain William Reynolds: Wyllie to Bowring, May 19, 1861, FO Ltr. Bk. 38.

The Hawaiian legislature ratified the treaty: Cabinet Council Minutes, Sep. 30, 1867.

Zephaniah S. Spalding: Spalding statement, 1868, USDS, Consular Ltrs., Honolulu; Varigny to Seward, Feb. 26, 1868, FO & Ex.

Kaona: Lyman to Lyons, Oct. 24, 1868, HMCS; Castle to Wife, Jan. 8, Feb. 2, 1874, HMCS; Kona Church Report, June 1, 1868, HMCS; Cabinet Council Minutes, Oct. 22, 1868; Lyman to Hutchison, Oct. 25, 1868, Int. Dept. Ltrs. Misc.; *Haw. Gaz.*, Feb. 12, Mar. 11, 18, June 10, Oct. 21, 28, Nov. 4, 18, 1868; *PCA*, Mar. 14, Oct. 10, 24, 31, Nov. 14, 21, 1868, May 15, June 5, 1869, Jan. 15, 1870; Hitchcock, generally.

The treaty was rejected: Envoy to Washington (E. H. Allen), 1869–1870, FO & Ex; *PCA*, July 2, 1870.

Canada and the British colonies: Tate, "Myth of Hawaii's Swing."

WHISKY BILL pp. 190–197

King Lot's successor: "Correspondence Relating to the Last Hours of Kamehameha V."

Lunalilo won an overwhelming victory: Emma to Hasslocher, Jan. 17, 1873, Hasslocher Papers; *PCA,* Dec 21–28, 1872; I. Bishop, pp. 194–195; Twain, *Sandwich Islands,* p. 13.

Reasons for looking toward the American market: Davies to Granville, Feb. 11, 1873, FO 58/136; Bishop to Hopkins, Apr. 30, 1873, FO Ltr. Bk. 52.

The government should lease Pearl Harbor: *Haw. Gaz.,* Feb. 22, 1873.

"Ascertaining the defensive capabilities": Belknap to Schofield, June 4, 1872, USDS, Misc. Ltrs.

Foreign Minister Bishop put a proposal: Cabinet Council Minutes, June 9, 1873.

To spill out their bitterness: *New York Evangelist,* June 7, 1873; *PCA,* Dec. 22, 1873.

"I am a messenger": *Nuhou,* Nov. 18, 1873.

The Royal Household Troops mutinied: Greer, "Mutiny"; Emma to Hasslocher, Feb. 17, 1873, Hasslocher Papers; Castle to Wife, Sep. 7 ff, 1873, HMCS; Emma to Young, Sep. 10, 1873, Emma Collection; Heuck to Beloved Ones, Sep. 10, 12, 1873, Heuck Papers; Cabinet Council Minutes, Sep. 12, 1873; *PCA,* Sep. 7–13, 20, 27, 1873; *Nuhou,* Sep. 9, 12, 16, 19, 1873; *Haw. Gaz.,* Sep. 10, 17, 1873.

Elisha H. Allen was commissioned: Cabinet Council Minutes, Sep. 11, 1874; Privy Council Record, Sep. 29, 1874.

He could not give his hearty support: Cabinet Council Minutes, Nov. 14, 1873.

He looked hopelessly ill: Emma to Young, Aug. 20, Sep. 2, 3, 1873, Emma Collection; Cabinet Council Minutes, Sep. 16, 1873.

The question of the succession: Bishop to Allen, Oct. 15, 1873, Allen Papers; Emma to Young, Oct. 27, 1873, Emma Collection; Castle to Wife, Jan. 7, 1874, HMCS; Kaleleonalani to Lucy, Jan. 19, 1874, Emma Collection; Cabinet Council Minutes, Sep. 7, 1873; Privy Coucil Record, Feb. 6, 1874.

Kalakaua and Young Hawaii: Emma to Young, Aug. 25 [?], Sep. 5, 20, 1873, Emma Collection; Peirce to Fish, Sep 2, 1873, USDS, Disp., Haw.

Lunalilo was dying: Kekelaokalani to Emma, Nov. 23, 1873, Emma Collection.

The right to choose a new king: Cabinet Council Minutes, Jan. 20, 29, Feb. 2, 1874.

Lunalilo died: Death certificate, Feb. 3, 1874, FO and Ex; Malo and others to Parke, Feb. 3, 1874, Parke Papers; Castle to Wife, Jan. 14, Feb. 3, 1874, HMCS; Trousseau to Judd, Feb. 11, 1874, in Cabinet Council Minutes; Lyons to Folks, Feb. 14, 1874, Lyons Papers; A. F. Judd, pp. 32–35.

A BURNING TORCH pp. 197–206

"Aole makou makemake": Lyons to Folks, Feb. 14, 1874, Lyons Papers.

"If elected": Parke to Everett, Feb. 9 [?], 1874, Marshal's Ltr. Bk. See also Parke to Fyfe, Feb. 10, 1874, Marshal's Ltr. Bk.; Allen to Allen, Feb. 23, 1874, Allen Papers.

On the great day: Wodehouse to Granville, Feb. 20, 1874, FO 58/143; Chamberlain to M. J. and Bella, Feb. 12, 1874, Chamberlain Papers; Parke to Everett, Feb. 14, 1874, Marshal's Ltr. Bk.

The "exquisite dignity" of the occasion: Lyons to Folks, Feb. 14, 1874, Lyons Papers.

The chagrin of the Emma-ites overflowed: Lyons to Folks, Feb. 14, 1874, Lyons Papers; Castle to Wife, Feb. 15, 1874, HMCS; Heuck to Beloved Ones, Feb. 12–22, 1874, Heuck Papers; *Kuokoa*, Feb. 14, 1874; *Nuhou,* Feb. 17, 1874.

"The court house is a perfect wreck": Parke to Severance, Feb. 16, 1874, Marshal's Ltr. Bk.

Armed troops ashore: Bishop to Peirce, Feb. 12, 1874, FO Ltr. Bk. 52; Green to Peirce, Feb. 19, 1874, FO Ltr. Bk. 52; Green to Wodehouse, Feb. 19, 1874, FO Ltr. Bk. 52.

Kalakaua and Emma did not trust each other: Kaeo to Emma, Apr. 3, 10, 1874, Emma Collection; Naone to Emma, Apr. 16, 1874, Emma Collection; Hartwell to Emma, Apr. 20, 1874, Emma Collection; Parke to Wilder, Aug. 6, 1874, Marshal's Ltr. Bk.; Parke to Dayton, Aug. 6, 1874, Marshal's Ltr. Bk.; Kaleleonalani to Lucy, Jan. 18, 1875, Henriques Collection; Emma to Kaeo, Feb. 4, 1876, Emma Collection; Kalakaua to Parke, May 31, 1877, Parke Papers; *PCA,* Apr. 25, 1874.

Treason trial: Zephyrin to Emma, Feb. 2, 1874, Emma Collection; Peirce to Fish, Sep. 10, 1874, USDS, Disp., Haw.; Ballieu to Kalakaua, Oct. 12, 1874, FO & Ex.

Peter Young Kaeo: Kaeo to Emma, May 29, 1874, Emma Collection.

"Pray that God would please place me": Korn and Pukui, "News," p. 29.

"Saturnalia": Peirce to Fish, Dec. 18, 1873, USDS, Disp., Haw. See also *Haw. Gaz.,* Dec. 31, 1873.

"The increase of the people": *PCA,* Apr. 18, 1874.

Merchants and others petitioned Peirce: Peirce to Fish, Feb. 17, Mar. 3, 1874, USDS, Disp., Haw.

"Human tigers": Peirce to Fish, Mar. 3, 1874, USDS, Disp., Haw.

W. L. Green had a much more temperate opinion: Green to Reeve, Apr. 8, 1874, FO Ltr. Bk. 52.

"Serious disaster": *PCA,* June 27, 1874.

A trip to the United States: Privy Council Record, Sep. 26, 1874; *PCA,* Oct. 24, Nov. 21, 1874; *Haw. Gaz.,* Nov. 18, 1874, Jan. 20, 1875.

Elisha Allen and Henry Carter were deep in discussion: Kuykendall, *Hawaiian Kingdom,* III, p. 24 ff; Stevens, p. 122 ff. See also Envoy to Washington, 1874–1876, FO & Ex.

Kalakaua arrived home: *Haw. Gaz.,* Feb. 17, 1875.

The Senate debate: Stevens, p. 132 ff.

Kalakaua ratified the treaty: Cabinet Council Minutes, Apr. 17, 1875.

Sugar refiners of San Francisco: *Haw. Gaz.,* Mar. 2, 1875.

J. C. Pfluger of Hackfeld & Co.: Pfluger to Green, Dec. 10, 1875, FO & Ex.

Extended debates in the House: Kuykendall, *Hawaiian Kingdom,* III, pp. 30–39.

Mary Belle Roberts arrived: *PCA,* May 27, 1876; *Haw. Gaz.,* May 31, 1876.

For a third time the old issues: Stevens, pp. 136–140.

The "ragged edge of uncertainty": *Haw. Gaz.,* July 26, 1876. See also *PCA,* July 29, 1876.

A "rainbow of bunting": *Haw. Gaz.,* Aug. 30, 1876.

"Hurrah!": *Haw. Gaz.,* Aug. 30, 1876.

The great occasion: *Haw. Gaz.,* Sep. 27, 1876.

Propaganda against reciprocity: Emma to Kaeo, Feb. 4, 1876, Emma Collection; Emma to Coz, May 10, 1876, Henriques Collection.
Claus Spreckels: Adler, *Claus Spreckels*, p. 3.
"So ends the year 1876": Sullivan, p. 142.

Chapter 6: Out in the Noonday Sun—1876–1887

THE PHILOSOPHY OF THE PLANTERS pp. 207–213

James Makee: *PCA*, July 2, 1864; *Haw. Gaz.*, Sep. 17, 1879; *Daily Hawaiian Herald*, July 3, 1884; Yates; *Hawaiian Annual for 1926*, pp. 80–87, 1927, pp. 27–39.
"Gentlemen, the birds": Stoddard, pp. 169–170.
Acreage under cane, total value, export crop: Bishop to Allen, Feb. 14, 1880, E. H. Allen Papers; *Hawaiian Annual for 1884*, p. 14, 1891, pp. 61–62; *Planters' Monthly* (Dec., 1908), pp. 485–507, (Jan., 1909), pp. 14–24; U. S. Dept. of Agriculture, *Yearbook*, 1898, p. 567.
Large plantations: Kuykendall, *Hawaiian Kingdom*, III, p. 52.
"It would be a God-send": *PCA*, June 16, 1884. See also *Haw. Gaz.*, July 31, 1878.
Laborers' quarters: Taylor to Mott Smith, Nov. 20, 1899, Immigration, Int. Dept. Ltrs. Misc.; Coman, pp. 20–21.
Money's worth: *Haw. Gaz.*, Feb. 7, Aug. 1, 1877, Oct. 26, 1886; Coman, p. 20.
Leprosy: *Haw. Gaz.*, Feb. 6, 1867, Sep. 23, 1885; *Leprosy. Report of President of Board of Health; Leper Settlement, on Island of Molokai; Molokai. Description of Leper Colony; Dedication of Kapiolani Home;* Mouritz, pp. 21–86; I. Bishop, pp. 250–251, 364, 366–377; Bushnell.
"That pity": *PCA*, July 20, Aug. 17, Oct. 19, 1872. See also *Haw. Gaz.*, Feb. 1, 1882.
William Ragsdale: *Damien Institute Monthly Magazine* (Aug., 1895), p. 117 ff; I. Bishop, pp. 364–366.
Koolau: Mouritz, pp. 72–75.
All kinds of doctors: Hopkins to Green, Jan. 23, 1875, FO & Ex; Akana to Moehonua, Apr. 21, 1875, Board of Health; Everett to Gulick, Aug. 3, 1875, Board of Health; Gulick to Arrowsmith, Mar. 20, 1876, Int. Dept. Ltr. Bk. 13; Board of Health Minutes, June 28, Aug. 5, 1873, Aug. 1, 1874; *Haw. Gaz.*, Aug. 6, 20, 1884.
Father Damien: Yzendoorn, *History of Catholic Mission*, pp. 197–221; *Haw. Gaz.*, Apr. 23, 1889.
The kingdom needed population: *Haw. Gaz.*, Jan. 4, 1882.
Servile laborers: Bishop to Brown, Jan. 2, 1874, FO Ltr. Bk. 52; Hillebrand to Minister of Interior, June 6, 1877, Immigration, Int. Dept. Ltrs.; *Haw. Gaz.*, Dec. 8, 1880, Nov. 7, 1883; *Planters' Monthly* (Apr., 1882), p. 30(Sep., 1882), pp. 123–125.
Immigrants as people: Address to His Majesty the King, Feb. 25, 1876, Int. Dept. Ltrs. Misc.; Privy Council Record, Feb. 29, 1876; *Haw. Gaz.*, Jan. 12, 1881, May 13, 27, June 17, 1885; Hörmann.

"Cognate race": *Haw. Gaz.*, May 10, 1882.

Chinese would never assimilate: *Haw. Gaz.*, Sep. 28, 1881, May 6, Oct. 27, 1885; *Friend*, Nov., 1885.

Yellow peril: *Haw. Gaz.*, June 24, 1885.

"Now, away with all these race antagonisms": Damon, pp. 90–91; *Haw. Gaz.*, Dec. 3, 1879.

Fitness to govern: *Saturday Press*, Oct. 9, 1880.

"The word in the beginning": *Planters' Monthly* (Nov., 1886), p. 199.

THE CONSCIENCE OF THE KING pp. 213–220

"An epidemic of gabble and gesture": Chaney, pp. 274–275.

Kalakaua played politics: S. Bishop Diary, Feb. 3, 9, 1886; Fornander to Dominis, Feb. 3, 1886, Kalanianaole Collection, BPBM; *Haw. Gaz.*, Nov. 30, 1881, Feb. 6, 13, 1884, Nov. 3, 1885, Feb. 16, 23, 1886, Feb. 28, 1888; Attorney General, *Report,* 1888, pp. 6–7.

The sugar industry was virtually the sole support: *PCA*, June 21, 1882; *Haw. Gaz.*, Sep. 14, 1881, June 21, July 19, 1882; *Saturday Press*, June 24, 1882; *Planters' Monthly* (Sep., 1883), pp. 121–122, (July, 1884), pp. 435–437, (Oct., 1889), p. 439; *Analysis of Taxation of Hawaiian Kingdom for 1881.*

"The life of my noble wife": Kalakaua to Moehonua, Mar. 24, 1876, Int. Dept. Ltrs. Misc. See also D. Forbes.

Second Iolani Palace: AH has a file of notes and photographs prepared by the Junior League of Honolulu. See also *Iolani Palace Register*, part of the same project.

Celso Caesar Moreno: Allen to Allen, Feb. 16, 1880, E. H. Allen Papers; Comly to Evarts, July 5, 1880, USDS, Disp., Haw.; *Haw. Gaz.*, Nov. 26, Dec. 10, 1879.

Moreno "had shown himself": Comly to Evarts, Aug. 21, 1880, USDS, Disp., Haw.

Legislature of 1880: Allen to Allen, Aug. 2, 1880, E. H. Allen Papers; *PCA*, June 5, 1880; *Haw. Gaz.*, Aug. 4, 1880.

"The indignation of the public": *PCA*, Aug. 7, 1880.

"The abdication of the King": Comly to Evarts, Aug. 21, 1880, USDS, Disp., Haw.; *Ko Hawaii Pae Aina*, Aug 21, 1880; *Haw. Gaz.*, Supplement, Aug. 25, 1880.

Asking for *their* removal: Bush to Allen, Aug. 27, 1880, FO Ltr. Bk. 57; Bush to Hopkins, Aug. 27, 1880, FO Ltr. Bk. 57; Bush to Martin, Aug. 27, 1880, FO Ltr. Bk. 57.

Secret powers: Kuykendall, *Hawaiian Kingdom*, III, pp. 220–221.

A royal tour: Kalakaua's Trip Around the World, 1881, FO & Ex; W. Armstrong.

Union and Confederation of Asiatic Nations: Mutsuhito to Kalakaua, Jan. 22, 1882, FO & Ex; Conroy, pp. 51–52.

"I am very reluctantly compelled": Sadawara to Kalakaua, Jan. 14, 1882, Kalanianaole Collection, BPBM; Kihara, pp. 427–428.

"My explanations": W. Armstrong, pp. 246–247.

Coronation ceremony: Coronation Documents, 1883, FO & Ex; *Coronation of Their Majesties.*

"Directly damaging to the property interests": *Planters' Monthly* (Mar., 1883), pp. 306–307.

The coronation itself was a flop: *Haw. Gaz.*, Feb. 14, 21, 1883.

"Truth compels us to declare": *Haw. Gaz.*, Feb. 28, 1883.

An obscene publication: *Kuokoa,* Mar. 3, 1883; *Haw. Gaz.*, Mar. 7, 14, Apr. 11, 1883; *Elele Poakolu,* Mar. 14, 1883.

Genealogists: *Haw. Gaz.*, Oct. 1, 1884, July 20, 1886.

Stripped bones: Smithers to Kalakaua, Oct. 27, 1884, Kalanianaole Collection, BPBM; *Haw. Gaz.*, June 22, 1886.

Kahunas: *Laws,* 1886, pp. 49–50.

Kumulipo: Beckwith.

Hale Naua: *Haw. Gaz.*, Nov. 29, 1887; *Constitution and By-Laws of Hale Naua.*

"Its by-laws": W. D. Alexander, *History of Later Years,* p. 16. See also Bishop to Gilman, Mar. 24, 1898, S. Bishop Ltr. Bk.

THE SHEPHERD SAINT pp. 220–225

Walter Murray Gibson: Sousa.

An unpardonable thing to say: Webster to My Dear Sir, Oct. 15, 1861, Kalanianaole Papers, AH; *PCA,* Aug. 15, 1861.

Outfitting a privateer: Wyllie to Lot Kamehameha, Sep. 27, 1861, FO Ltr. Bk. 35.

Some connection with the Mormon Church: Wyllie to Gibson, Oct. 15, 1861, FO Ltr. Bk. 37; Gregg to Kamehameha IV, Oct. 22, 1861, Kalanianaole Collection, BPBM; *PCA,* Oct. 24, 1861.

Mormon Church in disarray: Lewis to Young, Oct. 6, 1851, Int. Dept. Ltrs. Misc.; Hammond to Ana, Nov. 1, 1854, Int. Dept. Ltrs. Misc.; Thurston to Lewis and others, Nov. 15, 1854, Int. Dept. Ltr. Bk. 6; Gregg to Wyllie, Jan. 7, 1858, FO & Ex; Wyllie to Gregg, Jan. 8, 1858, FO & Ex; Wyllie to Board of Education, Mar. 12, 1858, FO & Ex; Armstrong to Wyllie, Mar. 18, 1858, FO & Ex; Miller to Wyllie, Aug. 26, 1858, FO & Ex; Wyllie to Kamehameha V, Aug. 4, 1865, FO & Ex; Cabinet Council Minutes, Nov. 15, 1854; Privy Council Record, Nov. 20, 1855; *Poly,* May 7, 1853; Bock, Ch. 2.

"Chief President": *Shepherd Saint,* p. 13.

Contributions: Documents in H. Judd Papers; *PCA,* Oct. 17, 1861.

"There are 10,000 acres": Gibson Diary, Nov. 5, 1861.

Land registered in the name of Gibson: Bock, p. 52; Sousa, p. 64.

A new settlement at Laie: *PCA,* Feb. 4, 1865; *Haw. Gaz.*, Apr. 12, 1882; Briggs, pp. 48–49.

"My heart leaps": Gibson Diary, Jan. 12, 1862.

Gibson's story of his birth: Hawthorne, pp. 26–30.

"Lines of power": Gibson Diary, Jan. 31, 1862.

Controlling the lines of power: Gibson Hearing; Gibson, *Prison of Weltevreden,* vii, pp. 22, 25, 392, 405; J. Gould, pp. 7–32.

Advice on how to vote: Gibson to Wyllie, Dec. 10, 1861, FO & Ex.

It became true later on: Gibson to Harris, Sep. 3, 1872, FO & Ex; *PCA,* Sep. 7, 14, 21, Oct. 5, 1872; *Haw. Gaz.*, May 15, 1878; Gibson, *He Mau Olelo.*

Sincere, frank, courteous: *PCA,* Aug. 3, 1878.

"He got up more special committees": *Haw. Gaz.*, Aug. 7, 1878.

In 1880 he was returned: *PCA*, Feb. 21, 1880.

Elele Poakolu: Comly to Evarts, Sep. 27, 1880, USDS, Disp., Haw.

Raking over Gibson's Mormon past: *Shepherd Saint*.

Fifteen electoral tickets: *Haw. Gaz.*, Jan. 18, 1882.

"The stupid and cowardly spirit": *PCA*, Feb. 4, 1882.

A "tall, thin old gentleman": Adee, p. 467.

"New departure": Gibson to Allen, Sep. 24, 1882, E. H. Allen Papers.

HIS ROYAL SACCHARINITY pp. 225–234

Dangerous leakage in the accounts: Wodehouse to Foreign Office, Aug. 6, 1883, FO 58/183; *Haw. Gaz.*, June 18, 1884.

A huge loan: Cabinet Council Minutes, Feb. 26, Mar. 5, 1874; *Haw. Gaz.*, Jan. 28, Aug. 11, 18, 1880, July 4, 1882; *Laws*, 1874, pp. 56–59, 1882, pp. 47–49.

"Let us be wide awake": *Haw. Gaz.*, Oct. 11, 1876.

More than seven thousand tons of sugar: Adler, *Claus Spreckels*, p. 3.

"A dreary expanse": I. Bishop, p. 330.

Hamakua Ditch: *PCA*, Aug. 26, 1876; Baldwin, generally.

"Schutzler & Spreckles replied": Harris to Allen, Oct. 4, 1878, E. H. Allen Papers.

Spreckels got his lease: Cabinet Council Minutes, July 3, 1878.

"Bills payable": His Majesty's Cash Book, July, 1878, AH.

A water course thirty miles long: Adler, *Claus Spreckels*, pp. 44–51.

Ruth's claim was doubtful: Spaulding, *Crown Lands*; Stokes, "Kaoleioku."

"There is something strange about this": *Haw. Gaz.*, July 26, 1882.

A royal patent in fee simple: *Hawaiian Reports*, VI, pp. 446–447; *Laws*, 1882, pp. 11–12.

"One of the smartest businessmen": *PCA*, Dec. 23, 1882.

"Mr. Spreckels naturally has something to say": *PCA*, Dec. 2, 1882.

Hawaiian coinage: Kuykendall, *Hawaiian Kingdom*, III, p. 86 ff.

A million dollars worth of silver coins: Cabinet Council Minutes, Sep. 20, 1882, Mar. 6, 1883.

He stood to make money: Carter to Kapena, June 7, 1883, H. A. P. Carter Papers; Cabinet Council Minutes, Mar. 6, 1883; *Daily Bulletin*, Jan. 9, 1884.

Spreckels' opponents went to law: *Hawaiian Reports*, V, pp. 27–38.

Spreckels and Irwin opened a bank: *PCA*, Jan. 19, 1884; *Saturday Press*, Jan. 19, 1884; Tilton.

A banking bill: *Daily Bulletin*, May 31, 1884.

"Shall we then sit tamely down": *Haw. Gaz.*, June 4, 1884.

The founders "do not carry their arguments": *PCA*, June 14, 1884.

Bank bill defeated: Journal of Legislature, June 26, 1884; *Haw. Gaz.*, July 2, 1884.

Gold Law: *Laws*, 1884, pp. 20–23.

Substantial political assets: *Haw. Gaz.*, Aug. 3, 1886; Adler, *Claus Spreckels*, p. 183.

His Majesty Spreckels or His Majesty Kalakaua: *Hawaiian Hansard*, pp. 447–448.

"This little shuffle of the knaves": *Haw. Gaz.*, July 6, 1886.

"If this were poker": *PCA*, Dec. 27, 1908.

"Enterprises of an exceptional and important character": *PCA,* May 1, 1886.

Loan of two million dollars: *Hawaiian Hansard,* pp. 55–56, 176, 180.

Loan act passed: *Daily Bulletin,* Sep. 1, 1886.

Amended version of the loan: *Laws,* 1886, pp. 57–59; *Hawaiian Hansard,* pp. 656–657, 694–696, 698–702.

Spreckels himself appeared again: *Haw. Gaz.,* Oct. 5, 1886.

"Mr. Spreckels on one or two occasions": Gibson to Carter, Oct. 22, 1886, FO & Ex.

Kalakaua could not be reached by calm reason: *Daily Bulletin,* Nov. 18, 1886. See also *Haw. Gaz.,* Nov. 23, 1886.

Freedom was costly: Adler, *Claus Spreckels,* pp. 204–213.

THE EMPIRE OF THE CALABASH pp. 235–239

"While former Cabinets": *Haw. Gaz.,* Oct. 26, 1886.

Wyllie and St. Julian: Horn, pp. 7–53.

"Guide the guardian and the National head": St. Julian to Wyllie, Oct. 2, 1854, FO & Ex. See also Wyllie to St. Julian, Apr. 15, 1863, FO & Ex.

"Primacy in the family of Polynesian States": *PCA,* July 3, 1880.

"Inflamed with the idea": Comly to Evarts, July 31, 1880, USDS, Disp., Haw.

"Hawaiian Protest": Gibson to Carter, Aug. 28, 1883, FO & Ex; Horn, pp. 69–74.

Another sheaf of documents: Horn, pp. 74–76.

Political reconnaissance: Gibson to Carter, Oct. 14, 1885, FO & Ex; Carter to Gibson, Dec. 4, 24, 1885, FO & Ex.

Ocean Island annexed: Cabinet Council Minutes, Sep. 14, 1886; *Haw. Gaz.,* Dec. 21, 1886.

Samoan Islands: Ryden.

John E. Bush, "Envoy Extraordinary": Consuls Commissions, Dec. 23, 1886, AH.

A confederation with the Hawaiian kingdom: Gibson to Bush, Dec. 24, 1886, Consular and Misc. Ltr. Bk., AH.

"My wits, this evening": Bush to King Kalakaua, Jan. 27, 1887, FO & Ex.

Great powers were much less enthusiastic: Horn, pp. 136–145.

"The friendly greeting": Gibson to Carter, Jan. 25, 1887, FO & Ex.

A gunboat: Cabinet Council Minutes, Jan. 19, 1887.

The *Kaimiloa*: Adler, "Hawaiian Navy."

"A drumstick on a crown": *Haw. Gaz.,* Mar. 22, 1887.

"How prospered the alliance grand": *Haw. Gaz.,* Jan. 25, 1887.

Influence of the *Kaimiloa* primarily moral: Gibson to Bush, Mar. 19, 1887, Consular and Misc. Ltr. Bk., AH.

Samoan landfall: Jackson to Gibson, June 16, 1887, Army & Navy, *Kaimiloa* File, AH.

Gibson had not been candid: Gibson to Carter, Jan. 18, 1887, FO & Ex; Gibson to Hoffnung, Jan. 18, 1887, FO & Ex.

Washington conference: Salisbury to Malet, Mar. 21, 1887, FO 58/226; Ryden, pp. 322–366.

"Discretionary powers with regard to Samoa": Poor to Webb, Apr. 10, 1887, H. A. P. Carter Papers.

Followed by Germans: Bush to Gibson, May 23, 1887, FO & Ex; Scott to Salisbury, July 28, 1887, FO 58/230.

Bush's "disreputable" conduct: Gibson to Webb, June 10, 1887, FO & Ex.

Some of her crew mutinied: Webb to Brown, July 18, 1887, FO & Ex.

Warnings from the great powers: Horn, pp. 136–145; Tansill, pp. 41–42.

"What was Prussia": *PCA*, July 24, 1886.

"To avoid any possible appearance": Gibson to Poor, June 10, 1887, FO & Ex.

A CLOUD ON THE SUN pp. 240–250

White men were overstepping themselves: *Ko Hawaii Pae Aina*, Aug. 21, 1880; *PCA*, Sep. 15, 16, 22, 23, 1882; *Haw. Gaz.*, June 20, 1883; *Daily Bulletin*, July 10, 1884.

Rough shod over the constitution: *Haw. Gaz.*, June 6, Oct. 17, Dec. 26, 1883, Oct. 15, 1884, Mar. 29, 1887; *Laws*, 1886, pp. 108–110.

"Mr. Gibson can govern": *Planters' Monthly* (Dec., 1885), p. 233.

News of revolution was played up: *Haw. Gaz.*, Aug. 25, 1880 and Supplement, June 14, 1882, June 13 1883.

"Low in mental culture". *Haw. Gaz.*, Nov. 30, 1886.

"Rottenness": *Haw. Gaz.*, Oct. 3, 1883.

A boil that should be halved: *Haw. Gaz.*, Mar. 11, 1885.

A political party of opposition: *Haw. Gaz.*, Aug. 4, 1880, Aug. 30, 1882, Nov. 24, 1885, Jan. 19, Feb. 9, 1886; *Planters' Monthly* (Nov., 1885), pp. 211–213, (Feb., 1886), p. 283.

"He does not yet realize": *Planters' Monthly* (Nov., 1886), p. 200.

Moral duty, racial right, self interest: *Haw. Gaz.*, Aug. 2, 1882; *Planters' Monthly* (Nov., 1886), p. 201. See also Andrade, generally.

Lorrin A. Thurston: L. A. Thurston, *Memoirs*, p. 16.

Reform politics: L. A. Thurston, *Memoirs*, pp. 95–114.

Habitual drunkards: Godfrey, p. 55; *Hawaiian Hansard*, p. 98.

"I consider that the presence of a member": Godfrey, p. 65.

Thurston "talked very loud": *Hawaiian Hansard*, p. 134.

"Thurston, how long": L. A. Thurston, *Memoirs*, p. 129.

A number of trustworthy men: L. A. Thurston, *Memoirs*, p. 130.

"Efficient, decent, and honest government": L. A. Thurston, *Memoirs*, p. 131.

The list Thurston kept: The notebook is in Thurston Papers.

Kill the king and have done: L. A. Thurston, *Memoirs*, pp. 135–139; Ashford, p. 24.

Honolulu Rifles: *Daily Bulletin*, Mar. 11, Apr. 1, 4, May 26, 1887.

Mrs. Thomas Lack's shop: *Haw. Gaz.*, July 12, 1887.

Opium: *Haw. Gaz.*, May 14, 1884.

Aki: Merrill to Bayard, May 31, 1887, USDS, Disp., Haw.; *Haw. Gaz.*, Jan. 4, Feb. 1, Apr. 19, May 10, 17, 31, June 28, 1887.

"These are incontrovertable facts": *Haw. Gaz.*, May 17, 1887.

"This beautiful emblem": *Haw. Gaz.*, Mar. 29, 1887.

"The tempest": Mellen, p. 193.

Iolani Palace was barricaded: Cabinet Council Minutes, May 23, 1887; *Haw. Gaz.,*
    May 24, 1887.
"Plunder and defiance": *Haw. Gaz.,* May 24, 1887.
The diplomats received petitions: Purvis and others to Wodehouse, May 7, 1887,
    FO 58/229; Cartwright and others to Merrill, June 6, 1887, USDS, Disp., Haw.
Merrill visited Kalakaua: Merrill to Bayard, July 30, 1887, USDS, Disp., Haw.
Gibson asked to resign: Cabinet Council Minutes, June 28, 1887; *Daily Bulletin,*
    June 29, 1887.
Calling for a public meeting: *Haw. Gaz.,* May 31, 1887.
Kalakaua ordered troops into the streets: Baker, p. 8.
"While the troops were patrolling": Dole, *Memoirs,* p. 50.
The public meeting: *Haw. Gaz.,* July 1, 1887; *Sketch of Recent Events.*
"I remember reading somewhere": *Haw. Gaz.,* July 1, 1887.
Diplomats advise Kalakaua to make peace: Wodehouse to Salisbury, July 5,
    1887, FO 58/229; Merrill to Bayard, July 30, 1887, USDS, Disp., Haw.; *Haw.
    Gaz.,* Extra, July 1; July 5, 1887.
He drew up a letter: *Haw. Gaz.,* July 5, 1887.
A big consignment of guns: *Haw. Gaz.,* Extra, July 1, July 5, 1887.
Ashford got ready to hang Gibson: L. A. Thurston, *Memoirs,* pp. 151–152;
    Haw. Gaz., Extra, July 1, 1887.
Gibson and Hayselden bound over for trial: *Haw. Gaz.,* Extra, July 1, July 5,
    12, 1887.
"The cabinet proceeded in a body": Ashford, pp. 25–26, 29.
No evidence to substantiate charges: *Haw. Gaz.,* Aug. 23, 1887.
Even-tempered interviews: *San Francisco Chronicle,* Aug. 7, 1887; *Haw. Gaz.,*
    Aug. 30, Dec. 6, 1887.
Breach of promise: *Haw. Gaz.,* Oct. 25, Nov. 1, 1887.
"Poor Gibsy's in a hospital": *Pa Gibby's Wooin'.*
"Thus we have seen the last on earth": *Daily Bulletin,* Feb. 20, 1888.
"So we joined the line": L. A. Thurston, *Memoirs,* p. 80.

Chapter 7: Aloha Oe—1887–1900

BULWARKS OF LIBERTY pp. 251–254

"I have an exalted idea": *Haw. Gaz.,* Oct. 26, 1886.
"Advocates of universal suffrage": *Haw. Gaz.,* Aug. 23, 1887.
Hawaiian voters: Lydecker, 159–170; Kuykendall, "Constitutions," pp. 47–52;
    Spaulding, "Cabinet Government."
Special election: *PCA,* Sep. 12, 19, 1887; *Daily Bulletin,* Sep. 13, 1887; *Haw. Gaz.,*
    Sep. 13, 20, 1887; *Planters' Monthly* (Nov., 1887), p. 495.
Cession of Pearl Harbor: Dozer, pp. 157–183.
Kalakaua would "never ratify that Treaty": Wodehouse to Foreign Office, Aug.
    2, 1887, FO 58/241.
Supplementary convention: Cabinet Council Minutes, Oct. 20, 1887; Minister of
    Foreign Affairs, *Report,* 1888, Appendix, pp. *i–iii.*

"All other things were equal": *Haw. Gaz.,* Aug. 16, 1887. See also Ashford to
    Everett, July 23, 1887, Attorney General Ltr. Bk.; L. A. Thurston, *Memoirs,*
    p. 139.
Kalakaua's favorite programs voted down: Cabinet Council Minutes, July 7, 13,
    1887; *Haw. Gaz.,* July 12, 27, Aug. 2, Nov. 8, 1887; *Laws,* 1887, 1888, gen-
    erally.
Opium license scandal: Record of Informal Meetings of the Cabinet Council,
    July 11, 1887; Document in Int. Dept. Ltr. Bk. 33, pp. 18–22; *Haw. Gaz.,*
    Dec. 6, 1887, Sep. 25, 1888; *Daily Bulletin,* Sep. 21, 29, Oct. 4, 29, 1888; *PCA,*
    Sep. 22, Oct. 30, 1888; *Hawaiian Reports,* VII, pp. 401–409.
Letters to the staff of the custom house: Attorney General, *Report,* 1888, pp.
    6–7; Record of the Informal Meetings of the Cabinet Council, Jan. 12, 1888;
    PCA, Apr. 26–28, 1888.
The court decided in favor of Kalakaua: *Hawaiian Reports,* VII, pp. 229–249;
    Daily Bulletin, Feb. 2–11, 1888.
"Any persons there": L. A. Thurston, *Memoirs,* pp. 213–214.

RED SHIRTS pp. 255–258

Castle and Dowsett asked Liliuokalani: Liliuokalani Diary, Dec. 20–23, 1887.
"Only respectful words": Liliuokalani Diary, Jan. 16, 1888.
Robert W. Wilcox: *Haw. Gaz.,* Oct. 29, 1889.
Salary "which would not keep a cat alive": *Haw. Gaz.,* June 17, 1890.
Liberal Patriotic Association: *Haw. Gaz.,* Apr. 30, 1889.
Wilcox led his revolutionary army: The story of the insurrection may be fol-
    lowed in: *Haw. Gaz.,* Aug. 6–20, 1889; Ashford to Austin, Aug. 13, 1889,
    Army and Navy, AH; Documents in Emma Taylor Papers.
Three were brought to trial on serious charges: *Haw. Gaz.,* Aug.–Dec., 1889;
    PCA, Aug.–Dec., 1889.
Two books celebrating his exploits: *Ka Buke Moolelo O Hon. Robert William
    Wilikoki; Duke Hao O Hawaii A Me Na Moolelo Pakui; Haw. Gaz.,* Dec. 9,
    1890.
Unsuccessful rebellion was always treason: *Haw. Gaz.,* Oct. 15, 1889.
"If the Revolution of June 30": *Friend,* Dec., 1889.
"Who are the murderers": *Haw. Gaz.,* Oct. 15, 1889.
Native militia company disbanded: *Haw. Gaz.,* Aug. 20, 1889.
Fence around the palace grounds lowered: *Haw. Gaz.,* Aug. 13, 1889.
Arms in the palace: Cabinet Council Minutes, July 29, 1889.

THE TORCH IS QUENCHED pp. 258–264

Opinion from the supreme court: Wodehouse to Foreign Office, Aug. 24, 1889,
    FO 58/242; Cabinet Council Minutes, Aug. 5, 1889.
"Despoiling the enemy": L. A. Thurston, *Memoirs,* pp. 158–161.
The divided cabinet: Ashford to McFarlane, Apr. 17, 1890, Attorney General
    Ltr. Bk.; Cabinet Council Minutes, Apr. 10, 1890.
"If it should become necessary": Austin to Carter, Mar. 8, 1889, FO & Ex.

A tentative arrangement: Carter to Blaine, Apr. 11, 1889, USDS, Notes from Hawaiian Legation.

A protectorate: Wodehouse to Foreign Office, Sep. 27, Oct. 19, 25, 1889, FO 58/242.

The usual round of mass meetings: *Daily Bulletin*, Sep, 25–27, 1889; *PCA*, Sep. 27–30, 1889.

Prosperity and independence: *Daily Bulletin*, Oct. 4, 1889.

"I have always been opposed": Carter to Kalakaua, Nov. 6, 1889, Cleghorn Collection.

The king refused to sign: Kalakaua to Liliuokalani, Dec. 27, 1889, Liliuokalani Collection, AH.

"I am willing, Let it come": Cabinet Council Minutes, Dec. 20, 1889.

A modified commission: Cabinet Council Minutes, Apr. 10, 1890; *Hawaiian Reports*, VIII, pp. 572–574.

"Plunged into the depths of despair": Castle, p. 669.

The National Reform Party: *Daily Bulletin*, Sep. 10, 14, 1889, Mar. 6, 1890; *PCA*, Sep. 14, 1889.

"We don't want these white men": *Haw. Gaz.*, Supplement, Jan. 28, 1890.

"A liberal modification": *Haw. Gaz.*, Jan. 7, 1890.

The white man had civilization behind him: *Haw. Gaz.*, Aug. 26, 1890.

A legislature almost equally divided: *Haw. Gaz.*, Feb. 18, 1890; Lydecker, p. 178.

"The voice of the People"; *PCA*, Feb. 10, 1890.

Wilcox was planning another insurrection: Ashford to Soper, May 28, 1890, Attorney General Ltr. Bk.; *Daily Bulletin*, May 28, June 6, 7, 1890; *PCA*, June 3, 7, 1890; *Haw. Gaz.*, June 10, 1890.

No confidence in the ministry: *Daily Bulletin*, June 14, 16, 1890; *PCA*, June 14, 16, 1890.

The cabinet looked "safe": *Daily Bulletin*, June 17, 1890.

Natives began talking about a new constitution: "Minutes of the Hawaiian National Committee," 1890, FO & Ex; *PCA*, July 21, 1890.

A matter of "duty": Wodehouse to Foreign Office, Aug. 29, 1890, FO 58/253.

"People say there will be no trouble": *Haw. Gaz.*, Sep. 16, 1890.

Kalakaua died: *Kalakaua Dead; Medical Report.*

"Very heathenish in looks and howling": S. Bishop Diary, Feb. 15, 1891.

LILIUOKALANI pp. 264–270

Liliuokalani was a complicated woman: Volumes of her diary are in AH and BPBM; see also letters in Liliuokalani Collection, AH, and Liliuokalani Papers, BPBM; Kalanianaole Collection, BPBM; Cleghorn Collection, AH; and *Hawaii's Story By Hawaii's Queen*.

"Kaleidoscopic": Thurston to Hopkins, Dec. 14, 1892, FO & Ex.

Native Sons of Hawaii: Blount Report, pp. 431–432; *PCA*, Dec. 29, 1891.

Robert Wilcox and John Bush: See Bush's newspaper *Ka Leo O Ka Lahui* generally; Robertson to Cleghorn, Sep. 21, 1891, Cleghorn Collection.

Thurston's "patriotic enthusiasm": Walker to Cleghorn, Sep. 21, 1891, Cleghorn Collection.

Cooper thought Liliuokalani was a dangerous woman: L. A. Thurston, *Memoirs,*
pp. 228–229.

Annexation Club: L. A. Thurston, *Memoirs,* p. 229.

A "pretty uppish sort of person": Morgan Report, p. 386.

"If conditions in Hawaii compel you to act": L. A. Thurston, *Memoirs,* p. 232.

Thurston put his views on paper: Thurston to Blaine, May 27, 1892, USDS,
Misc. Ltrs.

The elections of 1892: Lydecker, p. 182.

The Hawaiian Patriotic League: Stevens to Blaine, May 21, 1892, USDS, Disp.,
Haw.; Wodehouse to Foreign Office, May 24, 1892, FO 58/263; *Ka Leo O Ka
Lahui,* Mar. 16, 1892; *Daily Bulletin,* May 26–June 10, 1892; *PCA,* May 27–
June 13, 1892.

The legislative session of 1892: A. Loomis.

The appropriation bill: Journal of Legislative Assembly, June 14, 1892.

"She says I must have the House accept it": Liliuokalani Diary, July 8, 1892.

"No plan has ever been proposed": *Golden Era.*

A lottery bill and an opium licensing bill: Journal of Legislative Assembly, Aug.
29, 30, Dec. 8, 31, 1892; Jan. 10, 11, 14, 1893.

"What the Queen wanted": *PCA,* Jan. 13, 1893. See also *Daily Bulletin,* Jan. 12,
13, 1893.

Four new ministers: *PCA,* Jan. 14, 16, 1893.

A newspaper editor from San Francisco: *San Francisco Examiner,* Nov. 21,
1892.

"Very many of the best citizens": *PCA,* Nov. 30, 1892.

ROYALISTS AND REPUBLICANS pp. 270–280

She walked back to Iolani Palace: Blount Report, pp. 390–403.

The text of a new constitution: "Constitution of Jan. 14, 1893," Liliuokalani
Collection, AH; Blount Report, pp. 581–589.

"O, ye people who love the Chiefs": *Ka Leo O Ka Lahui,* Jan. 16, 1893; Blount
Report, pp. 538–539.

A Committee of Safety was formed: L. A. Thurston, *Memoirs,* p. 130; Blount
Report, pp. 495–498.

The "intelligent part of the community": Blount Report, pp. 496–497.

Wiltse seemed to approve: Blount Report, p. 496.

Stevens put no impediment in their path: Morgan Report, p. 448; Thurston to
Foster, Feb. 21, 1893, USDS, Notes from Hawaiian Legation.

The business of drafting papers: Blount Report, p. 497.

A proclamation that no new constitution would be invoked: Blount Report,
pp. 28–29, 34, 116, 442; *Daily Bulletin,* Jan. 17, 1893.

The queen could not get any assurance: Blount Report, pp. 82, 439; Morgan
Report, pp. 540, 572–573.

A simultaneous meeting in support of the queen: Morgan Report, p. 297.

"We, the undersigned": Blount Report, p. 118.

It was a subdued gathering: *Daily Bulletin,* Jan. 17, 1893.

"Consider the situation": *PCA,* Jan. 17, 1893. See also *Two Weeks of Hawaiian History.*

Troops from the *Boston:* Blount Report, pp. 583–594; Morgan Report, pp. 596–602.

Stevens took his time about replying: Cleghorn to Kaiulani, Jan. 28, 1893, Cleghorn Collection; Blount Report, pp. 495, 500, 548, 639, 1057–1059.

They decided that they needed more time: Blount Report, pp. 26, 966.

Thurston a "radical mover": Blount Report, p. 498.

The choice fell on Sanford Dole: Dole, *Memoirs,* p. 77; *Hon. Adv.,* Jan. 14, 1923.

"The constitutional evolution indicated": Morgan Report, pp. 1017–1019; W. D. Alexander, *History of Later Years,* p. 60.

A volunteer armed force at their disposal: Morgan Report, p. 611.

Liliuokalani was urged not to use force: Blount Report, pp. 82, 400–401, 569–570. But see McCarthy to Wilson, Jan. 16, 1893, Dole Collection.

Stevens gave no help at all: Morgan Report, pp. 547–549; Blount Report, pp. 28–29, 34, 82, 400–401, 439–440.

Good shot one of them: Morgan Report, pp. 624–625.

Captain Wiltse thought not: Blount Report, p. 673; Morgan Report, p. 488.

The royal troops: Blount Report, pp. 174–177.

A letter from Stevens: Stevens to Foster, Jan. 18, 1893, USDS, Disp., Haw.; *PCA,* Jan. 18, 1893; *Daily Bulletin,* Jan. 18, 1893.

The "superior force of the United States": Blount Report, p. 120; *Daily Bulletin,* Jan. 18, 1893.

Seek a treaty of union: Proceedings of Executive and Advisory Councils, Jan. 17, 1893.

Raise the Stars and Stripes: Stevens to Foster, Feb. 1, 1893, USDS, Disp., Haw.

The "ensign of Freedom": Alexander to Alexander, Feb. 1, 1893, HMCS.

The draft of an annexation treaty: Kuykendall, "Negotiation"; C. H. Hunter, "Statehood."

The queen's representatives: McFarlane to Cleghorn, Mar. 7, 8, 1893, Cleghorn Collection, Stenographic Report, Feb. 21, 1893, USDS, Notes from Hawaiian Legation.

Kaiulani: Cleghorn to Kaiulani, Jan. 28, 1893, Cleghorn Collection; McFarlane to Cleghorn, Feb. 24, 1893, Cleghorn Collection; W. D. Alexander, *History of Later Years,* pp. 77–78; Russ, *Hawaiian Revolution,* p. 164.

The treaty had been "precipitated upon the administration": Thurston to Dole, Mar. 10, 1893, FO & Ex.

James H. Blount: Blount Report, pp. 1–3.

"Her submission was thus coerced": Gresham to Bayard, Oct. 29, 1893, Gresham Papers.

Liliuokalani was in a harsh mood: Liliuokalani Diary, Nov. 13, 1893; Willis to Gresham, Nov. 16, 1893, USDS, Disp., Haw.; *Hawaii's Story By Hawaii's Queen,* pp. 247–248.

"We have done your government no wrong": Willis to Gresham, Dec. 23, 1893, USDS, Disp., Haw.

The Senate began its own hearings: These are published as the Morgan Report.

Resolutions passed in both House and Senate: *Congressional Record,* 53 Cong. 2 Sess., pp. 2001–2017, 5499–5500.

FAREWELL TO THEE pp. 280–285

"These Islands are totally unfit": Smith to Thurston, Feb. 18, 1894, Minister & Envoys.

Thurston was full of ideas: Thurston to Dole, Feb. 11, Mar. 10, 1894, Minister & Envoys.

The election of delegates: *Hawaiian Star,* Mar. 9, 1894; *PCA,* Apr. 3, 23, May 12, 1894.

The republican constitution that emerged: Spaulding, "Constitution;" Lydecker, pp. 190–205.

The inauguration of the republic: Willis to Gresham, July 9, 1894, USDS, Disp., Haw.; *Hawaiian Star,* July 5, 1894.

Cleveland sent a letter of recognition: Minutes of the Executive Council, Aug. 25, 27, 1894.

Queen Victoria followed suit: *Hawaiian Star,* Nov. 15, 1894.

The American Union party: *Daily Bulletin,* Oct. 10, 1894.

Liliuokalani's agents at Washington: Russ, *Hawaiian Republic,* pp. 49–51.

A strike against the republic: Towse; Girvin.

The biggest catch of all was Liliuokalani: S. Bishop Diary, Jan. 18, Feb. 7, 1895; *PCA,* Jan. 17, 1895.

A "forced abdication": *Hawaii's Story By Hawaii's Queen,* pp. 273–275. See also Willis to Gresham, Jan. 30, 1895, USDS, Disp., Haw.; Minutes of the Executive Council, Jan. 24, 1895.

She was in no position to abdicate: Willis to Gresham, Jan. 30, 1895, USDS, Disp., Haw.

No one died for royalist principles: Russ, *Hawaiian Republic,* pp. 78–87, 92–94.

A sensible compromise: Minutes of the Executive Council, Jan. 29, 1895. See also documents in Filibuster File, AH.

The royalists' arms: Russ, *Hawaiian Republic,* pp. 92–96.

Gresham had "repeatedly gone out of his way": Thurston to Hatch, Apr. 15, 1895, Minister & Envoys.

Liliuokalani freed: Minutes of the Executive Council, Sep. 3, 1895; Sealed copy of pardon, Oct. 23, 1896, in Henriques Collection.

The Reverend Sereno Bishop: Bishop's diary contains a running record of his publications in the United States. See especially *New York Herald,* Feb. 16, 1893; *Independent,* Feb. 2, Mar. 2, July 6, 1893, Jan. 4, 25, Feb. 8, Mar. 29, 1894; *Review of Reviews* (1891), pp. 147–163, 227–234.

MANIFEST DESTINY pp. 285–292

Japanese were admitted in great numbers: Conroy, pp. 54–80, 106–130; Rowland.

"Hawaii has reached the parting of the ways": Stevens to Foster, Nov. 20, 1892, USDS, Disp., Haw.

The laborers were forbidden to land: Conroy, p. 125.

An equal footing with the great powers: Conroy, pp. 137–141; Russ, *Hawaiian Republic*, pp. 130–177.

The Japanese war ship *Naniwa*: *PCA*, May 6, 1897; *Yamato Shimbun*, May 6, 1897.

"The difference between the attitude": Smith to Cooper, Mar. 26, 1897, Minister & Envoys.

A treaty ready for the Senate: Minister of Foreign Affairs, *Report*, 1897, Appendix A, pp. 1–5.

"Despite successive denials": Senate Reports, 55 Cong. 2 Sess., No. 681, p. 66.

"Hawaii may be regarded as a bride": *Hawaiian Star*, July 27, 1897.

The Hawaiian Senate ratified the treaty: *PCA*, Sep. 10, 1897.

Two groups of congressmen: *PCA*, Sep. 15, Nov. 19, 1897; *Hawaiian Star*, Sep. 22, 1897.

The good offices of President Dole: Minutes of the Council of State, Jan. 5, 1898; Minutes of the Executive Council, Jan. 8, 1898.

The larger question of the position of the United States: See Weinberg, LaFeber, H. Morgan, Pratt, *Expansionists*, generally.

"No mere sporadic effort": Mahan, *Interest Of America*, pp. 32–55.

Carl Schurz had a powerful and forbidding vision: Schurz.

Lorrin Thurston published his argument: L. A. Thurston, *Handbook*, generally.

Sugar: Stevens, pp. 227–229, 289; Weigle; Rowland.

The treaty commanded a majority: Hatch to Cooper, Feb. 10, 1898, Minister & Envoys; Russ, *Hawaiian Republic*, pp. 225–227.

Senate resolution: *Congressional Record*, 55 Cong. 2 Sess., p. 2853.

House resolution: *Congressional Record*, 55 Cong. 2 Sess., pp. 4600, 4989.

War with Spain: H. Morgan, LaFeber, generally.

The holding of the Philippines was essential: Pratt, *Expansionists*, pp. 317–360.

Hawaii would act as an undeclared ally: Sewall to Sherman, May 16, 1898, USDS, Disp., Haw.; *Independent*, Apr. 29, 1898.

"How can we endure our shame": *Congressional Record*, 55 Cong. 2 Sess., pp. 5788–5795.

The resolution passed: *Congressional Record*, 55 Cong. 2 Sess., p. 6019.

"The party of men": *Congressional Record*, 55 Cong. 2 Sess., p. 6157.

The annexationist press was delirious: *PCA*, July 14, 1898; *Hawaiian Star*, July 14, 1898; *Evening Bulletin*, July 14, 1898.

The Hawaiian Republic paid Japan: Cooper to Shimamura, July 27, 1898, Correspondence with Japanese Minister, AH; Minutes of the Council of State, July 27, 1898, AH.

"To the Hawaiian born it was pathetic": *PCA*, Aug. 13, 1898.

"Mission boys": L. A. Thurston, *Memoirs*, p. 277.

Church membership: *Haw. Gaz.*, Sep. 3, 1889.

The Hawaiian people were not badly off: W. Armstrong, pp. 276–277.

Chapter 8: The Territory—1900–1941

CHIEFS AND RETAINERS pp. 293–302

"Instead of using their vantage": L. A. Thurston, *Memoirs*, pp. 277–278.

As Sereno Bishop said: Bishop to Gilman, June 20, 1898, S. Bishop Ltr. Bk.

"Hater of things American": *Haw. Gaz.*, Apr. 17, 1900. See also Bishop to Gilman, June 20, 1898, May 23, 1899, S. Bishop Ltr. Bk.; *Honolulu Republican*, Nov. 11, 1900.

"Simply because they were grown up": *PCA*, Apr. 17, 1900.

Home Rule: Healy, p. 89 ff; *Hawaiian Star*, Sep. 10, 1900.

The first territorial legislature: Journal of Legislature, 1901, generally; Lydecker, pp. 264–265.

Jonah Kuhio Kalanianaole: AH has Kuhio's papers as delegate to Congress.

Ropes round the necks of the Republicans: *Hawaiian Star*, Sep. 10, 1903.

County government: Iaukea to Kuhio, Jan. 16, 1903, Kuhio Papers; Fuchs, p. 166.

Inundated by good advice: See letters in Kuhio Papers.

"If conditions remain": Rehabilitation Hearings, p. 70.

"This is our land": *HSB*, July 4, 1919.

"We are living on soil": *Hilo Tribune-Herald*, Dec. 17, 1919.

Earlier efforts to get homestead program: Dinell, pp. 4–6.

Leases would expire: Vause, pp. 17–22.

A territorial legislative commission: Rehabilitation Hearings, generally.

Hawaiian Homes Commission Act: 67 Cong. S. 1881.

"Personally": McCarthy to Payne, June 20, 1920, McCarthy Papers.

"Average acreage allowed": *Friend*, Dec., 1920.

On Molokai: Spitz, pp. 19–24.

Household lots: Spitz, pp. 25–26.

Under the terms of her will: The will is filed in probate court, Honolulu. Copy in Kalanianaole Collection, BPBM.

Hawaiians would "compete": *Official Prospectus—The Kamehameha Schools*.

William Brewster Oleson: Hudson, pp. 93–94.

No "general conception of honor": Hudson, pp. 185–186.

"The object of the Manual School": Hudson, pp. 152–153.

"Such as a man would choose": Bishop to Thompson, June 2, 1898, in Hudson, p. 106.

"The assumption is made": *PCA*, Dec. 1, 1916.

If he proved himself "deserving": *PCA*, Feb. 13, 1918.

THE RISING SUN pp. 302–311

Bubonic plague: Iwamoto, generally.

Not enough to prevent disaster: *PCA*, Jan. 22, 1900.

Claims for damages: *Hawaiian Annual for 1904*, p. 30. See also Banana Claims, AH.
"Asiatics pressed back": *PCA*, Jan. 26, 1900.
Strike for higher wages: Wakukawa, pp. 169–191.
"If a laborer comes from Japan": *Higher Wages Question*, pp. 5–6.
So they encouraged migrants: Figures are collected in *Hawaiian Annual* for appropriate years.
Filipinos: Cariaga; Dorita, generally.
They struck again for higher wages: Wakukawa, pp. 231–264.
"As completely the masters": *HSB*, Feb. 13, 1920.
Pablo Manlapit: *Nippu Jiji*, Jan. 3, 1920; *PCA*, Jan. 20, 1920; *Hawaii Hochi*, Jan. 21, 1920; Fuchs, pp. 216–218.
Pictures of Abraham Lincoln: Wakukawa, p. 252.
Reverend Albert W. Palmer: *HSB*, Feb. 23, 1920; *PCA*, Feb. 24, 1920.
The Japanese surrendered: Wakukawa, p. 259.
A commission was sent to Washington: Labor Hearings.
"We are subjects of Dai Nippon": *Yamato Shimbun*, Oct. 19, 1895.
"Supposing, for the sake of an example": Immigration Hearings, p. 100.
Not even if he served in the armed forces: Wakukawa, pp. 302–316.
"As an ethical system": *Friend*, Feb., 1889.
Planters encouraged Buddhist priests: L. Hunter, pp. 115, 152; Wakukawa, p. 131; *Hawaiian Star*, Aug. 1, 1904.
"The best future interests": Carter to Campbell, July 9, 1906, G. R. Carter Papers.
Christian missionaries did poorly: Hawaiian Evangelical Association, *Report*, 1916, p. 30; Scudder, p. 3.
Yemyo Imamura: *HSB*, Aug. 6, 1918; Imamura, pp. 7, 8, 22, 23.
"Unequivocally opposed": *Survey Of Education*, p. 135.
The fifteen-petaled chrysanthemum: *HSB*, Mar. 6, 1919.
"Time-honored reputation": Journal of Legislature, House, 1923, p. 26.
"Reasonable choice and discretion": Wakukawa, pp. 296–298.
"The Oriental races": Irwin, pp. 54–56.
Reverend Takie Okumura: Okumura, generally.

A QUOTA OF SWEETNESS AND LIGHT pp. 311–317

Sugar: See Hawaiian Sugar Planters' Association, *Proceedings*, for appropriate years.
Spreckels plantation interests: Adler, *Claus Spreckels*, pp. 82–84.
William Irwin: Adler, *Claus Spreckels*, pp. 102–103.
Hackfeld & Co.: W. Taylor, Ch. 3.
James D. Dole: Fuchs, pp. 241–242.
"These companies": U. S. Bureau of Labor Statistics, *Report on Hawaii*, 1906, p. 94.
"There is a government": Hawaiian Investigation, I, p. 10.
Interlocking directorates: Richardson Report, pp. 184–185.
An excess of money: Fuchs, p. 198.

"Up to the present time": U. S. Commissioner of Labor, *Report on Hawaii,*
   1902, p. 38.
"Trustworthy, upright and honored": *The Sugar Industry and the Labor Short-
   age,* p. 4.
"Little difference": Cooke to Prosser, July 24, 1930, in Aller, p. 32.
Pablo Manlapit: Johannessen, pp. 70–71.
"We are fond of saying": Irwin, p. 56.
A federal commission: *Survey of Education,* generally.
Why "blindly continue a system": Hawaiian Sugar Planters' Association, *Pro-
   ceedings,* 1925, p. 13.

THE HONOLULU MARTYRDOM pp. 317–327

Pearl Harbor: Snowbarger, generally.
Soldiers and sailors married local girls: R. Adams, generally.
Punti and Hakka: Glick, generally.
Japanese from southern prefectures: Conroy, pp. 90–118.
Korean: Kim, generally.
Filipinos: Cariaga, generally.
Pidgin: Reinecke, generally.
Brothels: Richardson Report, pp. 35–36, 70–72.
Myles Fukunaga: *HSB,* Sep. 19, 1928, and following issues.
Thalia Massie: The principal sources for the Massie case are—Ala Moana Case,
   Honolulu Police Files, 1931; *Territory v. Ahakuelo et al.,* County Attorney's
   Office, Honolulu; *Territory v. Grace Fortescue et al.,* County Attorney's Office,
   Honolulu; Ala Moana Papers in Houston Papers, AH; Report of Pinkerton
   Detective Agency to Governor Lawrence Judd, October, 1932, typescript in
   AH. Three published accounts—Van Slingerland; Wright; and Thomas and
   Packer, draw on these sources. Day to day coverage is in *HSB, Hon. Adv.,* and
   Hawaii Hochi.
A "white woman of refinement": *Hon. Adv.,* Sep. 13, 1931.
The "gangsters" of Hawaii: *Hon. Adv.,* Sep. 29, 1931.
No sign of pregnancy: Pinkerton Report.
"Enthusiastic priests": Stirling, *Sea Duty,* p. 234.
"Sordid people": Stirling, *Sea Duty,* p. 255.
"Seize the brutes": Stirling, *Sea Duty,* pp. 245–246.
A mistrial: *HSB,* Dec. 7, 1931.
Men "who might be given the benefit": Stirling, *Sea Duty,* p. 250.
"Swinging from trees": Stirling, *Sea Duty,* p. 253.
Horace Ida: *Hon. Adv.,* Dec. 13, 1931.
"Brutal, repulsive black face": Fortescue.
"Small, erect, dominating": Fortescue.
"But it wasn't murder!": Fortescue.
"People who take the law": *HSB,* Jan. 9, 1932.
"Now, of course": *The New York Times,* Feb. 8, 1932.
Grand jurors: *HSB,* Jan. 22–30, 1932.
Clarence Darrow: *Hon. Adv.,* Mar. 24, 1932.

"At times": Van Slingerland, p. 269.
"When I gazed into those dark faces": Stirling, *Sea Duty*, p. 262.
"The stoical Oriental faces": Fortescue.

ULTIMATE LOYALTY pp. 328–338

"The situation in Hawaii": *New York American,* Jan. 11, 1932.
Sex crimes at Honolulu: Richardson Report, pp. 29–33.
"Impotent, undisciplined": Richardson Report, p. *viii.*
City and county attorney: Richardson Report, pp. *ix,* 19.
Oahu Prison: Richardson Report, p. 23.
Crime commission: Richardson Report, pp. 24–25.
Special session of the legislature: Richardson Report, pp. 25–26; *Laws,* 1932, pp. 1–7, 15–16, 18–21, 25–28, 29–31.
Appointed by the President: Richardson Report, p. 45.
Congress taking proposals seriously: The Honolulu newspapers gave this full coverage in 1932 and 1933. See also *Congressional Record,* 73 Cong. 1 Sess., pp. 3889, 5606–5608, 6072–6080.
"The result of the miscarriage": Stirling, *Sea Duty*, p. 267.
"Scientists have stated": Richardson Report, p. 198–199.
"Bill of Rights": *Laws,* 1923, p. 86.
Evidence of economic discrimination: Crowe Hearings, pp. 93–96.
Jones-Costigan Act: *Hon. Adv.,* Apr. 27, June 1, 1934; *HSB,* June 1, 1934; Pratt, *America's Colonial Experiment,* pp. 253, 261.
Statehood: Dedmon.
"Those who have felt": Crowe Hearings, p. 64.
"The plantations and allied interests": Crowe Hearings, p. 164.
Social workers, teachers, university professors: Crowe Hearings, pp. 10, 16, 24, 34, 81–84, 117, 135–136, 154, 179, 227.
"One or two or three students": Crowe Hearings, pp. 39–40.
"We place national safety": Crowe Hearings, pp. 301–304.
Dual citizenship: Murphy, pp. 17–24.
Wilfred C. Tsukiyama: King Hearings, pp. 468–482.
A simple move: King Hearings, p. 323.
John F. G. Stokes: King Hearings, pp. 246–272.
Plebiscite: Roesch, generally; *Hon. Adv.,* Nov. 6, 1940; *HSB,* Nov. 14, 1940.

Chapter 9: Now We Are All Haoles—1941–1959

TORA, TORA, TORA pp. 339–343

"As much as we would hate": King Hearings, p. 315.
The American government knew an amazing amount: Wohlstetter, generally; Farago, generally.
As ready as they would ever be: Wohlstetter, pp. 71–169.

Carriers and their supporting ships disappeared: Pearl Harbor Hearings, Part 10, p. 4838, Part 17, p. 2638, Part 36, pp. 116–141.

The destroyer *Ward:* Pearl Harbor Hearings, Part 23, pp. 1033–1036, Part 36, pp. 59, 268–270.

Radar tracking station: Pearl Harbor Hearings, Part 22, pp. 221, 223, Part 27, p. 520.

"I don't know": Pearl Harbor Hearings, Part 22, p. 221.

"Tora, tora, tora": Lord, p. 67.

"The Star-Spangled Banner": Lord, pp. 70–71.

Battleship Row was a shambles: Pearl Harbor Report, pp. 58–62.

At the air bases: Pearl Harbor Report, pp. 62, 68–69.

The radar unit tracked them out: Pearl Harbor Report, p. 69.

"Military and naval forces": Pearl Harbor Report, p. 65.

WAR pp. 344–351

Joseph B. Poindexter: Lord, p. 171; *Hon. Adv.,* Dec. 9, 1941.

A proclamation: Proclamation Book, 1938–1943, AH.

The Honolulu switchboard: "Japs Fail," p. 16.

"Never hated doing anything so much": Hite, Dec. 7, 1941.

"Reasonably short time": Hite, Dec. 7, 1941.

Niihau: "Summary Of Events On Niihau"; Pearl Harbor Hearings, Part 24, pp. 1448–1553. See also Daws and Head, generally.

Loyalties still unproven: G. Allen, pp. 131–150.

Takeo Yoshikawa: Pearl Harbor Hearings, Part 35, pp. 355–368; Farago, pp. 156–157, 234–248.

Other men at the Japanese consulate: Farago, pp. 141–145, 147–151.

Local Japanese arrested: G. Allen, pp. 131–141.

Bernard Julius Otto Kühn: Farago, pp. 145–147, 242–244, 300–301; G. Allen, p. 133.

Segregating them all: Low to Poindexter, Dec. 30, 1941, Poindexter Papers.

Japanese guardsmen dismissed: Murphy, pp. 52–54.

"Watch the local Japanese": "History of Businessmen's Corps."

Varsity Victory Volunteers: Nakahata and Toyota.

Hawaiian Provisional Infantry Battalion: Murphy, pp. 61–72.

Internment camp: Murphy, p. 71.

Camp McCoy: Murphy, pp. 73–90.

Urging mass evacuation: Balch; Murphy, p. 100.

"A profound propaganda effect": Murphy, pp. 109–110.

"Open to distrust": *HSB,* Jan. 28, 1943; *Hon. Adv.,* Jan. 29, 1943.

442nd Infantry Regiment: Murphy, generally.

Casualty rate: G. Allen, p. 271.

"The highest aspiration": *Hawaii Times,* Nov. 27, 1945.

A COMMANDING GENERAL IS NEVER WRONG pp. 352–356

More than thirty thousand islanders: G. Allen, pp. 263–273.
Blackout and curfew: General Orders No. 16, HWRD; G. Allen, pp. 112–113;·
Anthony, pp. 58–59.
Table of organization: Anthony, pp. 36–37.
"Regulation of traffic": Anthony, p. 13.
"A commanding general is never wrong": Anthony, p. 12.
"A reign that is contrary": Anthony to Stainback, Dec. 1, 1942, Stainback Papers.
"I think," said Walter Dillingham: Pearl Harbor Hearings, Part 28, pp. 1444–
1445.
The military courts: General Orders No. 4, HWRD; Anthony, pp. 44–59.
"Test tube and a guinea pig": *Hon. Adv.*, Sep. 4, 1942.
Move out of Iolani Palace: Anthony, p. 25.
Stainback and Anthony flew to Washington: Ickes to Hicks, Jan. 9, 1943,
Chamber of Commerce File, HWRD; *Hon. Adv.*, Mar. 10, 1943; Anthony,
pp. 26–33.
Hans Zimmerman: Zimmerman v. Walker, 132 F. 2nd 442 (1942); Anthony, pp.
61–64.
Walter Glockner and Edwin Seifert: Ex parte Glockner, USDC (Hawaii), No.
295; Ex parte Seifert, USDC (Hawaii), No. 296; Anthony, pp. 64–77.
Lloyd C. Duncan: 327 US 304 (1946); Anthony, p. 77 ff.

LABOR PAINS pp. 357–367

Vibora Luviminda: Johannessen, pp. 72–73; Aller, p. 45.
The Industrial Association of Hawaii: Aller, pp. 50–51.
Violating the labor law: Aller, p. 52.
Members of west coast maritime unions: *Voice of Labor*, generally; Fuchs, p.
363.
"They shot us down": *Hawaii Sentinel*, Aug. 4, 1938. See also Walter Hearings,
Part 3, p. 1976, Part 4, pp. 13–14.
"The cops say in the papers": *Hawaii Sentinel*, Aug. 4, 1938.
They gave up and went back to work: Johannessen, p. 85.
Management was able to outwait the longshoremen: Johannessen, pp. 88–89.
American Federation of Labor: Fuchs, pp. 229–240; Johannessen, p. 88.
Labor agreements superseded by general orders: General Orders No. 38, 56,
91, 120, HWRD; Aller, p. 43; Johannessen, p. 94 ff.
The Hawaii Employers Council: Hawaii Employers Council, "Report of First
Annual Meeting," HWRD; Brooks, p. 13; Aller, p. 54 ff; *Hon. Adv.*, May 10,
1945.
The unions were determined to go ahead: Johannessen, p. 102.
The ruling favored the ILWU: Aller, p. 59.
Industry-wide contracts: Aller, pp. 60–61.
A strike in the sugar industry: Congdon, generally.
Undeniably the union had won: Aller, p. 87.

The perquisite system: HSPA, *Annual Report,* 1946; Aller, pp. 83–86.

More than thirty thousand members: Shoemaker, p. 184 ff; Johannessen, p. 110.

It was likely that union membership would fall: Johannessen, p. 110.

More citizens than ever before: U. S. Census, 1900–1950.

William P. Jarrett and Lincoln L. McCandless: AH has the McCandless Papers. Jarrett's papers have not been deposited.

Lucius E. Pinkham: AH has the Pinkham Papers.

Charles J. McCarthy: AH has the McCarthy Papers.

A violent factional fight: Fuchs, pp. 192–194.

Joseph B. Poindexter: AH has the Poindexter Papers. See also Lane, generally.

Wilson could see the obvious: Wilson to Farley, Mar. 22, 1937, Wilson Papers.

Certainly the figures were on Wilson's side: U. S. Census, 1900–1950.

The union was beginning to dabble in politics: Walter Hearings, Part 1, p. 1374; Fuchs, p. 239.

Political Action Committee: Walter Hearings, Part 1, pp. 1419–1420, 1451–1452, Part 3, p. 1981; Johannessen, pp. 141–142.

UNQUIET PEACE pp. 368–381

The ILWU was a nest of Communists: *HSB,* Jan. 25, 1954. See also Eastland Hearings, pp. 2285, 2718 ff.

The Truth About Communism in Hawaii: Izuka. See also Walter Hearings, Part 1, p. 1372 ff.

John E. Reinecke and his wife: *Hon. Adv.,* Nov. 26, 1947, Aug. 3, 9, Oct. 30, 1948.

Hawaii Civil Liberties Committee: HCLC Report, generally.

"The unseen Communist dictator": Butler Report, 1949, p. 1.

"By the well-known infiltration tactics": Butler Report, 1949, p. 1.

"Every aspect" of life: Butler Report, 1949, p. 2.

An "active Communist": Butler Report, 1949, p. 3.

He dismissed Ichiro Izuka's pamphlet: Walter Hearings, Part 1, p. 1439.

Everything was falling into the hands of Communists: Stainback to Chapman, May 14, 1948, Stainback Papers; Walter Hearings, Part 4, p. 35; Fuchs, pp. 311–312.

About two thousand dock workers walked off the job: Brooks, p. 189 ff.

A dock seizure act: *HSB,* Aug. 6, 1949.

On October 23 a settlement was reached: *HSB,* Oct. 23, 1949, and following issues.

When Harry Bridges arrived at Honolulu: *HSB,* June 1, July 1, Aug. 16, 1949.

Bridges and Jack Hall had secret and malign purposes: Eastland Hearings, pp. 2525–2530.

"This," he wrote, "is the familiar pattern": Butler Report, 1949, p. 11.

"For purposes revoltingly dishonest": *Hilo Tribune-Herald,* July 31, 1949.

A subversive activities commission: *HSB,* Oct. 26, 1949.

The hearings held at Honolulu: Walter Hearings. See also *Hon. Adv.,* Oct. 5, 1949; *HSB,* Oct. 5, 1949.

Ichiro Izuka: Walter Hearings, Part 1, p. 1372 ff.

"I could go ahead and do it": Walter Hearings, Part 2, p. 1670.

"Are you now or have you ever been": Walter Hearings, Part 2, p. 1538.

Francis E. Walter: Walter Hearings, Part 1, p. 1355.

The Reluctant Thirty-Nine were acquitted: *HSB*, Apr. 20, Aug. 11, 1950, Jan. 16, 19, 1951.

Jack H. Kawano: Walter Hearings, Part 4, pp. 1–53.

They were arrested at their homes: Eastland Hearings, p. 2756 ff; *HSB*, Aug. 28, 1951, and following issues; Bouslog; McNamara, generally.

The beginning of a legal battle: Eastland Hearings, p. 2756 ff.

The Seven were found guilty: *HSB*, June 19, 1953, and following issues.

The "hideous conspiracy": Walter Hearings, Part 1, p. 1354.

The number seemed to range from fifty to two hundred: Cordon Report, 1948, p. 6; Walter Hearings, Part 1, p. 1438; O'Mahoney Hearings, pp. 154, 162; Eastland Hearings, p. 2521; *HSB*, Jan. 5, 1950, Mar. 26, 1951.

Delbert Metzger and Paul Crouch: Johannessen, pp. 154, 159.

The unlikely items of information: Walter Hearings, generally; Eastland Hearings, generally.

Imua: *Spotlight*, generally; Johannessen, p. 155.

James O. Eastland: Eastland Hearings, generally.

The Seven were acquitted: McNamara, generally; C. H. Hunter, "Congress and Statehood," p. 363.

The ILWU was still very much alive: Aller, p. 95 ff; Johannessen, p. 119 ff; Fuchs, p. 372 ff.

Jack Hall dealt with setbacks and defections: *HSB*, Jan. 23, 1948, Aug. 30, 1950, Dec. 24, 1952; Johannessen, pp. 112–113.

A public testimonial dinner: Eastland Hearings, pp. 2465–2466; C. H. Hunter, "Congress and Statehood," p. 373.

Consolidate the various locals: Johannessen, p. 111; Fuchs, p. 362.

The ILWU staged short strikes: Eastland Hearings, pp. 2531–2532; *Honolulu Record*, Dec. 6, 1956; Johannessen, p. 132 ff.

"Certainly if a man were under question": Eastland Hearings, p. 2476.

Hall seemed to be mellowing slightly: Aller, p. 99 ff.

Kawano insisted on reading the names: Walter Hearings, Part 4, p. 52.

A betrayal by the Democrats: *HSB*, Nov. 7, 1956.

A place could be found in the party: Fuchs, p. 308 ff.

Immigrants were taking out citizenship papers: U. S. Census, 1900–1950.

The great exponents of the balanced ticket: Fuchs, p. 308 ff.

Electoral results: These may be followed in *Hon. Adv.* and *HSB*, for relevant years.

Joseph R. Farrington: AH has the Farrington Papers.

Samuel Wilder King: AH has the King Papers.

He used the veto seventy-one times: Fuchs, p. 326.

The old racial stereotypes: The periodical *Social Progress in Hawaii*, published at the University of Hawaii, contains a great amount of material. See also O'Mahoney Hearings, p. 20.

FIFTIETH STAR pp. 381–391

Nothing but a creature of the federal government: Larcade Hearings, pp. 31–32; O'Mahoney Hearings, p. 81; Cordon Report, 1954, pp. 6, 13.

No offshore possession had been given equal rights: Cordon Report, 1954, p. 7; Pratt, *America's Colonial Experiment,* generally; *Congressional Record,* 80 Cong. 1 Sess., p. 8079.

Hawaii was paying more federal tax: *Congressional Record,* 83 Cong. 2 Sess., p. 3479; Cordon Report, 1954, p. 4.

The population of the territory: U. S. Census, 1900–1950; O'Mahoney Hearings, p. 25; Cordon Report, 1954, p. 11.

The war wiped out all possible objections: Larcade Hearings, pp. 33–38.

"Any argument against statehood": O'Mahoney Hearings, pp. 268–269.

Walter F. Dillingham: Cordon Hearings, 1948, pp. 292 ff, 405–408; *Hilo Tribune-Herald,* July 7, 1952; *HSB,* July 7, 1952, July 4, 1953.

"Public Enemy No. 2": *HSB,* Apr. 14, 1959.

Alice Kamokila Campbell and bloc voting: Larcade Hearings, pp. 29, 330, 360, 463–465; Cordon Hearings, 1948, pp. 135, 138, 180, 410; O'Mahoney Hearings, p. 247; *Hon. Adv.,* Jan 15, 1938, Mar. 6, 7, 1945, Jan. 9, 18, 19, May 4, 1946, Feb. 4, 1948; *HSB,* Dec. 29, 1945, Jan. 7, Feb. 5, 1946.

In 1940 a plebiscite showed: *Hon. Adv.,* Nov. 6, 1940; *HSB,* Nov. 14, 1940.

Almost every organized group in the territory: Cordon Hearings, 1948, pp. 19–21; *HSB,* Feb. 2, Mar. 23, June 2, 1946; *Hilo Tribune-Herald,* June 15, 1946.

"A few craven souls": O'Mahoney Hearings, pp. 268–269. See also Larcade Hearings, pp. 31, 478; Cordon Hearings, 1948, p. 184.

An opinion poll published in *Fortune*: *Fortune,* Jan. 1940; *Hon. Adv.,* Jan. 29, 1940.

A poll taken early in 1946: *Hilo Tribune-Herald,* Mar. 8, 1946.

Seventy-eight per cent were said to be in favor: Cordon Report, 1954, p. 5. See also *HSB,* Feb. 2, 1952, Jan. 17, 1955, Apr. 14, 1959.

Important men were lending their names: Cordon Report, 1948, p. 7; Cordon Report, 1954, p. 5; *HSB,* Jan. 21, 1946, Feb. 21, 1955, Apr. 14, 1959; C. H. Hunter, "Congress and Statehood," p. 354.

A straight vote: *Congressional Record,* 81 Cong. 1 Sess., p. 10875.

Statehood resolutions by the dozen: *HSB,* Apr. 14, 1959.

Far more was known about Hawaii: Cordon Report, 1954, p. 23.

Non-contiguous territory: *Congressional Record,* 83 Cong. 1 Sess., p. 1859, 2 Sess., p. 2889; O'Mahoney Hearings, p. 26; Cordon Report, 1954, p. 13; *HSB,* Dec. 10, 1946.

"The senator from Scythia": Congressional Record, 83 Cong. 1 Sess., p. 1850.

"I fear for the future": *Congressional Record,* 83 Cong. 1 Sess., p. 1871.

Especially heavy commitments in the Pacific: Larcade Hearings, pp. 35–39; Cordon Hearings, 1948, pp. 166–173; Cordon Report, 1954, p. 4; *Congressional Record,* 81 Cong. 2 Sess., p. 2886.

A kind of moral leadership: Larcade Hearings, pp. 35, 37, 389, 473; O'Mahoney Hearings, p. 83; Cordon Report, 1954, p. 23; *HSB,* Feb. 8, 1954.

"Some of her people": Cordon Report, 1954, p. 4.

This was iniquitous: *Congressional Record,* 86 Cong. 1 Sess., pp. 3495–3496; Dedmon, pp. 351–352.

The matter had been resolved already: Cordon Report, 1954, p. 13; *Congressional Record,* 84 Cong. 1 Sess., p. 5960.

"To be dictated by the tools of Moscow": Butler Report, 1949, p. 14. See also Butler Report, 1950, p. 47; Butler Hearings, 1953–1954, p. 579.

Guy Cordon had made a trip: Cordon Hearings, 1948. See also *HSB,* June 25, 1949.

His exposure of Communism in Hawaii: Walter Hearings, p. 1354.

Hawaii had been making strenuous efforts: Cordon Report, 1954, generally. See also O'Mahoney Hearings, pp. 267–270; *Hon. Adv.,* Apr. 2, 1950; *HSB,* May 29, 1948, Apr. 11, 1950, Feb. 6, 1954.

Hugh Butler had reached the same conclusion: Cordon Report, 1954, pp. 8–9; *Hon. Adv.,* Nov. 23, 1952.

"Actually invite two Soviet agents": *HSB,* July 6, 1953. See also *Hon. Adv.,* Mar. 24, May 11, 1955, Apr. 14, 1958.

"As long as the boobs furnish us this material": *Hon. Adv.,* Dec. 28, 1953. See also *Hon. Adv.,* Dec. 8, 1957, Sep. 25, 1958.

The same small group of Southern senators: *Congressional Record,* 81 Cong. 2 Sess., p. 2871, 83 Cong. 2 Sess., pp. 3066–3068; Butler Hearings, 1954, Part 2, pp. 380–381; *HSB,* Apr. 4, 15, May 8, 1953, Dec. 28, 1955, Mar. 6, 1956, Mar. 2, 1957; *Hon. Adv.,* June 19, 1953, Mar. 21, 1956, Jan. 19, 1957.

"Tinctured with Communism": C. H. Hunter, "Congress and Statehood," p. 364.

"There are many shades and mixtures": *Congressional Record,* 86 Cong. 1 Sess., pp. 3461–3464.

The old fear of the Chinese senator: See Chapter 7, above.

Congress was not accustomed to move quickly: Cordon Report, 1954, p. 15; C. H. Hunter, "Congress and Statehood," generally; *Congressional Quarterly Fact Sheet,* Mar. 6, 1959, p. 369; *HSB,* Apr. 14, 1959.

Tying Alaska and Hawaii together: C. H. Hunter, "Congress and Statehood," p. 359 ff.

From 1953 to 1958: *Congressional Quarterly Fact Sheet,* Mar. 6, 1959, p. 360.

John A. Burns flipped a coin: *HSB,* Dec. 26, 1956.

Other proposals: *Maui News,* July 21, 1954; *Hon. Adv.,* Aug. 7, 1954, Oct. 2, 1955, July 12, 1956; *HSB,* July 11, 1956, Apr. 14, 1959; Dedmon, p. 297.

Benjamin F. Dillingham II: *HSB,* July 2, 1953, Apr. 25, 1955.

Harry Bridges: *HSB,* July 11, 1956.

Ingram Stainback: *HSB,* Jan. 20, 1948; *Hilo Tribune-Herald,* Feb. 11, 1948; *Maui News,* July 21, 1954; *Hon. Adv.,* Jan. 8, 1954; O'Mahoney Hearings, p. 78 ff.

Lorrin P. Thurston: *HSB,* Apr. 14, 1959.

"The Connally Caravan": *Hon. Adv.,* Mar. 9, 1952; *HSB,* Mar. 11, 1952.

The Statehood Honor Roll: *Hon. Adv.,* Feb. 8, 11, 23, 1954; *HSB,* Feb. 10, 1954.

Sending the entire territorial legislature: *Hon. Adv.,* Apr. 25, May 10, 19, 1954; *HSB,* Apr. 26, May 7, 1954.

The drivers of tourist buses: *HSB,* Nov. 1, 1955.

Dorothy Lamour: *Parade,* Jan. 11, 1959.

J. Frank McLaughlin: *HSB,* Jan. 19, 1959.

Burns came in for some abuse: *HSB,* Sep. 10, 1958, Apr. 14, 1959; C. H. Hunter, "Congress and Statehood," pp. 374–376.

Alaska was the forty-ninth state: *HSB,* July 1, 1958.

A last congressional committee: O'Brien Report.

The House began to consider a statehood bill: *Congressional Record,* 86 Cong. 1 Sess., pp. 4003–4096.

The Senate also had a statehood bill: *Congressional Record,* 86 Cong. 1 Sess., pp. 3806–3898.

Statehood for Hawaii was a reality: See *Hon. Adv.,* and *HSB,* Jan. 4–Mar. 12, 1959.

The balloting was held on June 27: *HSB,* June 29, 1959.

"The procedural requirements": *HSB,* Aug. 21, 1959.

EPILOGUE pp. 392–396

These remarks are based on personal observations by the author since 1959. No attempt has been made at formal documentation.

People and Places

Index